PUBLIC LAW

Public Law guides students through all the essential components of the Public Law module in a user-friendly structure that is ideal for visual learners.

Written by an experienced teacher of Public Law, the book takes an accessible and engaging approach to often complex areas of law, politics and the constitution. Incorporating recent developments, academic debate and commentary, the book introduces students to all the key concepts of this core subject. The text is grounded in context, explaining how Public Law operates in practice, and it thoroughly covers the spectrum of Constitutional Law, Human Rights and Administrative Law.

Integrated pedagogic features ease navigation of the text and reinforce key points. These include Public Law in Context, Recent Developments, Public Law in Practice, Practical Application and Academic Debate, and *Public Law* is also supported by online MCQs.

Public Law is essential reading for modules on public law and constitutional and administrative law on LLB degrees and conversion courses.

Chris Monaghan is a Principal Lecturer in Law at the University of Worcester, where he teaches and researches Public Law. He has taught Public Law for over a decade at a number of universities. His research interests include accountability mechanisms, prerogative powers and the Chagos litigation.

PUBLIC LAW

CHRIS MONAGHAN

Routledge
Taylor & Francis Group

LONDON AND NEW YORK

Cover image credit: Getty Image entitled 'Posterised or Pop Art styled Illustration of 10 Downing Street. Prime Minister' by **smartboy10**

First published 2022
by Routledge
2 Park Square, Milton Park, Abingdon, Oxon OX14 4RN

and by Routledge
605 Third Avenue, New York, NY 10158

Routledge is an imprint of the Taylor & Francis Group, an informa business

British Library Cataloguing-in-Publication Data
A catalogue record for this book is available from the British Library

Library of Congress Cataloging-in-Publication Data
A catalog record for this book has been requested

ISBN: 978-1-032-14595-2 (hbk)
ISBN: 978-0-367-26077-4 (pbk)
ISBN: 978-0-429-29349-8 (ebk)

DOI: 10.4324/9780429293498

Typeset in Stone Serif
by Apex CoVantage, LLC

Access the Support Material: www.routledge.com/Public-Law/
Monaghan/p/book/9780367260774

Contents

Preface

Public Law is a fascinating area that explores amongst many other things how the UK functions, the role of the government and monarch, the operation of the Westminster Parliament and the devolved legislatures, the importance of accountability and good government, the protection of human rights and the key role played by judges in reviewing decisions of public bodies.

I have been fortunate to have taught Public Law at UK universities since 2010. During this time, I have worked with colleagues who are passionate about teaching Public Law and have taught students who are willing to grapple with often complex issues and complicated concepts and who have made teaching this subject highly enjoyable. I have had the pleasure of teaching Public Law at the University of Worcester for five years now and have enjoyed teaching students who have made delivering lectures and seminars highly enjoyable.

The team at Routledge have been extremely supportive during the writing and production process. In particular I would like to thank Emily Kindleysides, Chloe James, Russell George, Katherine Carpenter and Pippa Whittle.

I would like to thank HH Toby Hooper QC, Josie Kemeys, Tom Bennett and Richard Glover for reading several chapters in this book and for their kind comments and suggestions. It goes without saying that all mistakes remain my own.

Finally, I would like to thank my family and in particular my wife, Nicola.

This book is dedicated to Katherine and Rebecca.

The law is stated as of April 2021.

Chris Monaghan

Table of Cases

International

European Legislation

International Legislation

Africa
African Charter on Human and Peoples' Rights

Australia

Table of Statutes

Statutory Instruments

Orders of Council

Osmotherly Rules

The United Kingdom's constitution

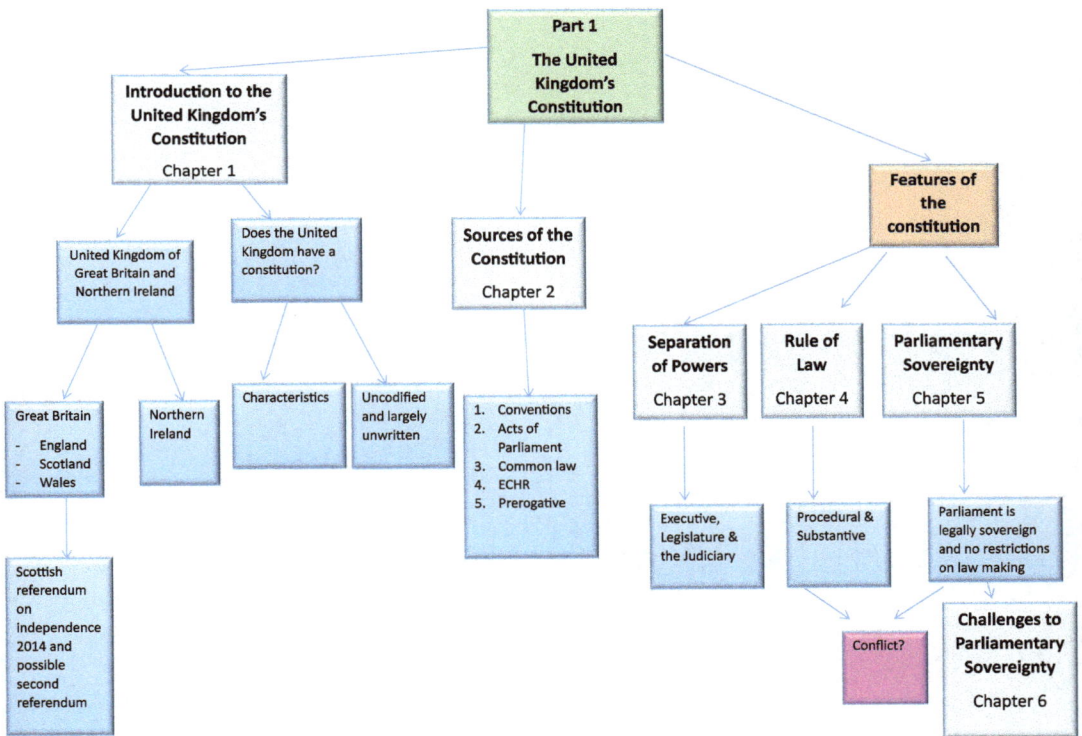

```
                                    Part 1
                                The United
                                 Kingdom's
                                Constitution

   Introduction to the
   United Kingdom's
     Constitution                                                          Features of
                                                                              the
      Chapter 1                                                           constitution


  United Kingdom of    Does the United        Sources of the
  Great Britain and    Kingdom have a          Constitution
  Northern Ireland     constitution?
                                                Chapter 2         Separation    Rule of    Parliamentary
                                                                  of Powers      Law       Sovereignty

                        Characteristics  Uncodified                Chapter 3   Chapter 4    Chapter 5
 Great Britain    Northern               and largely     1. Conventions
                  Ireland                unwritten       2. Acts of
 -  England                                                 Parliament
 -  Scotland                                             3. Common law
 -  Wales                                                4. ECHR          Executive,     Procedural &   Parliament is
                                                        5. Prerogative    Legislature &  Substantive    legally sovereign
                                                                          the Judiciary                 and no restrictions
                                                                                                        on law making
 Scottish
 referendum
 on                                                                                                      Challenges to
 independence                                                                           Conflict?       Parliamentary
 2014 and                                                                                                Sovereignty
 possible
 second                                                                                                   Chapter 6
 referendum
```

1 The United Kingdom's constitution

This chapter will

- define what is meant by a constitution;
- consider the nature of the United Kingdom's constitution;
- explore the history and the key constitutional developments of the United Kingdom; and
- consider the academic debate over whether the United Kingdom has a constitution.

BEFORE YOU BEGIN

It is important to understand that this chapter is intended to introduce you to a number of key themes and topics that will be explored in far more detail throughout this book. My advice to students when using any textbook is to read each chapter twice. The first time is the opportunity to navigate the text and get an overview of the subject-matter. The second time is usually where you should highlight key parts, take notes and possibly annotate the text.

In this chapter we will discuss concepts such as the Rule of Law, Parliamentary Sovereignty and the Separation of Powers, which together constitute four chapters in their own right. Therefore, my advice is to treat this chapter as an introduction and do not be put off by the scope of this chapter, as by its very nature it will need to explain the United Kingdom's Constitution.

1.1 Introduction

Many people use the word *constitution* without really knowing what it means. Indeed, if someone or an institution acts in a manner regarded by a particular newspaper or political opponent as against their own understanding of the constitution, then they are said to be acting unconstitutionally, or in an unconstitutional manner. This is not designed as a criticism because as you shall see the United Kingdom does not actually have a codified constitution. Therefore, it is not possible to visit London for the day and visit the British Library to see

DOI: 10.4324/9780429293498-2

the original written constitution or find it online via the parliament.uk website. This means that when the United Kingdom is faced with the political, economic and constitutional uncertainty that is the United Kingdom's departure from the European Union (or Brexit), then this causes questions to be raised about the constitution and the conduct of the actors working within it:

- What does Parliamentary Sovereignty mean within the United Kingdom's constitution and what will happen to the powers and 'sovereignty' repatriated from the European Union?
- Should Members of Parliament (MPs) vote to give effect to the people's decision (via the 2016 referendum) to leave the European Union, or do MPs in a representative democracy have the right to put the national interest over a non-binding advisory referendum?
- Should referendums be used to decide important constitutional questions given the seriousness of the decision and the resulting difficulty in the government reaching a position that could gain the support of the House of Commons?
- Are the judges really the 'Enemies of the People'[1] for holding that the government does not have the prerogative power to trigger Article 50 without parliamentary approval? The last question is important as the decision in *R (on the application of Miller) v Secretary of State for Exiting the European Union (Miller No. 1)*[2] is upholding the constitution and therefore this raises interesting issues regarding a clash between the constitution and popular opinion.
- Does the fact that a majority of the people of Scotland voted to remain within the European Union give support for greater devolution of legislative powers to the Scottish Parliament and possibly independence, which would then permit Scotland to reapply to join the European Union?
- What will be the long-term constitutional and political implications for Northern Ireland as part of the United Kingdom, given that it shares a land border with the European Union?

In this chapter, we will look at what the word *constitution* means and why every country, organisation or sports club will require a constitution to enable it to work effectively. The words effectively, or effective, are important as in a democratic society there would be no point in having a constitution if it served no purpose at all. The most famous constitution is that of the United States of America, which was drafted in 1787. The preamble to that constitution states:

> We the People of the United States, in Order to form a more perfect Union, establish Justice, insure domestic Tranquility, provide for the common defence, promote the general Welfare, and secure the Blessings of Liberty to ourselves and our Posterity, do ordain and establish this Constitution for the United States of America.[3]

We can see that the effective purpose behind the making of the constitution are spelt out quite clearly in the preamble. Not that the eventual constitution which came out of the constitutional convention held in Philadelphia in 1787 was uncontroversial, which is unsurprising given the fact that there were 13 separate states who would be voluntarily agreeing to cede a portion of their sovereignty when entering into a Union with each other.[4] It is useful to begin with the United States Constitution because it quite clearly sets out the relationship between the federal government which will be responsible for managing the new country and the individual states. The constitution gives certain powers to the three branches of the federal government: the executive[5], the legislature[6] and the judiciary[7].

PUBLIC LAW IN CONTEXT
NOT EVERY COUNTRY WITH A 'DEMOCRATIC' CONSTITUTION IS A DEMOCRACY

It is important to note that not every country is a democracy and even totalitarian states can have written constitutions. An example of this is the Democratic Republic of Korea (North Korea). The preamble of the North Korean constitution includes the following:

> Comrade Kim Il Sung regarded 'believing in the people as in heaven' as his motto, was always with the people, devoted his whole life to them, took care of and guided them with a noble politics of benevolence, and turned the whole society into one big and united family.
>
> The great leader Comrade Kim Il Sung is the sun of the nation and the lodestar of the reunification of the fatherland. Comrade Kim Il Sung set the reunification of the country as the nation's supreme task, and devoted all his work and endeavors entirely to its realization.'[8]

Article 4 of the North Korean constitution states that '[t]he sovereignty of the DPRK resides in the workers, peasants, working intellectuals and all other working people. The working people exercise power through their representative organs – the Supreme People's Assembly and local people's assemblies at all levels.'[9] Whilst Article 6 states '[t]he organs of State power at all levels, from the county People's Assembly to the SPA, are elected on the principle of universal, equal and direct suffrage by secret ballot.'[10] From reading the constitution, it is clear that the context in which it was first drafted and the fact that North Korea is still technically at war with South Korea and its allies, including the United States, have helped to shape the particular characteristics of the constitution. The effective purpose of the constitution in purporting to create a democracy is frustrated by reality and the realpolitik of the regime. However, it should be remembered that a dictatorship can have a constitution that provides the illusion of democracy without meaning that this reflects the reality. Equally, a country could be a fully functioning democracy and not have a written constitution.

This chapter is about the constitution of the United Kingdom and it is hoped that the above context will provide scope to reflect on what we mean by a

UK constitution. It is important to appreciate just how controversial an area this is. If you ask your lecturers whether the United Kingdom has a constitution, you might receive a number of very different responses. This is because many academics argue that the United Kingdom does not have a constitution. They argue that this is because it is not codified, i.e. written down in a single document such as the constitution of the United States of America. So, does this mean that the United Kingdom's constitution is unwritten? Technically large parts of what we consider constitutional sources are written down, such as important statutes (Acts of Parliament). However, other sources of the constitution are unwritten, such as constitutional conventions. Writing in 1996 Stephen M Griffin observed that '[s]ome scholars have seen a convergence . . . between the "written" American Constitution and the "unwritten" British constitution. As the British constitution became more written and formalized over time, the American Constitution became encrusted with political compromise and judicial interpretation.'[11] This means that over 20 years ago a leading US academic regarded the UK's constitution as becoming more written. Today this trend has greatly increased, and this will be addressed throughout this book. The following table provides some examples of this:

Table 1.1 Status of important constitutional principles

Important constitutional principle	Historically it was unwritten	Today it is written
The Prime Minister's ability to call a general election.	Historically unwritten as a constitutional convention.	This is now written as the rules about calling a general election are outlined in the Fixed-term Parliaments Act 2011. Please note the Fixed-term Parliaments Act 2011 will soon be repealed.
Holding a vote of no confidence in the government.	Historically unwritten as a constitutional convention.	This is now written as the rules about votes of no confidence are found in the Fixed-term Parliaments Act 2011. The obligations are outlined in the Cabinet Manual.
A duty upon the Prime Minister and Lord Chancellor to uphold the rule of law.	Historically unwritten although judicial decisions were clear as to the importance of the rule of law.	This is outlined in the Constitutional Reform Act 2005.
The UK Parliament will not legislate in devolved matters for Scotland.	Historically unwritten as a constitutional convention.	This is now written and set out in the Scotland Act 2016.
The convention of collective ministerial responsibility.	Historically unwritten as a constitutional convention.	The obligations are outlined in the Cabinet Manual.

This chapter will explore whether the United Kingdom has a constitution, and in doing this we will look at the key features of a constitution and see how these apply against the United Kingdom. We will also look at the history of the United Kingdom and consider how the country was created and the events that significantly impacted upon its constitutional system. In recent times the two most significant events have involved referendums which are very rare and only have been used since the 1970s.

PUBLIC LAW IN CONTEXT
TWO REFERENDUMS (2014 AND 2016)

In September 2014, the Scottish electorate voted to remain as part of the United Kingdom. Prior to the referendum on Scottish independence there was considerable uncertainty over what would happen if Scotland voted to become independent. This included whether the United Kingdom would require a new flag, whether Scotland would be able to join the European Union, and whether there would be a currency union between Scotland and the rest of the United Kingdom. The decision to vote 'no' means that Scotland will now have more powers devolved from the United Kingdom Parliament to the Scottish Parliament. Before the vote took place the leaders of the three main political parties promised to devolve more powers to Scotland. The Conservative party also wished to address the West Lothian question, which is where Scottish MPs are able to vote on matters that only affect England because this type of decision has been devolved to Scotland. One consequence of greater devolution is the English Votes for English Laws (EVEL) procedure in the House of Commons, whereby Members of Parliament (MPs) from non-English constituencies do not vote on laws that only affect England. Please note that EVEL is now being abolished. True this is not a significant step towards an English Parliament, but it was in itself a significant development in redressing the perceived unfairness of English MPs not getting to vote over devolved issues, but MPs for the devolved nations being able to vote on laws that affected England. Finally, greater devolution may lead to the creation of an English Parliament and the creation of regional assemblies or giving more power to local authorities. The recent pandemic caused by Covid-19 has seen the four nations that make up the United Kingdom each adopt separate rules for regulating how people behave (i.e. how far they could travel) and the Prime Minister was only responsible for England, not the whole United Kingdom.[12]

In June 2016, the British people were asked whether the United Kingdom should remain part of the European Union. The electorate by a narrow majority voted to leave (this decision is known as Brexit). The referendum was only advisory and was not legally binding. This meant that it would have been legally possible to remain a member of the European Union.

The constitutional history of the United Kingdom is relevant to the modern day and you will need to understand these key events and the impact of devolution to Scotland, Wales and Northern Ireland in 1998. We will explore below the key developments in the United Kingdom's constitutional history.

What is meant by a
'constitution'?

The constitutional history
of the United Kingdom

Key features of a
constitution

Does the United Kingdom
have a constitution?

Characteristics of a
constitution

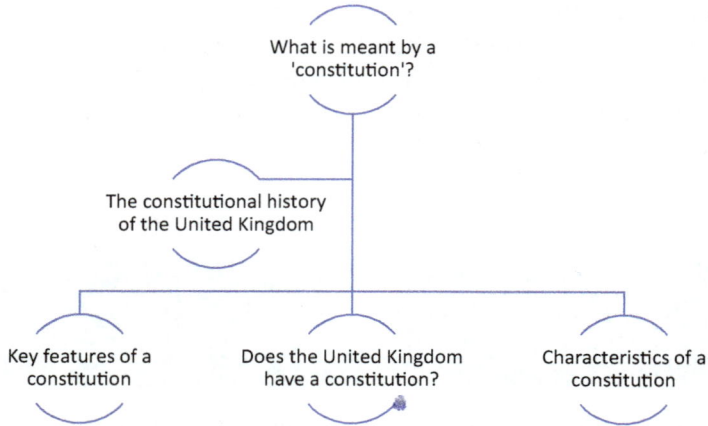

Figure 1.1
Chapter outline

1.2 What is meant by a constitution?

What is a constitution? A cricket club, a law society and a company can have a constitution; this word is not used exclusively in relation to a country and its institutions. On any level of its use, a constitution is the key rules and requirements by which the club, society or company are governed, and how the members, directors and shareholders understand their respective rights and duties. At a national level a constitution is a collection of rules, practices, laws which relate to the political life of a country and sometimes to the key rights enjoyed by its citizens. A constitution is intended to regulate government and it will contain the rules how the courts, the legislature and the executive operate, the rules about elections, the power of the head of state and protection from police and executive oppression.

Sir John Laws, a former Lord Justice of Appeal, observed that a constitution:

> [M]ean[s] that set of laws which in a sovereign State establish the relationship between the ruler and the ruled. It must therefore set the conditions by which the rule is defined, specify the principal organs of government (in Western models the legislature, executive and judiciary), and prescribe their powers and duties.[13]

Professor Anthony King questioned whether the United Kingdom has a constitution and stated that:

> A constitution is the set of the most important rules that regulate the relations among the different parts of the government of a given country and also relations between the different parts of the government and the people of the country.[14]

Viscount Bolingbroke, who was an important 18th-century politician, provided another definition of what is meant by a constitution:

By Constitution we mean, whenever we speak with propriety and exact-ness, that assemblage of laws, institutions, and customs, derived from certain fixed principles of reason . . . that compose the general system, according to which the community hath agreed to be governed.[15]

There are difficulties in defining what exactly falls within constitutional law and the academic writer FF Ridley noted that constitutional law textbooks 'cover a selection of laws that appear important to the author, together with important conventions and often a reduced version of the topics treated by institutionally oriented political scientists.'[16] There is some truth in this, as we shall see when we look at the sources of the constitution in **Chapter 2**.

Many people equate a constitution with a written document, which is codified and protected by the law. An example of this is the United States constitution, where the constitution is protected by a special status of con-stitutional law and cannot be amended unless through a special procedure.[17] If the federal government or Congress acts in a way that is incompatible with the constitution, then they are said to be acting unconstitutionally and the United States Supreme Court can challenge their actions. Importantly, the United States Supreme Court can declare an Act of Congress to be void.[18] The United Kingdom does not have a written codified constitution, and there is no special status of constitutional law.[19] This means that any legal features of the constitution, such as Acts of Parliament, can be repealed by Parliament. The United Kingdom Supreme Court has limited powers in comparison to the United States Supreme Court and cannot declare an Act of Parliament to be void. We shall see the reason for this in **Chapter 5**, where we will consider what is meant by Parliamentary Sovereignty.

PUBLIC LAW IN CONTEXT
WHAT PARLIAMENT COULD DO TO THE CONSTITUTION

If the United Kingdom does not accord 'constitutional law' a special status, then why do student lawyers need to study constitutional and administrative law? The answer is that much of what is covered in this book is of a legal nature, and the political material is essential to understanding how this law works. It is worth remembering that the law of the constitution (i.e. key statutes such as the Human Rights Act 1998) have the same legal status as any other law, despite their importance to our rights and political system. This means that no matter how important an Act of Parliament is – the Representation of the People Acts which extended the franchise so anyone aged over 18 (subject to exceptions) can vote – can be expressly repealed by another Act of Parliament.

This might seem outlandish as the very notion that a person because of their gender cannot vote is contrary to a modern democratic state. However, it was not until 1918 that women were permitted to vote, and it was only women aged 30, or over, who were given the vote by male politicians (the Representation of the People Act 1918). It would be perfectly possible (albeit unrealistic) for parliament to remove the ability of men to vote, to abolish human rights and to give the Prime Minister the power to sack any judges that she disagreed with.

Now that is not to say that the United Kingdom does not have a constitution; instead the sources of the constitution need to be identified from a range of sources. This will be explored below.

PUBLIC LAW IN CONTEXT
CONSTITUTIONAL 'IGNORANCE' OR TRYING TO DEFINE THE WORKINGS OF THE STATE?

Murray has considered the controversy surrounding the Article 50 litigation (*Miller (No. 1)*) and has questioned the extent to which people understand the nature of the United Kingdom's constitution:

> Among the lessons to be learned are that there was, and arguably remains, very considerable ignorance as to the fundamental principles of our constitution, as regards the nature of representative parliamentary sovereignty, the role of referendums and the role of the court in upholding the rule of law. This is a real weakness in our political system which needs to be corrected.[20]

This is not a criticism of the citizen, but rather the whole country, including the establishment and those who work within our government. It is always useful when first studying Public Law to ask yourself the following questions:

1. Prior to studying Public Law could I describe the features and characteristics United Kingdom's constitution?
2. Prior to studying Public Law was I aware that the United Kingdom did not have a written constitution?

Payne offered a similar criticism of the nature of the United Kingdom's constitution:

> The UK's constitution is obscure and open textured. The powers of the state are vested in the Crown, which is subject to diverse and contradictory interpretations of its identity. The obscurity of the UK constitution is dysfunctional and needs to be reformed by way of a written constitution. The shortcomings of the UK's unwritten common law constitution is illustrated in the Supreme Court's majority judgment in the 2017 Miller case.

1.3 The two types of constitutions

Whether the United Kingdom can be said to have a constitution will be discussed below, with reference to the features and characteristics of constitutions generally. At this point, it should be emphasised that we can identify the features of the constitution, and even if there were a written constitution on display at the British Library, then as Anthony King has argued, it would be unlikely that this formal document would contain the entire constitution.[21] King identified two types of constitution, the written Constitution (capital 'C'), and the unwritten constitution (small 'c'). King argued that there was an overlap between these two types of constitution in each state. King observed that a written constitution will cover much irrelevant material such as where the President must live, but will contain important omissions, such as how the electoral system would operate. However, these omissions are not left out of an unwritten constitution: '[n]o small-c constitution is, or could possibly be, silent on the subject: every democratic country has, and must have, some kind of electoral system.'[22] King observed that the United States' capital-C constitution makes no reference to the power of the United States Supreme Court to declare an Act of Congress void.[23]

1.4 The key features of the United Kingdom's constitution

The key features of the United Kingdom's constitution are the observance of the rule of law, the importance of the separation of powers and the fact that Parliament is legally sovereign. We shall briefly look at the key features of the United Kingdom's constitution.

1.4.1 Parliamentary sovereignty

Parliamentary Sovereignty means that the Acts of Parliament created by the United Kingdom Parliament are the highest source of law. These are higher than important judicial decisions, case law, or the royal prerogative. Parliamentary Sovereignty means that Parliament can make or change any law that it wishes, regardless of the subject matter of that. For example, Parliament could repeal the Human Rights Act 1998, abolish universal suffrage, or extend the lifetime of parliament to 50 years. Such legislation would be highly controversial, and the abolition of universal suffrage would be seen as anti-democratic and risk reducing a large number of people to becoming unequal in terms of their political rights. Parliament has extended the franchise, thus creating universal suffrage, and therefore in theory it could withdraw the franchise from certain sections of society. No matter what the Act of Parliament intends to do, the courts must give effect to an Act of Parliament and cannot declare it to be void. In **Chapter 5** we shall see the courts must apply an Act of Parliament no matter how repugnant that particular law is. However, there are legal and political limitations that arguably restrict Parliament's ability to make or unmake whatever law it wishes, and these shall be explored in **Chapter 6**. Parliamentary Sovereignty is traditionally regarded as the most important feature of the United Kingdom's constitution and reflected the supremacy of Parliament over the monarchy and its prerogative powers. It is really important to note that it is only an Act of Parliament that is legally supreme and not Parliament, as a resolution of both Houses of Parliament is not law.

1.4.2 Observance of the rule of law

The observance of the rule of law means that the executive cannot act unless their powers are derived from law or the prerogative powers. Acting beyond their powers makes executive action illegal. Although there is a debate over whether a government is permitted to do anything, so long as it is not expressly prohibited, and this is known as the Ram Doctrine. The rule of law is a very important feature of the United Kingdom's constitution and we shall see in **Chapter 4** that it means a variety of different things. According to Lord Reed in *R (on the application of UNISON) v Lord Chancellor*[24] it meant that:

> At the heart of the concept of the rule of law is the idea that society is governed by law. Parliament exists primarily in order to make laws for society in this country. Democratic procedures exist primarily in order to ensure that the Parliament which makes those laws includes Members of Parliament who are chosen by the people of this country and are accountable to them. Courts exist in order to ensure that the laws made by Parliament, and the common law created by the courts themselves, are applied and enforced. That role includes ensuring that the executive branch of government carries out its functions in accordance with the law.[25]
>
> Put simply, the rule of law means that not only must the government and it agencies act within the law, the laws that Parliament makes *must* be procedurally proper, there needs to be an independent judiciary to apply this law, and the law *must* be good law. You might appreciate that the last sentence raises a number of important questions. Firstly, if Parliament is legally sovereign then why *must* it create laws that are procedurally proper and good laws, as opposed to any law that it wishes to create? Secondly, what is a good law? Arguably some laws can be regarded by most people as good or bad, such as a law permitting genocide. However, it is not always that clear cut and certain laws will attract different interpretations as to whether they are to be considered good or bad. Thirdly, if the rule of law is a very important feature of the United Kingdom's constitution then what happens if Parliament creates legislation that is contrary to the rule of law? Lady Hale, the President of the Supreme Court, asked this question in 2019, '[b]ut might we sometimes have to stand up *to* Parliament? This is a much trickier question, as the two governing principles of our Constitution are the rule of law and the sovereignty of Parliament. The crunch comes when the two might be seen to be in conflict.'[26]

We shall see what happens when and if the 'two governing principles' clash in **Chapter 6**.

1.4.3 The separation of powers

The separation of powers sets out how the three governmental powers of a state are organised. According to the theory of the separation of powers, which is most associated with the French writer Montesquieu, the three branches of government – the executive (which is responsible for carrying out governmental functions), the legislature (which in the United Kingdom is Parliament and is responsible for making laws) and the judiciary (the courts which perform the judicial functions) – must be separate bodies and each of these comprising different people. The United Kingdom has never adhered to a strict version of the separation of powers and despite the enactment of the Constitutional Reform Act 2005 there remains considerable overlaps between the three powers and the functions they exercise and the personnel who carry out these functions. This is set out in **Chapter 3.**

1.4.4 Constitutional Monarchy

The United Kingdom's constitutional monarchy means that although the monarch is the head of state, the personal prerogative powers of the monarch are regulated by constitutional conventions. This is important because the monarch has a large number of important prerogative powers and if these were used in a way deemed to be unconstitutional, then this could lead to major political and social unrest or calls for a republic to be established. The important prerogative powers are regulated by constitutional conventions which are non-legal rules of the constitution and there are no legal sanctions in the event that they are broken. We will look at constitutional conventions in **Chapter 2** when we explore the sources of the United Kingdom's constitution.

PUBLIC LAW IN PRACTICE
THE IMPORTANCE OF THE CONSTITUTIONAL MONARCHY

An example of the importance of having a constitutional monarchy is that the monarch, Elizabeth II, has the prerogative power to appoint the Prime Minister. However, as a matter of constitutional convention she must appoint the person who commands the confidence of the House of Commons to lead her government. This means that if Party A gains a majority of seats in the House of Commons, then it would be unconstitutional for the monarch to appoint the leader of Party B as her Prime Minister. As a matter of constitutional convention, the monarch has little choice, albeit potentially such a choice would exist in the event of a hung Parliament where no political party could command the confidence of the House of Commons.

As we will see these key features are not established by a codified constitution; rather they have developed gradually as part of the United Kingdom's constitution.

1.5 The constitutional history of the United Kingdom

In order to understand the evolution of the constitution, it is important to appreciate the historical origins of the United Kingdom. The events discussed below will be relevant to the topics covered in this book, and so it is helpful to briefly consider some of the key constitutional events of the last thousand years (see Figure 1.2). It is important that you are familiar with the terminology used in this book. The Kingdoms of England and Scotland only united to form Great Britain in 1707. Prior to this they were separate countries, despite sharing the same monarch since 1603. England and Scotland had their own legal systems (which they still do), national Parliaments (note the creation of the Scottish Parliament in 1998), currencies and governments. In 1801, the Kingdom of Ireland and Great Britain united to form the United Kingdom of Great Britain and Ireland. This led to the abolition of the Irish Parliament and Irish parliamentarians sitting in the Westminster Parliament. In 1927, the country's name was changed to the United Kingdom of Great Britain and Northern Ireland, to reflect the independence of Southern Ireland. For a time, the new Irish state remained within the British Commonwealth and shared a monarch with the United Kingdom.

1.5.1 The Kingdom of England

England's first king was Egbert in 827. Prior to this England comprised a number of rival kingdoms ruled by Saxons and Vikings. A number of Saxon and

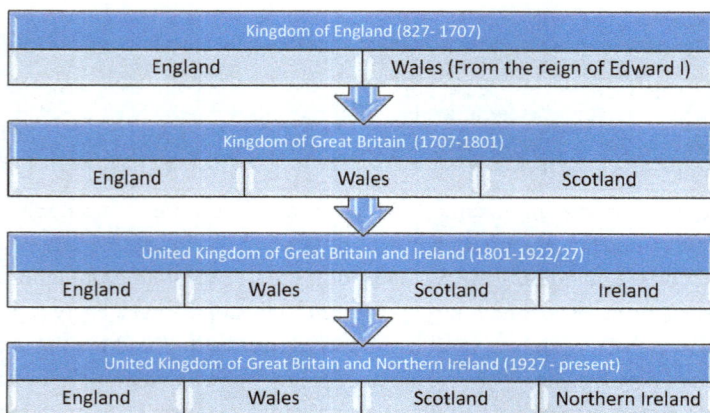

Kingdom of England (827- 1707)	
England	Wales (From the reign of Edward I)

Kingdom of Great Britain (1707-1801)		
England	Wales	Scotland

United Kingdom of Great Britain and Ireland (1801-1922/27)			
England	Wales	Scotland	Ireland

United Kingdom of Great Britain and Northern Ireland (1927 - present)			
England	Wales	Scotland	Northern Ireland

Figure 1.2
An overview of the key national developments

Danish kings ruled England until 1066, when Duke William of Normandy invaded England and seized the English throne. The Normans inherited a quite sophisticated English legal system, which did not exist in their Norman homeland. The Normans spoke French, whilst the native English spoke English and resented being ruled by a foreign power. The Plantagenet dynasty followed the Normans and the kingdom of Henry I included much of France, England and parts of Ireland. Henry's youngest son John managed to lose most of his French territory and from then onwards the focus of the kingdom was England. John was unpopular with his barons and faced a major revolt, which led to England being invaded by the French.

1.5.2 The Magna Carta

King John was forced to give his assent to the Magna Carta at Runnymede in 1215. The rebel barons wanted to prevent the king from abusing his power and stated that the king could not raise taxation without the barons' consent. The Magna Carta was annulled by the pope and John died whilst campaigning against the rebel barons. The Magna Carta was reissued by John's grandson Edward I, and is regarded as the first quasi-constitutional document in medieval history. John has a reputation as a 'bad king' and was viewed by later historians as oppressive.

1.5.3 The first Parliament

The first Parliament met in 1258 at Oxford and, as we will see in **Chapter 6**, the composition, freedoms and power of Parliament would gradually develop, so that soon no king could rule his country without the assent of Parliament. Parliament soon gained the important ability to approve the king's requests for taxation and therefore could hold royal advisors to account for how money was spent and military successes. In 1376, the first impeachments took place during the Good Parliament, whereby the House of Commons accused the king's advisors of essentially negligence and corruption and they were tried before the House of Lords.[27] Impeachment was a powerful device and could be

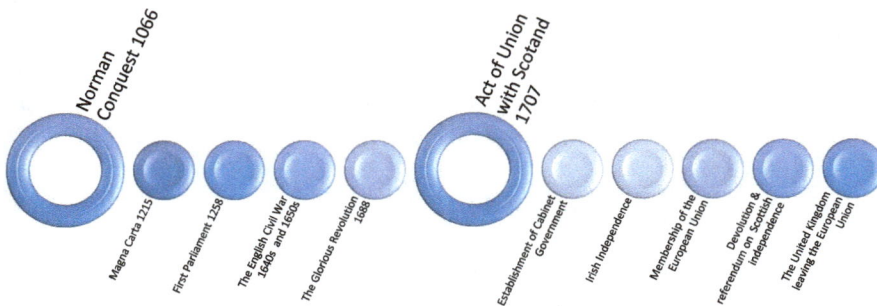

Figure 1.3
Key historical events

used independently of the monarch and against his most powerful advisors and friends. The last medieval impeachment took place in 1450 during the reign of Henry VI.

1.5.4 The Tudors

The Tudor dynasty lasted from 1485 to 1603. The first Tudor monarch Henry VII defeated Richard III at the Battle of Bosworth and claimed the throne. Henry VII did much to reform England and in 1509 he was succeeded by his son Henry VIII. Henry VIII merged Wales with England in the 1540s, and crowned himself as King of Ireland. This created a formal union between England and Wales, and a personal union with Ireland. Henry VIII created the Church of England when he broke with the Roman Catholic Church in the 1530s. Henry's death led to uncertainty over religion, as he was succeeded by his three children, Edward VI who was a Protestant, Mary I who was a Catholic and Elizabeth I who was a Protestant. The power of Parliament decreased during the reigns of Henry VII and Henry VIII, although it remerged during the reign of Elizabeth I, who governed through her Privy Council. Elizabeth's reign saw the excommunication of the queen by the pope, the execution of Mary Queen of Scots in 1587 and the defeat of the Spanish Armada in 1588.[28]

1.5.5 The Stuarts

After the death of Elizabeth I in 1603, the English Crown passed to James VI of Scotland. James was the son of Mary Queen of Scots, a granddaughter of Henry VII, who Elizabeth had executed in 1587. James ruled as King of England and King of Scotland. The kings of Scotland had successfully repelled English invasions and had maintained an independent nation. James I founded the Stuart dynasty in England and believed in the divine right of kings. This meant that the king believed he received his authority to rule directly from God and was thus superior to all laws. James failed to unite his thrones in a formal union and until 1707 the two kingdoms were only united by a personal union, which meant that they only shared a king.[29] Under James' son, Charles I, the Crown and the king's use of the prerogative clashed with Parliament and the supremacy of an Act of Parliament. Unable to work with Parliament, Charles I ruled without calling a Parliament for over a decade. During this time Charles relied on his prerogative powers to raise money, as direct taxation could only be raised with Parliamentary approval. This led to three Civil Wars in the 1640s and 1650s. Charles I was captured and tried for High Treason by Parliament. He was executed in 1649.

1.5.6 The Commonwealth and the Restoration

After Charles I's execution the monarchy was abolished, and Oliver Cromwell and Parliament ruled England and Scotland as one state during the Commonwealth. Cromwell was known as the Lord Protector and refused to be crowned as king. After Cromwell's death he was succeeded by his son Richard. However,

Richard's rule did not last long and the monarchy was restored in 1660. Charles II became king in 1660 and ruled until 1685. He had an uncomfortable relationship with Parliament. Charles II was succeeded by his Catholic brother, James II, who then attempted to repeal the Test Acts which discriminated against Catholics and used his prerogative powers to dispense with Acts of Parliament.

1.5.7 The Glorious Revolution

James II was forced to flee to France in 1688 when Parliament invited his son-in-law William of Orange to invade England. This was interpreted as James abdicating the English throne. This is known as the Glorious Revolution and marks the supremacy of Parliament over the monarchy. In 1689, Parliament offered the throne to William and his wife Mary upon acceptance of the Declaration of Right. From then on Parliament has determined the issue of royal succession. The 1689 Bill of Rights protected the right of Parliament and protected parliamentary privilege, which permits freedom of expression in Parliament. This means that an MP can speak in the House of Commons without fear of being prosecuted or sued. In Scotland, William and Mary were offered the Scottish throne in 1689 upon the acceptance of the Claim of Right.

1.5.8 The Kingdom of Great Britain

Great Britain was created by the English Union with Scotland Act in 1706, and the Scottish Union with England Act 1707 (this had been agreed under the Treaty of Union 1706). These Acts are collectively known as the Acts of Union 1707. England and Scotland were to be joined to create one country, with a shared Parliament and monarch. Anne I of England (who was also Anne I of Scotland), became Anne I of Great Britain. The Scottish and English Parliaments voted to abolish themselves and a new Parliament would meet at Westminster. It would comprise members from England and Scotland. Scotland and England were to have separate legal systems but would be ruled as one country. Many Scots were unhappy and there were claims that Scottish parliamentarians had to be bribed to vote in favour. The union was important to prevent the kingdoms of England and Scotland from having different monarchs in the future.

1.5.9 The Hanoverians and the development of Cabinet government

After Anne died, the throne passed to a distant relative, George of Hanover. George I spoke limited English and left the business of government to his Cabinet. Sir Robert Walpole presided over the Cabinet meetings and is generally known as the first Prime Minister. Under George II and George III, there was the development of Cabinet government with the business of state being run by the government, rather than under the monarch's direction. The political system which operated in the 1740s was admired by the French writer Montesquieu and influenced his writings on the separation of powers.[30]

1.5.10 The Kingdom of the United Kingdom of Great Britain and Ireland

The Union with Ireland Act 1800 created the United Kingdom of Great Britain and Ireland. The Irish Parliament was abolished, and Irish members were to join the Westminster Parliament. Many Irish nationalists were to resent being ruled from London and argued for Home Rule throughout the 19th and early 20th centuries.

During the 19th century there was a reform of the electoral system under the Reform Acts, which increased the electoral franchise and abolished the rotten boroughs. The enlargement of the electoral franchise has resulted in all men and women over the age of 18 (subject to limited restrictions) being able to vote. The legislation passed to achieve this will be discussed in **Chapter 6**. There was the development of the constitutional monarchy and the dominance of the political executive in governing the country. The legal system was transformed by the Judicature Acts 1873 and 1875, which merged the common law and equitable system. The Appellate Jurisdiction Act 1876 established the Appellate Committee of the House of Lords and created the Lords of Appeal in Ordinary, or the Law Lords. During this period the British Empire expanded to include one-quarter of the world, and eventually Canada, New Zealand, Australia and South Africa received their independence as self-governing dominions.

1.5.11 The Kingdom of the United Kingdom of Great Britain and Northern Ireland

In 1922, the Irish Free State received independence and in 1927 the Royal and Parliamentary Titles Act changed the name of the United Kingdom to the United Kingdom of Great Britain and Northern Ireland. Southern Ireland was independent and only Northern Ireland remained part of the United Kingdom.

1.5.12 Membership of the European Union

The United Kingdom finally became a member of the European Economic Community (now the European Union) in 1973, which was as a result of Parliament enacting the European Communities Act 1972. Parliament passed the European Communities Act 1972 to facilitate the United Kingdom's membership of the European Economic Community. Membership of the European Union has had an important impact on the United Kingdom's law and constitution. We shall see the significance of this in **Chapter 6**, when we discuss Parliamentary Sovereignty.

1.5.13 Devolution and the referendum on Scottish independence

In 1998, Scotland and Wales received devolved powers. In Northern Ireland, the Northern Ireland Act 1998 returned devolved powers, which had been suspended in 1974 as a consequence of the 'Troubles,' to Stormont.

The Scotland Act 1998 created a Scottish Parliament with the power to make legislation for Scotland, and a Scottish government which would govern Scotland using the powers devolved from Westminster. The Government of Wales Act 1998 created the National Assembly of Wales and a Welsh government. Devolution did not affect the integrity of the United Kingdom, as Scotland and Wales did not become independent. Rather, powers were being devolved from Westminster to a local level. However, post 1998, more powers have been devolved and there are calls for increased powers to be given to the Scottish Parliament.

In the 2011 elections for the Scottish Parliament, the Scottish National Party won a majority and called for a referendum on Scottish independence in 2014. In 2012, the United Kingdom and Scottish governments agreed that a referendum on Scottish independence would be held in 2014. In September 2014 the people of Scotland voted to remain as part of the United Kingdom. The leaders of the three main political parties (Conservatives, Labour and Liberal Democrats) have promised to devolve more powers to the Scottish Parliament. The Scotland Act 2016 increases the areas that are to be devolved to Scotland.

PUBLIC LAW IN CONTEXT
THE IMPLICATIONS OF SCOTTISH INDEPENDENCE

If the Scottish people had voted in support of independence, then an Act of Parliament would have been required to grant Scotland its independence. Scottish independence would have created an independent Scotland and a fully sovereign Scottish Parliament at Holyrood. The Scottish executive would have governed, and the Queen would have become Elizabeth I of Scotland. Civil servants working in Scotland would have been transferred from the United Kingdom's civil service to the Scottish civil service. The military would transfer assets and personnel to Scotland and the Queen would have become the head of the Scottish armed forces. Independence would not affect the judiciary (with the exception of the Supreme Court's current role), as Scotland has a distinct legal system to that of England and Wales. Scotland would either by default, or upon a formal application, have become a member of the European Union.

However, many opponents of Scottish independence warned that Scotland may have found it difficult to become a member of the European Union as the other 28 members would have to formally approve Scotland's membership. Scotland could have become a member of the Council of Europe (and, if it wished to, have the European Convention on Human Rights [ECHR] incorporated into domestic Scottish law).

1.5.14 Devolution for England?

England has not been affected by devolution in the sense that it does not have regional assemblies or a devolved Parliament. The West Lothian question remained unanswered at the time of the original devolution settlement and this meant that every MP can vote on matters that affect England and many people

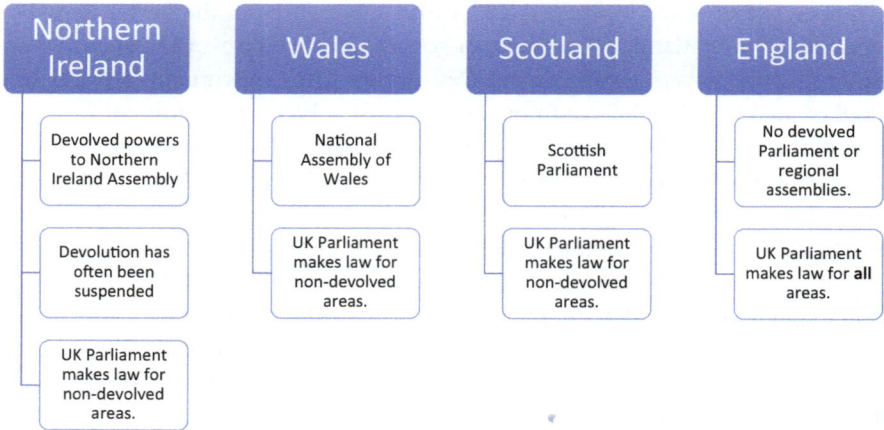

Figure 1.4
Devolution and England

regarded this as unfair, since English MPs could not vote on devolved matters in Scotland or Wales. Some commentators argued for the creation of an English Parliament to decide exclusively English matters. In 2018, Professor Meg Russell and Jack Sheldon wrote a detailed report 'Options for an English Parliament' on behalf of the Constitution Unit in which they inter alia 'explore[d] the issues that would need to be considered if seeking to create such a body, and some of the available options.'[31]

The decision of the Scottish electorate in 2014 to remain part of the United Kingdom inevitably led to the West Lothian question being addressed. The West Lothian question relates to questions asked by Tam Dalyell MP (West Lothian, Scotland) about whether in the event of devolution, Scottish Members of Parliament should be able to vote on matters which only concerned England – the point being that England would have been the only nation in the United Kingdom not to have had a devolved assembly. The creation of a devolved English Parliament may be one solution; however, it, like the other proposed solutions, remains controversial. However, a compromise in the form of English Votes for English Laws, which is known as EVEL, was introduced to allow only English MPs the right to vote on matters that only concerned England.[32] The introduction of EVEL has been criticised by the leading constitutional commentator, Professor Vernon Bogdanor.[33] Please note that EVEL has recently been abolished. There has also been an increase in the number of directly elected Mayors in English cities, such as in Bristol and in Birmingham.

1.5.15 Brexit or the United Kingdom leaving the European Union

Before the 2015 General Election, David Cameron, the Prime Minister, promised to hold a referendum on the United Kingdom's membership of the European Union in the event that the Conservative party won a majority and could govern without being in a coalition with the Liberal Democrats. To the surprise of commentators and perhaps the Prime Minister, the Conservative party won a majority and could govern alone. The House of Commons approved the 2016 referendum on the United Kingdom's membership of the European Union and there were two official groups representing the Remain and Vote Leave campaigns. The referendum was only advisory and was not binding on Parliament. The government campaigned for the United Kingdom to remain a member of the European Union. The Vote Leave campaign won by a narrow victory and in response David Cameron resigned as Prime Minister and was subsequently replaced by the then Home Secretary, Theresa May.

In order for the United Kingdom to leave the European Union the British government needed to trigger Article 50 of the Treaty on European Union. Once Article 50 was triggered the United Kingdom would automatically leave the European Union within two years. However, the problem was that many observers argued that the government could not use its residual prerogative powers to trigger Article 50. This was because Article 50 would remove many legal rights enjoyed by United Kingdom citizens and these rights were incorporated into domestic law by the European Communities Act 1972. As a matter of constitutional law the prerogative cannot be used in a way that would either impose new obligations or take away people's rights. The matter reached the High Court which held in *R (on the application of Miller) v Secretary of State for Exiting the European Union (No. 1)*[34] that the prerogative could not be used to trigger Article 50 and instead the government needed the approval of Parliament. The government appealed and a majority of the Supreme Court upheld the High Court's decision.[35] This meant that Parliament was required to enact the European Union (Notification of Withdrawal) Act 2017 to confer the authority upon the Prime Minister to trigger Article 50.

PUBLIC LAW IN CONTEXT
THE EUROPEAN UNION (NOTIFICATION OF WITHDRAWAL) ACT 2017

The European Union (Notification of Withdrawal) Act 2017 contained two sections and the first section stated:

1   The Prime Minister may notify, under Article 50(2) of the Treaty on European Union, the United Kingdom's intention to withdraw from the EU.
2   This section has effect despite any provision made by or under the European Communities Act 1972 or any other enactment.

The inclusion of subsection (2) was required to legislate contrary to the European Communities Act 1972. The reason for this will be outlined in **Chapter 6**, in which we will look at the decision in *Factortame (No 2)*[36] and the self-imposed restriction on Parliament's ability to impliedly legislate contrary to European Union law.

The European Union (Withdrawal) Act 2018 was intended to repeal the European Communities Act when the United Kingdom left the European Union. The date for exiting the European Union was stated to be 29 March 2019. However, the United Kingdom had to seek an extension from the European Union as the House of Commons could not agree on how the United Kingdom should leave.

1.6 Recent constitutional developments

This next section will look at recent constitutional developments that have taken place over the past 20 or so years.

1.6.1 The Labour government (1997–2010)

The Labour government (1997–2010) that came into power under Tony Blair in 1997 embarked on a series of important constitutional reforms.

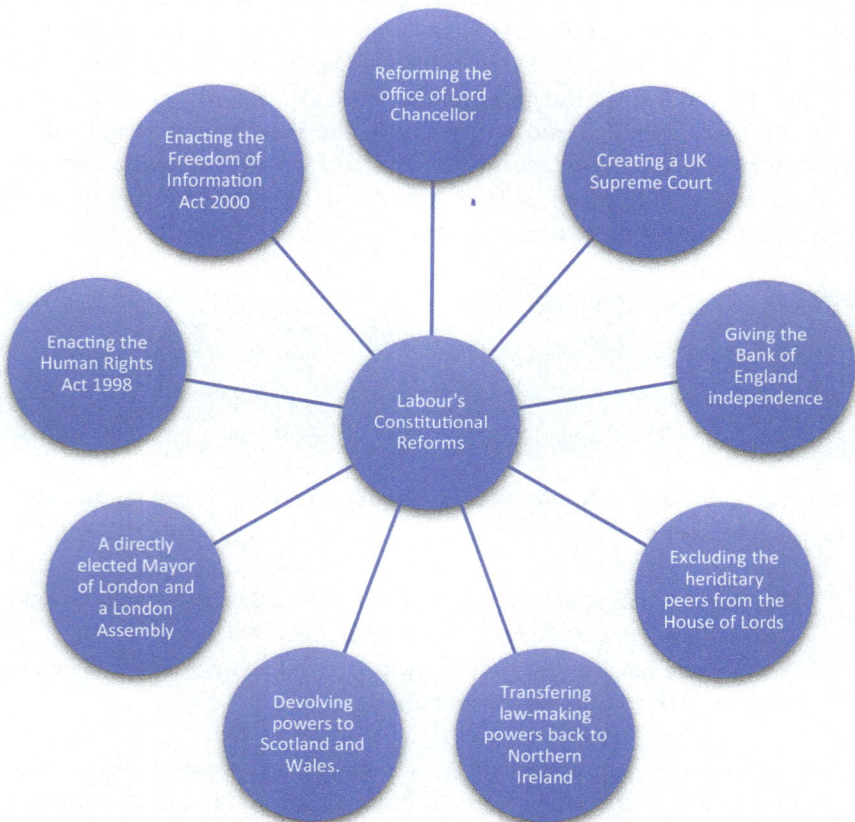

Figure 1.5
Labour's constitutional reforms

ACADEMIC DEBATE

Academics have commented on the significance of the reforms. Leyland observed that, '[t]he radical constitutional reform embarked upon by the Blair government elected in 1997 changed the complexion of the UK constitution. In many respects it has come to look much more like a codified constitution.'[37] Brazier rejected the idea that the reforms have brought the United Kingdom towards a codified constitution, as many key areas of the constitution were left untouched by the reforms.[38] Instead Brazier regarded the constitution as becoming more written:

> In implementing its range of reforms the Labour Government has caused Parliament to enact an additional and substantial corpus of statute law of a constitutional character. While, therefore, the United Kingdom still lacks a codified constitution, it has been given rather more of a written constitution by the addition of sixteen Acts of Parliament which, in whole or in part, add to the British constitution.[39]

The reforms introduced by the Labour government have changed many aspects of the constitution:

- The House of Lords Act 1999 resulted in the removal of all but 92 of the hereditary peers from the second chamber. Whilst this was an important reform as it meant that anyone who had inherited a title no longer could sit as a member of the House of Lords, the Act did not remove the Church of England Bishops who sit in the chamber, nor did it do anything to introduce an element of directly elected peers. Today there are still 92 hereditary peers in the House of Lords and in the event of a hereditary peer dying other hereditary peers can stand for election to become members of the House of Lords. The majority of peers are Life Peers who are appointed under the Life Peerages Act 1958 and are appointed for the duration of their lifetime. Upon their death their descendants do not inherit the title and therefore are not permitted to become members of the House of Lords. The majority of life peers are political appointments, having been nominated by a political party. However, a significant number of life peers sit as cross-benchers, i.e. the independent members of the House of Lords.
- The Constitutional Reform Act 2005. This Act created the Supreme Court, removed many of the powers of the Lord Chancellor, reinforced the independence of the judiciary and made the Lord Chief Justice of England and Wales the head of the judiciary in England and Wales. The Act did much to give effect to the separation of powers between the judicial and the other two branches of government. The original intention had been to abolish the office of Lord Chancellor. However, this proved too difficult and a new position was created, Secretary of State for Justice, to take over the Lord Chancellor's remaining duties. The Secretary of State for Justice and the

Lord Chancellor are the same person. The Constitutional Reform Act 2005 abolished the Appellate Committee of the House of Lords, which was then the highest court in the United Kingdom and replaced it with a Supreme Court. The Supreme Court is located in the former Middlesex Guildhall which is opposite the Houses of Parliament. Importantly the Lord Chancellor will no longer nominate judges and the role of recruiting judges has been taken over by the Judicial Appointments Commission.

- The Devolution Acts 1998 (Scotland Act 1998 and Government of Wales Act 1998). These Acts introduced devolution and created the Scottish Parliament and the National Assembly of Wales. The Northern Ireland Act 1998 reintroduced devolved powers to Northern Ireland, previously these devolved powers had been removed during the Troubles, and Northern Ireland been directly governed from Westminster.

- The Human Rights Act 1998. The Act was significant as it meant that much of the European Convention on Human Rights was directly incorporated into domestic law. Since October 2000, individuals no longer have to go to the European Court of Human Rights in Strasbourg to enforce their convention rights. This is important as public authorities are not permitted to violate Convention rights and if they do so, then they can be sued in domestic courts.

- The Freedom of Information Act 2000. This Act was intended to create open government and increase executive accountability.

- The Bank of England 1998 was important as it established the independence of the Bank of England to act independently of the Treasury. The Bank of England is responsible for setting the interest rate.

- The Greater London Authority Act 1999. This Act created the directly elected Mayor of London and the London Assembly. The mayor has a significant public profile and a former mayor, Boris Johnson, went on to become the Prime Minister. However, there is debate over how successful the reforms have been.[40]

- The Constitutional Reform and Governance Act 2010. This Act placed the Civil Service, who are the people responsible for helping elected politicians to run government departments, on a statutory footing. Previously the Civil Service, which is politically neutral, was organised under the prerogative. The Act has also placed a statutory requirement on the government to lay proposed treaties before Parliament, rather than just having this obligation as a matter of constitutional convention (see **Chapter 2**).

1.6.2 The Coalition government (2010–2015)

A coalition government will come into being when no one political party is able to form a government on its own; it will need to form a coalition with another party. Coalition governments are common in countries such as Italy and Germany. However, in the United Kingdom they are very rare and the formation of the Conservative and Liberal Democrat coalition in 2010 was the first peace-time coalition government since the 1930s. In the 2010 General Election

Figure 1.6
The Coalition government

no political party secured a majority of seats in the House of Commons. The incumbent Labour government was unable to form a coalition with the Liberal Democrats, and instead the Conservatives and Liberal Democrats decided to form a coalition government. The Prime Minister, Gordon Brown, resigned and the Queen invited the leader of the Conservative Party, David Cameron, to form the next government. Nick Clegg, the leader of the Liberal Democrats, became Deputy Prime Minister. The Coalition government consisted of Conservative and Liberal Democrats ministers. Both the Liberal Democrats and Conservatives had their own party-political manifestos and subsequently agreed on a common set of policies that are contained in the Coalition Agreement. This meant that ministers from both political parties would have agreed on legislation introduced by the government. If politicians from one particular political party wished to have introduced non-coalition legislation then this would have had to be in the form of a Private Members' Bill.

The Coalition government proposed some important changes to the constitution:

- In 2011, there was a referendum on the voting system. The referendum asked voters if they wished to replace First Past the Post with the Alternative Vote. A majority of voters voted against changing the voting system. The referendum was permitted by the Parliamentary Voting System and Constituencies Act 2011.
- The government's 2011 White Paper laid out the plans to reform the House of Lords. It was proposed that the House of Lords will either be wholly elected or consist of partly appointed and partly elected members. However, due to opposition from within the Conservative Party the reforms did not take place during the 2010–15 Parliament. This was criticised as a breach of the Coalition Agreement by the Conservative's coalition partners, the Liberal Democrats. The gradual reform of the House of Lords and the Coalition government's aborted reforms will be discussed in **Chapter 7**. The House of Lords reform was abandoned by the Coalition government in 2012.
- The Coalition Agreement contained plans to change the constituency boundaries in the House of Commons and reduce the number of MPs. This was not achieved during the lifetime of the 2010–15 Parliament due to the Conservative opposition to House of Lords reform.
- In 2011, the Coalition government established a Commission on a Bill of Rights. This commission sought views as to whether the United Kingdom requires a Bill of Rights which would expand upon the European

Convention on Human Rights (ECHR). This could have led to additional rights to those that existed under the Human Rights Act 1998. The Commission's final report was inconclusive, although it stated that a Bill of Rights could be introduced in the future.

- The Fixed-term Parliaments Act 2011. The government introduced the Fixed-term Parliaments Act 2011, which, subject to exceptions, prevented a general election from being called until May 2015. This restricts the Prime Minister's ability to ask the Queen to use her prerogative powers to dissolve Parliament and call a General Election. Please note that the Fixed-term Parliaments Act 2011 will be repealed.

- The Succession to the Crown Act 2013. This Act amended the rules relating to royal succession and permitted the first-born child of a monarch, regardless of their gender, to become the next monarch. This would have prevented the first-born child of the Duke and Duchess of Cambridge from being prevented from becoming monarch had it been female, and their younger sibling had been born male. Sweden had already reformed its law to allow the eldest child to inherit the throne, regardless of gender, and this meant that the younger son would no longer be king, as the heir would be his older sister.

- The Crime and Courts Act 2013. This Act transferred more of the Lord Chancellor's responsibilities to the Lord Chief Justice of England and Wales. Although the Act also gave the Lord Chancellor the ability to have more involvement with appointments to the Supreme Court.

- The publication of the Cabinet Manual in 2011. This was an attempt to describe the workings of the United Kingdom's constitution and its aim is to '[set] out the main laws, rules and conventions affecting the conduct and operation of government.'

- Holding of the referendum on Scottish independence. The people of Scotland narrowly voted to remain part of the United Kingdom.

1.6.3 The Conservative governments (2015–present)

In May 2015, David Cameron's Conservative Party won a surprise majority in the House of Commons. The victory was a shock to many as there had been an expectation that the Coalition government would have continued due to no party securing a majority. In 2017, the new Conservative leader, Theresa May, sought the House of Commons' permission under the Fixed-term Parliaments Act 2011 to hold an early general election. The result was that the Conservative party lost its majority in the House of Commons and had to enter into a supply and confidence agreement with the Democratic Unionist Party. The government survived a vote of no confidence in 2019. In 2019, Theresa May was succeeded as Prime Minister by Boris Johnson, who won a majority in that year's general election. There have been significant constitutional reforms and developments since 2015, most notably Brexit:

- In 2012, the Prime Minister promised that a referendum on membership of the European Union would be held in the lifetime of the next Parliament.

With the Conservative party securing a majority in the 2015 general election the party was able to form a government without the Liberal Democrats, who saw their number of MPs substantially reduced. The European Union Referendum Act 2015 permitted an advisory referendum to take place on whether the United Kingdom should remain as a member of the European Union.

- In June 2015, a narrow majority voted in favour of the United Kingdom leaving the European Union. The government had campaigned in support of the United Kingdom's continued membership of the European Union. As a result, the Prime Minister, David Cameron, resigned and was replaced by Theresa May. In March 2017, Theresa May's government triggered Article 50 and notified the President of the European Council that the United Kingdom would be leaving the European Union.
- The European Union (Withdrawal) Act 2018 set out how the United Kingdom's law would operate following the United Kingdom's departure from the European Union. The Act repealed the European Communities Act 1972.
- The Human Rights Act 1998 has proved controversial and there is a possibility that the United Kingdom may decide to change its relationship with the European Court of Human Rights. In 2013, the difficulties on deporting Abu Qatada to Jordan led senior figures in the government to discuss the possibility of temporarily withdrawing from the ECHR. In September 2014, the then Prime Minister, David Cameron, announced that a future Conservative government would repeal the Human Rights Act 1998 and replace it with a British Bill of Rights. In light of Brexit and the ongoing Covid-19 pandemic, it is unlikely that this will happen during the lifetime of the present Parliament.
- In 2019, the Conservative party's manifesto for the general election proposed constitutional reforms.[41] These reforms included promising to abolish the Fixed-term Parliaments Act 2011, reforming the size of boundaries for MPs constituencies, maintain First Past the Post as an electoral methods for the House of Commons, keeping the voting age at 18, promoting freedom of expression and establishing a Constitution, Democracy and Rights Commission. In addition, the manifesto provided that

> We will update the Human Rights Act and administrative law to ensure that there is a proper balance between the rights of individuals, our vital national security and effective government. We will ensure that judicial review is available to protect the rights of the individuals against an overbearing state, while ensuring that it is not abused to conduct politics by another means or to create needless delays.

1.7 Key features of a constitution

We will now look at some key features of constitutions (see Figure 1.7). It is important to note that every country has its own unique constitution. For example, the United Kingdom's constitution is similar to Australia's because

United Kingdom	United States of America
Flexible	Rigid
Traditionally Unitary, but since devolution increasingly Federal	Federal
Bicameral	Bicameral
Monarchy	Republic
Uncodified constitution	Codified constitution
Fusion	Separation of powers

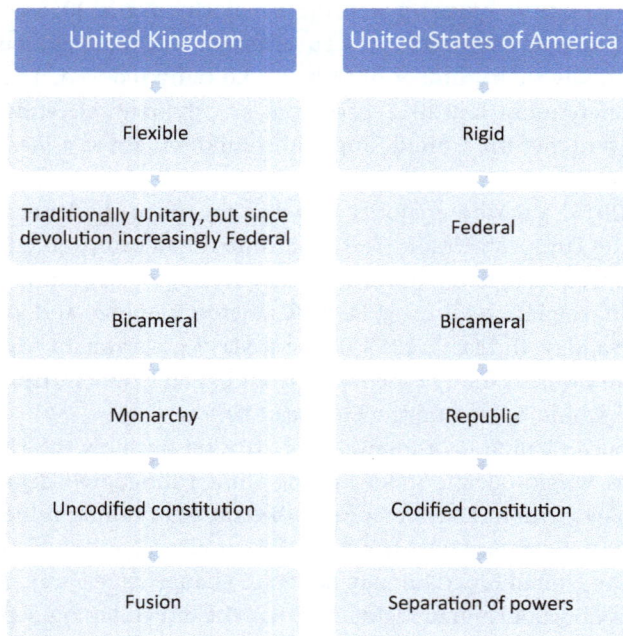

Figure 1.7
Key features of a constitution

there is a fusion between the executive and the legislature. However, there is also a key difference as, unlike the United Kingdom, Australia has a written constitution.

According to FF Ridley the characteristics of a constitution were that:

1   'It establishes, or constitutes, the system of government. Thus it is prior to the system of government, not part of it, and its rules can not be derived from that system.

2   'It therefore involves an authority outside and above the order it establishes. This is the notion of the constituent power. . . . In democracies that power is attributed to the people, on whose ratification the legitimacy of a constitution depends and, with it, the legitimacy of the governmental system.

3   'It is a form of law superior to other laws – because (i) it originates in an authority higher than the legislature which makes ordinary law and (ii) the authority of the legislature derives from it and is thus bound by it. The principle of hierarchy of law generally (but not always) leads to the possibility of judicial review of ordinary legislation.

4   'It is entrenched – (i) because its purpose is generally to limit the powers of government, but also (ii) again because of its origins in a higher authority outside the system. It can thus only be changed by special procedures, generally (and certainly for major change) requiring reference back to the constituent power.'[42]

ACADEMIC DEBATE

Having read the quote from FF Ridley above, we see that it is clear that he identified four necessary requirements for a constitution to exist. We shall see below that the United Kingdom does not meet all four requirements. Whether Ridley's four requirements are authoritative on what is essential for a constitution to exist has been vigorously debated. Ridley was dismissive of the United Kingdom having a constitution. He noted that the United Kingdom's Parliament created by the Acts of Union in 1707 'appears to have taken a sovereign power it was not given by the Act which constituted it.'[43] Therefore the United Kingdom's constitution does not establish the system of government, nor given Parliamentary Sovereignty can it be entrenched. We shall see in **Chapter 5** that Ridley's third characteristic does not exist, as Parliamentary Sovereignty negates the existence of superior form of constitutional law. After you have read this chapter it might be worthwhile considering whether you believe that Ridley's requirements must be met in order for there to be a constitution?

1.7.1 Rigid or flexible

A constitution can be rigid or flexible. A written constitution will more likely to be rigid, as the key provisions will often be 'entrenched.' This is less likely to be the case where the constitution is unwritten. Importantly, where the constitution is entrenched it will be harder to amend the constitution. This is because the constitution will often have a special legal status and cannot be amended by an Act of the legislature. The constitution will often lay down the requirements needed to amend the constitution. There might be a requirement for a referendum, where the electorate must vote in order to change the constitution. The referendum requirement is used in the Swiss constitution. The United Kingdom's constitution is flexible as it has evolved over hundreds of years. This flexibility can be viewed as a key strength of the constitution, meaning that it can develop to meet the requirements of a democracy. However, this flexibility can also be seen as dangerous because of the lack of safeguards to protect fundamental rights. As an alternative way of amending the constitution, there may be a requirement that there needs to a vote in the legislature of say 75 per cent to amend the constitution. Where such requirements exist, the constitution may not be amended unless these are complied with.

PUBLIC LAW IN CONTEXT
REFERENDUMS IN SWITZERLAND

The Swiss Federal Constitution establishes the use of referendums.[44] Article 138 of the constitution states that, 'Any 100,000 persons eligible to vote may within 18 months of the official publication of their initiative propose a total revision of the Federal Constitution' and that 'This proposal must be submitted to a vote of the People.' Article 139 deals with referendums for partial revisions of the constitution. There are certain times when particular reforms must be put before the electorate as a mandatory referendum[45], and those where it is optional to hold a referendum.[46] Article 142 sets out a referendum majority requirement of a majority of all voters and all Swiss Cantons, of which there are 23. The nearest that the United Kingdom has to the ability to debate changing the law is the petition system on Parliament's website.[47] Examples of referendums in Switzerland include the unsuccessful attempt to assert the supremacy of Swiss law over international law.[48]

The constitution may give the judiciary the power to ensure that the requirements are met and to prevent the legislature and executive acting in breach of the constitution. For example, the Israeli Supreme Court and the United States Supreme Court have given themselves the power to declare Acts of the legislature void. In *Marbury v Madison*[49], the United States Supreme Court claimed the power to declare an Act of Congress void, which is important as no such power had been conferred by the United States Constitution. However, the power of the Supreme Court to do this was accepted by those at the time and today is regarded as a key feature of the US Constitution, albeit it is not contained within the written constitution.

1.7.2 Federal or unitary

A constitution may be federal or unitary. Where a constitution is unitary there is only one level of government and that is at a national level. A federal constitution is one where all power is not controlled by the national government and Parliament; instead there is power sharing between the national state and the federal states which together form the country. Unlike devolution where these powers can be abolished by the national government, a federal system gives the states powers under the constitution.

In the United Kingdom there has traditionally been a unitary system (with the occasional exception of Northern Ireland), with power being centralised at Westminster and no separate layer of regional government for Scotland, Wales and the English regions. Prior to the creation of Great Britain in 1707, some commentators had argued for a different system to share power between Westminster and Edinburgh. This could have been done as a confederation between England and Scotland, rather than a full union.

The Labour government (1997–2010) devolved powers to Scotland, Wales, Northern Ireland and London. This has created a devolved system where Scotland, Wales and Northern Ireland have a legislature with devolved law-making powers. They each have a government to implement policy; however the powers conferred are determined by Westminster. London has a directly elected mayor, although elected mayors have not proved entirely positive elsewhere.

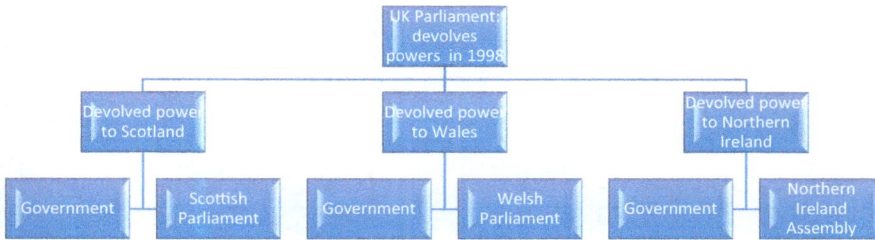

Figure 1.8
Devolution in the United Kingdom

The Mayor of London has been given devolved powers and there is an assembly with devolved legislative powers. Labour had intended to devolve powers to the English regions, but there was little public appetite for this idea. Brigid Hadfield has written that '[a] consideration of the devolved UK constitution may be placed within the perspective of the UK as a unitary state; this is, one in which popular power flows to and political power from the centrally located Parliament and government in London.'[50] Devolution has not created a federal system in the United Kingdom, as the powers are given and can be removed by Parliament (see Figure 1.7). This occurred in 1974 in Northern Ireland, and so legally the Scottish Parliament and government could be abolished by an Act of Parliament. However, the impact of devolution is that it might be more appropriate to describe the United Kingdom as somewhere between being a unitary and a federal state. In light of the outcome of the Scottish referendum in 2014, it is likely that there will be significant changes to the United Kingdom's constitution, which could possibly create a federal system and see powers devolved from the Westminster Parliament to England.

The impact of devolution has meant that it would not be correct to describe the United Kingdom as being a strictly unitary state. Instead, the United Kingdom would appear to be somewhere between unitary and federal. This is because of the existence of separate legislatures in Northern Ireland, Wales and Scotland.

The United States of America is a federal state

The United States of America has a federal constitution and each of the 50 states (California, New Jersey, etc.) has its own constitution (see Figure 1.9). The United States Constitution is based on power sharing between the federal and state government.

Before the American War of Independence (1776–83) each of the 13 American colonies had its own form of government. After gaining independence from Great Britain there were many people who wanted each colony to remain independent and not to create a federal state. They were known as anti-federalists, and consequentially, those who favoured unifying the 13 colonies were known as federalists. The United States constitution created a federal government with three distinct branches: the legislature, the executive and the judiciary.

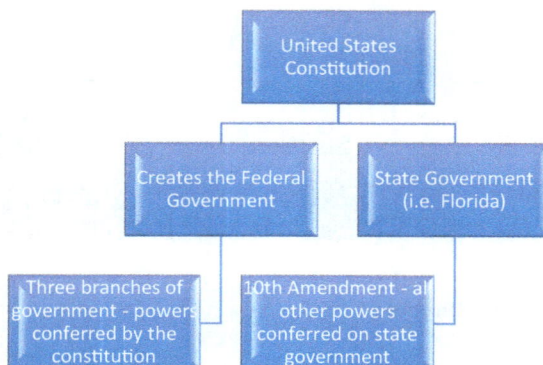

Figure 1.9
The federal structure of the United States of America

Article I of the constitution conferred legislative powers to Congress and limited the areas where Congress can make laws. Article II created the executive branch and the position of President. The President has powers conferred on him by the constitution. Article III created the judicial branch and the Supreme Court. The Tenth Amendment of the United States constitution states that all the remaining powers are conferred on individual states. Every state has its own constitution, with its own government, legislature and judiciary. Therefore, unlike the United Kingdom's system, it is the constitution that confers powers and has organised power sharing between state and federal government. Each state has its own legal system and can make its own laws. Therefore a state can abolish the death penalty, legalise same-sex marriage and impose its own immigration laws (see the controversy in Arizona in 2011).

1.7.3 Bicameral or unicameral

The legislature can either be bicameral, that is consisting of two chambers, or unicameral, that is consisting of only one chamber. The United Kingdom and United States both have bicameral legislatures. The two chambers in the United Kingdom are the House of Commons and the House of Lords. The House of Commons consists of 650 elected Members of Parliament who represent their local constituencies. The House of Lords is not elected and consists of life peers, the remaining hereditary peers, and Church of England bishops.

1.7.4 Monarchy or a republic

The United Kingdom has a constitutional monarchy. Queen Elizabeth II is the head of state. A constitution can be republican, that is, where there is no monarchy and a President will be the head of state. The United States is a republic and the President is the head of state.

The United Kingdom's constitutional monarch is Queen Elizabeth II of the House of Windsor. The House of Windsor was created in 1917, after the then monarch, King George V, changed his family's German name, Saxe-Coburg Gotha, to something more English sounding, Windsor. The reason for this was that the United Kingdom and Germany were at war at the time. The heir to the throne is Charles, Prince of Wales, Duke of Cornwall and Duke of Rothesay in Scotland. The monarch has an important ceremonial role and will open Parliament and read the Queen's Speech, which is written for her by the government. The present monarch is very popular and is regarded as having ensured the survival of the monarchy as an institution. The monarch still exercises some important prerogative powers, such as the appointment of the Prime Minister and royal assent to legislation so that it can become law.

PUBLIC LAW IN CONTEXT
AUSTRALIA HAS A CONSTITUTIONAL MONARCHY

Australia is a constitutional monarchy and its head of state is Queen Elizabeth II. In the 1990s, Australia held a referendum on whether it should become a republic. The referendum was unsuccessful, although it is clear that in the future there will be another referendum on Australia becoming a republic. The former Australian Prime Minister Malcolm Turnbull supported Australia becoming a republic, but declared upon becoming Prime Minister that this should not be during the lifetime of the present monarch. Turnbull had labelled himself as an Elizabethan, declaring, 'Even republicans like myself can be, and in my case are, very strong Elizabethans.'[51] This meant that he respected the present monarch, rather than the institution of monarchy.

1.7.5 Codified or uncodified constitution

Constitutions can be codified or uncodified. If a constitution is codified then the main features of the constitution are brought together in one document. The United Kingdom has an uncodified constitution. Although it would be incorrect to describe the United Kingdom as having a wholly unwritten constitution, the constitution is not codified. This means that the main provisions have not been consolidated into one document, in the same way that the German or US constitutions have. However, it is important to appreciate that parts of the United States' constitution is not codified, such as leading constitutionally important cases, such as *Roe v Wade*[52], which permitted access to abortion facilities for women and *Brown v Board of Education of Topeka*[53], which declared that it was unconstitutional to segregate schools on the basis of race.

1.7.6 The separation of powers or fusion of powers

A constitution can be based on the separation of powers or upon a fusion between the different branches of government. The United States constitution formally creates the separation of powers between the three branches of government. The United Kingdom's constitution is based on a fusion between the legislature and the executive, with the Constitutional Reform Act 2005 reinforcing the separation between the judiciary and the other two branches of government.

1.8 Does the United Kingdom have a constitution?

We have looked at the important historical and recent developments as well as the key features of the United Kingdom's constitution. The question remains whether the United Kingdom can truly be said to have a constitution. A constitution in the newer sense of the word is more than just a description of how the government works; rather it is the system that decides how the country will be governed, and as such will be established via a written document. This is a very interesting area and we shall see the arguments for and against whether the United Kingdom has a constitution.

1.8.1 Thomas Paine's critique

Thomas Paine was a radical writer and politician who wrote around the time of the American War of Independence. In *The Rights of Man* Paine criticised the British constitution and argued that there was no British constitution. Paine believed that government was formed from a compact between the rulers and governed, and that this compact was the constitution. The right to govern was dependent on the existence of a constitution. Paine was critical of the government of Britain and believed that it was based on the oppressive Norman Conquest in 1066, with the monarch and the lords exercising power without the consent of the people.

Many academics have questioned whether the United Kingdom has a constitution. Thomas Paine in *The Rights of Man* did not believe that the United Kingdom had a constitution:

We have now to review the governments which arise out of society. If we trace government to its origin, we discover that governments must have arisen either out of the people or over the people. In those which have arisen out of the people, the individuals themselves, each in his own personal and sovereign right, have entered into a compact with each other to produce a government; and this is the only mode in which governments have a right to arise.

This compact is the constitution, and a constitution is not a thing in name only, but in fact. Wherever it cannot be produced in a visible form, there is none. A constitution is a thing antecedent to government, and a government is only its creature. The constitution of a country is not the act of its government, but of the people constituting a government.[54]

Paine stated that as the Norman Conquest had created the government, there had been no founding document upon which the government was based. Therefore, there could be no constitution. It must be remembered that Paine was writing in support of the American republic and the new constitution that had created the United States of America. Paine thought that there needed to be a constitution on which the powers of government were based. Therefore, the government must not act unless in accordance with the powers conferred on it under the constitution. It is interesting to look at Paine's argument as he argued that: 'A constitution is a thing antecedent to government, and a government is only the creature of the constitution.'[55] This suggests that there needs to be a formal constitution upon which the legitimacy of the government is based. However, the United States of America was a new country constructed out of the t13 distinctly unique former British colonies, which needed to be fused into one unified state, whereas the British state had developed its system of governance incrementally. Paine argued that: 'Wherever [a constitution] cannot be produced in a visible form, there is none.'[56] Obviously his opponents could not produce a written document which contained the British constitution. However, the absence of a written document does not negate the fact that Britain in the 1790s had some sort of constitution. For instance, the behaviour of George III in the 1780s over his treatment of the Fox-North coalition government was attacked as unconstitutional. Even George III was restrained from vetoing a bill (Fox's India Bill in 1783) because it was recognised as unconstitutional to do so. Paine himself noted that England had a republican tradition (such as the power of the House of Commons), but declared, '[m]y is the constitution of England sickly, but because monarchy hath poisoned the republic, the crown hath engrossed the commons?'[57]

1.8.2 The absence of a written constitution

Does the fact that the United Kingdom's constitutional system is largely unwritten and uncodified mean that the United Kingdom does not have a constitution? Considering Anthony King's definition of a constitution we can see that the United Kingdom has 'a set of rules regulating the relations' between the executive, the legislature and the judiciary.[58] There are also rules which regulate these branches of the government. However, many of these rules are unwritten or are non-legal.

PUBLIC LAW IN CONTEXT
THE GANG OF THREE

The United Kingdom, New Zealand and Israel are the only countries which do not have a written constitution. However, it is important to consider whether the United Kingdom will be alone in due course as there have been calls to introduce written constitutions in both New Zealand and Israel.

Today every newly created country has a written constitution. For example, the Scottish government had proposed that if Scotland were to become independent that it would have a written constitution. A draft interim constitution had been prepared in the event that the Scottish electorate voted for independence in 2014.

New Zealand's constitution is a legacy of British rule and this is the reason why it is unwritten and uncodified. Sir Geoffrey Palmer, the former Prime Minister of New Zealand, is an advocate for introducing a written constitution. Palmer has written about his proposals for a new written constitution:

> In this project we have not contented ourselves by simply writing down the existing arrangements in one place. We have made suggestions for change in order to bring the Constitution up to date as well to improve accountability.
>
> . . .
>
> It needs also to be appreciated that a written, codified Constitution cannot save New Zealand or any nation from political disasters. A constitution can restrain the use of power but it cannot prevent intolerance, bad behaviour or cynicism about government. Nor can it stop all abuses of power.
>
> . . .
>
> While the written, codified Constitution we propose will be higher law, it does in the end give the last word to the House of Representatives where it can muster a 75 per cent majority in the House.[59]

Israel does not have a written constitution. However, it has 11 Basic Laws, which have a special legal status, and since the decision in *United Mizrahi Bank v Migdal*[60] it is unconstitutional to enact law that is contrary to the Basic Law. There has been attempts to introduce a written constitution in Israel.[61]

Many people have argued that the United Kingdom requires a written constitution. Some of the reasons for this are that:

- Parliamentary Sovereignty is incompatible with human rights and the rule of law. In the United Kingdom, Parliament can legislate to create any law it wishes and can act in a manner that is deemed unconstitutional or abolish key features of the constitution. Academics such as Vernon Bogdanor do not see Parliamentary Sovereignty as an obstacle to creating a codified constitution if the former is no longer the dominant principle of the constitution.[62]
- There is no clarity and certainty as to the operation of the United Kingdom's constitution. Too many features depend on non-legal rules being followed, or the executive and Parliament acting with restraint.

- The absence of a written constitution means that there is no special status of constitutional law. The judiciary cannot protect key features of the constitution from repeal by Parliament, or ensure that the executive does not act in a manner that is incompatible with the constitution.
- Human rights are not adequately protected as the Human Rights Act 1998 could be repealed.
- The powers of the monarch, the office and powers of the Prime Minister and government are not defined in law and rely on unwritten rules.

The judiciary have considered whether the United Kingdom has a constitution. The Supreme Court has had two recent opportunities to consider the status of the constitution. In the first decision, *R (on the application of Miller) v Secretary of State for Exiting the European Union (No. 1)*[63] the majority of the Supreme Court observed that:

> Unlike most countries, the United Kingdom does not have a constitution in the sense of a single coherent code of fundamental law which prevails over all other sources of law. Our constitutional arrangements have developed over time in a pragmatic as much as in a principled way, through a combination of statutes, events, conventions, academic writings and judicial decisions.[64]

Lord Thomas LCJ had in the High Court held that:

> The United Kingdom does not have a constitution to be found entirely in a written document. This does not mean there is an absence of a constitution or constitutional law. On the contrary, the United Kingdom has its own form of constitutional law, as recognised in each of the jurisdictions of the four constituent nations. Some of it is written, in the form of statutes which have particular constitutional importance. . . . Some of it is reflected in fundamental rules of law recognised by both Parliament and the courts. There are established and well-recognised legal rules which govern the exercise of public power and which distribute decision-making authority between different entities in the state and define the extent of their respective powers. The United Kingdom is a constitutional democracy framed by legal rules and subject to the rule of law. The courts have a constitutional duty fundamental to the rule of law in a democratic state to enforce rules of constitutional law in the same way as the courts enforce other laws.[65]

In *R (on the application of Miller) v The Prime Minister (No.2)*[66] Lady Hale, the President of the Supreme Court, and Lord Reed, the Deputy President, on behalf of the Supreme Court, reiterated its view as to the status of the constitution:

> Although the United Kingdom does not have a single document entitled 'The Constitution', it nevertheless possesses a Constitution, established

over the course of our history by common law, statutes, conventions and practice.

This is not to say that every senior judge was of the opinion that the United Kingdom had a constitution. Lord Neuberger, the then President of the Supreme Court, observed in 2015 that:

> [the Supreme Court is] *not, of course, a constitutional court*, because, in common with only Israel and New Zealand, *the UK has no constitution.* Some people like to say that we have constitutional conventions and some constitutional documents, and even that we have an unwritten constitution. To paraphrase Sam Goldwyn, I question whether an unwritten constitution is worth the paper it's written on. But more seriously, *I find it hard to accept that a few random conventions and a few disparate statutes, all or any of which can be removed or varied by a simple majority in Parliament can amount to much of a constitution.* But, as is so often the case with such arguments, it all depends on what you mean by 'constitution.'[67]

The following year, Lord Neuberger reconsidered whether the United Kingdom had a constitution, but was quite clear that it depended on which type of constitution you were talking about:

> I also am conscious that I address this topic after having been taken to task by some academic lawyers for saying that the United Kingdom has no Constitution. My critics undoubtedly have a point. However, as so often with a disagreement, whether about law or some other topic, the issue turns out, in the ultimate analysis, to be one of definition. And in this case it may depend on whether the word 'constitution' has an upper or lower case first letter. In one sense, a constitution (with a lower case "c") may be no more than the collection of rules or conventions by which a state is governed. On that basis, the UK has, *I accept, a constitution, much of which is in the form of unwritten conventions,* such as the notion that the House of Lords will not oppose a bill which was promised in the elected government's manifesto (the so-called Salisbury Doctrine), and the rest of which is in the form of some statutes or statutory provisions such as the Bill of Rights 1688/9.[68]

1.8.3 FF Ridley's critique

FF Ridley was dismissive of claims that the United Kingdom has a constitution. He argued that there was in fact no British constitution because there was not a wholly written constitution. Ridley was sceptical of the view the United Kingdom had a constitution:

> Not to be left out of the world of constitutional democracies, British writers define constitution in a way which appears to give us one too, even though there is no document to prove it. The argument is that a constitution need

not be embodied in a single document or, indeed, wholly written. We say instead that a country's constitution is a body of rules – some laws, some conventions – which regulate its system of government. Such a definition does not, however, bridge the gap between Britain and the rest of the world by providing us with a substitute for a documentary constitution: it simply shifts the ground, by using the word in an entirely different way.[69]

Ridley noted that the characteristics of a constitution required that there is a superior type of constitutional law and that this law was entrenched, both of which did not apply in the United Kingdom.[70] He noted that many people regarded this as a sign of the flexibility of the British constitution, which he dismissed. Ridley looked at the importance of constitutional conventions in the British system and observed that: '[c]onventions are considered binding so long as they are considered binding. That seems just another way of saying the British "constitution" is what people do, how the system works.'[71] Ridley stated that conventions are not constitutional and therefore could not form part of a constitution. We shall look at the sources of the United Kingdom's constitution in **Chapter 2**, including what is meant by constitutional conventions and why they serve an important purpose.

Ridley was critical that the misuse of the word *constitution* to describe the United Kingdom's collection of conventions and other sources might cause people to mislead 'themselves into thinking that there are parts of the system to which a special sanctity attaches. But in that normative sense the term is equally meaningless.'[72] What Ridley is emphasising is that Parliamentary Sovereignty results in the ability of Parliament to amend what is regarded as constitutional. It is certainly a persuasive argument.

However, it could be argued that the British constitution has developed over time to create a modern democracy. The powers of the monarch have been transferred to the Prime Minister and Cabinet without the need for a written constitution to do this. The British system has survived two world wars and the rise of fascism in the 1930s. Many countries that do have written constitutions are not democracies and do not adhere to the rule of law. A written constitution does not guarantee fundamental freedoms and good governance; instead the government of the country must be willing to govern in a manner that is compatible with a democracy. The British system does this, even if in the future a radical government could use the flexibility of the constitution to impose a dictatorship.

1.9 Why do most countries have a written constitution?

If most countries have written constitutions then it is important to understand why this is so. We can see that new written constitutions come about for a number of reasons, including military defeat, independence and political instability.

Table 1.2 Why countries have written constitutions

Country with a written constitution	The reason for having a written constitution
France	France was defeated by Germany in the Second World War and southern France (Vichy France) became an ally of Nazi Germany. The Fourth Republic was established in 1946 and it had a new constitution. The Fourth Republic collapsed as a result of the French province of Algeria's fight for independence, and the Fifth Republic was established in 1958. The new constitution was aimed at strengthening the power of the executive.
Germany	Germany was defeated by the allied powers in the Second World War. The western occupied zones were merged to create West Germany in 1949. The Germans wanted to prevent another dictatorship and therefore struck a balance between the federal government and the individual states.
Russian Federation	The break-up of the USSR in 1991 and the creation of the Russian Federation led to the creation of a new constitution. The current Russian constitution was created in 1993.
Kenya	Kenya was granted independence by the United Kingdom in 1963. The constitution was needed to ensure that the newly independent state could function effectively. The current Kenyan constitution was introduced in 2010.
United States of America	Drafted in 1787, the constitution created the federal United States of America. The 13 colonies had fought a war of independence against Great Britain. Under the constitution power is shared between the federal government and the 50 individual states. The constitution replaced the earlier Articles of Confederation which had been drafted after the 13 American colonies had declared independence from Great Britain.
Australia	The 1901 Commonwealth Constitution of Australia created Australia and united the separate states into a unified federal state. The constitution strikes a balance between federal government and the rights of the individual states.
Japan	The constitution was introduced by the United States following Japan's defeat in the Second World War. The constitution reformed the role of the Japanese Emperor and prevented Japan from using military force, except in the case of self-defence.

PUBLIC LAW IN PRACTICE

Imagine that Port Louis (fictitious) was until recently a province of the Republic of the East Coast. After 20 years of popular protests, the government of East Coast agreed that Port Louis could receive its independence. There are now a number of questions, namely, will Port Louis be a democracy? Who can vote? Will it have a President, or will a senior member of the old royal family be declared king? If Port Louis will have a Parliament, would this be unicameral or bicameral? These are important questions and it is likely that Port Louis will draft a written constitution which will create the system of government. The constitution will attempt to answer these big questions and will aim to avoid any future uncertainties over how the new country will operate. For example, if there is a relatively strong democratic tradition then the constitution need not focus on ensuring democratic safeguards, whereas a tradition of oppression and abuse of power would require entrenching the need to hold democratic elections and limiting the power of Parliament and the President.

1.10 Why does the United Kingdom not have a written constitution?

The United Kingdom's constitution is not wholly unwritten. There are written sources of the constitution, which include the common law and Acts of Parliament. It is important to appreciate that to say the United Kingdom's constitution is written, unwritten, codified or uncodified means very different things.

Parts of the constitution are written down, such as key statutes, the common law, the rules of Parliament and the Ministerial Code. The United Kingdom would be capable of drafting a constitution, as Parliament has previously drafted constitutions for former colonies when they have been granted independence. However, determining what should be included as part of a written constitution would be problematic.

Looking at the history, the only time of political crisis significant enough to trigger a written constitution has been the abolition of the monarchy in 1649 and the Glorious Revolution in 1688. During 1649–60, England was a republic and for much of this period there was a written constitution known as the Instrument of Government. In 1689, the Bill of Rights rebalanced the relationship between the monarch and Parliament. Whilst it guaranteed parliamentary privilege (granting MPs the freedom of speech inside Parliament), it could not be described as a written constitution.

1.10.1 Referendums as a way of protecting the constitution

Many constitutions such as Switzerland's require referendums to change parts of the constitution. In the United Kingdom there is no requirement that a referendum is used to introduce key constitutional changes. However, Professor Vernon Bogandor has noted that many of the key constitutional changes were preceded by a referendum (e.g. devolution and membership of the European Union).[73]

CHAPTER 1   THE UNITED KINGDOM'S CONSTITUTION

The European Union Act 2011 establishes a legal requirement for a referendum to be held before the government can agree to any significant changes to the United Kingdom's membership of the European Union. Whilst this offers a legal guarantee that there will be a popular vote, it would have been perfectly possible for a future government to repeal the referendum requirement by introducing a new Act of Parliament. This would have abolished the legal requirement to hold a referendum. The doctrine of Parliamentary Sovereignty states that Parliament has the ability to repeal any existing Act of Parliament. We shall see in **Chapter 6**, that Baroness Hale in the case of *R (on the application of Jackson) v Attorney-General*[74] made an obiter statement which indicated that the courts could potentially enforce a referendum requirement (this was not in the context of the European Union).

1.10.2 Advantages of having an unwritten constitution

An unwritten constitution has the advantage that it is flexible and can develop over time. Therefore, the constitution is not entrenched. The United Kingdom's constitution has seen the creation of a new state in 1707, 1801 and the independence of Southern Ireland. The creation of the office of Prime Minister and its importance in the British system has developed over the past 300 years.

In order to amend the United States constitution a complex procedure must be complied with (see Figure 1.10). Failure to comply with this procedure will mean that the amendment is ineffective.

An example of such an amendment is the 22nd, which turned a constitutional convention into a legally enforceable part of the constitution. The convention had prevented Presidents from seeking to serve more than two four-year terms in office. President Franklin D. Roosevelt had breached this convention in 1941 and 1945. Consequently, since the passing of the Twenty-second Amendment, even popular Presidents are unable to serve more than two terms.

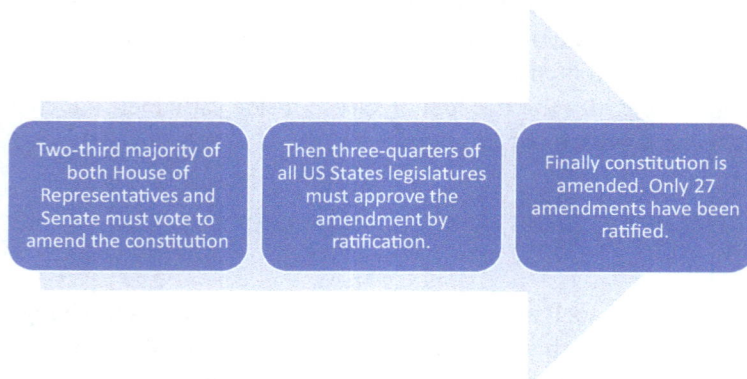

Two-third majority of both House of Representatives and Senate must vote to amend the constitution

Then three-quarters of all US States legislatures must approve the amendment by ratification.

Finally constitution is amended. Only 27 amendments have been ratified.

Figure 1.10
The procedure for amending the United States Constitution

Flexibility is important and an unwritten constitution can develop without the need of either popular referendums or majority votes in the legislature. Even the constitution of the United States of America relies on other rules apart from those contained in the written constitution, such as the requirement that during a general election each state's Electoral College will vote in accordance with their state's popular vote.

1.10.3 Disadvantages of having an unwritten constitution

There are a number of disadvantages of having an unwritten constitution. If a constitution is unwritten then the three branches of government may not adhere to strict separation of powers, as the government may have developed over a long period of time. It might be easier to amend the constitution, as there may be no special procedure or a requirement for a referendum to be held. If it is easier to amend, then the constitution will not be entrenched, and core constitutional features can be removed (e.g. key rights could be abolished). A written constitution may have a special legal status, and this will mean that the courts will be able to prevent any legislative or executive actions that are deemed to be unconstitutional. If a constitution is unwritten it is difficult to define what exactly is, or is not, part of the constitution, and therefore what sources should be protected.

1.10.4 The United Kingdom's constitution?

Professor Munro has written on whether the United Kingdom has a constitution. Munro takes the view that there is a constitution: 'Does the United Kingdom have a constitution, in the original sense of the word? Yes. Does the United Kingdom have a constitution, in the newer sense of the word? Perhaps not one as we know it, but up to a point.'[75]

Munro's position is interesting, as whilst the traditional meaning of constitution means a system of rules, the newer meaning equates to a written constitution. Munro has identified that much of the British constitutional system is written. Anthony King has questioned whether the United Kingdom still has a constitution and has concluded that it does, although the traditional constitution has been replaced by a more modern constitution. King notes that the new constitution is based on power sharing and power hoarding by the executive, with the Labour government having devolved powers to Northern Ireland, Wales, Scotland, London and the Bank of England.[76] King concluded by describing the United Kingdom's constitution as descriptive, that is a list of rules, practices and laws.[77]

Students will be required to engage with the academic debate on whether the United Kingdom has a constitution (see below). You should be able to present a balanced view, but ultimately your tutor will expect you to form your own informed opinion.

ACADEMIC DEBATE
DOES THE UNITED KINGDOM NEED A WRITTEN CONSTITUTION?

Does the United Kingdom need a written constitution? This is a question that divides academics and has led to much debate. The constitution has been tested over the last decade, with referendums on Scottish Independence and European Union Membership, and two landmark Supreme Court decisions of utmost constitutional importance (*Miller [No. 1]* and *Miller [No. 2]*). Therefore, the question is now of contemporary significance and you might be expected to understand the arguments on either side of the debate.

There have been calls to introduce a written constitution for the United Kingdom. The Political and Constitutional Reform Select Committee's second report of 2014, 'A New Magna Carta?' contained three blueprints for possible constitutions that had been drafted by Professor Robert Blackburn. The three blueprints were a written constitutional code that would list and describe the present workings of the constitution, a constitutional act that would consolidate the existing constitutional law, and a written constitution.[78] Professor Conor Gearty and Daniel Regan had also proposed a new written constitution. In 2013–15, Gearty and Regan invited members of the public to contribute to the proposed written constitution through the project 'Crowdsourcing the UK's constitution.'[79] Richard Gordon QC has also proposed a written constitution in *Repairing British Politics: A Blueprint for Constitutional Change*[80], in which he outlined the draft constitution and provided rationale for introducing such a written constitution. However, Nick Barber has argued 'Against a written constitution' and observed:

> Britain is one of a very few states which lack a written constitution, but this bare accident of history does not provide an argument for us to adopt one. Britain's constitution has, by and large, been a success. It has produced stable government and – in terms of democracy, transparency, human rights and the provision of social welfare – it compares reasonably favourably with many other constitutions.[81]

The decisions in *Miller (No. 1)* and *Miller (No. 2)* have seen calls for a new written constitution for the United Kingdom.[82] Sebastian Payne has argued that the Supreme Court's decision has shown that constitutional reform is needed:

> [T]he obscurity of the UK constitution is dysfunctional and needs to be reformed by way of a written constitution. The shortcomings of the UK's unwritten constitution (the common law constitution) can be seen in many contexts, but here I focus on the Supreme Court's majority judgment in the 2017 Miller case. . . . The common law constitution makes the judges the body that defines the constitution and so in effect the constituent power. This makes the judiciary especially vulnerable to criticism when dealing with intensely disputed political matters. In the absence of a written constitution designating the role of a top constitutional court, the Supreme Court may lack institutional confidence in its role and authority and seek to portray its decisions as merely technical applications of the law rather than assertions of creative and active constitutional law-making.[83]

Payne continued:

> I would suggest that the biggest improvement to be made would be for the UK to have a written constitution that identifies what the key concepts and principles of the constitution are. A written constitution that defined the powers of a supreme court and enshrined its status and independence would arguably empower a supreme court to act with confidence and set its own timetable when being harassed by politicians and the press. A written constitution would encourage the judges to think in deep terms about the constitutional structure of the country and give effect to that analysis in their judgments.[84]

A contrary view was taken by Adam Ramshaw:

> It isn't clear how, if the current constitution were written, this would, in itself, have helped the courts reach a decision in either of these Brexit-related cases [*Miller (No. 1)* and *Miller (No.2)*]. Rather than seeing suggestions for a written constitution as a call to consolidate the existing constitutional arrangements, they should instead be understood as calls for the constitution to be drastically changed to reflect the priorities of the people calling for the change.[85]

The question of whether the United Kingdom needed a 'proper' constitution was explored in a debate between Professor Sionaidh Douglas-Scott and Professor Adam Tomkins.[86] Douglass-Scott argued that is does need one: 'We need to codify our constitution to make it fit for today – to clarify its many obscurities, and to ensure the protection of rights both of UK individuals and its nations' and 'I agree that a good constitution balances and shares power. But I do not agree that the British constitution does this, nor that Brexit illustrates that the constitution is working well.' However, Tomkins took the contrary view: 'Britain has no need of a written constitution and, worse, for us to adopt one would do more harm than good' and 'Brexit has revealed unresolved tensions in the constitution. But a written constitution would not resolve them.'

1.11 Practical application

Imagine that you and the rest of the students in your School of Law were shipwrecked on a deserted island in the middle of the Pacific Ocean. Unfortunately, the island is unknown to the rest of the world and you have no hope of rescue. On the positive side you and the other students decide that you will use your knowledge from studying law to draft a constitution for the island. This constitution will set how you would like the island to function in the future, the type of government it will have and who will exercise power.

It would be useful to draft a diagram setting out how your constitution will function.

1.12 Key points to take away from this chapter

- The United Kingdom was created in 1801 and is a constitutional monarchy.
- Great Britain was created in 1707. Previously, England and Scotland were two independent kingdoms.
- Academics have questioned whether the United Kingdom actually has a constitution.
- There are a number of characteristics of a constitution, which can be used to describe a particular country's constitution.
- Whilst the United Kingdom's constitution is uncodified, it would be wrong to describe it as wholly unwritten.
- Parliamentary Sovereignty, the Separation of Powers and the Rule of Law are three of the key features of the United Kingdom's constitution.
- The United States of America serves as a useful comparison to the constitutional arrangements of the United Kingdom.

Notes

1 J Slack, 'Enemies of the People: Fury Over "Out of Touch" Judges Who Have "Declared War on Democracy" by Defying 17.4 Brexit Voters and Who Could Trigger Constitutional Crisis' *Daily Mail* (3 November 2016) <www.dailymail.co.uk/news/article-3903436/Enemies-people-Fury-touch-judges-defied-17-4m-Brexit-voters-trigger-constitutional-crisis.html>
2 [2017] UKSC 5.
3 Founding Fathers, *The Constitution of the United States* (Penguin 2017) 1.
4 For commentary on the convention see M Farrand, *The Framing of the Constitution of the United States* (Yale Press 1913); LW Levy (ed), *Essays on the Making of the Constitution* (2nd edn, OUP 1987).
5 Article I.
6 Article II.
7 Article III.
8 See <www.constituteproject.org/constitution/Peoples_Republic_of_Korea_1998.pdf?lang=en>
9 ibid.
10 ibid.
11 SM Griffin, *American Constitutionalism: From Theory to Politics* (PUP 1996) 55.
12 M Kettle, 'Boris Johnson Looks Increasingly Like the Prime Minister of England Alone' *The Guardian*, 13 May 2020, <www.theguardian.com/commentisfree/2020/may/13/boris-johnson-prime-minister-england-coronavirus>
13 J Laws, 'The Good Constitution' [2012] CLJ 567.
14 A King, *Does the United Kingdom Still Have a Constitution? Hamlyn Lecture 2000* (Sweet & Maxwell 2001) 1.
15 Viscount Bolingbroke, *On Parties* (1735) 108.
16 FF Ridley, 'There Is No British Constitution: A Dangerous Case of the Emperor's Clothes' [1988] Parliamentary Affairs 340–41.
17 To date there have been 27 amendments. See Article V of the US Constitution.

18 This important power of judicial review was declared by the Supreme Court in the landmark decision of *Marbury v Madison*. It is important to note that no such power was set out in the written constitution.

19 See **Chapters 5** and **6**.

20 R Murray, 'The Article 50 Legal Challenge: Clarifying the UK's Constitutional Requirements to Start Brexit' in DJ Galligan and P Dines (eds), *Constitution in Crisis: The New Putney Debates* (IB Tauris 2017) 104.

21 King (n 14).

22 ibid 4–5.

23 ibid 5.

24 [2017] UKSC 51.

25 ibid [68].

26 Lady Hale, 'Moral Courage in the Law: The Worcester Lecture 2019, Worcester Cathedral' 21 February 2019, 7 <www.supremecourt.uk/docs/speech-190221. pdf>.

27 See G Holmes, *The Good Parliament* (OUP 1975).

28 See J Guy, *Elizabeth: The Forgotten Years* (Penguin 2017).

29 See Chapter 3 'The Precedents: 1603–1660' in AI Macinnes, *Union and Empire: The Making of the United Kingdom in 1707* (CUP 2006).

30 See Book 11, Chapter 6 'Of the Constitution of England' in Charles Louis de Secondat and Baron de Montesquieu, *The Spirit of the Laws* (J Nourse 1748).

31 <www.ucl.ac.uk/constitution-unit/sites/constitution-unit/files/179-options-for-an-english-parliament.pdf>.

32 See 'English Votes for English Laws: House of Commons Bill Procedure' <www. parliament.uk/about/how/laws/bills/public/english-votes-for-english-laws/>; 'Project EVEL: Analysing English Votes for English Laws' <http://evel.uk>; R Kelly, 'English Votes for English Laws' House of Commons Library, Briefing Paper No. 7339, 2017, <https://researchbriefings.parliament.uk/ResearchBriefing/ Summary/CBP-7339>.

33 V Bogdanor, 'Why English Votes for English Laws Is a Kneejerk Absurdity' *The Guardian* (24 September 2014)) <www.theguardian.com/commentisfree/2014/ sep/24/english-votes-english-laws-absurdity-separatist>. See also, V Bogdanor, 'The West Lothian Question' (2010) 621 Parliamentary Affairs 156.

34 *R (on the application of Miller) v Secretary of State for Exiting the European Union* [2016] EWHC 2768 (Admin).

35 *R (on the application of Miller) v Secretary of State for Exiting the European Union* [2017] UKSC 5.

36 *R v Secretary of State for Transport ex p. Factortame (No 2)* [1991] 1 AC 603.

37 P Leyland, *The Constitution of the United Kingdom: A Contextual Analysis* (2nd edn, Hart Publishing 2012) 296.

38 R Brazier, 'How Near Is a Written Constitution' (2001) 52(1) NILQ 1.

39 ibid 3.

40 S Jenkins, 'Twenty Years On, What Has Having a Mayor Done for London?' *The Guardian* (7 May 2020) <www.theguardian.com/commentisfree/2020/may/07/ twenty-years-on-mayor-london-livingstone-johnson-skyline>.

41 See <https://assets-global.website-files.com/5da42e2cae7ebd3f8bde353c/5dda92 4905da587992a064ba_Conservative%202019%20Manifesto.pdf>.

42 Ridley (n 16) 342–43.

43 ibid 349.

44 <www.admin.ch/opc/en/classified-compilation/19995395/201809230000/101.
    pdf>.
45 Article 140.
46 Article 141.
47 <https://petition.parliament.uk>.
48 'Swiss Vote No in Sovereignty Referendum' *BBC News* (25 November 2018)
    <www.bbc.co.uk/news/world-europe-46335918>.
49 (1803) 5 US 137.
50 B Hadfield, 'Devolution a National Conversation?' in J Jowell and D Oliver
    (eds), *The Changing Constitution* (OUP 2011) 211.
51 'Malcolm Turnbull Meets the Queen: "Even Republicans Can Be Very Strong
    Elizabethans"' *The Guardian* (11 July 2017) <www.theguardian.com/australia-
    news/2017/jul/12/malcolm-turnbull-meets-the-queen-even-republicans-can-
    be-very-strong-elizabethans>.
52 410 US 113 (1973).
53 347 US 483 (1954).
54 T Paine, *Rights of Man* (HD Symonds 1792) 24.
55 ibid.
56 ibid.
57 T Paine, *Common Sense* (1776).
58 King (n 14) 101.
59 <https://constitution-unit.com/2016/08/18/new-zealand-needs-a-new-written-
    constitution/>
60 [1995] IsrSC 49.
61 'Constitution for Israel' <https://knesset.gov.il/constitution/ConstIntro_eng.
    htm>.
62 V Bogdanor, *The New British Constitution* (Hart Publishing 2009) 215.
63 [2017] UKSC 5.
64 [40] Lord Neuberger, Lady Hale, Lord Mance, Lord Kerr, Lord Clarke Lord Wil-
    son, Lord Sumption and Lord Hodge.
65 [2016] EWHC 2768 (Admin), [18].
66 [2019] UKSC 41.
67 Lord Neuberger, 'UK Supreme Court Decisions on Private and Commercial Law:
    The Role of Public Policy and Public Interest' Centre for Commercial Law Stud-
    ies Conference, 4 December 2015, [32] (emphasis added).
68 Lord Neuberger, 'The Constitutional Role of the Supreme Court in the Con-
    text of Devolution in the UK' (Lord Rodger Memorial Lecture 2016, 14 Octo-
    ber 2016), [4] (emphasis added).
69 Ridley (n 16) 349.
70 ibid 351.
71 ibid 358.
72 ibid 359.
73 See Bogdanor, *The New British Constitution*.
74 [2005] UKHL 56
75 C Munro, *Studies in Constitutional Law* (OUP 2005).
76 King (n 14) 99–100.
77 ibid 101.
78 See <www.parliament.uk/business/committees/committees-a-z/commons-select/
    political-and-constitutional-reform-committee/inquiries/parliament-2010/

mapping-the-path-to-codifying-or-not-codifying-the-uks-constitution/report-a-new-magna-carta/>.

79   See <https://blogs.lse.ac.uk/constitutionuk/2015/03/11/crowdsourcing-the-uk-constitution/>.

80   Richard Gordon QC, *Repairing British Politics: A Blueprint for Constitutional Change* (Hart Publishing 2010).

81   NW Barber, 'Against a Written Constitution' (2008) 1 PL 1, 18.

82   The decisions will be explored in Chapter 11.

83   S Payne, 'The Supreme Court and the *Miller* Case: More Reasons Why the UK Needs a Written Constitution' (2018) 107(4) The Round Table 441–42.

84   ibid 449.

85   A Ramshaw, 'A Written Constitution for the UK Would Not Have Resolved Recent Brexit Arguments – Here's Why' *The Conversation* (24 October 2019) <https://theconversation.com/a-written-constitution-for-the-uk-would-not-have-resolved-recent-brexit-arguments-heres-why-125597>.

86   S Douglass-Scott and A Tomkins, 'Does Britain Need a Proper Constitution?' *Prospect* (2 April 2019) <www.prospectmagazine.co.uk/magazine/does-britain-need-constitution-debate-sionaidh-douglas-scott-adam-tomkins>.

Further reading

Barber NW, 'Against a Written Constitution' (2008) 1 PL 11

Bogdanor V, *The New British Constitution* (Hart Publishing 2009)

———, *The Coalition and the Constitution* (Hart Publishing 2011)

Dicey AV, *Introduction to the Study of the Law of the Constitution* (Liberty Fund 1982)

Douglass-Scott S and A Tomkins, 'Does Britain Need a Proper Constitution?' *Prospect* (2 April 2019)

House of Commons, *Political and Constitutional Reform Select Committee, Second Report, A New Magna Carta?* (House of Commons 2014)

King A, *Does the United Kingdom Still Have a Constitution? Hamlyn Lecture 2000* (Sweet & Maxwell 2001)

———, *The British Constitution* (OUP 2007)

Leyland P, *The Constitution of the United Kingdom: A Contextual Analysis* (3rd edn, Hart Publishing 2016)

Lyons A, *Constitutional History of the United Kingdom* (2nd edn, Routledge 2016)

Maitland FW, *The Constitutional History of England* (CUP 1965)

Munro C, *Studies in Constitutional Law* (OUP 2005)

Payne S, 'The Supreme Court and the *Miller* Case: More Reasons Why the UK Needs a Written Constitution' (2018) 107(4) The Round Table 441–42

Ramshaw A, 'A Written Constitution for the UK Would Not Have Resolved Recent Brexit Arguments – Here's Why' *The Conversation* (24 October 2019)

Ridley FF, 'There Is No British Constitution: A Dangerous Case the Emperor's Clothes' [1988] Parliamentary Affairs 340

The sources of the United Kingdom's constitution

This chapter will

- outline the key sources of the United Kingdom's constitution, such as human rights and the prerogative;

- appreciate the key statutes that make up the legal constitution and engage with the debate over whether certain Acts of Parliament have a special constitutional and legal status;

- understand the importance of the common law as a constitutional source;

- explain the previous importance of European Union law as a source of the United Kingdom's constitution, the various types of European Union law and the impact of Brexit on the United Kingdom's constitution; and

- evaluate the importance of constitutional conventions and appreciate that, despite being very important, they are nonetheless not legally enforceable although their breach may result in political sanction.

2.1 Introduction

In **Chapter 1** we explored why the question of whether the United Kingdom has a constitution is a controversial issue. It is controversial for many reasons, including whether there is a constitution and even if we accept that there is, whether it ought to be contained in a single written document.

But if we accept that the United Kingdom does have a constitution, then what are the sources of the constitution? Alternatively, you may take the position that the United Kingdom does not have a constitution and that these sources are no substitute for a proper written constitution. This chapter will consider the sources of the United Kingdom's constitution and therefore what

DOI: 10.4324/9780429293498-3

they are and why they are considered to be so important. We shall see that it is not possible to locate just a single source of the constitution, or indeed to go to the British Library and view the 'United Kingdom Constitution' as you can do in many other countries. Even in countries that have a written constitution there are additional sources such as key judicial decisions or non-legal rules that actors within the constitution are expected to follow.

The central question this chapter will address is what exactly are the sources of the constitution? We will consider whether these sources are written or unwritten and if some are unwritten, is there uncertainty over their precise meaning? We will also consider whether these sources are legal or political in nature. This means whether they are law, i.e. can be legally enforced before the courts, or rather whether they are political, i.e. rules that are political in nature and impose non-legal obligations on those working within the constitution.

It is important to appreciate that the constitution has been traditionally regarded as being political in nature, i.e. with the most important rules that govern how it works being governed not by law, but by political rules known as constitutional conventions. These constitutional conventions are extremely important to the working of the constitution. An example of such a constitutional convention is that although the monarch has the prerogative power to refusal royal assent to proposed legislation, which would prevent a bill from becoming law, no monarch has refused royal assent for over 300 years. This inevitably leads to the questions of how a non-legal source can be protected and ultimately enforced, especially if, in the event of a breach, it cannot be enforced by the courts. Returning to the above example, what would happen if a future monarch were to refuse royal assent? This might seem far-fetched, but it is not completely inconceivable that a monarch might feel that a proposed bill violated their coronation oath.

The precise nature of the constitution and whether it is legal in nature or political is important. We will see that the sources are a mixture of both law and politics and therefore it is key that you appreciate why this is significant. The constitution is starting to resemble more of a legal than a political constitution, with key aspects of the constitution transferred from political practices into legal form. This will become apparent when we consider the Acts of Parliament that are regarded as part of the constitution, as these key Acts will include subject-matter that was once part of the political constitution. An example of this is the Constitutional Reform and Governance Act 2010 which made the constitutional convention of requiring the government to lay draft treaties before Parliament a legal requirement under the Act. This chapter will consider those statutes which are of constitutional significance and will feature throughout the rest of this book.

The other key sources that comprise the United Kingdom's constitution are the common law, the United Kingdom's previous membership of the European Union, the current membership of the Council of Europe, and the prerogative. We shall look at these in turn and explore why they are features of the constitution, and why these are so important.

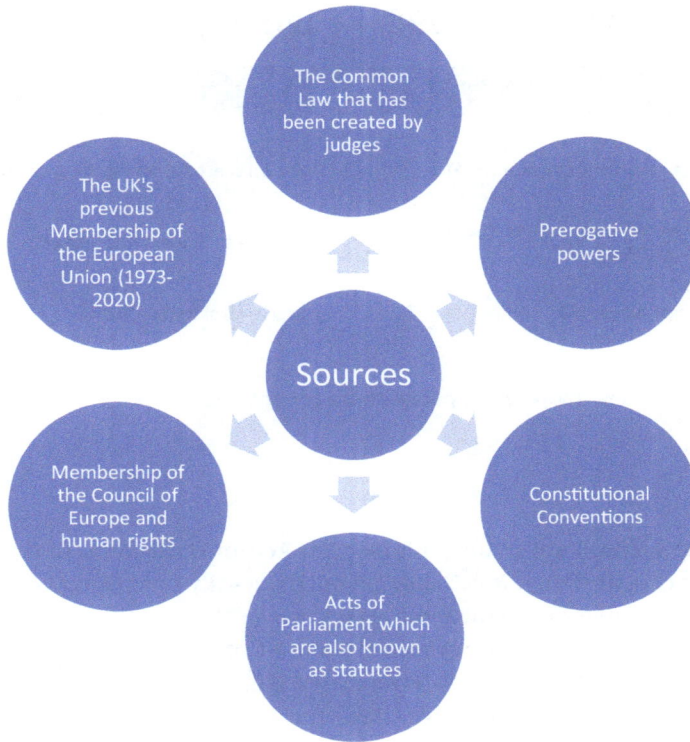

Figure 2.1
Key sources of the United Kingdom's constitution

2.2 Acts of Parliament

Acts of Parliament are an important source of the United Kingdom's constitution. An Act is primary legislation and the United Kingdom's Parliament will legislate on different areas such as criminal law, immigration, the regulation of companies and leaving the European Union. The legal basis for much of the United Kingdom's response to the Covid-19 pandemic was provided for by the Coronavirus Act 2020. This important Act provided a legal basis for the lockdown that was introduced in March 2020.

It is important to realise that because of devolution there are other bodies that can create legislation, namely, the Scottish Parliament, Northern Ireland Assembly and the National Assembly of Wales. We are concerned here with the legislation created by the United Kingdom Parliament. You shall see that devolution has created the sharing of law-making power between Parliament and the other legislative bodies, which are responsible for making laws for areas that have been devolved to them by an Act of the United Kingdom Parliament.

Another important point is that there is no special status of constitutional law in the United Kingdom (see Figure 2.2). However, some Acts of Parliament have come to be regarded as having a constitutional status. This will be considered below.

Human Rights Act 1998   Highways Act 1980

Special constitutional significance - **YES**	Special constitutional significance - **NO**
Gives effect to key rights under the ECHR - liberty, fair trial etc.	Regulates the use of the highways
Special legal status - **NO**	Special legal status - **No**

Figure 2.2
The traditional view: there is no special status of constitutional law

2.2.1 Constitutional statutes

There is no special legal status for important Acts of Parliament. In the United Kingdom's constitution it is Parliament which is legally sovereign and therefore all Acts of Parliament have the same legal status as they are the highest form of law. This means that there is no special status of constitutional law. According to the doctrine of Parliamentary Sovereignty, all Acts of Parliament, regardless of their constitutional importance, have the same legal status and therefore they can be repealed by a future Parliament. It does not matter how important an Act of Parliament is; it can be repealed, which includes all the key statutes listed below.

In *Thoburn v Sunderland City Council*[1] Laws LJ identified a list of constitutional statutes and in *obiter* stated that such statutes were superior to other statutes, as they could not be impliedly repealed. This means that any future act of Parliament which was inconsistent with a constitutional statute would not be taken to have impliedly repealed the earlier statute. This is simply an exception to the normal rule that a later inconsistent Act of Parliament is given precedence over an older Act of Parliament.

However, in any event all statutes can be expressly repealed by Parliament, because Parliament is legally sovereign. This means that in terms of express repeal the Human Rights Act 1998 has the same legal status as the Highways Act 1980. It must by emphasised that Laws LJ's view was only *obiter* and was not part of the actual decision.

In *Thoburn* Laws LJ observed that:

> The common law has in recent years allowed, or rather created, exceptions to the doctrine of implied repeal, a doctrine which was always the common law's own creature. There are now classes or types of legislative provision which cannot be repealed by mere implication. These instances are given, and can only be given, by our own courts, to which the scope and nature of parliamentary sovereignty are ultimately confided. The courts may say – have said – that there are certain circumstances in which the legislature

may only enact what it desires to enact if it does so by express, or at any rate specific, provision.[2]

What Laws LJ was saying here was that it was the courts that decided which statutes should be given special protection from implied repeal. This has an impact on the nature of Parliamentary Sovereignty, which we will explore in **Chapters 5** and **6**.

Laws LJ was clear that the time had come to accept that there should be a hierarchy and distinguish between ordinary and constitutional statutes: '[w]e should recognise a hierarchy of Acts of Parliament: as it were "ordinary" statutes and "constitutional" statutes.'[3]

The test to determine what was a constitutional statute was set by Laws LJ:

> The two categories must be distinguished on a principled basis. In my opinion a constitutional statute is one which (a) conditions the legal relationship between citizen and state in some general, overarching manner, or (b) enlarges or diminishes the scope of what we would now regard as fundamental constitutional rights. (a) and (b) are of necessity closely related: it is difficult to think of an instance of (a) that is not also an instance of (b). The special status of constitutional statutes follows the special status of constitutional rights.[4]

Laws LJ gave examples of what in his opinion would amount to a constitutional statute. These included the Human Rights Act 1998 and the Bill of Rights 1689.[5] He was clear that:

> Ordinary statutes may be impliedly repealed. Constitutional statutes may not. For the repeal of a constitutional Act or the abrogation of a fundamental right to be effected by statute, the court would apply this test: is it shown that the legislature's *actual* – not imputed, constructive or presumed – intention was to effect the repeal or abrogation? I think the test could only be met by express words in the later statute, or by words so specific that the inference of an actual determination to effect the result contended for was irresistible. The ordinary rule of implied repeal does not satisfy this test. Accordingly, it has no application to constitutional statutes.[6]

This meant that express words were needed to repeal a constitutional statute.

Laws LJ's reasoning in *Thoburn* was noted by Lord Hope in *H v Lord Advocate*[7] and by the Supreme Court in *R (on the application of HS2 Action Alliance Ltd) v Secretary of State for Transport*.[8] In *H v Lord Advocate* Lord Hope held that the Scotland Act 1998 must be a constitutional statute:

> It would perhaps have been open to Parliament to override the provisions of section 57(2). . . . But in my opinion only an express provision to that effect could be held to lead to such a result. This is because of the

fundamental constitutional nature of the settlement that was achieved by the Scotland Act. This in itself must be held to render it incapable of being altered otherwise than by an express enactment.

In the *HS2* case the decision involved the European Communities Act 1972 and the Bill of Rights 1689. The Supreme Court held that '[t]he United Kingdom has no written constitution, but we have a number of constitutional instruments.'[9] The court then continued to endorse *Thoburn*, as

> [i]t is, putting the point at its lowest, certainly arguable (and it is for United Kingdom law and courts to determine) that there may be fundamental principles, whether contained in other constitutional instruments or recognised at common law, of which Parliament when it enacted the European Communities Act 1972 did not either contemplate or authorise the abrogation.[10]

The decision in the *HS2* case will be explored in more detail in **Chapter 6**.

ACADEMIC DEBATE

The academic literature on constitutional statutes is interesting and addresses a number of points, including justification and definition of precisely what a constitutional statute is.

Professor David Feldman considered constitutional legislation and observed that Laws LJ's approach in *Thoburn* of '(t)ying the "constitutional" status of legislation to fundamental rights' was problematic for three reasons. The first was that 'the category of fundamental rights is not closed.' The second was that constitutional legislation is not 'always concerned with fundamental rights' and this includes legislation concerning state institutions and their relationships with each other. Finally, the third reason was that Laws LJ's test is 'over-inclusive' as '(m)ost legislation is concerned with the relationship between the state and the citizen.'[11]

In his conclusion, David Feldman observed:

> On reflection, it turns out to be unexpectedly tricky to separate constitutional from ordinary legislation. I have suggested that an approach based on fundamental rights is both over- and under-inclusive, and that a better approach is to concentrate on the contribution of Acts, subordinate legislation and individual provisions or groups of provisions to establishing institutions of the state, defining their roles and authority, and regulating their relationships with each other.[12]

Commenting on the *HS2*[13] decision Professor Paul Craig noted that the Supreme Court explored the possibility of a conflict between the European Communities Act 1972 and the

Bill of Rights 1689, the later might have also been a constitutional statute.[14] The Supreme Court endorsed the idea of constitutional statutes from *Thoburn*. Craig observed,

> [t]he Supreme Court's reasoning concerning constitutional instruments is technically an obiter dictum given that it held that there was no actual conflict with the Bill of Rights 1689 . . . [however] [t]he reasoning is to be welcomed, endorsing as it does the earlier ruling in *Thoburn*.'[15] Craig noted that the Supreme Court 'did not delve further into the principled foundation for the identification of such measures as constitutional.[16]

> Farrah Ahmed and Adam Perry have observed that '[i]t matters, in most other jurisdictions, whether a law is part of the constitution. Northing used to turn on that point in Britain, legally speaking.'[17] However, Ahmed and Perry have argued that decisions such as *Thoburn* and *HS2* have changed this.[18] The authors sought not just to list those statutes which were constitutional, but to produce a definition as to what made them such. They argued 'a constitutional statute is a statute that is about state institutions and which substantially influences, directly or indirectly, what those institutions can and may do.'[19]

2.2.2 Statutes of constitutional importance

The following subsection explores the statutes of constitutional importance which are of significance in the United Kingdom's constitution. This list includes some Acts that were passed by the old English Parliament as these are still of legal significance.

The Magna Carta 1215 and 1297

In 1215, King John was forced by his own barons to agree to the Magna Carta (great charter) at Runnymede on the banks of the River Thames. The meeting and the charter were an attempt to settle the grievances that the barons had against King John and how he ruled England. It was a complex charter that dealt with many issues, including the rights of freemen, or more specifically the barons. It is important to note that the Magna Carta was originally not a statute but was rather a charter and thus a constitutional instrument. John felt that his agreement had not been made voluntarily, as he had been forced by circumstances to agree to the charter. Therefore, the Magna Carta was promptly annulled by the pope and John reneged on its terms. Given its important constitutional status and powerful legacy the Magna Carta was reissued by Henry III and finally by Edward I in 1297. It is the 1297 legislative reissue that is partially in force today. The Magna Carta is constitutionally important, as it is regarded as establishing important protection for the subject from the arbitrary power of the monarch. It has also been argued that the Magna Carta established the right to trial by jury, although such a right has been dismissed by Lord Justice Auld in 2001.[20]

PUBLIC LAW IN CONTEXT
THE STATUS OF THE MAGNA CARTA TODAY

Today much of the Magna Carta has been repealed. The most important remaining clause is clause 29, which states that:

'No Freeman shall be taken or imprisoned, or be disseised of his Freehold, or Liberties, or free Customs, or be outlawed, or exiled, or any other wise destroyed; nor will We not pass upon him, nor condemn him, but by lawful judgment of his Peers, or by the Law of the Land. We will sell to no man, we will not deny or defer to any man either Justice or Right.'

From reading clause 29 it is clear why at the time it was so significant, as it restricted the power of the monarch to act outside of the law of England.

The Magna Carta is regarded as a constitutionally significant document in many countries, including the United States of America and Australia. Max Radin has written that the Magna Carta 'since at least 1297 . . . has been something more than a statute; it has been an assertion of the existence of fundamental rights of free men, however differently they might have been listed at different periods.'[21]

Petition of Right 1628

The Petition of Right 1628 is a construction instrument and was intended to limit the power of King Charles I and to prevent him from imprisoning people without trial and from raising taxation outside of Parliament. The king was forced to agree to the Petition of Right in order for Parliament to approve taxation.[22] Reeve has argued that despite earlier views that the petition was a judicial measure, 'the Petition was a legislative act of statutory character and effect, rather than a judicial measure which did not bind the king at law.'[23]

Bill of Rights 1689

The Bill of Rights 1689 was intended to protect the rights and liberties of the subject and to settle the matter of royal succession. The Bill of Rights was the result of the Glorious Revolution in 1688. The Bill of Rights covered the freedom of elections to the House of Commons, guaranteed MPs the freedom of speech in Parliamentary debates and proceedings, without fear of prosecution or impeachment. Importantly, the Bill of Rights protected individuals by stating that, 'excessive Baile ought not to be required nor excessive Fines imposed nor cruell and unusuall Punishments inflicted.'[24] Before the Glorious Revolution, the monarch and Parliament had clashed over the raising of money without the consent of Parliament. The Bill of Rights stated the monarch could no longer raise money through his prerogative powers. The power of the monarch to raise and keep an army was restricted by the need for Parliament's consent.

Act of Settlement 1701

The Act of Settlement 1701 is important, as it controls the succession of the monarchy. Under the Act of Settlement, a Roman Catholic cannot become the monarch nor can a member of the royal family marry a Roman Catholic without giving up their place in the line of royal succession. Note however the changes introduced by the Succession to the Crown Act 2013. The Conservative and Liberal Democrat Coalition Government[25] introduced the Succession to the Crown Act 2013, which has changed the rules of royal succession and has removed the preference in favour of men over women. The Act also permits a member of the royal family to marry someone who is a Roman Catholic, without having to give up their place in the royal succession.[26] The Act of Settlement 1701 also ensured judicial independence, as senior judges enjoy security of tenure and can only be removed as a judge by Parliament.

Union with Scotland Act 1706 and the Union with England Act 1707

The Union with Scotland Act 1706 allowed the way for the creation of Great Britain, whereby the Kingdoms of England and Scotland were unified into a single country. Prior to the union the two countries had been independent and had shared a personal union, as since 1603 they had a common monarch. The creation of Great Britain was significant and ensured that Queen Anne's successor, who would be George I, would become king of both England and Scotland. There was a risk that upon Anne's death the personal union would end and both countries would have different monarchs. It is important to note that although the Union with Scotland Act 1706 may have helped to create Great Britain many parts of the Act have been subsequently repealed. The Union with Scotland Act 1706 was an Act of the English Parliament, with the Scottish Parliament enacting the Union with England Act 1707. Together both Acts gave effect to the Treaty of Union agreed between negotiators from England and Scotland.[27]

Union with Ireland Act 1800

This Act created the United Kingdom, as Article 1 states, 'Great Britain and Ireland to be united for ever from 1 Jan. 1801.' Southern Ireland is no longer part of the United Kingdom. However, Northern Ireland remains part of the United Kingdom.

Representation of the People Acts (1832, 1867, 1884, 1918, 1928 and 1969)

This series of Acts has gradually increased the franchise (i.e. those people who are entitled to vote at a general election). Today, men and women aged 18 and over can vote (subject to limited restrictions). The first of the Acts, the Great Reform Act 1832, ended the system of rotten boroughs whereby a small village could have two Members of Parliament and a city, such as Manchester, could have none. It also increased the franchise, which broadened the electorate. Over the course of the 19th century the number of men who could vote was increased. However, it was not until 1918 that women aged 30 or above and who met a property qualification were permitted to vote. Men and women did not have equality in terms of the voting age until 1928. For a detailed overview of the effect of each of the Representation of the People Acts see **Chapter 7**. It might be interesting to work out in what year someone of your age and gender first became eligible to vote.

Parliament Act 1911 and Parliament Act 1949

The Parliament Acts 1911 and 1949 have transformed the relationship between the Houses of Commons and Lords. The House of Commons is now the superior House, and the ability of the House of Lords to block legislation has been restricted. The Parliament Act 1911 prevented the House of Lords from vetoing money bills and limited its power to block a bill to two years. The Parliament Act 1949 further limited the House of Lords ability to block a bill to one year. This had a significant ability on the power of the House Commons to enact legislation without the approval of the House of Lords. There are restrictions on the types of subject matter that can be legislated upon under the Acts.

Public Law in Context: the legal status of the Parliament Act 1949

The legal status of the Parliament Act 1949 has been questioned in *R (on the application of Jackson) v Attorney-General*[28]. This was because the 1911 Act was used to create the 1949 Act and therefore the 1949 Act was not approved by the House of Lords. In this case the House of Lords held that the Parliament Act 1949 was a primary piece of legislation and not delegated or secondary legislation.

European Communities Act 1972

The United Kingdom became a member of the European Economic Community (now the European Union) in 1973, and the European Communities Act 1972 gave legal effect to the United Kingdom's membership. The Act is very important as European law would apply in the United Kingdom and the judiciary must interpret domestic law in line with European law. The European Communities Act 1972 was needed before the United Kingdom would be able to fulfil its legal obligations as a member of the European Economic Community. This is because the United Kingdom has a dualist legal system and an Act of Parliament was required before European law could be enforceable in a domestic court. Section one of the European Union (Withdrawal) Act 2018 stated that the European Communities Act 1972 would be repealed on the day that the United Kingdom exited the European Union. The Act was abolished on 31 January 2020.

House of Commons Disqualification Act 1975

In order to prevent the government using a ministerial position as patronage (i.e. an incentive to support government policy), the House of Commons Disqualification Act 1975 limits the number of Members of Parliament (MPs) who can become ministers to 95. The limitation imposed on the number of MPs who can become ministers serves an important purpose. If an MP becomes a minister, then she will receive additional remuneration on top of her salary as an MP. The MP in her capacity as a minister will also have a role within the government and this will help her political career and chances of obtaining a more important position within government, such as Foreign Secretary. Therefore, ministerial office is used as a way to encourage MPs to support the government and, consequentially, is usually lost if the minister does not support the government.

Senior Courts Act 1981

The Senior Courts Act 1981 reiterated the important constitutional principle that senior judges enjoy security of tenure and can only be dismissed in limited circumstances and by following a clear procedure.

Police and Criminal Evidence Act 1984

The Police and Criminal Evidence Act 1984 (known as PACE) was enacted in response to Lord Scarman's report into the Brixton riots which occurred in 1981. PACE governs police powers and the admissibility of evidence. It provides a code of practice which offers guidance on how the police should use their powers. These codes cover stop and search, the search of vehicles and property, the interview of suspects, the treatment of suspects and how identification procedures should be conducted.

Bank of England Act 1998

The Bank of England Act 1998 gave the Bank of England independence from the government. The Bank of England is responsible for setting the interest rate, which has a significant impact on the economy and the lives of everyday people.

Human Rights Act 1998

The Human Rights Act 1998 incorporates most of the European Convention on Human Rights into domestic law. The Convention rights are now enforceable in domestic law against a public authority. The Act has increased the power of the courts to scrutinise an Act of Parliament and section 4 permits a court (High Court or above) to issue a declaration of incompatibility. It is important to note that section 4 does not permit a court to hold an Act of Parliament to be void.

PUBLIC LAW IN CONTEXT
REPEALING THE HUMAN RIGHTS ACT 1998?

In September 2014, the then–Prime Minister David Cameron promised that a future Conservative government would repeal the Human Rights Act 1998 and replace it with a British Bill of Rights. The Conservative government that was elected in 2019 promised in its manifesto that would update the Human Rights Act 1998. This may not happen during the lifetime of the current Parliament due to the Covid-19 pandemic.

Scotland Act 1998

The Scotland Act 1998 devolved powers from Westminster to Scotland. It created the Scottish Parliament and the Scottish government.

Government of Wales Act 1998

The Government of Wales Act 1998 devolved powers from Westminster to Wales. It created the National Assembly of Wales and a Welsh government. The Government of Wales Act 2006 further increased the legislative powers of the National Assembly of Wales.

Northern Ireland Act 1998

The Northern Ireland Act 1998 devolved powers to the Northern Ireland Assembly, after powers had been transferred back to Westminster in 1974. Devolved power is shared between the different political parties at Stormont, where the Northern Ireland Assembly meets.

Greater London Authority Act 1999

The Greater London Authority Act 1999 created the London Assembly and the office of the Mayor of London, a position that is directly elected by the people of London.

House of Lords Act 1999

The House of Lords Act 1999 reformed the second chamber, by removing all but ninety-two of the hereditary peers. However, the reform of the House of Lords remains incomplete.

Constitutional Reform Act 2005

The Constitutional Reform Act 2005 created the Supreme Court and removed many of the responsibilities and powers from the office of Lord Chancellor. The Act is very important as it reinforces the separation of powers between the judiciary and the other branches of government. The Lord Chancellor has been replaced as the head of the judiciary by the Lord Chief Justice, with whom he shares the power to discipline judges. The judicial appointment process has been transferred to the Judicial Appointment Commission, which is an independent body.

Equality Act 2010

The Equality Act 2010 defines protected characteristics (such as race, religion or belief, sex and disability) and lists a range of prohibited conduct which will amount to discrimination. The Equality Act 2010 has consolidated the previous legislation covering discrimination and seeks to ensure equality.

Constitutional Reform and Governance Act 2010

This Act places the civil service on a statutory basis, as opposed to the civil service being regulated under the prerogative. There is also now a statutory requirement that treaties entered into by the government under their prerogative powers must be laid before Parliament. This places the Ponsonby Rule on a statutory basis. These are two very important limitations on the prerogative.

Fixed-term Parliaments Act 2011

This Act states that the lifetime of the current Parliament will be fixed until May 2015. The Prime Minister is unable to use his discretion to ask the monarch to use her prerogative powers and to dissolve Parliament before May 2015. Prior to the introduction of this Act a Prime Minister could ask the monarch to dissolve Parliament at a date which benefited his party. Please note that the Fixed-term Parliaments Act will be repealed.

PUBLIC LAW IN CONTEXT
GORDON BROWN'S DECISION NOT TO CALL A GENERAL ELECTION IN 2007C

Gordon Brown became Prime Minister in 2007 (after the resignation of Tony Blair) two years into the lifetime of the 2005 Parliament. Brown decided to call a General Election to take advantage of his popularity with the electorate in 2007; however he eventually decided against it. The General Election finally took place in 2010 (as by law a General Election had to occur at least every five years, and the lifetime of the 2005 Parliament had nearly expired). Gordon Brown and the Labour Party failed to secure a majority in the House of Commons.

European Union Act 2011

The European Union Act 2011 states that a referendum must be held before any new powers can be transferred to the European Union. However, according to Parliamentary Sovereignty, the referendum requirement would not bind a future Parliament, which could transfer new powers without holding a referendum.

Scotland Act 2016

The Scotland Act 2016 devolved additional powers to the Scottish Parliament. It also sought to state that the Scottish Government and the Scottish Parliament were permanent and could not be abolished unless this was the wish of the Scottish people when voting in a referendum.[29] The Act referenced the Sewel Convention (see below) that the United Kingdom Parliament would not legislate for devolved areas onto a statutory footing. The only exception was where the Scottish Parliament consented to the legislation.[30]

Wales Act 2017

The Wales Act 2017 devolved further executive and legislative powers to the National Assembly of Wales. Section 2 of the Wales Act 2017 amended section 107 of the Government of Wales Act 2006 and gave statutory recognition to the Sewel Convention: 'But it is recognised that the Parliament of the United Kingdom will not normally legislate with regard to devolved matters without the consent of the Assembly.'

European Union (Withdrawal Act) 2018

The European Union (Withdrawal) Act was designed to repeal the European Communities Act 1972 when United Kingdom left the European Union (which it did in January 2020). The Act deals with issues such as the supremacy of European Union law by making it clear that this will no longer apply.[31]

2.3 The common law

The common law (or case law) is a record of judicial decisions. Judges today are not meant to make law, as their duty is to interpret Acts of Parliament. However, many areas of the law have been created by judges. This is especially true of areas of law such as contract law or tort law, where much of the law has been created and then developed by the courts. We need to understand that only those judicial decisions which have a special constitutional significance are said to be part of the United Kingdom's constitution.

    The common law is an important source of the constitution. Over the course of the last 500 years the courts have limited the powers of the monarch and government, by restricting the scope of the monarch's prerogative powers and then finally permitting the courts to be able to judicially review how the prerogative is used. More recently in *R (on the application of Miller) v Secretary of State for Exiting the European Union*[32], the Supreme Court held that the government could not trigger Article 50 of the Treaty on the European Union using the prerogative.

The courts have acknowledged the importance of the separation of powers, by deferring to the executive on matters of policy. In 2017, the Supreme Court upheld the importance of the rule of law by declaring employment tribunal fees to be illegal as they prevented people from accessing the courts.[33]

The courts have checked the power of the executive to act outside the law, such as in *Entick v Carrington*[34], where the court upheld the rule of law be setting limits on the powers of the Home Secretary and finding that he had no power to issue search warrants. Under section 6 of the Human Rights Act 1998 the courts are under a duty to prevent the executive breaching the European Convention on Human Rights. An important example of this was the House of Lords' decision in *A v. Secretary of State for the Home Department*[35], where the court held that detaining foreign nationals without trial breached their human rights.

The judges play an important role in interpreting statutes and, despite the doctrine of Parliamentary Sovereignty, the courts have considerable power to interpret an Act of Parliament in the way that the court presumes that Parliament would have intended (see Lord Hoffmann in *R v Secretary of State for the Home Department ex p. Simms*[36]).

In *R (on the application of Miller) v The Prime Minister*[37] the Supreme Court recognised and protected the importance of parliamentary accountability as a principle of the constitution, when holding that Prime Minister had not lawfully advised the monarch to prorogue Parliament for a long period of time. Traditionally, this aspect of accountability had been in part safeguarded through ministerial responsibility to Parliament. The Supreme Court also found that this the case because prorogation prevented Parliament from exercising its legislative sovereignty.

Finally, the common law has developed judicial review as a way of reviewing executive action. Judicial review provides an incredibly important check on the executive at a national and local level.

2.4 The United Kingdom's membership of the European Union (1973–2020)

The people of the United Kingdom voted to leave the European Union in 2016. The law of the European Union will be a source of the United Kingdom's constitution up until the United Kingdom exits. The European Union is a supranational organisation which was originally created after the Second World War (1939–45). It is separate from the Council of Europe, which is an intergovernmental organisation responsible for the European Convention on

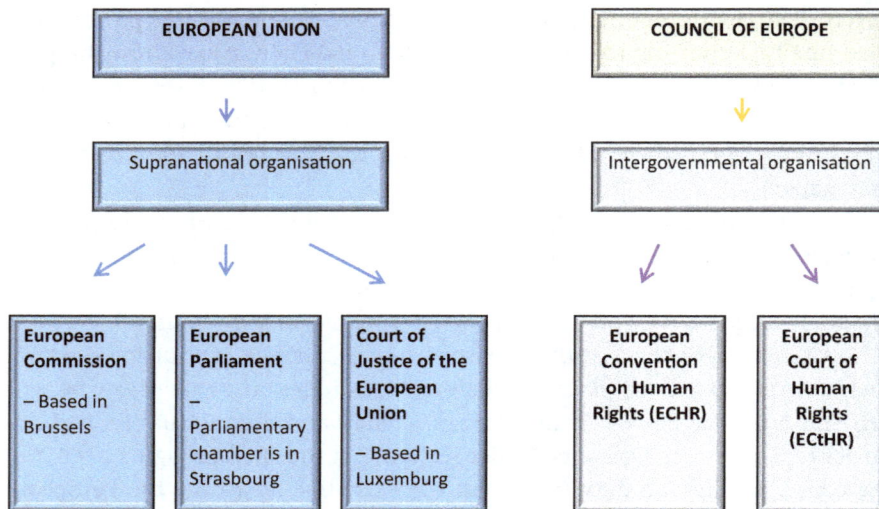

Figure 2.3
The European Union and the Council of Europe distinguished

Human Rights (see Figure 2.3). Today, there are 28 countries which are members of the European Union and its key institutions include the European Commission based in Brussels, the European Parliament based in Strasbourg and the Court of Justice of the European Union (CJEU) which is based in Luxembourg.

The United Kingdom joined the European Economic Community (now the European Union) in 1973. The European Communities Act 1972 gave effect to the United Kingdom's membership and made all present and future European law enforceable in domestic courts. The law of the European Union is an important source of the constitution, as citizens of member states are now also citizens of the European Union (see Article 20, The Treaty on the Functioning of the European Union). Citizens are entitled to travel and reside within any member state. Importantly, where the European Union has competence, then the law of the European Union has supremacy.

It was the Court of Justice of the European Union (then the European Court of Justice) that held that European law had supremacy over the domestic law of member states in *Van Gend en Loos v Nederlandse Administratie der Belastingen*[38]. This was confirmed in *Costa v ENEL*[39]. The consequence of this is that the constitutional courts of many member states have had to give way to the supremacy of European Union law.

In the United Kingdom the European Communities Act gave effect to this supremacy by instructing domestic courts to take into account European law and the decisions of the European Court of Justice. In *R v Secretary of State for Transport ex p. Factortame Ltd (No.2)*[40] the House of Lords set aside an Act of Parliament where the Act was inconsistent with European law.

There are a number of sources of European Union law. These include primary legislation, which includes the treaties which established and developed the European Union, and secondary legislation, which includes regulations, directives, decisions of the European Commission and the decisions of the Court of Justice of the European Union.

2.5 Membership of the Council of Europe

The Council of Europe is an intergovernmental organisation that is responsible for the European Convention on Human Rights. Member states agree to allow their nationals to enforce their Convention rights at the European Court of Human Rights, which is based in Strasbourg.

The United Kingdom's membership of the Council of Europe is important as it provides for the protection of human rights. The Council of Europe has 47 members and is separate from the European Union. The Council of Europe promotes human rights, democracy and the rule of law. It was founded in 1949 as a direct consequence of the horrors of the Second World War, where gross human rights violations took place and 6 million Jews were murdered by Germany.

The United Kingdom was an original member and helped to draft the European Convention on Human Rights. The convention outlined the key rights. The European Court of Human Rights (ECtHR) was established at Strasbourg in 1959 in order to rule on alleged breaches by member states. It was not until 1966 that British citizens were able to sue the United Kingdom at the European Court of Human Rights, and even then, it was not until October 2000 that many of the Convention rights were directly incorporated into domestic law when the Human Rights Act 1998 came into effect.

Today the Convention rights are directly enforceable in domestic courts against public authorities. Under section 2 of the Human Rights Act 1998 the decisions and opinions of the European Court of Human Rights must be taken into account, although the jurisprudence of the ECtHR is not binding on domestic courts.

2.6 Constitutional conventions

A constitutional convention is a key feature of the United Kingdom's constitution and is a rule which controls how the actors in the constitution use their powers. The operation of the United Kingdom's constitution depends heavily on the actors (such as the Queen, Prime Minister, ministers and Parliament) following constitutional conventions. In order to exist, a convention must have examples of it being followed, i.e. people must consider themselves bound by a particular convention and there must be a good reason for its existence.[41] If this were not the case then the actors within the constitution could feel justified to not follow a convention on the grounds that either no one else had followed it for a number of years, or even if it has been followed, that in hindsight there was no rationale for doing so now. In his famous account of the constitution Sir Kenneth Wheare stated that a convention 'meant a binding rule, a rule of behaviour accepted as obligatory by those concerned in the working of the constitution.'[42] We can see that this simply means that over time it has become accepted practice that the monarch will not do something, or that ministers will be responsible to Parliament, and although this practice is not a law, i.e. something that must occur, it is sufficiently important for the monarch or ministers to appreciate the ramifications of failing to abide by a convention.

At this stage it is important to distinguish between the legal and political constitution. A constitutional convention is part of the political constitution as these have emerged as a matter of political ethics. Whereas if the subject-matter of a convention were to be placed on a statutory footing as an Act of Parliament, then it would be part of the legal constitution and could be legally enforceable in a court of law. This will depend on whether the convention is being recognised by the statute or if there is now a legal obligation to do what had been required by the convention. For example the Scotland Act 2016 and the Wales Act 2017 simply give recognition to the Sewel Convention (which concerns the United Kingdom Parliament not legislating for devolved areas) and have not created a legally enforceable rule. As you will have seen above when we explored a number of constitutionally important Acts of Parliament, the constitution is becoming increasing legal in the manner of how recent governments have sought to codify key principles. Some of these principles were previously regulated by conventions and could be seem as part of the political constitution.

2.6.1 The importance of the Cabinet Manual and the Ministerial Code

This codification is not only limited to Acts of Parliament, as there has been an attempt to codify the key rules through which government operates by publishing the Ministerial Code (which describes a number of conventions) and the Cabinet Manual (which also describes a number of conventions). The Cabinet Manual appears to create new and amend some existing constitutional conventions. According to Professor Alison L. Young:

> The Cabinet Manual both establishes and recognizes conventions, leading to a form of codification of conventions. Whilst the Cabinet Manual may clarify the scope and application of conventions, it is clear that their enforcement is through political means, dominated by whether Parliament can exert sufficient political pressure to ensure that the convention is upheld.[43]

We can see that Young is arguing that the ultimate responsibility to enforce conventions lies with Parliament.

Andrew Blick has observed:

> The [Cabinet] manual can probably help bring conventions into being. But it cannot by itself create, alter or establish particular versions of conventions. Their emergence, sustenance and modification depend upon an interaction with political circumstances and the existence of sufficient levels of social consensus about their applicability.[44]

Blick is clear that the Cabinet Manual's role is persuasive and the version of the conventional landscape it presents will depend on wider support to ensure that it is accepted by those working within the constitution.

The Ministerial Code sets out wider duties than what was covered by the original conventions and sometimes a minister will have to resign if she is in breach of the Ministerial Code. An example of this is Damian Green, the First Secretary of State, who was found to have misled people over his knowledge that the police had found pornography on his office computer in the House of Commons. This conduct amounted to a breach of the Ministerial Code. However, we will be exploring the key conventions which regulate ministerial conduct in **Chapter 8**, which will consider individual ministerial responsibility and collective ministerial (or Cabinet) responsibility.

2.6.2 Understanding constitutional conventions

Constitutional conventions are an important source of the constitution and are crucial for the effective operation of the United Kingdom's constitutional system. Without the existence and observance of these conventions, the United Kingdom's uncodified constitution could not work for a number of reasons. In the United Kingdom key parts of the constitution have evolved over time, such as the office of Prime Minister, which is in essence a made-up position, as the office holder is technically the First Lord of the Treasury and the office of Prime Minister was only mentioned in statute at the beginning of the last century. The powers of the Prime Minister are in fact created by convention and many of the expectations that we have about how someone is appointed as Prime Minister or the powers that they have are actually conventions. It must be emphasised that not all conventions have the same importance and their breach will not always carry the same weight in terms of repercussions or political criticism.

Constitutional conventions regulate the conduct of the monarch, the government, individual minsters, Parliament and judges. Unlike the United States where there is a codified constitution which sets out how their constitutional system works and imposes legal restraints and obligation, the United Kingdom is heavily dependent on conventions, which are a non-legal part of the constitution. That is not to say that conventions are not a source of the United States constitution, even if they are not part of the codified constitution. For example, the way the President is elected in the United States is heavily dependent on a constitutional convention, which requires each state's Electoral College to vote in accordance with the popular vote of their state.

PUBLIC LAW IN CONTEXT
CONSTITUTIONAL CONVENTIONS AND THE UNITED STATES' CONSTITUTION

In the United States of America, the original constitution had not set any limits on the number of terms that a President could serve for. Instead, there had developed a constitutional convention that a President would only serve for two terms. This was a political rather than a legal restriction. It was intended to prevent the Presidency becoming a position for life and that a popular President might keep on getting elected. This could ultimately lead to an elected monarchy. However, President Franklin D Roosevelt ('FDR') had breached this convention by running for a third and then a fourth term during the Second World War. The Twenty-Second Amendment was ratified in 1951 and limited the number of terms that a President could serve to two:

> Section 1. No person shall be elected to the office of the President more than twice, and no person who has held the office of President, or acted as President, for more than two years of a term to which some other person was elected President shall be elected to the office of the President more than once. But this article shall not apply to any person hold-ing the office of President when this article was proposed by the Congress, and shall not prevent any person who may be holding the office of President, or acting as President, during the term within which this article becomes operative from holding the office of President or acting as President during the remainder of such term.

Therefore, it is now a legal requirement that a President cannot serve more than two terms. There has been debate amongst academics as to whether the Twenty-Second Amendment was needed.

Professor Gillian Metzger argued that:

> Fears that FDR destroyed the two-presidential-term convention seem overblown; the cri-sis and extreme circumstances of WWII may well have sufficed to reassert the two-term limit. The very example of FDR's breach of convention at the height of WWII proves the advantage of leaving a little flexibility in the joints. And simply constitutionalizing the convention ignores the important question of whether two terms is the right limit; per-haps a longer period – three terms, for example – would have been a better option once the flexibility of practice was traded for constitutional surety.[45]

Roosevelt's successor as President, Harry Truman, had argued against Roosevelt seeking a third term and had written that 'he could be elected again and continue to break the old precedent as it was broken by F.D.R., but it should not be done.'[46] However there has been much debate about amending the constitution to limit the number of terms that a President can serve to one six-year term. There have also been calls to repeal the Twenty-Second Amendment, such as by President Reagan in 1985.[47]

2.6.3 Dicey's definition of constitutional conventions

It is necessary to understand the importance of conventions to the United King-dom's constitution, how they are created and what purpose they serve. But first of all, it is necessary to define what we mean by a constitutional convention. Dicey argued that conventions were not law. He argued that

> [w]ith conventions or understandings [the lawyer] has no direct concern. They vary from generation to generation, almost year to year . . . The sub-ject . . . is not one of law but of politics, and need trouble no lawyer or the class of any professor of law.[48]

However, a constitutional lawyer needs to be concerned with conventions, because they are an important source of the constitution.

Many academics have debated whether conventions can become law and therefore whether they can be enforced in a court. AV Dicey argued that con-ventions were not law. His reasoning for this view was that:

> [There is an] essential distinction between the 'law of the constitution', which consisting (as it does) of rules enforced by the Courts, makes up a body of 'laws' in the proper sense of that term, and the 'conventions of the constitution', which consisting (as they do) of customs, practices, maxims, or precepts which are not enforced or recognised by the Courts, make up a body not of laws, but of constitutional or political ethics.[49]

2.6.4 Political enforcement of conventions

We can see from Dicey's definition of a convention, that they are 'customs, practices, maxims or precepts' which have developed, rather than laws which are capable of being enforced in courts.[50] Although Dicey wrote that breaches of a convention could not lead to breaches of the law, we can see that a breach of a convention may lead to a law being introduced to prevent its breach in the future. There are two examples of this actually happening. The first is the Parliament Act 1911 which restricted the House of Lords' power to veto bills relating to money bills and restricted the period of time that the Lords could delay a bill to two years. This was in response to the House of Lords refusing to vote for the 'People's Budget' of the Liberal Chancellor of the Exchequer, David Lloyd George. Importantly the House of Lords had breached a constitutional convention that had prevented them from refusing to pass money bills.

The second example is the Parliament Act 1949 which came about as a result of the House of Lords defeating bills that covered the subject-matter of the Labour government's election manifesto. As a result of the 1945 general election, which had seen a Labour government under Clement Atlee come to power, the then-leader of the Conservatives in the House of Lords, Viscount Cranborne, had promised that the Conservative Lords would not use their majority to veto bills that were in the election manifesto. This became known as the Salisbury Convention and was created in response to the fact that it would have been undemocratic for an unelected second chamber to prevent the government from implementing what it had promised voters in its election manifesto. However, the convention was breached when the Conservatives defeated a bill that had been in the manifesto and in response the government used the Parliament Act 1911 to enact the Parliament Act 1949. This hereby reduced the power to delay the passage of a bill to one year. We can see that in both instances the powers of the House of Lords were reduced in direct response to its breach of an important constitutional convention.

More recently it is clear that a convention has been established concerning the need to involve the House of Commons in the decision to use the armed forces. This came about as a result of Tony Blair, the then Prime Minister, permitting the House of Commons to vote on the invasion of Iraq in 2003[51] and the subsequent votes held by David Cameron on military action against Libya in 2011[52] (after military action) and Syria in 2013[53]. It is clear that this was an important convention as it gave the House of Commons, as the representatives of the voters, a role in debating whether it was right to take military action and Members of Parliament could ultimately vote to reject the government's proposed military action. This had been the case in 2013 when the House of Commons refused to support David Cameron's decision to take part in coalition airstrikes against the Syrian government in response to a chemical weapons attack on Syrian citizens. In 2018, the Trump administration sought United Kingdom military assistance in attacking the Syrian government by way of targeted airstrikes. Theresa May, the Prime Minister, used her powers under the prerogative to authorise the airstrikes and decided to not put the issue first to a vote in the House of Commons. During subsequent debates in the House of Commons the Prime Minister defended her decision and the government argued that the convention was limited to particular types of military action and in this instance a vote was not required. Arguably there should have been a vote, as the convention could be said to have applied to the airstrikes. However, if one takes this position the convention was breached and despite being an important convention and one that covered controversial subject matter, there was no immediate political fall-out beyond debates and a vote in the House of Commons which the government won.[54]

Does this mean that a government can argue that a particular convention will not apply in a given situation for a reason of its choosing? The answer is that because conventions are not written down in a definitive code (although some are in the Cabinet Manual[55]) this leaves uncertainty over the precise scope of a particular convention's application. However, it is important to note that in response to the Prime Minister's decision not to have a vote in the House of Commons before taking military action, the Leader of the Opposition, Jeremy Corbyn, proposed the introduction of a War Powers Act which would have placed the convention on a statutory footing.[56] Therefore, the long-term consequence of this alleged breach is that the prerogative power to deploy the armed forces may be superseded by an Act of Parliament.

Another example of uncertainty over whether a convention had been breached and the possible consequences if it had been breached was the decision of the House of Lords in October 2015 to defeat a statutory instrument on tax credits. This was said to have breached the convention that the House of Lords would not vote against a financial instrument. There was much debate over whether there was in fact a convention that the Lords would not vote against this type of instrument, with many in the Lords arguing that there was not one, whereas the government argued that there had been a breach of a constitutional convention. For example, Professor Lord Norton of Lough has argued that there was not such a convention.[57] David Cameron, the then Prime Minister, ordered Lord Strathclyde to carry out a review and to look into the matter. However, the defeat led to many claims that the government would respond by attempting to either reduce the power of the Lords over such matters by way of legislation or to create more Lords who would support the government and ensure that the instrument was passed.[58]

The distinction between conventions and law is important for two reasons. Firstly, there is no legal sanction for breaching a convention, as a breach cannot be enforced in a court. Whereas if a law is breached an application can be made to court to review the breach and determine whether a remedy will apply. Secondly, conventions have developed over time in response to changing social and political circumstances and the existence of a particular convention may negate the need to introduce an Act of Parliament to regulate the subject matter.

2.6.5 Why are constitutional conventions so important?

Conventions are a flexible way of changing the way the constitution operates, without the need to introduce laws to achieve this. For example, the use of conventions has:

Created modern Cabinet government as ministers are collectively responsible for the decisions the Cabinet makes and must keep Cabinet discussions confidential. The Cabinet is headed by the Prime Minister and has just over 20 members. The Cabinet exercises many of the prerogative powers of the monarch, such as going to war.

Made the government reliant on the confidence of the House of Commons as a matter of convention the government must hold another confidence vote within 14 days, and if it loses this to resign or hold a general election. Such votes are for the moment (as the act is in the process of being repealed) regulated by the Fixed-term Parliaments Act 2011 and the first such vote under the Act took place in 2019. This essentially means that the government can be removed by the House of Commons if it no longer has confidence in the Prime Minister and her Cabinet colleagues. However, it is important to note that the House of Commons could still hold a vote on a confidence vote outside of the provisions of the Fixed-term Parliaments Act 2011 and the government if loses would be expected to regain the House's confidence or resign, which means that the Prime Minster would advise the monarch to appoint the leader of the opposition as the next Prime Minister.[59]

Created the doctrine of ministerial responsibility to the House of Commons and that ministers are expected to be responsible for their departments and take responsibility for their private indiscretions. Ultimately a minister may be expected to resign if the breach of this convention is significant enough.

Created the office of the Prime Minister as this office has developed overtime from an informal 'nickname' to an official position. Conventions have been used to transfer powers to the holder of this position.

Reduced the power of the monarch as the monarch cannot use her prerogative powers in a way that is unconstitutional. The monarch's ability to choose her Prime Minister is limited by convention and the monarch must give royal assent to parliamentary bills.

Gave Parliament the opportunity to debate treaties before the government ratifies them as the Ponsonby Convention ensured this right. This has now been placed on a statutory footing by the Constitutional Reform and Governance Act 2010.

Dicey noted that conventions developed 'without any change in the law . . . because they meet the wants of a new time.'[60] Joseph Jaconelli argued that their existence is important as '[t]he "reasons" which animate many a constitutional convention are among the highest value of political theory.'[61] Jaconelli gives the example of non-judicial members of the House of Lords not taking part in the judicial function of the Lords (prior to the creation of the Supreme Court in 2009), or the Law Lords not taking part in politically contentious matters, and the House of Lords not challenging the House of Commons because of the importance of democracy.[62]

PUBLIC LAW IN CONTEXT
WHEN A GOVERNMENT MUST RESIGN

The forced resignation of a government is regulated by constitutional convention as the government is dependent on the confidence of the House of Commons. It is a matter of convention that a government that loses a General Election will resign as it can no longer command the confidence of the House of Commons. The Prime Minister's resignation will be expected if another person who can command the confidence of the House is in a position to form a new government (unless the Prime Minister believes that she can form a coalition government).

Dicey noted how this convention developed over the 19th century (after Benjamin Disraeli resigned as Prime Minister after losing the 1868 election) and argued that it was important, as it acknowledged the electorate as the political sovereign. Dicey observed:

> The new convention, which all but compels a Ministry defeated at a general election to resign office, is, on the face of it, an acknowledgment that the electorate constitutes politically the true sovereign power. It tends to convert a general election into a decision

that a particular party shall hold office for the duration of the newly-elected Parliament and, in some instances, into the election of a particular statesman as Prime Minister for that period.[63]

When Gordon Brown delayed resigning as Prime Minister for a few days after the 2010 General Election, many people argued that this was unconstitutional. There was a popular expectation that a government must resign, and so we can see that the existence of this convention has created an expectation amongst the electorate that a government in these circumstances must resign. However, despite the fact that Brown's Labour party had fewer MPs than the Conservatives, the Conservatives on their own could not command the confidence of the House of Commons. The support of the Liberal Democrat party could have meant that either Labour or the Conservatives, depending on who the Liberal Democrats supported, could command the confidence of the House of Commons. In 2010 Brown could not simply just resign, as there was no one else who could form a government that had the Commons' confidence. What Brown did was to try to gain the support of the Liberal Democrats, or see if the Conservatives were able to gain their support. The Cabinet Manual states that:

> Where an election does not result in an overall majority for a single party, the incumbent government remains in office unless and until the Prime Minister tenders his or her resignation and the Government's resignation to the Sovereign. An incumbent government is entitled to wait until the new Parliament has met to see if it can command the confidence of the House of Commons, but is expected to resign if it becomes clear that it is unlikely to be able to command that confidence and there is a clear alternative.[64]

It is possible for the House of Commons to withdraw its confidence during the lifetime of a Parliament. The Cabinet Manual states that 'The Prime Minister is expected to resign where it is clear that he or she does not have the confidence of the House of Commons and that an alternative government does have the confidence.'[65] There are two methods to do this:

Firstly, under section 2 of the Fixed-term Parliaments Act 2011 it is possible to trigger an early general election if the House of Commons passes a motion 'That this House has no confidence in Her Majesty's Government.' If this happens then the government has 14 days to regain the confidence of the Commons, or if it cannot do this another party could form a new government if it can command the confidence of the Commons. If this cannot happen, then there will be an early general election.

Secondly, as the Act has narrowed the scope but not prevented confidence votes outside of its statutory provisions, there could still be a vote of no confidence. If the government were to lose the vote then another party could form the next government, and if this cannot happen there would need to be an early general election under the Fixed-term Parliaments Act 2011. Please note that the Act is in the process of being repealed.

Conventions regulate the workings of the United Kingdom's constitution. Sir Ivor Jennings famously described conventions as 'the flesh which clothes the dry bones of the law; they make the legal constitution work; they keep it in touch with the growth of ideas.'[66] This is important, as conventions enable the United Kingdom's constitution to change with the time, without the necessity of complex reform by way of the introduction of laws or the need for a new written constitution. An example of this is that at no point since the Bill of Rights in 1689 has Parliament had to legislate in order to limit the powers of the monarch; instead conventions have developed to control the monarch's use of the prerogative. Another such example is that the office of Prime Minister has evolved over time and is regulated by convention. Conventions have been created to deal with new situations, such as devolution settlement in 1998.

Geoffrey Marshall observed that conventions could arise in a number of ways:

1   'Frequently they arise from a series of precedents that are agreed to have given rise to a binding rule of behaviour'; or
2   'They might arise quickly, such as a result of an agreement not to do something'; or
3   '[It] may be formulated on the basis of some acknowledged principle of government which provides a reason or justification for it.'[67]

Devolution has made it necessary for the Sewel Convention to be created, which is a promise by Parliament that it will not legislate for Scotland in areas that have been devolved. The Sewel Convention has not imposed a legal restraint – rather a constitutional restraint – which is necessary to ensure that devolution is effective and does not bring the Scottish and Westminster Parliaments into conflict. The Sewel Convention has now been given statutory recognition by the Scotland Act 2016 and the Wales Act 2017.

ACADEMIC DEBATE

Professor Lord Norton of Lough, a member of the House of Lords and an academic argued that:

Conventions do not become such by the words of a particular person, be it Viscount Cranborne in 1945 or Lord Sewel in 1998. They are not created, but develop. A convention exists once there is an invariable practice. That is not the same as standard or usual practice. If one deviates from it, it is not an invariable practice. Kenneth Wheare distinguished between conventions and usage. I think it more appropriate to distinguish between invariable and usual practice.[68]

We can see the importance of conventions when we consider that the following are governed by them:

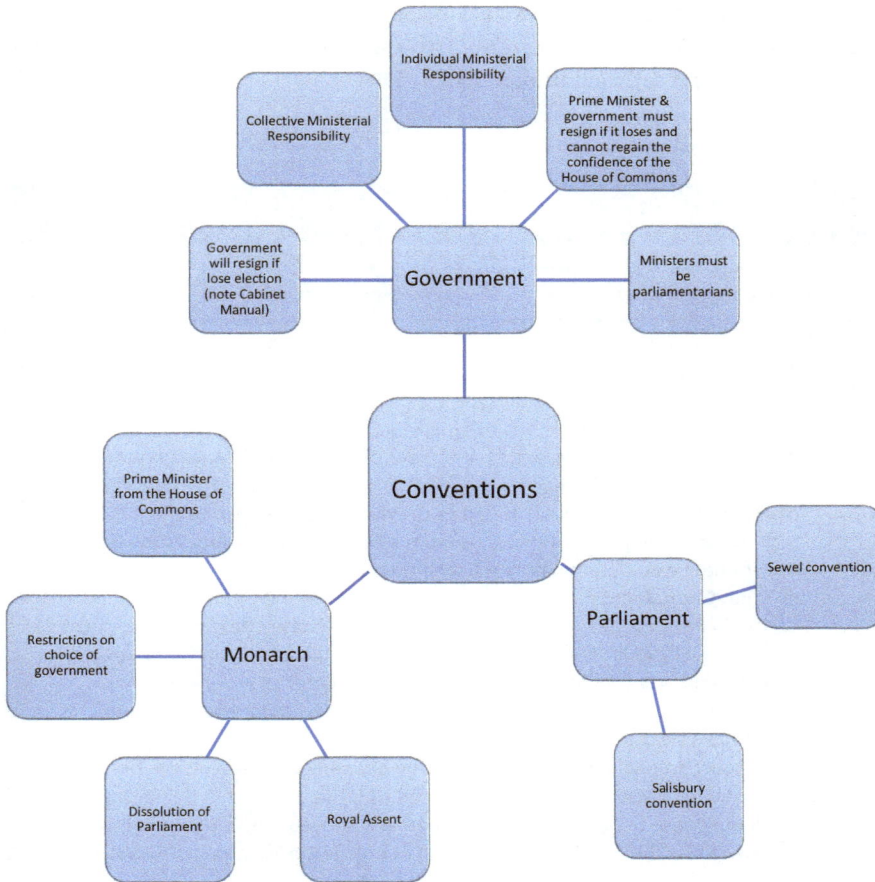

Figure 2.4
Important constitutional conventions

Looking at Figure 2.4 we can see that Parliament, the monarch and the government are restricted in their actions by the existence of constitutional conventions.

2.6.4 Who must follow conventions?

Conventions are only binding on the persons to whom they apply. But how do we know that a convention exists? The existence of a convention must be accepted by those persons who play an important role in the constitution. Jennings argued that we needed to distinguish between conventions and mere practices and established a test to see if a genuine convention existed.[69]

The test has three stages:

1   What are the precedents for the existence of the convention?
2   Did the actors in the precedents believe they were bound by a rule?
3   Is there a reason for the rule?

According to Jennings all three stages need to be satisfied in order for a convention to exist. We cam see from the two examples below how Jennings' test works and how it is satisfied in practice.

Table 2.1 Example: The monarch cannot refuse royal assent to legislation

Jennings' Test	The monarch cannot refuse royal assent to legislation
1 What are the precedents?	Yes – there are precedents for the existence of the convention: • The last time a monarch refused royal assent was Queen Anne in 1708. This was over the Scottish Militia Bill. It is important to note that assent was refused based on the advice of the queen's ministers. Queen Anne's predecessor, William III, had refused assent on a number of occasions. This was significant as Anne's successor, George I, relied heavily on his ministers and their control of the House of Commons. This led to the rise of Cabinet government and reduced the reality of a monarch being in a position to veto legislation as his government would dominate the Commons. • In 1783, George III did not veto Fox's India Bill, even though the king hated Charles James Fox, a leading member of the Fox-North coalition government and the bill. Fox's India Bill would have reformed the East India Company and the king was concerned that the government and its allies would have exploited the company's considerable wealth. It is evident that George III would have personally wished to veto the bill, but he realised that it would be unconstitutional for him to do so. As an alternative to vetoing the bill the king used his influence over members of the House of Lords to defeat the bill. In response the government resigned and subsequently legislation was introduced by the new Prime Minister, William Pitt the Younger, to reform the East India Company.
2 Did the actors in the precedents believe they were bound by a rule?	Yes – successive monarchs have believed themselves to be bound by the rule: • There has been no refusal of assent in over 300 years, although note that George V considered himself to have the power to veto the Irish Home Rule Bill before the onset of the First World War. Whether the king would have actually refused royal assent is a moot point and if he had, then it is likely that the refusal would have given rise to a constitutional crisis and potentially a statutory reform of the need for royal assent.
3 Is there a reason for the rule?	Yes – there appears to be very good reasons for the rule to exist: • It is needed to give effect to democracy and to restrict the monarch's use of the prerogative powers. • If a monarch was to refuse royal assent then there would certainly be calls to reduce the powers of the monarchy and this could include abolishing the prerogative power to give assent to legislation. • Mike Bartlett's play *Charles III* imagines a future King Charles, refusing royal assent over a bill that the king believes removes the freedom of the press. The result is that the king is forced to abdicate due to the unpopularity of his decision to refuse assent. There has been much speculation over whether Prince Charles when he becomes king would ever find himself in a situation where he could refuse royal assent. Professor Robert Blackburn has explored this in *King and Country: Monarchy and the Future King Charles III*.[70]

We will look in detail at the following conventions later on in this book:

- Choice of Prime Minister (**Chapter 7**)
- Individual ministerial responsibility (**Chapter 8**)
- Collective ministerial responsibility (**Chapter 8**)
- Royal assent (**Chapter 7**)
- Resignation upon being defeated in a vote of no confidence (**Chapter 8**)

PUBLIC LAW IN PRACTICE

Imagine that the highly popular Lord Petersfield (fictitious) held a senior Cabinet position and after several of his colleagues were forced to resign, including the Prime Minister, he wishes to stand as party leader and to become the new Prime Minister. Could a member of the House of Lords become Prime Minister? In order to see whether he could, we would need to see how Jennings' test works in practice and whether the convention that the Prime Minister must be a member of the House of Commons would prevent him from becoming Prime Minister.

Applying the three stages as identified by Jennings above, we can see that:

1   There is a precedent for the convention, as the last Prime Minister not to be from the House of Commons was the Marquis of Salisbury in 1902. Since then all other Prime Ministers have been MPs.

2   There are examples of people believing that they were bound by the rule. In order to succeed Harold Macmillan as Prime Minister, the Earl of Home renounced his peerage shortly after becoming Prime Minister 1963[71] and stood in a by-election for a seat in the House of Commons. From this point no Lord could be Prime Minister. Previously, in the 1920s King George V believed that he had to choose Stanley Baldwin MP over Lord Curzon, because of the convention. The choice of personality was also an important factor as the king preferred Baldwin to Curzon. In 1940, King George VI chose Winston Churchill MP over Lord Halifax as Prime Minister to head a wartime coalition government.

3   The reason for the rule is that the House of Commons is elected and it must hold the Prime Minister to account. Whereas the House of Lords is not elected and it would not be democratic for the Prime Minister to be in that chamber. If that was the case how would Prime Minister's Questions work? Importantly, the Prime Minister must be regarded as accountable to the House of Commons and the electorate, which is something that a member of the House of Lords is not.

Therefore, although there is no legal restriction on Lord Petersfield becoming Prime Minister, there is a rule established by convention that a member of the House of Lords cannot be the Prime Minister. Lord Petersfield will need to renounce his peerage and stand as a MP as soon as possible in order to become Prime Minister – which is exactly what the Earl of Home did in 1963, when he became the Prime Minister and leader of the Conservative party.

2.6.5 Are conventions enforceable?

Considering the constitutional importance of conventions, it might appear disconcerting that the monarch, Parliament or the government might choose not to follow a convention. The significance of the monarch refusing royal assent would be momentous and would have considerable constitutional implications. Conventions are not laws and a breach of a convention will not be enforceable in the courts. This was a point observed by Lord Reid in *Madzimbamuto v Lardner-Burke*[72]. In this case the Privy Council held that there was nothing illegal about the United Kingdom passing legislation for Southern Rhodesia, despite the existence of a convention that Parliament could not legislate without the consent of the colony. The legislation had been enacted in response to Southern Rhodesia's unilateral declaration of independence. Lord Reid held that the Board was not concerned whether something was unconstitutional as this was not a matter of law: '[t]hat is a very important convention but it had no legal effect in limiting the legal power of Parliament.'[73]

Likewise, in *Attorney-General v Jonathan Cape Ltd*[74] Lord Widgery CJ considered that a convention, here it was the convention of collective Cabinet responsibility, was not binding in law. His Lordship considered the parties' arguments as to the binding nature of the convention:

> In other words, the defendants submit that the confidential character of Cabinet papers and discussions is based on a true convention as defined in the evidence of Professor Henry Wade, namely, *an obligation founded in conscience only*. Accordingly, the defendants contend that publication of these Diaries is not capable of control by any order of this court.[75]
>
> . . .
>
> It seems to me, therefore, that the Attorney-General must first show that whatever obligation of secrecy or discretion attaches to former Cabinet Ministers, *that obligation is binding in law and not merely in morals*.[76]

Lord Widgery CJ is clearly observing that the obligation needs to be a legal one and not one founded in political morality.

This decision in *Attorney-General v Jonathan Cape Ltd* involved the publication of the dairies of Richard Crossman, a former Cabinet minister, which contained an account of Cabinet discussions. The Attorney-General argued that the contents of Cabinet discussions and the advice offered by civil servants should remain confidential as it was in the public interest to prevent publication. Importantly His Lordship recognised the existence of the convention, despite the fact that people sometimes breached it:

> It is convenient next to deal with Mr. Comyn's third submission, namely, that the evidence does not prove the existence of a convention as to collective responsibility, or adequately define a sphere of secrecy. *I find overwhelming evidence that the doctrine of joint responsibility is generally understood and practised and equally strong evidence that it is on occasion ignored*. The general

effect of the evidence is that the doctrine is an established feature of the English form of government, and it follows that some matters leading up to a Cabinet decision may be regarded as confidential. Furthermore, I am persuaded that the nature o[f] the confidence is that spoken for by the Attorney-General, namely, that since the confidence is imposed to enable the efficient conduct of the Queen's business, the confidence is owed to the Queen and cannot be released by the members of Cabinet themselves.[77]

The decision in *Attorney-General v Jonathan Cape Ltd* confirms Dicey's view that conventions are not law and are not enforceable in a court of law.

In *R (on the application of Miller) v Secretary of State for Exiting the European Union*[78] the majority of the Supreme Court followed the approach in *Attorney-General v Jonathan Cape Ltd* and recognised the existence of a constitutional convention, namely, the Sewel Convention. However, the majority of the court were clear that a convention was not a matter for the courts, as it was political and not legal in nature:

> Judges therefore are neither the parents nor the guardians of political conventions; they are merely observers. As such, they can recognise the operation of a political convention in the context of deciding a legal question (as in the Crossman diaries case – *Attorney General v Jonathan Cape Ltd* [1976] 1 QB 752), but they cannot give legal rulings on its operation or scope, because those matters are determined within the political world. As Professor Colin Munro has stated, 'the validity of conventions cannot be the subject of proceedings in a court of law' – (1975) 91 LQR 218, 228.[79]

Interestingly, the fact that the Scotland Act 2016 gave statutory recognition to the Sewel Convention did not make it a matter for the courts:

> As the Advocate General submitted, by such provisions, the UK Parliament is not seeking to convert the Sewel Convention into a rule which can be interpreted, let alone enforced, by the courts; rather, it is recognising the convention for what it is, namely, a political convention, and is effectively declaring that it is a permanent feature of the relevant devolution settlement. That follows from the nature of the content, and is acknowledged by the words ('it is recognised' and 'will not normally'), of the relevant subsection. We would have expected UK Parliament to have used other words if it were seeking to convert a convention into a legal rule justiciable by the courts.[80]

The majority of the Supreme Court were of the view that a convention was nonetheless important to the constitution, despite the fact it was not justiciable and therefore could not be enforced by the courts:

> [W]e do not underestimate the importance of constitutional conventions, some of which play a fundamental role in the operation of our constitution.

The Sewel Convention has an important role in facilitating harmonious relationships between the UK Parliament and the devolved legislatures. But the policing of its scope and the manner of its operation does not lie within the constitutional remit of the judiciary, which is to protect the rule of law.[81]

2.6.6 The Canadian perspective

The United Kingdom is not the only country which uses constitutional conventions. The Canadian Supreme Court considered the legal force of a convention in *Reference re Amendment of the Constitution of Canada*.[82] When the Canadian government sought to change its constitution it asked the United Kingdom's Parliament to enact legislation to achieve this. The Statute of Westminster 1931 had codified the convention that the Westminster Parliament would not pass legislation for the dominions (self-governing territories such as Canada, New Zealand and Australia) unless asked to do so. In Canada there was a complex procedure to change the constitution, with conventions governing the procedure. It was argued that there was a constitutional convention that the Canadian provinces would have to give their consent before the Canadian constitution could be amended. The question reached the Canadian Supreme Court in *Reference re Amendment of the Constitution of Canada*. The Supreme Court considered Jennings' test for establishing a constitutional convention. The court considered Sir Ivor Jennings' three-stage test[83] and found that:

1   there was a precedent for the convention that the consent of the provinces was required;
2   the actors treated the rule as binding on them; and
3   finally, there was a reason for the rule.

Therefore, a valid constitutional convention existed, and the Canadian government would be acting unconstitutionally if it did not obtain the consent of the provinces. However, the Supreme Court held that there was no legal sanction against the Canadian government for failing to act in accordance with the conventions. The Canadian Supreme Court also considered whether a convention could become crystallised, so that it became law. This argument was rejected by the Supreme Court:

> This conflict between convention and law which prevents the courts from enforcing conventions also prevents conventions from crystallizing into laws, unless it be by statutory adoption. It is because the sanctions of convention rest with institutions of government other than courts, such as the Governor General or the Lieutenant Governor, or the Houses of Parliament, or with public opinion and ultimately, with the electorate, that it is generally said that they are political.[84]

ACADEMIC DEBATE

Carissima Mathen considered the legacy of the Supreme Court's decision in *Reference re Amendment of the Constitution of Canada* and observed that:

> The Reference is a perfect example of the power of the declaration. The bald assertion of something as constitutional fact without attendant remedies or juridical consequences permits the Court to exert tremendous influence without engaging in a power struggle . . . stating something as "law" without stating a clearly binding rule. It did this, first, by recognizing a convention which admittedly had no legal force and, second, by providing an answer just binding enough to render the federal resolution unacceptable but sufficiently vague to leave future outcomes uncertain.[85]

The Court of Appeal in *Manuel v Attorney-General*[86] rejected the argument that a convention could restrict the Canadian government from asking the United Kingdom's Parliament to legislate to create a new constitution. The court held that Parliament could legislate for Canada under section 4 of the Statute of Westminster 1931. Slade LJ dismissed the argument that a convention could restrict this:

> The sole condition precedent which has to be satisfied if a law made by the United Kingdom Parliament is to extend to a Dominion as part of its law is to be found stated in the body of the Statute of 1931 itself (section 4). This court would run counter to all principles of statutory interpretation if it were to purport to vary or supplement the terms of this stated condition precedent by reference to some supposed convention, which, though referred to in the preamble, is not incorporated in the body of the Statute.[87]

Nonetheless, the existence of a convention can be relevant to support legal action. In *Attorney-General v. Jonathan Cape Ltd*[88] the convention of collective ministerial responsibility was used as evidence to support the argument that information discussed during Cabinet meetings, was protected by the tort of confidence. The convention had demonstrated the importance of Cabinet discussions remaining confidential.

PUBLIC LAW IN CONTEXT
'THE CONFIDENTIAL CHARACTER OF THE INFORMATION'

In *Attorney-General v. Jonathan Cape Ltd* Lord Widgery CJ made the following observations about the confidential nature of the information relating to discussions in Cabinet meetings:

In my judgment, the Attorney-General has made out his claim that the expression of individual opinions by Cabinet Ministers in the course of Cabinet discussion are matters of confidence, the publication of which can be restrained by the court when this is clearly necessary in the public interest.[89]

. . .

There must, however, be a limit in time after which the confidential character of the information, and the duty of the court to restrain publication, will lapse.[90]

. . .

It is unnecessary to elaborate the evils which might flow if at the close of a Cabinet meeting a Minister proceeded to give the press an analysis of the voting, but we are dealing in this case with a disclosure of information nearly 10 years later.

It may, of course, be intensely difficult in a particular case, to say at what point the material loses its confidential character, on the ground that publication will no longer undermine the doctrine of joint Cabinet responsibility. It is this difficulty which prompts some to argue that Cabinet discussions should retain their confidential character for a longer and arbitrary period such as 30 years, or even for all time, but this seems to me to be excessively restrictive.[91]

2.6.7 Non-legal consequences for breaching a convention

Dicey acknowledged that despite conventions not being law, there could still be sanctions for breaching a convention.[92] Dicey expressly referred to the passing of the Parliament Act 1911, when he noted the possibility of a non-legal sanction.[93] There had been a convention that the House of Lords would not veto money bills. This was breached when the Liberal Chancellor of the Exchequer David Lloyd George presented his budget to Parliament and the Conservative majority in the House of Lords rejected the budget. The government requested that the monarch create a large number of Liberal peers so that the Liberals would have a majority in the House of Lords. The threat worked and the Conservative peers voted in favour of the budget. By way of sanction, the Parliament Act 1911 was passed to restrict the ability of the House of Lords to veto money bills. Failure to follow a convention had resulted in the convention becoming law. Other conventions have become law, such as the convention that Parliament would not legislate for the dominions without their consent. This convention was established by 1926 and was given legal effect by the Statute of Westminster 1931. Failure to follow some conventions such as individual ministerial responsibility will result in no sanction, especially where the minister at fault has the support of the Prime Minister. However, a minister who refuses to resign may face dismissal. Dicey noted that some conventions were not always followed, but that many were enforced by public opinion.[94]

Given the importance of conventions it is unhelpful that each convention cannot be precisely defined. The conventions develop over time in order to respond to current issues (e.g. devolution resulted in the Sewel Convention). In the 1970s the Australian government attempted the codification of conventions and this proved problematic.[95] This was because conventions are flexible and develop over time in order to respond to new situations, whereas a code does not develop under its own violation and will become incomplete.[96] Andrew Blick has recently explored the impact of the publication of the Cabinet Manual in 2011 and its impact on conventions. The Cabinet Manual sets out many important conventions, although it also excludes others. Blick observes that '[c]onstitutional conventions do not lend themselves readily to codification' and notes the possible effects of having certain conventions set out in such a document. These include strengthening those included and weakening those which were excluded, preventing conventions from evolving to meet new situations and, interestingly, the Cabinet Manual being used in judicial review proceedings to challenge ministerial behaviour.[97]

2.7 Prerogative powers

The prerogative powers will be covered in detail in **Chapters 10** and **11**. The prerogative is an important source of the constitution because it forms the remainder of the monarch's discretionary powers – that is, powers which are recognised by the common law and are not given to the monarch by statute. Prerogative powers are largely exercised today by the government, although the monarch still possesses her personal prerogative powers. The prerogative powers cover:

- the deployment of British armed forces and the decision to declare war;
- foreign policy and dealings with other countries;
- the appointment of the Prime Minister, royal assent and the decision to dissolve Parliament (for now covered by the Fixed-term Parliaments Act 2011) and trigger a General Election.

Importantly the prerogative powers exist independently of Parliament and are subjected to limited parliamentary review.

2.8 Practical application

In light of the financial crisis that had engulfed the United Kingdom, the Prime Minister, had summoned an emergency Cabinet meeting at Downing Street. The meeting proved to be difficult, as many Cabinet ministers disagreed about the best way to respond to the crisis.

The Home Secretary had tweeted before the meeting about what he was going to say in Cabinet and how he hoped that his colleagues would 'do the right thing.'

The Prime Minister announced that he would ask the monarch to appoint Sandra Green to Cabinet due to her expertise in finance. Sandra Green is not a member of either House of Parliament.

The Chancellor of the Exchequer was unimpressed with her colleague's performance and told a television news programme that afternoon what had happened at Cabinet.

The Foreign Secretary had used social media to outline her version of the constitution, declaring 'a vote of no confidence is irrelevant today, if you are in government you govern the country, and you can ignore the House of Commons.'

With reference to constitutional conventions, case law, legislation and academic opinion, please outline the issues raised above.

2.9 Key points to take away from this chapter

- The United Kingdom's constitution comprises a number of different sources.
- The United Kingdom's previous membership of the European Union has had a significant impact on the constitution.
- The prerogative is an important source of non-statutory powers for ministers.
- Constitutional conventions play an important role in the workings of the United Kingdom's constitution.
- There are a number of constitutionally important statutes such as the Human Rights Act 1998.

Notes

1 [2002] EWHC 195 (Admin); [2003] QB 151.
2 ibid 185.
3 ibid 186.
4 ibid.
5 ibid.
6 ibid 186–87.
7 [2012] UKSC 24.
8 [2014] UKSC 3.

9   [207] (Lord Neuberger and Lord Mance).

10 ibid.

11 D Feldman, 'The Nature and Significance of "Constitutional" Legislation' [2013] LQR 343, 346–48.

12 ibid 357.

13 Above (n 8).

14 P Craig, 'Constitutionalising Constitutional Law: HS2' [2014] PL 373.

15 ibid 384.

16 ibid 389.

17 F Ahmed and A Perry, 'Constitutional Statutes' (2017) 37(2) OJLS 461.

18 ibid 462–65.

19 ibid 471.

20 Lord Justice Auld, 'Review of the Criminal Courts in England and Wales' <https://webarchive.nationalarchives.gov.uk/20070212075407/http://www.criminal-courts-review.org.uk/auldconts.htm>.

21 M Radin, 'The Myth of the Magna Carta' (1947) 60(7) HLR 1060.

22 For more details see <www.parliament.uk/about/living-heritage/evolutionof parliament/parliamentaryauthority/civilwar/overview/petition-of-right/>; LJ Reeve, 'The Legal Status of the Petition of Right' 29(2) The *Historical Journal* 257. For the precise text of the petition see www.legislation.gov.uk/aep/Cha1/3/1.

23 ibid 258.

24 Bill of Rights 1689.

25 2010–15.

26 For a detailed commentary on the significance of the Succession to the Crown Act 2013 see N Parpworth, 'The Succession to the Crown Act 2013: Modernising the Monarchy' (2013) 76(6) MLR 1070.

27 For a useful commentary on the union between England and Scotland see AI Macinnes, *Union and Empire: The Making of the United Kingdom* (CUP 2007).

28 UKHL 56.

29 Section 1 of the Scotland Act 2016 inserted a new section, section 63A into the Scotland Act 1998.

30 Section 2 of the Scotland Act 2016 inserted a new section, subsection 28(8) into the Scotland Act 1998.

31 For a detailed commentary on the European Union (Withdrawal) Act 2018 see P Craig, 'Constitutional Principle, the Rule of Law and Political Reality: The European Union (Withdrawal) Act 2018' (2019) 82(2) MLR 319.

32 [2017] UKSC 5.

33 *R (on the application of UNISON) v Lord Chancellor* [2017] UKSC 51.

34 (1765) 19 State Tr 1029.

35 [2004] UKHL 56.

36 [2000] 2 AC 115.

37 [2019] UKSC 41.

38 (26/62) [1963] ECR 1.

39 (6/64) [1964] ECR 585.

40 [1991] 1 AC 603.

41 I Jennings, *Law and the Constitution* (4th edn, UoL Press 1952).

42 K Wheare, *Modern Constitutions* (OUP 1951) 179.

43 AL Young, 'The Relationship Between Parliament, the Executive, and the Judiciary' in J Jowell and C O'Cinneide (eds), *The Changing Constitution* (9th edn, OUP 2019) 338.

44   A Blick, 'The Cabinet Manual and the Codification of Conventions' (2014) 67(1) Parliamentary Affairs 191, 205.

45   See G Metzger, 'Twenty-Second Amendment: Let It Be' <https://constitutioncenter.org/interactive-constitution/amendments/amendment-xxii/twenty-second-amendment-let-it-be-by-gillian-metzger/interp/50>.

46   HS Truman, *Memoirs* (Volume 2, Doubleday 1956) 488–89. Quoted in PS Davis, 'The Results and Implications of the Enactment of the Twenty-Second Amendment' (1979) 9(3) Presidential Studies Quarterly 289.

47   See 'For a One-Term, Six-Year Presidency' *The New York Times* (31 December 1985) <www.nytimes.com/1985/12/31/opinion/for-a-one-term-six-year-presidency.html>.

48   AV Dicey, *Introduction to the Study of the Law of the Constitution* (Originally published in 1915, reprinted edn, Liberty Fund 1982) cxlv.

49   ibid 276.

50   ibid.

51   M Tempest, 'Parliament Gives Blair Go-Ahead for War' *The Guardian* (18 March 2003) <www.theguardian.com/politics/2003/mar/18/iraq.iraq6>.

52   'MPs Debate Military Action Taken Against Libya' (UK Parliament, 22 March 2011) <www.parliament.uk/business/news/2011/march/debate-on-military-action-in-libya/>.

53   N Watt, R Mason and N Hopkins, 'Blow to Cameron's Authority as MPs Rule Out British Assault on Syria' *The Guardian* (30 August 2013) <www.theguardian.com/politics/2013/aug/30/cameron-mps-syria>.

54   P Walker, 'Government wins Commons Vote Over Syria Military Action' *The Guardian* (17 April 2018) <www.theguardian.com/politics/2018/apr/17/mps-should-take-back-control-of-military-action-jeremy-corbyn>.

55   The Cabinet Manual at [5.38] provides this outline 'In 2011, the Government acknowledged that a convention had developed in Parliament that before troops were committed the House of Commons should have an opportunity to debate the matter and said that it proposed to observe that convention except when there was an emergency and such action would not be appropriate.'

56   H Stewart, 'Corbyn Calls for "War Powers Act" as Check on Military Intervention' *The Guardian* (15 April 2018) <www.theguardian.com/politics/2018/apr/15/jeremy-corbyn-calls-for-war-powers-act-as-check-on-military-intervention>.

57   Lord Norton of Lough, 'The Strathclyde Recommendations Are Based on a False Premise That There Is a Convention That the Lords Does Not Reject Statutory Instruments' (Constitution Unit, 14 January 2016) <https://constitution-unit.com/2016/01/14/the-strathclyde-recommendations-are-based-on-a-false-premise-that-there-is-a-convention-that-the-lords-does-not-reject-statutory-instruments/>.

58   M Russell, 'The Lords and Tax Credits: Fact and Myth' (Constitution Unit, 22 October 2015) <https://constitution-unit.com/2015/10/22/the-lords-and-tax-credits-fact-and-myth/>.

59   For commentary see House of Commons Public Administration and Constitutional Affairs Committee, 'The Role of Parliament in the UK Constitution Interim Report: The Status and Effect of Confidence Motions and the Fixed-term Parliaments Act 2011 (Fourteenth Report of Session 2017–19), <https://publications.parliament.uk/pa/cm201719/cmselect/cmpubadm/1813/1813.pdf>.

60 Dicey (n 48) ixvi.

61 See the House of Commons Public Administration and Constitutional Affairs Committee (n 59).

62 J Jaconelli, 'The Nature of Constitutional Convention' (1999) 19(1) Legal Studies 24, 29.

63 Dicey (n 48) Lxvii.

64 Cabinet Manual [2.12].

65 ibid [2.19].

66 Jennings (n 41) 80–81.

67 G Marshall, *Constitutional Conventions: The Rules and Forms of Political Accountability* (OUP 1984) 8–9.

68 Lord Norton of Lough (n 57).

69 Jennings (n 41).

70 R Blackburn, *King and Country: Monarchy and the Future King Charles III* (Politico's Publishing Ltd, 2006).

71 Douglas-Home renounced his peerage using the procedure under the Peerages Act 1963. See 'Peers' Battle to Stay in the Commons' *BBC News* (26 July 2013) <www.bbc.co.uk/news/uk-politics-23447489>.

72 [1969] 1 AC 645.

73 ibid 723.

74 [1976] QB 752.

75 ibid 765 (emphasis added).

76 ibid 767 (emphasis added).

77 ibid 770 (emphasis added).

78 [2017] UKSC 5.

79 ibid 146.

80 ibid 148.

81 ibid 151.

82 [1981] 1 SCR 753. For an interesting commentary and consideration of the wider constitutional issues see PC Oliver, 'Constitutional Conventions in the Canadian Courts' (*UK Constitutional Law Association Blog*, 4 November 2011) <https://ukconstitutionallaw.org/2011/11/04/peter-c-oliver-constitutional-conventions-in-the-canadian-courts/>.

83 ibid 888.

84 ibid 882–83.

85 C Mathen, '"The Question Calls for an Answer, and I Propose to Answer It": The Patriation Reference as Constitutional Method.' (2011) 54 The Supreme Court Law Review: Osgoode's Annual Constitutional Cases Conference 143, 165–66.

86 [1983] 1 Ch. 77.

87 ibid [107].

88 [1976] QB 752.

89 ibid 771.

90 ibid.

91 ibid.

92 Dicey (n 48) 292.

93 ibid lxix.

94 ibid 295–97.

95 For detailed commentary see CJG Sampford, '"Recognize and Declare": An Australian Experiment in Codifying Constitutional Conventions' (1987) 7(3) OJLS 369.

96   See Jaconelli (n 62) 24.
97   Blick (n 44) 191.

Further reading

Ahmed F and A Perry, 'Constitutional Statutes' (2017) 37(2) OJLS 461

Blick A, 'The Cabinet Manual and the Codification of Conventions' (2014) 67(1) Parliamentary Affairs 191

Craig P, 'Constitutionalising Constitutional Law: HS2' [2014] PL 373

Dicey AV, *Introduction to the Study of the Law of the Constitution* (Originally published in 1915, reprinted edn, Liberty Fund 1982)

Feldman D, 'The Nature and Significance of "Constitutional" Legislation' [2013] LQR 343

Jaconelli J, 'The Nature of Constitutional Convention' (1999) 19(1) Legal Studies 24
——, 'Do Constitutional Conventions Bind?' [2005] CLJ 149

Jennings I, *Law and the Constitution* (4th edn, UoL Press 1952)

Marshall G, *Constitutional Conventions: The Rules and Forms of Political Accountability* (OUP 1984)

Munro C, *Studies in Constitutional Law* (OUP 2005)

Wheare K, *Modern Constitutions* (OUP 1951)

The separation of powers and the United Kingdom's constitution

This chapter will

- explain what is meant by the separation of powers;
- consider the importance of checks and balances between the different branches of government;
- evaluate the impact of the Constitutional Reform Act 2005 on the United Kingdom's constitution;
- engage with reforms to the judiciary such as the Constitutional Reform Act 2005 and the Crime and Courts Act 2013; and
- evaluate whether it can be said that the United Kingdom conforms to the separation of powers.

3.1 Introduction

Would it be acceptable in the 21st century for the same group of individuals who govern a country to also make its laws and to sit as judges? The answer is surely no, as having a system where governing a country, making its law and adjudicating upon legal disputes and dispensing justice as the judiciary is carried out by the same group of individuals could offer an opportunity for these individuals to act without restraint and to exercise their power in a way that serves their own purposes and to the detriment of their opponents and minority groups within society. The French academic Montesquieu identified this problem in the 18th century and his writings on the need for the separation of powers have proved extremely influential.

In this chapter we will look at the importance of the separation of powers as a constitutional theory. The powers that we are concerned with are the power to make law, the power to govern the country and the power to administer justice. Every country needs these three powers to be exercised in order for it to function. We shall see that academics and judges have argued that the three powers, or functions of government, should be exercised separately and that

DOI: 10.4324/9780429293498-4

a different branch of government, which comprises different people, should carry out each function (see Figure 3.1 below).

Why should a country's governmental system conform to the theory of the separation of powers? Is it necessary for the legislative, executive and judicial branches of government to comprise different groups of people and should each branch exercise distinctive functions? These are some of the questions that we will address. In this chapter we will focus on the United Kingdom and ask whether the United Kingdom's constitution and system of government conforms to the separation of powers. This is a controversial issue as many academics dispute whether the United Kingdom actually does have the separation of powers. However, as we shall see this is far from a simple yes, or no, answer. Therefore, for examination purposes it is essential that you understand the way that the United Kingdom's government operates.

This chapter serves an introduction to some of the key issues that we will address later on in this book, namely whether Parliament sufficiently holds the executive to account, whether the judiciary is sufficiently independent from the executive and Parliament and whether the Parliamentary system at Westminster means that the executive by the very nature of the United Kingdom's system of democracy dominates Parliament in terms of numbers of MPs and parliamentary time. We will also explore the impact of the Constitutional Reform Act 2005 and the Crime and Courts Act 2013 and look at whether further reform is needed. Finally, we will also look at the federal constitution of the United States of America by way of comparison to see how the separation of powers was used to frame the US constitution.

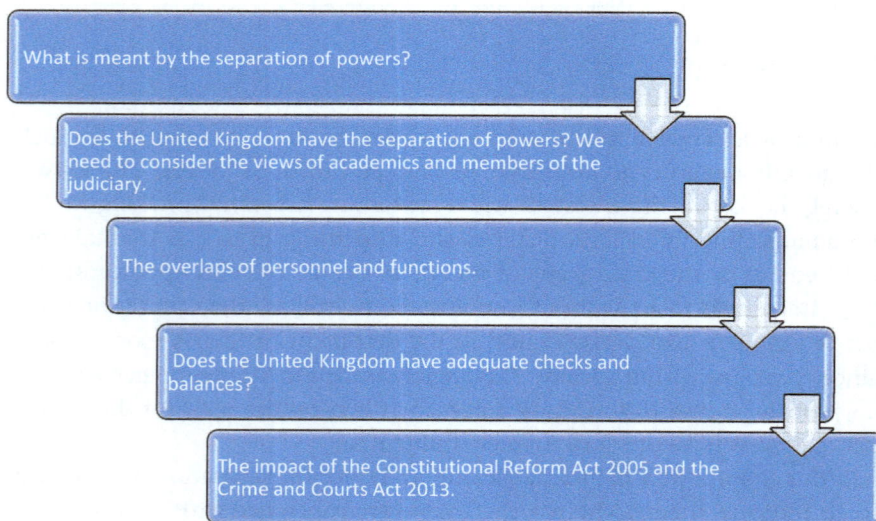

What is meant by the separation of powers?

Does the United Kingdom have the separation of powers? We need to consider the views of academics and members of the judiciary.

The overlaps of personnel and functions.

Does the United Kingdom have adequate checks and balances?

The impact of the Constitutional Reform Act 2005 and the Crime and Courts Act 2013.

Figure 3.1
Approaching the separation of powers

3.2 What is meant by the separation of powers

The separation of powers requires that the powers, or functions, of government which are law making, governing and administration of justice must be exercised by the three distinct branches of government: the executive, the legislature and the judiciary. The separation of powers can be explained as the division of the three key functions of any state between different groups of individuals. This, as we shall see below, could be set out in a written constitution, such as the constitution of the United States of America. The separation of powers has considerable constitutional importance and should not be seen as irrelevant or too dependent on theory. It serves a practical purpose, namely, to prevent tyranny and the abuse of power by an individual or group of individuals. For example, quite a few years ago in Pakistan, members of the judiciary and lawyers protested against the government of General Musharraf, who was the then President of Pakistan after coming to power as a result of a military coup.[1] The Chief Justice of Pakistan and other members of the Pakistani judiciary were arrested as a result of the protest. This protest symbolised the importance of the separation of powers in Pakistan.

We shall see that traditionally English judges have stated that there exists a form of the separation of powers in the United Kingdom. However, until recently there were very few academics that would support this view.

3.3 The three functions of government

In any state there are three identifiable functions of government that need to be carried out to ensure that the state operates effectively. The executive, the legislature and the judiciary should exercise these functions. It is important to understand the composition and function of the executive, legislature and the judiciary within the United Kingdom. In order to have a detailed understanding of this you may wish to refer to:

- **Chapter 7** Parliament
- **Chapter 8** The Executive
- **Chapter 9** The Judiciary

3.3.1 The executive

In the United Kingdom the executive is comprised of the monarch (Her Majesty Queen Elizabeth II, who is the head of state), the government (the Prime Minister, Boris Johnson MP, senior ministers who attend Cabinet and are known as Secretaries of State, and junior ministers who work in government departments), the emergency services such as the Metropolitan Police, the armed forces, local government, government departments (such as the Home Office headed by Priti Patel, or the Foreign Office headed by Dominic Raab) and the civil service which runs the day-to-day work of the government departments.

The civil service is politically neutral and is headed by the Head of the Civil Service and Cabinet Secretary, Sir Mark Sedwill. The Cabinet Office is based in Downing Street and serves an important role in ensuring the smooth operation of Cabinet government. Since 1916 the Cabinet Office has kept minutes of Cabinet meetings and it is responsible for drafting the Cabinet Manual

Additionally, as a result of Tony Blair's Labour government's policy of devolution following the 1997 general election, there are separate governments in Scotland, Wales and Northern Ireland. Each of these governments has responsibility for administering the powers that have been devolved since 1998. For example, as a result of the Scotland Act 1998, in Scotland there is a First Minister who is the head of government, ministers who are responsible for the departments, the Scottish emergency services and civil service.

PUBLIC LAW IN ACTION

It is important that you are able to understand the structure of the United Kingdom's government and the role of ministers in the running of government departments. Do you know what the Secretary of State for Foreign and Commonwealth Affairs is, or who the junior ministers are and what there particular areas of responsibilities are within the Foreign and Commonwealth Office? You can find this information by visiting the Foreign and Commonwealth Office's website: www.gov.uk/government/organisations/foreign-commonwealth-office

3.3.2 The legislature

The legislative function of creating laws is carried out by the United Kingdom's Parliament. Parliament comprises the House of Commons, the House of Lords and the Queen in Parliament. The United Kingdom's Parliament is based at Westminster and is bicameral which means that there are two chambers, the House of Commons and the House of Lords. Many other countries have bicameral legislatures, such as Canada that has a House of Commons and a Senate. Whereas, some countries have a unicameral legislature, which means that there is just one legislative chamber, such as Hungary's National Assembly. In the United Kingdom as a result of the Parliament Acts 1911 and 1949, the House of Lords has limited power to prevent legislation from being passed. Prior to the enactment of these Acts, the House of Lords had the same legislative powers at the House of Commons and as a matter of law could prevent any legislation from being enacted. According to the United Kingdom's constitution Parliament has legal sovereignty and an Act of Parliament is the highest source of law. This means that as a matter of law there are no restrictions on what laws Parliament may choose to enact. Although, as we shall see in **Chapter 6**, the United Kingdom's membership of the European Union had placed restrictions on the laws that Parliament can enact. This was because of the European Communities Act 1972. However, the European Communities Act 1972 has been repealed by the European Union (Withdrawal) Act 2018.

We will explore Parliamentary Sovereignty in **Chapter 5** and look at what this means in practice. We will also consider the changes that the result of the Referendum on the United Kingdom's membership of the European Union will have on the ability of Parliament to legislate on any subject matter.

There are 650 Members of Parliament (MPs) who sit in the House of Commons and their constituents directly elect them every five years under the Fixed-Term Parliaments Act 2011. There are 650 parliamentary constituencies in the United Kingdom and the system used to elect MPs is called First Past the Post. This system is controversial as the candidate with the most votes in their constituency will become that constituency's MP, even if they have one more vote than another candidate or in theory could have just 20 per cent of the overall vote. In 2011, there was a referendum on the alternative vote, which would have changed the way that MPs were elected. The public voted to keep First Past the Post.

Members of the House of Lords are not elected, and the three main political parties appoint most of its members. The members who are appointed under the Life Peerages Act 1958 are known as life peers and can sit in the House of Lords until their death or choose to retire under the House of Lords Reform Act 2014. Additionally, there are 92 hereditary peers who are members of the House of Lords because they have inherited a hereditary title and 26 Church of England Bishops. The House of Lords Reform Act 1999 removed the vast majority of hereditary peers. However, the 1999 Act did not decide whether members of the House of Lords should be elected, appointed or a mixture of both.

PUBLIC LAW IN CONTEXT
HOUSE OF LORDS REFORM

House of Lords reform has been proposed for since the beginning of 20th century. However, apart from the introduction of life peers under the Life Peerages Act 1958, the most significant reform occurred as a result of the House of Lords Reform Act 1999. In **Chapter 7** we will look in more detail at House of Lords reform and engage with the issue as to whether in a modern democracy it is still appropriate to have a non-elected second chamber.

3.3.2.1 Devolved legislatures

As a result of devolution the United Kingdom's Parliament has devolved many law-making powers to the Scottish Parliament under the Scotland Act 1998, to the National Assembly of Wales created by the Government of Wales Act 1998 and receiving law-making powers under the Governance of Wales Act 2006, and the Northern Ireland Assembly under the Northern Ireland Act 1998. These devolved legislative bodies have received significant law-making powers.

However, there are calls for further law-making powers to be devolved. As a result of the decision of the Scottish electorate in the referendum of Scottish independence to remain part of the United Kingdom in 2014 and 'the vow made' by the leaders of the main Westminster political parties, the Scotland Act 2016 has devolved further law making powers to the Scottish Parliament. Section 1 of the Act has also guaranteed the permanence of the Scottish Parliament and Scottish Government, whilst section 2 has given statutory recognition to the Sewel Convention (whereby the Westminster Parliament promises not to make laws for devolved areas without the consent of the Scottish Parliament).

The Northern Ireland Assembly was reinstated by the Northern Ireland Act 1998, having been suspended during the period known as the 'Troubles.' Since January 2017 the Northern Ireland Assembly had been suspended due to political difficulties, as unlike the other devolved governments there needs to be power sharing between the different political parties. The Assembly reopened in January 2020.

PUBLIC LAW IN CONTEXT
IN THE MATTER OF AN APPLICATION BY THE NORTHERN IRELAND HUMAN RIGHTS COMMISSION FOR JUDICIAL REVIEW (NORTHERN IRELAND)

This suspension means that the devolved legislature for Northern Ireland cannot make new laws and controversial issues such as abortion have been considered the United Kingdom Supreme Court. The majority in *In the matter of an application by the Northern Ireland Human Rights Commission for Judicial Review (Northern Ireland)*[2] held that the applicant did not have standing, despite the law being incompatible with Article 8 of the European Convention on Human Rights, which protects the right to a family life. The decision itself was controversial notwithstanding the subject-matter of the appeal, as if the applicant did have standing it would have led the Supreme Court to declare Acts of Parliament to be incompatible under section 4 of the Human Rights Act 1998 with Article 8 of the European Convention on Human Rights. Dissenting in part, Lord Reed warned:

> At national level, it is equally important that the courts should respect the importance of political accountability for decisions on controversial questions of social and ethical policy. The Human Rights Act and the devolution statutes have altered the powers of the courts, but they have not altered the inherent limitations of court proceedings as a means of determining issues of social and ethical policy. Nor have they diminished the inappropriateness, and the dangers for the courts themselves, of highly contentious issues in social and ethical policy being determined by judges, who have neither any special insight into such questions nor any political accountability for their decisions.[3]

His Lordship was clear that the question should be one for elected politicians and nor the courts. Therefore, the time for reforming law was when the Assembly was no longer suspended.

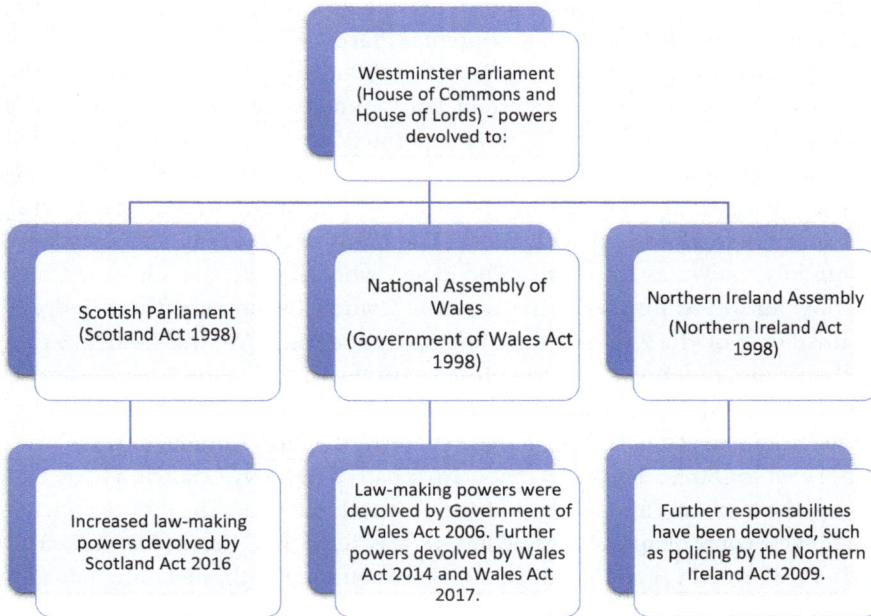

Figure 3.2
The effect of devolution within the United Kingdom

As a result of devolution within the United Kingdom there have been calls to establish an English Parliament to make laws that only concern England. Following the outcome of the 2014 referendum on Scottish independence the House of Commons introduced a system known as English Votes for English Laws, or EVEL, whereby the Standing Orders of the House of Commons were altered to require the consent of English MPs to bills which would only affect England. We will look at this in more detail in **Chapter 7** when we will consider how Parliament operates. Please note that the EVEL procedure has now been abolished.

3.3.3 The judiciary

Within the United Kingdom there are three distinct legal systems that have their own courts and judiciary. These are England and Wales, Northern Ireland and Scotland. This section will focus on England and Wales, although it is important to be aware of the different court structures in the other two jurisdictions. The most senior court in England and Wales for both criminal and civil law is the United Kingdom Supreme Court. The Supreme Court is situated in London in the former Middlesex Guildhall building. The Constitutional Reform Act 2005 created the Supreme Court and in October 2009 it replaced the Appellate Committee of the House of Lords as the highest court of appeal. The Supreme Court will hear appeals on matters of criminal and civil law from England and Wales, and from Northern Ireland. However, from Scotland, the Supreme Court is only the highest appeal court for civil law and not as a general rule for criminal law. As we shall see in **Chapter 9** when we explore the role of the judiciary there are exceptions when an appeal from Scotland regarding criminal law can be heard by the Supreme Court.

Prior to the Constitutional Reform Act 2005 the highest appeal court was the Appellate Committee of the House of Lords and its members were known as Lords of Appeal in Ordinary and were appointed to the parliamentary House of Lords as life peers in order to hear appeals. It is important to note that the House of Lords was the highest court within the United Kingdom, despite it being one of the two Houses of Parliament. The Lords of Appeal in Ordinary were commonly known as Law Lords. The judges who serve on the Supreme Court are now known as Justices of the Supreme Court. The Supreme Court judge is presided over by the President and the Deputy-President. We will see below that the Supreme Court must not be confused with the United States Supreme Court.

Another court, the Judicial Committee of the Privy Council, is also based in the former Middlesex Guildhall building. Previously, the Privy Council heard appeals at 10 Downing Street. This court (or board) is part of the Privy Council, a body that advises the monarch, and fulfils its historic judicial functions. The Privy Council is the highest court of appeal for British Overseas Territories, Crown Dependencies such as Jersey, and several countries in the Commonwealth, including Jamaica. Until quite recently the Privy Council was the highest appeal court for New Zealand, before the creation of the Supreme Court of New Zealand in 2004. You will encounter many Privy Council decisions in your studies and whilst they are not binding in England and Wales, they are nonetheless persuasive.

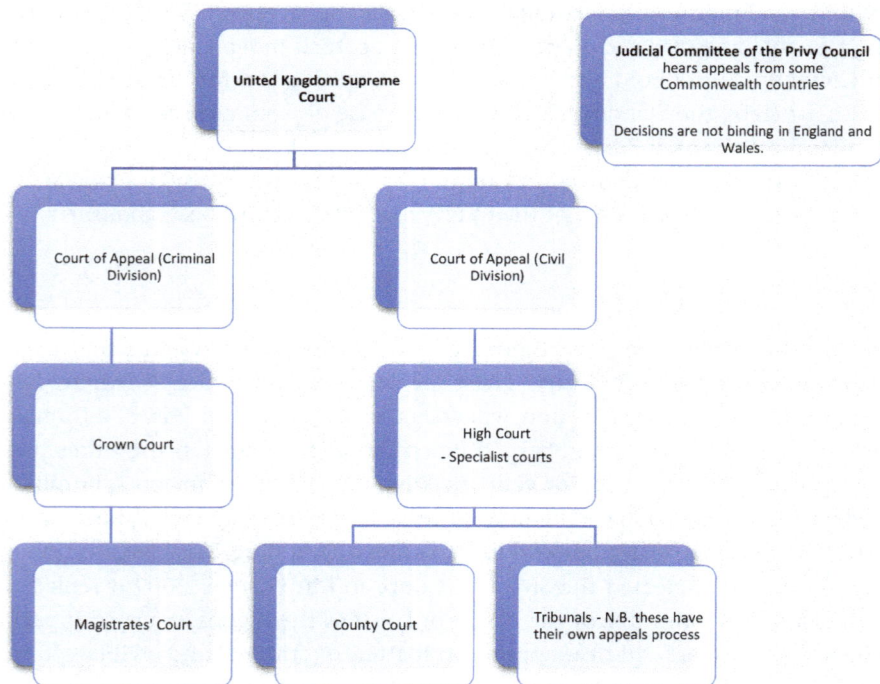

Figure 3.3
The court structure in England and Wales

The next senior court is the Court of Appeal. The Court of Appeal has a separate criminal and civil division. The head of criminal justice is the Lord Chief Justice, Lord Burnett, who is also head of the judiciary in England and Wales. The head of civil justice is the Master of the Rolls, Sir Geoffrey Vos. Then there is the High Court that comprises a number of specialised courts that deal with different areas of law, such as the Chancery Division and Family Division. The High Court was created by the Judicature Acts 1873 and 1875. The Acts merged the common law courts and the equitable Court of Chancery. In Chapters 15 and 16 we will see that applications for Judicial Review will be made at the High Court. Judicial Review is where the court will review government decision-making and determine whether the decision was legal, reasonable or procedurally fair.

The Crown Court will hear serious criminal cases and a circuit judge or recorder will preside over the case to determine questions of law, although the jury will determine questions of law. The courts which most people will have contact with are the County Courts and Magistrates' Courts. County Courts are located in most large towns and deal with smaller civil cases (usually under £50,000). Magistrates' Courts, which try summary only and triable either way offences, will hear over 95 per cent of criminal cases. Magistrates are volunteers and do not have any legal training, although they are assisted by a legally trained advisor. Additionally, there are a number of tribunals which are concerned with specific areas such as employment law, social security and immigration.

3.3 What does each of these branches of government do?

In **section 3.2** above we looked at the three branches of government within the United Kingdom and now we will look at what each branch does.

3.3.1 The executive

The executive is used to describe the function of governing a country. The executive includes the monarch, the government and the civil service. The government sets the legislative agenda of the new Parliament, which is set out in the Queen's Speech. The government uses the powers granted by Parliament to govern the country. The government will make decisions such as whether the build a new runway at a major airport and the annual budget. The government represents the Crown, hence it is 'Her Majesty's Government.' These decisions are by the Cabinet, which comprises senior ministers who are responsible for a government department, such as the defence, health and education. The electorate does not directly elect the Prime Minister. Instead, the political party who can command the support of the House of Commons (i.e. with the most MPs or is able to form a coalition) is invited by the monarch to form a government. The Prime Minister is usually the leader of the political party which has the most MPs in the House of Commons.

PUBLIC LAW IN ACTION

In 2007, Gordon Brown became Prime Minister after Tony's Blair resignation; in 2016, Theresa May became Prime Minister after David Cameron's resignation; and in 2019, Boris Johnson became Prime Minister after May's resignation and in all three cases there was no general election as a result of the country having a new Prime Minister. Should there have been a general election in both cases?

Imagine that you are an advisor to the Foreign Secretary who has just won her party's leadership contest. As the new party leader, she will become the Prime Minister because her political party is in government. Would you advise the new party leader to ask the House of Commons under the Fixed-term Parliaments Act 2011 to hold an early general election?

It is important to note that unlike Gordon Brown in 2007, Theresa May in 2016 could not request the monarch to use her prerogative powers to dissolve Parliament, because this power has been replaced by the Fixed-term Parliaments Act 2011. In 2017, Theresa May did ask the House of Commons to dissolve Parliament so that there could be a general election. However, the result was that Theresa May lost her majority in the House of Commons and was forced to enter into a Supply and Confidence agreement with the Democratic Unionists Party.

In 2019, after becoming Prime Minister, Boris Johnson attempted to ask the House of Commons to trigger an early general election under the Fixed-term Parliaments Act 2011. However, his request was unsuccessful (as you needed two-thirds of all seats in the House of Commons[4]) and eventually an early general election took place as a result of the Early Parliamentary General Election Act 2019.

The Monarch's role in the United Kingdom's constitutional monarchy is largely ceremonial. The important decisions that the monarch makes using her prerogative powers such as choosing a Prime Minister, approving ministerial appointments and giving royal assent to legislation so that it becomes law, are regulated by constitutional conventions. The monarch's role in dissolving Parliament has been limited by the Fixed-term Parliaments Act 2011. Please note the the Act will be repealed.

At a local level executive powers are used by local authorities to run services such as education, social services and transportation. Additionally, there are executive agencies such as the Highways Agency and the Crown Prosecution Service.

3.3.2 The legislature

The legislature makes law and exercises the legislative function. In the United Kingdom a bill does not become law before it receives Royal Assent. An Act of Parliament gives the executive the power to govern the country. For example, the powers of the Secretary of State for Health to build a new hospital or close a hospital is given to him by an Act of Parliament. The legislature will then hold the executive to account by using committees to oversee government policy and the way that the laws are administered. The legislature will also allow the executive to make legislation known as secondary or delegated legislation. Unlike an Act of Parliament, the courts can challenge this delegated legislation.

3.3.3 The judiciary

The function of the judiciary is to apply the law. There are two different types of law: case law and statute law. The judges will interpret an Act of Parliament and will apply it to a particular set of facts. There are a number of ways that judges can interpret legislation. However, judges must avoid going beyond what Parliament intended when it enacted the statue. Since the decision in *Pepper v Hart*[5] the courts, when confronted with an ambiguous statutory provision, have been permitted to refer to Hansard, which is a record of what has been said in Parliament, to look at the record of parliamentary debate and what the minister introducing the bill said, in order to interpret Parliament's intention.

Judges will create case law by interpreting the statute to different sets of facts. Additionally, large parts of the Law of Tort and Contract Law are judge-made with little influence from statute. In English and Welsh law there is a hierarchy known as precedent, which means that lower courts are bound by the decisions of the higher courts. This means that a lower court such as the High Court must apply the decision of a higher court, such as the Court of Appeal, unless it is possible to distinguish the two cases. The doctrine of precedent will ensure judicial certainty. Since the *Practice Statement (Judicial Precedent)*[6] the House of Lords and now its successor the Supreme Court are no longer bound by the previous decisions of the House of Lords. An interesting example of how the 1966 Practice Statement operates is in the decision in *R (Bancoult) v Secretary of State for Foreign and Commonwealth Affairs (No.2)*.[7]

PUBLIC LAW IN CONTEXT
THE DECISION IN *R (BANCOULT) V SECRETARY OF STATE FOR FOREIGN AND COMMONWEALTH AFFAIRS (NO.2)*[8]

In *R (Bancoult) v Secretary of State for Foreign and Commonwealth Affairs (No.2)*[9] the Supreme Court had to consider a previous decision of the House of Lords. The House of Lords in *R (Bancoult) v Secretary of State for Foreign and Commonwealth Affairs (No.2)*[10] had found in favour of the Secretary of State. The appellant Mr Bancoult argued before the Supreme Court that the Secretary of State had breached the duty of candour required by not disclosing information for use before the House of Lords in 2008. Lord Mance who had disagreed with the majority of the House of Lords in *Bancoult (No.2)* was clear that:

> I have not changed my opinion as to what would have been the appropriate outcome of the appeal to the House of Lords. But that is not the issue before us. The issue before us is whether the majority decision should be set aside, not on the grounds that it was wrong in law, but on grounds that the Secretary of State failed, in breach of his duty of candour

in public law proceedings, to disclose relevant documents containing information which it is said would have been likely to have affected the factual basis on which the House proceeded.... In addressing the issue now before us, we are bound by the legal reasoning which led the majority to its conclusion – indeed, strictly bound without possibility of recourse to the *Practice Statement (Judicial Precedent)*[11], since this is an application in the same proceedings.[12]

3.4 Who identified the classic Doctrine of the Separation of Powers?

In this section we will be exploring the historical origins of the separation of powers. It is important to appreciate the rationale for the theory and why a country's constitution would find it expedient to include it.

3.4.1 Aristotle

The Greek philosopher Aristotle in his book *Politics* identified the importance of having different people control the functions of the state. Having different people control each function is essential to the separation of powers. Aristotle wrote 'All states have three elements.

. . . When they are well-ordered, the state is well-ordered.[13] Aristotle defined the three elements as (a) deliberating over public affairs (which would be the executive), (b) choosing the magistrates and how to elect them and (c) the judiciary. Aristotle had reached this conclusion after exploring the different systems of government in the Greek world. Aristotle had taught Alexander the Great and Aristotle himself had been taught by the philosopher Plato, who had in turn had been taught by Socrates. Aristotle eventually fell out with both Alexander the Great and Plato.

3.4.2 Montesquieu and the separation of powers

The modern doctrine of the separation of powers comes from the French philosopher Charles, Baron de Montesquieu. Montesquieu, in his book *The Spirit of the Laws* in 1748, defined the separation of powers in a chapter 'Of the Constitution of England':

> In every government there are three sorts of power: the legislative; the executive in respect to things dependant on the laws of nations [this would be the executive]; and the executive in regard to matters that depend on the civil law [the judiciary].'[14]

Montesquieu was heavily influenced by John Locke's book, the *Two Treatises of Government*.[15] Locke argued that whilst the legislature should be the most important body in the state, the executive and the legislature should each exercise separate powers. It is important to note that for much of the 17th century, the conflict between the legislature and the executive had dominated English politics. It must be understood that there was much debate about how power should be shared between the monarch, the nobility and the House of Commons, which comprised landowners, merchants and professionals who represented their constituency. This conflict had marked the reign of James I[16] who struggled with his parliaments and their insistence on imposing restrictions on royal power. The idea that there should be a division of power between the monarch and Parliament, albeit controlled by the elite within the kingdom, is known as mixed government and influenced many people who looked for a compromise between the monarch and its prerogative powers and an assertive House of Commons.

This conflict resulted in three civil wars being fought between the supporters of the monarchy and Parliament in the 1640s and 1650s. Parliament triumphed militarily, and the monarchy was abolished upon the trial and execution of Charles I in 1649. Following the abolition of the monarchy the combination of the legislative and the monarch's previous executive functions in Parliament was not a success. This led to Oliver Cromwell becoming Lord Protector and the prospect that a monarchy would have been restored had he accepted the offer to become king. Eventually the monarchy was restored in 1660 when Charles I's son became Charles II. However, Parliament and the Crown continued to have an uneasy relationship and this marked the later part of Charles II's reign. Upon Charles' death in 1685, his brother James II became king and he soon fell out with Parliament and was forced to flee to France in 1688. Subsequently, Parliament invited James' son-in-law William and James' daughter Mary to become joint monarchs on its own terms by agreeing to accept the Bill of Rights in 1689. This now meant that Parliament was now superior to the executive, as the Crown was conferred on candidates of Parliament's own choosing. According to GC Moodie:

> Parliament has successfully asserted the right legally to define and sustain the Monarchy. Professor Chrimes, writing of the results of the Revolution Settlement, has pointed out that 'there was no question henceforth that the king was king by Act of Parliament.' Not only the succession to the throne, but the style and titles, and the revenues of the Crown have been the subject of successive parliamentary enactments.[17]

Montesquieu based his theory on the constitution of Great Britain as he saw it in the first part of the 18th century. It should be remembered that Montesquieu was writing before the rise of Cabinet government (i.e. before the monarch surrendered the day-to-day executive powers to his Prime Minister and other members of the Cabinet). Montesquieu admired the constitutional settlement in Great Britain, as in France there was not yet a national parliament:

> We have only to cast an eye on a nation that may be justly called a republic, disguised under the form of monarchy, and we shall see how jealous they are of making a separate order of the profession of arms, and how the military state is constantly allied with that of the citizen, and even sometimes of the magistrate, to the end that these qualities may be a pledge for their country, which should never be forgotten.[18]

The system created by the political upheavals of the 17th century had created in Great Britain a country that protected liberty:

> The English, to favour their liberty, have abolished all the intermediate powers of which their monarchy was composed. They have a great deal of reason to be jealous of this liberty. . . . [19] Liberty was safeguarded by the administration of justice in how the courts operated.[20]

The separation of powers is not simply an idea as to how the three branches of government in a state should be organised. There are very good reasons as to why there needs to be the separation of powers. Montesquieu believed that it was important for the liberty of the individual that these powers were not in the hands of one person or individual body. Montesquieu believed that where the executive and legislative powers were not separated, then there could be no liberty as a 'monarch or senate could enact tyrannical laws, to execute them in a tyrannical manner.'[21] Equally, Montesquieu believed that were the judicial and legislative powers were not separated, then peoples' lives 'would be exposed to arbitrary control.'[22] If the judicial and executive powers were not separated then 'the judge might behave with violence and oppression.'[23]

Montesquieu wrote that

> [t]he executive power ought to be in the hands of a monarch, because this branch of government, having need of despatch, is better administered by one than by many: on the other hand, whatever depends on the legislative power is oftentimes better regulated by many than by a single person.[24]

Montesquieu argued that '[t]hough, in general, the judiciary power ought not to be united with any part of the legislative, yet this is liable to three exceptions, founded on the particular interest of the party accused.'[25] These exceptions included the rights of nobility to be tried by their peers to avoid 'popular envy' from denying the nobility justice and the use of impeachment by Parliament to punish those who 'may infringe the rights of the people, and be guilty of crimes which the ordinary magistrates either could not or would not punish.'[26] Both of these exceptions permitted the House of Lords to exercise a judicial capacity (beyond that of hearing appeals). The last peer to be tried by his peers was the Lord de Clifford who was accused of manslaughter[27], whilst the last person to be impeached was Viscount Melville in 1805.

3.4.2.1 The requirement of 'checks and balances'

Montesquieu did not believe that there needed to be a strict separation of powers. We have seen that Montesquieu believed that there were times when it would be appropriate for the legislature to exercise a judicial function. This was because if each person or branch of government was left to use their power unchecked by the other branches, then there could be misuse of that power, which would result in oppression. Therefore, it is important that each branch is accountable to the others. This accountability is known as checks and balances.

For example, the legislature could not meet without the executives' consent. The legislature would make the laws, however the executive 'ought to have a share in the legislature by the power of rejecting, otherwise it would soon be stripped of its prerogative.' However, this did not mean that the legislature should 'usurp a share of the executive' as this would impact on the power of the executive.[28]

Montesquieu wrote that:

> Here then is the fundamental constitution of the government we are treating of. The legislative body being composed of two parts, they check one another by the mutual privilege of rejecting. They are both restrained by the executive power, as the executive is by the legislative.
>
> These three powers should naturally form a state of repose or inaction. But as there is a necessity for movement in the course of human affairs, they are forced to move, but still in concert.[29]

We can see that in order for each of the three powers to function there needed to be cooperation with the other two, hereby ensuring that there was a system of checks and balances to prevent abuse and to protect the powers of the other branches of government.

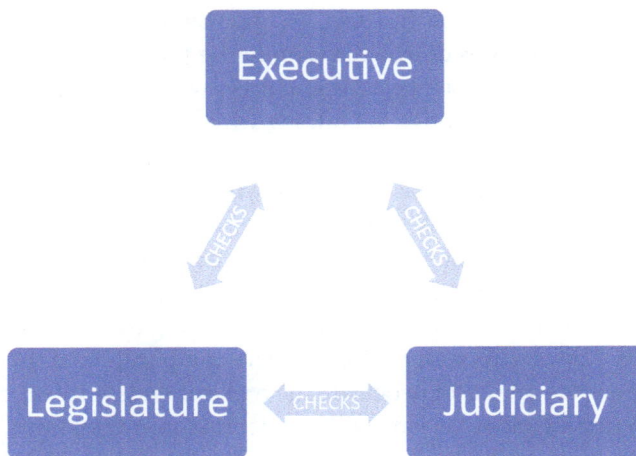

Figure 3.4
Checks and balances

Having checks and balances means that one branch of government will review the activities of the other branches to ensure that the power given to them is used properly. This makes sense as supervision ensures that there is accountability and good government. Arguably, too much interference is a bad thing, as interference in judicial decision-making by the government or Parliament, or parliamentary involvement in judicial appointments, might undermine the independence of the judiciary. However, the judiciary should respect Parliament's role in making law and should not seek to usurp that function. Montesquieu argued that the legislature should not have the power to summon itself, but instead should be summoned by the executive, which would regulate its meetings. Equally the executive should be able to check the legislature's power. Montesquieu argued that

> [w]ere the executive power not to have a right of restraining the encroachment of the legislative body, that latter would become despotic; for as it might arrogate to itself what authority it pleased, it would soon destroy all the other powers.[30]

3.4.2.2 The influence of Montesquieu on the drafters of the United States Constitution

Montesquieu influenced the drafters of the United States Constitution. The 'founding fathers' of the United States of America were former British subjects who wished to be independent of the British Parliament and eventually the Crown. The United States Constitution of 1787 creates a strong separation of powers in the United States. It is important to note that there is a separation between the federal government and the governments of the constituent states. This is important as it prevents the federal government from usurping the powers of each state. We are concerned here with the importance of the separation of powers between the three branches of the federal government.

The new US capital city, Washington, DC, was built after the American War of Independence and it was designed to emphasise the importance of the separation of powers. There is a presidential palace, which is now known as the White House, there is the Congress building which houses the House of Representatives and the Senate, and a distinct Supreme Court building which was created in the 20th century. It is clear that symbolically, as well as legally, a different body of people exercises each power.

The composition of the legislature and its functions are set out in Article I. The powers of the House of Representatives and Senate are clearly defined. There are strict term limits, with Representatives serving two years and Senators six years before having to seek re-election. The composition of the executive and its functions are set out in Article II. The office of President and the powers of the presidency are set out clearly with a strict four-year term limit. The composition of the judiciary and its functions are set out in Article III. The Supreme Court is the superior court for the United States and the judges enjoy security of tenure.

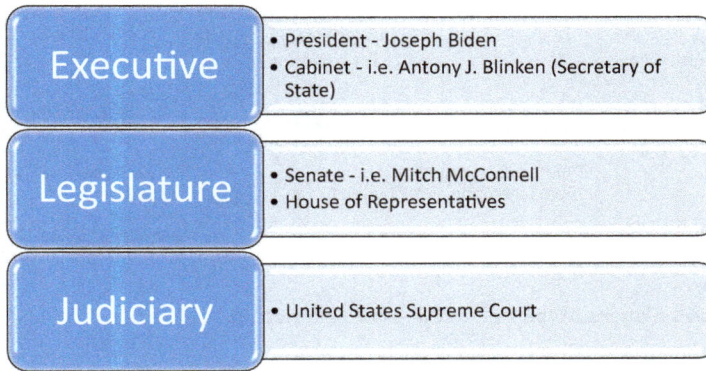

Figure 3.5
The separation of power in the United States of America

If you read the United States Constitution it is clear that the drafters intended there to be a separation of function between each branch of the state. Additionally, there is no overlap of personnel. In order to join the executive a member of the legislature must resign, such as when John Kerry resigned as a Senator in order to become Secretary of State (i.e. Foreign Minister). Although in the case of the Vice President, this role whilst originally intended to be part of the legislature as the President of Senate, has become part of the executive, with Vice Presidents such as Dick Cheney and Joe Biden being key advisors to the President. The evolution of the Vice Presidency and whether it offends the separation of powers as outlined in the constitution is an interesting point.[31]

3.4.2.3 Checks and balances

The United States Constitution does not follow the strict separation of powers at a federal level as there are checks and balances. This means that each branch can legitimately exercise a limited review of the power of the other branches. This prevents each branch from having a monopoly of power. For example, the legislature's function is to make law, but it is restrained from making any laws it likes by the limited power of the presidential veto which is contained in the 1787 US Constitution, and the power of the Supreme Court to strike down unconstitutional laws which was held to exist in *Marbury v Madison*.[32] The President is not immune when he abuses his power and can be impeached by the legislature, with the House of Representatives voting on whether there are grounds to impeach and the Senate acting as the court. The only Presidents to be impeached (albeit they were acquitted) were Andrew Johnson in 1868, Bill Clinton in 1998 and Donald Trump in 2019 and again in 2021. However, impeachment is an important check on the executive. When Barack Obama used his executive powers in 2014 to help illegal immigrants in order to bypass Congress, there were calls to impeach him.[33]

Congress can
propose legislation

Congress can
overide the
President's veto

The President can
veto legislation

The Supreme Court
can strike down
legislation as
unconstitutional

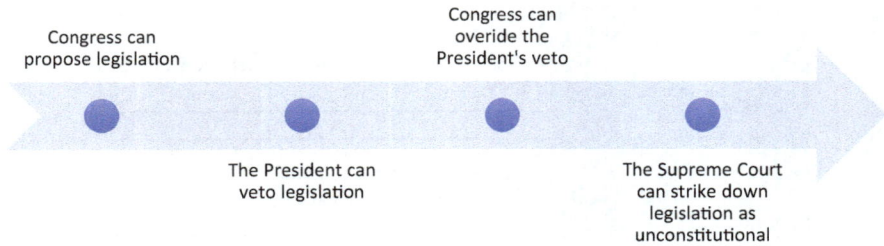

Figure 3.6
Checks and balances in the United States of America

The President has the power to veto legislation. However, unlike the United Kingdom (with the refusal of royal assent), the legislature can override the President's veto with a two-thirds majority in both Houses of Congress.

The United States Supreme Court has the power to strike down legislation which it holds to be unconstitutional. This power was held to exist in the case of *Marbury v Madison*,[34] where Chief Justice Marshall held that '[a] Law repugnant to the Constitution is void.' The case concerned the refusal of the Secretary of State to deliver a commission to Mr Marbury as a Justice of the Peace that had been authorised by the previous President. Marshall CJ held that when a law conflicted with the constitution, then the courts have a duty to decide which should be applied. Therefore, '[i]f, then, the courts are to regard the Constitution, and the Constitution is superior to any ordinary act of the legislature, the Constitution, and not such ordinary act, must govern the case to which they both apply.' This meant that the constitution would be protected from being amended by ordinary Acts of Congress that could expand the powers of the other branches of government as limited by the provisions of the constitution.

It is important to note that the United States Constitution did not give such a power to the courts. However, what was clearly motivating the Supreme Court here was the need to limit the power of the legislature and executive and uphold the legal superiority of the constitution. The United Kingdom Supreme Court cannot do this, as this would offend the constitutional principle of Parliamentary sovereignty. Judicial Review in England and Wales is limited to checking the validity of decisions made by the executive.

3.5 Historical support for the separation of powers within the United Kingdom

We have seen in **section 3.3** above that Montesquieu was influenced by Great Britain when writing about the need for the separation of powers. We will see below at **section 3.9** the views of prominent academics and members of the judiciary on whether the United Kingdom conforms, or has ever conformed, to the separation of powers. In this section we will look at historical support for separation of powers within the constitution.

The classic quote used to justify the separation of powers is that of Lord Acton, who said that, '[p]ower tends to corrupt, and absolute power corrupts absolutely. Great men are almost always bad men.'[35] A classic example of this is the man who is considered to have been the first Prime Minister, Sir Robert Walpole, who was notoriously corrupt and amassed a considerable personal fortune. Walpole famously remarked that 'Every man has his price.' Unsurprisingly, corruption was association with the politics of the 18th century.

3.5.1 The Instrument of Government 1653

We will begin by looking at the Instrument of Government from 1653 to see how Cromwell intended Britain to be governed following the abolition of the monarchy. The Commonwealth was established after the English Civil Wars. In 1653 the Protectorate was established and Oliver Cromwell ruled England, Scotland and Ireland[36]. The Protectorate was established by the Instrument of Government, which formed the basis of a constitution, outlining the powers of the Lord Protector and Parliament. It listed the functions of the state and who was responsible for carrying these out, with the executive power being in the hands of the Lord Protector[37] and the legislative power being in the hands of both Parliament and the Lord Protector.[38] Marchamont Needham observed that 'placing the legislative and executive powers in the same persons is a marvellous in-let of corruption and tyranny.'[39]

3.5.2 The development of parliamentary government

As a result of George I becoming king in 1714 it was parliamentarians who took over more responsibility for running the executive. During the 18th century the Cabinet comprised parliamentarians and met without the monarch. This led to parliamentary government whereby the government relied on Parliament for its continued support and would be forced from office should it lose a vote of no-confidence. Consequentially, there was an important change of views about the constitution from the 18th to 19th centuries. In the 18th century there was support for a system of checks and balances to exist within the constitution; however by the 19th century the general view was that Parliament was dominant. Earl Grey was of the view that the separation of powers had been superseded by a system of parliamentary government. This system relied on power being limited as opposed to being divided between different groups of individuals:

> [b]y this arrangement the Executive power and the power of the Legislation are virtually united in the same hands, but both are limited – the executive power by the law, and that of legislation by the necessity of obtaining the assent of Parliament to the measures brought forward.[40]

Earl Grey believed that this system was better, as the government could work effectively with Parliament to create laws and Parliament was able to hold ministers to account and review government policy. The future Prime Minister Benjamin Disraeli explored this system of government in his political novel *Coningsby*[41] that was published in 1844. His hero Coningsby called the system of government a Venetian Constitution, where power was dominated by the same individuals in Parliament since the reign of George I and the House of Commons exercised absolute power without checks.

3.5.3 'It was idle to talk of the separation of the legislative, executive, and judicial powers'

Whilst John Locke influenced Montesquieu, Montesquieu's theory as different as he treated the judiciary as a separate branch of government. According to FTH Fletcher, it was this 'feature of the theory which appealed most strongly to English thinkers.'[42] However, developments within the constitution meant that Montesquieu's theory did not reflect reality as 'defying the principle of the separation of powers, the three principal departments of state – executive, legislative and judiciary – have tended more and more to interpenetrate each other'[43] Fletcher observed that Bentham who had said that 'Montesquieu would not outlive his century would certainly seem to be justified insofar as constitutional theory in England was concerned,' but not in the United States and France, who 'placed the principle of the separation of powers at the very heart and centre' of their constitutions.[44]

Just over 50 years after the publication of *The Spirit of the Laws* the appointment of the Lord Chief Justice, Lord Ellenborough, to the Cabinet as a member of the executive in 1806 led to fierce parliamentary debate. The opposition argued that

> this association of a judge with the executive government . . . which . . . has a direct and alarming tendency to blend and to amalgamate those great elementary principles of political power, which it is the very object of a free constitution to keep separate and distinct. . . . The remarks of Montesquieu on this head are pointed and remarkable; and such value does he attach to the judicial power being kept separate and distinct,

otherwise the government risks being oppressive.[45] The government's response was '

> that we were not to take our principles of the English constitution from Montesquieu . . . but to gain our knowledge of it from study of precedents and from the practice of our forefathers. It was idle to talk of the separation of the legislative, executive, and judicial powers

as the reality was at odds with the theory.[46]

The response from the government is telling, as it is the overlaps that already existed by 1806 that we shall explore below in **Section 3.6**. We shall see that this system of parliamentary government still exists within the United Kingdom. However, in the United Kingdom is there a need to adhere to the theory of the separation of powers? The United States was a new country and could create a new system of government. The United Kingdom has evolved as a democracy with an independent judiciary, an elected House of Commons that enjoys universal suffrage and a constitutional monarchy. We shall see below that many academics have doubted whether the United Kingdom has ever had separation of powers.

3.6 Does the United Kingdom's constitution accord to the theory of the separation of powers?

This section considers whether the United Kingdom's constitution accords to the theory of the separation of powers.

3.6.1 The United Kingdom lacks a written constitution

Unlike most other countries the United Kingdom does not have a written constitution, although many sources of the constitution are written. This is not to say that the United Kingdom does not have a constitution, but rather that there is no one document that contains the key constitutional arrangements. Consequentially, the United Kingdom's constitution is far more fluid than a country that has a rigid codified constitution. The constitution existed prior to the imposition of a rigid set of rules which could incorporate the theory of the separation of powers. There is much debate over whether the United Kingdom has a constitution. Some academics such as FF Ridley have argued that there is no constitution, whereas Colin Munro refutes this view.[47] You may wish to refer back to **Chapter 1** for more detail on the debate as to whether the United Kingdom has a constitution and the unwritten and written sources of the constitution.

3.6.2 The United Kingdom has evolved constitutionally since Montesquieu

The country that Montesquieu observed in the 1720s is very different to the United Kingdom of today. The House of Lords and patronage dominated Parliament and the franchise was limited. Cities such as Manchester had no MPs, whilst many small villages had two MPs. The monarch dominated the executive, although it was in the reign of George I that the position of First Minister (or Prime Minister) developed under Sir Robert Walpole. Gradually the system of Cabinet government developed and the everyday running of the state was left to parliamentarians who could gain enough support in the House of Commons to form a government. The arrangement where parliamentarians carried out the executive function may offend the theory of the separation of powers, but it has proved constitutionally expedient. Academics have criticised Montesquieu, arguing that he wrongly described the British political and judicial system and that the United Kingdom has never conformed to the separation of powers.

ACADEMIC DEBATE

Many academics have been critical of Montesquieu's account of the British constitution in the mid-18th century and have argued that he misunderstood what he saw.

WA Robson was critical of Montesquieu's account and observed that the executive did execute both administrative powers as well as judicial powers 'as a matter of convenience.'[48] This dual function was explored in some detail by Stewart Jay in 'Servants of Monarchs and Lords: The Advisory Role of Early English Judges.'[49] Robson's was very critical:

> [t]he great majority of citizens were, indeed, unconscious that there was any lack of constitutional neatness and logical order in the prevailing governmental arrangements; for until Montesquieu misread the English system . . . the divine right of powers to be separated had hardly been asserted.[50]

Robson's view of the separation of powers was clear: '[an] antique and rickety chariot . . . so long the favourite vehicle of writers on political science and constitutional law for the conveyance of fallacious ideas.'[51]

Laurence Claus has argued that:

> Montesquieu did not appreciate the nature of the English common law and the mechanism that its doctrine of precedent established for authoritative judicial exposition of existing law. That empirical error caused him to distinguish and to trivialize the English judicial function as merely ad hoc determination of disputed facts. Consequently, Montesquieu failed to recognize the *lawmaking* character of English judicial exposition.[52]

Crucially with regards to judicial law-making, the key deficiency according to Claus was the lack of understanding of how the doctrine of precedent worked:

> He seems not to have appreciated how the English common law had been formed through deference to precedent. He did not notice the binding nature of precedent within a judicial hierarchy. He did not realize that the exercise of judicial power in one case had implications for other cases; that dispute resolution affected more than the parties before the court; that the doctrine of precedent could turn individual dispute resolution into law of general application. Most critically, he did not see that the doctrine of precedent applied to all judicial interpretation of authoritative texts.[53]

The problem with Montesquieu's account of the British constitution was that he was writing at a time when evolution was still taking place because of the shifting power of the monarch and politicians within the executive. Colin Munro noted that there was an overlap between the executive and the legislature. However according to Munro, '[i]t is easy, with hindsight, to criticise Montesquieu for paying insufficient attention to the developing Cabinet system. But when Montesquieu visited England, ministers still owed their positions more to the king's confidence in them than to the support in the House of Commons.'[54]

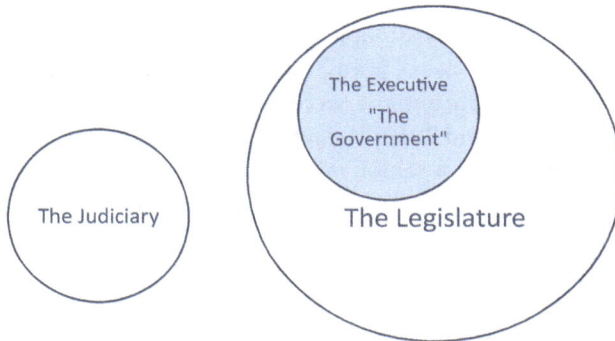

Figure 3.7
The overlap between the three branches of government

It is useful to consider how the United Kingdom's constitutional system changed since the 1720s–1740s. It will be important to have some familiarity with these changes and appreciate how these have impacted on whether the United Kingdom has the separation of powers.

We will now look at the overlaps of function and personnel between the three branches of government within the United Kingdom.

In the United Kingdom there is a fusion between the legislature and the executive. As a matter of constitutional convention the government must comprise parliamentarians and the Prime Minister must be a member of the House of Commons. The last member of the House of Lords to be Prime Minister was Marquis of Salisbury in 1902, although in 1963 the Earl of Home renounced his peerage under the Peerages Act 1963 in order to become Prime Minister.

In the rest of this section we will be exploring the overlaps of function and personnel in the United Kingdom. It is important to understand the extent of the overlaps and to be able to assess whether the United Kingdom has the separation of powers.

3.6.3 The overlap between executive and legislature

This subsection considers the overlap between the United Kingdom's executive and legislature.

3.6.3.1 An overlap of personnel

The government is part of the executive. The government comprises the Prime Minister, the Cabinet (e.g. Secretary of State for Foreign and Commonwealth Affairs), junior ministers, parliamentary private secretaries and government whips who must ensure that MPs vote in support of government-sponsored bills (public bills). As a matter of constitutional convention, the government is comprised entirely of parliamentarians from both Houses of Parliament. This means that there must be an overlap between the executive and legislature, as to have people in Cabinet who are not members of either House would be unconstitutional. The senior positions in government, such as the Chancellor of the Exchequer, are usually occupied by MPs. Although, Lord Mandelson, who is a member of the House of Lords, served in Gordon Brown's government as the First Secretary of State and the Secretary of State for Business, Innovation and Skills between 2008 and 2010. The rationale for this appointment was that Lord Mandelson had been a senior minister under Tony Blair and had then gone on to serve as the United Kingdom's member of the European Commission in Brussels. Therefore, when it had proved politically expedient for Gordon Brown to appoint Lord Mandelson to his Cabinet, he could nominate him as a Labour life peer and Mandelson therefore could avoid having to wait for a parliament constituency to become vacant in order to become an MP.

The Prime Minister as a matter of constitutional convention is a member of the House of Commons. Similarly, by convention the government is composed solely of parliamentarians. If the Prime Minister wishes to appoint an individual who is not a member of either House of Parliament, then this individual must then seek election as an MP, or more commonly will be appointed a life peer (as in the case of Peter Mandelson in 2008). This means that there is an overlap between the personnel in the legislature and the executive. For example, prior to the Constitutional Reform Act 2005, the Lord Chancellor was a senior government minister, who sat in Cabinet and was also a member of the legislature and acted as the speaker of the House of Lords.

At the moment there are 650 MPs although David Cameron's government had wished to reduce the number of constituencies. This means that any

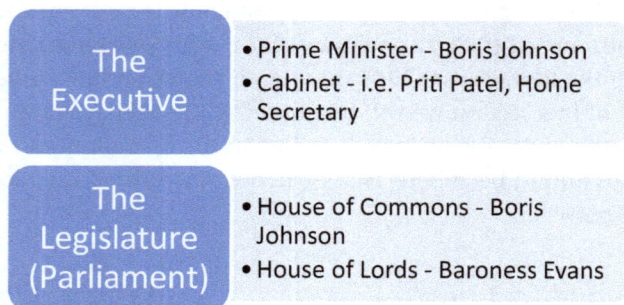

The Executive	• Prime Minister - Boris Johnson • Cabinet - i.e. Priti Patel, Home Secretary
The Legislature (Parliament)	• House of Commons - Boris Johnson • House of Lords - Baroness Evans

Figure 3.8
The overlap in personnel between Parliament and the executive

government requires at least 326 MPs to have a majority. The government can use ministerial offices as patronage, to ensure support from a MP in return for a position in government. The House of Commons Disqualification Act 1975 was introduced to restrict the number of ministers which a government may create. Section 2 of the Act limits the number of ministerial office holders to 95. This still gives the government guaranteed support of 95 MPs, or nearly one-sixth of the House of Commons.

PUBLIC LAW IN CONTEXT
SECTION 2 OF THE HOUSE OF COMMONS DISQUALIFICATION ACT 1975

1 Not more than ninety-five persons being the holders of offices specified in Schedule 2 to this Act (in this section referred to as Ministerial offices) shall be entitled to sit and vote in the House of Commons at any one time.
2 If at any time the number of members of the House of Commons who are holders of Ministerial offices exceeds the number entitled to sit and vote in that House under sub-section (1) above, none except any who were both members of that House and holders of Ministerial offices before the excess occurred shall sit or vote therein until the number has been reduced, by death, resignation or otherwise, to the number entitled to sit and vote as aforesaid.
3 A person holding a Ministerial office is not disqualified by this Act by reason of any office held by him ex officio as the holder of that Ministerial office.

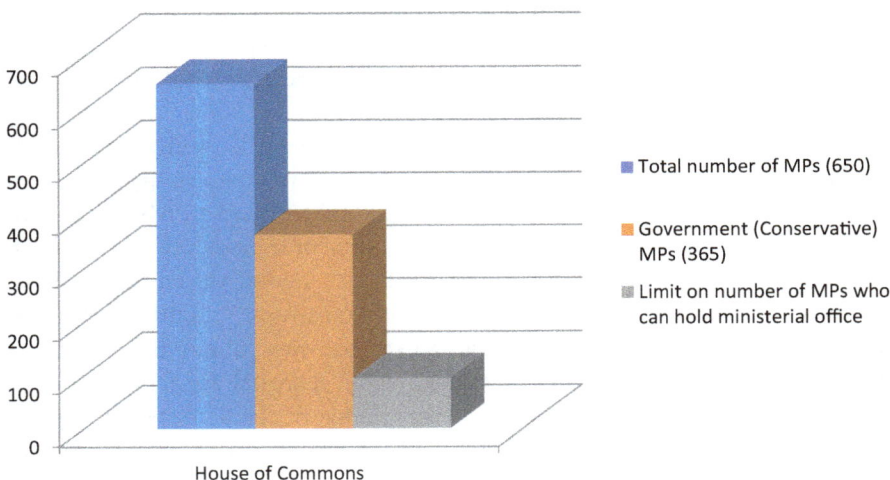

Figure 3.9
The impact of the House of Commons Disqualification Act 1975

An important question for people looking at how politics and the constitution operates is whether the fusion, which exists in the United Kingdom between the executive and legislature, is a good or bad thing? Walter Bagehot described the close union of the executive and legislature in their 'nearly complete fusion' as the '[t]he efficient secret of the English constitution.'[55] We have seen above that this was a viewed shared by the Prime Minister Earl Grey in the 19th century. Whereas, the former Lord Chancellor, Lord Hailsham, referred to this fusion as an elected dictatorship.[56] Lord Hailsham was concerned that a political party who won a majority in the House of Commons could legislate without restraint. Lord Hailsham was criticised by JAG Griffith in his article 'The Political Constitution.'[57]

As a result of modern political parties, the link between the government and MPs is strong. In order to build a career in politics, an MP will need the support of the Prime Minister in order to be promoted to the front bench (i.e. to become a minister). Therefore, Theresa May's reshuffle of the Cabinet in July 2016 involved much discussion of personality politics, such as the rationale for the dismissal of the Secretary of State for Justice, Michael Gove, and the Chancellor of the Exchequer, George Osborne. The government relies on whips to ensure that their MPs vote in support of the government. Therefore, a government that has won a large majority in the House of Commons effectively controls the legislative process and as a result of Standing Order 14 which was introduced in 1902, the government's business takes priority in the House of Commons. Where the government has a majority the other parties are unable to prevent legislation from being approved or have the opportunity of realistically proposing alternative legislation. This means that a government with a majority can legislate, in the House of Commons at least, as it wishes, free from any legal limitations, as the courts cannot question the validity of an Act of Parliament. Unlike the House of Commons, the government is not guaranteed to have a majority in the House of Lords and therefore is more likely to face defeats in the House of Lords than in the House of Commons.[58] That is not to say that a government with a majority is entirely safe, as there is always a risk of a backbench revolt, whereby MPs in the government's own party will vote against its legislation.

Many critics have argued that Parliament is rendered powerless under the current system. However, Conor Gearty has observed that whilst, '[t]here is certainly some truth in the deep-seated and frequently repeated criticism that Parliament has over many decades become the poodle of the executive,' he denies that 'things are not nearly so bad as is sometimes believed, particularly by lawyers and by advocates of strong human rights measures.'[59] Matthew Flinders has written that '[f]undamentally, parliament has two inherently contradictory roles – first, to sustain the executive, which it would appear to do well, and second, to hold the executive to account between elections, which it does rather less well.'[60] Flinders observed that '[c]ontrary to constitutional theory, the supremacy of parliament over the executive is thwarted by the latter's tight party management and procedural control of the House's timetable. In the face of executive obduracy the importance of the House is unequivocal.'[61] However, Flinders is clear that

> Parliament matters. . . . Those who suggest that the government is the real primary institution fail to appreciate parliament's enduring centrality within the constitution. . . . [M]inisters do take parliament seriously. Careers are still won and lost at the despatch box. The executive must treat parliament with respect to retain the support of their parliamentary party.[62]

There are however those who argue that it is wrong to assume that Parliament is weak. Meg Russell and Philip Cowley have argued that empirical evidence suggests that Parliament is not weak:

> In a recent book on policy failures in British government, two well-respected political Scientists claimed that as a legislative assembly, 'the parliament of the United Kingdom is, much of the time, either peripheral or totally irrelevant. It might as well not exist' (King and Crewe 2013, 361). This may be in line with the conventional 'parliamentary decline thesis' and comparative views of Westminster, but is inconsistent with the empirical evidence. The data that we have presented make clear that the British parliament has significant influence, at all stages of the policy process.[63]

PUBLIC LAW IN CONTEXT
BREXIT AND PARLIAMENT

The series of defeats suffered by Theresa May's government in 2019 on the United Kingdom left the European Union subject to the government's agreement with the European Union and the United Kingdom left the European Union without any deal. Such was the scale of the first defeat of the Prime Minister's agreement that she agreed to hold a vote of no confidence under the Fixed-term Parliaments Act 2011. The Prime Minister won the vote. This is significant because Parliament has asserted itself through the Brexit process and has demonstrated that a government, even with a majority based on a supply and confidence agreement with another political party, cannot be certain that the House of Commons will support its agenda.

3.6.3.2 The Queen in Parliament

The monarch appoints the government, although this prerogative power is restricted by convention. The power of Parliament to legislate is known as the Queen in Parliament. As a matter of constitutional convention the monarch must give her royal assent to legislation before a bill becomes law. The last time that a monarch seriously considered vetoing a bill was in 1913, when George

V disliked the Home Rule Bill which would have given Ireland home rule. This power is symbolic, as the political consequences of the monarch exercising the veto would be considerable. GC Moodie commented that if George V had vetoed the Home Rule Bill, then it is likely that the Liberal government would have resigned and the Conservative opposition would have been invited to form a new government and held a general election. If the Liberals had won the election the king would have been forced to give 'a pledge not to use the power of veto . . . again. It is not impossible that the Monarch's reign, or even the Monarchy, would have been at stake.'[64]

PUBLIC LAW IN ACTION

Can you think of any circumstances in which the monarch would refuse royal assent? What would be the consequences of a monarch refusing royal assent in the 21st century?

3.6.3.3 Delegated legislation and the prerogative

As a matter of expediency ministers are given powers by the legislative to create law. This secondary legislation is known as delegated legislation. The minister is effectively allowed to create legislation within the remit of the powers given to him by Parliament. Ministers need this power as it would be impossible for Parliament to legislate due to the amount of time this would take.

Additionally, ministers have non-statutory power under the prerogative. The prerogative is recognised by the common law and is the remnant of the historic powers of the Crown. The prerogative is simply the powers that were needed by the crown to govern the country. These powers include making treaties and deployment of the military.

PUBLIC LAW IN ACTION

Imagine that you and your seminar group were shipwrecked on a desert island and you have been appointed as the leader. What powers would you need to fulfil your role as leader?

During the 20th century there was limited parliamentary scrutiny on ministerial use of the prerogative as the government had little incentive to give up this power.[65] Recently, areas of the prerogative such as the civil service and Parliament's role in the scrutiny of treaties have been covered by legislation.[66] The ability of the Prime Minister to ask the monarch to use her prerogative power to dissolve Parliament and trigger a general election has been superseded by the Fixed-term Parliaments Act 2011 in order to allow the operation of a Coalition government between 2010 and 2015. The controversial use of the prerogative to engage in military action is now controlled by a constitutional convention that requires the consent of the House of Commons before military action such as airstrikes against ISIS in Iraq in 2014 and Syria in 2015 can be taken. However, in 2018 the United Kingdom government conducted airstrikes against the Syrian state without first having a vote in the House of Commons. This led to considerable disagreement over the existence of the convention and when it applied. Finally, as Parliament is legally sovereign where the prerogative and an Act of Parliament cover the same subject matter, the courts will give effect to the Act. We will look at importance of the prerogative powers and the limitations of effective parliamentary scrutiny in **Chapters 10** and **11**.

3.6.4 Executive and the judiciary

This subsection considers the overlap between the United Kingdom's executive and the judiciary.

3.6.4.1 An overlap of personnel

Prior to the Constitutional Reform Act 2005 the Lord Chancellor was the head of the judiciary. This meant that the Lord Chancellor could appoint judges, discipline judges and determine which judges could hear certain cases. Lord Hailsham argued that this overlap was necessary, as the Lord Chancellor 'is in the business of defending and preserving the independence and integrity of the judiciary. . . . To discharge this function it is necessary that he should be a member of all three traditional branches of government.'[67] Lord Hailsham regarded his role as

> the judges' friend at court, whether he is acting as their public defender in Parliament or as their private representative in Whitehall.[68] For this purpose he is to be regarded as the representative of the judicial body and not simply as a member of the executive.[69]

The Lord Chancellor was regarded as protecting judicial independence from Parliament as well as his colleagues in government. According to Professor Drewry, under the old system, 'Judges got on with their task of judging; parliamentarians looked nervously at a frontier guard-house marked "judicial-independence", occupied by the formidable figure of the Lord Chancellor, and kept their distance.'[70]

This system was problematic, as if a senior member of the executive was in charge of the judiciary, then the executive could be accused of undermining the independence of the judiciary. Furthermore, the Lord Chancellor could sit as a judge and took precedence in the House of Lords. According to Colin Munro, 'it has not been suggested that the executive has tried to interfere with the independence of judges trying cases. What has been in contention is the extent to which judges, rather than the executive, should have control over the administration of courts and legal processes.'[71] Lord Steyn argued extra-judicially in favour for the creation of a Supreme Court. His Lordship stated:

> The practice of the Lord Chancellor and his predecessors of sitting in the Appellate Committee is not consistent with even the weakest principle of separation of powers or the most tolerant interpretation of the constitutional principles of judicial independence or rule of law.[72]

The problem was that a defendant who has breached a law made by the legislature (of which the Lord Chancellor was a member), enforced by the executive (where the Lord Chancellor was a senior member) and applied by the judiciary (which the Lord Chancellor headed and could sit as a judge), could argue that he has not had a fair trial. Furthermore, the fact that a senior member of the executive and career politician, who could be dismissed by the Prime Minister, was responsible for appointing judges was seen as inconsistent with the separation of powers. It had sometimes been common practice to appoint judges on the basis of political persuasion up until the beginning of the 20th century; however this was no longer the case and appointments were made upon professional merit. In 1929, Lord Sankey LC 'abandoned the practice of appointing Law Lords by reference to party political criteria.'[73] One example of how politics played a party in judicial appointments was the case of John Donaldson (later a Law Lord) as a result of being President of the Industrial Relations Tribunal as viewed negatively by Labour MPs and believed that his promotion to the Court of Appeal was delayed due to political reasons, as he knew 'all along that elevation for him was unlikely so long as Labour remained in power. Lord Elwyn Jones, the Lord Chancellor, admitted in private that Donaldson deserved promotion, but that it would be more trouble than it was worth.'[74] Donaldson was promoted as soon as the conservatives came to power in 1979.

3.6.4.2 The Home Secretary's sentencing powers

Lord Steyn had criticised the Home Secretary's sentencing powers.[75] Writing extra-judicially, His Lordship stated that:

> The Home Secretary still retains the power to set the tariff of the term of imprisonment to be served in the case of mandatory sentences of life imprisonment for murder. Sentencing for any crime is a judicial function. The function of determining the tariff in the case of mandatory life sentences ought to be performed in public by neutral judges. That function ought not to be performed by the Home Secretary. The present opaque arrangements are in conflict with the principle of the separation of powers and with open justice. It ought to be brought into line with the position in regard to discretionary life sentences which is recognised to be a judicial function. I would hope that we can put our own house in order in

this respect rather than await a further ruling from the European Court of Human Rights.[76]

The Home Secretary as a result of section 269 of the Criminal Justice Act 2003 no longer has the power to set minimum tariffs for life sentences in cases involving an adult defendant. Section 269 has introduced a new scheme where the courts, instead of the Home Secretary, will determine the minimum term. Section 269 was introduced because of the judgments of the European Court of Human Rights in *Stafford v UK*[77] and the House of Lords in *R v Secretary of State for the Home Department Ex p. Anderson*.[78] Previously, the Home Secretary had lost the power to set the tariff for defendants under the age of 18.

The Prerogative of Mercy is used to give full pardons, partial pardons and to release prisoners early on compassionate grounds. The prerogative of mercy is exercised by the monarch on the advice of the Secretary of State for Justice. Previously, it was the Home Secretary who advised the monarch. The last pardon was that of the Liverpool Football Club fan, Michael Shields in 2009. This enables the executive to quash the sentence given by the courts.[79]

3.6.4.3 The Attorney-General

The Attorney-General is a member of both the legislature and executive and although not a member of Cabinet he sometimes does attend Cabinet. The Attorney-General is the government's chief legal advisor for England and Wales and he also serves as the Attorney-General for Northern Ireland. The Westminster government also has a separate legal advisor for Scotland, the Lord Advocate, and the devolved governments also have their own legal advisors. The Attorney-General is assisted by the Solicitor General who is also a parliamentarian.

There are a number of points to consider about the role of the Attorney-General. The Attorney-General can attempt to have a sentence reviewed where a trial judge has given a sentence which is considered unduly lenient. The Attorney-General has a limited power to refer the matter to the Court of Appeal.

The case of *Attorney General Reference No 16 of 2014*[80] is an example of when the Attorney-General will make a reference to the Court of Appeal. There was considerable public controversy surrounding the four-year sentence for manslaughter imposed by the trial judge on a man who had killed his victim by one punch with his fist. This was a so-called 'one-punch' killing. The Attorney-General made a reference under section 36 of the Criminal Justice Act 1988 to appeal the sentence on the grounds that it was unduly lenient. Giving judgment on behalf of the Court of Appeal, Treacy LJ held that the sentence

> was not one which can be described as unduly lenient. Indeed, it seems to us that the sentence imposed was one which was within the range reasonably available to a trial judge, properly weighing the relevant factors and the guidance of this court.[81]

The Attorney-General has the power to bring a prosecution under the Contempt of Court Act 1981 and the Criminal Justice and Courts Act 2015 where a juror is accused of misconduct. This may occur where a juror has conducted independent research during the trial and therefore has harmed the defendant's right to a fair trial, as this independent research has not been tested in court like the evidence adduced by the prosecution and defence.[82] The Attorney-General also has the prerogative power to stop a prosecution on indictment, this is known as *nolle prosequi*. Applications to the Attorney-General for *nolle prosequi* can be made by both the defence and the prosecution. Lord Wilson in *R (on the application of Gujra) v Crown Prosecution Service*[83] observed that 'in modern times, he makes rare use, indeed usually only when he considers that the defendant is unfit to plead.'[84] Additionally, if there has been an acquittal, the Attorney-General can refer a point of law to the Court of Appeal.

By convention the Attorney-General must be able to exercise his powers to prosecute independently of his colleagues in Cabinet. According to Geoffrey Marshall, 'since 1924 the holders of the Attorney-General's office . . . have asserted that by convention in matters relation to the institution and withdrawal of prosecutions the Attorney-General exercises his function independently of the Cabinet.'[85] However, the Attorney-General's position as chief legal advisor to the government, member of government and politician has led to criticism of the role. This criticism has increased following the controversy of the then Attorney-General Lord Goldsmith's legal advice to Tony Blair in 2003 on the legality of the invasion of Iraq. Alex Samuels has argued that the position needs to be abolished and the duties transferred to other people.[86] Samuels argues that the role of the Attorney-General leads to a perception of partiality:

> The Attorney General has been described as 'the bulldog of the Crown,' and as 'the corgi of the constitution.' . . . The basic problem is that the Attorney General is a politician and a minister and at the same time required to act objectively and impartially under the law in the public interest. The conflict of interest, or at least the perception of conflict of interest, is immediately apparent.[87]
>
> The office of Lord Chancellor was successfully reformed, so why not the office of Attorney General. Everything the Attorney General does at present should be passed to others, with the exception of the role of being the ministerial chief legal advisor to the government, and political head of the Government Legal Service, and renamed the Government Chief Legal Advisor.[88]

There have been previous calls to reform the role of Attorney-General, such as Sir Harry Woolf, who used his 1989 Hamlyn Lecture to argue for reform.[89]

3.6.5 *Legislature and the judiciary*

This subsection considers the overlap between the United Kingdom's legislature and the judiciary.

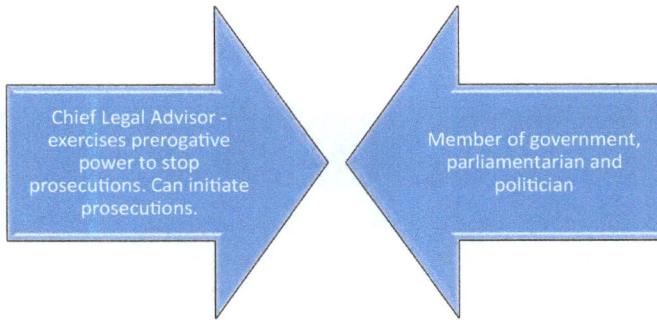

Figure 3.10
The inherent conflict of the Attorney-General's role

3.6.5.1 The legislature had a judicial function

Prior to the Constitutional Reform Act 2005 Parliament had a judicial function which was carried out by the Appellate Committee of the House of Lords. This arrangement was created by the Appellate Jurisdiction Act 1876. The Lords of Appeal in Ordinary (informally known as the Law Lords) were appointed by the Crown and performed this judicial function. The Law Lords were able to sit in the legislative chamber of the House of Lords and could take part in political debates. During passing of Human Rights Act 1998, Lord Brown-Wilkinson actively took part in debates and rejected the proposition that the jurisprudence of the European Court of Human Rights should be binding on the House of Lords. Thus, the Law Lords were members of the legislature and the highest court in the United Kingdom. Since the 1840s the other members of the House of Lords did not take part in the House's judicial function. The issue of who could hear an appeal arose during the trial of Daniel O'Conner, when the Prime Minister's supporters encouraged the non-judges to leave the chamber. The Court had its own rooms to hear cases, although it delivered its decision in the legislative chamber. Nonetheless, such an arrangement was quite confusing and did little to demonstrate the separation of powers.

Parliament could also issue Acts of Attainder which carried the death penalty, the last being passed in 1798. This was a legislative act and avoided a trial and the need to prove guilt, as all that was needed was a vote in Parliament. The Acts of Attainder required royal assent. Alternatively, Parliament could impeach an individual which unlike an Act of Attainder would involve a trial to determine guilt. The House of Commons would vote on whether to impeach and the House of Lords would vote on whether the defendant was guilty. In the House of Lords the defendant was prosecuted by Trial Managers, who were MPs acting on behalf of the House of Commons. This was a trial and required an offence to have been committed. During perhaps the most famous impeachment trial, that of Warren Hastings, the former governor-general of Bengal, the Lord Chancellor, Lord Thurlow, held that the usual laws of evidence applied. The last impeachment trial was that of Henry Dundas, Viscount Melville in

1806, who was accused of misusing public money. Impeachment had been used as way of making the executive accountable to Parliament.

PUBLIC LAW IN ACTION

Could Parliament still impeach today? Would there ever be a situation where Parliament would seek to try someone? Parliament has never formally abolished its power to impeach, although there is debate over whether the power still exists. Since 2003 there have been repeated calls by parliamentarians to impeach Tony Blair over the Iraq War.

3.6.5.2 Overlap of personnel

Prior to the Constitutional Reform Act 2005 judges could take part in parliamentary debates and the Lord Chancellor was a member of the legislature and the head of the judiciary. This was confusing and raised questions about the independence of the judiciary from the legislature. Lord Steyn supported reforming these arrangements and argued that for many people it was difficult to appreciate the distinction between the Parliamentary House of Lords and the Law Lords.[90] His Lordship stated:

> In 2002 the highest court in the land is still a committee of the legislature. . . . It has the appearance of a subordinate part of the Upper House. The sittings of the Appellate Committee therefore take place in a Committee room in the Palace of Westminster, and the Law Lords work on the Law Lords' Corridor. . . . A regular reminder of its status is also the theatrical performance in the chamber of Law Lords making speeches when they give their opinions after prayers with the mace on the woolsack. When judgments were delivered in *Pinochet No. 1* the crowded benches of the chamber apparently led foreign television viewers to believe that Lady Thatcher was part of the dissenting minority who opposed the extradition of General Pinochet![91]

We can see that the Law Lords delivered their judgments in the chamber of the House of Lords, and sitting in the same chamber were the non-judicial members of the House of Lords, which included Baroness Thatcher. Thatcher was a friend of General Pinochet, who was facing extradition to Spain to face charges of crimes against humanity. So to the casual observer it would appear that Thatcher *might* have been able to vote in the case before the Appellate Committee of the House of Lords – which we know was not the case.

3.6.5.3 Judges make law

According to the doctrine of the separation of powers the legislature should create law whilst the judiciary apply the law. However, the courts do create law. The law that the courts have made is known as the common law. Before Parliament began to create the vast number of laws that it does today, it was the decisions of the courts that were recorded and used to create a system of precedent. In your studies you will find that the vast majority of contract law and tort law was created by judges and is still relevant. However, many judges have argued that the courts do not create law; rather they just discover it. This can be criticised as a myth. We must distinguish between the common law (judge-made law) and the role of the judiciary today in interpreting statutes. Today the role of the courts is to interpret legislation and to give effect to the intention of Parliament.

According to the theory of the separation of powers judges should not make laws. However, in reality judges have been accused of law making. In the past it was regarded as acceptable for judges to state and refine our law, but today this is the role of Parliament. The orthodox view that judges do not make the law was stated by Lord Esher MR in *Willis v Baddeley*[92], where His Lordship stated:

> This is not a case, as has been suggested, of what is sometime called judge-made law. There is, in fact, no such thing as judge-made law, for the judges do not make the law, though they frequently have to apply existing law to circumstances as to which it has not previously been authoritatively laid down that such law is applicable.[93]

However, many judges have pointed out that the judiciary does make law. The common law is judge made and the judges are not merely finding law. This was the view of Lord Reid who argued:

> There was a time when it was thought almost indecent to suggest that judges make law. . . . Those with a taste for fairytales seem to have thought that in some Aladdin's cave there is hidden the Common Law in all its splendour and that on a judge's appointment there descends on him knowledge of the magic words Open Sesame. Bad decisions are given when the judge has muddled the password and the wrong door opens. But we do not believe in fairytales any more.[94]

We can see that Lord Reid was critical of the view that judges just discover the law.

There are a number of very important cases where judges have controversially made law. In *R v R (Rape: Marital Exemption)*[95] the House of Lords held that the Sexual Offences (Amendment) Act 1976 could be interpreted as to make marital rape unlawful.

PUBLIC LAW IN CONTEXT
R V R (RAPE: MARITAL EXEMPTION)[96]

In *R v R (Rape: Marital Exemption)*[97] the defendant was separated from his wife and forced his way into the victim's new abode and attempted to have sex with her. The defendant was charged with rape but the trial judge held that as a result of s.1(1) of the Sexual Offences (Amendment) Act 1976 a husband could not rape his wife as upon marriage she was deemed in law to have irrevocably consented. Section 1(1) had defined rape as:

1   For the purposes of section 1 of the Sexual Offences Act 1956 (which to rape) a man commits rape if-

(a) he has unlawful sexual intercourse with a woman who at the time of the intercourse does not consent to it; and

(b) at the time he knows that she does not consent to the intercourse or he is reckless as to whether she consents to it;

and references to rape in other enactment's (including the following provisions of this Act) shall be construed accordingly.'

The position that a wife impliedly consented to sexual intercourse was deemed to have been the case in the common law and accepted in cases such as *R v Miller*[98]. The House of Lords held that the husband could be guilty of raping his wife as the 1976 legislation that defined rape for the first time did not preclude the court from holding that it was unlawful. Lord Lane CJ held that:

> It seems to us that where the common law rule no longer even remotely represents what is the true position of a wife in present day society, the duty of the court is to take steps to alter the rule if it can legitimately do so in the light of any relevant Parliamentary enactment.[99]
>
> . . . .
>
> It may be on the other hand that the draftsman intended to leave it open to the common law to develop as it has done since 1976.
>
> The only realistic explanations seem to us to be that the draftsman either intended to leave the matter open for the common law to develop in that way or, perhaps more likely, that no satisfactory meaning at all can be ascribed to the word and that it is indeed surplusage. In either event, we do not consider that we are inhibited by the Act of 1976 from declaring that the husband's immunity . . . no longer exists. We take the view that the time has now arrived when the law should declare that a rapist remains a rapist subject to the criminal law, irrespective of his relationship with his victim.[100]

The House of Lords agreed with the Court of Appeal. Lord Keith held that:

> I am therefore of the opinion that section 1(1) of the Act of 1976 presents no obstacle to this House declaring that in modern times the supposed marital exemption in rape forms no part of the law of England. The Court of Appeal (Criminal Division) took a similar view. Towards the end of the judgment of that court Lord Lane C.J. said, ante, p. 611:
>
> "The remaining and no less difficult question is whether, despite that view, this is an area where the court should step aside to leave the matter to the Parliamentary process. This is not the creation of a new offence, it is the removal of a common law fiction which has become anachronistic and offensive and we consider that it is our duty having reached that conclusion to act upon it."
>
> I respectfully agree.[101]

ACADEMIC DEBATE

Marianne Giles was critical of the decision in *R v R (Rape: Marital Exemption)* and argued that the court went 'beyond the bounds of their legitimate law-making powers' and that it would be better for Parliament to reform the law, rather than a piecemeal development by judges.[102] Giles also criticised judicial law making in '[t]he law relating to recklessness . . . [which is a] another prime example of judicial law-making effecting major changes, and resulting in a state of confusion and disagreement for many years.'[103]

Nicola Padfield responded to Giles and argued that:

> [Giles] is right in saying that the House of Lords . . . came perilously close to creating a new criminal offence. . . . But she goes on to argue . . . that if judges resist the temptation to reform the law in piecemeal fashion. Parliament is more likely to be pressurised into passing reforms. Why should this be so? Where is the evidence for this? I doubt whether Parliament would have felt a greater pressure to act if Lord Keith had not spoken as he did.[104]

Giles responded that:

> It is never easy to pressurise Parliament into reform of the criminal law. Nicky Padfield rightly points out that judicial inaction can as easily be taken as a reason not to act as to act. Similarly, Parliamentary inaction can be a cause as much as a result of judicial failure to reform. I feel however that judicial creativity which goes beyond the bounds of the doctrine of precedent is generally unacceptable for constitutional reasons.[105]

There are many examples of judicial law-making in areas such as the Law of Tort. In *Donoghue v Stevenson*[106], Lord Atkins created the modern tort of negligence. Previously, in tort there was not a duty to avoid causing another loss as Victorian judges had restricted civil liability to contract law. Therefore modern negligence is a branch of law that has been created by judges. So to is the law relating to psychiatric injury in tort, which has been developed and restricted by case law. One example is the decision in *Alcock v Chief Constable of South Yorkshire*[107]. The House of Lords were motivated by public policy concerns, i.e. the risk that too many claimants might sue after a large-scale disaster. Parliament has yet to reform this area of the law.

Recently, Lord Hodge, a Justice of the Supreme Court, explored the scope of judicial law-making.[108] He acknowledged that judges do make law as it is required by their role in a common law legal system, where the law is largely not codified. Judge-made law was important as, '[w]hile statute law now impinges on many areas of private law, large tracts of our private law remain predominantly the product of judicial decisions.'[109] Lord Hodge identified seven constraints on judges in their law-making role. Of particular interest is his observation that:

> A fourth constraint is what I have described as role recognition. This is sometimes called judicial restraint but I will stick with my preferred

expression, because it points to an objective constraint rather than mere judicial self-denial. It has also been referred to as the separation of powers but that expression begs the question because it does not identify the boundary of the judicial power. . . . It has been suggested that judges are most ready to develop common law rules which are recognised as 'lawyer's law,' such as the immunity of an advocate or witness, or mistake of law, or the boundaries of the law of negligence, while leaving matters which affect large sections of the community and which raise issues which are the subject of controversy to the democratic legislature.[110]

Lord Hodge was commenting that the separation of powers has been referred to as a constraint on judicial law-making. However, he noted that there were problems with this, due to the questions on where the boundaries should be on judicial power. There were clearly limits on their ability to make law, as '[j]udges recognise that they are not permitted to develop the law in a direction which is contrary to the expressed will of Parliament. They may fill in gaps left by Parliament but must not create incongruity.'[111] It is important to note the infrequency of judges making law, even if there are benefits when they can: 'Judicial law-making is therefore constrained law-making. It is also a minority activity. The vast majority of judicial work, well over 90 percent, involves no law-making but is . . . "the disinterested application of known law."' The fact that judge-made law is an independent source of law contributes to its flexibility; and judges continue to adapt the common law to changes in commercial practice and social values.[112]

3.7 Does the United Kingdom's system have suitable checks and balances?

We have seen that there are many overlaps between the functions and personnel of the three branches of government. We will now consider whether in light of these overlaps, whether the United Kingdom's constitution has suitable checks and balances to prevent one branch, i.e. the executive, from abusing its position.

3.7.1 Executive and legislature

Given that over the past 30 years a majority of governments have enjoyed a majority (either outright, or in the form of a coalition or a supply and confidence agreement) in the House of Commons, there is scope for the executive to dominate the legislature. It is important that the legislature is able to check the power of the executive and review its actions.

3.7.1.2 Vote of no confidence in government

The government is accountable to the House of Commons. If the Prime Minister loses a vote of no confidence, then the government will resign and this will trigger a general election. Section 2 (4) of the Fixed-term Parliaments Act 2011 permits early general elections when the there is a motion 'That this House has no confidence in Her Majesty's Government.'

The government must command the support of the majority of the House of Commons. In this respect the government owes it survival to the continual support of the House of Commons. A vote of no confidence will as a matter of convention force the Prime Minister to resign. The Fixed-term Parliaments Act 2011 has introduced fixed-term parliaments which will last five years but has nonetheless preserved the ability of a vote of no confidence to trigger a general election. Given that apart from the general election in 2010 and in 2017, recent elections have seen the government gain a large minority, it is unlikely that a vote would succeed in bringing down the current government. This is because the development of the modern political party has made it more difficult for this to happen. The last successful vote of no confidence was in 1979, which brought down the Callaghan government and triggered a general election. Therefore, a vote of no confidence is only a risk to a government without a majority in the House of Commons. In 2019, Theresa May's government survived a vote of no confidence that was brought in the aftermath of a defeat over the meaningful vote on the Prime Minister's European Union exit deal.

3.7.1.3 Prime minister's questions

When Parliament is in session Prime Minister's Questions take place every Wednesday at 11 a.m. During this time the Prime Minister faces 30 minutes of questions from the Leader of the Opposition and from backbench MPs. Prime Minister's Questions (PMQs) is televised and the performance of the Prime Minister and the Leader of the Opposition is scrutinised by politicians and the media. Commentators will critique their performance and a weak speaker might face a backbench revolt from within their own party. However, success during PMQs does not necessary secure victory at the ballot box for the Leader of the Opposition (see William Hague's performance as leader of the Conservative Party). Critics regard PMQs as nothing more than a televised Punch and Judy show. The Hansard Society's report 'Tuned in or Turned Off? Public Attitudes to Prime Minister's Questions'[113] has proposed reforms to the current system and outlined the public's negative perception of PMQs and the behaviour of MPs.

The question which must be asked is just how effective are PMQs in holding the government to account? The answer is that it depends. The Prime Minister must make himself available for questions and this is televised. Although in 2013, David Cameron frequently missed PMQs and the Deputy Prime Minister, Nick Clegg, stood in for him. The performance of the Prime Minister matters, as it is reported in the media and ultimately may influence voters. PMQs give Parliament the opportunity to question the government's proposals and the Prime Minister is expected to defend his government's policies. When Theresa May took over as Prime Minister from David Cameron in July 2015, commentators made much of her first performance in PMQs and compared her style to that of former Prime Minister Margaret Thatcher.

Critics accuse PMQs as being just a sound bite and that they offer little in terms of accountability. However, the former Prime Minister Tony Blair revealed in his memoirs that he found PMQs to be a terrifying experience:

> PMQs was the most nerve-racking, discombobulating, nail-biting, bowel-moving, terror-inspiring, courage-draining experience in my prime ministerial life, without question. You know that scene in Marathon Man where the evil Nazi doctor played by Laurence Olivier drills through Dustin Hoffman's teeth? At around 11.45 on Wednesday mornings, I would have swapped 30 minutes of PMQs for 30 minutes of that.[114]

3.7.1.4 Ministerial question time

Senior government ministers have an opportunity to answer questions in the Parliament. This takes place during ministerial question time.

3.7.1.5 Select Committees and General/Standing committees

In the House of Commons Select Committees oversee the work of government departments. The committees have no power to compel ministers to attend. Ministers are not allowed to sit on the committees. This is important as the Committees serve to review executive action and to scrutinise policies. This means that Parliament can exercise independent scrutiny of the executive. The Committees focus on that department's policies, spending and administration. The work of the Committee is published. The House of Lords has five Select Committees that focus on the Constitution, the European Union, Communications, Science and Technology and Economic Affairs. The General or Standing Committees are involved with the progress through Parliament of particular pieces of legislation. Please refer to **Chapter 7** for a more detailed discussion on Select Committees in the House of Commons and their strengths and weaknesses in holding the executive to account.

3.7.2 Executive and judiciary

3.7.2.1 Security of tenure

The senior members of the judiciary enjoy security of tenure which prevents the judge from being dismissed unless the conditions outlined in section 11 of the Senior Courts Act 1981 are satisfied. The key subsection is (3) as this states that senior members of the judiciary 'shall hold that office during good behaviour, subject to a power of removal by Her Majesty on an address presented to Her by both Houses of Parliament.' It is important to note that all other judges can be dismissed in accordance to the Constitutional Reform Act 2005. This statutory protection from dismissal was first given to senior members of the judiciary by the Act of Settlement 1701.

PUBLIC LAW IN CONTEXT
SECTION 11 OF THE SENIOR COURTS ACT 1981

(1) This section applies to the office of any judge of the Senior Courts

(2) A person appointed to an office to which this section applies shall vacate it on the day on which he attains the age of seventy years unless by virtue of this section he has ceased to hold it before then.

(3) A person appointed to an office to which this section applies shall hold that office during good behaviour, subject to a power of removal by Her Majesty on an address presented to Her by both Houses of Parliament.

(3A) It is for the Lord Chancellor to recommend to Her Majesty the exercise of the power of removal under subsection (3)

. . . .

(8) The Lord Chancellor, if satisfied by means of a medical certificate that a person holding an office to which this section applies –

   (a) is disabled by permanent infirmity from the performance of the duties of his office; and

   (b) is for the time being incapacitated from resigning his office, may, subject to sub-section (9), by instrument under his hand declare that person's office to have been vacated; and the instrument shall have the like effect for all purposes as if that person had on the date of the instrument resigned his office.

(9) A declaration under subsection (8) with respect to a person shall be of no effect unless it is made –

   (a) in the case of any of the Lord Chief Justice, the Master of the Rolls, the President of the Queen's Bench Division, the President of the Family Division and the Chancellor of the High Court, with the concurrence of two others of them;

   (b) in the case of a Lord Justice of Appeal, with the concurrence of the Master of the Rolls;

   (c) in the case of a puisne judge of any Division of the High Court, with the concurrence of the senior judge of that Division.

Prior to the Act of Settlement monarchs such as Charles II[115] and James II[116] had dismissed judges so that the courts would find in their favour. As a result of the Act of Settlement 1701 the judiciary do not owe their continued employment to the support of the executive. This prevents the executive from dismissing judges who reach politically controversial decisions.

Lord Denning has recounted that after the decision in *Heatons Transport (St Helens) Ltd v Transport and General Workers Union*[117]:

I was told by one in a high place:

Your decision was a disaster for the country, which will last till the end of the century.

I was shaken to the core. But I was not downcast. I just thought:

Thank goodness, the judges of the Court of Appeal are independent. No government dare seek to influence them.[118]

Gavin Drewry has commented that:

[D]etachment, and independence from executive and parliamentary pressure is part of the heritage of the Act of Settlement: and, as Robson put it, an important element of judicial independence is that the judge 'can displease an indefinite number of persons an indefinite number of times without any personal consequences ensuing to himself, providing only that he remains sane and does not commit one of those enormities which constitute misconduct.[119]

Only one judge has been dismissed under the Act of Settlement, and this was Sir Jonah Barrington in 1830 for corruption. Barrington was a judge of the Irish High Court of Admiralty.[120] More recently in the 1970s, 181 Labour MPs attempted to have Sir John Donaldson MR dismissed from office.

The Lord Chancellor traditionally appointed judges and notwithstanding the Constitutional Reform Act 2005 and the creation of the Judicial Appointments Commission, the Lord Chancellor still has an important role in the appointment of members of the judiciary.

3.7.2.2 Judicial review

The judiciary can review the actions of the executive. This is known as judicial review. Judicial review allows the court to decide whether the executive's actions were unreasonable, irrational, or illegal or gave rise to a legitimate expectation and whether there was procedural impropriety. This means that where Parliament has given a minister the power to make secondary legislation or make decisions, that the minister must use the power for the intended purposes, must not make an unreasonable decision and must not be biased.

Judicial review is extremely important, as it is a key check on the use of statutory powers by the executive. Judicial review is not an appeal and the courts should not substitute its own opinion for that of the decision-maker. The courts can quash the original decision and order the decision-maker to make the decision again.

As discussed above the executive can make Orders using the Royal Prerogative. Traditionally it was held that the manner in which the prerogative was used was not reviewable. However, in the case of *Council of Civil Service Unions v Minister of State for Civil Service (GCHQ)*[121] the House of Lords held that the prerogative was reviewable. According to Lord Roskill there were certain areas which were non-justiciable. This was because the court was aware that the executive had the expertise and function of determining these issues, i.e. the decision to go to war. We will see in **Chapter 10** that the list of non-justiciable prerogative powers has been reduced by subsequent judicial decision.

Judicial review is an important check and balance by the judiciary. Where the executive is accused of breaching the European Convention on Human Rights the court may apply a higher standard of review to see whether the decision was proportionate. This risks substituting the decision of the court for that of the decision-maker. Arguably this offends the theory of the separation of powers. We shall look at this in more detail in **Chapters 16** and **17**.

3.7.2.3 Royal prerogative

As well as being reviewable, the prerogative's scope and existence can be determined by the courts. Parliamentary control of the prerogative is limited, as the executive has refused to disclose the full extent of its prerogative powers. Where an Act of Parliament and the prerogative cover the same area the courts will apply the Act and the prerogative will go into abeyance.[122] The courts have restricted the use of new prerogatives, as Diplock LJ stated in *British Broadcasting Corporation v Johns*[123] that 'it is 350 years and a civil war too late for the Queen's courts to broaden the prerogative.' However, the degree of judicial scrutiny depends upon the composition of the court.

3.7.3 Legislature and judiciary

3.7.3.1 No power to review the validity of an Act of Parliament

The United Kingdom's judiciary cannot set aside an Act of Parliament which is considered to be unconstitutional. Some members of the judiciary have questioned whether the courts could do this. The *obiter* in *R (Jackson) v Attorney-General*[124] demonstrates differing judicial attitudes to Parliamentary Sovereignty. Lord Steyn had argued that if Parliament should legislate to do the unthinkable, then the courts might have to reconsider the Judicial Rule of Recognition. This rule recognises that parliament is legally sovereign and as a consequence no one can question an Act of Parliament. To understand why judges have no power to review the validity of an Act of Parliament, please refer to **Chapter 6** on Parliamentary Sovereignty.

3.7.3.2 Human Rights Act 1998

Section 3 of the Human Rights Act 1998 allows the court to read down and interpret an Act so that it complies with the Convention rights. However, the power to do this is restricted, as the courts must not go beyond what Parliament intended when enacting legislation. This is a controversial power as some judges have been accused of going against what Parliament intended. Section 4 allows courts (High Court and above) to issue a Declaration of Incompatibility where an Act of Parliament breaches a Convention right that has been incorporated under the HRA 1998. A declaration of incompatibility does not allow the court to set aside an Act; however Parliament will usually amend the Act to remove the incompatibility with the Convention right. The importance of the HRA 1998 is that it allows the judiciary to challenge an Act of Parliament in a way that was impossible before. Whilst it may be argued that these powers are given by Parliament and can be removed by Parliament, nonetheless the judiciary have successfully challenged the previous government's controversial terrorism legislation in *A v Home Secretary*[125]. The Anti-Terrorism, Crime and Security Act 2001 allowed for indefinite detention of suspected terrorists without trial. The House of Lords issued a declaration of incompatibility and the government eventually responded by amending the offending legislation and introduced control orders.

3.7.3.3 Ouster clauses

The courts have refused to allow the legislature to prevent judicial review of executive actions. Where an Act of Parliament attempts to restrict judicial review the courts have managed to review the executive's use of the powers conferred by the statute.

PUBLIC LAW IN CONTEXT
ANISMINIC LTD V FOREIGN COMPENSATION COMMISSION[126]

In *Anisminic Ltd v Foreign Compensation Commission*[127] the House of Lords interpreted an ouster clause which prevented review of a decision made by the decision as inapplicable. This was because the decision reached was interpreted as a purported determination and not a proper determination. The court had construed the words of the statute to enable judicial review. The decision in *Anisminic* has been identified as a problematic case by the Judicial Power Project, which has argued that the House of Lords had embarked on 'judicial adventurism.'[128] The inclusion of *Anisminic* has been criticised by TT Arvind and Lindsay Stirton:

'Objectively viewed, therefore, *Anisminic* represents neither "judicial adventurism" nor an attack on Parliamentary sovereignty. It represents, instead, an attempt to understand what this idea – that only Parliament (not the executive, and not the judiciary) possesses unfettered power – means when it came to a claim by an executive body to possess unbounded power.'[129]

3.7.3.4 Parliamentary scrutiny of the judiciary

If a judge is accused of misconduct, then both Houses of Parliament can pass a resolution calling for that judge to be dismissed. According to the Subjudice Rule, Parliament cannot discuss forthcoming and current cases. There is a constitutional convention that states that members of the legislature should not criticise individual judicial decisions. However, Parliament can criticise judicial sentencing policy. This convention is repeatedly broken, such as when Margaret Thatcher in 1979 criticised the leniency of sentence for a defendant convicted of molesting a child.

3.8 Impact of the Constitutional Reform Act 2005

The Constitutional Reform Act 2005 has reformed the office of the Lord Chancellor, has changed the way that judges are appointed and has created the United Kingdom's Supreme Court. The impact on the separation of powers is considerable, although the Act does not attempt to reform the fusion between the legislature and executive in terms of the overlap of personnel which is essential to the system of parliamentary government which exists at Westminster. The main provisions of the Act will be discussed below with reference to the overlaps that existed previously.

3.8.1 Judicial independence

Under section 3 of the Constitutional Reform Act 2005 the Lord Chancellor and other ministers have a duty to uphold judicial independence.

PUBLIC LAW IN CONTEXT
SECTION 3 OF THE CONSTITUTIONAL REFORM ACT 2005

(1) The Lord Chancellor, other Ministers of the Crown and all with responsibility for matters relating to the judiciary or otherwise to the administration of justice must uphold the continued independence of the judiciary.

(4) The following particular duties are imposed for the purpose of upholding that independence.

(5) The Lord Chancellor and other Ministers of the Crown must not seek to influence particular judicial decisions through any special access to the judiciary.

(6) The Lord Chancellor must have regard to –
    (a) the need to defend that independence;
    (b) the need for the judiciary to have the support necessary to enable them to exercise their functions;
    (c) the need for the public interest in regard to matters relating to the judiciary or otherwise to the administration of justice to be properly represented in decisions affecting those matters.

3.8.2 The creation of a Supreme Court

Section 23 of the Constitutional Reform Act 2005 creates the Supreme Court. The Supreme Court is housed in the former Middlesex Guildhall. The building has been renovated and proceedings are televised and available online via the Supreme Court's website. The judges are now known as Justices of the Supreme Court. Crucially section 137 of the Constitutional Reform Act 2005 prevents serving judges from sitting or voting in the House of Lords. This prevents a blurring of the distinction between the Justices in their capacity as judge and politician. The creation of the Supreme Court is extremely symbolic.

The Constitutional Reform Act 2005 does nothing to empower the Supreme Court to strike down legislation which is considered unconstitutional or offends the rule of law. This is because of the doctrine of Parliamentary Sovereignty.

3.8.3 The reform of the role of Lord Chancellor

The position of the Lord Chancellor has been reformed. The Lord Chancellor is now also the Secretary of State for Justice. Nonetheless, the Lord Chancellor still has a role in all branches of government. Section 7 of the Constitutional Reform Act 2005 states that the Lord Chief Justice is now the head of the judiciary in England and Wales and is responsible for welfare, training and guidance. The Lord Chief Justice takes over these duties from the Lord Chancellor. Section 2 of the Constitutional Reform Act 2005 states that the Lord Chancellor must be qualified by experience but need not be a lawyer. Chris Grayling was the first non-lawyer to act as Lord Chancellor. Lord Falconer, who was a previous Lord Chancellor, had previously criticised the appointment of Grayling for not having any legal qualifications. More recently, the appointment of Liz Truss as Lord Chancellor in 2016 was criticised by Lord Falconer. Falconer argued that section 2 requires the Lord Chancellor to be qualified by experience: '[t]he 2005 reforms were made on the assumption that protections were needed to ensure the lord chancellor remained a powerful defender of the rule of law within government. I do not know whether May was aware of the provision before she appointed Liz Truss.'[130] When giving evidence to the House of Lords' Select Committee on the Constitution, Lord Judge, the former Lord Chief Justice was of the view that:

> I would be much happier if there was a statutory provision that required the Lord Chancellor and therefore the minister to have some legal qualification. It would not be a bad thing for someone to have a legal qualification if he is to be responsible for prisons. That is an area where there is quite a lot of law.[131]

PUBLIC LAW IN CONTEXT
SECTION 2 OF THE CONSTITUTIONAL REFORM ACT 2005

(1) A person may not be recommended for appointment as Lord Chancellor unless he appears to the Prime Minister to be qualified by experience.

(2) The Prime Minister may take into account any of these –
   (a) experience as a Minister of the Crown;
   (b) experience as a member of either House of Parliament;
   (c) experience as a qualifying practitioner;
   (d) experience as a teacher of law in a university;
   (e) other experience that the Prime Minister considers relevant.

When giving evidence before the Select Committee on the Constitution, Lord Woolf, the former Lord Chief Justice, was of the view that the reforms to the Lord Chancellor's role, which meant that he was now also the Secretary of State for Justice with responsibility for a larger portfolio including prisons, had changed

> the old style office of Lord Chancellor, and the special character of what came to be called the Lord Chancellor's Department and now the Ministry of Justice, has been diluted? I will not put it any stronger than that. Those who worked in the Lord Chancellor's Department tended to stay there. They realised that this what the situation required. It was part of the separateness of the Lord Chancellor from the general political hurly-burly. It had a special character.[132]

According to section 1 of the Constitutional Reform Act 2005 the Lord Chancellor must protect the rule of law. The Lord Chancellor no longer has any judicial functions and no longer sits as a judge. This is very important as this removes the potential for breaching Article 6 of the European Convention on Human Rights, which guarantees a fair and impartial tribunal. Although Lord Falconer[133] who replaced Lord Irvine[134] as Lord Chancellor, had promised not to sit as a judge, it is important that the judiciary are seen to be independent of the executive.

We have seen that Lord Hailsham had defended the role of the Lord Chancellor as the judiciary's friend in government. This role of representing the judiciary falls to the Lord Chief Justice, who under section 5 of the Constitutional Reform Act 2005 is permitted to make representations to Parliament. Lord Judge, the former Lord Chief Justice, has commented that the Constitutional Reform Act 2005 has removed a valuable link between the judiciary and the government: 'There's nobody in the Cabinet who is responsible for representing – to those members of the Cabinet who may need advice on an issue – how a particular proposal may impact on the judiciary.' Lord Judge also commented that there were political restrictions on the ability to make representations under section 5 to Parliament, as this risked being seen to take sides against the government.[135]

In July 2014, Lord Judge appeared before the House of Lords' Select Committee on the Constitution. His Lordship made some very interesting comments about section 5 of the Constitutional Reform Act 2005 and the fact that the Act played 'lip service' to the separation of powers.[136] His Lordship viewed the power under section 5 as 'a feeble nuclear option'[137]:

> I always took the view that the written representation was neither fish nor fowl. You introduce dramatic changes to the constitution on the basis of the separation of powers, and how wonderful that is, *without acknowledging that the executive fills the legislature.* It has quite a few members in the upper House. *So we do not have a separation of powers; we are paying lip service to it.* But the result ignored the situation that the head of the judiciary was no longer in the Cabinet, and the right of the Lord Chief Justice . . . to address Parliament, went. *This is all part of the lip service paid to the separation of powers.* You are then left with the ability to write a letter. I am sorry to say this, but in a system where orality is fundamental, the idea of writing a letter saying, 'Dear House of Lords. I am really rather worried about such and such. Please will you do something about it?', *strikes me as being on the side of the absurd.* I think that the Lord Chief Justice should be able to address Parliament if he has the sort of concerns which he would expect to write a letter about. Moreover, I am more convinced now than I was that there are times when I have heard the minister – there is no criticism of him – speak about what the judges might think. If anyone should be speaking about what the judges might think, assuming it matters, it should be the Lord Chief Justice or his equivalent. Again, the idea of him writing a letter saying, 'I don't think the minister quite understood what I was saying, and anyway he is wrong about this and that,' simply makes it absurd. *So whereas I always regarded the opportunity to write to the House of Lords as my nuclear option, to be exercised only in very exceptional circumstances, because you do not use your nuclear option more than once, there is something to be said for the following. If the House wants to know the views of the Lord Chief Justice – and if they matter – on issues of practicality, then he should have the right to speak in the House.*[138]

Lord Judge was concerned that the Lord Chief Justice must not be seen as taking political sides, as '[t]hat would be terrible. We would go down a long route of saying, "Judges cannot be appointed without hearing their political views", and the like.'[139]

The appointment of the judiciary has been reformed. Section 14 transfers the right of appointment of High Court Judges and District Judges from the Lord Chancellor to the Queen. This is very important. Equally, the establishment of the Judicial Appointments Commission under section 61 of the Constitutional Reform Act 2005 opens up the judicial appointment process. The Lord Chancellor no longer appoints candidates and under section 29 can only reject the nominees presented by the Judicial Appointments Commission. Section 27 states how the Judicial Appointment Commission will select the Supreme Court Justices. The Lord Chancellor and the Lord Chief Justice are both responsible for disciplining judges.[140] The Crime and Courts Act 2013 has transferred some of the Lord Chancellor's role in the appointment of judges to the Lord Chief Justice. Schedule 13 of the 2013 Act has amended the Constitutional Reform Act 2005:

- Section 27A of the Constitutional Reform Act 2005 now gives the Lord Chancellor the power to make regulations that could give him the power to require the commission established to appoint new members of the Supreme Court to reconsider a candidate or to reject the commission's candidate.
- Section 29 has been amended to transfer much of the Lord Chancellor's responsibility for the appointment of junior judges to the Lord Chief Justice. Under section 29 the Judicial Appointments Commission will report to the Lord Chief Justice with their selection of candidates.
- Sections 36 and 38 transfer the power of appointing Deputy District Judges from the Lord Chancellor to the Lord Chief Justice.

Section 18 of the Constitutional Reform Act 2005 removed the Lord Chancellor as speaker of the House of Lords. The House of Lords elects its own speaker. The Lord Chancellor is still a member of the legislature. Since 2007, all Lord Chancellors have been members of the House of Commons.

Table 3.1 A comparison of the situation before and after the Constitutional Reform Act 2005

Who sits in Parliament?	Prior to CRA 2005	Post CRA 2005
Legislature	Yes	Yes
Executive	Yes (Government)	Yes (Government)
Judiciary	Yes, in the House of Lords	No

Who makes laws?	Prior to CRA 2005	Post CRA 2005
Legislature	Yes	Yes
Executive	Yes, through delegated legislation	Yes, through delegated legislation
Judiciary	Yes, through case law	Yes, through case law

PUBLIC LAW IN ACTION

Imagine that a barrister was appointed to the judiciary. Prior to the CRA 2005 her appointment would have been managed by the Lord Chancellor and was not a transparent process. Post the CRA 2005 judicial appointments are managed by the Judicial Appointments Commission. Once appointed the new judge would be managed by the Lord Chief Justice who is the head of the judiciary in England and Wales. If she misbehaves in office, she will be disciplined by both the Lord Chancellor and the Lord Chief Justice. Eventually, she might become a member of the Supreme Court. As a Justice of the Supreme Court she would no longer have the right to sit in the House of Lords. As a Justice of the Supreme Court she would not have the power to strike down Acts of Parliament, however repugnant the Act may be.

3.9 What do the experts think?

It is important to appreciate that academics have different views as to whether the United Kingdom's constitution conforms to the requirements of the separation of powers.

ACADEMIC DEBATE

Professor Barendt argued that Montesquieu's understanding of the British constitution was flawed.[141] Barendt stated that '[t]he truth is that there is no effective separation of powers between legislature and executive in the United Kingdom in the sense of a system of 'checks and balances.' The advent of mass political parties has destroyed the semblance of such a system which existed a century ago.[142]

Barendt argued that, '[t]here is, however, an effective separation of the judicial power from the other branches. Judges may not sit in the House of Commons and they are protected from summary removal under the Act of Settlement 1701.'[143] Barendt continued to state the role of the Lord Chancellor and the Law Lords involvement with the House of Lords 'contravene the principle, albeit moderately and perhaps acceptably.'[144] Barendt argued that, 'While there is in practice a fusion of legislative and executive *powers*, there is in principle a distinction between the two *functions*.'[145]

Professor Munro observed that the separation of powers 'h[as] shaped constitutional arrangements and influenced our constitutional thinking. . . . The separation in the British Constitution, although not absolute, ought not to be lightly dismissed.'[146] Other academics such as Griffith and Street were critical and argued 'the doctrine is so remote from the facts that it is better to disregard it altogether.'[147] Equally hostile are SA De Smith and R Brazier who argued that 'no writer of repute would claim that it is a central feature of the modern British constitution.'[148]

Lord Steyn writing extra-judicially considered the separation of powers and observed, 'in *Duport Steels Ltd v. Sirs*, Lord Diplock repeated that "it cannot be too strongly emphasised that the British Constitution, though largely unwritten, is firmly based on the separation of powers". I respectfully agree with those observations. But, given that all members of the political executive are members of the legislature, the concept applies in a qualified form in this country.'[149]

Lord Bingham observed that '[w]hile the British constitution does not, quite obviously, provide for the separation of legislative and executive authority, it does . . . Lord Bingham noted that prior to the CRA 2005 there were two exceptions: the Lord Chancellor and the House of Lords] provide for an absolute separation of judicial from legislative and executive authority.'[150]

Other members of the judiciary have highlighted the importance of judicial independence and the fact that judiciary and legislature both have different functions. Lord Donaldson stated in *R v HM Treasury, Ex p Smedley*[151] that it is 'of the highest importance that the legislature and the judicature are separate and independent of one another. . . . It therefore behoves the courts to be ever sensitive to the paramount need to refrain from trespassing on the province of Parliament . . .'[152]

In *R (on the application of Tigere) v Secretary of State for Business, Innovation and Skills*[153] the Supreme Court had to consider the issue of whether refusing student finance to a student was illegal on the basis of her immigration status. A majority of the court held that it was illegal. However, in their dissenting judgment Lords Sumption and Reed had observed,

[i]n a case where a range of rational and proportionate policy options is open to the decision-maker, the decision which provides the best allocation of scarce resources is a question of social and economic evaluation. These are matters of political and administrative judgment, which the law leaves to those who are answerable to Parliament. They are not questions for a court of law. It is enough to justify the Secretary of State's choice in this case that discrimination on the basis of residence and settlement are not manifestly without foundation.[154]

This demonstrates the awareness of the judiciary to the separation of powers and whether the court should interfere in what the dissenting judges referred to as 'matters of political and administrative judgment.'[155] The Supreme Court's decision in *Tigere* has been highlighted as a problematic case by the Judicial Power Project.[156]

3.10 Conclusion

Does the United Kingdom have the separation of powers? It is important that after reading this chapter that you feel confident to answer this question. We have seen that the separation of powers has been acknowledged as important to prevent tyranny and abuse of power. Historically, the legislature and the executive have struggled for mastery. Since the 17th century the law-making powers of the executive have been checked by Parliament. What does the separation of powers actually mean? Does the existence of checks and balances, which necessitate interference by the other branches of government into the workings of a particular branch, prevent there being separation of powers? Can the United Kingdom's system of government be regarded as conforming to what is required the separation of powers, or does the overlap of personnel and function prevent this? The Constitutional Reform Act 2005 has created the Supreme Court and reformed the role of Lord Chancellor. However, the fusion of the executive and legislature has not been reformed by the Constitutional Reform Act 2005.

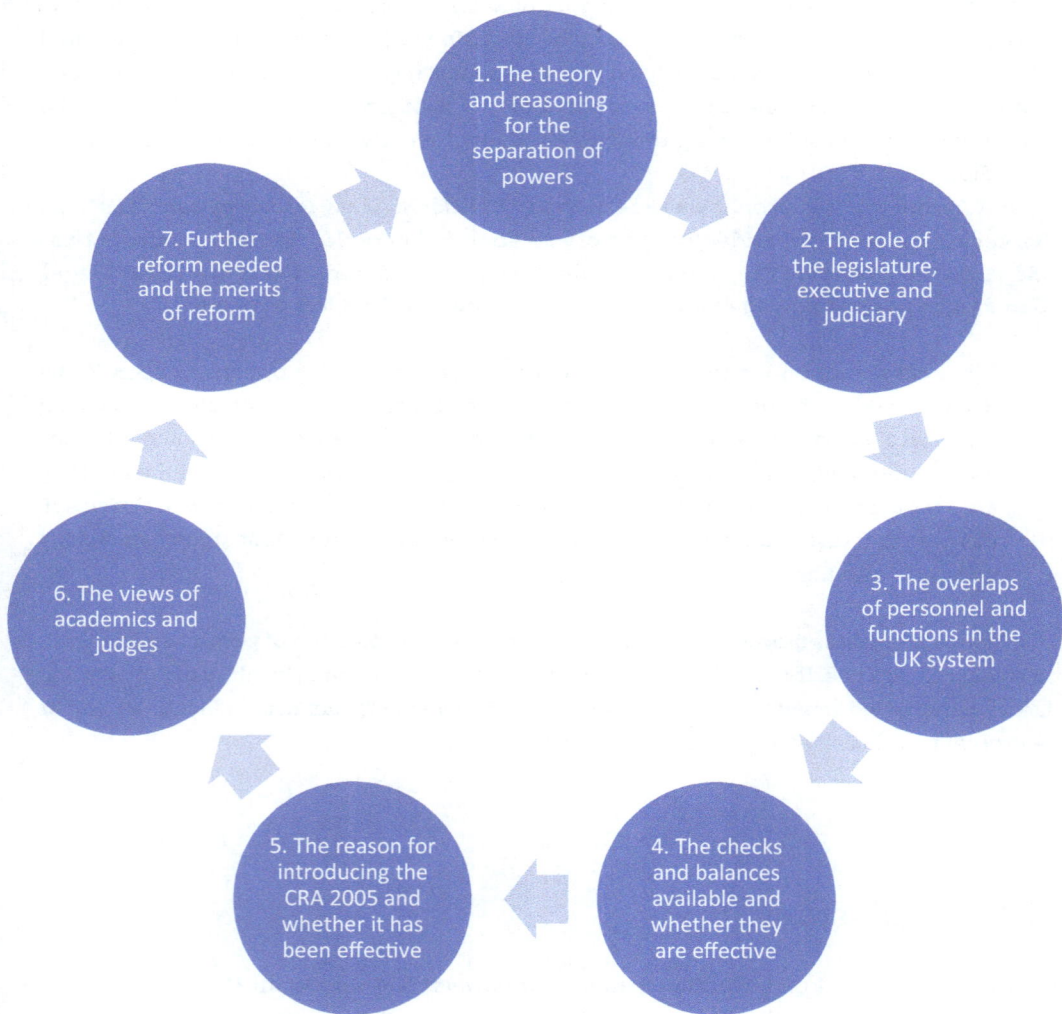

Figure 3.11
The key areas of the separation of powers

3.11 Practical application

1   Was the creation of the United Kingdom Supreme Court something that was required or rather was it an unnecessary development given the independence enjoyed by senior members of the judiciary since 1701?
     You should make reference to legislation, case law and academic opinion in your answer.
2   To what extent has the Constitutional Reform Act 2005 strengthened the separation of powers within the United Kingdom?
     You should make reference to legislation, case law and academic opinion in your answer.

3.12 Key points to take away from this chapter

- The separation of powers is regarded as important to ensure the effective running of a country and to avoid the risk of tyranny and the abuse of power.
- The separation of powers requires the three powers, making laws, governing the country and administering justice to be exercised by three distinct bodies, each of which is composed of different people.
- The strict separation of power without check and balances would risk good government and would permit abuse of power.
- The classic account was written by Montesquieu, whose writings influenced the drafters of the United States Constitution.
- It is controversial as to whether the United Kingdom's system has separation of powers. Although the Constitutional Reform Act 2005 has changed the relationship between the judiciary and the other branches of government.

Notes

1   J Perlez and D Rohde, 'Pakistan Attempts to Crush Protests by Lawyers' *The New York Times* (6 November 2007).
2   [2018] UKSC 27.
3   ibid 344.
4   Section 2(1) of the Fixed-term Parliaments Act 2011.
5   [1992] UKHL 3.
6   [1966] 3 All ER 77.
7   [2016] UKSC 35; [2016] 3 WLR 157.
8   ibid.
9   ibid.
10 [2008] UKHL 61.
11 [1966] 1 WLR 1234.
12 ibid 2.

13   Aristotle's, *Politics* (Clarendon Press 1905) 1297b, 1–1298 a, 150).

14   Charles Louis de Secondat and Baron de Montesquieu, *The Spirit of the Laws* (J Nourse 1748) 173.

15   (1689).

16   (1603–25).

17   GC Moodie, 'The Crown and Parliament' [1957] Parliamentary Affairs 256, 256–57.

18   Above (n 13) 84.

19   ibid 33.

20   ibid 195.

21   ibid 199.

22   ibid.

23   ibid.

24   ibid 181.

25   ibid 180.

26   ibid.

27   See R Paley, 'The Dying Embers of an Outdated Privilege: The 1935 Trial of Lord de Clifford in the House of Lords' in *Institutional Practice and Memory: Parliamentary People, Records and Histories. Essays in Honour of Sir John Sainty* (Wiley-Blackwell 2013).

28   de Secondat and de Montesquieu (n 14) 181.

29   ibid.

30   ibid 179.

31   See JK Goldstein, 'Constitutional Change, Originalism, and the Vice Presidency' [2013] IJCL 369; RE Brownell, 'A Constitutional Chameleon: The Vice President's Place Within the American System of Separation of Powers' (2014–2015) 24 KJLPP 1.

32   [1803] 5 U.S. 137.

33   See PH Schucknov, 'Why Congress Can Impeach Obama: The Impeachment of Obama on Immigration May Be Legal – But It's Wrong' *The New York Times* (21 November 2014).

34   [1803] 5 U.S. 137.

35   Lord Acton to Bishop Creighton, 1887.

36   1653–58.

37   Article II.

38   Article I.

39   M Needham, *A True State of the Case of the Commonwealth* (1654) 10.

40   HJ Hanham, *The Nineteenth Century Constitution 1815–1914: Documents and Commentary* (CUP 1969) 13.

41   B Disraeli (1844).

42   FTH Fletcher, *Montesquieu and English Politics (1750–1800)* (Porcupine Press 1980) 137.

43   ibid 150.

44   ibid 151.

45   ibid 147.

46   ibid 148.

47   C Munro, *Studies in Constitutional Law* (2nd edn, OUP 2005); FF Ridley, 'There Is No British Constitution: A Dangerous Case the Emperor's Clothes' [1988] Parliamentary Affairs 340.

48 WA Robson, *Justice and Administrative Law: A Study of the British Constitution* (2nd edn, Stevens and Sons Ltd 1947) 18.

49 S Jay, 'Servants of Monarchs and Lords: The Advisory Role of Early English Judges' (1994) 38(2) AJLH 117.

50 Robson (n 48) 18.

51 ibid 14.

52 L Claus, 'Montesquieu's Mistakes and the True Meaning of Separation' (2005) 25(3) OJLS 419–20.

53 ibid 431.

54 Munro (n 47) 303–4.

55 W Bagehot, *The English Constitution* (OUP 2001) 11.

56 Lord Hailsham, 'Elective Dictatorship' (1976) 120 SJ 693.

57 JAG Griffith, 'The Political Constitution' (1979) 42(1) MLR 1 at 7–10.

58 See 'Government Defeats in the House of Lords' <www.parliament.uk/about/faqs/house-of-lords-faqs/lords-govtdefeats/>.

59 C Gearty, *Principles of Human Rights Adjudication* (OUP 2004) 210.

60 M Flinders, 'Shifting the Balance? Parliament, the Executive and the British Constitution' (2002) 50 PS 23.

61 ibid 31.

62 ibid 38.

63 M Russell and P Cowley, 'The Policy Power of the Westminster Parliament: The "Parliamentary State" and the Empirical Evidence' (2016) 29(1) Governance: An International Journal of Policy, Administration, and Institutions 121, 132.

64 Moodie (n 17) 256, 260.

65 See A Tomkins, *Our Republic Constitution* (Hart Publishing 2005).

66 See the Constitutional Reform and Governance Act 2010.

67 Lord Hailsham, 'The Office of Lord Chancellor and the Separation of Powers [1989] CJQ 308, 311.

68 ibid 314.

69 ibid.

70 G Drewry, 'Parliamentary Accountability for the Administration of Justice' in A Horne, G Drewry and D Oliver (eds), *Parliament and the Law* (Hart Publishing 2013) 359.

71 Above (n 54) 316.

72 Lord Steyn, 'The Case for a Supreme Court' [2002] LQR 382, 388.

73 G Drewry, 'Judicial Inquiries and Public Reassurance' [1996] PL 368.

74 'Obituary: Lord Donaldson of Lymington' *The Telegraph* (2 September 2005).

75 Lord Steyn, 'The Weakest and Least Dangerous Department of Government' [1997] PL 84.

76 ibid 93.

77 [2002] 35 EHRR 32.

78 [2002] 3 WLR 1800.

79 See Ministry of Justice, *The Governance of Britain Review of the Executive Prerogative Powers: Final Report* (Ministry of Justice 2009).

80 [2014] EWCA Crim 956.

81 ibid 36.

82 See 'Jurors Given Suspended Jail Terms for "Serious" Contempt of Court' *The Guardian* (9 June 2015).

83 [2012] UKSC 52; [2013] 1 A.C. 484.

84 ibid 11.

85 G Marshall, *Constitutional Conventions: The Rules and Forms of Political Accountability* (OUP 1987) 113.

86 A Samuels, 'Abolish the Office of Attorney-General' [2014] PL 609.

87 ibid 610.

88 ibid 614.

89 H Woolf, *Protection of the Public – A New Challenge* (Steven & Sons 1990).

90 Above (n 72).

91 ibid 382.

92 [1892] 2 QB 324.

93 ibid 326.

94 Lord Reid, 'The Judge as Lawmaker' (1972) 12 JSPTL 23.

95 [1992] 1 AC 599.

96 ibid.

97 ibid.

98 [1954] 2 Q.B. 282.

99 Above (n 95) 610.

100 ibid 611.

101 ibid 623.

102 M Giles, 'Judicial Law-Making in the Criminal Courts: The Case of Marital Rape' [1992] Crim LR 407.

103 ibid.

104 N Padfield, 'Letter: Judicial Law-Making' [1992] Crim LR 680.

105 Giles (n 102) 680.

106 [1932] AC 562.

107 [1992] 1 AC 310.

108 Lord Hodge, *The Scope of Judicial Law-Making in the Common Law Tradition* (Max Planck Institute of Comparative and International Private Law 28 October 2019) <www.supremecourt.uk/docs/speech-191028.pdf>.

109 ibid 1.

110 ibid 33.

111 ibid 36.

112 ibid 39–40.

113 (2014).

114 T Blair, *A Journey* (Arrow 2011) 109.

115 (1660–85).

116 (1685–1688).

117 [1972] 3 WLR 73.

118 Lord Denning, *The Closing Chapters* (Butterworths 1983) 177.

119 Drewry (n 73) 368–69.

120 For an interesting commentary see P O'Brien, 'When Judges Misbehave: The Strange Case of Jonah Barrington' (*UK Constitutional Law Blog*, 7 March 2013) <http://ukconstitutionallaw.org>.

121 [1985] AC 374.

122 See *Attorney-General v De Keyser's Royal Hotel Ltd.* [1920] AC 508.

123 [1964] WLR 1071.

124 [2005] UKHL 56.

125 [2004] UKHL 56.

126 [1969] 2 AC 147.

127 ibid.

128 See <http://judicialpowerproject.org.uk/50-problematic-cases/>.

129 TT Arvind and L Stirton, 'Why the Judicial Power Project Is Wrong About *Anisminic*' (*UK Constitutional Law Blog*, 20 May 2016) <https://ukconstitutionallaw.org/>.

130 'This Row Over Liz Truss as Lord Chancellor Isn't About Gender: It's About the Law' *The Guardian* (25 July 2016).

131 House of Lords, *Select Committee on the Constitution, The Office of Lord Chancellor, Oral and Written Evidence* (The Stationery Office 2014) 152.

132 ibid 144.

133 (2003–7).

134 (1997–2003).

135 J Rozenberg, 'Lord Chief Justice Changes to Judiciary "Eroding Something Important"' *The Guardian* (30 January 2013) <www.theguardian.com/law/2013/jan/30/lord-chief-justice-changes-judiciary>.

136 Above (n 131) 145.

137 ibid 148.

138 ibid 145–46 (emphasis added).

139 ibid 147.

140 Sections108 and 109.

141 E Barendt, 'Separation of Powers and Constitutional Government' [1995] PL 599.

142 ibid 614.

143 ibid 615.

144 ibid.

145 ibid.

146 Munro (n 47) 332.

147 JAG Griffith and H Street, *Principles of Administrative Law* (5th edn, Pitman, 1973) 16.

148 H Barnrett, *Constitutional and Administrative Law* (8th edn, Penguin 1998) 18.

149 (1997).

150 T Bingham, *The Lives of the Law: Selected Essays and Speeches 2000–2010* (OUP 2011) 71–72.

151 [1985] QB 657.

152 ibid 666.

153 [2015] UKSC 57.

154 [100].

155 ibid.

156 See <http://judicialpowerproject.org.uk/50-problematic-cases/>.

Further reading

Barber NW, 'The Separation of Powers and the British Constitution' Legal Research Paper Series, University of Oxford, Paper No 3/2012, January 2012

Barendt E, 'Separation of Powers and Constitutional Government' [2005] PL 599

Bingham T, *The Lives of the Law: Selected Essays and Speeches 2000–2010* (OUP 2011)

Claus L, 'Montesquieu's Mistakes and the True Meaning of Separation' [2005] OJLS 419

Drewry G, 'Judicial Inquiries and Public Reassurance' [1996] PL 368

————, 'Parliamentary Accountability for the Administration of Justice' in A Horne, G Drewry and D Oliver (eds), *Parliament and the Law* (Hart Publishing 2013)

Fletcher FTH, *Montesquieu and English Politics (1750–1800)* (Porcupine Press 1980)

Giles M, 'Judicial Law-Making in the Criminal Courts: The Case of Marital Rape' [1992] CLR 407

Hailsham, Lord, 'Elective Dictatorship' (1976) 120 SJ 693

————, 'The Office of Lord Chancellor and the Separation of Powers' [1989] CJQ 308

The Hansard Society, *Tuned in or Turned off? Public Attitudes to Prime Minister's Questions* (The Hansard Society 2014)

Hodge, Lord, *The Scope of Judicial Law-Making in the Common Law Tradition* (Max Planck Institute of Comparative and International Private Law 28 October 2019)

House of Lords, *Select Committee on the Constitution, The Office of Lord Chancellor, Oral and Written Evidence* (The Stationery Office 2014)

Lester A, 'English Judges as Law Makers' [1993] PL 269

Montesquieu B and C de Secondat, *The Spirit of the Laws* (J Nourse 1748)

Munro C, *Studies in Constitutional Law* (OUP 2005)

Padfield NM and M Giles, 'Letter: Judicial Law-Making' [1992] CLR 680

Reid, Lord, 'The Judge as Lawmaker' (1972) 12 JSPTL 23

Samuels A, 'Abolish the Office of Attorney-General' [2014] PL 609

Steyn, Lord, 'The Weakest and Least Dangerous Department of Government' [1997] PL 84

————, 'The Case for a Supreme Court' [2002] LQR 382

Windleman, Lord, 'The Constitutional Reform Act 2005: Ministers, Judges and Constitutional Change: Part 1' [2005] PL 806

The rule of law and the United Kingdom's constitution

This chapter will

- consider what is meant by the rule of law;
- appreciate the relationship between the rule of law and the United Kingdom's constitution;
- understand the challenges facing the rule of law within the United Kingdom; and
- distinguish between different academic versions of the rule of law.

4.1 Introduction

Imagine that the government has announced that from now on ministers – that is those individuals running government departments – can act with legal immunity and will face no sanction if they break the law. Does this sound right? Should ministers, by virtue of their position, be above the law? This is contrary to the rule of law. The purpose of this chapter is to give an understanding of what is meant by the rule of law. However, it will become apparent that there are many different possible interpretations of what is required for a country and its laws to meet the standards required to comply with this important constitutional principle. The observance of the rule of law is an important characteristic of the United Kingdom's constitution. Although, as we have discussed in **Chapter 1**, the United Kingdom does not have a fully written constitution, the rule of law is an integral concept to the operation of the United Kingdom's constitutional system and plays an important part in the English and Welsh legal system.

The rule of law means many different things and there are various theories as to what is expected in order for a country to conform to the rule of law. It can mean that the government and its agencies must act in accordance to the

DOI: 10.4324/9780429293498-5

law, that the government is not above the law, and that the law should be sufficiently certain and accessible. It is also said to mean that there can be no action by the executive, unless there is legal authority to do so, and that the laws created by the courts (through common law) and Parliament (Acts of Parliament) must meet certain conditions, otherwise they do not comply with the rule of law. It can also mean that the government cannot decide the extent of its own authority, otherwise the government would potentially wield arbitrary power and there would be no certainty. The rule of law holds that the state is governed in accordance with the law, not by the arbitrary whim of its current rulers. This is important as the law and the value attached to the observance of it by every one of us, regardless of our position or status, is vital.

In the United Kingdom even members of the royal family, with the exception of the Queen, as Head of State, are subject to the law and will be held to account in the event that their conduct is deemed to be illegal. For example, in 2002 Princess Anne was prosecuted after her pet dog attacked children in Windsor Great Park.[1] The Princess Royal was convicted of a criminal offence. In 2019, Prince Philip, the Duke of Edinburgh was involved in a car accident in which a woman was injured. Prince Philip could have faced prosecution for causing the accident; however, the decision was taken not to prosecute the Prince after he voluntarily

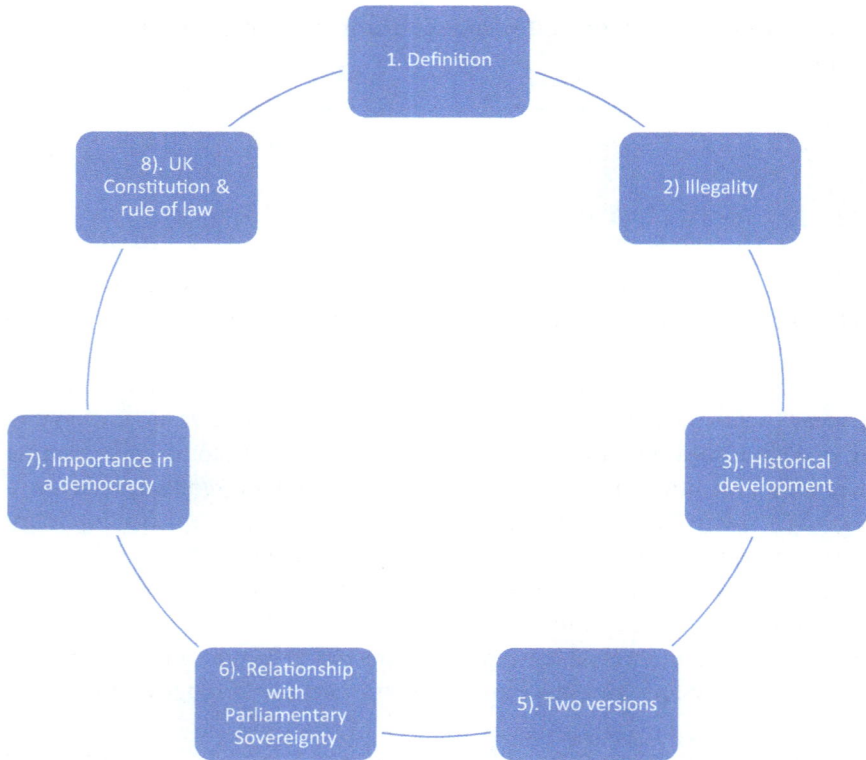

Figure 4.1
Chapter overview

surrendered his driving licence.[2] There would be public outrage if certain individuals were permitted to break the law without facing a sanction. The monarch's immunity is a legal prerogative of the Crown. It is difficult to envisage a monarch embarking on a wave of criminal activity and if this were to occur, then the fact that there would be no legal sanction could be seen as contrary to the rule of law.

The rule of law is not just a public law issue, it is important to other branches of the law from criminal law to commercial law. We will look at the definition and different versions of the rule of law and see why it matters that the United Kingdom's laws are compatible with this important characteristic of the constitution. This chapter will firstly look at the rule of law and why it is important, before secondly looking at the development and the protection of the rule of law in UK constitutional history. It will thirdly consider the differing ideas put forward by academics and judicial commentators for what is meant and required by the rule of law, before finally considering some contemporary UK challenges to the rule of law.

4.2 Definition of the rule of law

How do we define the rule of law? This is problematic, as we shall see below, because the rule of law can mean different things to different people. Many of the definitions provided by academics and judges have similarities, but also important differences. The purpose of this section is to introduce you to some broad definitions of what is meant by the rule of law, which we can then expand on throughout this chapter.

FA Hayek's definition of the rule of law provides a useful start. Hayek in *The Road to Serfdom* gave a famous and authoritative definition of the rule of law. Hayek stated

> [the rule of law] stripped of all technical formalities . . . means that government in all its actions is bound by rules fixed and announced beforehand – rules which make it possible to foresee with fair certainty how the authority will use its coercive powers in given circumstances, and to plan one's individual affairs on the basis of this knowledge.[3]

Hayek is describing a system of limited government, whereby the government's power is limited by law, and members of the executive are not permitted to act outside of the law in the name of expediency or their own interest. An example of this was the lockdown introduced by the government in March 2020, with rules stipulating what you could or could not do. This lockdown had a lawful basis, the Coronavirus Act 2020. However, when the rules were first announced it was not clear that they had any legal basis, as the Act was not yet in force, leading to legal commentators looking for the source of the government's authority for introducing these rules.[4] To Hayek we all must know what the law is so that we can make sure that we can abide by it. We can see that it is possible in theory for everyone in the United Kingdom to find out what the law is, such as through websites like www.legislation.gov.uk which contains an up-to-date account of statutory law.

Another way to understands the rule of law is provided by Professor Jeremey Waldron, who has observed that

> [t]he Rule of Law is one ideal in an array of values that dominates liberal political morality: others include democracy, human rights, social justice, and economic freedom. The plurality of these values seems to indicate that there are multiple ways in which social and political systems can be evaluated, and these do not necessarily fit tidily together.[5]

Waldron sees the rule of law as one of the important values in liberal a society. Finally, Brian Tamanaha provided another definition of what is meant by the rule of law:

> The rule of law means that government officials and citizens are bound by and abide by the law. I repeat: government officials and citizens are bound by and abide by the law. This definition requires that there must be a system of laws – and law by its nature involves rules set forth in advance that are stated in general terms. A particular decision or an order made for an occasion is not a rule. The law must be generally known and understood. The requirements imposed by the law cannot be impossible for people to meet. The laws must be applied equally to everyone according to their terms. There must be mechanisms or institutions that enforce the legal rules when they are breached.[6]

Tamanaha has placed considerable emphasis on the fact that the government and the citizens must follow the law. The law that they are bound by must be certain, possible to follow and be applied to everyone. Tamanaha explored the importance of being able to enforce laws and to provide ways of getting redress if the law is breached.

Whilst we consider below three different versions or definitions of the rule of law, it is important to appreciate that there are many more. The first that we will look at is AV Dicey's classic three-stage definition of the rule of law.[7] The second is the formal, or procedural, version of the rule of law as defined for the purposes of this chapter by Joseph Raz.[8] The third is the substantive version of the rule of law that has been defined amongst others by Lord Bingham, the former Senior Law Lord in the United Kingdom.[9] These three versions of the rule of law are different and it is important that as you read this chapter you appreciate the differences between them.

4.3 Illegality

A central component of the rule of law is that the government must act in accordance with the law. The government is not above the law and should the Prime Minister commit a criminal offence then he will be arrested. The Crown Prosecution Service and the police cannot refuse to prosecute the Prime Minister, unless they are legally allowed to do so under the Code for Prosecutors.[10] This is important as we shall see below, because equality before the law is of upmost importance. Today the Prime Minister is responsible, as the head of government, for running the country; whereas, historically this power had been exercised by the monarch. Even 800 years ago legal commentators were clear that monarch must govern according to the law.[11] An example of a senior politician being subject to the law is Chris Huhne, who was a senior Cabinet minister in the 2010–15 Coalition Government, and was convicted of conspiracy to pervert the course of justice.[12] Despite his position in government, Huhne was not immune from being prosecuted and went to prison.

Legality means more than the Prime Minister, should he steal a packet of biscuits from a supermarket, being treated like everyone else. It means that the government and those responsible for exercising power must act in accordance to the law and ensure that decisions are legal and do not exceed their lawful authority. The government is given the power to take decisions and implement policy by Parliament (through Acts of Parliament). The government also has power under the prerogative, which is a non-statutory power, recognised by the courts and enjoyed by the government by virtue of holding office. When ministers exceed the powers given to them by acting illegally, or use those powers for an improper purpose, then it is possible to bring an application for judicial review. This enables the High Court to quash an illegal decision (see Chapter 15).

An important decision in the courts defending the rule of law is *M* v. *Home Office*[13], where a minister who ignored a court order was held to be in contempt of court. In *M* v. *Home Office*[14] the Home Secretary was found to be in contempt of court because the Home Office had deported a Zairian national, notwithstanding a court order preventing him from being deported. The issue was whether a government department could, unlike an ordinary citizen, ignore a court order without facing consequences. This is important, as contempt of court is a serious offence and can result in a fine and/or a custodial sentence. Lord Woolf, who was one of the judges in *M* v. *Home Office*, was of the opinion that finding the Secretary of State to be liable on behalf of the Home Office would ensure that court orders were taken seriously and not flouted with impunity. The fact that a fine would not be imposed did not make the finding of contempt of court to be pointless: 'The very fact of making such a finding would vindicate the requirements of justice. In addition an order for costs could be made to underline the significance of a contempt.'[15] Lord Woolf was clear that 'the object of the exercise is not so much to punish an individual as to vindicate the rule of law by a finding of contempt.'[16] *M v Home Office* was a landmark decision. Perhaps, if the facts were to be repeated today, the judgment would have expanded on the importance of the rule of law, and the need to ensure that the government governs according to the law, but for a decision that is almost 30 years old, it demonstrated an important statement of constitutional principle.

4.4 Development of the rule of law in England and the United Kingdom

The rule of law has been important in the development of English (and then British) constitutional history. This section is designed as a brief overview of the development of the rule of law, which is important to appreciate in order to understand its origins, and why it so important today within the constitution. The Magna Carta of 1215 was forced on King John by his barons (see **Chapter 1**). Although the Magna Carta was annulled by Pope Innocent III at John's request, it was reissued by John's son, Henry III, and grandson, Edward I. The most important surviving clause is clause 29, which stated that the king did not have the arbitrary power to condemn a man and that the only way a man could be condemned was by lawful judgment which required a trial to take place. The semblance of justice and the absence of the exercise of arbitrary royal rule were deemed by the drafters of the Magna Carta to be essential.

The monarch's power under the prerogative (that is the power to govern, make treaties, declare war etc.) was limited by the developing role of Parliament in the 13th and 14th centuries. During the reign of Edward I it was accepted that the king could not use his prerogative to impose taxes; rather taxation had to be approved by the Commons, which represented the country. The power to make arbitrary decision was further limited by the importance attached to the common law and procedural fairness. For example, it had been possible for the monarch to condemn a person based on the king's record (that is the presumption that the king could determine who was guilty). However, by the mid-1300s the king could no longer do this, and the monarch had to ensure that his enemies received a trial (often before Parliament) before guilt could be determined.

A central theme of English constitutional history is that the monarch had to rule through law and not by arbitrary means. The importance of Parliament and the need for the monarch to rule in conjunction with this institution representing important groups of society ensured that the monarch's powers were limited, and he had to rule according to the law. Henry VIII (1509–47) was a powerful monarch who reformed religion in England and Wales and obtained two divorces so that he could remarry. Despite Henry's considerable power he ruled through Parliament and the great innovations of his reign took the form of Acts of Parliaments. An often-cited example is when Henry VIII wanted to punish Richard Roose, a cook, for poisoning a Bishop. The king wished to have the Roose killed using a method that the law did not recognise. However, the law did not recognise this as a punishment, and therefore Parliament needed to create a law to permit the king to kill Roose using this method in 1531. This is a minor example, but it does illustrate a point that even a monarch with the historical legacy of Henry VIII governed according to the law. However, it is important to note that Henry VIII was granted considerable power by Parliament to use his personal prerogative powers to make law, which gave the king the power to impose obligations upon his subjects without the need for parliamentary legislation and undermined the rule of law. This extra-parliamentary law-making power was repealed when Henry died. Professor Sir John Baker has observed the importance of the rule of law in Tudor England:

> Henry [VIII]'s determination always to act within legal forms was itself of consequence in shaping attitudes. Since the rule of law is incapable of precise definition, the question of its prevalence in a particular age must be a matter of degree and opinion. Of the general attitude of the Tudor age there seems no room for doubt. Whatever lapses and failures may have occurred from time to time at moments of crisis, 'Tudor thinking and practice on the law subordinated everybody, the king included, to the rule of law.[17]

Baker's observations are important, as he is clear that even if we could say that a particular definition of the rule of law applied during Henry VIII's reign, there was an expectation that the king would rule according to the law and that everyone would follow the law.

An example of the importance attached to following the law, and the proscribed procedures for trying someone accused of breaching it, is demonstrated by the following example. When King James I (1603–25) succeeded to the English throne in 1603, while on his way to London he and entourage caught a thief.[18] The king wanted the man killed straightaway and the thief was hanged. Subsequently, the king was informed that in England a man could only be condemned if he was found guilty after a trial. The importance of the accused receiving a trial before being punished extends to the need for the people administering justice to be impartial, and that the trial, so much as was possible at the time, was fair.

During the reign of James I, the king clashed with his most senior common law judge, Sir Edward Coke, who asserted a degree of judicial independence and rebuked the king for claiming to have the right to act as a judge.[19] Coke also held that the king could not impose legal obligations, or take away his subject's rights, by using his prerogative powers as this could only be imposed by the law and not by the king's discretionary powers.[20] This was an important step in developing the rule of law. However, Coke was dismissed as a judge in 1616.[21] The dismissal of Coke demonstrated that judges were servants of the monarch and could be dismissed from their posts at the king's pleasure. Judges continued to be dismissed by the monarch during the rest of the 17th century. This undermined the rule of law, as in order to the law to be applied and enforced fairly, and without bias, the judiciary had to be seen as impartial. Judicial independence was safeguarded by the Act of Settlement 1701 even if this was not always the reality.[22]

James I's successor, Charles I (1625–49), was accused of royal absolutism and attempted to raise money without asking Parliament to approve taxation. This was done using the king's prerogative powers and was viewed by many contemporaries as unlawful, as the king was acting outside the scope of the law. Those who refused to pay were often arrested and imprisoned. Their recourse was to argue before the courts that their detention was unlawful using the prerogative writ of Habeas Corpus.[23] In response to the king's policies Parliament introduced the Petition of Right 1628, which was intended to limit Charles' extra-legal power. This petition was resented by the king, who then dissolved Parliament and ruled for 11 years without summoning Parliament. During this time Charles relied on his prerogative powers and loyal officials, such as administrators and judges, to raise money in often dubious circumstances. Importantly, this was seen as unlawful by his opponents, but as the courts supported the king, the policies were held to be lawful. James Hart has observed the conflict that existed between the king's supporters, who held that his actions were lawful, and his opponents, who held that he was acting unlawfully:

> Governments laid claim to an ever expanding range of powers, frequently justifying their actions on grounds of simple expediency . . . a position perhaps best exemplified by the declaration, allegedly made by Justice Robert Berkeley in the case of Richard Chambers in 1637, that 'There is a rule of law and a rule of government and things that might not be done by the rule of law might be done by the rule of government[24]'

The issue was reconciling the government's discretionary powers 'with the traditions and forms of English law.'[25]

What does this mean for the rule of law? This period of English history is important as it demonstrates that people were willing to stand up to a monarch's policy of acting outside of the law. Charles I was clearly acting contrary to the rule of law, even if the courts were not in a position to acknowledge this. Charles' policies led to several civil wars and a republic being established. Eventually, the monarchy was restored in 1660 with Charles II as king (1660–85) and in 1685, James II (1685–88) became king. James challenged the rule of law by declaring that he had the prerogative power to dispense, that is treat as void, Acts of Parliament. This was controversial, as the king was declaring that the law of the land could be ignored, if the king did not agree with it. As a result, the Bill of Rights 1689, which was introduced after the king was overthrown, declared that the monarch cannot dispense with Acts of Parliament using the prerogative.

The most important case of the 18th century which concerned the rule of law, was the decision in *Entick v Carrington*.[26]

PUBLIC LAW IN CONTEXT
ENTICK V CARRINGTON[27]

The rule of law is an important feature of the constitution. The courts have held the executive could not act outside the law. An important example is the decision of Lord Camden CJ in *Entick* v *Carrington*. In *Entick v Carrington* the Secretary of State had sent his agents to search the house of John Entick, who was a supporter of the radical politician and journalist John Wilkes. Entick was accused of producing libellous material which criticised the government. The agents broke into Entick's house and searched his papers for four hours. Entick sued the agents for trespass. The agents had entered and searched the property under a warrant authorised by the Secretary of State. Lord Camden CJ found in favour of Entick and held that the Secretary of State was not a magistrate and therefore did not have the authority to issue a warrant. Consequentially, the actions of the agents were illegal and amounted to trespass.

Lord Camden's judgment supports the rule of law, as the executive may only act in accordance to the powers given to them under the law: '[i]f any such power in a Secretary of State, or a Privy Counsellor, had ever existed, it would appear from our law-books; all the ancient books are silent on this head.'[28]

Lord Camden made the following points:

- There was no authority for the government being able to search a house of a person accused of libel. The consequences of such a power would be that anyone suspected could have their house searched.
- Such a general power would give the Secretary of State arbitrary and discretionary power to decide whose house to search.
- Lord Camden noted that if there was a need to seize libellous material before it was published, then this decision should be taken by Parliament: 'if the Legislature be of that opinion they will make it lawful.'[29]
- The government should prosecute Entick for libel and let a jury try him.

It is interesting to note that Lord Camden CJ indicated that if Entick were guilty, then he was a dangerous man; but nonetheless, the government could not act illegally, even if it they were acting to prevent anarchy. Richard Gordon QC has written about the decision and its impact. He noted that:

Although *Entick v Carrington* applied the law of trespass to the particular set of facts before it, the court applied it to what would now be treated as an exercise of public law power amenable to judicial review. In public law terms, Lord Camden's ruling was in substance to the effect that the rule of law compelled the conclusion that a *public body* was only empowered to act within the law and could not, without legal authority, claim power merely because it was desirable to have that power or even because the executive considered it necessary to have the power in the national interest.[30]

This demonstrates the importance of the rule of law in ensuring that the government acts lawfully and does not seek to claim powers that there is no legal basis for.

PUBLIC LAW IN PRACTICE

In light of the decision in *Entick* v. *Carrington*, imagine that the Secretary of State had received permission from the king to issue the warrant. Would this have made a difference?

The answer would be no. However, had the Secretary of State received the authority to issue the warrant from an Act of Parliament, then he could have lawfully issued the warrant and no trespass would have been committed by his agents.

4.4.1 Judicial Review and the Rule of Law

Today the courts prevent the government from acting illegally (i.e. from violating those parts of the European Convention on Human Rights given effect to by the Human Rights Act 1998), even where the government considers a group, or an individual, to be a danger to national security. Judicial Review is an important check on the abuse of power by the executive, or those exercising public law powers, as to permit such abuse, whether this is intentional such as a deliberate breach, or unintentional such as a consequence of government policy, would undermine the rule of law.[31] Ordinary citizens, subject to the requirement of standing (which as we shall see in **Chapter 15** can be liberally applied where there is a perceived threat to the rule of law), can make an application to the High Court to challenge decisions made by public bodies. This review of public decision making by the courts is the bedrock of judicial review. In *R (on the application of Cart) v The Upper Tribunal*[32] Lady Hale observed:

> the scope of judicial review is an artefact of the common law whose object is to maintain the rule of law – that is to ensure that, within the bounds of practical possibility, decisions are taken in accordance with the law, and in particular the law which Parliament has enacted, and not otherwise.[33]

In *Cart* Lord Phillips also commented that, 'The rule of law requires that the laws enacted by Parliament, together with the principles of common law that subsist with those laws, are enforced by a judiciary that is independent of the legislature and the executive.'[34] A person affected by a public law decision (such as that of local council, a governmental department or even a decision of the Prime Minister) can bring an application for judicial review. Even someone who is considered by the government to be a threat to the country can review the legality of governmental decisions which concern them. Examples of this include the attempts to deport the radical cleric Abu Qatada (*Othman* v. *Secretary of State for the Home Department*[35]) and the Belmarsh case, where suspected terrorist suspects were detained without trial (*A* v. *Secretary of State for the Home Department*[36]).

4.4.2 Review of executive decisions even where there is an emergency threatening the life of the nation

In *A* v. *Secretary of State for the Home Department* the Home Secretary had used his powers under section 23 of the Anti-terrorism, Crime and Security Act 2001 to indefinitely detain foreign nationals who were suspected of being terrorists. As Lord Bingham observed in his opinion, '[n]one has been the subject of any criminal charge. In none of their cases is a criminal trial in prospect.'[37] Lord Nicholls remarked, '[i]ndefinite imprisonment without charge or trial is anathema in any country which observes the rule of law.'[38] The detained individuals were being held at Belmarsh high security prison in London. They argued that indefinite detention without charge or trial violated their rights under Article 5 of the European Convention on Human Rights (ECHR), which protects the right to liberty and security of the person. Article 5 is a limited right and can only be restricted in certain prescribed circumstances. The Human Rights Act 1998 had given effect to the vast majority of the ECHR and this meant that the domestic courts could review the decision. The government had argued that there were good reasons for detaining the individuals and that there was evidence that they posed a risk to the United Kingdom. Parliament had given the Home Secretary the power to detain individuals

The United Kingdom had sought to derogate from its obligations under Article 5 of the ECHR.

Article 15 of the ECHR permitted the United Kingdom to derogate from certain rights (including Article 5) where there was a time of emergency:

> In time of war or other public emergency threatening the life of the nation any High Contracting Party may take measures derogating from its obligations under this Convention to the extent strictly required by the exigencies of the situation, provided that such measures are not inconsistent with its other obligations under international law.

However, the power to derogate is not without restriction and needs to be proportionate, i.e. it must not go beyond what is strictly required by the circumstances.

In *A v. Secretary of State for the Home Department* the majority of the House of Lords held that the government's decision to decide that there was an emergency which threatened the life of the nation, whilst open to challenge and review by the courts, could be justified. The problem was that legislation only applied to non-UK nationals:

* Someone who was a suspected terrorist, but who was a UK national, could not be detained under the 2001 Act.
* Importantly, this distinction on the grounds of nationality was discriminatory and violated Article 14 of the ECHR, that protects people from suffering discrimination, and which the government had not derogated from.

Furthermore, not only did the legislation make this distinction, but the purpose of the legislation was to detain individuals without charge or trial, and then to deport them to the country that they were a national of. This was important as once a person was removed from the United Kingdom, he or she would be free to engage in terrorist activities. Lord Hope observed:

> [S]ection 23 of the 2001 Act is not rationally connected to the legislative objective. If the threat is as potent as the Secretary of State suggests, it is absurd to confine the measures intended to deal with it so that they do not apply to British nationals, however strong the suspicion and however grave the damage it is feared they may cause. There is also the point that foreign nationals who present the same threat are permitted, if they can safely do

so, to leave this country at any time. Here too there is a clear indication that the indefinite detention of those who remain here as a means of countering the same threat is disproportionate.[39]

The decision was disproportionate and discriminatory, and the House of Lords made a declaration of incompatibility under section 4 of the Human Rights Act 1998. As we shall see in **Chapter 6** a declaration of incompatibility respects the sovereignty of Parliament by not declaring the legislation (here the offending sections of the 2001 Act) to be void; rather the court is declaring that they are incompatible with the United Kingdom's obligations under the ECHR.

In *A* v. *Secretary of State for the Home Department* the government had sought to argue that the courts should not review the validity of the decision due to institutional deference, i.e. it was government and not the courts who were entrusted by the electorate with taking decisions of this nature. This argument was rejected by the House of Lords. Any restriction on the grounds of deference was contrary to the rule of law:

> But the function of independent judges charged to interpret and apply the law is universally recognised as a cardinal feature of the modern democratic state, a cornerstone of the rule of law itself. The Attorney General is fully entitled to insist on the proper limits of judicial authority, but he is wrong to stigmatise judicial decision-making as in some way undemocratic.[40]

There are considerable merits in the court, whilst respecting the notion of institutional competences (i.e. the respective roles of Parliament, the executive and the courts), not permitting undue institutional deference and to decide that the government should, on the basis of the gravity of the subject-matter, not on the ability to determine who to detain without judicial scrutiny. The reason why the House of Lords' decision in *A* v. *Secretary of State for the Home Department* remains important is that even when the United Kingdom faced a new terrorist threat following the attacks on the United States of America on 11 September 2001 (which were followed by other attacks, including in Madrid in 2003), the rights of those individuals detained to challenge the legality of their detention should be protected.

Lord Hoffmann had dissented in part in *A* v. *Secretary of State for the Home Department*, as he had taken the view that the government's claim, that there was an emergency threatening the life of the nation, could not be justified. His Lordship placed the decision under greater scrutiny and held that there was no such emergency as to justify a derogation under Article 15 ECHR:

> This is a nation which has been tested in adversity, which has survived physical destruction and catastrophic loss of life. I do not underestimate the ability of fanatical groups of terrorists to kill and destroy, but they do not threaten the life of the nation. Whether we would survive Hitler hung in the balance, but there is no doubt that we shall survive Al-Qaeda. The Spanish people have not said that what happened in Madrid, hideous

crime as it was, threatened the life of their nation. Their legendary pride would not allow it. Terrorist violence, serious as it is, does not threaten our institutions of government or our existence as a civil community.[41]

Before we leave the House of Lords' decision it is important to consider a number of points:

- Why was the rule of law in issue here?
- Could the detention without charge or trial of the detainees be justified?
- Was the decision to only permit the detention of non-UK nationals proportionate?
- Was there really an emergency threatening the life of the nation, as to justify the derogation?

4.4.3 Can Judicial Review be 'ousted' (that is prevented) by Parliament?

We have seen that the rule of law requires that the courts must be able to review decisions made by the government (and other public bodies); this is in order to ensure that they are using their statutory, or prerogative, powers lawfully. Therefore, protecting the ability of individuals to have a right of access to the courts in order to challenge such a decision, is an essential part of the rule of law. However, there have been attempts by Parliament to restrict the courts from reviewing a particular decision made by a specific body. In **Chapter 15** will see how statutory attempts to oust the supervisory role of the courts have been treated by the courts. The most famous decision remains *Anisminic Ltd v Foreign Compensation Commission,*[42] where the House of Lords held that section 4(4) of the Foreign Compensation Act 1950 did not oust judicial review of decisions made pursuant to the Act, as the ouster clause only applied to proper decisions, not purported decisions (i.e. attempted decisions) where there was a complaint that the body in question had acted beyond its jurisdiction. *Anisminic* was an important decision with regards to the protection of the rule of law.[43]

More recently in *R (on the application of Privacy International) v Investigatory Powers Tribunal*[44] the issue in question was whether section 67(8) of the Regulation of Investigatory Powers Act 2000 prevented a decision of the Investigatory Powers Tribunal from being reviewed by the courts. Section 67(8) purported to prevent judicial review. It is important to note that here the Act had purported to restrict the ability of the ordinary courts from reviewing a decision made by the Investigatory Powers Tribunal. The Supreme Court was divided over the issues in the appeal. This is hardly surprising given the importance of Parliamentary Sovereignty and the importance in following Parliament's clear intention when interpreting legislation.

A majority of the Supreme Court held that section 67(8) of the Regulation of Investigatory Powers Act 2000 did not oust the supervisory jurisdiction of the ordinary courts and the decision of the tribunal could be reviewed. The court was clear that the only decision which could not be reviewed by the courts was a decision that was legally valid and properly related to jurisdiction. Therefore, a purported decision could still be reviewed by the courts. The Supreme Court was alive to the importance of the rule of law and the need for courts to have a supervisory jurisdiction.

Lord Carnwath (with whom Lady Hale and Lord Kerr agreed) observed:

> In accordance with established principles, the ultimate safeguard of judicial review remains essential if the rule of law is to be maintained. The special status of the IPT (like that of the Upper Tribunal) may be a reason for restricting the grant of permission for judicial review, but not for excluding it altogether.[45]
>
> The legal issue decided by the IPT is not only one of general public importance, but also has possible implications for legal rights and remedies going beyond the scope of the IPT's remit. Consistent application of the rule of law requires such an issue to be susceptible in appropriate cases to review by ordinary courts.[46]

It is important to consider the following points:

- It was always open to Parliament to restrict judicial review. However, the courts would ensure that only proper decisions as to jurisdiction would fall within this.
- Purported decisions would not be excluded from judicial review.
- The rule of law required that decisions made by public bodies could be judicially reviewed by those affected by them.

4.4.4 Shortcomings in judicial protection

We can see that the judiciary recognise and protect access to the courts (i.e. to have the ability to judicially review a decision made by a public body) as essential to the rule of law. We shall see below how being able to afford to bring legal action is also an integral part of the rule of law and one recognised by the courts. However, judicial protection of the rule of law has not always been satisfactory. One example of the shortcomings in how the rule of law was protected in England and Wales is the decision in *Malone v Metropolitan Police Commissioner*[47] where the police had tapped Malone's telephone. Malone argued that this was unlawful as there was no law ('either statute or common law') that permitted the police to do. Sir Robert Megarry VC held that the telephone tapping was lawful. It did not matter that there was no law which permitted the police to act as they did. Megarry VC observed and equated the police's actions to someone smoking, that is they could act in this way as there was no law which prevented the action, but neither was there a law that permitted it: 'England is not a country where everything is forbidden except what is expressly permitted. One possible illustration is smoking.'[48] Commenting on the decision Professor Ewing observed, '[t]he principle is, however, impossible to define in a way that commands universal agreements, with "thin" and "thick" versions. . . . There is no thinner a version of the rule of law than that expressed by Vice Chancellor Sir Robert Megarry.'[49]

Subsequently, Malone brought a case against the United Kingdom at the European Court of Human Rights. In *Malone v United Kingdom*[50] the European Court of Human Rights found that there was a violation of Article 8 of the European Convention on Human Rights, namely, the right of respect for a private and family life. Any interference with Article 8 needed to be prescribed by law and here the phone tapping was not. The Court was clear that:

> Since the implementation in practice of measures of secret surveillance of communications is not open to scrutiny by the individuals concerned or the public at large, it would be contrary to the rule of law for the legal discretion granted to the executive to be expressed in terms of an unfettered power. Consequently, the law must indicate the scope of any such discretion conferred on the competent authorities and the manner of its exercise with sufficient clarity, having regard to the legitimate aim of the measure in question, to give the individual adequate protection against arbitrary interference.[51]

In response to the judgment of the European Court of Human Rights, Parliament enacted the Malicious Communications Act 1988. This Act provided a lawful basis for phone tapping.

4.4.5 Judicial views as to the importance of the rule of law and public confidence in the judiciary: reconsidered in the aftermath of Miller (No. 1) and Miller (No. 2)

In recent years the judiciary have reiterated the importance of the rule of law within the United Kingdom's constitution. Lord Neuberger, the former President of the Supreme Court, gave an extra-judicial speech in which he stated 'that the rule of law and democracy are the twin constitutional foundation stones, or pillars, of our society.'[52] To Lord Neuberger the rule of law required open justice:

> Unless what goes on in court can be seen by the public, by those in government, and by the media, there is a real risk that public confidence in the courts will start to wane, and, indeed, a real risk that we Judges will gradually start to get sloppy in our ways. Sunlight has been famously been said to be the best disinfectant, and without public access to the courts, there is a real danger that justice is neither done nor seen to be done.[53]

The rule of law required the public to be able to visit the courts and see the judges in action, to ensure that the public had confidence in the work that the judges were doing, and also to keep the courts in check. Transparency was a key element to Lord Neuberger's understanding of the rule of law. Continuing with this theme, Lord Hodge observed that

> [t]he rule of law, and judicial independence as its essential component, is a political achievement. All judges have a duty to take care to preserve political and public support for the rule of law; senior judges in particular

have a duty to explain. For the rule of law is based ultimately on society's confidence in and consent to our judicial institutions.[54]

Lord Hodge is emphasising the need to for the public to have confidence in the judges and the courts, as citizens need to be able to accept a judgment of the court without feeling that it is untenable and illegitimate. This extends to maintaining the confidence of the political class, as to apply what Lord Hodge was stating to recent litigation before the Supreme Court in *R (on the application of Miller) v Secretary of State for Exiting the European Union (No. 1)* and *R (on the application of Miller) v The Prime Minister (No. 2)*, the courts need to ensure that politicians (and the public) have confidence in their judicial decisions. In both *Miller (No. 1)* and *Miller (No. 2)* certain sections of the political establishment clearly did not have confidence in the judiciary and this public criticism arguably undermined the rule of law and will have long-term consequences for the relationship between the legislature, executive and judiciary and the developing role of the Supreme Court.[55] This criticism extended to the press, with the *Daily Mail* declaring that the High Court judges in *Miller (No. 1)* were 'Enemies of the People.'[56]

However, in all instances in the *Miller (No. 1)* and *Miller (No. 2)* litigation the courts explained the reasons for their decision in considerable detail, the hearing was televised (for the Supreme Court) and the public had access to proceedings. This demonstrates the need for the courts to do as much as possible to explain their decisions and protect the rule of law and the importance of an independent judiciary from political and media criticism.[57] What was particularly controversial was that the Lord Chancellor, Liz Truss, who has a constitutional duty to protect the rule of law and judicial independence (see below), did not immediately intervene and defend the judiciary.[58] Sir Stephen Sedley, a retired Court of Appeal judge, was critical of the Lord Chancellor, observing, '[t]he failure of . . . Liz Truss . . . to do anything to defend the three senior judges . . . is evidence enough of the fragility of judicial independence.'[59] Given that an independent judiciary, free to rule against the government without

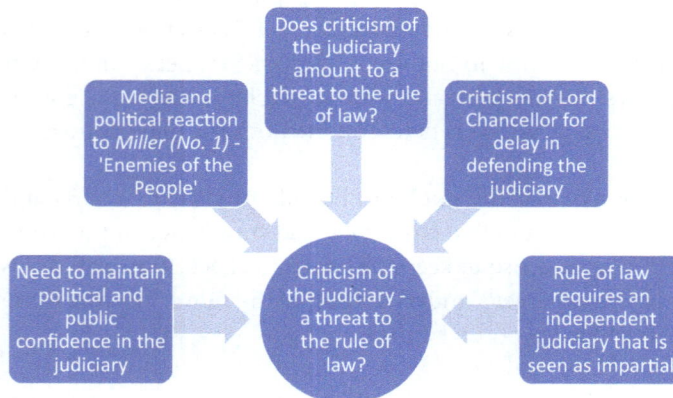

Figure 4.2
Some issues relating to criticism of the judiciary

fearing the consequences from the media or from political criticism, is essential to the rule of law, Sedley's critique is a warning to the dangers of officehold-ers not upholding the rule of law. Lord Dyson, a retired Supreme Court Justice, called Truss's time as Lord Chancellor as 'disastrous' and was of the view that Truss favoured appeasing the press over upholding her statutory duty of upholding judicial independence.[60]

Joshua Rozenberg has given a thorough account of how the judiciary reacted to the *Daily Mail*'s 'Enemies of the People' frontpage headline.[61] Rozenberg recounts one of the High Court judges, Sales LJ's experiences of the aftermath of the decision,

> the sense of threat felt most real when I received a visit from two police officers of the anti-terrorism unit of the Metropolitan Police to conduct a security review at my home. Fortunately, they assured me that their review of online activity and social media did not indicate an especially height-ened threat of physical attack. . . . I have to say that I was rather naïve in terms of what was likely to happen when we handed down our judgment.[62]

The 2019 decision in *Miller (No.2)* has proved equally controversial. We will look at the Supreme Court's decision in **Chapters 10** and **11** when we look at the prerogative. At this stage it is sufficient to say that *Miller (No.2)* concerned the Supreme Court finding that the Prime Minister had unlawfully advised the monarch to prorogue Parliament. The consequences of this was that Parliament, whose proceedings had been suspended, was held to be session and MPs could challenge the government's Brexit policy. Some commentators and politicians have criticised the Supreme Court's decision.[63]

QUESTION

Do you think the criticism of the Supreme Court's decisions in *Miller (No.1)* and *Miller (No.2)* undermined the rule of law?

4.4.6 The Supreme Court defends the rule of law

In *R (on the application of Unison) v Lord Chancellor*[64] the issue of access to justice and the constitutional importance of the rule of law was considered by the Supreme Court. The decision related to the issue of tribunal fees, which meant that people bringing a claim against their employer would have to pay increased fees in order to access the rights given to them by Parliament, the courts and the European Union. The Lord Chancellor had used his statutory power under section 42(1) of the Tribunals, Courts and Enforcement Act 2007 to set fees for employment tribunals and the employment appeals tribunal using the Employment Tribunals and Employment Appeal Tribunals Fees Order 2013. The fees for single claimants ranged from £390 to £1,200.[65] This compared unfavourably

Figure 4.3
The *Unison* decision

with the relatively modest fees for the County Court, which were between £50 and £745.[66] Unison argued that the 2013 Fees Order had the effect of reducing access to justice, as many potential claimants were put off from making a claim due to the high costs. The Supreme Court observed:

> Comparing the figures preceding the introduction of fees with more recent periods, there has been a long-term reduction in claims accepted by ETs of the order of 66–70%.[67]
>
> The fall in the number of claims has in any event been so sharp, so substantial, and so sustained as to warrant the conclusion that a significant number of people who would otherwise have brought claims have found the fees to be unaffordable.[68]
>
> Furthermore, it is not only where fees are unaffordable that they can prevent access to justice. They can equally have that effect if they render it futile or irrational to bring a claim.[69]

Lord Reed relied upon the rule of law in finding for Unison. His Lordship was clear that '[t]he constitutional right of access to the courts is inherent in the rule of law' and the rule of law included access to the courts.[70] The courts played a vital role and were important to society, rather than just the parties appearing in the proceedings or the lawyers. Lord Reed observed that:

> At the heart of the concept of the rule of law is the idea that society is governed by law. . . . Courts exist in order to ensure that the laws made by Parliament, and the common law created by the courts themselves, are applied and enforced. That role includes ensuring that the executive branch

of government carries out its functions in accordance with the law. In order for the courts to perform that role, people must in principle have unimpeded access to them. Without such access, laws are liable to become a dead letter, the work done by Parliament may be rendered nugatory, and the democratic election of Members of Parliament may become a meaningless charade. That is why the courts do not merely provide a public service like any other.[71]

Academic commentary on the decision has been quick to highlight the practical significance of the rule of law being used as a constitutional principle in order to defend the right to access to justice. Professor Mark Elliot observed that

> In a tour de force that ought to be compulsory reading for every Minister and parliamentarian, the Court elucidates the true value of independent courts and tribunals, illuminates the common law's potential as a guarantor of basic rights, and reiterates an axiomatic set of constitutional home truths.[72]

Professor Michael Ford writing in the *Industrial Law Journal* provided a thorough analysis of the decision and its implications for the theoretical and practical understanding and conceptions of the rule of law.[73] We will consider the academic theory and different concepts of what is the rule of law below. However, at this stage it is important to appreciate the practical significance of the rule of law. Ford was clear that the context of the decision was important coming after *Miller (No.1)*[74]. Ford made reference to the Supreme Court's decision in *Miller (No.1)* and the earlier High Court decision in *Miller (No.1)*, which had been heavily criticised by some sections of the press and by certain politicians.

4.4.7 The Constitutional Reform Act 2005

Tony Blair's New Labour government in the late 1990s and early 2000s embarked on wholesale constitutional reform, which in the Constitutional Reform Act 2005 culminated in the creation of the UK Supreme Court and reforms to the role of the Lord Chancellor. We have considered the impact of the Constitutional Reform Act 2005 on the separation of powers in **Chapter 3**. However, another important aspect of the Act is the statutory recognition of the importance of the rule of law. Section 1 of the Constitutional Reform Act 2005 is concerned with the rule of law, stating that, 'This Act does not adversely affect – (a) the existing constitutional principle of the rule of law, or (b) the Lord Chancellor's existing constitutional role in relation to that principle.' The Lord Chancellor now takes an oath under section 17 of the Constitutional Reform Act 2005, in which she promises to respect the rule of law and defend judicial independence.

4.5 Definitions of the rule of law

The next sections will consider the academic definitions of the rule of law. As you shall see there are many different views as to what is required by the rule of law and each academic will put forward different interpretations.

4.6 Dicey and the rule of law

Dicey claimed that the rule of law or the supremacy of law had been a key feature of English law and politics since 1066. The concept of the rule of law existed before Dicey, but it was Dicey who, if not responsible for inventing the phrase, was responsible for ensuring that it is recognised as a key part of the constitution. Dicey defined the rule of law as meaning 'at least three distinct though kindred concepts.'[75] The first meaning of the rule of law was that no one could be punished or deprived of their goods unless they had breached a law, which has been established in an ordinary way and applied by an ordinary court. This meant that the state could not act in an arbitrary manner which was unlawful.

The second meaning of the rule of law was that no man is above the law, and that anyone (the Prime Minister or a billionaire) 'is subject to the ordinary law of the realm and amenable to the jurisdiction of the ordinary tribunals.'[76] This means that no one is above the law and that anyone can be tried by the courts. So, for example, the Prime Minister could be prosecuted for shoplifting and could not prevent himself from being tried before a court. The law is supreme, and no one is immune from their legal obligations. Writing over 100 years ago Dicey was critical of the French use of administrative courts and believed that administrative issues should be tried by ordinary courts. Today English law has developed administrative law, with judicial review as a key part of administrative law, which enables citizens to challenge the executive's decisions.

The third meaning of the rule of law is that 'the general principles of the constitution (as for example the right to personal liberty, or the right of public meeting) are with us the result of judicial decisions determining the rights of private persons in particular cases brought before the courts.'[77] This means that the constitutional principles which safeguard our freedoms have been created by the common law (i.e. previous judicial decisions). The rule of law requires the law to protect our key liberties and prevent tyranny.

PUBLIC LAW IN CONTEXT
AN EARLY 20TH CENTURY UNDERSTANDING OF THE RULE OF LAW

Lord Hewart CJ considered the meaning of the rule of law in his book, *The New Despotism*:

What is meant here by the 'Rule of Law' is the supremacy or the predominance of law, as distinguished from mere arbitrariness, or from some alternative mode, which is not law, of determining or disposing of the rights of individuals. It is, or at any rate it was until quite recently, a commonplace to say that the 'Rule of Law' is one of the two leading features which distinguish our Constitution.[78]

Lord Hewart feared that the developing bureaucratic state, i.e. the growth of government, was undermining the rule of law: 'That there is in existence, and in certain quarters in the ascendant, a genuine belief that Parliamentary institutions and the Rule of Law have been tried and found wanting, and that the time has come for the departmental despot, who shall be at once scientific and benevolent, but above all a law to himself, needs no demonstration.'[79] We can see Lord Hewart's assessment of the rule of law was tempered by bureaucratic developments in the early 20th century.

4.7 Two versions of the rule of law

Many different academics have attempted to define the rule of law and we will look at two versions which have received particular attention and have proved influential (see the Figure below).

4.7.1 Joseph Raz and the formal (procedural) version of the rule of law

The formal or procedural version of the rule of law is concerned with how the law is made, how it is applied, and the procedure that is used. It is not concerned with whether a law is good or bad. This essentially means that a law which is intentionally discriminatory could perhaps comply with the requirements set out by this version of the rule of law. Joseph Raz is the academic who is probably most associated with the formal or procedural version of the rule of law. Outlining what was meant by the rule of law, Raz stated:

'The rule of law' means literally what it says: the rule of the law. Taken in its broadest sense this means that people should obey the law and be ruled by it. But in political and legal theory it has come to be read in a

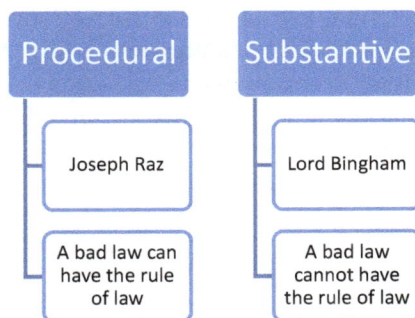

```
Procedural              Substantive

Joseph Raz              Lord Bingham

A bad law can           A bad law
have the rule           cannot have
of law                  the rule of law
```

Figure 4.4
Different versions of the rule of law

narrower sense, that the government shall be ruled by the law and subject to it (which is expressed as) 'government by law and not by men.'[80]

Raz considered the rule of law to be a formal concept. The procedure must be certain, the law accessible and capable of being understood.[81] Raz argued that the rule of law had nothing to do with democracy, the protection of human rights, justice or equality. Instead, it was a political idea. An important question to consider is whether a country ruled by a dictator could be regarded as having the rule of law. Raz considered whether a dictatorship could be considered as having the rule of law:

> A non-democratic legal system, based on the denial of human rights, on extensive poverty, on racial segregation, sexual inequalities and religious persecution may, in principle, conform to the requirements of the rule of law better than any of the legal systems of the more enlightened western democracies.[82]

This is interesting, as Raz is arguing that potentially a dictatorship might conform to the rule of law better than a democracy. Examples of countries where the legal systems discriminated on grounds of race include South Africa during apartheid, where there were courts, judges, law makers and a white only electorate, and the United States of America during segregation. The United States of America was a democracy, but this did not prevent many states in the south of the country from introducing laws to segregate individuals on the basis of race. Therefore, possibly South Africa and certainly the United States of America could have met, as we shall see below, Raz's version of the rule of law. Raz elaborated further on this point:

> It is evident that this conception of the rule of law is a formal one. It says nothing about how the law is to be made: by tyrants, democratic majorities or any other way. It says nothing about fundamental rights, about equality or justice. It may even by thought that this version of the doctrine is formal to the extent that it is almost devoid of content. This is far from the truth.[83]

Raz believed that the formal version of the rule of law does have content, namely, the important procedural requirements which he identified. These requirements are necessary to ensure that people are able to follow the law.

We will now consider these requirements in turn and consider how these apply to the United Kingdom.

Requirement 1: All laws should be prospective, open and clear

The first requirement that all laws should be prospective, open and clear prohibits the use of retrospective laws. This means that Parliament cannot make laws criminalising an action that you did yesterday. If this was the case, then your

1	•All laws should be prospective, open and clear
2	•Laws should be relatively stable
3	•The making of particular laws (particular legal orders) should be guided by open, stable, clear and general rules
4	•The independence of the judiciary must be guaranteed
5	•The principles of natural justice must be observed
6	•The courts should have review powers over the implementation of the other principles
7	•The courts should be easily accessible
8	•The discretion of the crime prevention agencies should not be allowed to pervert the law

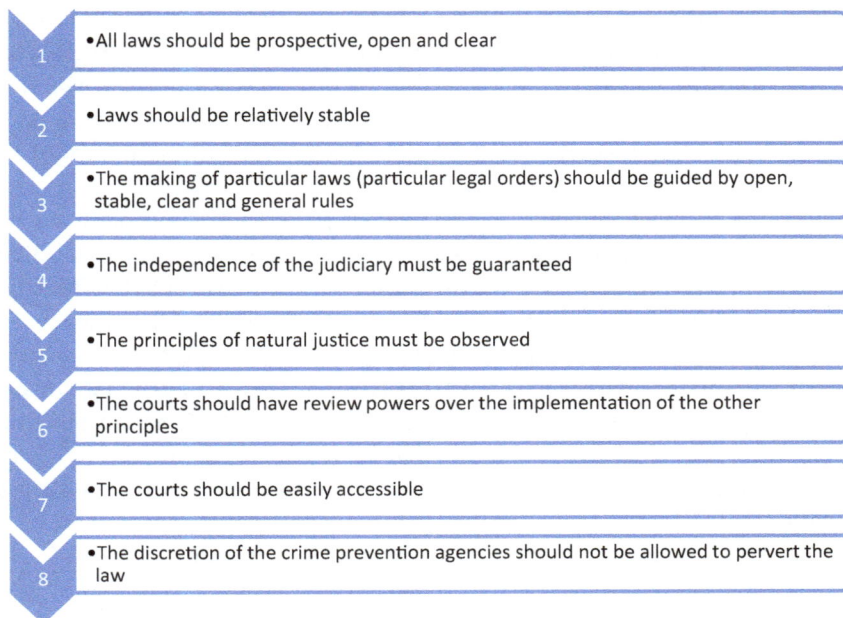

Figure 4.5
Requirements of the procedural rule of law

lawful actions on Monday would, on Tuesday, be considered a criminal offence; and therefore, you could then be prosecuted for what you did on Monday.

PUBLIC LAW IN PRACTICE

An example of this could be omissions in the criminal law, which often proves controversial amongst law students. There is no general duty to act to protect others, and so if you stood by and watched someone drown you have not committed a criminal offence. Imagine that Barbara were to watch as someone drowned in just a foot of water. There understandably might be a press campaign condemning her omission to act. However, whatever the public mood calling for her to be punished, Parliament should not pass a law to punish Barbara, as her failure to act was not unlawful.

There are some examples of retrospective legislation:

• War Crimes Act 1991 – this retrospectively criminalised any war crimes committed in mainland Europe during the Second World War.
• War Damages Act 1965 – this reversed the House of Lords' decision in *Burmah Oil Co (Burma Trading) Ltd* v. *Lord Advocate*[84] and denied the claimants compensation.

It is important that laws need to be clear and unambiguous. It should be possible to know what will amount to a criminal offence. However, the Fraud Act 2006 and its use of the previous test for dishonesty from *R* v. *Ghosh*[85] had been criticised for creating much uncertainty, as has the decision in *R* v. *Hinks*[86] which potentially makes the acceptance of a valid gift amount to theft.

Therefore, to meet this first requirement, legal obligations should not be applied retrospectively. We have seen that there are examples of retrospective legislation being used in the United Kingdom, but that this applied to specific circumstances and is not widely used. We need to know that what the law is, and this means that it must be open and clear. It cannot be hidden behind a costly paywall, i.e., you need to pay a £2,000 fee to find out what constitutes the offence of bribery under the Bribery Act 2010. Furthermore, the law should not be drafted in such a way as to be confusing or open to many possible interpretations as to render it impossible to comply with one's legal obligations.

As Lord Neuberger has observed in an extra-judicial lecture:

> One access aspect of the rule of law which is sometimes overlooked is access to the law itself, in other words access to statutes, secondary legislation and case law. It is of course a fundamental requirement of the rule of law that laws are clearly expressed and easily accessible. To put the point simply, people should know, or at least be able to find out, what the law is.[87]

Requirement 2: Laws should be relatively stable

The second requirement that laws should be relatively stable requires the law to be stable and not to change too quickly as to lead to confusion. People need to know what is legal and what is not. Ignorance of the law is no defence; however, as Raz observes we need knowledge of the law for both short-term and long-term decision-making.[88] This is an important procedural requirement as it can be confusing where the law and our obligations under it change too quickly, an example of this being the controversy over the requirements in the laws and regulations introduced to combat Covid-19 in 2020 and 2021.[89]

Requirement 3: The making of particular laws (particular legal orders) should be guided by open, stable, clear and general rules

The third requirements requires that the making of particular laws should be guided by open, stable, clear and general rules. Raz identifies the use of orders made by the executive and its agencies, such as the police. These laws are designed to be flexible but must be made in accordance with a general framework which is laid down by the law.

Requirement 4: The independence of the judiciary must be guaranteed

The fourth requirement is of utmost importance as the judiciary must be independent and capable of applying the law consistently. Raz argued that people rely on case law to understand how the law will apply to them. Raz also argued that judicial independence was 'essential for the preservation of the rule of law.'[90] The Act of Settlement 1701 and the Constitutional Reform Act 2005 guarantee judicial independence and provide judges with a salary and security of tenure, meaning that the judiciary are independent of the executive. Certainty of the law is important, and English commercial law has a good reputation because of this legal certainty. Lord Mansfield first identified this importance of certainty in *Vallejo* v. *Wheeler*.[91] Ralf Dahrendorf stated that the independence of the judiciary was vital for the existence of the rule of law:

> independence of the 'judicial department' may indeed be regarded as the very definition of the 'rule of law'; it is certainly an important part of it. . . . [T]he partisan administration [under the control of the government or Parliament] is in fact the prevision of the law, and the denial of the rule of law.[92]

Requirement 5: The principles of natural justice must be observed

In his fifth requirement Raz argued that for natural justice to be observed meant that there needed to be an '[o]pen and fair hearing [and the] absence of bias.'[93] In the United Kingdom any decision taken by a public body must be procedurally proper and that the decision-maker, whether administrative or judicial, should not be biased. We shall see in **Chapter 15** that if this is not the case then a decision can be judicially reviewed.

Requirement 6: The courts should have review powers over the implementation of the other principles

In his sixth requirement Raz stated the courts should have 'a very limited review – merely to ensure the conformity to the rule of law' over primary and secondary legislation, as well as executive administrative action. This is interesting as the court:

- can judicially review secondary legislation and executive administrative action;
- cannot judicially review primary legislation. Parliamentary Sovereignty states that the courts cannot review an Act of Parliament; and
- can interpret an Act of Parliament to ascertain Parliament's intention where there is confusion as to the Act's meaning.

Requirement 7: The courts should be easily accessible

Raz stated that the courts needed to be accessible. There should not be long delays and the costs should not be excessive. The legal system can be expensive and, especially with the reduction of legal aid, many people cannot afford to bring claims or to defend themselves. On 5 March 2013, *The Times* had an article on its front page which read 'Top judge warns of risk to rule of law.'[94] This article explored the government's reduction of the legal aid budget and the 'top judge' referred to in the headline was Lord Neuberger, the then President of the Supreme Court. Lord Neuberger warned that the reform to legal aid could undermine the rule of law. In 2017, Lord Neuberger delivered an extra-judicial lecture and warned against the risks to the rule of law.[95] What was important was the access to affordable legal advice and representation in court:

> While access to law is important, access to legal advice and representation is equally important but more challenging. Access to legal advice and representation is of course a fundamental ingredient of the rule of law, and the rule of law together with democracy is one of the two principal columns on which a civilised modern society is based. It is simply wrong, and fundamentally wrong at that, if ordinary citizens and businesses are unable to obtain competent legal advice as to their legal rights and obligations, and competent legal representation to enforce and protect those rights and test those obligations in court. Obtaining advice and representation does not merely mean that competent lawyers exist; it also must mean that their advice and representation are sensibly affordable to ordinary people and businesses: access to justice is a practical, not a hypothetical, requirement. And if it does not exist, society will eventually start to fragment.[96]

Lord Neuberger was highly critical of people having legal rights without the means of enforcing them: 'It verges on the hypocritical for governments to bestow rights on citizens while doing very little to ensure that those rights are enforceable.'[97]

Requirement 8: The discretion of the crime prevention agencies should not be allowed to pervert the law

This eighth and final requirement demands that the prosecution does not have the discretion to refuse to prosecute certain offences or offenders. Equally, the police should not decide which crimes to investigate or to enforce. The Attorney-General does have the power to initiate or stop prosecutions, and the Director of Public Prosecutions, who manages the Crown Prosecution Service (CPS), can offer guidance on which offences to prosecute (e.g., assisted suicide). The CPS, under the Code of Practice for Prosecutors, has the discretion to refuse to prosecute where it is not in the public interest to do so.

PUBLIC LAW IN PRACTICE

Imagine that Parliament passes the Inequality Act (fictitious) which gives public bodies and private companies the right to discriminate on the grounds of race, religion, sex and age. The Act stipulates that anyone who is unemployed and aged over forty can face compulsory euthanasia. Would such a law meet the eight requirements above? Potentially this Act of Parliament would satisfy Raz's eight requirements.

4.7.2 *The substantive version of the rule of law*

The substantive version of the rule of law is concerned with the quality of the law, rather than just the procedural requirements. The law must be a good law. Andrei Marmor has argued that, '[t]he most common mistake about the rule of law is to confuse it with the ideal of the rule of good law, the kind of law, for instance, that respects freedom and human dignity.'[98] According to the procedural version, the rule of law has nothing to do with whether the law is considered to be a good one; instead, it is concerned with the procedural requirements. This means that Parliament could enact laws (i.e. permitting sex discrimination) that we, the vast majority of the population, would consider repugnant and this law could still qualify as being compatible with the rule of law. There have been many academics who have argued that the rule of law should relate to the quality of the law, i.e. the rule of law should mean more than the narrower version that was defined by Raz. Instead, these academics argue that the rule of law should have a wider meaning and that a law must be considered a good law in order to qualify. Therefore, a country's law must not just meet the procedural requirements but must also be viewed objectively as a good law.

Writing extra-judicially Lord Bingham outlined the sub-rules which he believed comprised the rule of law.[99] It is interesting to see that Bingham's sub-rules initially seem familiar to those proposed by Raz. However, there are fundamental differences between the two:

- Sub-rule 1: The law needs to be accessible, 'intelligible, clear and predictable.'
- Sub-rule 2: Questions of law and liability need to be decided by application of law and not discretion.
- Sub-rule 3: The law must apply to everyone, unless differences can be justified.
- Sub-rule 4: There must be adequate protection of fundamental human rights.
- Sub-rule 5: People must be able to resolve legal disputes without facing a huge legal cost or excessive delays.
- Sub-rule 6: The executive must use the powers given to them reasonably, with good faith, for the proper purpose and must not exceed these powers.

- Sub-rule 7: There must be procedural fairness.
- Sub-rule 8: The state must comply with the obligations of international law.

Sub-rule 4 is interesting, as Lord Bingham is rejecting the procedural version of the rule of law. This is important as a

> state which savagely repressed or persecuted sections of its people could not in my view be regarded as observing the rule of law, even if the transport of the persecuted minority to the concentration camp . . . were the subject of detailed laws duly enacted and scrupulously observed.[100]

This raises the question, what do fundamental human rights mean? Lord Bingham acknowledged this and noted that the definition is vague.

The compliance with international law in sub-rule 8 raises some important questions. Governments who act illegally in times of war may try and justify their actions on the grounds of necessity; however, if they breach international law then they are acting in violation of the rule of law. Lord Bingham refused to say whether the United Kingdom had breached the rule of law when it invaded Iraq in 2003. However, His Lordship would later state in his 2010 book *The Rule of Law* that there was no legal justification for the invasion.[101]

RECENT DEVELOPMENTS

Would Parliament ever legislate contrary to international Law? In 2020, the government introduced the United Kingdom Internal Market Bill to Parliament. The clauses, 42, 43 and 45 of the bill was accused of breaching the rule of law as it was contrary to the United Kingdom's obligations under international law.[102] In the House of Lords, Lord Judge, the former Lord Chief Justice of England and Wales, was successful in getting a motion of regret passed. It is interesting to observe what Lord Judge was concerned about:

> The rule of law is a bulwark against authoritarian incursion, and even the smallest incursion threatens it. When those responsible for making the law – that is, us the Parliament, we the lawmakers, who expect people to obey the laws we make – knowingly grant power to the Executive to break the law, that incursion is not small. The rule of law is not merely undermined, it is subverted. There is one consequence, and the damage is to our standing in the world. We have no real power now, except soft power – the English language and an understanding that we in this country have a traditional belief in the rule of law and we respect it. We hope that, one day, all the countries in the world that do not have respect for the rule of law will have it. Yet here we are, about to tear it into tatters. Our contribution to happier days around the world will be diminished. . . . We need to be careful to distinguish between the rule of law and rule by laws. It is the rule of law that carries us and gives us the protection that we need from the abuse or misuse

of the constitutional power that is enjoyed by Parliament. It is our safest shield against authoritarianism. It is a phrase that was conjured up by the Commons for the first time in 1610 to tell an overweening king that he was seeking to exercise overmuch power. It is a phrase we should use to remind an overweening Executive that they are going too far.[103]

Eventually the offending clauses were amendment and the final legislation, the United Kingdom Internal Market Act 2020, did not breach international law and the rule of law.

PUBLIC LAW IN CONTEXT
IT IS CLEAR THAT A BAD LAW IS NOT COMPATIBLE WITH THE SUBSTANTIVE VERSION OF THE RULE OF LAW

A law which violates human rights such as religious freedom and prohibits marriages between people of different racial groups is a bad law. As such it would not be compatible with the substantive version of the rule of law. However, in some countries mixed-faith marriages might be considered detrimental to the society and there might be an attempt to justify this restriction. Therefore, whether a law is good or bad is subjective.

4.8 Parliamentary sovereignty and the rule of law

The United Kingdom's Parliament is legally sovereign and can make any law it wishes. There are no legal restraints to prevent Parliament from violating human rights, as the Human Rights Act 1998 gives the courts no power to declare an Act void, as this would be impossible under the traditional doctrine of Parliamentary Sovereignty (see Chapters 5 and 6). According to Lord Hoffmann, 'Parliamentary sovereignty means that Parliament can, if it chooses, legislate contrary to fundamental principles of human rights. The Human Rights Act 1998 will not detract from this power.'[104] However, in accordance with the principle of legality there is a presumption by the courts that Parliament would not intend to do this. Therefore, clear words and clear expression would be required on the part of the legislature.

The present constitutional system may not be sufficient to protect human rights and prevent bad laws from being passed as was noted by Ralf Dahrendorf, who stated, '[i]n Britain, some greater emphasis on the rule of law may not come amiss, including possibly the explicit recognition that the sovereignty of parliament is not a sufficient guarantee of human rights.'[105]

So, is Parliamentary Sovereignty compatible with observance of the rule of law? In *R (on the application of Jackson) v. Attorney-General*[106] the House of Lords made some interesting *obiter* comments about the relationship between the rule of law and Parliamentary Sovereignty. In **Chapter 6** we will look at the impact of the rule of law on Parliamentary Sovereignty. It is interesting to note the obiter comments in the judgment. Lord Hope stated that '[t]he rule of law enforced by the courts is the ultimate controlling factor on which our constitution is based.'[107] Baroness Hale commented that '[t]he courts will treat with particular suspicion (and might even reject) any attempt to subvert the rule of law by removing governmental action affecting the rights of the individual from all judicial scrutiny.'[108] Whilst Lord Steyn stated that if Parliament did the unthinkable then the courts would be forced to qualify the principle of Parliamentary Sovereignty.[109] Such judicial comments would suggest that Parliamentary Sovereignty and the substantive version of the rule of law are incompatible. Lord Steyn writing extra-judicially went further and argued that a sufficiently serious violation of the rule of law would result in the courts qualifying the principle of Parliamentary Sovereignty:

> For my part the dicta in *Jackson* are likely to prevail if the government tried to tamper with the fundamental principles of our constitutional democracy, such as five-year Parliaments, the role of the ordinary courts, the rule of law, and other such fundamentals. In such exceptional cases the rule of law may trump parliamentary supremacy.[110]

ACADEMIC AND JUDICIAL DEBATE
CAN A 'BAD LAW' BE COMPATIBLE WITH THE RULE OF LAW?

What is a bad law? Section 23 of the Anti-terrorism, Crime and Security Act 2001 permitted the government to detain suspected terrorists without trial for an indefinite period of time. This violated Articles 5 and 6 of the European Convention on Human Rights (ECHR). However, it was possible to derogate under Article 15. The government had been given these powers by Parliament under the Act. The powers were justified on the grounds of national security. Was this a bad law, even if it was purporting to defend the lives of citizens? The House of Lords ruled in *A v. Secretary of State for the Home Department*[111] that section 23 breached the ECHR, as no derogation was permitted in the circumstances.

In South Africa during apartheid, the White African ruling elite discriminated against the Black and Asian population. Those in power and the majority of the electorate (albeit with most of the population prohibited from voting) considered that the apartheid laws were good laws. It would appear that South Africa met the procedural requirements of the rule of law. Writing extra-judicially Lord Steyn observed that:

> In the apartheid era millions of black people in South Africa were subjected to institutionalised tyranny and cruelty in the richest and most developed country in Africa. What

is not always sufficiently appreciated is that by and large the Nationalist Government achieved its oppressive purposes by a scrupulous observance of legality. If the judges applied the oppressive laws, the Nationalist Government attained all it set out to do. That is, however, not the whole picture. In the 1980s during successive emergencies . . . almost every case before the highest court was heard by a so-called "emergency team" which in the result decided nearly every case in favour of the Government. Safe hands were the motto. In the result the highest court determinedly recast South African jurisprudence so as to grant the greatest possible latitude to the executive to act outside conventional legal controls.'[112]

It is clear that a 'bad law,' which does not protect fundamental human rights, will violate the substantive version of the rule of law that was advocated by Lord Bingham.

It is important to contrast how the two versions of the rule of law operate. We can do this by demonstrating whether in the following scenarios a given country would conform to the rule of law:

Table 4.1

Country	The relevant law	Violation of the procedural version of the rule of law?	Violation of the substantive version of the rule of law?
South Africa	There were apartheid laws until the early 1990s, which separated people of different racial groups. There were no voting rights for Black Africans, etc. Today apartheid has ended and there is equality for people of all racial groups.	No violation.	Yes, there is a violation.
United States of America	In the southern states there was segregation until the 1960s. This led to restrictions on the rights of African Americans.	No violation.	Yes, there is a violation.
China	There are restrictions on political freedoms, religious freedoms and human rights violations.	Yes, for a number of reasons, including that the judiciary are not independent.	Yes, there is a violation.
United Kingdom	Detention without trial was introduced by the Anti-terrorism, Crime and Security Act 2001. This has now been repealed.	Initially no. The government was legally able to derogate from Article 5 of the ECHR; however, the House of Lords in *A v. Secretary of State for the Home Department* [2004] UKHL 56 held that it was not proportionate to detain only foreign terrorist suspects.	Yes, there is a violation.

4.9 Importance of the rule of law in a democracy

Does a democracy need to adhere to the rule of law? Does adherence to the rule of law make a country democratic? In the United Kingdom the courts have at times shown considerable deference to the government and have held that in the absence of a law against doing something, the government would be legally allowed to do it. The decision in *Malone* v. *Metropolitan Police Commissioner (No.2)*[113] is an example of this. In *Malone* the government was allowed to tap people's phones. As we have seen, Raz' version of the rule of law permits an authoritarian state to have the rule of law, providing that it abides by the procedural requirements. Ralf Dahrendorf noted that

> [d]emocracy is precious, but the rule of law is indispensable, and the two often do not go together. . . . However, at no time can it be acceptable to cross the boundary between expediency and morality, and suspend the rule in the sense of leaving elementary human rights in the partisan and often soiled hands of government.[114]

Dahrendorf noted that a country can have the rule of law but that does not mean that it is a democracy. The rule of law is important as it prevents a government from abusing human rights. Dahrendorf looked at Germany and noted that Bismarck's Germany (late-19th century) was not a democracy, but abided by the rule of law, whereas Hitler's Germany (1933–45) was also not a democracy, but it violated fundamental human rights.

Finally, it is important to note that when people use the term 'the rule of law' they often mean different things. Therefore, in defining the rule of law you must be aware of the many different versions which we have discussed above.

4.10 The rule of law and the United Kingdom's constitution: some challenges

This final section seeks to show difficulties with the protection of the rule of law, even in the United Kingdom.

4.10.1 Can a government ignore an Act of Parliament that instructs them how to conduct policy?

The rule of law is perhaps the most important feature of the United Kingdom's constitution. We expect individuals to abide by the law, such as paying taxes, obeying speed restrictions on a motorway and not committing theft as they simply decide that they are not in the mood to pay their taxes, not to speed, or not to pay for the goods. We have seen above that a government minister can be found in contempt of court for not obeying a court order, even if it is the department, and not him personally, who will face financial sanctions. However, what if a government is minded not to comply with a law as it disagrees with it for political-cum-policy reasons? It must be stated that the government must command the confidence of the House of Commons and it derives its ability to govern and formulate policies by virtue of the Commons.

Would a UK government ever refuse to apply a law that it disagreed with? There has been debate whether a government could advise the monarch to refuse royal assent under the prerogative and it is unlikely that the monarch would agree to do this. Therefore, a bill opposed by the government, but enacted by both Houses of Parliament, would receive royal assent.

It has been implied that a UK government might refuse to comply with such a law. In August 2019, the Prime Minister received the monarch's approval to prorogue Parliament for five weeks. Many people argued that this was done to prevent the House of Commons having sufficient time to prevent a no-deal Brexit taking place on 31 October 2019. In response the government's opponents in the House of Commons planned to introduce legislation to prevent a no-deal Brexit. It was in this context that Michael Gove, a member of the Cabinet, was interviewed by Andrew Marr on the BBC:

Gove: Let's see what the legislation says. You're asking me about a pig in a poke. And I will wait to see what legislation the opposition may try to bring forward.

Marr: We are in constitutional times, but for a government to say that we won't abide by legislation is impossible surely?

Gove: We will see what the legislation says when it is brought forward. For me the point is that we already have legislation in place which an overwhelming majority of MPs voted for.[115]

Gove was accused of implying that the government would not comply with the rule of law. A day later a draft bill[116] was published by Hillary Benn, which if adopted, would force the Prime Minister to seek an extension to Article 50 in the event of a no-deal Brexit. Later that day, the Prime Minister, Boris Johnson, made a speech outside Downing Street in 2019 in which he stated: 'I want everybody to know – there are no circumstances in which I will ask Brussels to delay. We are leaving on 31 October, no ifs or buts. We will not accept any attempt to go back on our promises or scrub that referendum.'[117] Johnson's speech was taken to imply that the government in the event of Benn's bill becoming law would refuse to comply with the statutory requirements.

On 5 September 2019, the Prime Minister seemed to confirm that he would not comply with the law, with the *Guardian* reporting '[Johnson] vowed not to go back to Brussels to request a delay to Brexit beyond 31 October, despite the likelihood of him being obliged to do so by parliament, via a bill expected to pass the House of Lords on Friday. "I'd rather be dead in a ditch," he said.'[118] Furthermore, the Prime Minister informed his supporters, 'They just passed a law that would force me to beg Brussels for an extension to the Brexit deadline. This is something I will never do.'[119]

In the anticipation that the Prime Minister might have refused to comply with the law, Robert Buckland QC, the Lord Chancellor, made a public statement on Twitter regarding his future in Cabinet: 'Speculation about my future is wide of the mark. I fully support the Prime Minister and will continue to serve in his Cabinet. We have spoken over the past 24 hours regarding the importance of the Rule of Law, which I as Lord Chancellor have taken an oath to uphold.'[120] There was then an emergency debate on the Rule of Law in the House of Commons on Monday 9 September 2019 in response to concerns that the Prime Minister might not comply with the law.

In the event the bill which would have required the Prime Minister to request an extension became law, the European Union (Withdrawal) (No.2) Act 2019, which the Prime Minister did comply with. The debate surrounding whether the Prime Minister would comply with the legislation is not just political hot air, as it demonstrates the frailty of a respect for the rule of law, and how an impression can be given that it will be violated by the government.

4.11 Practical application

1   To what extent is it correct to say that the United Kingdom's constitution and the actors within the constitution always conform to the rule of law?
2   To what extent are the procedural and substantive versions of the rule of law incompatible?

4.12 Key points to take away from this chapter

- The rule of law is an important feature of the United Kingdom's constitution.
- There can be many different definitions of the rule of law, with Raz' procedural or formal version and Lord Bingham's substantive version.
- Dicey is credited with coming up with the phrase 'the rule of law' and he identified three meanings of the rule of law.
- There is a potential for conflict between Parliamentary Sovereignty and the rule of law.

Notes

1   'Princess Anne Guilty Over Dog Attack' *The Guardian* (21 November 2002) <www.theguardian.com/uk/2002/nov/21/monarchy>.
2   O Bowcott, 'Prince Philip Will Not Be Prosecuted Over Car Crash, Says CPS' *The Guardian* (14 February 2019) <www.theguardian.com/uk-news/2019/feb/14/prince-philip-will-not-be-prosecuted-over-car-crash-cps>.
3   FA Hayek, *The Road to Serfdom* (Routledge 1944) 54.
4   For commentary see R Hogarth, *The Government Must Draw a Clear Line Between Law and Guidance During the Coronavirus Crisis* (Institute For Government 1

April 2020) <www.instituteforgovernment.org.uk/blog/government-law-and-guidance-coronavirus-crisis>.

5   J Waldron, 'The Rule of Law' in EN Zalta (ed), *The Stanford Encyclopedia of Philosophy* (Summer edn, 2020) <https://plato.stanford.edu/cgi-bin/encyclopedia/archinfo.cgi?entry=rule-of-law>. This is a highly accessible account of the rule of law and offers an insight into the theoretical elements to this important aspect of law and the constitution.

6   BZ Tamanaha, 'The History and Elements of the Rule of Law' [2012] SJLS 232–33.

7   AV Dicey, *Introduction to the Study of the Law of the Constitution* (Liberty Fund 1982).

8   J Raz, 'The Rule of Law and Its virtue' (1977) 93 LQR 195.

9   Lord Bingham, 'The Rule of Law' (2007) 67 CLJ 1.

10 <www.cps.gov.uk/publication/code-crown-prosecutors-2018-downloadable-version-and-translations>

11 See for example the jurist Henry de Bracton writing in the 1200s: 'Nothing is more fitting for a sovereign than to live by the laws, nor is there any greater sovereignty than to govern according to the law, and he ought properly to yield to the law what the law has bestowed upon him, for the law makes him king' (*De Legibus et Consuetudinibus Angliae*). See also Lord Denning MR in *Gouriet v Union of Post Office Workers* [1977] 2WLR 310: 'To every subject in this land, no matter how powerful, I would use Thomas Fuller's words over 300 years ago: "Be you ever so high, the law is above you." ' 761–62. Finally, see Lord Bingham, *The Rule of Law* (Allen Lane 2010) 4–5, where Bingham provided an interesting account of the importance of equality before the law.

12 M Gordon, 'Ministerial Responsibility After Huhne' (*UK Constitutional Law Association Blog*, 25 March 2013) <https://ukconstitutionallaw.org/2013/03/25/mike-gordon-ministerial-responsibility-after-huhne/>.

13 [1994] 1 AC 377.

14 [1994] 1 AC 377.

15 425 (Lord Woolf).

16 425–26.

17 J Baker, 'Human Rights and the Rule of law in Renaissance England' (2004) 2(1) NJIHR <https://scholarlycommons.law.northwestern.edu/cgi/viewcontent.cgi?article=1006&context=njihr>. This is a really interesting article which you may find useful by way of gaining an understanding of the rule of law during the 16th century. See also J Baker, *An Introduction to English Legal History*, (5th edn, OUP 2019).

18 L De Leanda, *After Elizabeth: How James, King of Scots, Won the Crown of England in 1603* (HarperCollins 2005) 181.

19 *Prohibitions Del Roy* (1607) 12 Co. Rep 63.

20 *Case of Proclamations* (1611) 12 Co. Rep 74.

21 See Chapter 10 for a discussion of Sir Edward Coke's judicial career and his dismissal by King James I. See also JS Hart, *The Rule of Law 1603–1660: Crowns, Courts and Judges* (Routledge 2003) 46–47.

22 R Stevens, *The English Judges: Their Role in the Changing Constitution* (Hart Publishing 2005) 12. See Lord Mansfield's judgment in *R v Wilkes* (1700) 4 Burr 2527; 98 ER 327, 2562–63, where the Lord Chief Justice was clear that, 'If, during this King's reign, I have ever supported his Government, and assisted

his measures; I have done it without any other reward, than the consciousness of doing what I thought right. If I have ever opposed, I have done it upon the points themselves; without mixing in party or faction, and without my collateral views.'

23 For example, see the *Five Knight's Case* (or *Darnel's Case*) (1627) 3 St Tr 1, 59.

24 J Hart, *The Rule of Law 1603–1660: Crown, Courts and Justice* (Routledge 2003).

25 ibid.

26 (1765) 19 State Tr 1029.

27 ibid.

28 ibid 286.

29 ibid 292.

30 R Gordon, '*Entick v Carrington* [1765] Revisited: All the King's Horses' in S Juss and M Sunkin (eds), *Landmark Cases in Public Law* (Hart Publishing 2017) 10. See also A Tomkins and P Scott (eds), *Entick v Carrington: 250 Years of the Rule of Law* (Hart Publishing 2015).

31 See TT Arvind and L Stirton, 'The Curious Origins of Judicial Law' (2017) 133 LQR 91 for an interesting discussion of the importance of judicial review to upholding the rule of law and a critique of the accepted narrative that judicial protection of the rule of law has been continuous.

32 [2011] UKSC 28; [2011] All ER 127.

33 ibid 37.

34 ibid 64.

35 [2013] EWCA Civ 277.

36 [2004] UKHL 56.

37 ibid 3.

38 ibid 74.

39 ibid 133.

40 ibid 42.

41 ibid 96.

42 [1969] 2 AC 147.

43 Arvind and Stirton have responded to the inclusion of the *Anisminic* by the Judicial Power Project as a problematic case on the basis of judicial overreach. They argue that, 'The Project's description of *Anisminic* becomes even more problematic when we look at the case's actual effects. Far from being an example of judicial overreach, *Anisminic* presents an outstanding example of how a judicial decision can improve the quality of administrative decision when all parties approach its implications in a spirit of commitment to the rule of law.' See TT Arvind and L Stirton, 'Why the Judicial Power Project Is Wrong About Anisminic' (*UK Constitutional Law Blog*, 20 May 2016) <https://ukconsti tutionallaw.org/>. For the Judicial Power Project see <http://judicialpowerproj ect.org.uk/50-problematic-cases/>.

44 [2019] UKSC 22.

45 ibid 126.

46 ibid 139.

47 [1979] Ch 344; [1979] 2 WLR 700.

48 ibid 366.

49 KD Ewing, *Bonfire of the Liberties: New Labour, Human Rights, and the Rule of Law* (OUP 2010).

50 (1985) 7 EHHR 14.

51   ibid 68.

52   Lord Neuberger, 'Justice Innovation Programme Lecture for the Northern Ire-
     land Assembly Committee for Justice' (3 March 2016) <www.supremecourt.uk/
     docs/speech-160303.pdf>, [12].

53   ibid 20.

54   Lord Hodge, *Upholding the Rule of Law: How We Preserve Judicial Independence in
     the United Kingdom* (Lincoln's Inn Denning Society, 7 November 2016) <www.
     supremecourt.uk/docs/speech-161107.pdf>, [33].

55   For example see a ministerial view on the High Court's decision in *Miller (No.1)*:
     'Brexit Case "Attempt to Block Will of People" Says Sajid Javid' *BBC News* (4
     November 2016) <www.bbc.co.uk/news/uk-politics-37866411>. Javid 'said he
     was not criticising the judges, but the people who brought the case: "This is an
     attempt to frustrate the will of the British people and it is unacceptable."' For
     coverage of the media's reaction see G Davies and D Wincott, 'Brexit, the Press
     and the Territorial Constitution' [2020] *Social and Legal Studies* (online access).
     See also G Davies and D Wincott, 'Brexit, the Press and the Territorial Constitu-
     tion' (*UK Constitutional Law Blog*, 10 June 2020) <https://ukconstitutionallaw.
     org/>. Finally see, P O'Brien, '"Enemies of the People"" Judges, the media and
     the mythic Lord Chancellor' for an interesting account of the reaction to *Miller
     (No.1)*. O'Brien observed that, 'As a systemic threat – to the rule of law or to the
     authority of judiciary – "enemies of the people" is a genuine worry but a minor
     one; a short-lived problem that will pass and has probably already done so.'
     He continued, 'Criticism will be of more concern if it plausibly threatens the
     impartiality of the judiciary.' The article is <https://radar.brookes.ac.uk/radar/
     file/a7666467-7a26-4600-89b5-da16ecda5055/1/fulltext.pdf>.

56   See 'Enemies of the People: Fury Over "Out of Touch" Judges Who Have
     "Declared War on Democracy" by Defying 17.4m Brexit Voters and Who Could
     Trigger Constitutional Crisis' *Daily Mail* (4 November 2016) <www.dailymail.
     co.uk/news/article-3903436/Enemies-people-Fury-touch-judges-defied-17-4m-
     Brexit-voters-trigger-constitutional-crisis.html>.

57   For further comment see C Monaghan, 'The Prorogation Litigation: "Which Was
     if the Commissioners Had Walked into Parliament with a Blank Piece of Paper"'
     (2019) 24(2) Cov LJ 7; J Simpson Caird, 'Miller 2, the Supreme Court and the
     Politics of Constitutional Interpretation' *Counsel Magazine* (November 2019)
     <www.counselmagazine.co.uk/articles/miller-2-the-supreme-court-and-the-
     politics-of-constitutional-interpretation>; 'Attacks on Judges Undermines
     Law – Supreme Court President' *BBC News* (16 February 2017) <www.bbc.co.uk/
     news/uk-38986228>.

58   See R Burgon, 'Liz Truss Swore to Defend the Judiciary: But She Stood by as
     They Got a Roasting' *The Guardian* (8 November 2016) <www.theguardian.
     com/commentisfree/2016/nov/08/liz-truss-defend-judges-article-50-stood-by>.

59   S Sedley, 'Judicial Independence Is a Fragile Thing' *The Financial Times* (27 Jan-
     uary 2017) <www.ft.com/content/abd56378-e3e0-11e6-9645-c9357a75844a>.

60   J Dyson, *A Judge's Journey* (Hart Publishing 2019) 174–75.

61   See Chapter 2 'The Miller Tale' in J Rozenberg, *Enemies of the People? How Judges
     Shape Society* (Bristol Press 2020).

62   ibid 33.

63   R Ekins, 'Judgment Day: The Dangers of Courts Taking Over Politics' *The Spectator*
     (21 September 2019) <www.spectator.co.uk/article/judgment-day-the-danger-

of-courts-taking-over-politics>; 'Boris Johnson Hits Back at Supreme Court Ruling Saying People Want to "Frustrate Brexit" and "Stop This Country Coming Out of the EU"' *The Telegraph* (24 September 2019) <www.telegraph. co.uk/politics/2019/09/24/brexit-latest-news-supreme-court-ruling-boris-johnson-prorogue/>.

64 [2017] UKSC 51.

65 ibid 11.

66 ibid 20.

67 ibid 39.

68 ibid 91.

69 ibid 96.

70 ibid 66.

71 ibid 68.

72 M Elliot, 'The Rule of Law and Access to Justice: Some Home Truths' (2018) 77(1) CLJ 5–6.

73 M Ford, 'Employment Tribunal Fees and the Rule of Law: R (Unison) v Lord Chancellor in the Supreme Court' (2018) 47(1) ILJ 1.

74 ibid 23–24.

75 Dicey (n 7).

76 ibid.

77 ibid.

78 Lord CJ Hewart, *The New Despotism* (The Cosmopolitan Book Company 1929) 23.

79 ibid 14.

80 Raz (n 8) 195.

81 ibid.

82 ibid.

83 ibid.

84 [1965] AC 75.

85 [1982] QB 1053.

86 [2001] 2 AC 241.

87 'Access to Justice' Welcome address to Australian Bar Association Biennial Conference, 3 July 2017 <www.supremecourt.uk/docs/speech-170703.pdf>.

88 Raz (n 8) 195.

89 For an interesting account see J Grogan, *Rule of Law and Covid-19: The Need for Clarity, Certainty, Transparency and Coordination* (LSE British Politics and Policy 26 October 2020) <https://blogs.lse.ac.uk/politicsandpolicy/rule-of-law-and-covid19/>.

90 Raz (n 8) 195.

91 (1774) 1 Cowp 143.

92 R Dahrendorf, 'Confusion of Powers: Politics and the Rule of Law' (1977) 40(1) MLR 1.

93 Raz (n 8) 195.

94 F Gibbs, 'Top Judge Warns of Risk to Rule of Law' *The Times* (5 March 2013).

95 'Access to Justice' (n 87).

96 ibid 7.

97 ibid.

98 A Marmor, 'The Rule of Law and Its Limits' [2004] Law & Philosophy 1.

99 Bingham, 'The Rule of Law' (n 9) 1.

100 ibid.

101 Bingham, *The Rule of Law* (n 11).

102 R Hogarth, *Internal Market Bill Breaks International Law and Lays the Ground to Break More Law* (Institute of Government 9 September 2020) <www.institutefor government.org.uk/blog/internal-market-bill-breaks-international-law>; R Cormacain, 'The United Kingdom Internal Market Bill and Breach of Domestic Law' (*UK Constitutional Law Blog*, 23 September 2020) <https://ukconstitutionallaw. org/>; M Hunt, 'The House of Lords Should Remind the Government That the Rule of Law Is Not Negotiable' *Prospect* (19 October 2020) <www.prospectmag-azine.co.uk/politics/brexit-internal-market-bill-lords-rule-of-law-parliament>.

103 HL Deb 19 October 2020, col 1287.

104 R v. Secretary of State for the Home Department ex p. Simms [2000] 2 AC 115 at 131.

105 Dahrendorf (n 92) 1.

106 [2005] UKHL 56.

107 ibid 107.

108 ibid 159.

109 ibid 102.

110 Lord Steyn, 'Democracy, the Rule of Law and the Role of Judges' [2006] EHRLR 243.

111 [2004] UKHL 56.

112 Steyn J, 'Democracy, the Rule of Law and the Role of Judges' [2006] EHRLR 243.

113 [1979] 2 All ER 620.

114 Dahrendorf (n 92) 1.

115 <www.theguardian.com/politics/2019/sep/01/brexit-gove-refuses-rule-out-ignoring-law-passed-stop-no-deal>

116 The European Union (Withdrawal) No. 6 Bill 2019.

117 <www.gov.uk/government/speeches/prime-ministers-statement-2-september-2019>

118 K Proctor and P Walker, 'Boris Johnson: I'd Rather Be Dead in Ditch Than Agree Brexit Extension' *The Guardian* (5 September 2019) <www.theguardian. com/politics/2019/sep/05/boris-johnson-rather-be-dead-in-ditch-than-agree-brexit-extension>.

119 C Duffield, 'Boris Johnson Tells Conservative Members He Will Break the Law Rather Than Extent Article 50' *I News* (7 September 2019) <https://inews.co.uk/ news/politics/boris-johnson-brexit-article-50-law-extension-break-mps-for-deal-group-conservative-tory-members/>.

120 Robert Buckland QC, 'Twitter' (8 September 2019) <https://twitter.com/Robert-Buckland?ref_src=twsrc%5Egoogle%7Ctwcamp%5Eserp%7Ctwgr%5Eauthor>.

Further reading

Bingham, Lord, 'The Rule of Law' (2007) 67 CLJ 1

———, *The Rule of Law* (Allan Lane 2010)

Dahrendorf R, 'Confusion of Powers: Politics and the Rule of Law' (1977) 40(1) MLR 1

Dicey AV, *Introduction to the Study of the Law of the Constitution* (republished, Liberty Fund 1982)

Elliot M, 'The Rule of Law and Access to Justice: Some Home Truths' (2018) 77(1) CLJ 5

Ewing KD, *Bonfire of the Liberties: New Labour, Human Rights, and the Rule of Law* (OUP 2010)

Ford M, 'Employment Tribunal Fees and the Rule of Law: R (Unison) v Lord Chancellor in the Supreme Court' (2018) 47(1) ILJ 1

Marmor A, 'The Rule of Law and Its Limits' [2004] Law & Philosophy 1

Neuberger, Lord, 'Access to Justice' Welcome Address to Australian Bar Association Biennial Conference, 3 July 2017

Raz J, 'The Rule of Law and Its Virtue' (1977) 93 LQR 195

Steyn, Lord, 'Democracy, the Rule of Law and the Role of Judges' [2006] EHRLR 243

Tamanaha BZ, 'The History and Elements of the Rule of Law' [2012] SJLS 232

Waldron J, 'The Rule of Law' in EN Zalta (ed), *The Stanford Encyclopedia of Philosophy* (Summer edn, SU 2020)

5 Parliamentary Sovereignty I

The foundations

This chapter will

- define what is meant by Parliamentary Sovereignty;
- consider the origins for why Parliament is legally sovereign;
- explore what Parliamentary Sovereignty meant to AV Dicey and his three requirements for Parliament to be legally sovereign;
- examine the significance of the decision in *R (on the application of Jackson) v Attorney General* [2005] UKHL 56 relating to the status of the Parliament Act 1949 and the Hunting Act 2004.

5.1 Introduction

Imagine that a radical government has been swept to power last year after a major financial crisis and has a majority of 100 Members of Parliament in the House of Commons. In its manifesto the government promised to introduce three specific policies: mandatory microchipping for the entire population in order to deter crime, to remove any welfare support from people who are not in employment, and to make it a criminal offence to support anyone not in employment.

The Economic Response Act (fictitious) is now law and people are being dragged from the street by enforcement officers and are having microchips fitted against their will. The Act has also removed welfare benefits and criminalised supporting those not in employment. There have been reports of food banks being raided and people starving to death. There has been an attempt to challenge the Economic Response Act (fictitious) in court and the High Court has rejected the challenge on the basis of Parliamentary Sovereignty.

The Economic Response Act (fictitious) is certainly repugnant and demonstrates that it would be possible for a sovereign Parliament to enact such legislation. However, it is important to realise that in the above scenario, the legal challenge failed because of Parliamentary Sovereignty.

DOI: 10.4324/9780429293498-6

This chapter will consider what is meant by Parliamentary Sovereignty and why it is the most important doctrine in the United Kingdom's constitution. In order to explain this, the traditional doctrine of Parliamentary Sovereignty as outlined by AV Dicey will be considered, with reference to case law and to the three requirements that Dicey attributed to a legally sovereign Parliament. This chapter will explain why Parliament is the highest law-making body in the United Kingdom and why each new Parliament has the ability to make, or unmake, any law that it wishes. The ability of Parliament to enact legislation on any subject matter will be explored.

This chapter will outline how an Act that would impose compulsory euthanasia on people aged over 30 would be considered legal and could not be challenged by the courts. In reality, Parliament does not legislate to impose compulsory euthanasia or kill all babies with blue eyes, and so it might be tempting to dismiss the full effect of the doctrine as somewhat academic.

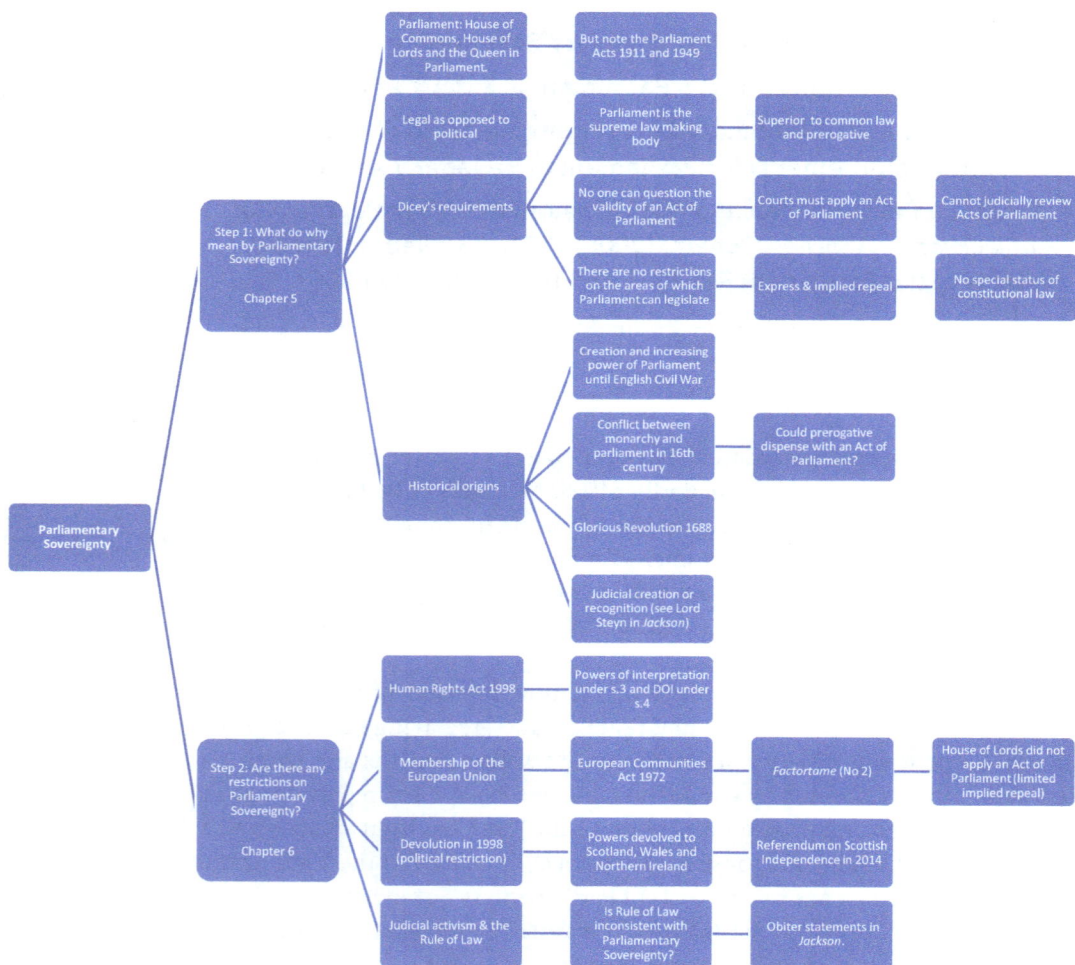

Figure 5.1

Chapter overview for **Chapters 5** and **6**

However, in *R (on the application of Jackson) v Attorney General*[1] several leading judges have rejected this argument and have stated in *obiter* that Parliament's sovereignty is not unlimited. This and other legal challenges to Parliamentary Sovereignty will be considered in **Chapter 6**.

It is important to consider that the doctrine of Parliamentary Sovereignty is English in tradition, as opposed to Scottish, and in *MacCormick v Lord Advocate*[2] it was suggested that we should not presume that the United Kingdom's Parliament had inherited every characteristic of the old English Parliament and none of the Scottish. Had Scotland received its independence in the 2014 referendum, the interim constitution for an independent Scotland explicitly rejected Parliamentary Sovereignty.

5.2 Defining Parliamentary Sovereignty

It is important to define what is meant by Parliament. According to Dicey: 'Parliament means . . . the King, the House of Lords, and the House of Commons; these three bodies acting together may be aptly described as the "King in Parliament."'[3] Since the creation of the Scottish Parliament under the Scotland Act 1998 it is important to state it is only the UK Parliament that is legally sovereign.

Lawyers and politicians will state that the UK Parliament is legally sovereign,[4] but what does this mean? It means that Parliament can legislate in any way that it wishes. There are no limitations on the Acts that Parliament can pass, save the requirement that the monarch needs to give royal assent in order for a bill to become an Act. Importantly, a bill is not sovereign as it is not law; neither is a resolution by both Houses of Parliament. This seems unproblematic, especially if Parliament enacts legislation that is not considered to be bad or immoral. But there would be nothing to stop Parliament from enacting legislation that would ban freedom of religion or the wearing of religious symbols and clothing. Legislation effectively banning certain religious clothing has already been passed by the French legislature and has proved to be controversial. In 2018, Denmark's legislature created a law that made it illegal to cover your face with an item of clothing. This legislation was perceived as targeting the wearing of the burqa or the niqab in public.

PUBLIC IN PRACTICE
HOW PARLIAMENT COULD MAKE 'BAD' LAW

Imagine if such a law were to be passed by the United Kingdom's Parliament. Arguably this would be considered by many to be a bad law. However, could this law be challenged in the courts? The answer is that according to the traditional doctrine of Parliamentary Sovereignty, the courts could not challenge the validity of the Act of Parliament. **Chapter 6** will look at the possible challenges to this Act (see Figure 5.2 for an overview of these challenges). For the purposes of this example whilst the courts could rely on the Human Rights Act 1998 to review the compatibility of the Act to the European Convention on Human Rights, they could not question the legality of the Act. Equally, prior to the United Kingdom leaving the European Union, if the Act contravened the Law of the European Union, then the courts would be empowered by the European Communities Act 1972 to give effect to European Union Law, unless Parliament has clearly intended to legislate contrary to European Union Law through the use of express language. Finally, there is a possibility, albeit a controversial one, that the courts could decide to impose limits on Parliamentary Sovereignty, by arguing that the Act goes against the rule of law.

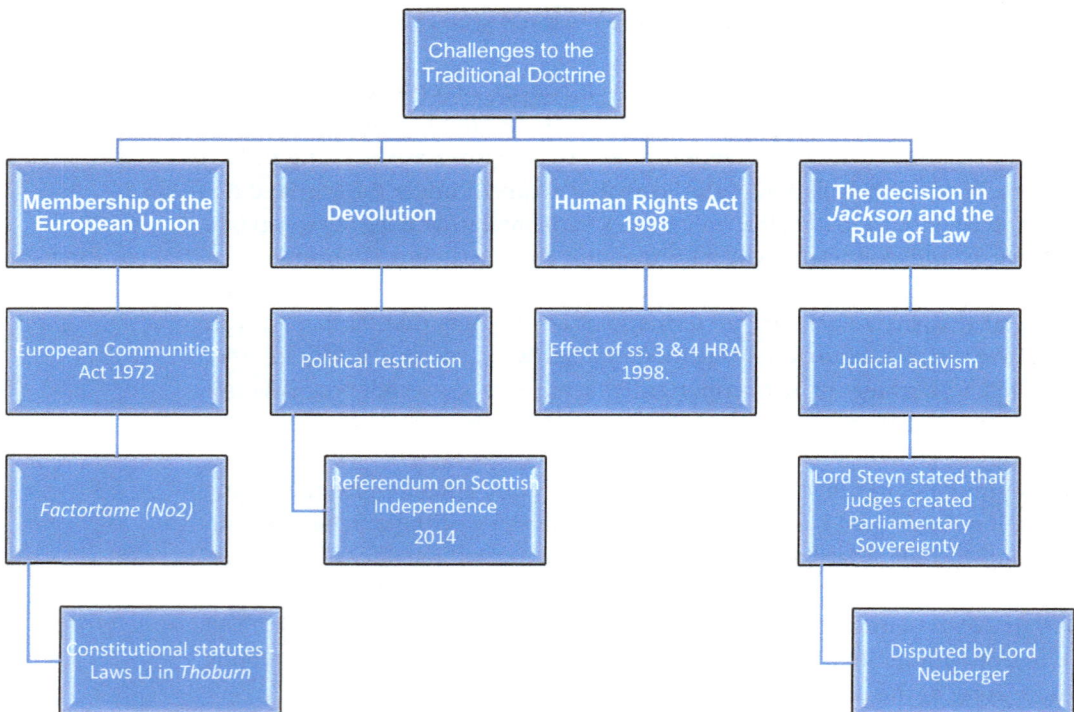

Figure 5.2
Challenges facing Parliamentary Sovereignty

It is important to consider whether Parliament actually enacts bad laws. Is the Identity Cards Act 2006 an example of a 'bad law'? This Act would have introduced compulsory identification cards. The Identity Cards Act 2006 has now been repealed and is no longer law. At the time the introduction of compulsory identification cards was extremely controversial and its opponents argued that it would have a negative impact on civil liberties. Professor KD Ewing criticised identification cards as the 'nasty offspring' of the 2006 Act and would permit 'a bewildering amount of personal information to be recorded by a State authority (for what purpose?).'[5] The Identity Cards Act 2006 was enacted with the aim to benefit the state and amounted to a compromise between civil liberties and the perceived public benefit. Whilst the Identity Cards Act 2006 was controversial and perhaps could be regarded by some as a bad law, it is extremely difficult to imagine that there could be in instance where the majority of the population could agree that a given Act of Parliament was a bad law. This is because labelling a given Act as a good or bad law is a subjective exercise, albeit often underpinned by evidence and expertise. Some groups in society might regard an Act of Parliament as a bad law because of what the Act intends to do, or because of the possible consequences it may have. Ultimately, whether a law is good or bad is subjective, as is it depends on a particular individual's point of view. Returning to the fictitious Economic Response Act that was used in the introduction, it is arguable that anyone reading this chapter would determine that this Act was a bad law. However, whilst the Economic Response Act was an extreme example, it is a direct result of a majority of the electorate voting for the government's manifesto, so within the fictional scenario, the person on the street might not necessarily regard this as a bad law. Parliaments can enact laws that could at the time be justified by some groups in society, such as legislation enacted in Germany following Adolf Hitler becoming Chancellor in 1933, or the legislation underpinning segregation in the Southern US States, or apartheid in South Africa.

5.3 The reason for Parliament being legally sovereign

This section will look at why an Act of Parliament is the highest source of law in the UK. Parliament is not the only law-making body in the United Kingdom. Firstly, the monarch historically used their prerogative powers to govern the country. Whilst today the prerogative powers are not a law-making power, i.e. capable of passing legislation, there was a time when the monarch did claim law-making powers. The prerogative powers were last treated as being able to pass legislation equivalent to that of Parliament during the reign of Henry VIII. Parliament had granted these powers to the king and they were repealed after his death. The monarch can still issue proclamations and create Orders in Council through the Privy Council, albeit these will be upon the advice of her government.

PUBLIC LAW IN CONTEXT
DID THE MONARCH HAVE LAW-MAKING POWERS?

The prerogative does not make law and neither can it impose any new legal obligations. However, Sir Edward Coke CJ in *Case of Proclamations*[6] had declared that the prerogative could not be used to impose new legal obligations upon subjects, unless these obligations were to be found in statute or the common law. Coke had stated, 'the king hath no prerogative, but that which the law of the land allows him.'[7] This is important because the prerogative is viewed as the remaining discretionary powers of the monarch. The prerogative cannot be used in new situations, i.e. where there is no precedent of it being used in the past. This means that the prerogative, which is today largely exercised by the government, cannot be used to create new laws or legal obligations.

Secondly, the judges have created the common law. According to Dicey, '[a] large proportion of English law is in reality made by the judges.'[8] Large parts of the law of contract and the law of tort are judge made. The impact of Parliament on the law of contract is limited and in your studies there will be few areas of contract law where the focus is on an Act of Parliament, as opposed to the common law.[9] The concept that judges make law is controversial as it offends the theory of the separation of powers. However, today the courts do not often 'make law' and their role is to interpret Acts of Parliament to determine Parliament's intention.

It is important to understand why Parliament is held to be legally sovereign, which means that Parliament is the supreme law-making body in the United Kingdom and no other body can question or declare an Act of Parliament to be invalid. The origins of Parliamentary Supremacy can be found in the political and constitutional disturbances in the 17th century, when the monarch, the courts and Parliament found themselves in both theoretical and military conflict (see Figure 5.3).

In the early 17th century the common law did not accept that Parliament could make any law that it wished and that the courts had the legal right in certain circumstances to declare an Act to be void. The circumstances were restricted to when an Act of Parliament was contrary to a fundamental right of the common law. The most famous expression of this willingness to declare that there were limitations upon an Act of Parliament, was that of Sir Edward Coke, the Chief Justice of the Court of Common Pleas in *Dr Bonham's Case*.[10]

PUBLIC LAW IN CONTEXT
SIR EDWARD COKE AND THE LIMITATIONS ON AN ACT OF PARLIAMENT IN THE 17TH CENTURY

In *Dr Bonham's Case*, Dr Bonham was a physician and had been detained for seven days and 'evilly treated' by those who had imprisoned him. The individuals who had imprisoned him relied on an Act of Parliament from the reign of Henry VIII, which empowered them to detain and punish members of the faculty at the University of Cambridge for 'their offence or disobedience, contrary to any article or clause contained in the said grant or Act.' Dr Bonham's offence was to have practiced medicine in the City of London without the permission of his College. Dr Bonham was bringing an action for unlawful imprisonment and therefore the questions to be determined by the court were whether the Act of Parliament could prevent him from practicing medicine in the City of London, whether he could rely upon an exception in the Act and finally whether he had been unlawfully imprisoned. The court found for Dr Bonham. The key part of the court's judgment was Sir Edward Coke's observation that 'And it appeareth in our Books, that in many Cases, the Common Law doth controll Acts of Parliament, and somtimes shall adjudge them to be void: for when an Act of Parliament is against Common right and reason, or repugnant, or impossible to be performed, the Common Law will controll it, and adjudge such Act to be void.'[11]

In *Day v Savadge*[12] the case concerned an action for trespass. The claimant had brought an action against the defendant for removing a bag of nutmegs in connection to the costs of transporting goods from a wharf. It was argued by Savadge that he could rely on a custom to remove the nutmegs. The court rejected this argument as it could not properly be considered a custom of the entire City of London, as it only applied to a certain area. The court was clear that even if there had been a custom to permit him to do this, it would be void as it went against natural equity.[13] The key part of the judgment is the observation by Sir Henry Hobart, the Chief Justice of the Court of Common Pleas, that 'even an Act of Parliament, made against natural equity, as to make a man Judge in his own case, is void in it self.'[14] It is clear that it was not just Sir Edward Coke who was of the opinion that the common law could declare an Act of Parliament to be void. According to Glenn Burgess, even one of Sir Edward Coke's opponents, Lord Ellesmere, the Lord Chancellor, had accepted Coke's reasoning for why an Act of Parliament could be declared void by the courts.[15] However, it is important to appreciate that Coke's judgment in Dr Bonham's Case was controversial and prior to his dismissal in 1616, he was instructed to clarify what he had meant and to amend his Reports. Coke refused to do this.[16] Burgess observed that Coke appeared to be suggesting that the courts could review an Act of Parliament on the basis of the common law.[17]

It was not just the common law that could in limited circumstances declare an Act to be void. Coke argued that the king could use his prerogative power to dispense with an Act of Parliament. In the *Case of Non Obstante, or Dispensing Power*,[18] Coke argued that this would occur where an Act attempted to 'bind the King from any Prerogative which is sole and inseparable to his person.' In *Calvin's Case*[19] the court considered the question of whether a Scottish subject of the king could own land in England. It was argued that Robert Calvin was an alien and could not own land as he was Scottish. The court rejected this argument as although England and Scotland were separate countries, they both shared a monarch, and as the king's subject, Calvin could own land in England. As part of his judgment, Coke had held that the king could dispense with an Act of Parliament: 'the King should expressly dispense with the said Statute: howbeit it is agreed in 2 Hen. 7. that against the expresse purview of that act, the king may by a special Non obstante dispense with that act, for that the act could not barr the King of the service of his subject, which the law of nature did give unto him.'[20]

Finally, it is not to say that Coke did not place considerable emphasis on the powers of Parliament. Sir William Blackstone observed that '[t]he power and jurisdiction of parliament, says Sir Edward Coke, is so transcendent and absolute, that it cannot be confined, either for causes or persons, within any bounds.'[21]

The 17th century was dominated by a series of conflicts between the Stuart kings and Parliament. After encountering opposition from Parliament to his policies Charles I[22] ruled England without summoning a Parliament. This meant that from 1629 until 1640 the king had to rely upon his prerogative power to impose new obligations, such as taxation, upon his subjects, without parliamentary approval. The constitutional implications of the king's policy and Parliament's response and the statutory limitations placed on the monarch's prerogative powers are considered in **Chapter 9**. Considering the judgments of Sir Edward Coke and the view that an Act of Parliament could in certain circumstances be limited by the common law and the prerogative, it is clear that it was not accepted that Parliament had the power to legislate without limits nor was an Act of Parliament immune from legal challenge. However, this is not to say that many people did consider Parliament to have the power to make any law that it wished and that an Act of Parliament was the highest form of law in England. What is important to consider is how, and why, this view was accepted as orthodoxy over the arguments adopted by Coke and others.

According to Jeffrey Goldsworthy, '[e]ven before the 1640s, many . . . lawyers described Parliament's legislative authority as legally unlimited.' Goldsworthy continued to argue that during the English Civil War, Royalists and Parliamentarians disagreed on whether it was the King in Parliament (i.e. the king giving royal assent) or only both Houses of Parliament acting on their own that was legally sovereign.[23] The dispute between Parliament and King Charles I led to three civil wars in the 1640s and 1650s. Parliament won the first civil war (1640–46) and the second civil war (1647–49). As a consequence of losing the second civil war in 1649 Charles I was executed after being tried for treason and convicted by a majority of Parliament. The abolition of the monarchy was not unpopular and a third civil war took place between 1649 and 1651, when Charles' son, Charles II, and his supporters unsuccessfully attempted to re-establish the monarchy. The result was that England was a republic and Oliver Cromwell, the leading general during the civil wars, ruled as the Lord Protector during the Protectorate. There had been an attempt to re-establish a monarchy with Cromwell as king; however, Cromwell declined the offer and eventually after his death, the monarchy was restored and Charles II became king.[24] What is crucial was that his brother James II succeeded Charles II as king in 1685 and this new monarch was indirectly responsible for the acceptance that Parliament was legally sovereign. The reasons for this were that:

1   James was a Catholic and his country was predominately Protestant.
2   James sought to use his prerogative power to dispense with an Act of Parliament in order to circumvent the legal restrictions on Catholics holding office or military commissions. The legality of this was upheld in *Godden v Hales*.
3   As Parliament had been dissolved (that is suspended by James II), a group of former parliamentarians arranged for James' son-in-law William of Orange and his wife Mary to invade England to depose James II. This is known as the Glorious Revolution.

4   James II fled to France and Parliament offered the crown to William and
     Mary on the condition that they accepted the Bill of Rights 1688. The Bill
     of Rights abolished many of the more controversial powers, including the
     power to dispense with an Act of Parliament.

5   The choice of who became monarch was now Parliaments and this was
     confirmed by the Act of Settlement 1701. This established the requirement
     that the monarch must be a Protestant and removed James II's Catholic
     children from the line of succession, restricted the ability of the monarch
     to pardon in an impeachment and established the independence of the
     English judiciary.

6   Parliament extended its own lifetime to seven years under the Septennial
     Act 1716.

7   Therefore in terms of the political and constitutional battle between the
     monarch, Parliament and to a lesser extent the courts, the clear winner was
     Parliament.

From 1688 Parliament has been regarded as legally sovereign. According to
Jeffrey Goldsworthy,

> [a]fter the Revolution of 1688, Parliament's sovereign power was used
> to control both the royal succession and the prerogatives of the Crown,
> which some royalists had previously deemed sacrosanct. Parliamentary
> sovereignty was central to the ideology of . . . Whigs, and . . . (most) Tories
> as well.[25]

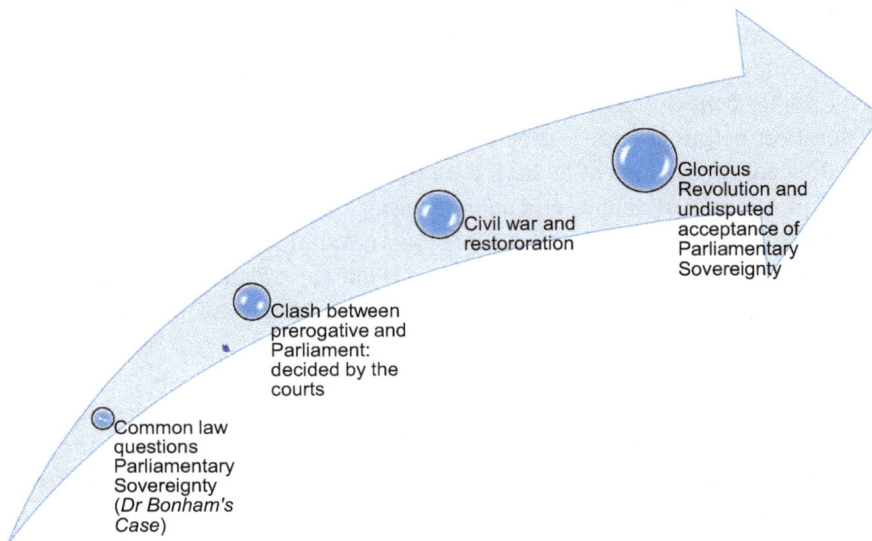

Figure 5.3
The important development of Parliamentary Sovereignty in the 17th century

The majority in the Supreme Court in *R (on the application of Miller) v Secretary of State for Exiting the European Union (No. 1)* were of the view that 'Parliamentary sovereignty is a fundamental principle of the UK constitution, as was conclusively established in the statutes [such as the Bill of Rights 1689 and the Act of Settlement 1701].'[26] However, it has not always been accepted that there are no restrictions on Parliament's legislative sovereignty. Even after 1688 the courts observed that there were some restrictions. In *City of London v Wood*[27] Holt CJ stated,

> And what my Lord Coke says in Dr. Bonham's case in his 8 Co. is far from any extravagancy, for it is a very reasonable and true saying, that if an Act of Parliament should ordain that the same person should be party and Judge, or, which is the same thing, Judge in his own cause, it would be a void Act of Parliament. . . . An Act of Parliament may not make adultery lawful, that is, it cannot make it lawful for A. to lie with the wife of B. but it may make the wife of A. to be the wife of B. and dissolve her marriage with A.[28]

In 1701, the common law was still maintaining that common law principles of natural justice, i.e. a man cannot be a judge in his own cause, would be protected from parliamentary legislation. Equally, adultery was deemed immoral and could not be legalised by Parliament. This is no longer the case as according to Parliamentary Sovereignty as it understood today, Parliament could do exactly that.

Theodore Plucknett observed that argument presented by Coke and others that there could be limitations placed on Parliament, 'was slowly abandoned – not so much because the mediaeval authority for it adduced by Coke is unconvincing as because subsequent events had proved that there were no legal limitations upon the powers of Parliament.'[29] Plucknett regarded Chief Justice Holt as 'the last great judge to accept the principle whole-heartedly,' as in *R v Earl of Banbury*[30] Holt had observed that 'yet when this comes incidently in question before [a court], they ought to adjudge and intermeddle with it, and they adjudge things of as high a nature every day; for they construe and expound Acts of Parliament, and *adjudge them to be void.*'[31] Another example of this residual belief that there were limits on an Act of Parliament, is evidenced in *Thornby, on the Demise of the Duchess of Hamilton v Fleetwood*[32] where there was suggestion that the court still had the power to find that an Act to be void. The claimant's counsel argued that

> In the case of Day v. Savage it is indeed said, that an Act of Parliament may be void from its first creation, as an Act against natural equity; for jura naturæ sunt immutabilia, sunt leges legum. But this must be a very clear case, and Judges will strain hard rather than interpret an Act void ab initio.[33]

This is significant as it meant that there was still an acceptance that there were limits on Parliament's legal sovereignty. The reluctance of some common lawyers to accept that the common law could never be used to declare an Act to be void is unsurprising and in 1871 in the decision in *Lee v Bude and Torrington Junction Railway*[34] Willes J expressly rejected the court's ability to do this. However, in the 2005 decision in *R (on the application of Jackson) v Attorney-General*[35] Lord Steyn argued in obiter that the common law still had this power.[36]

There is no Act of Parliament that establishes Parliamentary Sovereignty. Given that the United Kingdom lacks a codified constitution, it is unsurprising that there is no statute which declares Parliament to be legally sovereign. The Declaratory Act 1766 is an example of an Act that described the power of Parliament to legislate without restriction. The Declaratory Act 1766 was enacted to counter the claims of the American colonists that Parliament did not have the right to levy taxes on the American colonies, as this would amount to taxation without representation. The Act stated

> that the king's Majesty, by and with the advice and consent of the Lords Spiritual and Temporal, and Commons, of *Great Britain*, in Parliament assembled, had, hath, and of right ought to have, full power and authority to make laws and statutes of sufficient force and validity to bind the colonies and people of *America*, subjects of the crown of *Great Britain*, in all cases whatsoever.

To the drafters of the Declaratory Act 1766 it was just restating the obvious, rather than attempting to claim a new and novel power for the British Parliament. The reason for this lack of founding document or Act of Parliament declaring Parliament to be legally sovereign is that in 1688 it was a political fact that Parliament had defeated the Crown. Over the past 300 years the courts have recognised and given effect to this political fact.

5.2.1 Preventing the prerogative from undermining Parliamentary Sovereignty

As we shall see in **Chapters 10 and 11** when the prerogative and an Act of Parliament cover the same subject matter, it will be the prerogative which must make way for the Act (see *Attorney-General v De Keyser's Royal Hotel Ltd*).[37] The courts have protected the sovereignty of Parliament from being effectively undermined by the executive's use of the prerogative. In *Attorney-General v De Keyser's Royal Hotel Ltd* a hotel had been occupied by the Royal Flying Corps during the First World War and the owners sought compensation. The House of Lords held that compensation was payable under the Defence Act 1842, notwithstanding the fact that the government had sought to rely on the prerogative to negate the need to compensate under the Act.

The courts have not only protected the supremacy of an Act of Parliament over the prerogative, but have prevented the prerogative from being used in a manner that would undermine Parliamentary Sovereignty. In *R (on the application of Miller) v The Prime Minister (No. 2)* and *Cherry v Advocate General for Scotland*[38] the Supreme Court held that the use of the prerogative power to prorogue Parliament was unlawful as it prevented Parliament from exercising its sovereignty, as in order for Parliament to be legal sovereign it needed to be able to be in session. By proroguing Parliament, the Prime Minister had suspended Parliament for six weeks.

PUBLIC LAW IN CONTEXT
THE PROROGATION LITIGATION

In 2019, the Prime Minister requested that the monarch use her prerogative powers to prorogue (suspend) Parliament for six weeks. The decision to prorogue Parliament was challenged before the courts. The Supreme Court held in *R (on the application of Miller) v The Prime Minister (No. 2)* and *Cherry v Advocate General for Scotland* that the Prime Minister's advice to the monarch was unlawful. Part of the reason for deciding that decision was unlawful was that it placed a restriction on Parliamentary Sovereignty. The following passages are extracts from the judgment given on behalf of the court by Lady Hale and Lord Reed:

> [T]he principle of Parliamentary sovereignty [means] that laws enacted by the Crown in Parliament are the supreme form of law in our legal system, with which everyone, including the Government, must comply. However, the effect which the courts have given to Parliamentary sovereignty is not confined to recognising the status of the legislation enacted by the Crown in Parliament as our highest form of law. Time and again, in a series of cases since the 17th century, the courts have protected Parliamentary sovereignty from threats posed to it by the use of prerogative powers, and in doing so have demonstrated that prerogative powers are limited by the principle of Parliamentary sovereignty.[39]
>
> The sovereignty of Parliament would, however, be undermined as the foundational principle of our constitution if the executive could, through the use of the prerogative, prevent Parliament from exercising its legislative authority for as long as it pleased. That, however, would be the position if there was no legal limit upon the power to prorogue Parliament (subject to a few exceptional circumstances in which, under statute, Parliament can meet while it stands prorogued). An unlimited power of prorogation would therefore be incompatible with the legal principle of Parliamentary sovereignty.[40]
>
> It must therefore follow, as a concomitant of Parliamentary sovereignty, that the power to prorogue cannot be unlimited.[41]

The Supreme Court were able to use the importance of Parliamentary Sovereignty to place a limit on the Prime Minister's ability to request a potentially unlimited prorogation of Parliament. We will explore the decision in more detail in **Chapters 10** and **11** when we consider the relationship between the prerogative and the courts.

5.4 The traditional doctrine

According to the traditional doctrine of Parliamentary Sovereignty, it has been accepted since 1688 that an Act of Parliament is the highest form of law and therefore Parliament is legally sovereign. Professor AV Dicey is the academic most closely associated with the view that Parliament is legally sovereign. According to Dicey Parliament can make or unmake any laws and no one in the United Kingdom can challenge an Act of Parliament. This includes the courts, which may only interpret an Act of Parliament but cannot question its validity. According to Dicey there were three principles that underpinned Parliamentary Sovereignty:

1   Parliament is the supreme law-making body and could make or unmake any law it wished, no matter what the subject-matter was;
2   No person or court could question the validity of an Act of Parliament; and
3   Parliament is not bound by its predecessors, nor can it bind its successors.[42]

These requirements will be considered in turn.

5.4.1 First requirement: Parliament is the supreme law-making body

It is important to appreciate that although Parliament is the supreme law-making body in the UK, it is only an Act of Parliament that is legally sovereign. The concept of sovereignty is often used to describe many things and in many contexts. However, Parliament is the supreme law-making body, whereas according to Dicey the political sovereign is the electorate. It is important to note that only a valid Act of Parliament is sovereign and not a bill. The bill must receive royal assent before it becomes an Act. The monarch has the prerogative power to decide whether to give her assent. As a matter of constitutional convention the monarch will give her assent, as the last time that royal assent was refused was in 1708 when Queen Anne on the advice of her ministers refused her assent to the Scottish Militia Bill. Therefore Parliament can only make law if the monarch gives her assent. In other words, whilst it is extremely unlikely that assent would be refused, it is feasible that in exceptional circumstances a monarch might refuse assent.

It is possible for an Act of Parliament to be made by the House of Commons without the need for the approval of the House of Lords. While it is clear that one House acting on its own, such as the House of Commons, is not legally sovereign, the Parliament Act 1911 and Parliament Act 1949 permit the House of Commons to effectively bypass the House of Lords. This would occur where the House of Lords has previously refused to vote for a bill and after a year, the bill is introduced into the House of Commons. It is important to appreciate that the power of the House of Commons is limited; for example a bill extending the lifetime of Parliament could not be enacted under the 1911 and 1949 Acts. In the event that the Acts apply, the bill will receive royal assent and become an Act of Parliament. Examples of Acts made this way include the War Crimes Act 1991 and the Hunting Act 2004.

A resolution of the House of Commons (and indeed both Houses) is not law. In *Stockdale v Hansard*[43] the High Court held that a resolution of the House of Commons (and indeed both Houses) was not law. The case involved an action for defamation and a defence that the House of Commons had authorised the publication of documents via a resolution. In dismissing the defence, Lord Denman CJ stated that, 'the House of Commons is not the Parliament, but only a co-ordinate and component part of the Parliament . . . the resolution of any one of them cannot alter the law, or place any one beyond its control.'[44]

5.4.1.1 There is no special status for constitutional law

In the United Kingdom there is no special status of constitutional law. This means that the Highways Act 1980 and the Constitutional Reform Act 2005 are treated the same by the courts; they are both normal Acts of Parliament and it is irrelevant the Constitutional Reform Act 2005 has any special constitutional significance. In a 21st-century democracy it might appear to be strange that statutes which establish or preserve fundamental constitutional rights hold no special legal status and could be repealed in the same manner as any other statute. However, it is not universally accepted that there is no distinction between an ordinary statute (the Highways Act 1980) and a constitutional statute (the Constitutional Reform Act 2005). Laws LJ's judgment in *Thoburn v Sunderland DC*[45] argued in *obiter* that there was such a distinction. Laws distinguished between ordinary and constitutional statutes, setting out those statutes which could be considered to have a special constitutional status, and arguing that unlike an ordinary statute, that there were restrictions on how Parliament could repeal a constitutional statute. The restriction being that a constitutional statute could not be repealed by implication and required express words to do so. This will be considered below.

5.4.1.2 There are no restrictions on the areas on which Parliament can legislate

It is important to distinguish between legal and political limitations on Parliament's ability to legislate as it wishes. Although there are no legal restrictions

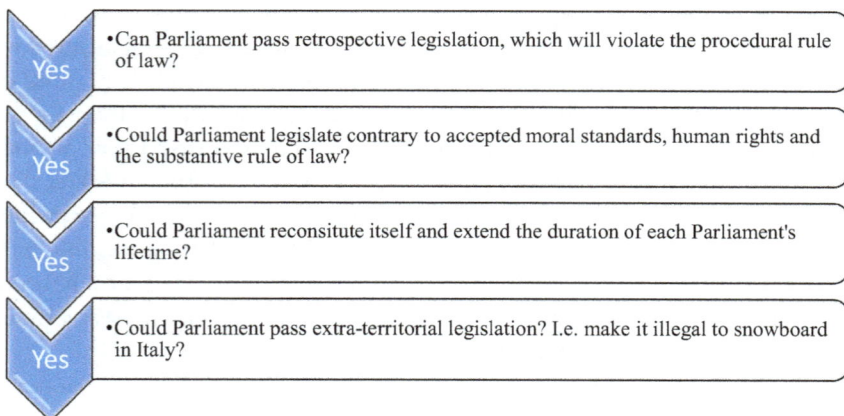

Yes • Can Parliament pass retrospective legislation, which will violate the procedural rule of law?

Yes • Could Parliament legislate contrary to accepted moral standards, human rights and the substantive rule of law?

Yes • Could Parliament reconsitute itself and extend the duration of each Parliament's lifetime?

Yes • Could Parliament pass extra-territorial legislation? I.e. make it illegal to snowboard in Italy?

Figure 5.4
No restrictions of Parliament's legislative ability

on areas which Parliament may legislate on, there will be political restrictions such as public opinion and the consequences of enacting such a law.

PUBLIC LAW IN CONTEXT
NORTHERN IRELAND AND THE RIGHT TO HAVE AN ABORTION

A recent example of a political restriction is the debate surrounding access to abortions in Northern Ireland. There is a difference in the laws relating to abortion between Northern Ireland and the rest of the United Kingdom. The Abortion Act 1967 allows women in the rest of the UK to have abortions, whereas in Northern Ireland the ability to have an abortion was extremely limited. This meant that a woman from Northern Ireland wishing to have an abortion would have to have travelled to mainland Britain. Following the referendum in the Republic of Ireland in favour of reforming Ireland's abortion laws, which meant that abortion will be legalised, focus shifted to Northern Ireland. Parliament is legally sovereign, and it could legislate to bring Northern Ireland's abortion laws into line with the rest of the United Kingdom. However, the power to make laws in this area has been devolved to the Northern Ireland Assembly and although it has been suspended due a failure between the political parties to reach a power sharing agreement, there was an argument that Parliament was restricted politically (and constitutionally) from enacting legislation. However, the United Kingdom Parliament enacted the Northern Ireland (Executive Formation etc) Act 2019 and the laws relating to abortion were brought into line with the rest of the United Kingdom by section 9 of the Act.[46] The change in the law followed the Supreme Court's decision in *In the matter of an application by the Northern Ireland Human Rights Commission for Judicial Review (Northern Ireland)*[47], where a majority of the court held the validity of Northern Ireland's abortion laws could not be challenged under the Human Rights Act 1998, because the applicants lacked the necessary standing. But for this lack of standing, a majority of the court would have issued a declaration of incompatibility under section 4 of the Human Rights Act 1998.

According to Sir William Blackstone, '[Parliament] can, in short, do everything that is not naturally impossible; and therefore some have [called] . . . its power the omnipotence of Parliament.'[48] The traditional doctrine of Parliamentary Sovereignty claims that there are no legal restrictions on Parliament's ability to legislate. This is not to say that there might be political or practical restrictions on the ability of Parliament to legislate in any way it chooses. In *Lee v Bude and Torrington Junction Railway*[49] Willes J was clear that there were no legal restrictions:

> I would observe, as to these Acts of Parliament, that they are the law of this land; and we do not sit here as a court of appeal from parliament. It was once said, – I think in Hobart, – that, if an Act of Parliament were to

create a man judge in his own case, the Court might disregard it. That dictum, however, stands as a warning, rather than an authority to be followed. We sit here as servants of the Queen and the legislature. Are we to act as regents over what is done by parliament with the consent of the Queen, lords, and commons? I deny that any such authority exists. If an Act of Parliament has been obtained improperly, it is for the legislature to correct it by repealing it: but, so long as it exists as law, the Courts are bound to obey it.[50]

Lord Steyn had written extra-judicially that, '[t]he courts acknowledge the sovereignty of Parliament. And in countless decisions the courts have declared the unqualified supremacy of Parliament. There are no exceptions.'[51] This is at odds with His Lordships' obiter comments in *Jackson* which suggest the opposite (see below).[52] The courts have no discretion to prefer their own interpretation over that which Parliament intended. Lord Edmund-Davies in *Duport Steel Ltd v Sirs*[53] advised judges to avoid the urge to do the following:

My Lords, a judge's sworn duty to 'do right by all manner of people after the laws and usages of this realm' sometimes puts him in difficulty, for certain of those laws and usages may be repugnant to him. When that situation arises, he may meet it in one of two ways. First, where the law appears clear, he can shrug his shoulders, bow to what he regards as the inevitable, and apply it. . . . Alternatively, a judge may be bold and deliberately set out to make new law if he thinks the existing legal situation unsatisfactory. But he risks trouble if he goes about it too blatantly, and if the law has been declared in statutory form it may prove too much for him, dislike it though he may. . . . From time to time some judges have been chafed by this supremacy of Parliament, whose enactments, however questionable, must be applied.[54]

Lord Edmund-Davies was clear in that judges are not free to impose limitations upon an Act of Parliament and ought to be careful before attempting to reform the law through the common law.

The decision in *Madzimbamuto v Lardner-Burke*[55] concerned the unilateral declaration of independence by Southern Rhodesia in 1965. The United Kingdom responded by passing the Southern Rhodesia Act 1965, which declared that Southern Rhodesia was still part of the British Empire and that Acts of Parliament still applied. Lord Reid held that despite the existence of a constitutional convention that the United Kingdom would not legislate for Southern Rhodesia, Parliament could still legislate as although it 'was a very important convention . . . it had no legal effect in limiting the legal power of Parliament.'[56] Lord Reid stated that, '[i]t is often said that it would be unconstitutional for the United Kingdom Parliament to do certain things, meaning that the moral, political and other reasons against doing them are so strong that most people would regard it as highly improper if Parliament did these things. But that does not mean that it is beyond the power of Parliament to do such things.

If Parliament chose to do any of them the courts could not hold the Act of Parliament invalid.'[57]

It is now necessary to consider what Parliament is capable of doing and has done previously.

1 Parliament can legislate to pass retrospective legislation which offends the procedural requirements of the rule of law

The rule of law is an important feature of the UK's constitution although there is no one definition of what is meant by the rule of law. Broadly speaking the rule of law can be defined as procedural or substantive. Each of these share many characteristics and will be considered in **Chapter 4**. However, it will become apparent that there is one crucial distinction between them. According to Professor Joseph Raz the procedural version of the rule of law requires there to be no retrospective legislation[58] Nonetheless, Parliament has enacted retrospective legislation. Retrospective legislation is where an Act of Parliament is enacted to change the law as it applied before the Act was created. It criminalises actions that were not regarded as criminal offences at the time that they took place. This begs the question as to why Parliament would enact retrospective legislation and whether it could be justified.

There are a several examples of retrospective legislation. One of these is the War Crimes Act 1991, which allowed the prosecution for 'murder, manslaughter or culpable homicide' which was 'committed during the period beginning with 1st September 1939 and ending with 5th June 1945 in a place which at the time was part of Germany or under German occupation [which] . . . constituted a violation of the laws and customs of war.'[59] The Act only applied to individuals who later became British citizens or a resident of the United Kingdom, the Isle of Man or the Channel Islands. Professor Michael Hirst has commented that, '[The War Crimes Act 1991] is unusual in that it has retrospective effect, creating offences under English law in respect of conduct that, when originally committed, was incapable of amounting to any such offence.'[60] In terms of justification it is possible to argue that there was a need to prosecute war criminals who might otherwise have escaped justice. Ronald Cottrell observed that prior to the enactment of the Act, there had been '[a]rguments based on the overwhelming gravity of the alleged crimes, the moral case for bringing people to book for such outrages have been weighed against the repugnancy to the Rule of Law of retrospective legislation, the age of both the alleged offences and the potential defendants.'[61] There have been prosecutions under the War Crimes Act 1991, including of Anthony Sawoniuk for the murder of Jewish people in 1942.[62] The murders had taken place during the German occupation of the Soviet Union.

Parliament is able to retrospectively set aside a judicial decision by enacting legislation. The House of Lords were asked to rule on whether compensation was payable where the prerogative had been used to destroy private property, in order to prevent it falling into the hands of the enemy. In 1942, the oil wells belonging to Burmah Oil had been destroyed to prevent these being captured by the Japanese Army. In *Burmah Oil Co Ltd v Lord Advocate*[63] a majority of the House of Lords ruled that compensation was payable. Parliament enacted the War Damage Act 1965 to reverse this decision and held that compensation was not payable. Section 1 abolished the common law right to compensation and subsection 2 states that

> [w]here any proceedings to recover at common law compensation in respect of such damage or destruction have been instituted before the passing of this Act, the court shall, on the application of any party, forthwith set aside or dismiss the proceedings, subject only to the determination of any question arising as to costs or expenses.

This had the effect of reversing the decision of the House of Lords. This was a controversial use of legislation to reverse a judicial decision.

PUBLIC LAW IN CONTEXT
THE DEBATE SURROUNDING RETROSPECTIVE LEGISLATION AND THE WAR DAMAGE ACT 1965

The War Damage Act 1965 was a controversial statute as it was intended to reverse the decision of the House of Lords in *Burmah Oil Co Ltd v Lord Advocate*. Paul Jackson observed that:

> Seldom can a statute of any length have led to such controversy as attended the passing of this Act of two sections. When last did a Lord Chief Justice of England express himself as forcefully as Lord Parker who felt "I should not be able to hold my head again were I not to come here and remonstrate as strongly as possible against this Bill?" The Act is of interest not merely for the change it effects in the law but also for the controversies it provoked concerning the Rule of Law and retrospective legislation.[64]

During a debate in the House of Lords, the former Lord Chancellor, Viscount Dilhorne, had defended the proposed legislation:

> In the controversy over this Bill a great deal has been said about the rule of law and about the Executive reversing a decision of the Judiciary. There is surely nothing contrary to the rule of law in reversing a judicial decision for the future. Revision of judge-made law is, after all, one facet of law reform. It is also said that the effect of this Bill on our interests overseas will be very serious; and this argument, if I understand it correctly, and so far as I can appreciate it, is put in two ways.[65]
>
> . . .
>
> To some, the mere words "retrospective legislation" are like a red rag to a bull, but I certainly could not agree with the proposition, if anyone sought to put it forward, that all

retrospective legislation is necessarily bad. It must depend on its content and on what it does.[66]

Viscount Dilhorne noted that a law would be bad if 'to quote from the judgment of Mr. Justice Wills in the well-known case of Phillips v. Eyre ought not to change the character of past transactions carried on upon the faith of the then existing law. Such legislation is always bad.'[67] However, this was not the case here, as prior to the judgment, the Burmah Oil Company were not understood to have such a right. It is clear that at the time the Act was controversial and it divided opinion. To have the former Lord Chancellor, Viscount Dilhorne, and the current Lord Chief Justice, Lord Parker, engaged in opposite sides of the debate in the House of Lords demonstrates this controversy and the strength of feeling as to the constitutional probity of the War Damage Act 1965.

An Act of Parliament is superior to the common law and Parliament can legislate to effectively reverse decisions of even the Supreme Court. It should be noted that this would not change the outcome for the parties involved in the decision; rather it would legislate to avoid the future application of the decision. Examples of this included decisions of the House of Lords in in *YL v Birmingham City Council*[68] and *Malcolm v Lewisham LBC*[69]. In both instances the decision was controversial and limited the rights of the claimants. In *YL v Birmingham* the House of Lords held that a private care home did not come within the definition of a public authority for the purposes of section 6 of the Human Rights Act 1998. The owner of the care home, Southern Cross Healthcare Ltd, had provided the care on behalf of Birmingham City Council pursuant to the council's legal obligations under the National Assistance Act 1948. In response to the House of Lords' decision Parliament enacted section 145 of the Health and Social Care Act 2008. Section 1(1) of the Act states that 'A person ("P") who provides accommodation, together with nursing or personal care, in a care home for an individual under arrangements made with P under the relevant statutory provisions is to be taken for the purposes of subsection (3)(b) of section 6 of the Human Rights Act 1998 (c. 42) (acts of public authorities) to be exercising a function of a public nature in doing so.'

2   Parliament can legislate against accepted moral standards and violate human rights (which offends the substantive version of the rule of law)

The substantive rule of law maintains that in order for a law to be regarded as complying with the rule of law, it must be a good law and not contravene human rights and be discriminatory. According to Dicey

[t]here is no legal basis for the theory that judges, as exponents of morality, may overrule Acts of Parliament. . . . A modern judge would never listen to a barrister who argued that an Act of Parliament was invalid because it was immoral, or because it went beyond the limits of Parliamentary authority.[70]

This means that Parliament can legislate contrary to acceptable moral standards. The most drastic statement to this effect is from Leslie Stephens, who wrote that, '[i]f a legislature decided that all blue-eyed babies should be murdered, the preservation of blue-eyed babies would be illegal.'[71] Over 100 years later in *R v Secretary of State for the Home Department ex p. Simms*[72], Lord Hoffmann reiterated that the unfettered legislative ability of Parliament remained unchanged by the passing of the Human Rights Act 1998, as

> Parliamentary sovereignty means that Parliament can, if it chooses, legislate contrary to fundamental principles of human rights. The Human Rights Act 1998 will not detract from this power. The constraints upon its exercise by Parliament are ultimately political, not legal. But the principle of legality means that Parliament must squarely confront what it is doing and accept the political cost.[73]

Lord Hoffmann noted that the restraints on Parliament are political and not legal. Would a government remain in power for long if Parliament enacted legislation that was repugnant to the majority of the population? However, as Dicey observed, Parliament is not limited in its actions as an agent of the electorate or by the idea of trusteeship; rather it is sovereign in its own right.[74] Even if Parliament does not owe a duty to the electorate there is still a risk that an MP might be voted out of office by her constituents. Lord Hoffmann continued to observe that:

> Fundamental rights cannot be overridden by general or ambiguous words. This is because there is too great a risk that the full implications of their unqualified meaning may have passed unnoticed in the democratic process. In the absence of express language or necessary implication to the contrary, the courts therefore presume that even the most general words were intended to be subject to the basic rights of the individual. In this way the courts of the United Kingdom, though acknowledging the sovereignty of Parliament, apply principles of constitutionality little different from those which exist in countries where the power of the legislature is expressly limited by a constitutional document.[75]

This is important, as the principle of legality places an inherent limitation on implicit interference with fundamental rights. Hence the need for express words and not a reliance on deliberate vagueness that can in the future be interpreted by agents of the state to impede the protection of rights.

3   Parliament could legislate to remove key constitutional rights

As there is no special status of constitutional law and it is not possible to entrench an Act of Parliament, no matter how constitutionally significant the Act is, it is perfectly possible for Parliament to repeal legislation that provides for important constitutional rights, or to introduce legislation that would remove rights recognised by the common law. For example, the Habeas Corpus

Act 1679 prevents an individual from being unlawfully detained. If the state wishes to detain someone, the law must permit this detention, such as where an individual is charged with committing a criminal offence and is prosecuted before the courts. However, the Habeas Corpus Act 1679 has been suspended in 1793 when Britain was at war with revolutionary France and during the First and Second World Wars. In the United States the Supreme Court can declare legislation to be void if it is held to be unconstitutional. The UK Supreme Court cannot do this.

However, that is not to say that certain Acts of Parliament will not have a special constitution status. In *Thoburn v Sunderland City Council*[76] Laws LJ distinguished between ordinary statutes and statutes of constitutional importance. This was in *obiter*. However, the idea has had traction. In *R (on the application of Miller) v Secretary of State for Exiting the European Union*[77], the majority observed that '[t]he 1972 Act accordingly has a constitutional character.'[78] Previously the Supreme Court in *R (on the application of HS2 Action Alliance Limited) v Secretary of State for Transport*[79] had distinguished between ordinary and constitutional statutes, identifying the European Communities Act 1972 and the Bill of Rights 1689 as constitutional instruments:

> Important insights into potential issues in this area are to be found in their penetrating discussion by Laws LJ in the Divisional Court in *Thoburn v Sunderland City Council* [2002] EWHC 195 (Admin), [2003] QB 151, (*The Metric Martyrs* case) . . . although the focus there was the possibility of conflict between an earlier 'constitutional' and later 'ordinary' statute, rather than, as here, between two constitutional instruments, which raises yet further considerations.[80]

4   Parliament can reconstitute itself, extend its own duration and the procedural requirements for passing a bill

Parliament has the ability to reconstitute itself and change the procedures for enacting legislation. The courts will look to the parliamentary roll and are only concerned with whether the legislation has received royal assent. It is possible for Parliament to legislate to extend the lifetime of each Parliament. The Triennial Act of 1694 limited the life of each Parliament to three years. The Septennial Act 1716 extended the lifetime of each Parliament to six years. This was very controversial as Parliament was viewed as usurping the power of the electors. Today, the lifetime of Parliament is five years. Subject to a number of exceptions, the Fixed-term Parliaments Act 2011 restricts the Prime Minister from requesting that the monarch dissolve Parliament before the expiry of the five-year fixed term. A general election can only take place before the expiry of the fixed five-year term when two-thirds of MPs vote to trigger an early General Election, or where there has been a vote of no confidence.[81]

5   Parliament can pass extra-territorial legislation and make laws for other countries without their consent

Parliament can pass legislation that will apply beyond the territory of the United Kingdom. In English law there is a presumption that when Parliament creates a criminal statute that its application is limited to England.[82] Parliament could enact legislation that criminalises conduct that takes place in other countries. One example of this is the War Crimes Act 1991 which criminalised acts that took place in continental Europe during the Second World War. Another example is the Continental Shelf Act 1964 which applies to the exploration and exploitation of the sea.

PUBLIC LAW IN PRACTICE
EXTRA-TERRITORIAL LEGISLATION

Imagine that Parliament decides that it is an offence to drive on the right-hand side of the road and enacts legislation which expressly states that it will apply throughout the world. A British citizen who goes on holiday to the United States and abides by the local law and drives on the right-hand side of the road could upon her return home face prosecution. An American citizen who travels on holiday to the United Kingdom could also be prosecuted, having been arrested at the airport by police officers who have evidence that she has previously driven on the right-hand side.

The theoretical, if legally possible, ability of Parliament to enact such legislation was considered by Sir Ivor Jennings who famously stated that Parliament could legislate to make it an offence to smoke on the streets of Paris.[83] The obvious answer to this is that a French court would not uphold an Act of Parliament, nor would it prosecute anyone who did smoke on the streets of Paris. But this is not a legal restriction on the ability of Parliament to legislate beyond the United Kingdom; rather it is a political or practical restriction.

Parliament has granted independence to the former colonies of the British Empire. In doing this it has lost the ability to legislate for over a quarter of the world. Years ago, an Act of Parliament could be applied from Vancouver to Auckland, and from Toronto to Cape Town. However, because British colonies gradually gained autonomy and developed their own legislatures to make law, the UK Parliament enacted the Colonial Laws Validity Act 1865 to avoid inconsistency between a UK Act and an Act of a colonial legislature. The Colonial Laws Validity Act 1865 ensured that a UK Act of Parliament would not automatically apply to a colony, and that express words were needed for it to apply. Most of the UK's colonies have gained political and legislative independence and even if Parliament expressly stated that an Act should apply to, say, South Africa, the South African courts would refuse to apply it. The granting of independence is a political and diplomatic restriction, rather than a legal one.

The Statute of Westminster 1931 granted the Dominions of the British Empire (such as the Irish Free State and the Dominion of Canada) legislative independence from the Westminster Parliament. Section 4 of the Statute of Westminster 1931 prevented an Act of Parliament from applying to a Dominion:

> No Act of Parliament of the United Kingdom passed after the commencement of this Act shall extend, or be deemed to extend, to a Dominion as part of the law of that Dominion, unless it is expressly declared in that Act that that Dominion has requested, and consented to, the enactment thereof.

The purpose of section 4 was to give further independence to the Dominions and to ensure that the UK Parliament would no longer legislate for a Dominion, unless at the request of the Dominion. The Act was a product of the 1926 Imperial Conference when the British government agreed that the UK and the Dominions enjoyed equal status.[84] In terms of its impact, the Act was regarded as giving legal independence to the Dominions, such as the Australian Federal Parliament when Canberra eventually adopted it in 1942.[85]

Despite the constitutional importance of the Statute of Westminster 1931, the UK Parliament could still legislate for a Dominion without its consent. In *British Coal Corporation v The King*,[86] Viscount Sankey LC observed that section 4 did not prevent Parliament from choosing to legislate for a Dominion in the future. His Lordship stated that, '[i]t is doubtless true that the power of the Imperial Parliament to pass on its own initiative any legislation that it thought fit extending to Canada remains in theory unimpaired: indeed, the Imperial Parliament could, as a matter of abstract law, repeal or disregard section 4 of the Statute.'[87] The UK Parliament did legislate for Canada in 1982 in order to introduce a new constitution. The Canada Act 1982 was enacted at the request of the Canadian government. The Act incorporated the Constitution Act 1982 into Canadian law, which contained the new constitution. The Canada Act 1982 states that '[n]o Act of the Parliament passed after the Constitution Act, 1982 comes into force shall extend to Canada as part of its law.' This is significant as it could be regarded as the final abandonment of the UK Parliament's ability to legislate for Canada.

PUBLIC LAW IN CONTEXT
'LEGAL VALIDITY IS ONE THING, ENFORCEABILITY IS ANOTHER'[88]

It was argued in *Manuel v Attorney General*[89] that by 1931 there was a constitutional convention that Parliament would not legislate for Canada, 'By 1926 it had become recognised as a clear constitutional convention that the United Kingdom Parliament would not legislate for a Dominion without the consent of that Dominion.'[90] Despite the convention, Parliament could still legislate to change the Canadian constitution. The case concerned a request by the

Canadian government for the Westminster Parliament to change the Canadian constitution. Sir Robert Megarry VC was clear that. '[i]t matters not if a convention had grown up that the United Kingdom Parliament would not legislate for that colony without the consent of the colony. Such a convention would not limit the powers of Parliament, and if Parliament legislated in breach of the convention, "the courts could not hold the Act of Parliament invalid."'[91] Megarry VC confirmed that Parliament could legislate for another country that had never been a UK colony (i.e. such as Poland) and that Act would be enforceable in UK courts, but the courts of the other country would not recognise the Act. 'I do not think that any English court would or could declare the Act ultra vires and void. No doubt the Act would normally be ignored by the foreign state and would not be enforced by it, but that would not invalidate the Act in this country . . . Legal validity is one thing, enforceability is another.'[92] Finally, Meggary VC observed that if Parliament 'legislated for [other countries], I do not see how the English courts could hold the statute void, however impossible it was to enforce it, and no matter how strong the diplomatic protests.'[93]

6   Each Parliament is legally sovereign and it can make or unmake any law

Each Parliament is legally sovereign and therefore can repeal any laws that have been passed by its predecessors. According to the orthodox account of Parliamentary Sovereignty it is not possible to entrench an Act of Parliament, which is to impose requirements that prevent a future Parliament from repealing the Act.

5.4.2 Second requirement: no one can question the validity of an Act of Parliament

The second of Dicey's requirements was that no person or body can question the validity of an Act of Parliament. Once a bill has received royal assent then the courts must apply the Act of Parliament. The courts cannot question the Act with regards to the procedure that Parliament followed to pass the bill, or whether Parliament may have been misled by a party who had an interest in seeing the bill passed. This was acknowledged by Sir William Blackstone who had argued that, '[t]rue it is, that what the Parliament doth, no authority upon earth can undo.'[94] Under the traditional doctrine of Parliamentary Sovereignty neither the courts nor the monarch's prerogative powers can set aside an Act of Parliament. This is important as it gives Parliament considerable freedom to legislate without being restricted by the other key constitutional principle that is the rule of law. Crucially Parliament can change its composition; for example it could pass legislation to abolish the House of Lords, which would mean that Parliament would no longer be bicameral.

1   No one can question the way that an Act of Parliament was made, in terms of procedure or whether Parliament was misled

The courts cannot question the validity of an Act of Parliament, nor can they enquire into the way in which the bill was passed by Parliament. According to Lord Campbell in *Edinburgh and Dalkeith Railway Company v Wauchope*[95] the courts are restricted to looking at the parliamentary roll. As long as a bill has passed both Houses (however, note the effect of the Parliament Acts 1911 and 1949) and has received royal assent, then the courts cannot investigate further. Lord Campbell stated

> [a]ll that a court of justice can look to is the parliamentary roll; they see that an Act has passed both Houses of Parliament, and that it has received the royal assent, and no court of justice can inquire into the manner in which it was introduced into Parliament, what was done previously to its being introduced, or what passed in Parliament during the various stages of its progress through both Houses of Parliament.[96]

This means that the courts are restricted from questioning the background of an Act.

2   The decision in *British Railway Board v Pickin*

In *British Railway Board v Pickin*[97] the House of Lords restated a key constitutional principle that the courts cannot declare an Act invalid or ineffective because of the manner in which the Act was passed or any irregularity in the procedure used. The decision concerned ownership of land as Pickin claimed that he owned the land in the middle of the track because of the Bristol and Exeter Railway Act 1836. This Act was repealed by the British Railways Act 1968, which was a private Act and not a Public Act of Parliament. The claimant alleged that the Act was ineffective because the British Railway Board, who had wanted the new Act, had misled Parliament. The House of Lords held that courts could not investigate this allegation, because they could not examine the procedure by which Parliament passed the Act. Lord Wilberforce famously declared that an Act of Parliament could not be declared invalid because of an alleged irregularity in the procedure used. According to Lord Wilberforce, '[t]he remedy for a Parliamentary wrong, if one has been committed, must be sought from Parliament, and cannot be gained from the courts.'[98] In his judgment Lord Morris stated that the courts can only resolve issues such as the correct interpretation of a statute. Once an Act of Parliament is on the statute book it cannot be questioned by the courts:

> It is the function of the courts to administer the laws which Parliament has enacted. In the processes of Parliament there will be much consideration whether a Bill should or should not in one form or another become an enactment. When an enactment is passed there is finality unless and until it is amended or repealed by Parliament. In the courts there may be argument as to the correct interpretation of an enactment: there must be none as to whether it should be on the Statute Book at all.[99]

3   The decision in *R (on the application of Jackson) v Attorney-General*

In *R (on the application of Jackson) v Attorney-General*[100] the House of Lords (the Appellate Committee) was asked to consider the validity of the Hunting Act 2004. The Hunting Act 2004 was extremely controversial as it banned hunting in the United Kingdom. The House of Lords (the legislative chamber) had opposed the Hunting Bill and had rejected it on two occasions. The Parliament Act 1911 as amended by the Parliament Act 1949, had allowed the House of Commons after one year to pass the Hunting Bill without the consent of the House of Lords. The Hunting Bill had received royal assent and the Hunting Act had become law.

It is important to appreciate that in 1911 the House of Lords had not voluntarily surrendered its ability to block a bill from becoming law. The passing of the Parliament Act 1911 had been achieved after the overwhelmingly Conservative House of Lords had been effectively 'blackmailed' by the Liberal government and the king into voting for the 1911 Act. If the House of Lords had refused, then the king had promised the government that he would create more Liberal peers in order to remove the Conservative majority and vote for the bill. The Parliament Act 1949 was the result of a Labour government being unable to implement its manifesto promises due to resistance of a overwhelmingly Conservative House of Lords. What is significant is that rather than compel the House of Lords to vote for a new limitation on its ability to delay legislation, which would refuse the period that the Lords could delay a bill from two years to one year, the government used the Parliament Act 1911 to bypass the need for the House of Lords' approval.

In *Jackson* the applicants argued that the Hunting Act 2004 was invalid because it had been passed under the procedures established by the Parliament Act 1949. The applicants argued that the Parliament Act 1949 was an invalid Act. They also argued that legislation passed under the Parliament Act 1911 was delegated legislation and not primary legislation; thus it could be reviewed by the courts. Finally, they argued that the legislative power under the Parliament Act 1911 was not unlimited. The House of Lords dismissed the appeal. The House held that legislation passed under the Parliament Act 1911 was an Act of Parliament and not delegated legislation. This was not like where Parliament delegates to a government minister the power to create secondary legislation for a particular area, such as asylum or education. In 1911, Parliament had not simply delegated law-making power to the House of Commons; rather Parliament had decided that in certain circumstances an Act of Parliament could be enacted without the consent of the House of Lords. In other words the Parliament Act 1911 did not create delegation legislation; rather it was a new way of enacting primary legislation, whereby the House of Commons could legislate without the consent of Lords. In *Jackson* the House of Lords held that the Parliament Act 1911 could be amended by the Parliament Act 1949, and therefore the Hunting Act 2004 was a perfectly valid Act of Parliament. Therefore, the House had rejected the argument that the provisions under section 2 of the

Parliament Act 1911 could not be used to enlarge the power of the House of Commons.

4   Why did the House of Lords find Jackson distinguishable from *Pickin*?

Lord Bingham justified the review of the 1949 Act and the Hunting Act 2004 by distinguishing the facts of *Jackson* from those in *Pickin*. This was because unlike in *Pickin*, the House of Lords was not investigating 'the internal workings and procedures of Parliament to demonstrate that it had been misled and so had proceeded on a false basis,'[101] and in the present case it involved a question of law, which only the court and not Parliament could resolve. Lord Bingham agreed with the Attorney-General that the Parliament Act 1911 could be amended to enable Parliament to legislate to extend the life of Parliament.[102] Lord Nicholls noted the constitutional principle from *Pickin* and justified the House of Lords' decision to review the legislation:

> Their challenge to the lawfulness of the 1949 Act is founded on a different and prior ground: the proper interpretation of section 2(1) of the 1911 Act. On this issue the court's jurisdiction cannot be doubted. This question of statutory interpretation is properly cognisable by a court of law even though it relates to the legislative process. Statutes create law. The proper interpretation of a statute is a matter for the courts, not Parliament. This principle is as fundamental in this country's constitution as the principle that Parliament has exclusive cognisance (jurisdiction) over its own affairs.[103]

The House of Lords rejected the appeal and refused to declare that the Hunting Act 2004 was invalid. However, it was the obiter comments of the Law Lords that proved controversial with regards to parliamentary sovereignty. The impact of the *obiter* comments in *Jackson* on Parliamentary Sovereignty will be considered below.

PUBLIC LAW IN PRACTICE
THE SQUIRREL CULLING ACT 2014 (FICTITIOUS)

Imagine that Parliament enacted the Squirrel Culling Act 2014 (fictitious) to respond to the threat posed by grey squirrels to native red squirrels. Because of opposition in the House of Lords, the government used the procedure under the Parliament Acts 1911 and 1949 to pass the bill without the support of the House of Lords. The Act states that all local councils in England must actively take steps to eliminate all grey squirrels. Friends of Grey Squirrels, which is a pressure group, attempt to challenge the validity of the Act. They argue that the

Parliament Act 1949 is invalid and therefore the Squirrel Culling Act 2014 is also invalid. They also argue that the procedure used to pass the bill was flawed. In light of the decision in *Jackson* their arguments would be rejected, as in the Parliament Act 1949 is valid. Furthermore, the *Pickin* in confirmed that the courts cannot question parliamentary procedure.

5   The courts must apply an Act of Parliament

The courts must apply an Act of Parliament, as it has no discretion under the doctrine of Parliamentary Sovereignty to declare an Act to be invalid or to ignore the intention of Parliament. Over 300 years ago in *City of London v Wood*[104] Holt CJ stated that 'an Act of Parliament can do no wrong, though it may do several things that look pretty odd.'[105] The courts are tasked with interpreting Acts of Parliament and rely upon a number of different rules to do this. What is crucial is when interpreting an Act of Parliament the courts must not go against what Parliament intended when it enacted the Act. This is a delicate balancing act and as will be explored below, the courts need to be mindful when using section 3 of the Human Rights Act 1998 to avoid usurping Parliament's legislative function. The courts have often reiterated the different roles of the judiciary and Parliament. In *Duport Steels Ltd v Sirs*[106] Lord Diplock considered the relationship between Parliament and the courts. In *Duport Steels Ltd* the House of Lords had to decide the correct interpretation of section 13 of the Trade Union and Labour Relations Act 1974 as amended by the Trade Union and Labour Relations (Amendment) Act 1976. Lord Diplock was clear that Parliament makes the law and that the court must interpret the law:

> My Lords, at a time when more and more cases involve the application of legislation which gives effect to policies that are the subject of bitter public and parliamentary controversy, it cannot be too strongly emphasised that the British constitution, though largely unwritten, is firmly based upon the separation of powers; Parliament makes the laws, the judiciary interpret them.[107]

His Lordship warned that judges must not be tempted to use their powers of interpretation to refuse to give effect to Parliament's intention, no matter how controversial the Act may be:

> Where the meaning of the statutory words is plain and unambiguous it is not for the judges to invent fancied ambiguities as an excuse for failing to give effect to its plain meaning because they themselves consider that the consequences of doing so would be inexpedient, or even unjust or immoral. In controversial matters such as are involved in industrial relations there is room for differences of opinion as to what is expedient, what

is just and what is morally justifiable. Under our constitution it is Parliament's opinion on these matters that is paramount.[108]

6   The courts cannot review an Act of Parliament

The courts can review delegated legislation and since the decision in *Council of Civil Service Unions v Ministers for the Civil Service*,[109] the courts can also review the prerogative. If for example the Welfare Reform Act 2018 (fictitious) gave ministers the power to make delegated legislation to help relieve fuel poverty, and the minister made delegated legislation under the Act to help tackle obesity, then the courts could review the delegated legislation and hold it to be ultra vires and quash the delegated legislation. Judicial review is an important check on the executive's power. The courts cannot judicially review an Act of Parliament nor can they hold it to be void on the grounds of irrationality and ultra vires. This is because there is an important distinction between primary and secondary legislation. According to the orthodox theory of Parliamentary Sovereignty primary legislation cannot be reviewed by the courts.

This can be contrasted with the position in the United States. Although the United States constitution does not permit the Supreme Court to do this, the United States Supreme Court has claimed the right to review primary legislation. In the key case of *Marbury v Madison*[110] the court held that it could declare an Act of Congress to be unconstitutional. Such a right was deemed to be essential to ensure the supremacy of the constitution as the highest form of law and to prevent the constitution from being violated by ordinary law. The Supreme Court's decision was accepted and is now an established part of US constitutional law. Finally, it should be noted that UK Parliament has given the courts the power to review the compatibility of an Act of Parliament with the European Convention on Human Rights. Section 4 of the Human Rights Act 1998 permits a court to issue a Declaration of Incompatibility where an Act is incompatible with a Convention Right. The issuing of such a declaration does not impact upon the validity of the Act and it remains good law.

5.4.3 Third requirement: Parliament cannot be bound by its predecessors, nor can Parliament bind its successors

The third of Dicey's requirements is that Parliament cannot be bound by its predecessors, nor can Parliament bind its successors. This section will consider what this means.

1   The requirement of express repeal

According to Dicey, Parliament is prevented from 'entrenching' a particular piece of legislation. This means that Parliament cannot prevent future Parliaments from expressly repealing legislation that it has enacted. Express repeal means that each Parliament must have the ability to expressly repeal legislation

Figure 5.5
An example of express repeal

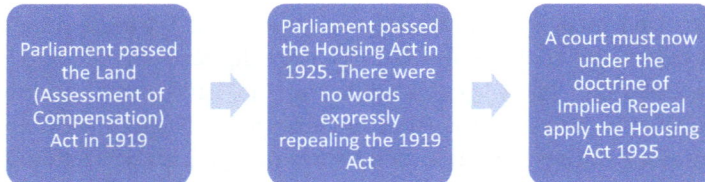

Figure 5.6
An example of implied repeal

enacted by previous Parliaments. By using express words Parliament can repeal existing legislation (see Figure 5.5).

2   The requirement of implied repeal

Implied repeal means that where there are two Acts of Parliament which cover the same subject matter, the courts must apply the later Act of Parliament. Implied repeal does not require there to be express words in the newer Act of Parliament. Implied repeal is important, as in order to be legally sovereign the current Parliament must be able to impliedly repeal legislation enacted by a previous Parliament (see Figure 5.6).

In *Vauxhall Estates Ltd v Liverpool Corporation*[111] landowners were seeking compensation and they sought to argue that the higher measure of compensation payable by the Land (Assessment of Compensation) Act 1919 should apply, rather than the lower measure of compensation available under the Housing Act 1925. The landowners argued that the 1919 Act should apply because of section 7(1), which stated that:

> [t]he provisions of the Act or order by which the land is authorised to be acquired, or of any Act incorporated therewith, shall, in relation to the matters dealt with in this Act, have effect subject to this Act, and so far as inconsistent with this Act those provisions shall cease to have or shall not have effect.

The landowners had argued that:

1   the 1925 Act was inconsistent with the 1919 Act;
2   the 1919 Act had not been impliedly repealed by the 1925 Act (this was because section 7(1) stated that where a later Act was inconsistent with the

1919 Act, the 1919 Act would still have effect and the newer provisions would be ineffective);

3   the 1919 Act had been entrenched by Parliament and required express repeal; and

4   the 1919 Act had not been expressly repealed.

Their argument was dismissed by the High Court. Mr Justice Avory stated that there could be no restrictions on Parliament's ability to impliedly repeal an earlier Act of Parliament, no matter what the language of the previous Act suggested:

> [W]e are asked to say that by a provision of this Act of 1919 the hands of Parliament were tied in such a way that it could not by any subsequent Act enact anything which was inconsistent with the provisions of the Act of 1919. It must be admitted that such a suggestion as that is inconsistent with the principle of the constitution of this country. . . . I should certainly hold, until the contrary were decided, that no Act of Parliament can effectively provide that no future Act shall interfere with its provisions . . . if they are inconsistent to that extent, then the earlier Act is impliedly repealed by the later.

The court made reference to the decision in *Brown v The Great Western Railway Company*[112], where implied repeal was used to give effect to a later Act of Parliament. In *Brown* Field J had observed that implied repeal existed as part of statutory interpretation,

> [i]f an Act of Parliament is passed containing clauses which are repugnant to and inconsistent with prior legislation, the legislature cannot have two minds at one and the same time, and therefore the subsequent mind must alter the first mind. Therefore, if even in an affirmative Act there is a clause which is repugnant to and inconsistent with a previous Act, the two cannot stand together; the subsequent Act repeals the prior Act, and, à fortiori, when it is negative.[113]

It is important to appreciate that despite the constitutional importance of implied repeal, it can viewed in decisions such as *Brown* as straightforward statutory interpretation. However, the use of language to indicate a restriction on the operation of implied repeal in the Land (Assessment of Compensation) Act 1919 complicates matters, as it appears to suggest that there is a manner and form restriction that requires Parliament to expressly repeal the Act. However, this was rejected by the High Court in *Vauxhall Estates Ltd* and again by the Court of Appeal in *Ellen Street Estates Ltd v Minister of Health*.[114]

The decision in *Ellen Street Estates Ltd* involved an attempt by a local authority to compulsorily purchase land in Stepney, London. An argument similar to Vauxhall Estates Ltd was submitted on behalf of the landowner. The landowner argued that the 1925 Act could not impliedly repeal the 1919 Act and that Parliament was required to use express words in order to repeal the 1919 Act. The Court of Appeal rejected the proposition that Parliament could bind a successor as to the form of subsequent legislation. Maugham LJ held that an Act of Parliament could not bind a previous Parliament as to the manner and form of future legislation:

> The Legislature cannot, according to our constitution, bind itself as to the form of subsequent legislation, and it is impossible for Parliament to enact that in a subsequent statute dealing with the same subject-matter there can be no implied repeal. If in a subsequent Act Parliament chooses to make it plain that the earlier statute is being to some extent repealed, effect must be given to that intention just because it is the will of the Legislature. This second point also fails.[115]

3   The manner and form debate

The decisions in *Ellen Street Estates Ltd* and *Vauxhall Estates Ltd* are important as they support Dicey's third principle that it is not possible for Parliament to bind future Parliaments. Based on Dicey's third principle, an Act cannot be entrenched by requiring (i) only express repeal, or (ii) that it cannot be repealed at all. Academics have debated whether Parliament could be bound to comply with manner and form requirements. This means that an Act of Parliament cannot restrict its future repeal, i.e. by requiring a particular percentage of the House of Commons to vote for repeal, or the holding of a national referendum. It has been argued that if Parliament has the ability to redefine the requirements for passing a bill under the Parliament Acts 1911 and 1949, which exclude the House of Lords, it would be able to set further requirements which require additional requirements to be met before particular legislation could be amended or enacted. According to the orthodox doctrine of Parliamentary Sovereignty all that is required to repeal existing legislation is a simple majority in both Houses of Parliament.

However, there is some academic support for the ability of a Parliament to impose restrictions on its successors through the use of manner and form requirements. The academic most associated with this argument is Sir Ivor Jennings.

ACADEMIC DEBATE
MANNER AND FORM THEORY

In *The Law and the Constitution*[116], Sir Ivor Jennings explored what was meant by Parliamentary Sovereignty. Jennings considered the fact that sovereignty did not mean supreme power: 'if sovereignty is supreme court, Parliament is not sovereign. For there are many things, as Dicey and Laski both point out, which Parliament cannot do ... Parliament passes many laws which many people do not want. But it never passes any laws which any substantial section of the population violently dislikes.'[117] The reason for this was that Members of Parliament needed to be re-elected. Jennings considered whether Parliament could introduce manner and form requirements to limit its ability to amend the law using the existing bare majority procedure in both Houses of Parliament. He considered New South Wales, where its legislature had introduced an Act in 1929 which stated that the legislative council could not be abolished by an Act, unless there had been a referendum beforehand.[118] This referendum requirement was upheld in *Attorney-General for New South Wales v Trethowan*[119] when the legislature sought to abolish the legislative council without holding the referendum. The Privy Council held that

> In the result, their Lordships are of opinion that section 7 A of the Constitution Act, 1902, was valid and was in force when the two Bills under consideration were passed through the Legislative Council and the Legislative Assembly. Therefore these Bills could not be presented to the Governor for His Majesty's assent unless and until a majority of the electors voting had approved them.[120]

Jennings observed that Parliament's powers come from the law. Any manner and form requirement would be provided for by law, observing

> [t]hat manner and form is provided, at present, either by the common law or by the Parliament Acts of 1911 and 1949. But Parliament may, if it pleases, provide another manner and form. Suppose, for instance, that the present Parliament enacted that the House of Lords should not be abolished except after a majority of electors had expressly agreed to it, and that no Act repealing that Act should be passed except after a similar referendum. There is no law to appeal to except that Act. The Act provides a new manner and for which must be followed unless it can be said that at time of its passing that Act was void or of no effect.[121]

The decision as to whether this requirement must be satisfied is one to be determined by the courts.[122] Michael Gordon has sought to explain how the manner and form theory as originally proposed by Jennings can be justified, and according to Gordon this justification is 'rooted in the democratic virtue of parliamentary sovereignty itself.'[123] Gordon argues that 'that potential concerns as to the use of the legislative power to alter the future manner and form can – and should – be dealt with as matters of political justification, rather than questions of legal validity.'[124]

According to Geoffrey Marshall,

> [t]he power to modify the manner and form of law-making is one which may in certain circumstances (as Australian experience has shown) be used as a political weapon. It could, in certain situations, be so used as to bring into conflict the principle that a sovereign authority is uncircumscribed as to the topics which it may legislate, and the principle that the rules governing the manner and form of legislation must be followed.[125]

Marshall considered the hypothetical requirement for preventing any statutory amendment to the Upper house, unless 80 per cent of all voters agreed to do this in a referendum, which would mean that a future Parliament could never amend the Upper House and would be a restriction as to the substance of what Parliament can do.[126] Marshall noted that some commenters had argued for the courts to determine whether something was manner and form, or 'a bar on future policy.'[127]

Marshall commented on the then contemporary debate surrounding the impact of the Parliament Acts 1911 and 1949, observing that HWR Wade did not regard these as creating 'a different manner and form,' but just 'a form of delegated legislation.'[128] However, Marshall observed, that if this were the case, then if the House of Lords were to be abolished, the House of Commons would only be making delegated legislation.[129]

In terms of the use of manner and form in the Commonwealth, Marshall considered the decision of the Supreme Court of the Union of South Africa in *Harris v Minister of the Interior*[130], where the court held that an Act removing the right to vote from non-white South Africans was invalid. This was because Parliament had failed to comply with section 152 of the South Africa Act 1909. Section 152 stipulated the requirements for amending or repealing section 35, which stated that the right to vote applied to people regardless to their race. The South African Parliament had failed to pass a bill with 'both Houses of Parliament sitting together, and at the third reading be agreed to by not less than two-thirds of the total number of members of both Houses.'[131]

Imagine if there were a referendum requirement in statute X, which stated that in order to pass a law to do Y, there would need to be a referendum in favour of doing this. According to the orthodox approach to the doctrine of Parliamentary Sovereignty Parliament could simply pass an Act to do Y without first holding the referendum. The use of referendums is very rare in the UK, even when taking into account those that only applied to particular geographic areas for the purposes of devolution.[132] To date the UK-wide referendums have been on membership of what is now the European Union in 1975 and 2016, and changing the voting system in General Elections in 2011.

According to the orthodox view the only limitation on Parliament legislating without first having held a referendum would be political. An example of a statute containing a referendum requirement is the European Union Act 2011. This Act was intended to place a restriction on future governments by limiting their prerogative power to transfer more power to the European Union. The Act had its origins in speeches by David Cameron, then Leader of the Opposition in 2009, and by William Hague, the Foreign Secretary, at the Conservative Party's conference in 2010. Hague had told delegates, that '[a] sovereignty clause on EU law will place on the statute book this eternal truth: what a sovereign parliament can do, a sovereign parliament can also undo. . . . [T]his clause will enshrine this key principle in the law of the land.'[133] Importantly, section 2 of the European Union Act 2011 states that the United Kingdom cannot ratify a treaty which amends or replaces either the Treaty of the European Union or the Treaty for the European Union, unless:

1 Parliament has approved such this by passing an Act of Parliament; and
2 there has been a referendum.

Section 2 was in response to criticisms by some politicians and members of the public that the Labour government had not held a referendum on the UK's ratification of the Lisbon Treaty.

PUBLIC LAW IN PRACTICE
AVOIDING THE REFERENDUM REQUIREMENT IN THE EUROPEAN UNION ACT 2011

The United Kingdom has left the European Union. However, imagine that this was not the case and the government wished ratify a new treaty to replace the Treaty of the European Union. As a matter of law the government could not do this without holding a referendum and then asking Parliament to vote to permit the ratification. The government could either comply with the European Union Act 2011 or it could ask Parliament to repeal the Act. Consequentially, once the European Union Act 2011 is repealed there is no longer a requirement to hold the referendum.

However, what would happen if the European Union Act 2011 contained the following words: 'in order to repeal the European Union Act 2011 there is a requirement that before any bill seeking to repeal the Act is presented for royal assent, that there must be a referendum asking the electorate whether the Act should, or should not, be repealed.' This raises a number of important questions: would the government decide to ignore this requirement and seek royal assent, would the monarch give assent if the referendum requirement is not complied with, what would be the legal status of the Act repealing the European Union Act 2011, would the referendum requirement in the European Union Act 2011 remain valid law, and how would the courts resolve this and would this involve a decision that the new Act is void for non-compliance with the referendum requirement?

This is not just hypothetical, as the idea of a manner and form requirement that required that a referendum took place was addressed by Baroness Hale in *Jackson* and will be considered below.[134]

4   It is not possible to entrench legislation

According to Dicey's orthodox account of Parliamentary Sovereignty it is not possible to entrench an Act of Parliament. Each Parliament must have the ability to repeal any previously enacted legislation. If this were not the case then a future Parliament would be less sovereign than its predecessors and its ability to enact legislation would be limited. Unlike the United States, there is no special status of constitutional law in the United Kingdom. Therefore, even if an Act of Parliament concerned the constitution, an attempt to entrench such an Act would be invalid. The Statute of Westminster 1931 could not prevent a later Parliament from legislating for a Dominion without its consent. This point was made by Slade LJ in *Manuel v Attorney General*, a decision that concerned Parliament legislating to change the Canadian constitution (albeit at the request of the Canadian government). Slade LJ reiterated that Parliament could not bind its successors by enacting legislation such as the Statute of Westminster in 1931.

There have been attempts by Parliament to prevent future Parliaments from amending legislation. Dicey gave the Acts of Union as one example, where Parliament had 'endeavoured to pass Acts which should tie the hands of their successors.'[135] However, Dicey noted that 'the endeavour has always ended in failure.'[136] Prior to the Acts of Union, England and Scotland had been separate nations. The Acts had intended to lay down the future workings of Great Britain. Yet key provisions of the Acts that created the United Kingdom have been repealed. If the Act which founded the British Parliament (since the English and Scottish Parliaments had ceased to exist) could be repealed, despite the clear intention of an earlier Parliament, then it is clear entrenchment will be ineffective. For example, Article I of the Act of Union with Scotland 1706 states that England and Scotland shall 'for ever after be united into one Kingdom by the name of Great Britain.' Had the outcome of the referendum on Scottish independence resulted in a yes vote, then Scotland would have left the United Kingdom and the Acts of Union would have been repealed. This can be evidenced by Southern Ireland leaving the United Kingdom to form the Irish Free State, despite Article 1 of the Act of Union with Ireland 1800, which stated that the Kingdoms of Great Britain and Ireland were for 'ever after, be united into one kingdom, by the name of the United Kingdom of Great Britain and Ireland.'

Some Scottish lawyers have argued that Parliament was not born unfree and that there are restrictions on its legislative freedom. In *MacCormick v Lord Advocate*[137] Lord Cooper had stated '[t]he principle of the unlimited sovereignty of Parliament is a distinctively English principle which has no counterpart in Scottish constitutional law.'[138] His Lordship did not rule on whether the Act of Union could bind Parliament, but it is interesting to question whether we should assume that English constitutional principles, rather than Scottish ones, should apply as of right to the new British Parliament:

> Considering that the Union legislation extinguished the Parliaments of Scotland and England and replaced them by a new Parliament, I have difficulty in seeing why it should have been supposed that the new Parliament of Great Britain must inherit all the peculiar characteristics of the English Parliament but none of the Scottish Parliament, as if all that happened in 1707 was that Scottish representatives were admitted to the Parliament of England. That is not what was done.[139]
>
> I have not found in the Union legislation any provision that the Parliament of Great Britain should be 'absolutely sovereign' in the sense that that Parliament should be free to alter the Treaty at will.[140]

In 2014, the Scottish Government published 'The Scottish independence Bill: A Consultation on an Interim Constitution for Scotland,' which would have potentially been used as Scotland's constitution in the event that the Scottish people had voted to leave the United Kingdom in September 2014's referendum.[141] Clause 2 states that '[i]n Scotland, the people are sovereign' and clause 10(2) states that 'The Parliament's power is subject to the constitution.'

5.5 Practical application

Earlier this year the Great Reform Act came into force. The relevant sections are as follows:

Section 1: The judiciary shall be appointed by the Prime Minister and shall serve at his pleasure.

Section 2: It is now a criminal offence to have driven a diesel car anywhere in the world. Anyone who has driven a diesel car in the past three years shall now be guilty of having committed a criminal offence.

Section 3: The United Kingdom hereby revokes the independence of the United States of America.

Section 4: This Act shall only be capable of repeal by express words in a statute and not by implication.

Please consider sections 1–4 and explore the extent to which these might affect Parliamentary Sovereignty.

An outline answer is available on the companion website.

5.6 Key points to take away from this chapter

- Parliamentary Sovereignty arose as a consequence of the conflict between the Crown and Parliament in the 17th century.
- The courts have protected Parliamentary Sovereignty from the executive's use of the prerogative powers.
- Dicey is associated with the view that Parliament has unlimited legal sovereignty and can make or unmake whatever law it wishes.
- The courts give effect to Parliamentary Sovereignty through the doctrines of express and implied repeal.

Notes

1   [2005] UKHL 56.
2   [1953] SC 396.
3   AV Dicey, *Introduction to the Study of the Law of the Constitution* (reprint edn, Liberty Fund 1915) 3.

4   'Parliament Should Reassert Its Sovereignty' *The Telegraph* (10 January 2011).

5   KD Ewing, *Bonfire of the Liberties* (OUP 2010) 9.

6   (1611) 12 Co. Rep 74.

7   ibid 76.

8   Dicey (n 3) 18.

9   Examples of Acts of Parliament include the Misrepresentation Act 1967 and the Law Reform (Frustrated Contracts) Act 1943.

10   (1609) 8 Coke Reports 113b.

11   ibid 118a.

12   (1614) Hobart 85; 80 ER 235.

13   ibid 87, 237.

14   ibid.

15   G Burgess, *Absolute Monarchy and the Stuart Constitution* (Yale Press 1996) 182. Lord Ellesmere to Montague CJ.

16   ibid 185–86.

17   ibid 193.

18   12 Co Reports 18.

19   (1608) 7 Co Reports 1a.

20   ibid 14a.

21   W Blackstone, *Commentaries on the Laws of England* (reprint of 1765 edn, UCP 1979) 156–57.

22   Reigned 1625–49.

23   J Goldsworthy, *The Sovereignty of Parliament: History and Philosophy* (OUP 1999) 231.

24   Reigned 1660–85.

25   Goldsworthy (n 23).

26   [2017] UKSC 5, [43]. See [41] for the complete list of statutes referred to by the majority.

27   (1701) 12 Mod Rep 669.

28   ibid 687–88.

29   T Plucknett, *A Concise History of the Common Law* (5th edn, Butterworth & Co 1956) 337.

30   (1694) Skin 517; Plucknett (n 29) 337.

31   *R v Earl of Banbury* (1696) Skin 517, 526–27 (emphasis added).

32   (1712) 10 Modern 114.

33   ibid 115.

34   (1871) LR 6 CP 576.

35   [2005] UKHL 56; [2005] 3 WLR 733.

36   ibid 102 (Lord Steyn).

37   [1920] AC 508; [1920] All ER 508.

38   [2019] UKSC 41, for commentary on the decision see C Monaghan, 'The Prorogation Litigation: "Which Was as if the Commissioners Had Walked into Parliament with a Blank Piece of Paper"' (2019) 24(2) Cov LJ 7.

39   ibid 41.

40   ibid 42.

41   ibid 44.

42   Dicey (n 3).

43   (1839) 112 ER 1112.

44   ibid 1153–54.

45 [2002] EWHC 195 (Admin); [2003] QB 151.

46 C Page, 'Northern Ireland Abortion and Same-Sex Marriage Law Change' *BBC News* (22 October 2019) <www.bbc.co.uk/news/uk-northern-ireland-50128860>.

47 [2018] UKSC 27.

48 Blackstone (n 21) 160–61.

49 (1871) LR 6 CP 576.

50 *Lee v Bude and Torrington Junction Railway* 582.

51 See Lord Steyn, 'The Weakest and Least Dangerous Department of Government' [1997] *Public Law* 84, 85.

52 See *R (on the application of Jackson) v Attorney General* [2005] UKHL 56.

53 [1980] 1 WLR 142.

54 ibid 164.

55 [1969] 1 AC 645.

56 ibid 723.

57 ibid.

58 J Raz, 'The Rule of Law and Its Virtue' (1977) 93 LQR 195.

59 Section 1 of the War Crimes Act 1991.

60 M Hirst, *Jurisdiction and the Ambit of the Criminal Law* (OUP 2003) 241.

61 R Cottrell, 'The War Crimes Act and Procedural Protection' (1992) Crim LR 173.

62 *R v Sawoniuk (Anthony)* [2000] 2 Cr App R 220.

63 [1965] AC 75.

64 P Jackson, 'War Damage Act 1965' (1965) 28 MLR 574.

65 HL Deb Vol 584 Col 753.

66 ibid 754.

67 ibid.

68 [2007] 3 All ER 957.

69 [2008] UKHL 43. Following the decision in *Malcolm v Lewisham LBC* the Equality Act 2010 amended the law.

70 Dicey (n 3) 19–20.

71 L Stephens, *The Science of Ethics* (GP Putnam 1882).

72 [2000] 2 AC 115.

73 ibid 132.

74 Dicey (n 3) 9.

75 Above (n 65) ibid.

76 [2002] EWHC 195 (Admin).

77 [2017] UKSC 5.

78 ibid 67.

79 [2014] UKSC 3.

80 [208] (per Lord Neuberger and Lord Mance).

81 Section 2.

82 See Lord Reid in *Treacy v DPP* [1971] AC 537, 551.

83 I Jennings, *The Law and the Constitution* (4th edn, UoL Press 1952) 154.

84 D Lee, 'States Rights and Australia's Adoption of the Statute of Westminster, 1931–1942' (2016) 13(2) History Australia 258, 260.

85 ibid 259.

86 [1935] AC 500.

87 ibid 520.

88 [1982] 3 WLR 821, 87–88 (Sir Robert Meggary VC).

89 [1982] 3 WLR 821.

90 ibid 96–97.

91 ibid 87–88.

92 ibid.

93 ibid.

94 Blackstone (n 21) 161.

95 (1842) 8 Cl & Fin 710.

96 ibid 725.

97 [1974] AC 765.

98 ibid 792–93.

99 ibid 789.

100 [2005] UKHL 56.

101 ibid 27.

102 ibid 32.

103 ibid 51.

104 (1701) 12 Mod. Rep. 669.

105 ibid 687–88.

106 [1980] 1 WLR 142.

107 ibid 157.

108 ibid.

109 [1985] AC 374.

110 [1803] 1 Cr 137.

111 [1932] 1 KB 733.

112 (1882) 9 QBD 744.

113 ibid 753.

114 [1934] 1 KB 590.

115 ibid 597.

116 Jennings (n 83).

117 ibid 143.

118 Section 7A of the Constitution Act 1902, as amended by the Constitution (Legislative Council) Amendment Act, 1929 (New South Wales).

119 (1932) AC 526.

120 ibid.

121 Jennings (n 83) 149.

122 ibid 150.

123 M Gordon, *Parliamentary Sovereignty in the UK Constitution: Process, Politics and Democracy* (Hart Publishing 2015) 3.

124 ibid 8.

125 G Marshall, *Parliamentary Sovereignty and the Commonwealth* (Clarendon Press 1957) 41.

126 ibid 41.

127 ibid 41–42.

128 ibid 43–44.

129 ibid 44.

130 [1952] 1 TLR 1245.

131 Section 152 of the South Africa Act 1909.

132 For example there have been two Scottish referendums on devolution (in 1979 and 1997) and one referendum on whether Scotland should leave the UK (in 2014).

133 H Mulholland, 'William Hague Outlines Plans for UK Sovereignty Clause in EU Bill' *The Guardian* (6 October 2011) <www.theguardian.com/politics/2010/oct/06/william-hague-uk-sovereignty-law>.

134 *R (on the application of Jackson) v Attorney General* [2005] UKHL 56, [163].

135 ibid.

136 Dicey (n 3) 21.

137 [1953] SC 396.

138 ibid 411.

139 ibid.

140 ibid 412.

141 See <www.gov.scot/Resource/0045/00452762.pdf>.

Further reading

Bogdanor V, *The New British Constitution* (Hart Publishing 2009)

Dicey AV, *Introduction to the Study of the Law of the Constitution* (Liberty Fund 1982)

Goldsworthy J, *The Sovereignty of Parliament: History and Philosophy* (OUP 1999)

Gordon M, *Parliamentary Sovereignty in the UK Constitution: Process, Politics and Democracy* (Hart Publishing 2015)

Parliamentary Sovereignty II

The challenges

This chapter will

- consider the political and legal challenges facing Parliamentary Sovereignty;

- evaluate the impact of the Human Rights Act 1998 and the effect of sections 3 and section 4 on Parliamentary Sovereignty;

- understand judicial views as to the possible limitation of Parliamentary Sovereignty; and

- examine to what extent it can be argued that Parliament is still legally sovereign.

6.1 Introduction

Imagine that Parliament enacted legislation that would permit the construction of internment camps for followers of a proscribed religion, or that people were stripped of their citizenship and rights based on their religion or sexuality. According to the traditional doctrine of Parliamentary Sovereignty it would be perfectly possible for Parliament to enact legislation that would do this. This chapter is concerned in part with whether the courts would hold that there are certain things that Parliament cannot do and place a restriction on Parliamentary Sovereignty.

In **Chapter 5** we looked at the foundations of Parliamentary Sovereignty. This chapter will consider the four challenges to Parliamentary Sovereignty. The first is devolution, which is a political restriction. The second was the UK's previous membership of the European Union, which was a legal restriction. The third is the Human Rights Act 1998 which some have argued places a legal restriction on Parliamentary Sovereignty. The fourth is common law constitutionalism and the rule of law. Each of the above will be explained and then evaluation in order to gauge to what extent it is a serious challenge to the traditional doctrine of Parliamentary Sovereignty.

DOI: 10.4324/9780429293498-7

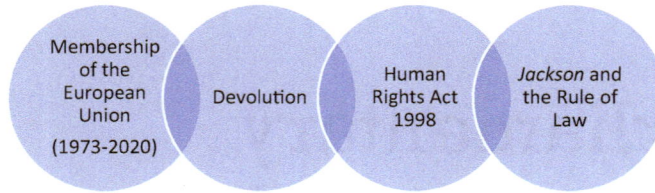

Figure 6.1
Possible limitations on Parliamentary Sovereignty

In this chapter we will consider the limitations on the doctrine of Parliamentary Sovereignty. It is a moot point as to whether any of the below are actual limitations, as opinion is divided.

6.2 Membership of the European Union (1973–2020) and the broader constitutional implications

As a result of the 2016 referendum on whether the UK should remain a member of the European Union, the UK left the European Union in 2020. This is known as Brexit, which stands for Britain exiting the EU. The perceived impact that the UK's membership of the EU had on Parliamentary Sovereignty was one of the criticisms made against remaining in the EU. While the UK left the EU in 2020 it is still important to appreciate the constitutional implications of the UK's membership between 1973 and 2020 and the wider ramifications that this had on our understanding of Parliamentary Sovereignty. The purpose of this section will be to:

1   consider the effect of what being a member of the European Union had on Parliamentary Sovereignty and the development of the United Kingdom's constitution
2   consider what is the legacy of this membership on how Parliamentary Sovereignty is understood today

The United Kingdom joined the European Economic Community (now the European Union) in 1973. As the United Kingdom is a dualist state (that is a state which makes a distinction between national and international law) an Act of Parliament was required to give legal effect to membership of the EEC. The European Communities Act 1972 was enacted to facilitate the United Kingdom's membership. The European Communities Act 1972 was an important statute as it states how domestic courts should apply European Union law. Section 2, General Implementation of Treaties stated:

(1)   All such rights, powers, liabilities, obligations and restrictions from time to time created or arising by or under the Treaties, and all such remedies

and procedures from time to time provided for by or under the Treaties, as in accordance with the Treaties are without further enactment to be given legal effect or used in the United Kingdom shall be recognised and available in law, and be enforced, allowed and followed accordingly; and the expression and similar expressions shall be read as referring to one to which this subsection applies. Similar expressions shall be read as referring to one to which this subsection applies.

. . .

(4) The provision that may be made under subsection (2) . . . includes, subject to Schedule 2 to this Act, any such provision (of any such extent) as might be made by Act of Parliament, and any enactment passed or to be passed, other than one contained in this part of this Act, shall be construed and have effect subject to the foregoing provisions of this section; but, except as may be provided by any Act passed after this Act.'

Prior to the United Kingdom's departure, the European Union had 28 member states and had ever-increasing competence to legislate over new areas. The Court of Justice of the European Union (the CJEU), formerly the European Court of Justice (the ECJ), remains the highest court and is tasked with ensuring compliance, enforcement and the uniformity of European law. The CJEU will ensure that individuals can enforce their rights under European law and that member states meet their obligations. It must be emphasised that this is only where member states have agreed to give the EU competence over certain areas.

In order to ensure that the EU functioned and that the fundamental freedoms of free movement of goods, services, capital and people applied uniformly in every member state, it was important that the law of each member state would not impose different restrictions or interpretations. Put simply, if it was left to different national courts to determine the rights of free movement of goods, then there would be discrepancies and differing approaches. This would defeat the purpose of free movement. Equally, if a national court were able to challenge certain parts of EU law on the basis that it contravened national law or its constitution, then there would be lack of uniformity. Therefore, for those areas that member states had decided the EU should be given competence for, it was necessary that EU law should have precedence over national law and even the constitutions of member states. This is the principle of the supremacy of EU law. The supremacy of EU law was not established in a Treaty, but by ECJ in the decisions of *Van Gend en Loos v Nederlandse Administratie der Belastingen*[1] and *Costa v ENEL*.[2] Where there is a conflict between the two then it will be European law that must be applied.

Article 2 of the Treaty on the Functioning of the European Union sets out how competence operates within the EU and how it can sometime be shared between the EU and member states. This has led to conflict with the constitutional courts in other member states. For example, in Germany EU law was in conflict with German law and the ECJ held that EU law took supremacy.[3] The German Constitution permits the transfer of sovereignty to the EU[4] and permits the supremacy of EU law.[5]

6.2.1 The position prior to Factortame (No.2)

In *Bulmer v Bollinger*[6] Lord Denning MR considered the implications for the UK's membership of the European Communities. His Lordship stated, '[b]ut when we come to matters with a European element, the Treaty is like an incoming tide. It flows into the estuaries and up the rivers. It cannot be held back. Parliament has decreed that the Treaty is henceforward to be part of our law. It is equal in force to any statute.'[7] In *McCarthys Ltd v Smith*[8] Lord Denning MR held that it was the duty of the national court to give priority to European law where the national law was inconsistent. Lord Denning stated that in doing this the courts were having regard to Parliament's intentions under section 2(1) and (4) of the European Communities Act 1972. However, Lord Denning held that if there was a repudiation of the European Communities Act 1972, or express inconsistency with European law (such as if Parliament deliberately intended to legislate contrary to European law), then the courts would have to apply national law. Nonetheless, the European Communities Act 1972 obliged national courts to interpret UK law so that it was consistent with EU law. The extent of this interpretive power was considered in *Garland v British Rail Engineering Ltd*[9] and *Lister v Forth Dry Dock and Engineering Co Ltd*.[10]

6.2.2 The decision in Factortame (No.2)

The decision in *R v Secretary of State for Transport ex p. Factortame Ltd (No.2)*[11] has been regarded as limiting Parliamentary Sovereignty. The decision concerned Spanish fishermen who sought to utilise the fishing quota that had been granted to British fisherman by the EEC (see Figure 5.7). The fishermen established a company that was registered in the United Kingdom. The company was majority owned by the Spanish fishermen and had a fleet of 95 vessels. The UK government enacted the Merchant Shipping Act 1988 to prevent the fishermen from exploiting the quota. The Merchant Shipping Act 1988 imposed conditions and the 95 vessels failed these since they were owned by a majority of Spanish nationals and were controlled by Spanish nationals. The Act required that at least 75 per cent of the ownership of the company's shares and its directors had to be British. The fisherman alleged that the Act contravened their EEC rights, which were given effect in English law by the European Communities Act 1972.

The case reached the House of Lords and in *R v Secretary of State for Transport ex p. Factortame Ltd (No.1)*[12] the House was asked by the fishermen to grant interim relief. This was whilst a decision of the ECJ was pending on the matter. The House ruled that it could not grant interim relief, as this would mean overturning an Act of Parliament. According to Lord Bridge:

> [t]he effect of the interim relief granted would be to have conferred upon them rights directly contrary to Parliament's sovereign will and correspondingly to have deprived British fishing vessels, as defined by Parliament, of the enjoyment of a substantial proportion of the United Kingdom quota of stocks of fish protected by the common fisheries policy. I am clearly of the

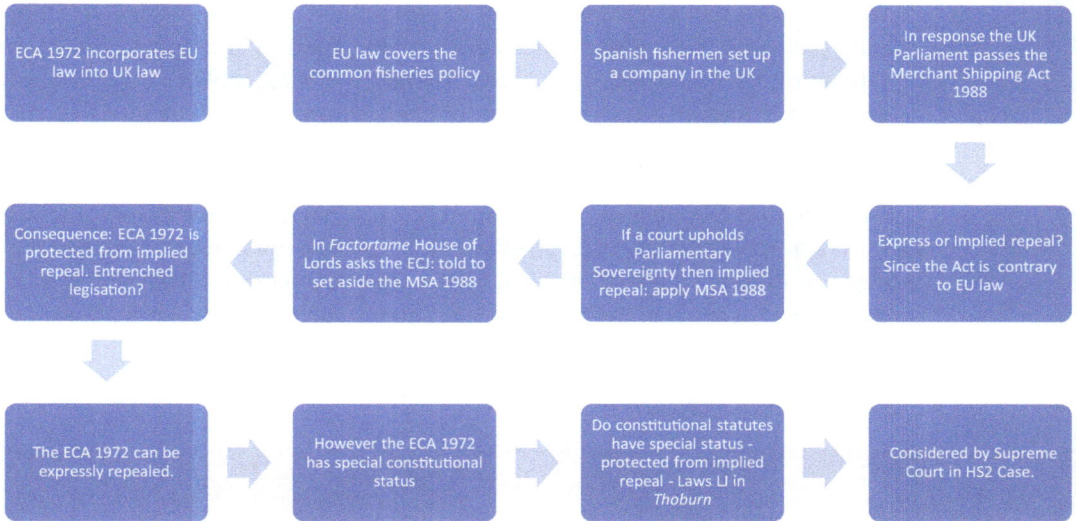

Figure 6.2
The decision in *Factortame (No. 2)*

opinion that, as a matter of English law, the court has no power to make an order which has these consequences.[13]

The House asked the ECJ by way of a preliminary reference whether it must set aside the Merchant Shipping Act 1988. In *R v Secretary of State for Transport ex p. Factortame Ltd and Others*[14] the ECJ held that the Act must be set aside, because it was the only obstacle to granting interim relief. In response the House of Lords ruled in *Factortame (No.2)* that section 2 of the European Communities Act 1972 gave the court the authority to disapply an Act of Parliament. Lord Bridge noted that Parliament in 1972 had accepted that European law was supreme over national law; 'whatever limitation of its sovereignty Parliament accepted when it enacted the European Communities Act 1972 was entirely voluntary.'[15] The Act made it clear that 'the duty of a United Kingdom court, when delivering final judgment, to override any rule of national law found to be in conflict with any directly enforceable rule of Community law.'[16] It is important to appreciate that Lord Bridge viewed any limitation on Parliamentary Sovereignty as entirely voluntary. This was because Parliament understood that EU law was supreme and the European Communities Act 1972 gave effect to this. The courts were following the instructions of Parliament when it had effectively agreed to give supremacy to EU law.

Lord Bridge justified the House of Lords' decision by reference to Parliament enacting the European Communities Act 1972. It is important to note that if there was a limitation of sovereignty, then it was Parliament that had ordered the courts to give supremacy to European Union law (where it had competence). His Lordship specifically referred to the jurisprudence of the ECJ, which has consistently held European law to be supreme. Unsurprisingly the decision was controversial, as Parliament had intentionally created the Merchant Shipping Act 1988 to deal with the actions of the Spanish fishermen who were relying on their European law rights. Therefore it is arguable that Parliament had always intended to legislate contrary to European law. The effect of the Merchant Shipping Act 1988 was inconsistent with section 2 of the European Communities Act 1972. Returning to Dicey's view as to what was meant by Parliamentary Sovereignty, if Parliament was sovereign then the House of Lords must apply the doctrine of implied repeal. If the House of Lords had applied the doctrine of implied repeal, then no matter what answer the ECJ gave by way of preliminary reference, the House would have applied the later Act. Instead the House of Lords applied the older Act (the European Communities Act 1972) to set aside the newer Act (the Merchant Shipping Act 1988).

ACADEMIC DEBATE
THE IMPACT OF *FACTORTAME (NO.2)*

The European Communities Act 1972 appears to be protected from implied repeal. As a matter of constitutional law this is not only novel, but also it presents a significant departure from how Dicey envisaged Parliament Sovereignty. It should be noted that the House of Lords did not hold that the European Communities Act 1972 was entrenched, meaning that it could never be repealed. Rather the judgment in *Factortame (No.2)* was that the doctrine of implied repeal would not operate to apply a newer Act of Parliament that was inconsistent with the European Communities Act 1972. This made the European Communities Act 1972 unique, as it was the only Act that could only be repealed by express words alone.

The decision in *Factortame (No.2)* was extremely controversial. Professor Wade responded to the decision by asserting that '[t]he Parliament of 1972 had succeeded in binding the Parliament of 1988 and restricting its sovereignty, something that was supposed to be constitutionally impossible.'[17] This was, Professor Wade stated, 'at least in a technical sense . . . a constitutional revolution.'[18] Wade argued that:

> It is obvious that sovereignty belongs to the Parliament of the day and that, if it could be fettered by earlier legislation, the Parliament of the day would cease to be sovereign. . . . Nothing in Lord Bridge's language suggests that he regarded the issue as one of statutory construction. He takes it for granted that Parliament can "accept" a limitation of its sovereignty which will be effective both for the present and for the future. It is a statement which could hardly be clearer: Parliament can bind its successors. If that is not revolutionary, constitutional lawyers are Dutchmen.[19]

Professor Wade regarded this as a political rather than legal revolution brought about by membership of a new political order which is the European Union. It is the courts and Parliament which can change this rule of recognition and decide whether a future Parliament can be fettered. It is clear that Wade believes that the judges are able to adapt Parliamentary sovereignty to deal with a new political reality. Wade viewed the decision as a legal revolution.

The recognition of legal sovereignty is 'a political fact which the judges themselves are able to change when they are confronted with a new situation which so demands.'[20]

Responding to Wade's article, Professor TRS Allan questioned the argument that *Factortame (No.2)* had brought about a legal revolution and that the 1972 Act had bound newer Acts of Parliament.[21] Allan observed that Wade had rejected as implausible the argument that 'the 1972 Act creates only a rule of construction for subsequent statutes, requiring such statutes to be read as compatible with rights arising under European Community law in the absence of express words to the contrary.'[22] Allan questioned whether Parliamentary Sovereignty is a matter for the judges, i.e. legal, as opposed to politicians, i.e. political. Allan remarked that to '[t]alk of revolution falsely implies that the courts' role is merely to accept, on grounds of expediency, whatever the politicians decide.'[23]

What does this mean? It can be argued that *Factortame (No.2)* was based on expediency. The House of Lords had no choice other than to follow the 1972 Act whilst (a) the United Kingdom was a member of the European Union and (b) unless the 1972 Act was expressly repealed. Putting aside academic arguments, Allan stated that '[f]or all practical purposes . . . it is certainly true that the sovereignty of Parliament has been curtailed during continued membership of the European Community.'[24]

6.2.3 Can the common law modify Parliamentary Sovereignty to restrict implied repeal and as a consequence protect constitutional statutes?

It would appear that one Parliament can be bound by a decision of a previous Act of Parliament. However, the only decision which supports this is *Factortame (No.2)* and the European Communities Act 1972 is the only Act which is protected from implied repeal.

However, Laws LJ considered this special treatment of the European Communities Act 1972 in *Thoburn v Sunderland City Council*.[25] The decision in *Thoburn* involved the so-called Metric Martyrs, who were convicted of breaking the law by selling goods in imperial weights rather than by metric. The sellers were obliged by law to indicate the price of the food per kilogram; however their machines were not calibrated to do this. Laws LJ dismissed the sellers' appeal against their convictions. However, what was interesting from a constitutional perspective was Laws LJ's *obiter* statements concerning Parliamentary Sovereignty after *Factortame (No.2)*.

Laws LJ stated that Parliament cannot bind its successors by restricting implied repeal or express repeal. This is because the law will not allow them to do it. Neither can the European Union bind future Parliaments. Parliament is unable to abandon its legal sovereignty. Laws LJ stated that Parliamentary Sovereignty was still controlled by the United Kingdom, but it was not the politicians but rather the common law which can modify it. It is the common law that has created the exceptions to implied repeal and can decide whether an Act has succeeded in binding future Parliaments. Addressing the problems created by membership of the European Union, the courts have resolved the problem by creating two supremacies, that of Parliament and the European law where it has competence. Laws LJ took the view that the decision in *Factortame (No.2)* demonstrates that,

> '[t]he conditions of Parliament's legislative supremacy in the United Kingdom necessarily remain in the United Kingdom's hands. But the traditional doctrine has in my judgment been modified. It has been done by the common law, wholly consistently with constitutional principle.[26]

Laws LJ noted that

> Parliament cannot bind its successors by stipulating against repeal, wholly or partly, of the 1972 Act. It cannot stipulate as to the manner and form of any subsequent legislation. It cannot stipulate against implied repeal any more than it can stipulate against express repeal.[27]

His Lordship clearly regarded the decision in *Factortame (No.2)* as holding that section 2(4) cannot be impliedly repealed. What is interesting is that Laws LJ extends the effect of the decision, by stating that where the common law recognises rights as constitutional or fundamental then implied repealed could be modified to protect Acts which are of a constitutional significance. This is a bold statement. Firstly, according to Parliamentary Sovereignty all Acts are the same and should be capable of being impliedly repealed by a later Act; secondly, there is no special status of constitutional law in the United Kingdom; and thirdly, the common law cannot impose limitations on Parliament's legislative ability. Therefore Laws LJ's *obiter* comments are a radical reconsideration of the traditional doctrine of Parliamentary Sovereignty.

Laws LJ argued that constitutional statutes should be protected from implied repeal:

> In the present state of its maturity the common law has come to recognise that there exist rights which should properly be classified as constitutional or fundamental and from this a further insight follows. We should recognise a hierarchy of Acts of Parliament: as it were 'ordinary' statutes and 'constitutional' statutes. The two categories must be distinguished on a principled basis. In my opinion a constitutional statute is one which (a) conditions the legal relationship between citizen and state in some general, overarching manner, or (b) enlarges or diminishes the scope of what we would now regard as fundamental constitutional rights. . . . Ordinary statutes may be impliedly repealed. Constitutional statutes may not . . . *A constitutional statute can only be repealed, or amended* in a way which significantly affects its provisions touching fundamental rights or otherwise the relation between citizen and state, *by unambiguous words on the face of the later statute. . . . (This) preserves the sovereignty of the legislature and the flexibility of our uncodified constitution. . . .* [T]he courts (in interpreting statutes and, now, applying the

Human Rights Act 1998) will pay more or less deference to the legislature, or other public decision-maker, according to the subject in hand.[28]

This is significant as Laws LJ's argument drew a distinction between ordinary and constitutional statutes, something that is contrary to the view that there is no special status of constitutional law. Laws LJ gave examples of constitutional statutes, including the Human Rights Act 1998. Laws LJ was clear that this approach was justified by the constitution, observing that, '[t]he common law has in recent years allowed, or rather created, exceptions to the doctrine of implied repeal, a doctrine which was always the common law's own creature.'[29] However, Laws LJ acknowledged that Parliament could expressly repeal an Act that was protected by implied repeal. It is important to note that Laws LJ's distinction between ordinary and constitutional legislation is *obiter* and is not binding.

6.2.3.1 *R (on the application of HS2 Action Alliance Limited) v The Secretary of State for Transport and another* [2014] UKSC 3

The Supreme Court had an opportunity to explore the issue of constitutional statutes in *R (on the application of HS2 Action Alliance Limited) v The Secretary of State for Transport and another*.[30] The decision concerned the government's decision to build a high-speed railway, known as HS2, linking London and Manchester and Leeds. In his judgment Lord Carnwath observed that:

> Neither the Bill of Rights nor any of the authorities I have mentioned was however referred to in the parties' printed cases; nor was this issue mentioned before us until it was raised by the court. Nevertheless, it follows that the claimants' contentions potentially raise a question as *to the extent, if any, to which these principles may have been implicitly qualified or abrogated by the European Communities Act 1972.*[31]
>
> Contrary to the submission made on behalf of the claimants, *that question cannot be resolved simply by applying the doctrine developed by the Court of Justice of the supremacy of EU law,* since the application of that doctrine in our law itself depends upon the 1972 Act. If there is a conflict between a constitutional principle, such as that embodied in article 9 of the Bill of Rights, and EU law, that conflict has to be resolved by our courts as an issue arising under the constitutional law of the United Kingdom. *Nor can the issue be resolved, as was also suggested, by following the decision in R v Secretary of State for Transport, Ex p Factortame Ltd (No 2) (Case C-213/89) [1991] 1 AC 603, since that case was not concerned with the compatibility with EU law of the process by which legislation is enacted in Parliament.*[32]

This is interesting as any conflict between a key constitutional statute, the Bill of Rights and the process that law was made by Parliament and the UK's obligations under EU law, as given effect to by the European Communities Act 1972, would be determined by the UK courts.

Lord Neuberger and Lord Mance's judgment contained an interesting discussion on the conflict between the European Communities Act 1972 and another constitutional instrument, such as the Bill of Rights:

> Under the European Communities Act 1972, United Kingdom courts have also acknowledged that European law requires them to treat domestic statutes, whether passed before or after the 1972 Act, as invalid if and to the extent that they cannot be interpreted consistently with European law. . . . But it is difficult to see how an English court could fully comply with the approach suggested by the two Advocates General without addressing its apparent conflict with other principles hitherto also regarded as fundamental and enshrined in the Bill of Rights . . .[33]
>
> *The United Kingdom has no written constitution, but we have a number of constitutional instruments.* They include Magna Carta, the Petition of Right 1628, the Bill of Rights and (in Scotland) the Claim of Rights Act 1689, the Act of Settlement 1701 and the Act of Union 1707. The European Communities Act 1972, the Human Rights Act 1998 and the Constitutional Reform Act 2005 may now be added to this list. The common law itself also recognises certain principles as fundamental to the rule of law. It is, putting the point at its lowest, certainly arguable (and it is for United Kingdom law and courts to determine) *that there may be fundamental principles, whether contained in other constitutional instruments or recognised at common law, of which Parliament when it enacted the European Communities Act 1972 did not either contemplate or authorise the abrogation.*[34]
>
> We are not expressing any view on whether or how far article 9 of the Bill of Rights would count among these, but the point is too important to pass without mention. . . . [35]
>
> Important insights into potential issues in this area are to be found in their penetrating discussion by Laws LJ in the Divisional Court in *Thoburn v Sunderland City Council* [2002] EWHC 195 (Admin), [2003] QB 151, (*The Metric Martyrs* case), especially paras 58–70, *although the focus there was the possibility of conflict between an earlier "constitutional" and later "ordinary" statute,* rather than, as here, *between two constitutional instruments,* which raises yet further considerations.[36]

PUBLIC LAW IN CONTEXT
EXTRA-JUDICIAL VIEWS ON CONSTITUTIONAL STATUTES AND WHETHER THESE ARE PROTECTED FROM IMPLIED REPEAL

In an extra-judicial lecture Lord Reed considered the influence of *Thoburn* on identifying constitutional statutes:

The basis for identifying such instruments was not discussed in HS2, but some valuable ideas were put forward by Laws LJ in the Thoburn case and have been developed in the academic literature, particularly by Prof David Feldman. The category of common law constitutional principles has been discussed to some extent in recent cases concerned with human rights and in academic commentary on those cases, and lies beyond the scope of this lecture, but it would include such matters as open justice and judicial independence.[37]

It is interesting to consider whether Laws LJ's *obiter* has now been endorsed and if now there are broadly accepted categories of constitutional statutes, which are to be protected from implied repeal. The answer to can be deduced from Lady Hale's extra-judicial lecture in July 2017, where this was viewed as a potential limitation:

A second *potential limitation* lies in the rules of statutory construction . . . (the second rule) is more recent. This is that *certain Acts of Parliament* are so *constitutionally important* that where later legislation appears inconsistent it is *presumed not impliedly to have repealed the constitutional statute*. This was articulated in the so-called 'metric martyrs' case, where Laws LJ held that the European Communities Act itself was such a statute. The primacy it gave to EU legislation (requiring the use of metric measures) prevailed over a later statute (allowing for the use of imperial measures).[38]

6.2.4 Has Parliament voluntarily surrendered part of its sovereignty?

In *Thoburn* Laws LJ argued that Parliament cannot surrender its sovereignty as the only limitations can be imposed by the common law. In *Jackson* Lady Hale stated that 'Parliament has . . . for the time being at least, limited its own powers by the European Communities Act 1972.'[39] In 2017, Lady Hale observed 'of course, Parliament can voluntarily surrender some of its sovereignty, as it undoubtedly did in the European Communities Act 1972.'[40] Lord Neuberger writing extra-judicially has argued that

[w]hen the courts scrutinise the validity of Acts of Parliament, and refuse to apply them where they are in conflict with European Union law, as happened in *Factortame (No.2)*, they do not so in the teeth of Parliament. They do so precisely because that is what Parliament has chosen to give the courts the power to do.[41]

His Lordship said that the decision was not 'a refutation of Parliamentary sovereignty: on the contrary, it is an instance of its operation.'[42] Finally, in his 2013 Hamlyn Lecture, 'The Common Law and Europe,' Laws LJ argued that the supremacy which European law possesses in this jurisdiction is entirely given by the United Kingdom Parliament. . . . And so, because the supremacy which European law possesses in this jurisdiction is given by the United Kingdom Parliament, the reach of European law is ultimately a function of Parliament's will; and it is of course not to be assumed that Parliament has given the European legislature *carte blanche*.'[43]

Finally, because of the 2016 referendum on the UK's membership of the EU, and the decision to leave the EU, Parliament will expressly repeal the European Communities Act 1972. This will be achieved by the European Union (Withdrawal) Bill when it becomes law. The consequence of the UK leaving the EU is addressed by Lady Hale: '[t]here was a time when our constitutional experts debated whether Parliament could take back the sovereignty it had yielded to the EU or whether it was gone forever. That time is long past.'[44]

6.3 Devolution

The next limitation on Parliamentary Sovereignty is devolution. This is not a legal restriction; rather it is a political restriction on Parliament's ability to make law for Scotland, Northern Ireland and Wales, where certain law-making powers have been devolved from the UK Parliament to each nation's legislative assembly or Parliament. In 1997, the Labour government wanted to devolve power from Westminster and to allow the home nations to have a say over local issues. Brigid Hadfield observed that

> [d]evolution has been presented by successive Labour Governments in terms of the needs to preserve the union, on the one hand, and, on the other, to enhance accountability, responsiveness, inclusiveness and transparency as reflected in new forms of governance for the devolved nation.[45]

The devolution settlement was achieved through the Devolution Acts 1998, which are the Scotland Act 1998, the Government of Wales Act 1998 and the Northern Ireland Act 1998. These Acts created the Scottish Parliament and the National Assembly of Wales (now known as the Welsh Parliament or Senedd Cymru) and the Northern Ireland Assembly was re-established (see Figure 5.8). It is important to appreciate that not all legislative powers have been transferred. The United Kingdom remains a unitary state as power is devolved from Westminster and could be revoked. However, in reality devolution has created more of a quasi-unitary system, with the appearance of an increasingly federal structure. This move towards an increasingly federal structure will continue and could be acknowledged in any future attempt to introduce a written constitution for the UK.

Whilst the Scotland Act 1998 gave the Scottish Parliament law-making powers, it was not until the Government of Wales Act 2006 that the National Assembly of Wales received law-making powers. Despite being able to create

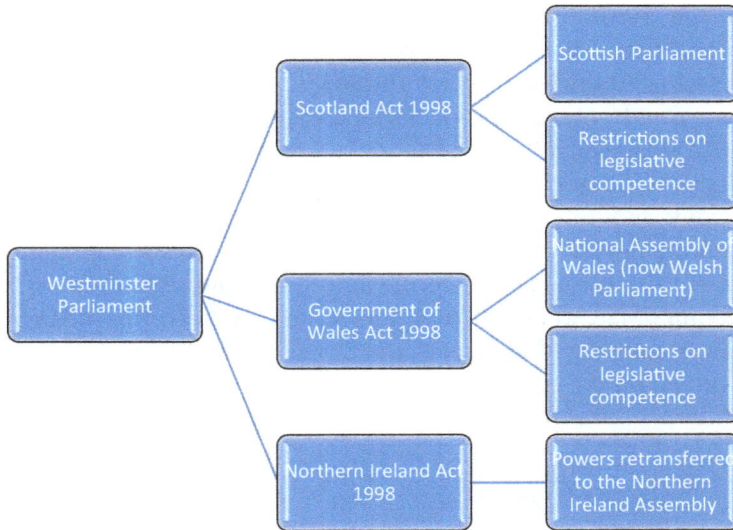

Figure 6.3
Devolution in the United Kingdom

legislation, these new legislative bodies cannot legislate where they have no competence to do so as the Westminster Parliament has restricted their legislative capability. Any attempt to enact legislate that fell outside of the lawmaking powers devolved would be ultra vires.

6.3.1 The Scotland Act 1998

Section 1 of the Scotland Act 1998 created the Scottish Parliament, which sits at Holyrood. Section 28 concerns legislation passed by the Scottish Parliament which are known as Acts of the Scottish Parliament. As with Acts of the Westminster Parliament, section 28(5) states that, '[t]he validity of an Act of the Scottish Parliament is not affected by any invalidity in the proceedings of the Parliament leading to its enactment.' Crucially, Section 28(7) states that, '[t]his section does not affect the power of the Parliament of the United Kingdom to make laws for Scotland.' Section 29(1) clearly states that, '[a]n Act of the Scottish Parliament is not law so far as any provision of the Act is outside the legislative competence of the Parliament.' If an Act of the Scottish Parliament legislates for section 29(1)(b) reserved matters, or breaches the restrictions in schedule 4 (s.20(1)(c)), or importantly is 'incompatible with any of the Convention rights or with Community law'[46] then the Act will be invalid. As we shall see below, unlike an Act of the Westminster Parliament, the Scottish Parliament cannot legislate contrary to the Convention rights which are incorporated into domestic law by the Human Rights Act 1998. The task of reviewing Scottish legislation will fall to the courts.

An Act of the Scottish Parliament is not legally sovereign. The Scottish Parliament can only legislate where Westminster holds that it has competence to do so. The Westminster Parliament could still legislate for areas where the Scottish Parliament has been given competence. In *AXA General Insurance Ltd and others v HM Advocate and others*[47] the Supreme Court held that the Scottish Parliament could only legislate in those areas that had been devolved to it by the UK Parliament. Whilst the Supreme Court could ensure that the Scottish Parliament did not exceed the limits from section 29 of the Scotland Act 1998, it could judicially review whether the Scottish Parliament in creating law within the devolved areas had acted irrationally. This was because it was up to the Scottish Parliament to decide how to legislate and the courts had no role at common law to review an Act. Craig and Walters, who had observed that there is authority that Acts of the Scottish Parliament cannot be judicially reviewed on the grounds of irrationality, had previously advocated this approach.[48]

6.3.1.1 The Scottish Parliament

As with the UK Parliament, the party with a majority in the Scottish Parliament will form a government (although in the past there have been coalition governments). The current government formed by the Scottish National Party and is headed by Nicola Sturgeon, the First Minister of Scotland. Barry Winetrobe observed that the UK government wanted the Scottish government to be based on the Westminster model, which permits a single party government and does not require power sharing between all the political parties who are represented in Parliament, as is the case in Northern Ireland. Winetrobe noted that 'the relationship between the Scottish Executive and the Scottish Parliament will be similar to the relationship between the UK Government and the UK Parliament.'[49] In *AXA General Insurance Ltd* Lord Hope drew an analogy between the relationship of the UK Government and UK Parliament (where the government normally enjoys a majority) and the relationship between the Scottish Government and Scottish Parliament:

> We now have in Scotland a government which enjoys a large majority in the Scottish Parliament. Its party dominates the only chamber in that Parliament and the committees by which bills that are in progress are scrutinised. It is not entirely unthinkable that a government which has that power may seek to use it to abolish judicial review or to diminish the role of the courts in protecting the interests of the individual. Whether this is likely to happen is not the point. It is enough that it might conceivably do so. The rule of law requires that the judges must retain the power to insist that legislation of that extreme kind is not law which the courts will recognise.[50]

This is interesting as it draws upon the concern that exists about the UK Parliament and the *obiter* from the House of Lords' decision in *Jackson* (see below), to suggest that the court could decide that it could review an Act of the Scottish Parliament.

6.3.1.2 The 2014 independence referendum and the Scotland Act 2016

In 2011, the Scottish National Party won an overwhelming majority in the elections for the Scottish Parliament and argued that they had secured a mandate for holding a referendum on Scottish independence. The referendum took place on 18 September 2014 and voters were asked '[s]hould Scotland be an independent country?' For the first time, young adults aged 16–17 were permitted to vote. The outcome was narrowly in favour of remaining as part of the UK. If there had been a 'yes' vote, then legally it would have been the Westminster Parliament which would have had to give Scotland its independence. This would have been achieved by repealing the Act of Union with Scotland 1706.

What effect does Scottish devolution have on Parliamentary Sovereignty? Parliament is still the superior law-making body in the United Kingdom. The Scotland Act 1998 did not prevent Parliament from legislating for Scotland. Even if it did, Parliament could still expressly repeal the Act at a later date. There is a convention established known as the Sewel Motion, which states that the Westminster Parliament would not legislate for devolved matters As a result of the referendum outcome and the promise made by the main UK political parties to devolve more powers to Scotland, the Scotland Act 2016 transferred more law-making areas to the Scottish Parliament. The Scotland Act 2016 contains several constitutionally significant provisions.

PUBLIC LAW IN CONTEXT
THE SCOTLAND ACT 2016

Section 1 of the Scotland Act 2016 concerns the permanence of the Scottish Parliament and the Scottish Government and inserts section 63A into the Scotland Act 1998. It states:

1   The Scottish Parliament and the Scottish Government are a permanent part of the United Kingdom's constitutional arrangements.
2   The purpose of this section is, with due regard to the other provisions of this Act, to signify the commitment of the Parliament and Government of the United Kingdom to the Scottish Parliament and the Scottish Government.
3   In view of that commitment it is declared that the Scottish Parliament and the Scottish Government are not to be abolished except on the basis of a decision of the people of Scotland voting in a referendum.

This is a clear statement by the UK Parliament that the Scottish Parliament and Scottish Government are permanent and will not be abolished by Westminster. However, Parliament could legislate to repeal this section and unilaterally abolish both institutions.

Section 2 of the Scotland Act 2016 concerns the Sewel Convention. It has inserted subsection (8) into section 28 of the Scotland Act 1998: 'But it is recognised that the Parliament of the United Kingdom will not normally legislate with regard to devolved matters without the consent of the Scottish Parliament.' This is an example of a convention being placed on a statutory footing. Comparisons could be drawn here with the Statute of Westminster 1931, which could not prevent a future Parliament from unilaterally legislating for a former UK Dominion.

Would Parliament legislate contrary to the Scotland Act 1998? This not a legal question but rather a political one. The consequence of such legislation might ultimately result in Scottish independence. If there were to be a violation of the powers devolved to Scotland, then this would lead to calls for a second referendum to be held on Scottish independence. Any government will be wary of introducing legislation that would seek to legislate for devolved matters. The Scotland Act 1998 reserves all constitutional matters to the Westminster Parliament. Therefore, the Scottish government and Scottish Parliament, as devolved bodies, would be acting illegally if they attempted to hold their own referendum. If Scotland had pressed ahead and held a referendum and subsequently declared unilateral independence, then this would be legally ineffective. However, this would demonstrate a practical limit to the sovereignty of the Westminster Parliament. In order to hold a referendum there needed to be an agreement between the British and Scottish governments. This is known as the Edinburgh Agreement and increased the legislative competence of the Scottish Parliament to hold a referendum.[51] However, the only way Scotland can receive its independence is through an Act of Parliament.

Finally, Professor John McEldowney has observed that '[t]he legal sovereignty of the UK Parliament has not been diminished by devolution, but democratically and politically the devolved institutions have rival and strong claims to legitimacy within their areas and these affect the politics of UK parliamentary sovereignty.'[52] Therefore, whilst Scotland remains part of the United Kingdom this will lead to more powers being devolved to Holyrood from Westminster.

6.3.2 The Government of Wales Acts 1998 and 2006

The Government of Wales Act 1998 created the National Assembly of Wales. The National Assembly of Wales has been renamed as the Welsh Parliament or Senedd Cymru of Wales and sits in Cardiff. The party who can command the support of the Welsh Parliament will form a government. The Government of Wales Act 2006 devolved more powers to the Welsh Parliament. According to section 81 the Welsh Parliament cannot legislate contrary to Convention rights, which are now incorporated under the Human Rights Act 1998. Similarly, section 82 reiterates this restriction with regards to international obligations (such as international law). Therefore, the Welsh Parliament is not a sovereign legislative body. The Government of Wales Acts have not legally restricted Parliamentary Sovereignty, but rather have placed political restrictions on areas that the UK Parliament can legislate on.

6.3.2.1 The Wales Act 2017

The Wales Act 2017 has introduced several constitutionally significant amendments to the Government of Wales Act 2006. The Wales Act 2017 has inserted Part A1 into the Government of Wales Act 2006. This states that '(1) The Assembly established by Part 1 and the Welsh Government . . . are a permanent part of the United Kingdom's constitutional arrangements' and '(2) The purpose of this section is, with due regard to the other provisions of this Act, to signify the commitment of the Parliament and Government of the United Kingdom to the Assembly and the Welsh Government.' This promise as to the permanence of the Welsh devolved institutions is further reinforced, '(3) In view of that commitment it is declared that the Assembly and the Welsh Government are not to be abolished except on the basis of a decision of the people of Wales voting in a referendum.' However, this is not a legal restriction on Parliamentary Sovereignty, as a future UK Parliament could legislate to abolish both devolved institutions. Whilst section 107(5) of the Government of Wales Act 2006 was explicit in stating that the UK Parliament still had the power to makes law for Wales, the Wales Act 2017 creates a new constitutional convention, which states '[b]ut it is recognised that the Parliament of the United Kingdom will not normally legislate with regard to devolved matters without the consent of the Assembly.'[53]

6.3.3 The Northern Ireland Act 1998

The Northern Ireland Assembly is based at Stormont and is not based on the Westminster model. The parties are required to share power, rather than the largest party forming a government. During the Troubles in Northern Ireland the powers of the Assembly were revoked and the province was ruled from Westminster. Powers were devolved in 1998 as a result of the Good Friday peace agreement that brought the Troubles to a close.

6.4 The Human Rights Act 1998

On 10 October 2000 the Human Rights Act 1998 came into force. It had the effect of directly incorporating most of the European Convention on Human Rights into English law. The Human Rights Act 1998 allows Convention rights to be directly enforced by domestic courts where there has been a breach of these rights by a public authority.[54] Prior to 2000, Convention rights were not enforceable in domestic courts and British citizens had to take their case to the European Court of Human Rights which is based at Strasbourg. If the party were successful at Strasbourg the United Kingdom would be under an obligation to pay damages. The rights contained in European Convention on Human Rights are very important.

The Human Rights Act 1998 was never intended to limit Parliamentary Sovereignty. Unlike the fundamental rights protected by the Canadian constitution[55] the domestic courts do not have the power to strike down or dissapply an Act of Parliament which is held to be incompatible with the Human Rights Act 1998. There if the intention of Parliament was that the HRA 1998 would not limit Parliamentary Sovereignty, then does the effect of the Act in practice impose any limitation? To answer this question it is necessary to consider sections 3 and 4 of the Human Rights Act 1998. Section 3 concerns the interpretation of legislation and gives courts the following instruction: '[s]o far as it is possible to do so, primary legislation and subordinate legislation must be read and given effect in a way which is compatible with the Convention rights.' Section 3 gives the courts extremely wide interpretive powers to read primary legislation as though it were Convention compliant. This means that the courts can read words into a statute to give effect to Convention rights. This interpretive power is novel (with the exception of ECA 1972) in domestic law and the courts can go beyond the words used by Parliament when it passes an Act. Section 3 'does not affect the validity, continuing operation or enforcement of any incompatible primary legislation,' which means that the Act will remain unchanged and it is still valid. The courts can question an Act of Parliament and have considerable scope to amend the effect of an Act.

ACADEMIC DEBATE
THE IMPACT OF SECTION 3 OF THE HUMAN RIGHTS ACT 1998

The use of section 3 raises the problem of judges becoming lawmakers and reading down words into a statute that are contrary to what Parliament intended. The use of section 3 has proved to be controversial in practice. Alison Young questions whether Parliament, as a result of section 3, has given the courts considerable power to restrict Parliamentary Sovereignty:

Section 3(1) appears to limit the powers of the court, allowing them to interpret statutes in a manner compatible with Convention rights only when it is possible to do so. However, in practice, Parliament has given the judiciary carte blanche to determine when it is impossible to interpret statutes in a manner compatible with Convention rights. The express words of section 3(1) are so vague that they do not provide a clear outline of the limits of possibility. . . . Moreover, it raises issues as to the reality of parliamentary supremacy, particularly when delineating the respective roles of the judiciary and the legislature. How can the judiciary respect Parliament's intention with regard to its role under section 3(1) of the Act, if Parliament has made its intentions so unclear as to place the court fully in charge of delineating its own power? Parliamentary sovereignty has given way to judicial sovereignty.[56]

The courts need to ascertain the intention of Parliament and ensure that its interpretation of statutes respects this. Section 3 requires the courts to look for the key intention of Parliament, and not just the natural and ordinary meaning of the words used. Sir Philip Sales explained this approach:

> [t]he limit of the interpretative obligation is whether it is "possible" to construe the domestic legislation compatibly with . . . Convention rights. . . . It will not be "possible" to construe domestic legislation in this way if to do so would distort or undermine some important feature of the legislation. Parliamentary sovereignty is thus preserved, but in a somewhat attenuated sense. . . . The application of the relevant test calls for a value judgment on the part of the court, to assess whether Parliament has expressed some sort of fundamental intention in the legislation which it must be presumed from the scheme of the legislation and the language it has used it would not have been willing to sacrifice if confronted at the time with objections based on . . . Convention rights. Since the court is required not to confine itself to determining the intention of Parliament simply from the words used and the usual canons of construction, but has to try to assess whether the intention derived from the words of the legislation is of an essential character or not, this is not a straightforward exercise. In effect, the courts have to examine whether some departure from what has hitherto been regarded as the natural meaning of the statute is justified, having regard to the general objective of producing compatibility with Convention rights set by s.3 of the HRA, but balancing that objective against the general long-stop preservation of parliamentary sovereignty inherent in the HRA: can a compatible construction be produced without generating excessive friction or dissonance in terms of the Parliamentary intent to be derived from the words of the legislation to be construed?[57]

One of the most controversial uses of section 3 to read down words into a statute was in *R v A (Complainant's Sexual History)*[58]. This case concerned whether the defendant in a rape trial could adduce evidence as to the victim's sexual history. Section 41 of the Youth Justice and Criminal Evidence Act 1999 stated that the defendant was unable to do this unless the court could rely on one of the three narrow exceptions. Parliament had intended to restrict the discretion of the trial judge in controlling when such evidence was admissible. In *R v A (Complainant's Sexual History)* the House of Lords held that section 41 of the Youth Justice and Criminal Evidence Act 1999 breached Article 6 of the European Convention on Human Rights and deprived the defendant of a fair trial. The House of Lords used section 3 to read down words and interpreted section 41 to allow evidence of the victim's previous sexual history to be admitted.

Aileen Kavanagh contrasted the supposedly different approaches of Lord Hope and Lord Steyn and has argued that the academic criticism ignores the fact that the House of Lords' decision to rely on section 3 was unanimous.[59] In *R v A (Complainant's Sexual History)* it was Lord Steyn's judgment that was the most controversial. As Kavanagh argued,

Lord Steyn was clear at the outset of his judgment in *A* that the interpretative obligation under s.3 is a strong one, which applies even if there is no ambiguity in the language. This point is uncontroversial. It was endorsed by Lord Hope in *R. v. A*, and has been followed in subsequent decisions of the House of Lords and supported by many of the senior judiciary.[60]

What was more controversial was Lord Steyn's statement that

[i]n accordance with the will of Parliament as reflected in s.3 it will sometimes be necessary to adopt an interpretation which linguistically may appear strained. The techniques to be used will not only involve the reading down of express language in a statute but also the implication of provisions.'[61]

Kavanagh observed that:

The most prominent reason given by critics of *A* for its illegitimacy is that it went against what Parliament intended when they enacted s.41 YJCEA. . . . There is no denying that the interpretation in *A* is contrary to Parliament's intention to control the admissibility of sexual history evidence by way of the narrowly circumscribed gateways alone. Parliament decided against the 'safety valve approach' which would allow judges a residual discretion to admit evidence it would be unsafe to exclude, and the judges nonetheless read this discretion into the legislation. Does this render the decision in *R. v. A* illegitimate?[62]

Gavin Phillipson and Conor Gearty have debated how section 3 should be used by the courts, based of their respective interpretations of the Human Rights Act 1998.[63] Commenting on *R v A*, Phillipson remarked, 'it may tentatively be hazarded that the real reason for the markedly activist stance taken in *R. v A* was a judicial desire to protect the judges' own sphere of discretion over an area traditionally jealously preserved – the admissibility of evidence – from interference by Parliament.'[64]

In *Re S, Re W (Minors)*[65] Lord Nicholls held that the Court of Appeal had overstepped a constitutional boundary and had disregarded the intention of Parliament. The Court of Appeal had used section 3 to read words into section 31 of the Children Act 1989 in order to make the provision Convention compliant. His Lordship stated that the courts should not ignore Parliament's intention and observed that, 'a meaning which departs substantially from a fundamental feature of an Act of Parliament is likely to have crossed the boundary between interpretation and amendment.'[66] Lord Nicholls held that the courts had to have regard to the fundamental purpose of the Act. If the court's interpretation of the statute is different than what Parliament had intended, then the courts will have overstepped the mark, by having used section 3 to amend rather than to interpret the legislation. His Lordship's approach allows the court to interpret an Act to give the victim a remedy, whilst still upholding the doctrine of Parliamentary Sovereignty:

> But the reach of this tool is not unlimited. Section 3 is concerned with interpretation. . . . In applying section 3 courts must be ever mindful of this outer limit. The Human Rights Act reserves the amendment of primary legislation to Parliament. By this means the Act seeks to preserve parliamentary sovereignty. The Act maintains the constitutional boundary. Interpretation of statutes is a matter for the courts; the enactment of statutes, and the amendment of statutes, are matters for Parliament.[67]

The decision in *R (on the application of Anderson) v Secretary of State for the Home Department*[68] concerned the Home Secretary's power to fix the tariff of a prisoner's sentence. Anderson had been sentenced for a tariff at imprisonment for 15 years. The Home Secretary raised the tariff to 20 years under section 29 of the Crime (Sentences) Act 1997. The House of Lords held that this power being used to increase the tariff was a violation of Article 6 of the ECHR. The House of Lords refused to use section 3 of the Human Rights Act 1998 to interpret the Crime (Sentences) Act 1997 to make it compatible with Article 6 ECHR. The rationale for this was not to infringe upon what Parliament had quite clearly intended, with Lord Steyn observing 'In this way Parliamentary sovereignty was preserved.'[69] Lord Bingham was clear that,

> To read section 29 as precluding participation by the Home Secretary, if it were possible to do so, would not be judicial interpretation but judicial vandalism: it would give the section an effect quite different from that which Parliament intended and would go well beyond any interpretative process sanctioned by section 3 of the 1998 Act.[70]

Lord Steyn observed that, 'Section 3(1) is not available where the suggested interpretation is contrary to express statutory words or is by implication necessarily contradicted by the statute.'[71] However, because section 29 of the Act was inconsistent with Article 6 ECHR, the House of Lords used its powers under section 4 of the Human Rights Act 1998 to issue a declaration of incompatibility.

The decision in *Ghaidan v Godin-Mendoza*[72] concerned whether a homosexual partner fell within the protection afforded by the Rent Act 1977. The defendant's partner had died, and he wanted to become a protected assured tenant, which protected 'spouses' in the event of a tenant's death. Did a homosexual partner fall within the definition of spouse? The House of Lords relied on section 3 and interpreted spouse to include homosexual partners. Lord Steyn defended his approach to section 3. His Lordship stated that, '[i]f Parliament disagrees with an interpretation by the courts under section 3(1), it is free to override it by amending the legislation and expressly reinstating the incompatibility.'[73] His Lordship stated that if the Convention rights were to be 'brought home' then UK citizens would need to be able to rely on the courts using section 3, as opposed to section 4. This was because:

In enacting the 1998 Act Parliament legislated 'to bring rights home' from the European Court of Human Rights to be determined in the courts of the United Kingdom. . . . That is what Parliament was told. The mischief to be addressed was the fact that Convention rights as set out in the ECHR, which Britain ratified in 1951, could not be vindicated in our courts. Critical to this purpose was the enactment of effective remedial provisions. . . .[74]

The linch-pin of the legislative scheme to achieve this purpose was section 3(1). Rights could only be effectively brought home if section 3(1) was the prime remedial measure, and section 4 a measure of last resort.[75]

Where it is not possible to use section 3 to give effect to Convention rights, a court (from the High Court to the Supreme Court) may instead issue a section 4 declaration of incompatibility. A declaration of incompatibility declares to Parliament that the Act violates a Convention right. The courts cannot declare the Act to be invalid and it remains good law. The courts have no power to strike down incompatible legislation. The person whose rights have been violated will not usually have a remedy if the courts are unable to use section 3 and instead issue a section 4 declaration of incompatibility. It is for this reason that Lord Steyn preferred the use of section 3 rather than section 4.

Shona Wilson Stark has observed that the reason for this preference for section 3 over section 4 can be deduced from the background to the Human Rights Act 1998:

> During the Human Rights Bill's passage through Parliament, Lord Irvine (then Lord Chancellor, and architect of the Bill) said that declarations of incompatibility would be unnecessary 'in 99 per cent. of cases that will arise.' Such statements have set the tone for judicial caution around s.4, and what has been criticised as overreliance on s.3. But why did the Lord Chancellor feel the need to all but strangle s.4 at birth?[76]

Shona Wilson Stark argues that the judges have 'shown reluctance and confusion towards their novel power' and need to be more consistent in how they use this power.[77] It is not a strike down as enjoyed by the US Supreme Court and therefore would not result in an Act becoming void. There have been only been 29 Declarations of Incompatibility made since October 2000.[78] The majority of these have resulted in the Act being amended to remove the incompatibility. The only time that the government has not done this is in regards to the declaration made in *Smith v Scott*[79], which concerned a blanket ban on prisoner voting. In 2013 the UK Supreme Court in *R (on the application of Chester) v Secretary of State for Justice*[80] held that the ban was incompatible with the European Convention on Human Rights and for the reasons giving in the two judgments, did not issue a declaration.

It is important to appreciate that section 10 of the Human Rights Act 1998 gives the government the power to take remedial action where a section 4 declaration has been issued. This avoids the need for Parliament to amend the offending legislation and permits a fast-track process to make an Act of

Parliament compatible with the European Convention on Human Rights. The Human Rights Act 1998 is not just concerned with whether an Act of Parliament complies with the Convention, as section 19 requires the minister who is in charge of introducing a bill into Parliament to provide a statement that the bill is compatible with the Convention rights. This requirement would not prevent Parliament legislating in a manner that clearly breaches the Convention; however it places a requirement on the government to flag up this violation at the moment the bill is introduced into Parliament.

Finally, Adam Wagner and Gideon Barth have reviewed the use of section 3 by the courts and have observed that '[d]espite the reach of s. 3 elucidated in *Ghaidan*, the courts have also demonstrated a reluctance to undermine the apparent intention of Parliament'[81] and '[i]n recent years, the courts have been willing to use s. 3 but the activist approach of *R v A* and *Ghaidan* seen in the early years has receded'[82]. Furthermore, '[i]f the limits of the power of s. 3 remain elusive, the courts at least have clarified to which legislation s. 3 applies. It does not apply to an Order in Council giving royal assent to legislation passed by the legislature of the Channel Islands. . .'[83] An example of this is the Court of Appeal's decision in *Adesina v Nursing and Midwifery Council*[84], where the court was clear that any reading down using section 3 must be 'to the minimum extent necessary to secure compliance with Convention.'[85]

6.5 The decision in *R (Jackson) v Attorney-General* [2005] UKHL 56 and the rule of law

This chapter has previously discussed the background to the House of Lords' decision in *Jackson*. In reaching their decision the members of the House of Lords made some very interesting *obiter* comments on the nature of Parliamentary Sovereignty in the 21st century. Lord Bingham reiterated that

> [t]he bedrock of the British constitution is, and in 1911 was, the supremacy of the Crown in Parliament. . . . Then, as now, the Crown in Parliament was unconstrained by any entrenched or codified constitution. It could make or unmake any law it wished. Statutes, formally enacted as Acts of Parliament, properly interpreted, enjoyed the highest legal authority.'[86]

This is clearly the traditional view of the doctrine. However, there were other very different views expressed

6.5.1 The potential validity of a manner and form requirement

Lord Steyn challenged the traditional doctrine of Parliamentary Sovereignty. His Lordship did so in a number of ways. According to the traditional doctrine, Parliament is not bound by manner and form, which means that an Act which

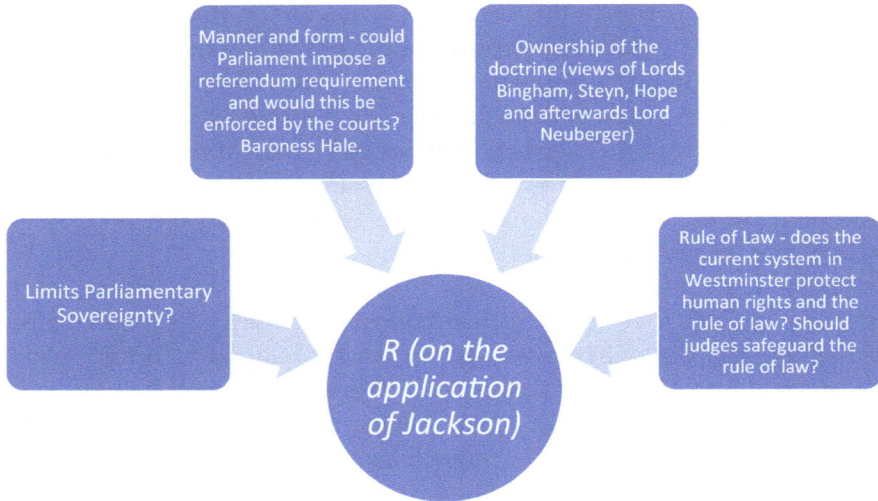

Figure 6.4
Issues arising out of the decision in *Jackson*

established special procedural or voting requirements to repeal it could not prevent these requirements from being ignored at a later date. However, Lord Steyn stated that,

> [a]part from the traditional method of law making, Parliament acting as ordinarily constituted may functionally redistribute legislative power in different ways. For example, Parliament could for specific purposes provide for a two-thirds majority in the House of Commons and the House of Lords. This would involve a redefinition of Parliament for a specific purpose. Such redefinition could not be disregarded.[87]

This is important as His Lordship is suggesting that a manner and form requirement could bind future Parliaments and that the courts would not disregard such requirements when enquiring into the validity of a future Act. Lord Steyn referred to an article written by Owen Dixon in 1935:

> [t]he very power of constitutional alteration cannot be exercised except in the form and manner which the law for the time being prescribes. Unless the legislature observes that manner and form, its attempt to alter its constitution is void. It may amend or abrogate for the future the law which prescribes that form or that manner. But, in doing so, it must comply with its very requirements.[88]

His Lordship referred to *Attorney General for New South Wales v Trethowan*[89], where the court had ruled that as legislation required a referendum to abolish the Upper House of the New South Wales Parliament, any Act purporting to do this without having first held a referendum would be invalid. Lord Steyn then referred to *Harris v Minister of the Interior*[90] which was a South African decision that concerned the voting rights of non-white nationals in South Africa who were protected by a requirement that any changes to the legislation required a two-thirds majority. The Supreme Court found that an Act that did not fulfil the requirement was void. It is clear that His Lordship was keen to point out that in other common law jurisdictions manner and form requirements have been held to be effective.

Baroness Hale argued that if Parliament could remove the requirement for the consent of the House of Lords, then a binding manner and form requirement could be possible. If that were so, then a court could require Parliament to comply with such a requirement. However, Her Ladyship does not attempt to provide a definitive answer. Baroness Hale had observed:

> What the Commonwealth cases do suggest, however, is the contrary proposition: that if Parliament is required to pass legislation on particular matters in a particular way, then Parliament is not permitted to ignore those requirements when passing legislation on those matters, nor is it permitted to remove or relax those requirements by passing legislation in the ordinary way. . . . If the sovereign Parliament can redefine itself downwards, to remove or modify the requirement for the consent of the Upper House, it may very well be that it can also redefine itself upwards, to require a particular parliamentary majority or a popular referendum for particular types of measure. In each case, the courts would be respecting the will of the sovereign Parliament as constituted when that will had been expressed. But that is for another day.[91]

This is powerful *obiter* as it suggests that if Parliament were to do this, then the courts could uphold the manner and form requirement. This is only *obiter*, although it is important to appreciate that if such a scenario were to reach the new Supreme Court then it would be the court that would determine the enforceability of manner and form requirements.

6.5.2 Parliamentary Sovereignty is not absolute

Lord Steyn observed that Parliamentary Sovereignty was the general principle of the United Kingdom's constitution, but rejected the view that it was absolute and without restriction. His Lordship believed that the courts can qualify Parliamentary Sovereignty and could potentially declare an Act void. Importantly, His Lordship viewed the doctrine as a common law construct – one that is a common law rule. The consequence of this is important, as if we follow His Lordship's interpretation, then the courts could legitimately modify their own rule. Lord Steyn did not accept that there could be no qualifications on Parliament's legislative sovereignty. It is important to break down Lord Steyn's argument to appreciate exactly what he is saying: 'The classic account given by Dicey of the doctrine of the supremacy of Parliament, pure and absolute as it was, can now be seen to be out of place in the modern United Kingdom.'[92]

It is clear that Lord Steyn views Dicey's account is outdated and does not reflect the modern understanding of Parliamentary Sovereignty. 'Nevertheless, the supremacy of Parliament is still the general principle of our constitution. It is a construct of the common law.'[93]

Lord Steyn is arguing that it is a general principle, which implies that there are qualifications. He is also arguing that it was created by the judges. 'The judges created this principle. If that is so, it is not unthinkable that circumstances could arise where the courts may have to qualify a principle established on a different hypothesis of constitutionalism.'[94] Therefore, Lord Steyn is arguing that if the judges created the principle of Parliamentary Sovereignty, then they are capable of deciding to impose limits.

> In exceptional circumstances involving an attempt to abolish judicial review or the ordinary role of the courts, the . . . new Supreme Court may have to consider whether this is constitutional fundamental which even a sovereign Parliament acting at the behest of a complaisant House of Commons cannot abolish.[95]

Finally, it is important to appreciate that Lord Steyn is not advocating giving the courts a wide power to qualify what Parliament may do; rather such a power is consigned to where Parliament attempts to do things that adversely impact upon the rule of law. Lord Steyn is also drawing attention to the danger of the government's majority in the House of Commons dominating Parliament and passing whatever law the government wishes. Whether the government does in fact dominate and whether Parliament is subservient is a moot point.

PUBLIC LAW IN CONTEXT
A JUDICIAL WARNING

Writing extra-judicially former Lord Chief Justice of England, Lord Woolf, had previously argued something very similar to Lord Steyn:

> But what happens if a party with a large majority in Parliament uses that majority to abolish the courts' entire power of judicial review in express terms? . . . Do the courts then accept that the legislation means what it says? . . . my own personal view is that they do not. . . Our parliamentary democracy is based on the rule of law. One of the twin principles upon which the rule of law depends is the supremacy of Parliament in its legislative capacity. The other principle is that the courts are the final arbiters as to the interpretation and application of the law. As both Parliament and the courts derive their authority from the rule of law so both are subject to it and can not act in manner which involves its repudiation. . . . [I]f Parliament did the unthinkable, then I would say that the courts would also be required to act in a manner which would be without precedent. Some judges might chose to do so by saying that it was an unrebuttable presumption that Parliament

could never intend such a result. I myself would consider there were advantages in making it clear that ultimately there are even limits on the supremacy of Parliament which it is the courts' inalienable responsibility to identify and uphold.[96]

Lord Hope agreed with Lord Steyn and observed that,

[o]ur constitution is dominated by the sovereignty of Parliament. But Parliamentary sovereignty is no longer, if it ever was, absolute. . . . It is no longer right to say that its freedom to legislate admits of no qualification whatever. Step by step, gradually but surely, the English principle of absolute legislative sovereignty of Parliament which Dicey derived from Coke and Blackstone is being qualified.[97]

His Lordship is describing an incremental process where Parliamentary Sovereignty is being reconsidered and will evolve over time.

6.5.3 *The importance of the rule of law*

Lord Hope stated that

[t]he rule of law enforced by the courts is the ultimate controlling factor on which our constitution is based. The fact that your Lordships have been willing to hear this appeal and to give judgment upon it is another indication that the courts have a part to play in defining the limits of Parliament's legislative sovereignty.[98]

Observance of the rule of law may appear to be at odds with the unqualified supremacy of Parliament. This is because the Parliament could legislate contrary to what is required by both the procedural and substantive versions of the rule of law. This raises the possibility that the Supreme Court in the future might be asked to choose between the two.

6.5.4 *Judicial treatment of the* obiter *in* Jackson

In *Moohan v Lord Advocate*[99] Lord Hodge considered whether the common law could ever declare legislation to be unlawful:

While the common law cannot extend the franchise beyond that provided by parliamentary legislation, I do not exclude the possibility that in the very unlikely event that a parliamentary majority abusively sought to entrench its power by a curtailment of the franchise or similar device, the common law, informed by principles of democracy and the rule of law and international norms, would be able to declare such legislation unlawful. The existence and extent of such a power is a matter of debate, at least in the context of the doctrine of the sovereignty of the United Kingdom Parliament. . . . But such a circumstance is very far removed from the present case, and there is no need to express any view on that question.[100]

The Court of Appeal of Northern Ireland considered the *obiter* in *In the matter of application by JR80 for Judicial Review*.[101] It had been argued at first instance that legislation (the Northern Ireland [Executive Formation and Exercise of Functions] Act 2018) was of an 'extreme, offensive or repugnant nature contemplated by Lords Steyn and Hope.'[102] The court observed:

> It can be seen that *Jackson* did not decide that there was a common law exception to the principle that 'the courts in this country have no power to declare enacted law to be invalid' but even if there was such an exception the threshold for its operation is extraordinarily high. It is on the basis of these obiter comments in *Jackson* that Mr Macdonald contends that the 2018 Act is in breach of such constitutional fundamentals or is so absurd or so unacceptable leading to the populace at large refusing to recognise it as law that this court should declare it to be invalid.[103]

6.5.5 Putting Jackson *into context*

Lord Carswell struck a note of caution in *Jackson* and observed that '[a]s a judge I am very conscious of the proper reluctance of the courts to intervene in issues of the validity of Acts of Parliament. I should be most unwilling to decide this or any other case in a way which would endanger that tradition of mutual respect.'[104] Lord Neuberger, writing extra-judicially, rejected Lord Steyn's proposition that the courts created Parliamentary Sovereignty:

> I cannot accept the accuracy of the claim that Parliamentary sovereignty is a product of the common law, or that, because common law existed prior to Parliament's 'legislative supremacy' . . . I am not aware of any authority which supports, let alone establishes, the proposition that the common law created Parliamentary sovereignty. Nor am I aware of any significant authority which suggests that the common law can justify the courts lawfully setting aside or invalidating a statute. . . . I doubt that Lord Steyn would suggest that that provides much of a foundation for his doubts about Parliamentary sovereignty.'[105]

Lord Bingham in his book *The Rule of Law* rejected the idea that the judges established Parliamentary Sovereignty, stating that they have just accepted its existence: '[t]he judges did not by themselves establish the principle, and they cannot, by themselves, change it.'[106] In 2011, in an extra-judicial lecture Lord Hope responded to Lord Neuberger's comments on the decision in *Jackson*:

[Lord Neuberger] concluded that the doctrine of Parliamentary sovereignty remains as it was declared to be by Dicey. Although he recognised that the judges have a vital role to play in protecting individuals against the abuses and excesses of an increasingly powerful executive, he said that we cannot go against Parliament's will as expressed through a statute. That, with respect, seems to be to a dangerous doctrine unless one can be absolutely confident that the increasingly powerful executive will not abuse the legislative authority of a Parliament which, ex hypothesi, it controls because of the absolute majority that it enjoys in the House of Commons.[107]

Lord Hope was aware that Parliament could choose to legislate contrary to the rule of law and that the judiciary should remind the government that there are limits on what it could do. This is a clear warning that the courts could limit the legislative ability of Parliament. Furthermore, Lord Hope remarked that, '[t]he absence of a general power to strike down legislation which it has enacted does not mean that the courts could never fashion a remedy for use in an exceptional case where the survival of the rule of law itself was threatened because their role as the ultimate guardians of it was being removed from them.'[108] This indicates that the courts reserve the right to limit Parliamentary Sovereignty should the need arise. Is Lord Hope correct? Could the United Kingdom's Supreme Court declare an Act of Parliament to be invalid on the grounds that it is repugnant to the rule of law, i.e. unconstitutional? Professor Dawn Oliver considered the outcome of a judicial strikedown of an Act of Parliament and noted that such action would prove to be counter-productive.[109] Oliver argued that

[i]n my view therefore it could well be extremely unwise, damaging to the authority of the judiciary and the rule of law itself and to the stability of our constitutional arrangements, and counter-productive for the courts to strike down a provision in an Act, however much it is contrary to some of the elements of the rule of law and other constitutional 'principles.'[110]

This is a clear warning to the courts on claiming such a power, even if could be argued in principle, it would not work in practice and would weaken the judiciary.

PUBLIC LAW IN PRACTICE

Considering the fallout from the High Court's decision in *R (on the application of Miller) v Secretary of State for Exiting the European Union*[111], where the *Daily Mail* branded the judges as the 'Enemies of the People,' it might be useful to imagine what might happen where a future Parliament passes an Act that is popular with those members of the public that support the government's radical stance on X, but is deemed to be a serious contravention of the rule of law. In this case could the Supreme Court deploy such a strikedown power? Imagine that it did and gave a reasoned judgment that sought to provide a constitutional basis for the decision. It would not be difficult to imagine that a radical government with a majority in the House of Commons to respond by proposing reforms on how judges are appointed and removed from office, nor that as in the case of *Miller*, where the Lord Chief Justice of England and Wales, Lord Thomas, sought police protection,[112] there would be serious questions about the role of the judiciary within the UK's constitution.

Therefore would the potential fallout of a judicial strikedown of an Act of Parliament be enough to prevent the Supreme Court from adopting the approach of Lords Hope and Steyn? Arguably, this could depend on the legislation in question and the political and constitutional climate that existed at the time. For example a judicial strikedown of an Act that imposed draconian press regulation would likely be met with considerable media support.

The *obiter* in *Jackson* explored the conflict between Parliamentary Sovereignty and the rule of law. Lord Neuberger observed that

> Professor Bogdanor has, as noted by Lord Bingham, stated that it is 'clear that there is a conflict between the two constitutional principles, the sovereignty of parliament and the rule of law.' Might this conflict justify or require the courts to place limits on Parliamentary sovereignty?[113]

Lord Neuberger noted that Lord Hope and Baroness Hale appeared to suggest that 'the courts might reject legislation if it contravened' the rule of law.[114] His Lordship noted that there were two types of rule of law, procedural and substantive. It is the substantive version that is problematic since it protects human rights. Lord Neuberger found such a proposition to be problematic, as 'it cannot be the case that any aspect of a statute which is contrary to an aspect of the rule of law to be overruled by the courts.'[115] If Lord Steyn is correct then the courts could modify Parliamentary Sovereignty to allow limitations. This is very controversial. Goldsworthy considered whether the judges could repudiate Parliamentary Sovereignty. He argued that judges had no grounds for doing this based upon 'a venerable tradition of English law, a golden age of constitutionalism, in which the judiciary enforced limits to the authority of Parliament imposed by common law or natural law. There never was such an age.'[116]

6.6 The different views on what is now meant by Parliamentary Sovereignty

The beginning of this chapter explored the origins and what Parliamentary Sovereignty means. However, the *obiter* in *Jackson* presents a significant opportunity to reassess whether the traditional account is still correct. It is important to understand that the challenges faced are not fatal to Parliamentary Sovereignty; rather it has been regarded as subject to limitations, whether these are imposed by the common law constitution (such as the rule of law) or by Parliament itself (manner and form and legislation such as the European Communities Act 1972). Vernon Bogdanor has observed that 'the doctrine of parliamentary sovereignty clearly means something very different from what it meant before Britain entered the European Community in 1973. It remains in form, but not substance. In practice, therefore, if not in law, parliamentary sovereignty is no longer the governing principle of the British constitution.'[117]

ACADEMIC DEBATE
'PEOPLE ARE FREE TO USE THE PHRASE "PARLIAMENTARY SOVEREIGNTY" AS THEY CHOOSE'

Nick Barber considered the debate surrounding manner and form in 'The afterlife of Parliamentary Sovereignty.'[118] Barber argued that:

> People are free to use the phrase 'Parliamentary sovereignty' as they choose; the earlier authors have no proprietary rights in the term. But some, at least, of the controversy surrounding the continuing health of Parliamentary sovereignty turns on a confusion of the pre- and post-1991 senses. In the pre-1991 sense, Parliamentary sovereignty was legally unchangeable, a rule of the United Kingdom's Constitution that placed serious limits on the ambitions of constitutional change. The constraints imposed by post-1991 sovereignty are far more limited. The old rule of sovereignty no longer prevents Parliament from placing limits of substance, as well as form, on itself.[119]

This is an interesting argument and highlights the impact of the decision in *Factortame (No.2)* on what is meant by a legally sovereign Parliament. Barber also noted that much remains open about whether Parliament could permanently prevent another Parliament from repealing legislation, or whether it Parliament could give up the sovereignty that it enjoys. However, Barber noted that '[t]here is a broad consensus that Parliament is, at present, the supreme legal authority in the United Kingdom constitution; there is no piece of legislation beyond its reach.'[120] There is a range of different views surrounding the nature of Parliamentary Sovereignty and this will become evident from engaging in wider reading. Vernon Bogdanor has argued that it is wrong to focus on 'what Parliament "can" or "cannot" do, than to ask what are the rules that regulate Parliament, and whether these rules prescribe any limits in form or in substance on legislation.'[121]

6.7 Practical application

Earlier this year the Equalities and Rights Reconsideration Act came into force. The relevant sections are as follows:

Section 1: The Home Secretary shall have the power to deport any foreign national from the UK and the courts cannot review the decision.

Section 2: The Human Rights Act 1998 and the European Convention on Human Rights shall not apply to anyone currently serving a prison sentence or who has been released from prison within the last five years.

Section 3: This Act cannot can be repealed unless a two-thirds majority of both Houses of Parliament vote to repeal the Act.

Section 4: The Prime Minister shall have a discretionary power to suspend the Scottish Government and Scottish Parliament.

Please consider sections 1–4 and explore the extent to which these might affect Parliamentary Sovereignty.

An outline answer is available on the companion website.

6.8 Key points to take away from this chapter

- Parliamentary Sovereignty arose as a consequence of the conflict between the Crown and Parliament in the 17th century.
- Dicey is associated with the view that Parliament has unlimited legal sovereignty and can make or unmake whatever law it wishes.
- The courts give effect to Parliamentary Sovereignty through the doctrines of express and implied repeal.
- Devolution is a political restriction on Parliamentary Sovereignty.
- Until the UK left the European Union, membership of the EU and the supremacy of EU law was an important restriction on the traditional understanding of Parliamentary Sovereignty.
- The rule of law and Parliamentary Sovereignty are ultimately incompatible and the *obiter* in *Jackson* suggests that judges may be willing to place limitations on Parliament's legislative ability in order to safeguard important freedoms and the rule of law.

Notes

1 (26/62) [1963] ECR 1.
2 (6/64) [1964] ECR 585.
3 See *Internationale Handelsgesellschaft GmbH v Einfuhr- und Vorratsstelle fur Getreide und Futtermittel* (No.2, BVL 52/71) [1974] 2 C.M.L.R. 540.

4   Article 23.

5   Article 25.

6   [1974] Ch 401.

7   ibid 418.

8   [1979] 1 WLR 1189.

9   [1983] 2 AC 751.

10   [1988] SC 178.

11   [1991] 1 AC 603.

12   [1990] 2 AC 85.

13   ibid 143.

14   (C-213/89) [1991] 1 All ER 70.

15   *R v Secretary of State for Transport, Ex Parte Factortame Ltd (No. 2)* [1991] 1 AC 603, 659.

16   ibid 658–59.

17   HWR Wade, 'Sovereignty – Revolution or Evolution?' [1996] LQR 568.

18   ibid.

19   ibid 573.

20   ibid 574.

21   TRS Allan, 'Parliamentary Sovereignty: Law, Politics, and Revolution' (1997) 113 LQR 443.

22   ibid.

23   ibid 451.

24   ibid 447.

25   [2002] EWHC 195 (Admin); [2003] QB 151.

26   ibid 184–85.

27   ibid 184.

28   ibid 186–87 (emphasis added).

29   ibid 185.

30   [2014] UKSC 3.

31   ibid 78 (emphasis added).

32   ibid 79 (emphasis added).

33   ibid 206.

34   ibid 207.

35   ibid 208.

36   ibid.

37   Lord Reed, 'EU Law and the Supreme Court' The Sir Thomas More Lecture for 2014, 12 November 2014.

38   Lady Hale, 'The United Kingdom Constitution on the Move' The Canadian Institute for Advanced Legal Studies, Cambridge Lectures 2017, 7 July 2017.

39   *R (on the application of Jackson) v Attorney-General* [2005] UKHL 56.

40   ibid.

41   Lord Neuberger, 'Who Are the Masters Now?' Second Lord Alexander of Weedon Lecture, 6 April 2011.

42   ibid.

43   Lord Justice Laws, 'Lecture III: The Common Law and Europe' Hamlyn Lecture 2013.

44   Hale (n 38).

45   B Hadfield, 'Devolution and the Changing Constitution: Evolution in Wales and the Unanswered English Question' in J Jowell and D Oliver (eds), *The Changing Constitution* (6th edn, OUP 2007) 272.

46   Section 29(1)(d) of the Scotland Act 1998.

47   [2011] UKSC 46; [2011] 3 WLR 871.

48   P Craig and M Walters, 'The Courts, Devolution and Judicial Review' [1999] PL 274.

49   B Winetrobe, 'Scottish Devolution: Developing Practice in Multi-Layered Governance' in J Jowell and D Oliver (eds), *The Changing Constitution* (6th edn, OUP 2007) 213.

50   *Axa General Insurance Ltd* [51].

51   See section 30 of the Scotland Act 1998.

52   J McEldowney, 'The Impact of Devolution on the UK Parliament' in A Horne, G Drewry and D Oliver (eds), *Parliament and the Law* (Hart Publishing 2013) 219.

53   Section 107(6) of the Government of Wales Act 2006.

54   Section 6 of the Human Rights Act 1998.

55   See the Canadian Charter of Rights and Freedoms.

56   A Young, 'Judicial Sovereignty and the Human Rights Act 1998' [2002] CLJ 53.

57   P Sales, 'A Comparison of the Principle of Legality and Section 3 of the Human Rights Act 1998' [2009] LQR 598.

58   [2001] UKHL 25.

59   A Kavanagh, 'Unlocking the Human Rights Act: The "Radical" Approach to Section 3(1) Revisited' [2005] EHRLR 259.

60   ibid 265.

61   *R v A (Complainant's Sexual History)* [2001] UKHL 25, [67]–[68].

62   Kavanagh (n 60) 259, 267.

63   See C Gearty, 'Reconciling Parliamentary Democracy and Human Rights' (2002) 118 LQR 248; G Phillipson, '(Mis)-Reading Section 3 of the Human Rights Act' (2003) 119 LQR 183; C Gearty, 'Revisiting Section 3(1) of the Human Rights Act' (2003) 119 LQR 551.

64   Phillipson (n 64) 183, 188.

65   [2002] UKHL 10.

66   ibid 40.

67   ibid 38–39.

68   [2002] UKHL 46.

69   ibid 58.

70   ibid 30.

71   ibid 59.

72   [2004] UKHL 30; [2004] 2 AC 557.

73   ibid 43.

74   ibid 42.

75   ibid 46.

76   S Wilson Stark, 'Facing Facts: Judicial Approaches to Section 4 of the Human Rights Act 1998' [2017] LQR 631, 647.

77   ibid 654.

78   See <https://publications.parliament.uk/pa/jt201415/jtselect/jtrights/130/13006.htm#note53>.

79   [2007] CSIH 9.

80   [2013] UKSC 63.

81   A Wagner and G Barth, 'Judicial Interpretation or Judicial Vandalism? Section 3 of the Human Rights Act 1998' (2016) *Judicial Review* 99, [6].

82 ibid 11.

83 ibid 14.

84 [2013] 1 WLR 3156.

85 ibid 15.

86 *R (on the application of Jackson) v Attorney-General* [2005] UKHL 56, [9].

87 ibid 81.

88 O Dixon, 'The Law and the Constitution' (1935) 51 LQR 590, 601.

89 (1931) 44 CLR 394.

90 [1952] (2) SA 428 (AD).

91 *R (on the application of Jackson) v Attorney-General* [2005] UKHL 56, [163].

92 ibid 102.

93 ibid.

94 ibid.

95 ibid.

96 Lord Woolf, 'Droit Public – English Style' [1995] PL 57.

97 *R (on the application of Jackson) v Attorney-General* [2005] UKHL 56, [104].

98 ibid 107.

99 [2014] UKSC 67; [2015] AC 901.

100 ibid 35.

101 [2019] NICA 58.

102 ibid 44.

103 ibid 52.

104 ibid 168.

105 ibid 42.

106 Lord Bingham, *The Rule of Law* (Allen Lane 2010) 267.

107 Lord Hope, 'Sovereignty in Question: A View from the Bench' Delivered at the WG Hart Legal Workshop, 28 June 2011 <www.supremecourt.gov.uk/docs/speech_110628.pdf>.

108 ibid.

109 D Oliver, 'Parliamentary Sovereignty: A Pragmatic or Principled Doctrine?' (2012) <http://ukconstitutionallaw.org/2012/05/03/dawn-oliver-parliamentary-sovereignty-a-pragmatic-or-principled-doctrine/>.

110 ibid.

111 [2016] EWHC 2768 (Admin).

112 See <https://www.huffingtonpost.co.uk/entry/brexit-supreme-court-high-court-ruling-lord-thomas-liz-truss_uk_58d24f72e4b02d33b746f575?guccounter=1>.

113 Neuberger (n 41).

114 ibid.

115 ibid.

116 J Goldsworthy, *The Sovereignty of Parliament: History and Philosophy* (OUP 1999) 235.

117 V Bogdanor, *The New British Constitution* (Hart Publishing 2009) 283.

118 N Barber, 'The Afterlife of Parliamentary Sovereignty' (2011) 1(1) IJCL 144.

119 ibid 154.

120 ibid.

121 V Bogdanor, 'Imprisoned by a Doctrine: The Modern Defence of Parliamentary Sovereignty' (2011) 32(1) OJLS 179, 194.

Further reading

Barber N, 'The Afterlife of Parliamentary Sovereignty' (2011) 1(1) IJCL 144

Bingham, Lord, *The Rule of Law* (Allen Lane 2010)

Bogdanor V, *The New British Constitution* (Hart Publishing 2009)

——, 'Imprisoned by a Doctrine: The Modern Defence of Parliamentary Sovereignty' (2011) 32(1) OJLS 179

Dicey AV, *Introduction to the Study of the Law of the Constitution* (Liberty Fund 1982)

Goldsworthy J, *The Sovereignty of Parliament: History and Philosophy* (OUP 1999)

Gordon M, *Parliamentary Sovereignty in the UK Constitution: Process, Politics and Democracy* (Hart Publishing 2015)

Hope, Lord, 'Sovereignty in Question: A View from the Bench' Delivered at the WG Hart Legal Workshop, 28 June 2011

Kavanagh A, 'Unlocking the Human Rights Act: the "Radical" Approach to Section 3(1) Revisited' [2005] EHRLR 259

Neuberger, Lord, 'Who Are the Masters Now?' Second Lord Alexander of Weedon Lecture, 6 April 2011

Oliver D, 'Parliamentary Sovereignty: A Pragmatic or Principled Doctrine?' (*Constitutional Law Association Blog*, 2012)

Sales P, 'A Comparison of the Principle of Legality and Section 3 of the Human Rights Act 1998' [2009] LQR 598

Wade HWR, 'Sovereignty – Revolution or Evolution?' [1996] LQR 568

Wagner A and G Barth, 'Judicial Interpretation or Judicial Vandalism? Section 3 of the Human Rights Act 1998' [2016] Judicial Review 99

Wilson Stark S, 'Facing Facts: Judicial Approaches to Section 4 of the Human Rights Act 1998' (2017) LQR 631

Young A, 'Judicial Sovereignty and the Human Rights Act 1998' [2002] CLJ 53

The three branches of government

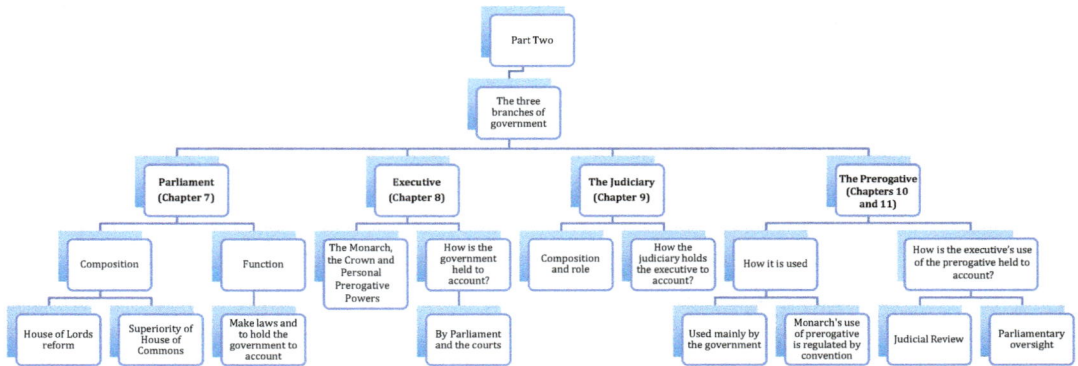

```
                          ┌──────────────┐
                          │   Part Two   │
                          └──────┬───────┘
                          ┌──────┴───────┐
                          │  The three   │
                          │  branches of │
                          │  government  │
                          └──────┬───────┘
```

Parliament (Chapter 7)	Executive (Chapter 8)	The Judiciary (Chapter 9)	The Prerogative (Chapters 10 and 11)

Parliament (Chapter 7)
- Composition
  - House of Lords reform
  - Superiority of House of Commons
- Function
  - Make laws and to hold the government to account

Executive (Chapter 8)
- The Monarch, the Crown and Personal Prerogative Powers
- How is the government held to account?
  - By Parliament and the courts

The Judiciary (Chapter 9)
- Composition and role
- How the judiciary holds the executive to account?

The Prerogative (Chapters 10 and 11)
- How it is used
  - Used mainly by the government
  - Monarch's use of prerogative is regulated by convention
- How is the executive's use of the prerogative held to account?
  - Judicial Review
  - Parliamentary oversight

Parliament

Composition and functions

This chapter will

- discuss what is meant by Parliament and explain the bicameral nature of the UK's legislature;

- explore the functions of Parliament and its role in making law and to what extent does Parliament hold the executive to account; and

- consider the composition of Parliament and the arguments for reforming or abolishing the House of Lords.

7.1 Introduction

The United Kingdom's Parliament is known as the Westminster Parliament and sits in the Palace of Westminster, which is situated beside the River Thames in London. Parliament has met at this location for hundreds of years. A fire destroyed the original royal palace in 1834 and the site was rebuilt during the 1830s.[1] The 'new' Palace of Westminster is an imposing gothic building, and its most famous landmark is the Elizabeth Tower, which contains a bell called 'Big Ben.' Despite its impressive appearance the Palace of Westminster is in a poor condition and is undergoing refurbishment. At time of writing the Elizabeth Tower is cladded in scaffolding and it is likely that Parliament may have to temporarily relocate to an alternative venue. The United Kingdom's Parliament consists of two chambers, the House of Commons with its green leather seats and the House of Lords with its red leather seats. This chapter is concerned with the role and composition of each chamber and how they work together.

The parliamentary business which took place in the House of Commons, with the indicative votes, and the regular defeats faced by the government, during the recent Brexit process saw the House of Commons attempt to settle for itself the United Kingdom's future relationship with the European Union. This amounted to an example of an independent and proactive House of Commons, which because of the then government's absence of a majority in the House of Commons could on its own initiative propose legislation and put forward its own (not that there was one common view) often cross-party policy

DOI: 10.4324/9780429293498-9

on Brexit. The present Conservative government (2019–) and the Prime Minister, Boris Johnson, currently enjoy a large majority in the House of Commons. This does not mean that the government can ignore the House of Commons, as even though it enjoys a majority of Members of Parliament (MPs), it still faced opposition from 38 of its MPs over the government's decision to allow Huawei, the Chinese technology company, to help build the United Kingdom's 5G network.[2]

Even though Parliament is located in a gothic building, surrounded by barriers and protected by armed-police, the public can still access the parliamentary chambers and in terms of public engagement the proceedings in Parliament are televised and broadcast on television and there is even a dedicated BBC Parliament television channel. This means that it is possible for members of the public to follow parliamentary proceedings at home and follow for example the House of Commons' role in the Brexit process.

The public's respect for and confidence in Members of Parliament and the House of Commons was badly affected by the parliamentary expenses scandal. Professor Flinders observed that

> [u]nlike other scandals this did not involve a rogue politician or a couple of scoundrels on the make. This was systemic in nature and tarred just about every MP with the same brush and, as a result, a large number lost their careers – some even lost their freedom and ended up in prison.[3]

There are concerns that MPs lie, with examples of politicians providing misleading information to colleagues and the public. One commentator observed, 'So do people in public life lie? Yes, copiously and consistently.'[4] The most famous example of a politician being accused of lying was Boris Johnson, who was accused of knowingly claiming that the NHS would receive an extra £350 million a week after the United Kingdom left the European Union[5], and also for allegedly misleading the Queen over the reason for proroguing Parliament in 2019[6] (something the Supreme Court did not concern itself with).[7] MPs are not permitted to call each other liars, an exception being Chris Bryant MP who claimed that Jeremy Hunt MP was a liar.[8] So what does this mean for public confidence in Parliament? A good source is the *Hansard Society's* 'Audit of Political Engagement 16' that was published in 2019 which found that, '[o]pinions of the system of governing are at their lowest point in the 15-year Audit series – worse now than in the aftermath of the MPs' expenses scandal' and '[o]nly 25% of the public have confidence in MPs' handling of Brexit.'[9]

It is in this context that this chapter will explore the workings of Parliament and the role of its members as parliamentarians. This chapter is broadly divided into a number of parts. The first part is concerned with the history of Parliament, from its creation and its transfer from a purely English institution to a British and finally a United Kingdom Parliament. This history is important as in 1707 the English and Scottish Parliaments were dissolved, and the new British Parliament sat at Westminster. The British Parliament was united with the Irish Parliament in 1801, when the personal union between the British and Irish Crown was formalised by the Act of Union. Whilst Northern Ireland remains part of the United Kingdom, Southern Ireland is independent. We will look at 'recent' developments such as the legislative bodies created by the Devolution Acts in 1998.

The second part will then consider the composition and function of Parliament and the possibility of further reform. It will address how effective parliamentarians are in holding the government to account. The relative ability of MPs to hold the government accountable divides opinion and will depend on the circumstances. For example, previous Conservative governments (2017–2019) lost their majority in the House of Commons and this led to MPs being able to become more independent and pursue their own Brexit policy and initiate legislation to steer the government's position on Brexit. In their book, *The Blunders of Our Governments*, two political scientists Professors King and Crewe argued that we had a peripheral Parliament, stating that:

> [a]nyone who investigates government blunders is bound to be made aware . . . that parliament as an institution occasionally barks, frequently nips at its master's heels but very seldom bites. . . . As a legislative assembly, the parliament of the United Kingdom is, much of the time, either peripheral or totally irrelevant. It might as well not exist.[10]

In this chapter, we will consider the truth of this assertion and consider alternative arguments regarding the ineffectiveness or effectiveness of Parliament to hold the government to account.

We will also consider the calls to reform Parliament. The second chamber, the House of Lords. has been the subject of calls for reform since the beginning

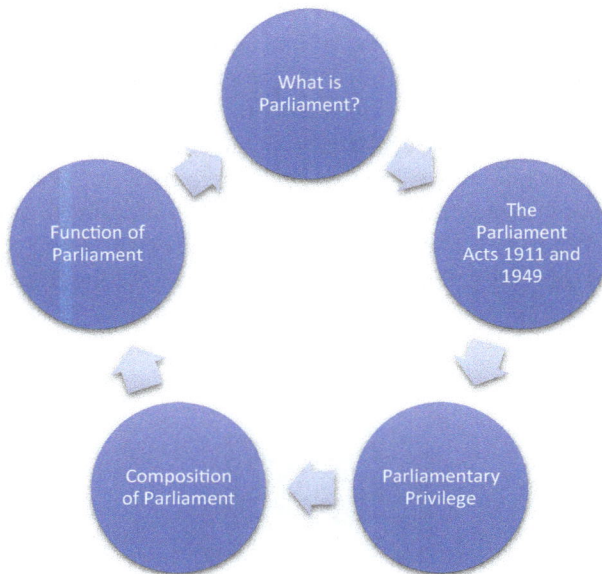

Figure 7.1
Chapter overview

of the 20th century and is accused of being 'out of touch.'[11] One report concluded that 'the current members lack all democratic accountability and legitimacy.'[12] This is because the membership of the House of Lords is appointed, hereditary or based on religious affiliation (the Church of England Bishops) and not elected by the public.

Therefore, this chapter will hopefully not just provide an account of the composition and function of the United Kingdom's Parliament but will also engage in controversial and relevant areas of debate.

7.2 The United Kingdom's Parliament

The United Kingdom has a bicameral Parliament. This means that Parliament is composed of two legislative chambers. These are known as the House of Commons and the House of Lords. They owe their name to their respective historical origins (which we will discuss below). In the United Kingdom, both Houses are known as the Houses of Parliament. Each House comprises different types of members.

Together the House of Commons, the House of Lords and the Queen in Parliament form Parliament (see Figure 7.2). The monarch plays an important role as her approval is required before proposed legislation, a bill, can become law, an Act of Parliament. Royal assent is one of the personal prerogative powers of the monarch and we shall look at the prerogative in **Chapters 10** and **11**. Therefore this means that the law-making power of Parliament is exercised through the legislative supremacy of the Queen in Parliament.

In order to make law, a bill (as legislation is known before it takes effect as an Act), needs to debated and voted for by the House of Commons and the House of Lords. The bill, if supported by both Houses, will then be presented to the monarch for royal assent. Once the bill receives royal assent it will become an Act. The participation of all three elements is required in order to make a valid Act of Parliament. However, we should at this stage emphasise that this is subject to the Parliament Act 1911 and the Parliament Act 1949. We will discuss the impact of these Acts below. However, it is important to note that it is possible for an Act to be made without the approval of the House of Lords. The justification for this is that the House of Commons unlike the House of Lords is

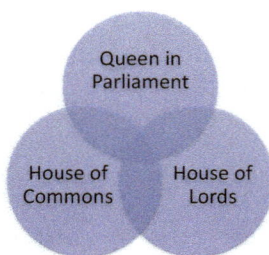

Figure 7.2
The composition of Parliament

the elected chamber, and the unelected House of Lords should not be permitted (subject to the ability to delay a bill) to have an effective veto on essentially what are government supported bills.

PUBLIC LAW IN CONTEXT
BICAMERAL AND UNICAMERAL LEGISLATURES

It is possible for a Parliament (or legislature) to have one or two chambers. If a country has two parliamentary chambers, this is known as a bicameral system. Whereas, if a country only has one parliamentary chamber, then it has as a unicameral system. Countries may decide to have one or two parliamentary chambers for a variety of reasons. Some countries, which originally had two chambers, have decided to abolish the upper chamber and adopt a unicameral system. Denmark's Parliament, the Rigsdag, has one chamber, the Folketing. Originally, the Danish constitution of 1849 (the Constitutional Act of Denmark) established a bicameral Parliament with the Folketing (the lower house) and the Landstinget (the upper house). The Landstinget was abolished as a result of a referendum in 1953. The Landstinget had been established to give a voice to the landowners and it was deemed to have served its purpose as an institution by the early 1950s. The Danish Rigsdag performs its functions in enacting legislation and holding the government to account with only one parliamentary chamber. More recently in 2013, there was a referendum in the Republic of Ireland to abolish the upper chamber, the Senate. This was unsuccessful, as a small majority of voters wished to retain the Senate.[13]

Many countries have a bicameral system such as France and the United States of America. In the United States of America the legislative body is known collectively as Congress. There are two Houses in Congress, the House of Representatives and the Senate. The House of Representatives has over 500 individuals is composed of members who represent districts in their states, which are allocated to mirror the population, and serve a two-year term before seeking re-election. The Senate has 100 members and each state (regardless of its population) is represented by two Senators, who will each serve a six-year term. It was not until the beginning of the 20th century that the electorate directly elected Senators. The reason for the inclusion of a Senate, when it would have been possible to have just one chamber for the United States, was to protect the rights of states, i.e. there was a fear that more populous state would dominate and drown out less populous states, and to balance the potential for a more radical directly elected House of Representatives. The Senate's webpage notes that the '[t]he framers of the Constitution created the United States Senate to protect the rights of individual states and safeguard minority opinion in a system of government designed to give greater power to the national government.'[14] One such framer, James Madison, argued that the 'use of the Senate is to consist in its proceeding with more coolness, with more system, and with more wisdom, than the popular branch.'[15]

7.2.1 Parliament's legislative sovereignty

It is the cornerstone of the United Kingdom's constitution that the United Kingdom's Parliament is the supreme law-making body in the United Kingdom. This was a point emphasised by Lord Bingham of Cornhill, the then

Senior Law Lord, in *R (on the application of Jackson) v Attorney-General*, where he said 'the bedrock of the British constitution is . . . the supremacy of the Crown in Parliament. . . . the Crown in Parliament was unconstrained by any entrenched or codified constitution. It could make or unmake any law it wished.'[16] This point was reiterated in the *Miller (No.1)* litigation which concerned the issue of whether the Prime Minister could use the prerogative to trigger Article 50 of the Treaty on European Union to start the two-year period for the United Kingdom to leave the European Union. At first instance the High Court observed that, '[i]t is common ground that the most fundamental rule of UK constitutional law is that the Crown in Parliament is sovereign and that legislation enacted by the Crown with the consent of both Houses of Parliament is supreme.'[17] The majority of the Supreme Court reiterated that 'Parliamentary sovereignty is a fundamental principle of the UK constitution.'[18]

In **Chapter 5** we have seen that an Act of Parliament is legally sovereign and cannot be challenged by the courts. The courts' role is to interpret and apply the statute and not to question the validity of what Parliament wishes to do. However, there are said to be a number of challenges to Parliamentary Sovereignty. We have addressed these in **Chapter 6**. These are:

1   The impact of the Devolution settlement in 1998.
2   The enactment of the Human Rights Act 1998.
3   The rule of law and the *obiter dicta* in *R (on the application of Jackson) v Attorney-General*.
4   The then United Kingdom's membership of the European Union. Please note that as of 2020 the United Kingdom is no longer a member of the European Union.

The High Court in *R (on the application of Miller) v Secretary of State for Exiting the European Union (No. 1)*[19] noted the impact of the then membership of the European Union: 'There is no superior form of law than primary legislation, save only where Parliament has itself made provision to allow that to happen. The ECA 1972[20], which confers precedence on EU law, is the sole example of this.'[21] In **Chapter 6**, we considered whether membership of the European Union had restricted Parliament's legislative supremacy. Nonetheless, Parliamentary Sovereignty is the key principle of the United Kingdom's unwritten constitution.

Parliament is legally sovereign as a result of winning the long-running conflict with the Crown over the issue of legal supremacy. Today, the Crown's remaining discretionary powers, known as the prerogative, are inferior to an Act of Parliament. Equally, the common law is inferior to an Act of Parliament. Unlike in the United States or Canada, the United Kingdom's Supreme Court cannot strike down Acts that are held to be unconstitutional. Indeed, unless Parliament permits otherwise, the courts cannot question the validity of an Act of Parliament. If Parliament has legislative sovereignty then, according to Dicey, it is the electorate who has the political sovereignty.[22]

7.2.2 The Parliament Acts 1911 and 1949

The House of Commons and the House of Lords fulfil the legislative function of the United Kingdom. The House of Commons is an elected body and the House of Lords comprises hereditary and appointed peers. The House of Commons is the most powerful House, as it can pass legislation without the agreement of the House of Lords under the Parliament Acts 1911 and 1949.

7.3 Devolved legislative bodies

The Devolution Acts of 1998 created the National Assembly for Wales[23] (Government of Wales Act 1998) and the Scottish Parliament (Scotland Act 1998). Since their creation, more power has been devolved to these legislative bodies. Following the creation of Northern Ireland in 1922 the Northern Ireland Assembly was abolished and has been reconstituted over the course of the last 90 years. This was as a result of the 'Troubles' in Northern Ireland which saw almost 30 years of sectarian strife and terrorism which was responsible for a great many deaths. Powers have been retransferred to the Northern Ireland Assembly under the Northern Ireland Act 1998.

The devolved legislative bodies in Northern Ireland, Wales and Scotland have been given power to create legislation for their respective area. This legislation does not enjoy legal sovereignty and can be declared invalid by the courts, such as where an Act was not compatible with the European Convention on Human Rights (as given effect to by the Human Rights Act 1998). These devolved legislatures have been given devolved powers to make legislation in certain policy areas, such as education. They may not exceed the powers devolved by the Westminster Parliament.

7.4.1 The Scottish Parliament and the Sewel Convention

In a referendum in 1997, 74.3 per cent of Scottish voters supported devolving powers to Scotland. This was an improvement on the 51.6 per cent who voted in support of devolution in 1979. The Scottish Parliament is responsible for legislating under the devolved powers. The Westminster Parliament legislates for non-devolved matters in Scotland. According to the Sewel Convention the Westminster Parliament will not legislate for devolved matters. The Sewel Convention was recognised in statutory form by the Scotland Act 2016. As noted in Chapter 5 there is nothing legally that could prevent Westminster legislating on devolved matters, or indeed abolishing the Scottish Parliament. The 2014 referendum on Scottish independence asked the Scottish electorate whether they wished to leave the United Kingdom. As over 55 per cent of the electorate voted to remain as part of the United Kingdom, partly as a result of the three main UK political parties promising to devolve more powers to Scotland, further powers were devolved under the Scotland Act 2016. It is likely that there will be a second independence referendum in the near future, and this could see the breakup of the United Kingdom. If Scotland does vote to remain as part of the United Kingdom, then this will inevitably lead to further devolution. This could mean that eventually, if powers are also devolved to an English Parliament or regional English assemblies, that the Westminster Parliament will just be responsible for truly national matters such as defence and foreign affairs.

7.4.2 The Welsh Parliament or Senedd Cymru

A referendum in Wales in 1997 saw a tiny majority of Welsh voters (50.3 per cent) support the creation of the National Assembly of Wales. This was hardly a strong endorsement of devolving powers from Westminster. However, this was a significant improvement on the 20.3 per cent who voted in favour of devolution in 1979. The Government of Wales Act 1998 and the Government of Wales Act 2006 have devolved powers from Westminster to Cardiff. The 2006 Act established the National Assembly and the Welsh Government as two distinct institutions. Following a referendum in 2011 where people in Wales voted for law-making powers, the National Assembly received additional powers. Further powers were devolved from Westminster to the National Assembly of Wales by the Wales Act 2014 and Wales Act 2017. The Wales Act 2017 gives statutory recognition to the Sewel Convention, whereby the Westminster Parliament will not legislate for devolved areas. In 2020, the National Assembly of Wales was renamed as the Welsh Parliament or Senedd Cymru.

7.4.3 The Northern Ireland Assembly

The Good Friday Agreement and the Northern Ireland Act 1998 led to the creation of the Northern Ireland Assembly in 1998. There are 90 members of the Assembly. In light of the Troubles, the appointment of minsters in Northern Ireland is different than in the rest of the United Kingdom, as different political parties will share power as ministers will be appointed based on the strength of each party in the assembly. The Northern Ireland Executive is headed by a First Minister and Deputy First Minister who will represent different political parties. This means that the main parties will have to govern together. The Northern Ireland Assembly has full powers to make law over many areas, including education and social security.

7.4.4 The West Lothian question and an English Parliament

As part of its devolution programme, the Labour government had intended to devolve powers to the English regions. There were plans, for instance, to create a North East regional assembly, but this proved unpopular with over three-quarters of voters rejecting the proposals in 2004 and this has not been proceeded with. It was always controversial that Scottish, Welsh and Northern Irish MPs can vote on matters that affect England, whereas English MPs cannot vote on devolved matters. This is known as the West Lothian Question. Many people now support the creation of an English Parliament to decide English affairs. If this were to occur, then the Westminster Parliament would have devolved most of its law-making powers. As a consequence of more powers being devolved to Scotland following the independence referendum, the Conservative Party wished to address the West Lothian question through some sort of English devolution. There were many options available for increased devolution in England, such as powers being devolved to regional assemblies, non-English MPs being excluded from voting on laws which only concern England, the creation of directly elected mayors for major urban areas and cites, or the creation of an English Parliament. The government used the Local Government Act 2000 to create directly elected mayors for cities such as Bristol, Liverpool and Manchester.

7.4.5 English Votes for English Laws

A solution to the West Lothian Question was the creation of a procedure in the House of Commons known as English Votes for English Laws (or EVEL). This has now since been abolished. This meant that where a proposed law or part it (such as clause or schedule of a bill) applies to England (and also Wales) it needs to be approved by a majority of English (or Welsh) MPs. The job of determining whether a proposed bill came within the EVEL procedure fell to the Speaker of the House of Commons, who if they believed that EVEL applied would grant a certificate. The bill (or parts of it) would need to have been approved by a legislative committee of MPs from England (or Wales) before the bill could receive its third reading in the House of Commons and become law. This need for the committee to give a consent motion was an important procedural development to the law-making process at Westminster. The legislative committee could have withheld its consent, and this could prevent the bill from receiving its third reading in the House of Commons. We will look what is meant by a third reading later on in this chapter.

ACADEMIC DEBATE

It is interesting to note whether EVEL had been a success and whether it has countered calls for more English devolution. Daniel Gover and Michael Kenny argued that, 'EVEL was intended, in part, to assuage such feelings within England. Yet whether it can provide a sustainable answer in the long term is an increasingly open question. While EVEL may have introduced an English veto right, this remains a long way short of the forms of devolved representation enjoyed by other parts of the UK. It is unclear for how long such a limited set of reforms will be able to satisfy those with concerns about England's governance within the UK.'[24] However, was EVEL ever a solution for increased English devolution and maintaining the United Kingdom? There were criticisms of EVEL in Scotland with MPs representing the Scottish National Party critical of being excluded from voting on the NHS Funding Bill as part of the EVEL procedure.[25] The concern was that although the bill applied to England, it would have a consequential impact on how much money could be spent in Scotland.

PUBLIC LAW IN CONTEXT

One example of the key differences between England and Scotland is the cost of healthcare for the elderly and university tuition fees. The Scottish Parliament has voted to make university tuition fees free for Scottish students, whereas Scottish MPs were able to vote on raising English tuition fees.

For more information on EVEL see R Kelly, 'English Votes for English Laws' House of Commons Library, Briefing Paper No. 7339, 20 June 2017, https://commonslibrary.parliament.uk/research-briefings/cbp-7339/.

7.5 Secondary or delegated legislation

An Act of Parliament can delegate law-making powers to individual ministers. This delegated legislation is not primary legislation but rather is secondary legislation, which means that the courts can review ministerial use of their delegated legislative powers.

An Act of Parliament will allow a minister to create new law without requiring additional Acts of Parliament. This permits a minister to develop policies in line with the aims set out in the Act, which will just set out a framework and it is for the minister to develop the required legislation to give effect to what Parliament intended. Ministerial use of delegated legislation is controlled by Parliament, with two House of Lords committees reviewing ministerial use of delegated legislation (the House of Lords Delegated Powers Scrutiny Committee and the House of Lords Secondary Legislation Scrutiny Committee).

Each year far more delegated legislation is created than primary legislation. Delegated legislation is required because it would not be possible for Parliament to spend its time passing all the required legislation. Primary legislation cannot be judicially reviewed by the courts, whereas secondary legislation can be reviewed. For the constitutional reasons for this distinction see **Chapter 5**. Otherwise secondary legislation can be created by a minister using the powers conferred on him by Parliament. Statutory instruments are the most common type of delegated legislation

7.5.1 Henry VIII clauses

Sometimes a bill will contain a clause which will give the government the power to repeal or amend that bill in the future using delegated legislation. Such a clause is known as a Henry VIII Clause, as Parliament gave Henry VIII the power to legislate using his prerogative by the Statute of Proclamations. Parliament will give a minister the power to create further legislation (i.e. to amend) in a bill (or to repeal parts of a bill), but if this secondary legislation will impose new legal obligations on people then the consent of Parliament is needed. Controversially, during the United Kingdom's withdrawal from the European Union, the European Union (Withdrawal) Act 2018 contained Henry VIII clauses that had the purpose of giving ministers the authority to amend primary and secondary legislation, where it would be necessary to amend those laws to give effect to Brexit.

7.6 History of the United Kingdom's Parliament

Parliament has been called every year since 1689. The Bill of Rights in 1689 stated that the King and Queen must summon Parliament every year. The King was restricted from making or unmaking laws without the consent of Parliament. The Bill of Rights can be seen as an assertion of the legislative supremacy of Parliament over the monarch. We must remember that the legislative supremacy of Parliament involves the Queen in Parliament and the monarch's assent is required before a bill can become law.

7.6.1 The English Parliament

The Magna Carta, which was presented to King John by his barons in 1215, established the idea that the barons in a representative capacity were needed to consent before the king could raise taxation. This was significant as it restricted the power of the Crown to govern without the consent of the barons and introduced the idea of governing by consensus. Although the Magna Carta was annulled by the pope it was later reissued by Edward I.

In the decades after Magna Carta, the barons rebelled once more against John's son, Henry III, who was forced to hold the first meeting of Parliament at Oxford in 1258. Crucially, the barons wanted to advise the king and consent to taxation. This established regular meetings of Parliament, whose role was to consult with the monarch on taxation.

It was only in 1295 that two distinct groups of representatives were summoned, the Lords and members representing counties and towns. Parliament's consent was required in 1362 for all taxation that the monarch wished to raise. The role of Parliament was soon extended to formally disposing monarchs and finally to consenting to all the laws that the monarch wished to make in 1414. It is clear that medieval monarchs appreciated that they needed to consult with Parliament and a weak monarch, such as Edward III (albeit this was due to old age illness), could face parliamentary attempts to impeach his advisors and dismiss members of the council. Parliament approved the English reformation and granted considerable law-making powers to Henry VIII.

Parliamentarians did not enjoy freedom of speech in the chamber and soon clashed with the monarch. During the reign of Charles I the relationship between monarch and Parliament deteriorated and the king ruled without summoning one for 12 years, attempting to govern using his prerogative powers instead. Eventually the king was forced to recall Parliament, and this led to civil war. The king raised an army and Parliament did the same. Parliament defeated the king and voted to execute Charles I in 1649. Parliament then ruled without a king, with Oliver Cromwell having dictatorial powers as the Lord Protector. Upon his death the monarchy was restored. The relationship between Parliament and Charles II and James II was not a happy one. James II was deposed by Parliament in 1688 and William of Orange and his wife Mary were invited to become joint monarchs.

In 1689 the Bill of Rights helped establish the supremacy of Parliament over the executive as it prohibited the raising of taxes and an army without parliamentary consent. The Bill of Rights also established parliamentary privilege which ensured that parliamentarians enjoyed free speech inside the chamber. The English Parliament was legally sovereign, but this power could only be exercised by the King or Queen in Parliament.

7.6.2 The United Kingdom Parliament

The Acts of Union in 1707 created Great Britain and the new Parliament was composed of members from England and Scotland. It met at Westminster and continued to enjoy legal sovereignty. The Union with Ireland Act 1800 incorporated Ireland into the new United Kingdom. The Irish Parliament was dissolved and Irish parliamentarians joined the Westminster Parliament.

During the 18th century parliamentarians took over the governance of the country from the monarch. The development of Cabinet government saw the government being composed of members of the Houses of Commons and Lords. Matters of great importance would be debated in the chambers of both Houses and oratory was an important skill. Speeches were reproduced as pamphlets and sold to the public.

PUBLIC LAW IN CONTEXT

In the 18th and 19th centuries not everybody could vote. The franchise (i.e. those who could vote) was limited to very wealthy men, and not every town or city had a Member of Parliament. We will see below how the franchise was eventually expanded to include most men and women aged over 18.

7.7 Parliament Acts 1911 and 1949

The Parliament Acts 1911 and 1949 altered the relationship between the House of Commons and the House of Lords. The Acts have limited the ability of the House of Lords to prevent bills from becoming law.

The passing of the Parliament Act 1911 was an important development and resulted from the House of Lords rejecting the government's budget. At this time the House of Lords could vote to reject any legislation and there was noth-ing that the House of Commons could do about this. A constitutional conven-tion regulated money bills and the House of Lords rejected the budget and only relented when the government threatened to create new peers that would vote in their favour. As a consequence of breaching a convention, the Parliament Act 1911 was passed. This Act restricted the House of Lords' ability to delay the passing of a bill by more than two years after the bill's second reading in the House of Commons. This applied to all bills except those to extend the lifetime of Parliament (see Figure 7.3). The House of Lords is unable to veto money bills as these will be automatically passed one month after being introduced to the House of Lords.

The Parliament Acts 1911 and 1949 gave the House of Commons supremacy over the House of Lords. It is important to understand why they were intro-duced and what the restrictions are on using these Acts today. The Parliament Act 1949 reduced the ability of the House of Lords to delay the passing of a bill one year after the bill's second reading in the House of Commons. The new Act was needed to introduce key legislation, including the Iron and Steel Bill. This amendment to the Parliament Act 1911 was considered necessary as the House of Lords could still block the Labour government's legislation during the last two years of the lifetime of a Parliament. The House of Lords were acting in breach of the Salisbury Convention.

The Salisbury Convention exists to ensure that the House of Lords does not veto bills which were contained in the government's election manifesto. It came about in 1945 when the Labour government wished to legislate to give effect to its manifesto but were in a minority in the House of Lords. The Labour

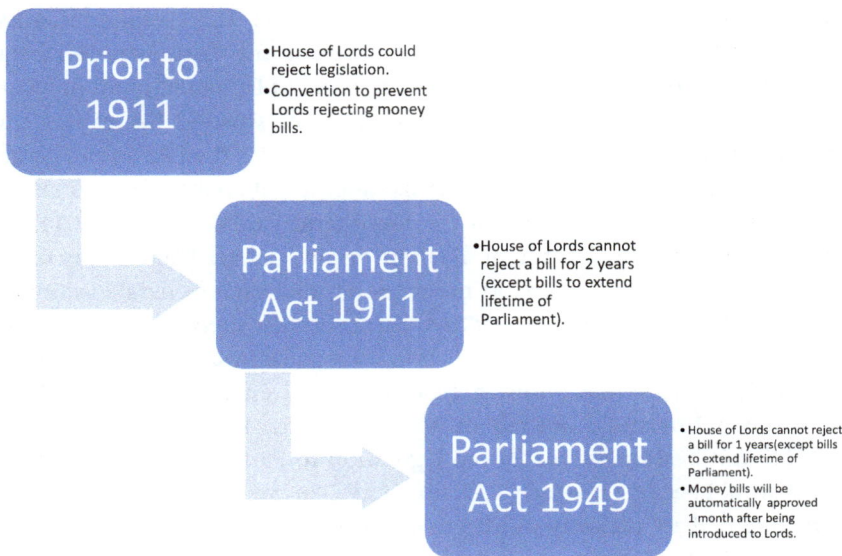

Figure 7.3
The Parliament Acts 1911 and 1949

Leader of the Lords, Viscount Addison, remarked that, 'in the House of Lords the Labour Benches are, as it were, but a tiny atoll in the vast ocean of Tory reaction.' This convention helped to ensure that Labour could introduce key manifesto commitments. For more information see 'The Salisbury Doctrine' House of Lords Library Note (2006).[26]

As a consequence of the Salisbury Doctrine being breached, the Parliament Act 1949 was passed using the procedure set out in the 1911 Act, thus removing the need for the House of Lords to consent.

The House of Lords still has the power to veto bills that will extend the lifetime of Parliament, or bills which were originally introduced in the House of Lords. The validity of the Parliament Acts 1911 and 1949 was questioned in *R (Jackson) v. Attorney-General*[27] (see **Chapter 6**). The House of Commons is now the most important House and the power of the Lords is limited. However, the House of Lords can still scrutinise bills and provide important amendments. Lord Bingham observed that, '[t]he Parliament Acts mitigated the affront to democracy inherent in the power of an unelected, unaccountable chamber to thwart the will of the elected chamber answerable to the electorate.'[28] The House of Lords does scrutinise proposed legislation and the government routinely suffers defeats in the House of Lords; for example the government suffered over 70 defeats on the 2019–21 parliamentary session.[29]

7.8 The lifetime of each Parliament and the Fixed-term Parliament Act 2011

The lifetime of each Parliament was shortened from seven to five years by the Parliament Act 1911. Previously, the Septennial Act 1715 had stated that the maximum lifetime of each Parliament was seven years. The Fixed-term Parliaments Act 2011 was enacted by Parliament during the Conservative–Liberal Democrat coalition government to fix the lifetime of Parliament and prevents the calling of a General Election until the five years period has expired. In May 2015 a General Election was held in accordance with the Fixed-term Parliaments Act 2011. However, the five-year fixed-term will apply unless an exception applies under the section 2 of the Fixed-term Parliaments Act 2011. An example of this was the decision of the then–Prime Minister Theresa May to ask the House of Commons to support her request for an early General Election in 2017. As May received the required two-thirds of MPs supporting the request for any early General Election, an election took place in 2017. Boris Johnson, May's successor as Prime Minister, held an early General Election in 2019. Unlike May, Johnson did not rely on section 2 of the Fixed-term Parliaments Act 2011, and he instead introduced legislation to Parliament in the form of bill that would become the Early Parliamentary General Election Act 2019. This just required a bare majority of MPs to support the bill, unlike the two-thirds majority under the Fixed-term Parliaments Act 2011.

Under Section 3 of the Fixed-term Parliaments Act 2011 an early General Election can take place where the House of Commons by a bare majority supports a motion stating, 'That this House has no confidence in Her Majesty's Government.' A General Election will take place unless within 14 days of the motion under section 3, there is another motion supported by a bare majority of MPs stating 'That this House has confidence in Her Majesty's Government.'

The monarch will dissolve Parliament in accordance with the Fixed-term Parliaments Act 2011 and call a General Election. Once dissolved, parliamentarians are prevented from entering Parliament. The Fixed-term Parliaments Act 2011 has removed the ability of the Queen to dissolve Parliament using her prerogative power. Previously, as a matter of constitutional convention the monarch would use her prerogative power to dissolve Parliament upon the request of the Prime Minister. There is much debate about whether the Fixed-term Parliaments Act 2011 has abolished the prerogative power, or whether it has placed it in abeyance, which means that if the Fixed-term Parliaments Act 2011 were to be repealed, then the prerogative power would be revived.

Section 6 of the Fixed-term Parliaments Act 2011 is clear that the Act does not affect the Queen's power to prorogue Parliament, that is. bring a parliamentary session to an end. The monarch will prorogue Parliament, that is, use her prerogative power to do so, upon the advice of her Prime Minister. Prorogation is usually for a short period and was uncontroversial. However, the decision in 2019 to advise the monarch to prorogue Parliament for five weeks proved highly controversial and was challenged in the courts. The Supreme Court in *R (on the application of Miller) v Prime Minister (No.2)*[30] ruled that the Prime Minister's advice was unlawful.

Parliament will be opened every year by the Queen in a ceremony known as the State Opening of Parliament. Today the monarch is not allowed to enter the House of Commons. During the State Opening of Parliament an official known as Black Rod will be sent from the House of Lords to summon MPs in the House of Commons. The door to the Commons is already open until Black Rod approaches. It is then slammed in Black Rod's face. Black Rod will bang on the door with his official staff three times before it's opened again. This rather strange tradition originates from the time when Charles I had entered the chamber of the House of Commons to arrest several MPs.

RECENT DEVELOPMENTS

Was the Fixed-term Parliaments Act 2011 a good piece of legislation? Was it an improvement on the monarch's power to dissolve Parliament using her prerogative? The prerogative gave the Prime Minister considerable flexibility to request that the monarch dissolve Parliament at a time that was politically expedient, such as where the Prime Minister believed that it was advantageous to call a General Election. However, this flexibility can also be criticised as creating uncertainty and bringing the monarch into what is essentially a political decision. Raphael Hogarth considered the arguments for and against repealing the Fixed-term Parliaments Act 2011 and returning to the prerogative: 'Neither keeping the FTPA nor trying to restore the old system is without risk. A possible middle way might be to modify the Act, trying to preserve what is good and amend away what is bad. . . . No solution is perfect. The situation pre-FTPA was a mess in some ways; the FTPA is a mess in others. If the next government is going change the system again, it needs to make sure it doesn't mess up the constitution further still. A one-line bill to repeal the FTPA is no panacea.'[31]

In its 2019 election manifesto the Conservative Party promised to repeal the Fixed-term Parliaments Act 2011. A bill was introduced to Parliament in 2020 to do this. The Fixed-term Parliaments Act 2011 (Repeal) Bill was intended to repeal the Fixed-term Parliaments Act 2011 and revive the monarch's prerogative power to dissolve Parliament. The lifetime of Parliament would not be more than five years, as under the bill Parliament was automatically dissolved at the end of five years. Importantly, the government were keen to prevent the monarch's power to dissolve Parliament could not be judicially reviewed (after what had happened in *Miller (No.2)* with prorogation) and the Bill contained a statutory exclusion of judicial review for this specific purpose. A government minister, Lord True, was of the opinion that '[t]he Fixed-term Parliaments Act was brought forward under unique circumstances and was an exception, not the rule. As we saw last year, it resulted in far more confusion than the tried-and-tested constitutional arrangements it had hastily swept aside.'

Robert Hazell commented on the government's proposals and observed that: 'Meg Russell [the Director of the Constitution Unit] and I strongly supported the central principle of the FTPA, to shift power from the executive to parliament. It is a myth that the FTPA came into being simply to shore up the Lib Dem-Conservative coalition. The proposal had been made for decades previously, in several private members' bills, before appearing in the 2010 Labour and Liberal Democrat election manifestos.'[32] This is important, as the repeal of the Fixed-term Parliaments Act 2011 could be regarded as a retrograde step. The onus of placing the decision whether to accept or refuse a Prime Minister's request to the monarch was criticised by Hazzell, 'If the Crown is left as the only check on improper or untimely requests for dissolution, it would inevitably be drawn into controversy if such requests are refused.'

7.9 Parliamentary privilege

The Bill of Rights 1689 gave parliamentarians certain privileges. Article 9 of the Bill of Rights 1689 states '[t]hat the Freedome of Speech and Debates or Proceedings in Parlyament ought not to be impeached or questioned in any Court or Place out of Parlyament.' Parliamentarians enjoy freedom of speech and can speak freely in the Houses of Parliament. This enables parliamentarians to speak without risk of criminal or civil sanction. An example of this privilege being used is when MPs have revealed the names of those persons protected by super injunctions without facing the prospect of being prosecuted under the Contempt of Court Act 1981. Equally, statements can be made which if made outside the chamber could give rise to a claim for defamation in tort. This right of free speech is essential in a modern democracy and parliamentarians should have the freedom to incite debate. However, on the other hand parliamentarians have been criticised by the judiciary for misusing parliamentary privilege. Parliamentary privilege also means that Parliament has exclusive competence over its own proceedings. The courts have determined the extent of parliamentary privilege. One such example is the Supreme Court's decision in *R v. Chaytor*,[33] where the court ruled that parliamentarians could not invoke parliamentary privilege to prevent prosecution for false accounting.

7.9.1 R v. Chaytor *[2010] UKSC 52 and the expenses scandal*

It is important at this point to highlight the recent controversy surrounding parliamentary expenses. As a result of a newspaper investigation it was revealed that both MPs and Lords had been abusing the expenses system. This revelation resulted in the then Prime Minister, Gordon Brown, and other leading politicians repaying money which they had received, and a new expenses regime being introduced. Both MPs and Lords have been convicted and have served custodial sentences. Initially those parliamentarians accused had argued that they could rely on parliamentary privilege as a defence. The Supreme Court in *R v. Chaytor* unsurprisingly rejected this. The result is that the reputation of Parliament has been tarnished.

7.10 Link with the executive

In the Westminster system there is a strong link between Parliament and the executive. The United Kingdom has a parliamentary system of government and this means that the government and its members must be from Parliament. This is to ensure that Parliament can hold ministers to account through a number of parliamentary accountability mechanisms and within the constitution, as a matter of constitutional convention, Minsters are responsible to Parliament. This means that there is a strong relationship between the legislature and executive. In order for a political party to form a government and exercise the powers of the executive, that party needs to gain a majority in, or have the confidence of, the House of Commons. Therefore, a government which loses the confidence of the House of Commons (subject to the Fixed-term Parliaments Act 2011) could lose office.

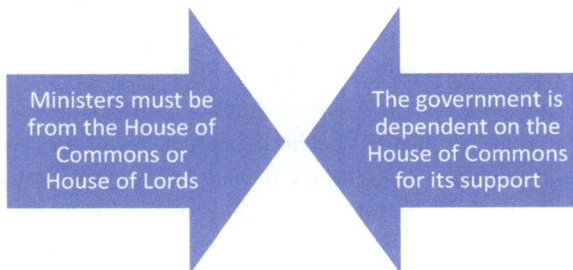

Ministers must be from the House of Commons or House of Lords

The government is dependent on the House of Commons for its support

Figure 7.4
The relationship between the executive and Parliament

PUBLIC LAW IN CONTEXT

The Prime Minister as a matter of constitutional convention must be from the House of Commons. If the Prime Minister wishes to appoint a person to a ministerial position, then that person by convention will have to become a member of either House of Parliament. During the Second World War the Prime Minister wanted Ernest Bevin, who was the leader of a trade union, to join the Cabinet. Bevin had to first become an MP before he could take up his ministerial position. However, Field Marshall Jan Smuts was a member of Churchill's wartime Cabinet during the Second World War, without being a member of the UK Parliament. The commonest method is to appoint someone who is not parliamentarian as a member of the House of Lords. More contemporary examples include the retired admiral, Alan West, who upon being appointed to the House of Lords became Security Minister under a previous Labour government and Peter Mandelson was appointed as a member of the House of Lords and became a member of Gordon Brown's Cabinet. Lord Mandelson was viewed as one of the most powerful members of Cabinet, despite not being an MP. In 2021, Lord David Frost, a former civil servant, was appointed to Cabinet as the minister responsible for the United Kingdom's relationship with the European Union

7.11 Composition of Parliament

We will now have a look at the composition of Parliament and who exactly the members of both Houses are. The members of both Houses are known as parliamentarians. They all have offices in the parliamentary estate and have access to staff, libraries and other resources.

7.11.1 The House of Commons

We will look first at the composition of the House of Commons and how MPs are elected.

7.11.1.1 The Member of Parliament

Members of Parliament (MPs) represent their local constituencies. There are 650 MPs in the House of Commons from constituencies across the United Kingdom. There were 220 female MPs elected in 2019. By way of comparison, out of the 650 MPs elected in the 2010 General Election only 147 were women. The first female MP to take her seat in the House of Commons was Nancy Astor in 1919. Interestingly, Countess Constance Markievicz was the first woman to be elected to Parliament in 1918 but as a member of Sinn Fein she did not take her seat. The practice of Sinn Fein MPs not taking their seats in the House of Commons continues to this day.

In 2019 65 MPs from ethnic minority backgrounds were elected; this is a significant increase from 2010 when only 28 MPs were from ethnic minorities.

The first Asian MP took his seat in the 1890s. All MPs are elected and none are appointed. Everyone is entitled to vote in the constituency where they live (subject to some restrictions). Most MPs are members of a political party and support that party's policies; however, an extremely small number of MPs are independents and do not align themselves to any political grouping.

7.11.1.2 The constituency

The MP will represent the constituency in Parliament and will serve as a link between the legislature and the electorate. The MP will hold surgeries in their constituency to enable their constituents to raise important issues and to seek their help. The MP will be expected to use their time to benefit their constituency, for example by protesting against plans to build a waste disposal site or the closure of a local factory.

7.11.1.3 How MPs are elected

MPs are elected at the General Election (or through a special by-election). Candidates will put themselves forward and will pay a deposit. Almost anyone can stand as an MP, with the notable exception of Lords who cannot do so unless they renounce their peerage (see Tony Benn who campaigned to be permitted to renounce his hereditary peerage to stand as a Labour MP). The main political parties field candidates who stand for election. The local party association has power over who is nominated to stand as their party's candidate. The Labour Party and Liberal Democratic Party have in some constituencies introduced all-female shortlists for candidates because only a minority of MPs were female. In 2019, over half all Labour MPs were women. In terms of context, before the 2010 General Election the Conservative Party decided to change the rules about how candidates were selected. This experiment only applied to two constituencies. Firstly, they allowed anyone to stand as the Conservative candidate, and secondly, they permitted any constituent to vote for who became the local Conservative candidate. Although the Conservative party did not use all female shortlists in 2019, the party had its highest number of female MPs elected.

The method of electing an MP is called First Past the Post. This allows the person with the most votes to become the MP. This system is controversial for many reasons, namely, that it permits an MP to be elected without having a majority of the total votes. For example, an MP could be elected with just 33 per cent of the vote or a majority of just one vote. This means that there are a large number of MPs who were not elected by a majority of their constituents. Many people feel that their vote is wasted if they live in a constituency where most people will vote for a particular political party. One example of this is Luton South where the local MP is almost guaranteed to be a member of the Labour Party, or neighbouring Dunstable where the local MP will almost be guaranteed to be a member of the Conservative Party. The Ballot Act 1872 introduced secret voting, which means that you do not need to tell anyone who you voted for.

This ensures that people have the freedom to vote without being influenced by the candidate's supporters, or indeed their own friends and family.

As well as voting at a polling station, it is possible to register to vote via the post. Postal voting has led to allegations of election fraud. However, as voter turnout is low in the United Kingdom with only two-thirds of those entitled to vote doing so in 2019, many people see postal voting as a good way to try to encourage more people to vote. In Australia people are obliged by law to vote and every election will see a debate in the press on whether the United Kingdom should introduce compulsory voting.

7.11.1.4 The need for reform

The First Past the Post system means that the number of MPs a political party has at Westminster does not actually reflect the share of the popular vote that the party received. It must be remembered that voters do not vote for a political party; rather they vote for their local MP. Nonetheless, the United Kingdom's system of modern political parties means that First Past the Post will usually lead to either a Labour or a Conservative government. The Liberal Democrats have as a political party always supported reforms to the way that MPs are elected. The opportunity for reform came after the 2010 General Election, which led to the first coalition government since the Second World War, and is the exception rather than the norm. In 2010 the Liberal Democrats received almost 7 million votes, but despite their share of the vote (23 per cent), the Liberal Democrats only managed to win 8.8 per cent of the seats (57). The fact

Table 7.1 The House of Commons after the May 2010 General Election

Party	Seats	Percentage of votes
Conservative	306	36.1%
Labour	258	29%
Liberal Democrat	57	23%
Democratic Unionist	8	0.6%
Scottish National	6	1.7%
Sinn Fein	5	0.6%
Plaid Cymru	3	0.6%
Social Democratic & Labour	3	0.4%
Alliance	1	0.1%
Green	1	1%
Independent	1	
Speaker	1	
Total	650	

that the number of MPs did not reflect the actual percentage of votes is a major criticism of the system used to elect MPs in the United Kingdom. The Liberal Democrats supported changing the voting system and replacing it with proportional representation.

Proportional representation is used in many different countries such as Germany. The number of seats a political party has in the legislature is based on their overall share of the national vote. Whilst proportional representation ensures that the legislature represents the voting intentions of the electorate, many critics allege that introducing this system into the United Kingdom would lead to weak and unstable coalition governments. Italy is often referred to as there have been 61 governments since 1945. There is a fear that fringe parties such as the British National Party might gain seats in the House of Commons. Critics also point to the Weimar Republic in Germany during the 1920s and 1930s, where proportional representation was blamed for weakening the government of Germany and allowing the NSDAP (Nazis) to take power in 1933.

7.11.1.5 The 2011 referendum on changing the method of voting

As a result of the Liberal Democrats being in government as part of the coalition, in May 2011, there was a referendum on proposals to replace First Past the Post with the Alternative Vote (AV). The AV system allows voters to list their candidates by preference. If a candidate achieves 50 per cent he will win outright. If no candidate receives 50 per cent of the votes, then the weakest candidate is eliminated, and their votes are given to the voter's second favoured candidate. The process will continue until one candidate achieves the important 50 per cent required. The nation voted in favour of retaining First Past the Post.

7.11.1.6 The 2019 General Election

The 2019 General Election provides an opportunity to understand why the current United kingdom government is a Conservative one.

It is certainly true that the existing system means that the number of votes does not necessarily reflect the number of seats in the House of Commons. On a breakdown of the 2019 General Election results it took 38,264 votes to elect a Conservative MP, 59,719 to elect a Labour MP and 336,038 votes to elect a Liberal Democrat MP (see Figure 7.5).

The following table shows the number of seats each political party gained in the 2019 General Election:

7.11.1.6 Who can vote?

We take it for granted that if we are aged over eighteen then we are entitled to vote and although this is generally true, there are a few exceptions.

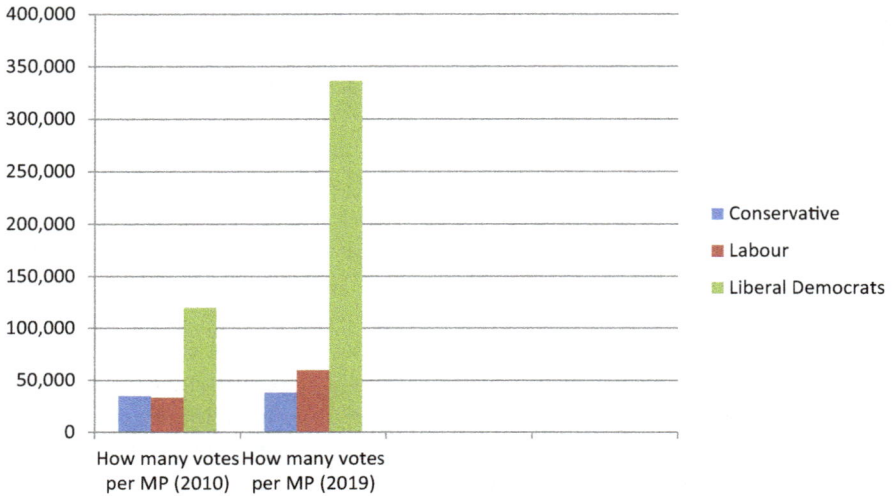

Figure 7.5
How many votes does it take to elect an MP?

Table 7.2 The House of Commons after the May 2019 General Election		
Party	Seats	Percentage of votes
Conservative	365	43.6%
Labour	203	32.2%
Liberal Democrat	11	11.5%
Democratic Unionist	8	0.8%
Scottish National Party	48	3.9%
Sinn Fein	7	0.6%
Plaid Cymru	4	0.5%
Social Democratic & Labour	2	0.4%
Alliance Party	1	0.4%
Green	1	2.7%
Total	**650**	

Can prisoners vote?

Prisoners are not entitled to vote but the European Court of Human Rights in *Hirst v. United Kingdom (No.2)* (2005) 42 EHRR 849 held that a blanket ban on all prisoners voting was unlawful. The UK Supreme Court in *R (Chester) v. Secretary of State for Justice* [2013] UKSC 63 applied the decision in *Hirst* but refused to issue a declaration of incompatibility, as the matter was being considered by the UK Parliament and a declaration had been issued on a previous occasion.

In 2013 the Joint Committee on the Draft Voting Eligibility (Prisoners) Bill recommended that prisoners should be allowed to vote unless there was a good reason to restrict certain types of prisoners from voting. If the recommendations become law then the UK will no longer be in breach of the European Convention on Human Rights.

PUBLIC LAW IN CONTEXT

Historically only a small number of people could vote at a General Election. Voting rights were restricted to men who owned land and had a certain income. The constituencies were not spread evenly over the United Kingdom so, for example, despite being a large city Manchester did not have any MPs. When the American colonists declared independence because of Britain's attempt to tax them without the Americans being represented by the body that made the law, some commentators could point to Manchester to show that their situation was not unique. On the other hand, small villages might have two MPs. These were known as rotten boroughs.

The universities of Oxford and Cambridge both had their own MP and former students could return to take part and vote (as well as voting in their own constituency). This meant that the nobility controlled a large number of consistencies and could build up their own followings in Parliament. The ability of the nobility to secure patronage through their ownership of these constituencies resulted in placing considerable power in their hands.

The reforms in the 19th century increased the number of men who could vote by lowering the income requirement. This happened through the Representation of the People Acts. The most significant was the Great Reform Act of 1832. However, the creation of voting parity between men and women would take almost another hundred years to achieve. Most women over the age of 30 only received the vote in 1918. There was only fully voting equality between men and women in 1928. The result of universal franchise saw the creation of the Labour Party and the first Labour government in 1922. There have been calls to reduce the voting age to 16 and a private members' bill which attempted to achieve this was unsuccessful in 2008.

Looking at Figure 7.6 and taking into account your current age, in what year were you able to vote at your current age? For example, Jasmine who is 34 could only vote in 1918, and Delia who is 21 could only vote in 1928.

7.11.1.7 The House of Commons creates the government

A government is created in the House of Commons. The political party or coalition that has the most seats in the House of Commons will form the next government. Theresa May's Conservative government depended on a supply

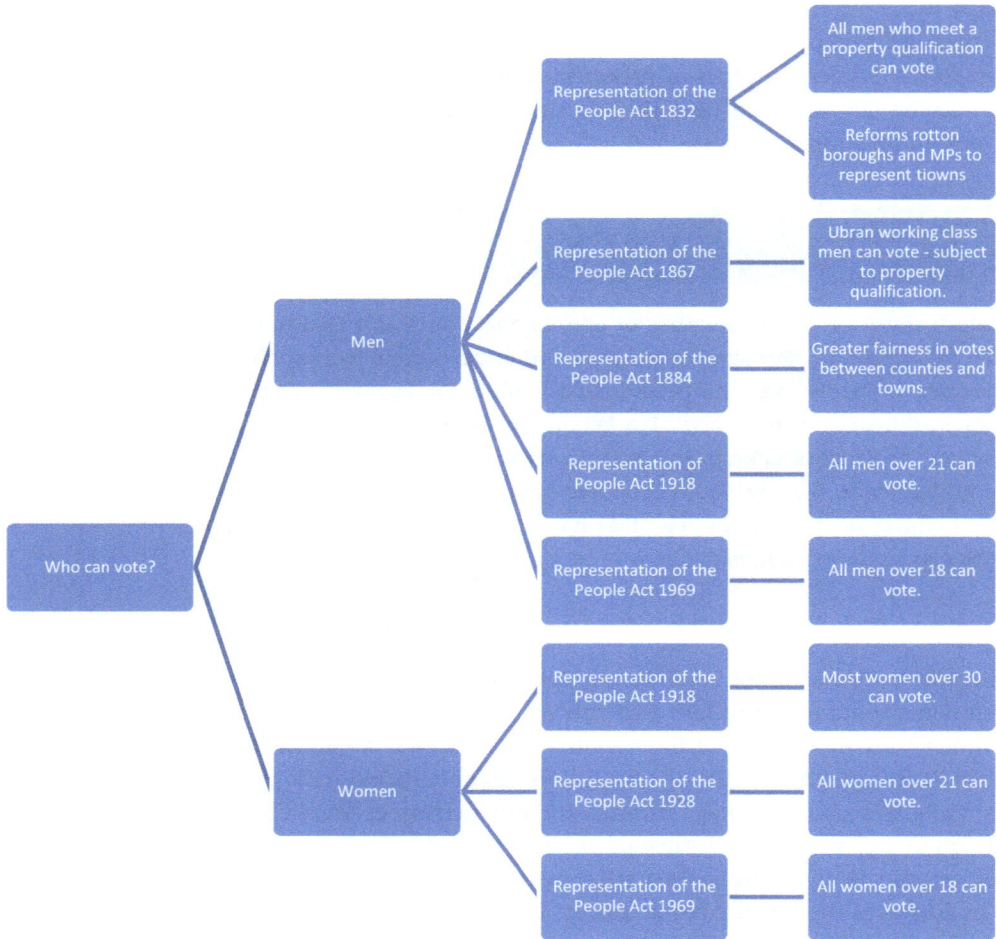

Figure 7.6
The expansion of the franchise

and confidence agreement with the Democratic Unionist Party after the 2017 General Election. The current Conservative government under Boris Johnson enjoys a large majority in the House of Commons.

7.11.1.8 Only an MP can become the prime minister

By convention only an MP can become the Prime Minister. The last Prime Minister from the House of Lords was the Marquis of Salisbury who resigned in 1902. Had Churchill inherited the family Dukedom of Marlborough then he would not have been able to become Prime Minister in 1940. The convention has been shown to exist because whenever there has been a choice between an MP and a Lord, the monarch has chosen the MP to become Prime Minister. The choice in 1940 was between Churchill and Lord Halifax. In 1924 it was between Stanley Baldwin MP and Lord Curzon, and the king chose Baldwin.

In 1963, the Prime Minister Harold Macmillan resigned due to ill health. At that time there was no internal way to select the next leader of the Conservative Party, and therefore Macmillan's successor as Prime Minister. This meant that the Queen had to make a choice between two Conservative Cabinet ministers, Rab Butler and the Earl of Home. On the advice of Macmillan, the Queen chose the Earl of Home, who after becoming Prime Minister considered himself bound by convention and renounced his peerage. He was able to become an MP as there was a vacant seat and Home won the by-election.

PUBLIC LAW IN PRACTICE

Lord Poplar (fictitious) sits in the House of Lords and is a member of the Conservative Party. He has been made Foreign Secretary and is very popular with the electorate. The Prime Minister is forced to resign due to ill health. Lord Poplar wishes to put himself forward to become leader of the Conservative Party (and therefore Prime Minister). Would the convention that the Prime Minister must come from the House of Commons prevent him from becoming Prime Minister? Lord Poplar could renounce his peerage, although there is nothing legally which would prevent a member of the House of Lords from becoming Prime Minister. Ultimately, it may well depend on public and press opinion.

7.11.1.9 The vote of no confidence

Ultimately the House of Commons can vote to bring down the government. The last government to be defeated by a vote of no confidence was that of James Callaghan in 1979. Upon losing the vote the Prime Minister will as a matter of convention ask the monarch to dissolve Parliament.

It is important to note that the ability to trigger an early General Election is now on a statutory footing under the Fixed-term Parliaments Act 2011. Section 3 of the Fixed-term Parliaments Act 2011 provides for a confidence vote. It is still possible to have a vote of no confidence outside of the Fixed-term Parliaments Act 2011, but this will not bring about an early General Election.

7.11.1.10 Speaker of the House of Commons

The business of the House of Commons is presided over by the Speaker of the House. The speaker is an MP who is elected by his colleagues to chair debates and run the proceedings in the House. The speaker is elected by way of a secret ballot and the normally the two largest political parties will take in turns to have a speaker appointed from their party. The Speaker is accorded significant respect by the House and can keep order during noisy debates. The Speaker lives in the Palace of Westminster and continues to represent his constituency but is no longer associated with his or her political party. The Speaker is a high-profile position and carries significant authority. By convention no other political party will field candidates against the speaker. This convention was broken when the Conservative government said that they would field a candidate against John Bercow in September 2019.[34] This did not happen as Bercow resigned as speaker. Previously, Nigel Farage, the then leader of UKIP, stood against John Bercow in 2010.

7.11.1.11 Reforming the House of Commons

The 2010–15 Coalition government introduced plans to reduce the number of MPs and to make the size of constituencies more consistent. This was contained in the 2010 Coalition Agreement. Due to political reasons, it was not achieved during the lifetime of the 2010–15 Parliament. This was controversial as a number of high-profile MPs will risk losing their seats. However, the House of Commons has arguably too many MPs when contrasted with the House of Representatives in the United States, which has fewer members who each in their districts represent a larger population.

The Boundary Commissions in each UK nation are responsible to advising on distribution of seats. The proposal to reduce the number of MPs to 600 was rejected by the current government though legislation enacted through Parliament (Parliamentary Constituencies Act 2020). The Boundary Commissions are currently carrying out another review the conclusions of which will be implemented in the future.

7.11.2 The House of Lords

7.11.2.1 Membership of the House of Lords

The House of Lords is the upper chamber in the United Kingdom. Its members are all appointed or entitled to seats through their position, and importantly none are elected by the electorate.

The House of Lords is a controversial body as it is seen by many as lacking any democratic legitimacy, because unlike the House of Commons it holds considerable law-making power and yet is not accountable to the British people. According to Alexandra Kelso, '[i]t is perhaps ironic that the House of Lords is, on the one hand, condemned for its undemocratic composition, and, on the other hand, applauded for the important contribution it makes to the broad work of parliament.'[35] Members of the House of Lords are not paid a salary, but receive expenses. There are about 800 members which is a very large number, especially when we consider that the Senate in the United States only has 100 members. The discussion of the different types of members will be looked at alongside the continuing reform of the House of Lords (see Figure 7.7).

The hereditary peers

Traditionally all hereditary peers were entitled to sit in the House of Lords. The House of Lords Act 1999 has removed this right, and instead only 92 peers were allowed to remain. Those 92 hereditary peers were selected by their fellow

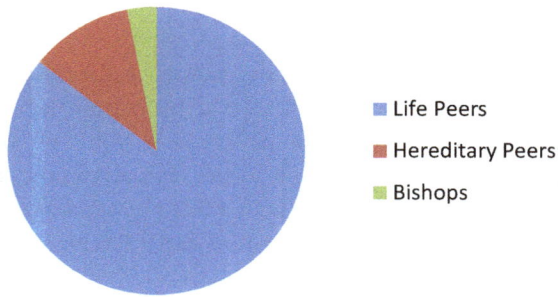

Figure 7.7
The composition of the House of Lords

hereditary peers. Hereditary peers had traditionally played an important part in government, as many Prime Ministers and leading ministers were from the nobility.

The life peers

The majority of the members of the House of Lords are life peers. There are about 700 in total. Life peers were introduced by the Life Peerages Act 1958. Life peers have no fixed term and are appointed for life. It is not a hereditary peerage and so the peerage ceases to exist upon death. Life peers are appointed via the House of Lords Appointments Commission. The Commission will nominate individuals for life peerages and will vet nominations made by political parties. Life peerages are given to senior politicians upon retiring from the House of Commons, or upon losing their seats, to distinguished persons in the arts, sciences, broadcasting and the Civil Service, etc. Distinguished peers include Lord Sugar, star of television's The Apprentice, Lord Coe, who was responsible for the London 2012 Olympic Games, and the former Deputy Prime Minister, Lord Prescott.

PUBLIC LAW IN CONTEXT

There has been controversy over peerages being given to those who give money to political parties. Tony Blair, the then Prime Minister, was interviewed twice by police in 2006 over allegations that peerages were being given in return for donations to the Labour Party.

　　The increase in the number of life peers being appointed by successive governments has proved controversial. For example, Boris Johnson appointed 36 life peers in July 2020.[36] Lord Fowler, the Lord Speaker, was critical of the additional number of life peers created: 'Boris Johnson has now created 52 new peers this year – taking the total size of the Lords to more than 830 – despite a cross-party agreement three years ago that numbers should over time be reduced to 600.'[37] Lord Fowler observed, 'The truth is that a vast amount of good work takes place in the House of Lords. The trouble is that this is often hidden by some of the decisions not of peers, but of governments.'[38]

The Bishops

The United Kingdom unlike most other countries gives the leaders of a religious faith seats in its legislative chamber. This is a historical quirk. There are 26 Church of England Bishops who are members of the House of Lords. The Bishops play an important role and take part in the legislative process. Other faith groups are not formally represented by such a fixed quota, but religious leaders have been made life peers such as the previous Chief Rabbi.

The Law Lords

As we shall see below, historically the House of Lords had a judicial function and was the highest court in the United Kingdom. Traditionally any member of the House of Lords could sit and judge a case. This ceased in the 1840s when only Lords who had legal training would try the case. David Lewis Jones observed:

> By the late 1830s the membership of the House (of Lords) included seven peers with judicial experience, and they were sufficient for a quorum to hear appeals. In the appeal of Daniel O'Connell from a decision of the Irish Queen's Bench in 1844, five of these Law Lords sat, with the assistance of 12 judges from the common law courts. This appeal was controversial on political grounds and lay peers wished to support.'[39]

In a speech in 2019, Lord Reed, then the Deputy President of the United Kingdom Supreme Court, made reference to the philosopher Jeremey Bentham's criticism of the House of Lords' judicial function:

> Bentham's principal objection was that the judges who sat in the House of Lords at that time also served in the courts below, and appear from what he says to have had no compunction about participating in appeals against their own decisions. He was also critical of the practice of lay peers taking part in the consideration of appeals, despite their being, in his words, 'ignorant of the law' and 'destitute of judicial aptitude, by indolence and carelessness.'[40]

We can see that this criticism of lay peers being able to vote on cases was a sound one, and was addressed in the middle of the 19th century.

The Appellate Jurisdiction Act 1876 created the Lords of Appeal in Ordinary, commonly known as the Law Lords. However, as a matter of convention the Law Lords would not normally sit in the legislative chamber of the House of Lords. Since the creation of the new United Kingdom Supreme Court in 2009, members of the Supreme Court do not sit in the legislative House of Lords (even if entitled to as peers), whilst new Supreme Court Justices are not automatically made members of the House of Lords. For example, Lord Dyson, Lord Hughes and Lord Sumption were not made life peers. However, others such as Lord Reed were given a life peerage

The crossbenchers

Members of the House of Lords (with the exception of the Law Lords and Bishops) can be members of political parties. The Labour Party currently has 180 peers, the Conservatives 262 and the Liberal Democrats 87. Significantly there are 183 crossbench peers who are independent and do not belong to a political party. The crossbenchers are important and play an important role in ensuring that debates are not always dominated by politics. There are also 48 non-affiliated members.'

The Lord Speaker of the House of Lords

Prior to the Constitutional Reform Act 2005, the Speaker of the House of Lords was the Lord Chancellor. The Lord Speaker is now elected by the members of the House.

7.11.2.2 Further reform of the House of Lords

Reforming the House of Lords was first seriously considered by the Liberal government at the beginning of the 20th century. In 1999, the Labour government introduced the House of Lords Act 1999 to remove the majority of the hereditary peers. Whilst this removed the vast majority of hereditary peers, it did nothing to introduce an element of democracy into the second chamber. As a result of the Parliament Acts 1911 and 1949 the House of Lords is inferior to the House of Commons. Consequentially, there was a concern that further reform that legitimised the House of Lords as a democratic legislative chamber would change the relationship between the two Houses.

Wakeham Commission Report

The Wakeham Commission delivered its report in 2000. The commission was composed of senior politicians and academics. The commission suggested that there should be further reform of the House of Lords. The main proposals were:

- The balance of power between the two Houses should be unchanged. The Parliament Acts 1911 and 1949 would remain.
- The House of Lords would have a proportion of regional members who would represent the regions.
- The new chamber should be wholly or substantially elected.
- Those appointed should be chosen by a genuinely independent appointment commission. This would prevent the system from being abused by the government.
- Other religious groups should be represented in the chamber.
- All members would serve 15-year terms.

Whilst the Wakeham Commission's recommendation for an independent appointment commission was taken up, no further reform of the House of Lords has been carried out since then.

The 2007 White Paper on House of Lords reform was followed by Parliament having a free vote on how to reform the House of Lords in March 2007. The House of Commons voted against a wholly appointed House of Lords (66 per cent against). The House of Commons voted for an 80 per cent elected and 20 per cent appointed House of Lords (53 per cent in support). The House of Commons also voted to support a wholly elected House of Lords (60 per cent in support). The House of Lords voted overwhelmingly in favour of a fully appointed House of Lords (75 per cent in support).

2008 White Paper

The Labour government's White Paper in 2008 'An Elected Second Chamber: Further Reform of the House of Lords' looked at further ways to reform the House of Lords. The government supported the findings of the Wakeham Commission that suggested introducing elections to the House of Lords. Elected members would serve a 12–15-year non-renewable term. The government stated that an appointed element could exist in the reformed House of Lords, whilst the Church of England Bishops would still have a place amongst the appointed members.

In its 2008 White Paper, 'The Role of the Reformed House of Lords?' the Labour government put forward its opinion that:

> The reformed second chamber should be confident in challenging both the executive and the House of Commons. The second chamber should be able to make the government pause and reconsider. Ultimately, however, the government should be able to get its business through the legislature, through effective resolution of disagreements between the two Houses and, if necessary in the most exceptional cases, by using the Parliament Acts. This ensures the primacy of the House of Commons and means that, ultimately, any gridlock between the two Houses can be resolved.[41]

It was clear that the then government was determined to secure the supremacy of the House of Commons and to prevent the House of Lords from having increased powers to veto legislation. The reforms would increase the legitimacy of the House of Lords.

Lord Bingham argued that appointment 'no matter how enlightened and wise the process of selection, can never yield a House which is either democratic or representative or constituted on a popular basis.' Whereas His Lordship highlighted that an elected House would raise other problems, namely how the members would be elected. If the members were elected by proportional representation then the Lords would feel 'more truly representative of opinion in the country than the Commons.' His Lordship stated that an elected House might see the members being drawn from second-rate politicians and the House would lose its current distinguished membership.[42]

It is interesting to look at House of Lords reform from the viewpoint of a senior member of the judiciary. Lord Bingham proposed that the House should be replaced by a Council of the Realm:

- It would be similar to the House of Lords and wholly appointed.
- Its role would be to review legislative proposals and not law-making. Parliament would be unicameral and the Council would not be a second chamber.
- It could not recommend the contents of a bill, but could make recommendations to the Commons.
- The Council could not veto legislation and would have fewer powers than the current House of Lords.
- The Council would choose its own members.
- Members could become ministers.
- The Commons would take heed of the recommendations made by the Council.

These proposals would protect the experience, reputation and knowledge of the current House of Lords, which would be lost by having an elected House of Lords.

The coalition government's proposals (2010–15)

The Coalition government proposed further reform of the House of Lords. The draft bill was presented to the Parliament along with the government's White Paper. These reforms were considered by the Joint Committee on the Draft House of Lords Reform Bill. However, the Prime Minister, David Cameron, decided not to proceed with House of Lords reform. This was a political decision because of the lack of support from Conservative backbenchers and the amount of time that would have to be spent debating the proposals in the House of Commons. Whether there will be an attempt at further reform of the House of Lords after the 2015 General Election remains to be seen (note the Fixed-term Parliaments Act 2011).

The draft House of Lords Reform Bill 2011 contained the following proposals:

- Initially the name 'The House of Lords' would be retained – although some favour renaming it as the Senate.
- The chamber would contain 300 members. The membership could be wholly elected, or have a majority elected (240) and 60 appointed. There would be 12 Church of England Bishops. Although there would be no

hereditary peers in the reformed House. They could stand for election as elected members.

- The supremacy of the House of Commons would be preserved, with the Parliament Acts 1911 and 1949 unchanged. The elections to the House of Lords would be staggered, with a third elected every five years. This is similar to the United States Senate.
- Each member would serve for one 15-year term. This would be non-renewable.
- The appointed members would be chosen along a similar process as today.
- A peerage would not be given to members of the House of Lords.
- Unlike the present House of Lords the members would receive a salary.
- Members would be elected by proportional representation. The bill suggested using the single transferable vote.

It is perhaps ironic that the Coalition government intended to reform the House of Lords at the same time that the House proved to be extremely effective at checking the government's reforms. During 2011–12 the government suffered a number of defeats in the House of Lords.[43]

The House of Lords Reform Act 2014, which had been a private member's bill, introduced the possibility of retirement for members of the House of Lords and permitted the House of Lords to expel members. An example of a peer resigning from the House of Lords is Lord Carswell, who was a Lord of Appeal in Ordinary. The powers to expel members were increased by the House of Lords (Expulsion and Suspension) Act 2015.

Conservative government(s) and reform (2015–present)

In 2016 the Lord Speaker's Committee on the Size of the House was established in 2016. The committee was chaired by Lord Burns. In its first report, the committee recommended reducing the number of peers to 600.[44] Individuals appointed to the House of Lords would retire after a fixed-term. This would mean that the numbers of the House would not exceed a certain number as current members serve for the rest of their life. The committee supported 15-year terms. In 2018 the House of Commons Public Administration and Constitutional Affairs Committee delivered a report, 'A Smaller House of Lords: The Report of the Lord Speaker's Committee on the Size of the House,' in which it endorsed the Burns Report. The committee noted:

> The effect of implementing the Burns Report recommendations is the very minimum reform which should be contemplated. We support the objective of reducing the size of the House of Lords and capping the Chamber's size at a maximum of 600 members, but we recommend that this be achieved more quickly that the rate set out in the Burns Report. We recognise that gaining consent for this reform depends upon avoiding unreasonable pressure on existing members to retire, but we urge the leaders of the party groups in the House of Lords to agree to strict retirement targets. We hope

a faster rate of retirements is possible while maintaining the equal contribution basis outlined in the Burns report'

The Conservative Party's 2019 election manifesto made reference to looking at
House of Lords reform. However, there have been proposals from other politicians, including abolishing the House of Lords, introducing a retirement age,
relocating the House of Lords to York, or creating a body representing the different regions that make up the United Kingdom.[45]

PUBLIC LAW IN PRACTICE

You have been asked to vote on the future of the House of Lords; please vote for the option
that you find most preferential. What were your reasons for choosing this option?

The House of Lords should be abolished as we require only one chamber []
The House of Lords should be 100 per cent elected []
The House of Lords should stay as it is now []
The House of Lords should be 70 per cent elected and 30 per cent appointed []
The House of Lords should be 70 per cent appointed and 30 per cent elected []

7.12 Function of Parliament

We shall now look at the function of Parliament. We will look at the law-making
powers of Parliament, the recently reformed judicial function of Parliament
and the role of Parliament in providing a check on the power of the executive.

7.12.1 Law-making

The most important function of Parliament is making law. We will look at how
laws are made.

7.12.1.1 Different types of bills

The most common types of bills are public bills (see Figure 7.8 for the different
types of bills). Public bills are introduced to Parliament by the government.
We shall see below the procedure used for public bills. Examples of public bills
include the Constitutional Reform Act 2005.

Private members' bills are unlikely to succeed because being independent
of government policy, they are unlikely to attract the support of a majority
of parliamentarians. Either an MP, or a member of the House of Lords, can
introduce private members' bills. The ways that a private members' bill can be

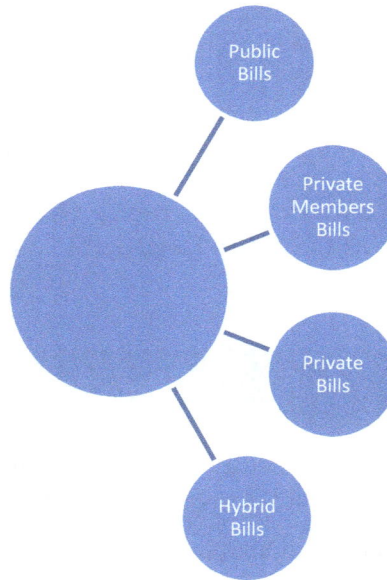

Figure 7.8
Different types of Bills

introduced include by ballot, by the ten-minute rule and by presentation. The method most likely to be successful is by the ballot procedure. For the 2012–13 parliamentary session MPs were given the chance to put themselves forward to introduce a private members' bill. Twenty MPs were chosen randomly by a ballot and were allowed to put forward a private members' bill.

Alternatively, an MP can use the ten-minute rule which allows parliamentarians a short period of time to raise issues, but this is not enough time to seriously introduce a bill. Equally presentations are unlikely to succeed, as there is insufficient opportunity for the parliamentarian presenting the bill to gain support. Members of the House of Lords can also introduce a private members' bill. An example of a private members' bill introduced in the House of Lords in 2012 is the Airports (Amendment) Bill. Successful examples of private members' bills include the Hunting Act 2004 and the Abortion Act 1967.

Private bills are bills that will only change the law for a particular organisation which will promote the bill. It is not a way of changing the law for the entire country, but only the law in relation to a particular private or public body. An example of a recent private bill is the Canterbury City Council Bill which was introduced in the 2007–8 parliamentary session. The purpose of this bill was to regulate trading in Canterbury and to increase the powers of the police and council officials to issue enforcement notices.

Finally, there can be a bill which is a hybrid (i.e. part private and public bill). It is hybrid because it will concern certain groups or individuals (like a private bill) but will also affect the public (like a public bill). Hybrid bills are introduced by the government or a backbencher and will often attempt to undertake a large project, such as the Channel Tunnel Bill. An example of a hybrid bill is the Crossrail Bill. Crossrail is a major construction project which will link Essex and Heathrow through a high-speed train and underground link. A bill which is hybrid will undergo a lengthier procedure than a public bill.

Public bills: procedure and stages

It is important to consider that before a bill can become law it must be supported by the majority of those voting in the House of Commons and, subject to the Parliament Acts 1911 and 1949, the House of Lords. Finally, before a bill can become an Act it must receive royal assent.

Prior to introducing a bill to Parliament, the government will issue a draft bill. This is designed to invite comment from the public. A Green Paper will seek consultation from interested groups and this can influence the bill that will be introduced to Parliament. A White Paper states government policy and is far more precise. The Law Commission will often provide draft bills for the government to consider and many of these have become law, such as the Contracts (Rights of Third Parties) Act 1999 and the Fraud Act 2006.

PUBLIC LAW IN PRACTICE

How does a bill become law? We have seen the different types of bills and most are introduced as public bills by the government. The government can introduce a bill in either the House of Commons or Lords (see Figure 7.9) Where a bill is introduced in the House of Commons it receives its first reading, which is an opportunity of introducing the bill to the House. The bill will then be debated by the House in the second reading. If the House votes in support of the bill, then it can proceed to the committee stage. The Public Bill Committee will consider whether amendments need to be made to the bill. They will seek the views of experts on the proposed legislation. The amended bill will then proceed to the report stage where MPs can debate whether there should be additional amendments. If the bill is controversial this can be lengthy. Finally, the bill will proceed to its third reading. At this stage no new amendments can be proposed and the House must vote on the amended bill. If the House votes in support of the bill then the bill goes to the House of Lords. The procedure in the House of Lords is very similar to the House of Commons. The role of the House of Lords is to provide an important check on the Commons, as the House is less partisan and there are a considerable number of Lords who are independent (crossbenchers). The quality of the debate is better and more informed. The House of Lords will propose amendments and will often vote against the bill.

What happens if the House of Lords votes against a bill? In this case it must be remembered that the House of Commons is the superior House because of the Parliament Acts 1911 and 1949. The bill will be reintroduced in the Commons and then proceed to the Lords. The bill can be passed after one year despite the House of Lords refusing its consent. However, whilst the Hunting Act 2004 and the War Crimes Act 1991 were passed without the consent of the

Bills introduced in House of Commons

House of Commons	House of Lords	Consolidation	Royal Assent
• First Reading • Second Reading • Committee Stage • Report Stage • Third Reading	• First Reading • Second Reading • Committee Stage • Report Stage • Third Reading	• Ping Pong • Amendments consolidated • Both Houses must agree	• Royal assent given by convention. • Commencement order required? Or automatic?

Bills introduced in House of Lords

House of Lords	House of Commons	Consolidation	Royal Assent
• First Reading • Second Reading • Committee Stage • Report Stage • Third Reading	• First Reading • Second Reading • Committee Stage • Report Stage • Third Reading	• Ping Pong • Amendments consolidated • Both Houses' must agree	• Royal assent given by convention. • Commencement order required? Or automatic?

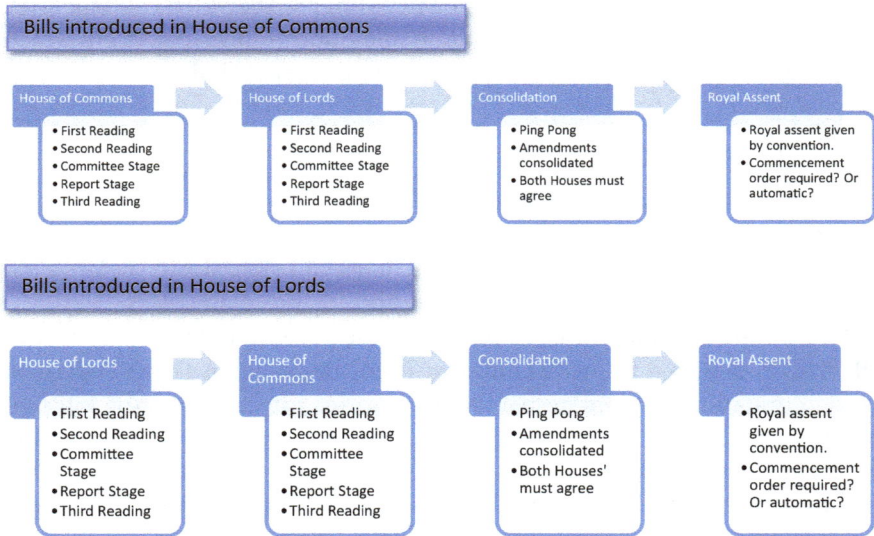

Figure 7.9
The procedure for bills in Parliament

Lords, the Mode of Trial Bill in 1999/2000 was dropped by the then government after being defeated on many occasions by the House of Lords.

Normally the House will propose amendments and the bill will then proceed to the stage known as consideration of amendments. Both Houses must consider the other's amendments and this is known as the 'ping-pong' stage. Once both Houses have agreed on the wording of the bill it will proceed to the monarch for royal assent. Only then will the bill become an Act. As we will see in **Chapter 9**, the monarch does not have to give her assent to a bill, but assent will be given as a matter of convention. However, the Act must be brought into force by a commencement order made by a government minister, or automatically if there is none. It is not uncommon that sections of an Act will never be introduced.

Resolutions

A resolution of either House of Parliament is not law. Rather it is the House voting to express its opinion on a certain matter.

7.12.2 Executive accountability

An important function of Parliament is to hold the executive to account. In the United Kingdom the executive is very powerful and will dominate Parliament through the governing party controlling a majority of the seats in the House of Commons. Nonetheless, Parliament must hold the executive to account and challenge the bills introduced by the government and secondary legislation made by ministers. The key question is whether the executive dominates

Parliament. In *R (on the application of Jackson) v. Attorney-General*[46] Lord Steyn observed the government's dominance of the House of Commons:

> My Lords, the power of a government with a large majority in the House of Commons is redoubtable. That has been the pattern for almost 25 years. In 1979, 1983 and 1987 Conservative Governments were elected respectively with majorities of 43, 144 and 100. In 1997, 2001 and 2005 New Labour was elected with majorities of respectively 177, 165 and 67. As Lord Hailsham of St Marylebone explained in The Dilemma of Democracy (1978), p 126, the dominance of a government elected with a large majority over Parliament has progressively become greater. This process has continued and strengthened inexorably since Lord Hailsham warned of its dangers in 1978.[47]

7.12.2.1 The House of Commons and executive accountability

The House of Commons is the superior House. Under the Parliament Acts 1911 and 1949 it can pass legislation without the consent of the House of Lords.

Party control and a government majority

Ultimately the House of Commons can make and destroy a government. If defeated in a vote of no confidence a government must resign. However, as noted by Lord Steyn above, the British political system has had a tradition of returning governments with a majority. Even the coalition government enjoys a majority and has been able to pass what has been controversial legislation through the House of Commons. This means that the government can control the House of Commons and pass whatever legislation is required.

The vast majority of MPs belong to a political party and therefore will owe their loyalty to that party. The government whips (who are MPs that actively encourage other MPs to vote with the party) will try to prevent an MP from abstaining from or voting against government legislation. Therefore, it is fair to say that most MPs will vote according to party allegiances.

The quality of debate

The quality of debate in the House of Commons is inferior to that of the House of Lords. Debate is often political and avoids real discussion of the issues. The purpose of debate is to review legislation and to propose amendments. The debate is recorded in *Hansard* and is available to read online. Debates are televised and can be watched on BBC Parliament.

This is not to say that a government with a large majority is immune from being defeated. For example, although Tony Blair's Labour government had enjoyed a large majority in the House of Commons it still suffered defeats in the Commons. An example of this was in 2005, when 49 Labour MPs voted against the government over its proposed anti-terror legislation. This defeat was the first suffered by the then Prime Minister, Tony Blair, in the House of Commons. On other occasions the Labour government had to rely on the support of opposition MPs in order to counter its own backbench MPs. An example of this was in 2003, when 139 Labour MPs supported a rebel amendment to the British government's position on Iraq.

Questioning government policy

Members of Parliament can ask questions of the government. The most well-known is Prime Minister's Question Time [PMQs]. PMQs take place when Parliament is sitting every Wednesday at midday for thirty minutes. How effective PMQs are at holding the government to account is questionable, but it is important for both the Prime Minister and the Leader of the Opposition to perform well.

Ministerial question time is an opportunity for MPs to question ministers from different government departments. An MP can ask written questions and will send these to the relevant government department. These can be more effective than oral questions. The answer they receive can be given on a particular named day, or received at some point in the future.

There are other ways of MPs raising issues or questioning government policy. Adjournment debates relate to a discussing a particular topic, either chosen by the speaker or by MPs. The MP whose topic is chosen by the ballot procedure can ask a question, and the minister will respond to it. Adjournment debates take place either in the House of Commons or Westminster Hall. Another way of raising an issue is through an Early Day Motion. An Early Day Motion will attract signatures of support from other MPs, although it is very rare for these to be debated in the House of Commons. Nonetheless, they are a way of raising important issues.

The committee system

We will look at the committee system in the House of Commons. We should note that there are different types of committees:

- select committees;
- general or standing committees; and
- joint committees.

Select committees

Select committees in the House of Commons investigate the work of a particular government department. A select committee is composed of 11 members from across the political parties which are represented at Westminster.

Membership of select committees is based on the number of seats a political party has in the House of Commons, i.e. the bigger parties will have a larger representation on committees. A minister is not allowed to be a member of a select committee. There are different ways to appoint members to committees, but most are elected by fellow MPs. The select committee's main function is to review the work of the relevant government department and it will have access to important information. It will seek written and oral evidence and then will publish its recommendations. The government then has 60 days to respond. The work of the committee is important to ensure that the department is accountable to Parliament. The proceedings of the committee are televised and although ministers and civil servants cannot be compelled to attend when summoned by the committee, it is advisable that they do attend to face questioning.

PUBLIC LAW IN CONTEXT

In November 2001, the independence of the select committees was seriously questioned when the Labour government deliberately prevented the reappointment of Gwyneth Dunwoody to a committee, which she had chaired in the previous Parliament. Had she been nominated then she would probably have been elected as the chairperson. Previously in July 2001, Dunwoody had been stripped of her position as the chair of the Transport Select Committee by government whips. Dunwoody was not the only Labour MP to be stripped of such a position. The government's treatment of Dunwoody illustrates the problems MPs face when they attempt to hold their own government to account.

The House of Commons Reform Committee delivered its first report in 2009, entitled 'Rebuilding the House.' The committee noted that in response to the Dunwoody controversy, 'the Parliamentary Labour Party agreed a procedure for Labour nominations of Chairs and select committee members to be agreed by their backbench Parliamentary Committee.' The committee discussed the strengths and weaknesses of the select committee system:

Table 7.3

Strengths	Weaknesses
Party balance in the select committees. This means that the opposition parties can nominate MPs to sit on committees and overview the work of the government.	Power of the whips to control the appointment of chairperson. This should be a matter for the House of Commons. MPs in order to be nominated have to agree to the parties' choice of chair.
Split between the government and opposition parties between the positions of committee chairs. This means that the government will not have a monopoly over the chairs of the committees.	It is wrong that the executive can prevent 'maverick' MPs from becoming members of a committee, or that 'former Ministers, and that favoured candidates are parachuted into committees when a vacancy occurs.'
Some power for committees in theory to choose their chairperson. Although the committee noted that this is limited in practice.	Lack of transparency as all political parties will decide on how to divide up position of chairs and whips will decide who to nominate as members.

Table 7.3 (Continued)	
Strengths	Weaknesses
Full membership of committees. There are many MPs willing to serve.	The committee system is used as a source of party-political patronage. Membership of committees is 'largely controlled and influenced by the whips [and] might on occasion be less an "alternative career path" and more of an extension of the massive patronage that already exists through the appointment of ministers.'

The committee proposed that chairs of select committees should be elected by MPs. This was adopted and today the chairperson for most select committees is elected by MPs. This takes place through the use of a secret ballot.

We can see why it is very important that the select committees are able to exercise independently from government. The committees need to review the executive and hold ministers to account. The committee noted that the use of committee membership as patronage meant that committee membership would not be regarded as an 'alternative career path.' This means that unlike in the United States where committee membership and ultimately chairing that committee is considered as a valid and important political career, in the United Kingdom it could be regarded as a steppingstone to a ministerial position.

PUBLIC LAW IN CONTEXT

In the United States, committees exercise considerably more power than they do in the United Kingdom. Serving on a committee is attractive to senior politicians. For example, John Kerry chaired the Senate Foreign Relations Committee after losing the 2004 presidential election against George W. Bush. In 2012 Kerry succeeded Hillary Clinton as US Secretary of State and is currently the Climate Change envoy for President Joseph Biden.

General committees

General committees are focused around particular bills that are going through Parliament. They play an important part in a bill becoming law. The task of members of a general or standing committee is to consider the merits of a bill and then to write a report which is then presented to Parliament. In order to do this the committee will seek written and oral evidence from civil servants and third parties. The House of Commons will consider the report and any amendments which the committee has proposed.

Joint committees

Joint committees comprise members from both Houses of Parliament. They will focus on an area such as House of Lords reform, human rights and the ongoing review of delegated legislation.

Accountability?

Prior to joining the Supreme Court, Lord Sumption delivered a lecture in which he held that the House of Commons does hold the government to account. His Lordship was rejecting the view raised by Lord Steyn in *Jackson* (see above):

> There is a widespread perception that Parliament is no longer capable of holding ministers or officials to account, because party discipline enables ministers with a majority in the House of Commons to control it. . . . [However] the degree of ministerial control over the House of Commons has if anything declined in recent years. Departmental committees of the House of Commons have proved to be a moderately effective method of holding ministers and public officials to account, and a highly effective method of exposing their inadequacies to politically damaging publicity. Even on the floor of the House, where proceedings are naturally more partisan, MPs have defied the party whip more often and in greater numbers in the last two decades than at any time since the war. Individual ministers are vulnerable to Parliamentary sentiment, however large the government's majority.[48]

The previous Prime Minister, Theresa May, suffered numerous defeats in the House of Commons. The current Prime Minister, Boris Johnson, has also suffered defeats in the House of Commons.

ACADEMIC DEBATE

The House of Commons does to some extent hold the government to account. The House of Lords plays a considerably more vocal role in ensuring accountability. Writing in 2013, Anthony King and Ivor Crewe observed, 'As a legislative assembly, the parliament of the United Kingdom is, much of the time, either peripheral or totally irrelevant. It might as well not exist.'[49] This rather pessimistic position was countered by Meg Russell and Philip Cowley, who were clear that this was not supported by the evidence.[50]

7.12.2.2 The House of Lords and executive accountability

Limited power to veto/delay legislation: The Parliament Acts and the Salisbury Convention

As noted above, the House of Lords has a limited power to veto legislation and the House of Commons can pass legislation under the Parliament Acts 1911 and 1949 without the consent of the House of Lords. The Salisbury Convention has further limited the House of Lords' ability to vote against governmental policy that was in its election manifesto. Whilst it may appear correct that the House of Lords has limited powers, it must be remembered that the House of Commons is dominated by a government that enjoys a majority of MPs. The House of Lords has voted against many bills and has successfully forced the government to change its policy on occasion. However, even if the Lords cannot prevent a bill from becoming law, their opposition can highlight flaws in the bill and offer amendments, which can be incorporated into the final bill.

The independent crossbenchers, the experience of members and informed debate

The crossbenchers play an important role in preserving the non-partisan environment of the House of Lords. In the House of Commons there are very few members who are not members of a political party. The ability to have a large a number of independent Lords which are not members of either the government, or the opposition, is important as it offers a non-political perspective on proposed legislation. The members of the Lords tend to have a lot of experience in different areas of society, as a debate on a particular topic will benefit from having Lords with experience in that area. This mixture of highly qualified and respected people in the House of Lords has built a reputation of experience and high-quality debate. Debate in the Lords tends to be better and more considered than in the House of Commons. The crossbenchers serve to make debate less partisan. Any reform of the House of Lords would need to preserve this important strength. Ultimately, the House of Lords does serve as an important and vocal check on the government's legislative agenda.

Questioning government policy

Just as in the House of Commons, government ministers in the House of Lords are questioned during ministerial question time.

The committee system

The House of Lords select committees each focus on a particular area such as economics, sciences, the United Kingdom's constitution and the European Union. The committees' proceedings are televised. The role of the general committee is conducted in the chamber of the House of Lords by all members, rather than a distinct group of members as happens in the Commons.

7.12.2.3 Judicial function

Prior to 2009, Parliament (or more specifically the House of Lords) was the highest court in the United Kingdom (see the Constitutional Reform Act 2005). Over time the Judicial House of Lords had developed into a separate court, and only specially appointed Lords could hear appeals (Lords of Appeal in Ordinary). The United Kingdom Supreme Court is now distinct both in location and name from the legislative House of Lords.

The creation of the Supreme Court was seen as an important way of helping to create the separation of powers in the United Kingdom. Importantly, it was confusing if not questionable to have the highest court and the legislative chamber sharing the same name, members (as the Law Lords could take part in debates and vote) and building.

ACADEMIC DEBATE
THE USE OF IMPEACHMENT

Historically, Parliament used impeachment to hold the executive to account for high crimes and misdeameanours. The House of Commons would vote on whether there were sufficient charges to impeach and the trial would take place before the House of Lords. Impeachment originated during the Good Parliament of 1376 and the first person to be impeached was Lord Latimer. Impeachment fell into disuse during the 15th century and was rediscovered by parliamentarians (including Sir Edward Coke) in 1621. It was often accused of being used for partisan purposes and the impeachments that took place during the beginning of the 18th century were politically partisan. The most famous impeachment and subsequent trial was that of Warren Hastings, the former governor-general of Bengal, who was impeached by the House of Commons in 1787 and his subsequent trial lasted seven years.

The last impeachment, that of Viscount Meville, took place in 1805 and he was acquitted by the House of Lords in 1806. Impeachment still takes place in the United States of America and President Donald Trump was impeached twice by the House of Representatives, in 2019 and 2021, although on both occasions he was acquitted by the Senate.

There is an interesting debate about whether impeachment could ever be used again in the United Kingdom. In 2004, there was an attempt to impeach the then Prime Minister, Tony Blair, in relation to the invasion of Iraq. The attempt did not proceed and was supported by approximately 20 MPs, including Boris Johnson, Edward Garnier and Douglas Hogg (now Viscount Hailsham).

Have a read of the briefing paper from Jack Simson Caird from of House of Commons Library. Do you think that impeachment could ever serve a way to enhance the powers of the House of Commons and improve how the executive is held to account?

The briefing paper, 'Impeachment' Number CBP7612, 6 June 2016, can be found at: https://commonslibrary.parliament.uk/research-briefings/cbp-7612/.

7.13 Practical application

1   Do you think that the House of Commons effectively holds the government to account?
2   Do MPs have sufficient freedom to raise matters and start debates in the House?

Key points to take away from this chapter

- Parliament is composed of the House of Commons, the House of Lords and the Queen in Parliament.
- Reform of the House of Lords has been proposed since the beginning of the 20th century. The House of Lords Act 1999 left considerable scope for further reform.
- The Parliament Acts 1911 and 1949 have limited the power of the House of Lords to veto legislation.
- Members of Parliament who represent their constituents in the House of Commons are elected by a system known as First Past the Post. Members of the House of Lords are not elected by the electorate.
- Parliament is the supreme law-maker in the United Kingdom and is responsible for holding the executive to account.

Notes

1   C Shenton, *The Day Parliament Burned Down* (OUP 2012).
2   'Huawei: Government Wins Vote After Backbench Rebellion' *BBC News* (10 March 2020) <www.bbc.co.uk/news/uk-politics-51806704>.
3   M Flinders, 'MPs' Expenses: The Legacy of a Scandal' *BBC News* (7 May 2018) <www.bbc.co.uk/news/uk-politics-48187096>.
4   D McKie, 'Do Our MPs Lie? Yes, Copiously and Consistently' *The Guardian* (26 May 2015) <www.theguardian.com/commentisfree/2015/may/26/mps-lies-sliding-scale-alistair-carmichael>.
5   B Quinn, 'Judge Rejects Court Action Against Boris Johnson Over £350m Brexit Claim' *The Guardian* (14 August 2019) <www.theguardian.com/politics/2019/aug/14/johnson-quashes-supreme-court-action-over-350m-brexit-claim>.
6   S Carrell and O Bowcott, 'Did Johnson Lie to the Queen? Key Questions in the Supreme Court Verdict' *The Guardian* (24 September 2019) <www.theguardian.com/law/2019/sep/24/uk-supreme-court-ruling-key-issues-behind-judges-decision-boris-johnson-suspension-parliament>.
7   *R (on the application of Miller) v The Prime Minister* [2019] UKSC 41. The court stated that '[w]e are not concerned with the Prime Minister's *motive* in doing what he did' [58].
8   McKie (n 4). Mckie observed 'Chris Bryant said in the house that Jeremy Hunt, then culture secretary, had lied to the house about his connections with the forces of Rupert Murdoch.'

9   See <https://assets.ctfassets.net/rdwvqctnt75b/7iQEHtrkIbLcrUkduGmo9b/
    cb429a657e97cad61e61853c05c8c4d1/Hansard-Society__Audit-of-Political-
    Engagement-16__2019-report.pdf>.

10 ibid 361.

11 D Hughes, 'Revealed: The Lords Is Increasingly Out of Touch with Modern
    Britain' (*Electoral Reform Society*, 18 June 2019) <www.electoral-reform.org.uk/
    revealed-the-lords-is-increasingly-out-of-touch-with-modern-britain/>.

12 'How Undemocratic Is the House of Lords?' *Democratic Audit* (2 October 2018)
    <www.democraticaudit.com/2018/10/02/audit2018-how-undemocratic-
    is-the-house-of-lords/>.

13 'Seaned Vote: Public Vote to Keep Irish Senate' *BBC News* (5 October 2013)
    <www.bbc.co.uk/news/world-europe-24404157>.

14 See United States Senate <www.senate.gov/artandhistory/history/common/
    briefing/Origins_Development.htm>.

15 See United States Senate <www.cop.senate.gov/about/origins-foundations/idea-
    of-the-senate/1787Federalist62.htm>.

16 [2005] UKHL 56, [9].

17 *R (on the application of Miller) v Secretary of State for Exiting the European Union
    (No. 1)* [2016] EWHC 2768 (Admin) [20].

18 *R (on the application of Miller) v Secretary of State for Exiting the European Union
    (No. 1)* [2017] UKSC 5 [43].

19 [2016] EWHC 2768 (Admin).

20 European Communities Act 1972.

21 [2016] EWHC 2768 (Admin), [20].

22 AV Dicey, *Introduction to the Study of the Law of the Constitution* (Liberty Fund
    1982).

23 Now known as the Welsh Parliament.

24 D Gover and M Kenny, 'Five Years of "EVEL"' (*The Constitution Unit*, 23 Octo-
    ber 2020) <https://constitution-unit.com/2020/10/23/five-years-of-evel/>.

25 E Arnold et al, 'SNP Lead "Speak No EVEL" Commons Protest Against English-
    Only NHS Funding' (*Daily Record*, 4 February 2020) <www.dailyrecord.co.uk/
    news/politics/snp-mps-lead-speak-no-21430827>.

26 See <www.parliament.uk/globalassets/documents/lords-library/hllsalisburydoctrine.
    pdf>.

27 [2005] UKHL 56.

28 T Bingham, *The Lives of the Law: Selected Essays and Speeches 2000–2010* (OUP
    2011) 113.

29 See www.parliament.uk/about/faqs/house-of-lords-faqs/lords-govtdefeats/.

30 [2019] UKSC 41.

31 R Hogarth, *The FTPA Is a Bad Law – but It Should Not Be Replaced with Something
    Worse* (Institute for Government 27 November 2019) <www.instituteforgovern
    ment.org.uk/blog/ftpa-should-not-be-replaced-something-worse>.

32 R Hazell, 'The Fixed-Term Parliaments Act: Should It Be Amended or Repealed?'
    (*The Constitution Unit*, 11 December 2020) <https://constitution-unit.com/2020/
    12/11/the-fixed-term-parliaments-act-should-it-be-amended-or-repealed/>.

33 [2010] UKSC 52.

34 <www.telegraph.co.uk/politics/2019/09/03/tories-tear-convention-plan-
    contest-john-bercows-seat-general/>.

35 Alexandra Kelso, 'Parliament' in *The Oxford Handbook of British Politics* (OUP
    2011) 232.

36   P Walker and B Quinn, 'Boris Johnson "Still Committed to Lords Reduction" Despite 35 Peerages' *The Guardian* (3 August 2020) <www.theguardian.com/politics/2020/aug/03/no-10-boris-johnson-pm-still-committed-lords-reduction-despite-36-peerages>.

37   N Fowler, 'The House of Lords Is Bloated: We Need an Inquiry into the Peerages System' *The Guardian* (23 December 2020) <www.theguardian.com/commentisfree/2020/dec/23/house-of-lords-peerages-appointments>.

38   ibid.

39   D Lewis Jones, 'Judicial Role of the House of Lords Before 1870' in L Blom-Cooper, B Dickson and G Drewry (eds), *The Judicial House of Lords: 1876–2009* (OUP 2009) 11.

40   Lord Reed, 'The Supreme Court Ten Years On' The Bentham Association Lecture 2019, University College London, 6 March 2019 <www.supremecourt.uk/docs/speech-190306.pdf>.

41   at [3.1].

42   Bingham (n 28) 116–18.

43   For more details on government defeats in the House of Lords see the UCL Constitution Unit's ongoing research at <www.ucl.ac.uk/silva/constitution-unit/research/parliament/house-of-lords/lords-defeats>.

44   Report of the Lord Speaker's Committee on the Size of the House (31 October 2017) <https://old.parliament.uk/documents/lords-committees/size-of-house/size-of-house-report.pdf>.

45   M Russell, 'Lords Reform Is Back on the Agenda: What Are the Options?' (*The Constitution Unit*, 23 February 2020) <https://constitution-unit.com/2020/02/23/lords-reform-is-back-on-the-agenda-what-are-the-options/>.

46   [2005] UKHL 56.

47   ibid 71.

48   J Sumption, 'Judicial and Political Decision-Making: The Uncertain Boundary' The FA Mann Lecture, 2011.

49   A King and I Crewe, *The Blunders of Our Governments* (Oneworld 2013) 361.

50   M Russell and P Cowley, 'The Policy Power of the Westminster Parliament: The "Parliamentary State" and the Empirical Evidence' (2015) 29(1) Governance: An International Journal of Policy, Administration and Institutions 121.

Further reading

Bingham T, *Lives of the Law: Selected Essays and Speeches 2000–2010* (OUP 2011)

Gay O and H Tomlinson, 'Parliamentary Privilege and Freedom of Speech' in A Horne, G Drewry and D Oliver (eds), *Parliament and the Law* (Hart Publishing 2013)

Gover D and M Kenny, 'Answering the West Lothian Question? A Critical Assessment of "English Votes for English Laws" in the UK Parliament' (2018) 71(4) Parliamentary Affairs 760

House of Lords Briefing, 'Reform and Proposals for Reform Since 1900' (2006) <www.parliament.uk/documents/lords-information-office/hoflbpreform.pdf>

Leyland P, *The Constitution of the United Kingdom: A Contextual Analysis* (3rd edn, Hart Publishing 2016)

Lipscombe S and A Horne, 'Parliamentary Privilege and Criminal Law' in A Horne, G Drewry and D Oliver (eds), *Parliament and the Law* (Hart Publishing 2013)

McHarg A, 'Devolution in Scotland' in J Jowell and C O'Cinneide (eds), *The Changing Constitution* (9th edn, OUP 2019)

Norton P, *Parliament in British Politics* (2nd edn, Palgrave Macmillan 2013)

———, 'Parliament: The Best of Times, the Worst of Times' in J Jowell and C O'Cinneide (eds), *The Changing Constitution* (9th edn, OUP 2019)

Oliver D, 'The Parliament Acts, the Constitution, the Rule of Law, and the Second Chamber' (2012) 33(1) SLR 1

Rawlings R, 'The Welsh Way/Y Ffordd Gymreig' in J Jowell and C O'Cinneide (eds), *The Changing Constitution* (9th edn, OUP 2019)

Sumption J, 'Judicial and Political Decision-Making: The Uncertain Boundary' The FA Mann Lecture, 2011

Wakeham L (Chairman), *A House for the Future: Royal Commission on the Reform of the House of Lords* (The Stationery Office 2000)

White Paper, 'An Elected Second Chamber: Further Reform of the House of Lords' (2008) <https://assets.publishing.service.gov.uk/government/uploads/system/uploads/attachment_data/file/228706/7438.pdf>

———, 'The House of Lords Reform Draft Bill' in *Erskine May's Treatise on the Law, Privileges, Proceedings and Usage of Parliament* (25th edn, 2019) <https://erskinemay.parliament.uk> <www.parliament.uk>

The executive

Crown, government and accountability

This chapter will

- consider the role of the Crown in the United Kingdom;

- explore the functions of the monarch and the monarchy as an institution;

- define what is meant by the executive and accountability;

- examine the office of prime minister, the role of the Cabinet and civil service; and

- review the effects of devolution upon executive responsibility for the United Kingdom.

8.1 Introduction

Henry VIII[1] had two of his chief ministers charged with treason and another escaped execution by dying whilst in custody. Henry also had two wives executed by having their heads chopped off, and he was granted powers by Parliament to create law using his prerogative powers and to decide royal succession on the basis of his own will. By contrast Elizabeth II[2] is a constitutional monarch who has weekly audiences with her prime ministers and reads state papers, but strives to remain above party politics and the business of government. Almost 500 years separate Henry VIII and Elizabeth II and the nature of the executive has changed significantly since the days when members of the government could be killed (albeit after a trial) because they fell out of royal favour. This chapter will explore what is meant by the executive today and examine the relationship between the monarch and her prime minister.

The executive is responsible for the governance of the United Kingdom. When we talk about the executive we could mean the government, the Cabinet, the Prime Minister or the Crown. Equally we could be referring to the civil servants who run the government departments, local authorities, government

DOI: 10.4324/9780429293498-10

agencies such as the Crown Prosecution Service or the Highways Agency, or the armed forces. The growth of the executive in the 20th century has been considerable, with the executive now responsible for many areas of our lives. We will all encounter the state and its agencies on a daily basis, and our day-to-day freedoms are monitored and in some ways restricted by the state. For example, our telephone calls may be tapped, our journey to work recorded by CCTV cameras, our private information collated and until in the early 2000s it looked likely that we would all require a compulsory identity card. This proposal was never implemented due to the wartime connotations of compulsory identification, although it is worth noting that this system applies in much of continental Europe.

The two people arguably most associated with the executive are the Prime Minister, who is the head of government, and the Queen, which is the head of state. Today it is the Prime Minister who is most powerful in terms of their actual day-to-day powers in directing the business of state, whereas hundreds of years ago it would have been the monarch. The monarchy is largely ceremonial, with the monarch playing a significant role in terms of tradition, such as the State Opening of Parliament, or formal Prorogation at the end of each session of Parliament. However, as we shall see the monarch does have significant

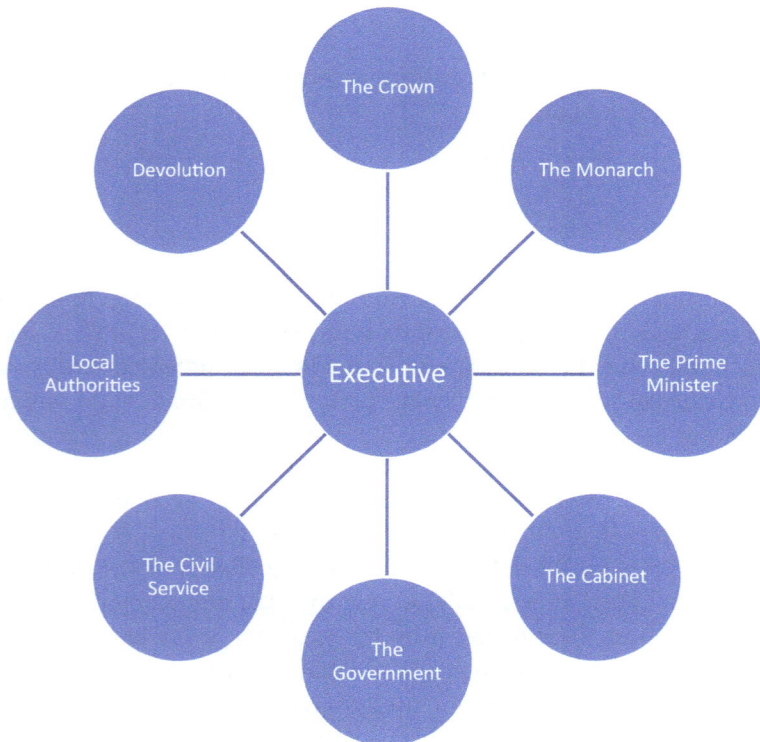

Figure 8.1
Chapter Overview

power and could, however unrealistically, exercise real power, as opposed to acting as a constitutional monarch. Returning to the Prime Minister it is the Queen who appoints her, and the two have weekly audiences in which they discuss government policy, for it is the Queen's government and it carries on business in her name.

In this chapter we will focus on the roles of the monarch, the government, the Cabinet, the Prime Minister and government departments. Consideration will also be given to the executive bodies which have been created by devolution in Wales, Scotland and Northern Ireland, as well as a directly elected mayor in London. Given that the executive is responsible for the running of the United Kingdom and will make important decisions, such as the closing of hospitals, the decision to invade a foreign country and indeed which schools will receive funding to replace existing buildings, we will look at how the executive is held to account. Accountability is important to prevent the executive from dominating public life and taking arbitrary decisions. We will look at how the executive is held to account, politically by Parliament, and legally by the courts.

8.2 The Crown

The Crown is a term which is misleading, as Maitland famously wrote,

> There is one term against which I wish to warn you, and that term is 'the crown.' You will certainly read that the crown does this and the crown does that. As a matter of fact we know that the crown does nothing but lie in the Tower of London to be gazed at by sight-seers.[3]

The Crown is an important symbol of the state, as during the State of Opening of Parliament by the Queen, the Crown will be brought to Parliament in its own carriage and will be accompanied by an escort of the Household Cavalry. Maitland observed that in order to see who exercises the power we needed to look at whether the power was being exercised under the prerogative or statute. The Crown is shorthand for the power which is exercised by the government, though prerogative and statutory powers. The Crown can be used to describe the monarch's powers or those powers which are exercised by the government.

It is important to note that the monarch is expected to use her constitutional powers responsibly and to act upon the advice of her Prime Minister. Professor Blackburn has noted that

> [t]he legal context within which the monarch reigns but does not rule remains a mystery to most people. Operating in an unwritten and uncodified system of government even the very concept of the Crown as a legal entity is open to uncertainty and ambiguity. . . . The Crown as executive and Crown as monarch are distinct concepts in law for certain purposes.'[4]

8.2.1 The monarch

The head of state of the United Kingdom is the monarch. The monarchy is a constitutional one, meaning that the monarchy's role is regulated by the constitution. The monarch's power is restricted by the constitution. We need to appreciate that the restrictions are not written down nor are they legal, instead constitutional conventions regulate the monarch's role within the United Kingdom's constitution.

Over the last several hundred years the monarch's power has been reduced. The monarch's ability to make laws was challenged by Parliament and the courts during the 17th century. Today the monarch plays a largely ceremonial role carrying out duties such as opening Parliament, receiving ambassadors and giving formal assent to legislation. The monarch is also head of the Commonwealth and is still head of state of many Commonwealth nations including Australia, Canada and Jamaica.

The current monarch is Elizabeth II who has reigned since 1952. Elizabeth II is Queen of the United Kingdom (although to be accurate she should be Elizabeth I, as Elizabeth I, who ruled from 1558 to 1603, was only Queen of England). The heir to the throne is Prince Charles, Prince of Wales (see Figure 8.2 for a list of monarchs since 1714).

The monarch has personal prerogative powers and could theoretically refuse to give her assent to legislation, to choose her government and Prime Minister. Legally the monarch could do these things. However, the monarch will follow constitutional conventions which state that her power will be controlled by established constitutional principles. The existence of the monarchy is owed to the monarch's voluntary surrender of power.

The choice of monarch is determined by Parliament and the rules are laid out in the Succession to the Crown Act 2013. The current monarch could not determine, as Henry VIII did, the succession to the Crown in her will, as Parliament

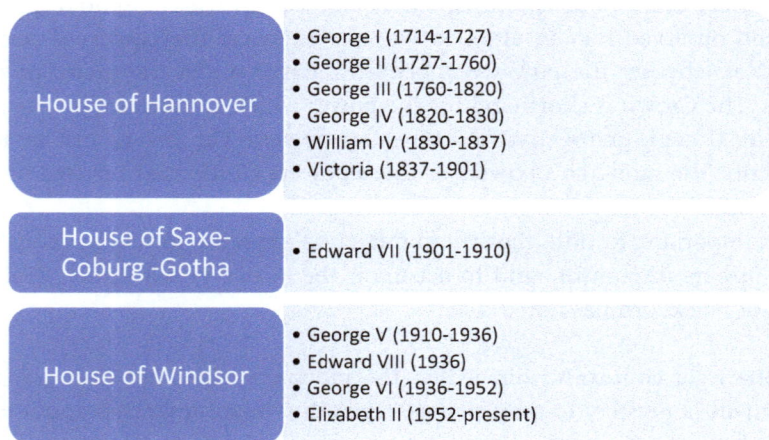

House of Hannover	• George I (1714-1727) • George II (1727-1760) • George III (1760-1820) • George IV (1820-1830) • William IV (1830-1837) • Victoria (1837-1901)
House of Saxe-Coburg -Gotha	• Edward VII (1901-1910)
House of Windsor	• George V (1910-1936) • Edward VIII (1936) • George VI (1936-1952) • Elizabeth II (1952-present)

Figure 8.2
The monarchs of the United Kingdom since 1714

has removed this power. The Act of Settlement 1701 restricts a Roman Catholic from becoming the monarch, although the Succession to the Crown Act 2013 has removed the requirement that upon marriage to a Roman Catholic, a member of the royal family can no longer succeed to the crown.[5] Section 1 of the Succession to the Crown Act 2013 states that, '[i]n determining the succession to the Crown, the gender of a person born after 28 October 2011 does not give that person, or that person's descendants, precedence over any other person (whenever born).' This means that a first-born child who happened to be female would no longer lose their place in the list of succession in the event of the second-born child happening to be male. The effect of the Act of Settlement can be seen in Figure 8.2 below, whereby the Roman Catholic half-brother of Queen Anne was prevented from succeeding to the Crown, and instead, as stipulated by the Act, the Crown was inherited in 1714 by George I (the ruler of Hannover in what is now Germany) who was a distant relation and most importantly a Protestant.

8.2.2 The Queen's role in the Commonwealth

The Queen is also the monarch of those Commonwealth countries where she is also head of state. For example, Elizabeth II is Queen of Australia and is represented by a governor-general who gives formal assent to legislation. The Queen of Australia has prerogative powers and these are regulated by constitutional conventions. The Succession to the Crown Act 2015 is an Australian Act that governs the succession to the Crown. It mirrors the UK Act, as section 6 removes gender inequality and section 7 removes the disqualification of marrying a Roman Catholic.

8.2.3 A constitutional monarchy

The United Kingdom is a constitutional monarchy and over time the monarch's actual power has been gradually eroded. The fact that the monarchy still exists is a remarkable achievement. Most other European monarchies were swept away at the end of the First World War. Germany, France, Russia, Italy and Poland are republics, while Spain and several other northern European countries, such as Denmark and Norway, are monarchies.

PUBLIC LAW IN CONTEXT

The monarchy under the Stuarts was one of absolute monarchs who claimed to have the divine right of kings. James I and Charles I believed themselves to have superior law-making powers to Parliament and Charles I ruled for much of his reign without there being a Parliament. Charles I fought a civil war against Parliament, but was defeated and executed. Eventually the monarchy was restored under Charles II, who clashed with Parliament, as did his brother James II, who eventually fled to France. Parliament gave the crown to William III and Mary II and from then on Parliament was acknowledged as legally sovereign, and was superior to the executive. The monarchy retained considerable power, however, until the succession of the German-speaking George I in the 18th century and the creation of Cabinet government. Then George I handed over the day-to-day running of the country to his first minister, Sir Robert Walpole, who is regarded as the first Prime Minister. Thenceforth, it was parliamentarians who dominated the executive and exercised most of the monarch's prerogative powers.

The monarchy has been good at evolving to survive. The modern House of Windsor was created by George V in 1917 to distance himself from his German relatives. George V was determined that the monarchy would be connected to the British people and he recorded the first Christmas Day broadcast which continues today. Commenting on how the monarchy has survived as a legitimate system in a democracy, Professor Vernon Bogdanor observed,

> [t]he most remarkable feature in the history of the monarchy remains the skill with which it has adapted itself to changing conditions. In the United Kingdom the monarchy has been an institution which, behind unchanging forms, has seemed almost infinitely adaptable, even if at times this adaption seemed somewhat unwilling.[6]

Recently, Parliament has enacted legislation that will permit the first-born child of the monarch to succeed to the throne regardless of gender. This is important as it shows that the monarchy as an institution is not sexist. The monarchy must be relevant if it is to survive and it must serve its important purpose that according to Bogdanor is to represent the United Kingdom.[7] The present monarch, Elizabeth II, has represented the United Kingdom abroad and serves as an important symbol of continuity with the past, and as a head of state the monarch is above party politics.

Walter Bagehot in *The English Constitution* noted that, '[a] family on the throne is an interesting idea. . . . It brings the pride of sovereignty to the level of petty life. No feeling could seem more childish than the enthusiasm of the English at the marriage of the Prince of Wales.'[8] Bagehot was writing in the 1860s, but this surely applies to the royal wedding of Prince William and Catherine Middleton in 2011, or Prince Harry and Meghan Markle in 2018.

8.2.4 The personal power of the monarch

The monarch exercises those prerogative powers which are personal to her (see **Chapters 10** and **11**). The monarch has the power to refuse assent to legislation, to choose her next government and Prime Minister and to dissolve Parliament (subject to the Fixed-term Parliaments Act 2011). These powers are very import-ant and it might seem strange that in a democracy, a person who is unelected would exercise these. However, the constitution controls the exercise of these powers through the existence of constitutional conventions and these powers are only used after taking advice from the Prime Minister and government The last monarch to refuse to give her assent to a bill was Queen Anne in 1708, and George III understood that in the early 1780s that he could not refuse assent to legislation which he disliked.

The monarch cannot exercise her prerogative powers unless acting upon the advice of her ministers. Obviously, she could act without such advice, but this would mean that the monarch would be acting unconstitutionally.

ACADEMIC DEBATE

The last monarch to refuse royal assent to legislation was Queen Anne, who on the advice of her ministers, refused her assent to the Scottish Militia Bill in 1708. Refusing royal assent on the advice of democratically elected ministers, who command the confidence of the House of Commons, is different to refusing royal assent where the government and the monarch are not in agreement. In **Chapter 2** we explored the reason why there is a constitutional convention, which restricts the ability of the monarch to use her prerogative powers to refuse royal assent. However, is it constitutional for ministers to advise the monarch to withhold royal assent? This is arguably a moot point for it means that Parliament has voted to introduce a bill despite the opposition of the government, and the government in order to prevent this bill from becoming an Act, will seek to advise the monarch to withhold royal assent. In light of the fact that a government must command the confidence of the House of Commons in order to remain in power, it would be in the most exceptional circumstances that a government would be unable to prevent the House of Commons from voting for legislation that the government opposed. Commentators believed that this might occur within the context of the Brexit debates on indicative motions in the spring of 2019, when the government could not effectively command its own MPs (or even some ministers) from voting to support the then prime minister's Brexit deal. There might have been a possibility that the House of Commons would propose legislation that was contrary to the prime minister's own Brexit deal, which if this bill passed the House of Lords, feasibly, however unlikely, could have seen the prime minister advise the monarch to refuse royal assent.

Professor Richard Ekins and Stephen Laws QC argued that in the context of the Brexit process the government could advise the monarch to refuse royal assent.[9] It is an interesting argument and is based on the fact that the government whilst not able to prevent legislation would nonetheless retain the confidence of the House of Commons. Ekins and Laws argued:

'What can the government do about it? Well, it is perfectly legitimate for the government to resist so long as it retains the confidence of the House. The logic of our constitution is clear: provided the Commons does not withdraw its confidence, Her Majesty's ministers can and should insist on retaining the power to discharge their responsibility to govern. Legislation designed to usurp the government's functions should be blocked. If the Speaker were to subvert the normal rules – as past events suggest he might – the government might even prorogue parliament, ending a session prematurely to stop a bill being passed. The process of royal assent has become a formality, but if legislation would otherwise be passed by an abuse of constitutional process and principle facilitated by a rogue Speaker, the government might plausibly consider advising Her Majesty not to assent to the bill in question: it would be MPs, not the government, that had opened up the question of whether an executive veto on legislation should be revived.'

Professor Thomas Poole argued against this position and was clear that this was not constitutionally correct:

'What Ekins and Laws suggest, in effect, is getting the monarch to thwart Parliament in the interests of the executive. At the level of principle, this is little short of monstrous. It invents for the 21st-century executive, out of the archaic form of the monarch's 'negative voice,' a power to veto legislation. They invoke a principle that the law should not be changed until both the government and Parliament have agreed that it should be. There is no such principle.'[10]

Professor Jeff King took the view that if the government did seek to advise the monarch to refuse royal assent, then the monarch was under no constitutional obligation to follow the government's advice.

'Royal Assent is an instance of a prerogative power to which ministerial advice does not apply but to which other constitutional conventions apply.

'Here, as with the convention of Royal Assent in respect of her legislative function, the constitutional convention goes with the grain of a representative democracy and governs her use of the prerogative power entirely independently of Government views. My claim is therefore that there is no convention that ministerial advice be accepted in relation to exercise of Royal Assent, for the Queen follows, as the preamble to all enactments states, the advice of the two Houses of Parliament and not the advice of the Government. The proffering of ministerial advice may in some kinds of cases be permissible.

'In the UK, however, the Monarch is not bound to accept that advice. It is a separate question, in fact, and not explored seriously here, whether in circumstances such as the present, it would be unreasonable and hence unlawful for ministers to advise the Queen to withhold consent.'[11]

This is interesting as we can see this is far from a clear-cut issue, and one where academics hold very different opinions. It is submitted that the argument advanced by Ekins and Laws is unconvincing, either as a matter of constitutional principle, or one that would be likely to happen in reality. That is not to say that a prime minister might be tempted to advise the monarch, however unlikely such a situation were to occur, although King is quite clear that the monarch would be free to refuse such advice. To conclude if the government were to advise that assent should be refused and the monarch was to follow such advice, then it is questionable how long the government would retain the confidence of the House of Commons.

Exceptionally, there may be times that the monarch will exercise her powers without the advice of her ministers. Elizabeth II in her capacity as Queen of Fiji sent two messages in 1987; these messages were sent without the advice of her

Fijian ministers who had been deposed by a military coup. It is clear why the monarch acted without ministerial advice and if the government of the United Kingdom were to be removed through an act of terrorism, then it is conceivable that the monarch may have to use her prerogative powers without royal assent.

This means that the choosing of a government, the dissolution of Parliament (subject to the Fixed-term Parliaments Act 2011) and the giving of royal assent is decided for the monarch by the electorate, the Prime Minister and Parliament. Where the monarch has exercised her powers to make a choice without first having received advice, then such an exercise of choice might prove controversial. An example of this is where the monarch had to choose between two leading members of the Conservative Party to become Prime Minister in 1957 and 1963. In 1963, the monarch had appointed Alec Douglas-Home as Prime Minister, rather than Rab Butler. However, Thorpe rejects the notion that the monarch remained impartial:

> [t]he Palace made it clear that the choice of a new leader should be for the Conservative Party alone, a process known as "You Choose, We Send For". Far from colluding, the Queen maintained the monarchy's political impartiality, waiting for a name to be brought to her.[12]

Today the internal rules of the Conservative Party would decide the leadership of the party, so that the monarch would not be required to make such a choice again. The Cabinet Manual is clear on this point: '[w]here a Prime Minister chooses to resign from his or her individual position at a time when his or her administration has an overall majority in the House of Commons, it is for the party or parties in government to identify who can be chosen as the successor.'[13] In 2019, when Theresa May resigned as leader of the Conservative Party, the choice of her successor as both the leader of the party and the Prime Minister was determined by the party's own internal leadership election rules, which involved MPs voting to reduce the number of candidates to two and the final choice elected by the membership of the party.

Bagehot noted that the monarch had the prerogative power to veto legislation, but in reality '[s]he must sign her own death-warrant if the two Houses unanimously send it up to her,' and that the monarch no longer controlled the executive, as ministers pursue policies independently of the monarch.[14] Bagehot defined the rights of the monarch as being the right to be consulted, the right to encourage and the right to warn:

> To state the matter shortly, the sovereign has, under a constitutional monarchy such as ours, three rights – the right to be consulted, the right to encourage, the right to warn. And a king of great sense and sagacity would want no others. He would find that his having no others would enable him to use these with singular effect. He would say to his Minister: 'The responsibility of these measures is upon you. Whatever you think best must be done. Whatever you think best shall have my full and effectual support. BUT you will observe that for this reason and that reason what you propose

to do is bad; for this reason and that reason what you do not propose is better. I do not oppose, it is my duty not to oppose; but observe that I WARN.' Supposing the king to be right, and to have what kings often have, the gift of effectual expression, he could not help moving his Minister. He might not always turn his course, but he would always trouble his mind.[15]

The monarch today still has weekly meetings with the Prime Minister and offers advice and encouragement, and may well warn against particular government proposals. These meetings are private and so we do not know what is said. Sarah Bradford has described the relationship between the monarch and her prime ministers:

She never talks about her PMs and they never talk about her. It is said that she raises an eyebrow when she agrees with a view preferred and that her face remains motionless when she does not. Yet we know from what former prime ministers have intimated that she makes each one feel they have a confidante in her; more than that, that they have the ear of the Queen in a way that none of their predecessors ever had. This is very skilfully done, the frontier between monarch and Prime Minister is never actually crossed.[16]

PUBLIC LAW IN CONTEXT
ROYAL CONSENT AS OPPOSED TO ROYAL ASSENT

Royal consent is a constitutional convention whereby the consent of either the monarch or the Prince of Wales is needed before a bill will be introduced to Parliament. Consent is required where a bill would affect the Queen's prerogative powers, her personal or royal interests, or in her capacity as the Duke of Lancaster, or the Prince of Wales in his capacity as the Duke of Cornwall. The monarch and the Prince of Wales have given their consent to 20 draft bills and on no occasion has consent been refused.[17] This is different from royal assent. The Office of the Parliamentary Counsel is clear that '[t]he granting of Queen's or Prince's consent for a bill is merely a consent for Parliament to debate the bill and does not affect the theoretical right of the monarch to withhold Royal Assent to the bill. That said, Royal Assent is of course never refused for a bill that has successfully made its way through Parliament.'[18]

8.2.5 The monarch's roles

The monarch is the head of state of the United Kingdom and whilst this role is heavily ceremonial, the monarch's assent is needed before legislation becomes law. The monarch chairs the Privy Council and exercises important prerogative powers. The monarch is also the head of the Commonwealth, which includes countries such as India and Canada. The monarch does not have any powers as the head of the Commonwealth; rather this role is ceremonial, but the monarch will use her position to conduct personal diplomacy with other heads of state. The head of the Commonwealth is not a hereditary position and the monarch's successor need not have been a member of the royal family. However, in 2018 the leaders of the Commonwealth agreed that her eldest son, Charles, Prince of Wales, would succeed the queen. The monarch is also the Supreme Governor of the Church of England. This role is inherited from Henry VIII breaking links with the Roman Catholic Church in the 1530s.

8.2.6 Should the United Kingdom become a republic?

Most countries are republics and there have been calls for the United Kingdom to become a republic and for the abolition of the monarchy. In 2000, *The Guardian* newspaper supported attempts for the United Kingdom to become a republic:

> We declare our hand: we hope that in time we will move – by democratic consensus – to become a republic. We are gradualists: we accept that it will not happen tomorrow. Let the Queen remain Queen for as long as she lives, or she wishes, or she remains able. But in the meantime there should be a long, vigorous and grown-up debate – both inside and outside parliament – as to who, or what, should succeed her.[19]

If the United Kingdom were to become a republic then either the Prime Minister would become the head of state, or we might have an elected President who would take on many of the monarch's powers, as is the case in Germany or Italy. Polls suggest that the monarchy is still very popular, and it was telling that Alec Salmond, who was the then First Minister of Scotland during the 2014 referendum campaign on Scottish independence, wanted to keep the monarch as the head of state of an independent Scotland.[20] In 2015, one poll conducted by YouGov revealed that 68 per cent of respondents believed that the monarchy was good for the United Kingdom and some 62 per cent of respondents believed that the monarchy would still be here in 100 years' time.[21]

8.2.7 Prince Charles and the future of the monarchy

Some constitutional commentators have questioned whether Charles, when he succeeds his mother as monarch, will be able to carry out the duties of king without causing some constitutional difficulties.[22] This is due to Prince Charles' activist nature and his Royal Highness' willingness to make his views known to members of the government. *The Guardian* newspaper obtained after a lengthy legal battle letters that the prince had written to government ministers.[23] The letters were known as the Black Spider memos due to the nature of the prince's handwriting. These show that the correspondence between the prince and the then Prime Minister where Charles gave his advice on policy: 'I discussed with you some relatively simple steps which I think could be taken to ameliorate the situation and ensure that help is given to ease the transition to the new world. If I may, I shall list them.'[24]

8.3 The formation of a government

The United Kingdom is governed by the executive. The government manages the country and is responsible for national matters such as transportation, health and defence. Many of these areas will be managed on a more local level by National Health Service Trusts and local authorities. However, it is the government that is ultimately responsible and takes key national decisions.

A political party will get to form the next government if at a General Election:

1   They can command the confidence of the House of Commons by having a *majority of all* MPs, or
2   They are able to form a formal coalition with another party and then have a majority of all MPs, or
3   They are able to form a formal inter-party agreement with another party and then have a majority of all MPs, or
4   They can enter into a supply and confidence agreement with another party and then although they are a minority government they will notionally be supported by a majority of all MPs.

However, it is important to note that the Cabinet Manual states that:

> [w]here an election does not result in an overall majority for a single party, the incumbent government remains in office unless and until the Prime Minister tenders his or her resignation and the Government's resignation to the Sovereign. An incumbent government is entitled to wait until the new Parliament has met to see if it can command the confidence of the House of Commons, but is expected to resign if it becomes clear that it is unlikely to be able to command that confidence and there is a clear alternative.[25]

In 2010, the May general election saw the incumbent Labour government lose its majority in the House of Commons and gain the second largest number of MPs, 258. The Conservative opposition gained the largest number of MPs, 306, but did not have a majority of all MPs. The then Prime Minister, Gordon Brown, did not immediately resign and both the Labour and Conservative Parties sought to enter into a coalition with the Liberal Democrat Party, who had 57 MPs. Some commentators in the press accused Gordon Brown of squatting in Downing Street during this time; however, we can see that it was constitutionally appropriate for him to stay on as Prime Minister until it was clear that another party could command the confidence of the House of Commons. In the event, the Liberal Democrats agreed to enter into a formal coalition with the Conservatives and Gordon Brown then resigned as prime minister.

PUBLIC LAW IN CONTEXT
SQUATTING IN DOWNING STREET?

Based on pure parliamentary arithmetic it appeared in 2010 that Gordon Brown's Labour government had lost the general election and in some quarters of the press there was a view that he should immediately get into his government limousine, be driven to Buckingham Palace and tender his resignation to the monarch. To do otherwise would be squatting in Downing Street, as he had lost the popular mandate that the Labour Party had won in the 2005 general election under Tony Blair. Gordon Brown remaining in Downing Street was reported as 'Mr Brown, who has effectively been a "squatter" at Number Ten since the election delivered Labour's worst result in decades and ended in a hung parliament, at last gave in to the inevitable.'

However, David Cameron's Conservative party did not have a majority in the House of Commons despite having the last number of MPs and therefore had Brown resigned straightaway he would have had to advise the monarch to summon Cameron to form the next government. Cameron would not have been able to command the confidence of the House of Commons and any Conservative government would have been a minority government and could have faced an immediate vote of no confidence.

Therefore what was Gordon Brown to do? The only viable option was for either the Labour government or Conservative party to form a coalition government or other arrangement with the Liberal Democrats, the third largest party. This would have created a majority in the House of Commons. The problem was that to enter into negotiations would take time and in the meantime Brown felt he had to stay on as Prime Minister to avoid a situation whereby the United Kingdom would have had no effective government.

Petra Schleiter and Valerie Belu has reviewed the controversy and observed that, '[w]hen Brown remained in office pending the completion of the coalition talks, he was widely decried as the "squatter in Downing Street". There seemed to be little understanding of the government's caretaker status.'[26]

Schleiter and Belu discussed the difficulties for the incumbent Prime Minister: '[i]nadequate caretaker conventions give rise to considerable costs and risks. As the "squatter in Downing Street" episode illustrates, they can generate high-profile political controversy. As a result, parties were forced into unwisely frantic government formation negotiations in 2010, under tremendous public and media pressure.'[27]

Lord Adonis has provided a first-hand account of the days following the election result. According to Adonis, when it was clear that Nick Clegg of the Liberal Democrats were going to try to form a coalition with the Conservatives, Brown had decided to resign: '"Nick [Clegg][28] . . . I have to resign as people don't understand my clinging on to power."'[29] In a later conversation between the two men after Clegg had requested Brown not to resign, Brown said '"I can't delay. I've got to resign now, Nick. I need to go to the Palace."'[30]

In light of what happened in 2010, Schleiter and Belu have advised that:

> To ensure effective governance in the transition period, it is essential that the Prime Minister and government do not resign until the next regular government has been formed.

Clear expectations about the identity of the government during caretaker periods are critical in effectively managing political and economic uncertainty during those periods. The UK should therefore follow the example of other parliamentary democracies and affirm the first principle of all caretaker conventions: a caretaker government cannot resign until an alternative government has taken office because the country cannot be left without a functioning executive. If the Cabinet Manual is not the appropriate vehicle to introduce such an innovation, it could be securely established by legislation.[31]

After a general election the leader of the political party that meets the conditions in 1–4 above will become the Prime Minister and she will be invited by the monarch to form her next government. The Prime Minister will then choose members of either Houses of Parliament to serve as members of the government. The most senior positions in government entitle their holder to become a member of Cabinet and most are known as Secretaries of State and will be responsible for running a government department. The Cabinet will control the most important areas of government policy and should be the forum where government decisions are made. In addition to those members of the government that can attend Cabinet, there will also be other members of government such as the attorney general, or those who hold junior ministerial positions within government departments. The House of Commons Disqualification Act 1975 limits the number of MPs that may become ministers. This is important as becoming a minister entitles the MP to a higher salary and other important benefits. Consequently, it could be argued that many MPs are loyal to their party because they are aiming to become a minister in the future.

The actual government department will be run by the civil service which is independent of the political party in power and whose employees will remain in their jobs no matter what political party is in government. The independence and neutrality of the civil service is very important and we shall see how this is both enforced and protected below.

The political party with the next largest number of MPs will take on the role as the Official Opposition. Members of the opposition will be selected as shadow government ministers and are effectively a government in waiting (see Figure 8.3).

By convention all members of the government must be members of either the House of Commons or Lords.[32] This means that in the United Kingdom there is a weak separation of powers between the executive and the legislature, as the same people will serve as a government ministers and as MPs. The situation in the United Kingdom can be contrasted with the United States of America, where the constitution expressly prohibits members of the legislature from serving as members of the executive (see Figure 8.4). The government relies on whips, who are MPs, to encourage their fellow MPs from the governing party to vote in line with the government. The whips are sometimes accused of bullying

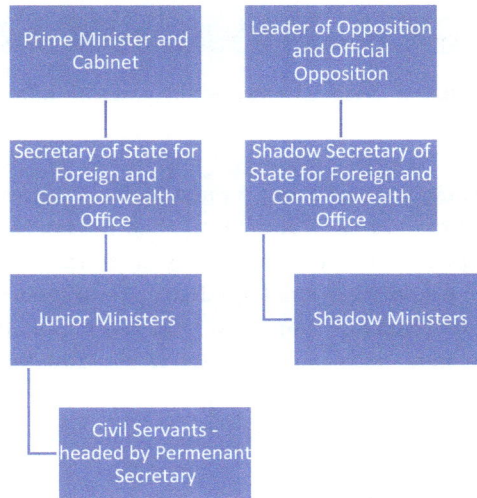

Figure 8.3
The government and the official opposition

MPs and threatening sanctions in the event that they do not vote to support government bills. MPs who are members of the governing party, but do not vote in accordance with the government's instructions, are known as rebels.

PUBLIC LAW IN CONTEXT
THE WHIPS AND BULLYING AT WESTMINSTER

The political party machine relies on MPs voting inline with their party. The government will need its MPs to vote to support government bills, otherwise the government will be defeated and its policies not introduced. The opposition requires that its MPs vote with the leadership's position, which could be against the government. In order to ensure that several hundred people will all vote the same away, each party relies on a system of whips, who are also MPs, to manage the voting.[33] The whips need to have certain skills: '[t]hey have to care enough about the politics that they can form and transmit strong messages via their team. And yet they must not be afraid to cajole, flatter and threaten. As the best Mafia dons are fond of saying – "I am not a man of violence. However, I cannot account for the actions of my associates."'[34] The whips have been accused of creating a culture of bullying, as one article in The Guardian observed:

> Dark rumours have been circulating around Westminster this week about the government whipping operation, with talk of misdemeanour lists to keep troublesome MPs in line, and alleged attempts to put pressure on those threatening to rebel on Brexit. The Conservative party was forced to deny the suggestion that one politician had been

reduced to tears by "bullyboy tactics" before being gently steered through the desired voting lobby by a Cabinet minister.

. . .

Back in the 1990s, the imposing physique and reputation for robust methods led to one Conservative whip being branded 'the Terminator.' [The person in question] was simply a party devotee, who expected the same level of loyalty from his colleagues (and would happily escort them to the smoking room for a drink after a stern word), according to one friend. But others described him pinning at least one potential rebel against the wall, warning him of the consequences of a vote in the wrong direction.'[35]

8.3.1 The Prime Minister

The Prime Minister's official residence is 10 Downing Street, which is a badly built and a rather small London townhouse, which once belonged to Sir Robert Walpole. Compared to the Kremlin and the White House, the official residence of the Prime Minister seems quite inappropriate to the importance of the office. However, the role of Prime Minister originates from the dominance of Robert Walpole during the reign of George I and George II. Walpole had become the first minister of George I, the German-speaking king who ascended the British throne after the death of Queen Anne. Walpole oversaw Cabinet meetings in the king's absence from 1721 to 1742. Walpole is known as the first Prime Minister, although the term Prime Minister was not recognised as an official title until much later. It originally was used as a term of abuse, i.e. having too much power. There have been many Prime Ministers who have shaped the office and defined its importance: these include William Pitt the Younger, Benjamin Disraeli and the Marquess of Salisbury. During Disraeli's premiership the ability of the Prime Minister to dominate government was limited by the importance of Cabinet ministers, who could develop their own policy. Salisbury attempted to combine the roles of Prime Minister with that of Foreign Secretary, and had to be forced to abandon the latter when he became older. Professor Vernon Bogdanor considered the evolutionary nature of the position of Prime Minister, and made reference to the opinion of a former Prime Minister: 'Asquith (Prime Minister 1908–1916) realised that, precisely because the premiership was a product of historical evolution rather than a constitutional document, "There is not, and cannot be, from the nature of the case, any authoritative definition of the precise relation of the Prime Minister to his colleagues." "The office of Prime Minister,' Asquith went on, 'is what its holder chooses and is able to make of it.'[36] Every Prime Minister will have a different approach to the office and their ability to lead the Cabinet will be vital to ensuring that they can implement their policies. Recent examples of Prime Ministers include those who had very different styles of governing and varying abilities to command the loyalty and obedience and colleagues around the Cabinet table. We shall see that Tony

Blair (1997–2007) was considered to be too presidential and ignored his Cabinet colleagues, which was regarded as a breakdown in collective Cabinet government. However, Blair had a permanent rival in his Cabinet, the Chancellor of the Exchequer Gordon Brown, who wanted to, and finally did, replace Blair as Prime Minister. Theresa May (2016–2019) struggled to get her Cabinet to back her withdrawal agreement with the European Union and this led to resignations from key ministers, David Davis and Boris Johnson.

The Prime Minister is the public face of the government and many voters believe that at a General Election they are voting for who becomes the next Prime Minister (see Figure 8.4 for a timeline of UK Prime Ministers since 1976). This misconception is not helped by the first televised leadership debates in 2010 between the leaders of the three main political parties. However, as we have seen in **Chapter 7**, the electorate are actually voting for who will become their local MP and represent their constituency in the House of Commons.

The Prime Minister has considerable power and dominates the Cabinet. The Prime Minister determines the choice of his Cabinet (subject to party rules), and can dismiss Cabinet ministers and reshuffle important posts. Very few ministers can successfully oppose the Prime Minister and keep their position inside the Cabinet. One who did was Gordon Brown, who as the Chancellor, opposed many of Tony Blair's policies from 1997 to 2007. Gordon Brown was able to do this because he was supported by many Labour MPs and had a popular image as a very competent chancellor.

The Cabinet Office assists the Prime Minister, and civil servants are based in 10 Downing Street. Recently, the Prime Minister has relied on special advisors who will advise on media issues, government policy and will act as spokespersons for the Prime Minister. There have been accusations that this reliance on political advisors will exclude the Civil Service and risks making the office presidential in nature.

Where do we find the law which created this office? In the United States of America the office of President was created by the constitution. However, in the United Kingdom the Prime Minister is a constitutional development, which has seen power shift from the monarch to the leader of the largest political party. The monarch has the prerogative power to choose the Prime Minister, but this choice is regulated by convention. The leader of the political party that can command the confidence of the House of Commons will become Prime Minister.

By convention the Prime Minister must be a parliamentarian and a member of the House of Commons. The last Prime Minister to be a member of the House of Lords was the Marquess of Salisbury in 1902. Since 1902, the monarch (before the day when leaders of political parties are chosen by their party) always chose an MP over a peer to become Prime Minister. The Prime Minister is the First Lord of the Treasury and is Minister for the Civil Service.

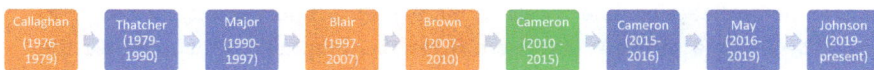

Callaghan (1976-1979) → Thatcher (1979-1990) → Major (1990-1997) → Blair (1997-2007) → Brown (2007-2010) → Cameron (2010-2015) → Cameron (2015-2016) → May (2016-2019) → Johnson (2019-present)

Figure 8.4
Prime Ministers since 1976 (n.b. David Cameron led a coalition government)

ACADEMIC DEBATE

Each Prime Minister can determine her style of leadership; some may attempt to devolve responsibility to their Cabinet colleagues and act as an equal, whilst others might wish to centralise the governing of the country from 10 Downing Street. In any event the allegation that a Prime Minister dominates his colleagues and exercises presidential powers is not a new one. Blick and Jones have written that:

> 'From Walpole's time onwards observers have frequently accused either individual Prime Ministers or the office itself of excessive dominance within government. In 1806 the incoming Prime Minister, Lord Grenville, described his immediate predecessor, William Pitt the Younger, as having led "a Cabinet of cyphers and a government of one man alone ... [a] wretched system".

One critic of the Duke of Wellington as Prime Minister from 1828 to 1830 called him a 'Dictator.' Sidney Low argued in 1904 that for 'the greater part of the past half century ... The office of premier has become more than ever like that of an elective President.' David Lloyd George was described by Harold Laski in 1920 as "virtually the President of a State". In the 1960s John Mackintosh held that the "position and power of the Prime Minister has been the focal point of modern Cabinets"; and Richard Crossman that "the post war epoch has seen the final transformation of cabinet government into prime ministerial government."'[37]

According to Professor Peter Hennessy: 'George Jones, writing in 1965, took on ... Crossman, stressing the ministerialism (as opposed to prime ministerialism) of British central government. . . . "The Prime Minister is the leading figure in the Cabinet . . . But he is not the all-powerful individual which many have recently claimed him to be. . . . A Prime Minister who can carry his colleagues with him can be in a very powerful position, but his is only as strong as they let him be."'[38] Hennessy noted that debates in 1960s reappears 'whenever a Prime Minister pushes – or appears to push – his or her own policy in such a way that Cabinet colleagues seem cowed or overridden,' an example being Tony Blair.[39] Hennessy observed that Blair's approach to government resulted in 'the demise of anything approaching a genuine system of Cabinet government.'[40]

Blair himself observed in an interview: 'I think most Prime Ministers who have a strong programme end up expecting their Secretaries of State to put it through. . . . [I]f you have a strong idea of what you want to do and believe in pushing it through, then you're, in inverted commas, a "dictator."'[41] Blair denied not consulting his ministers and said he expected ministers to raise concerns with him.[42] However, Blair said, 'I think a lot of things that I've done – a strong centre, making sure that the writ of the Prime Minister runs throughout – I think that's just an inevitable part of modern government.'[43]

Bogdanor considered the argument that Prime Ministers were becoming presidential in their approach to the office, and that they were thus at risk of being too powerful at the expense of their Cabinet colleagues: 'the thesis of increasing prime ministerial power to "presidentialisation" of the role of prime ministers is far too simplistic to account for the complex facts of modern political life. The power of the prime minister depends, and always has depended, upon vicissitudes, electoral and personal, and no clear evolutionary trend is discernible. Those who believe that there has been a progressive accretion of prime ministerial power are ahistorical. They overrate the power of a modern prime minister and underrate that of prime ministers of the past'[44]

Giddens had considered whether Blair could be considered Presidential and assessed his relationship with the House of Commons and his Cabinet colleagues:

> Although an outstanding speaker and debater, [Blair] was not by nature a parliamentarian. He had no particular fondness for the arcane details of parliamentary procedure, and as Prime Minister avoided the Commons whenever he could.[45]
>
> Blair's mode of government was termed 'Presidential' by critics – with his inner cadre of advisors, he took decisions of key importance well away from public scrutiny. Debate in Parliament was assessed mostly in terms of how far he could get a majority for what he had already decided. His dominance in Cabinet meetings was such that little of note was actively discussed in Cabinet meetings. Top civil servants found the Blair style of government challenging, and many felt they had been sidelined. Were these criticisms justified? In some part they were. Political leaders in current times have to be quick on their feet and must often respond to media stories in a direct way. Yet the Cabinet should be more than a cipher, while Parliament should remain at the core the of democratic process.'[46]

What about Theresa May, was her style of government any different from Tony Blair's? One commentator observed that:

> Theresa May restored the form of cabinet government, but not the substance. Even as her premiership draws to a close, cabinet meetings often go on for three hours as she ensures that everyone has their say. But the really big decisions have continued to be taken elsewhere. The red lines that May set out for the Brexit talks were decided well away from the Cabinet. The 2017 Tory manifesto was launched with almost no one in her Cabinet having seen the whole document. The joke then was that May's Cabinet acted as a rubber stamp – hit by a hammer.[47]

In any event the Prime Minister is held accountable to the media, the public, his own party and the House of Commons. A Prime Minister will be forced (or expected) to resign if:

- his government loses a vote of no confidence (Callaghan 1979 – technically did not resign but requested that Parliament was dissolved);
- she loses the leadership of her own political party (Thatcher 1990);
- his government does not obtain a majority of the seats in the House of Commons (Major 1997, Brown 2010) or cannot form a coalition (Brown 2010, Heath 1974);

- there is a major disaster such as a military/diplomatic crisis (Eden 1957);
- he loses a referendum campaign (Cameron 2016);
- internal party politics necessitates their resignation (Blair 2007, May 2019).

PUBLIC LAW IN PRACTICE

What would happen if Boris Johnson was forced to stand down as leader of the Conservative Party; would he also have to stand down as Prime Minister? And if so, who would decide the person who would succeed Johnson as the next Prime Minister?

8.3.1.1 Cameron, May and Johnson

In 2015, after winning a majority in the House of Commons, David Cameron, the then Prime Minister, promised to hold a referendum on the United Kingdom's continued membership of the European Union. The Prime Minister and the majority of the Cabinet, including the then Home Secretary, Theresa May, campaigned for the United Kingdom to remain as a member of the European Union. The government sent literature to every household stating that '[t]he Government believes it is in the best interest s of the UK to remain in the EU. This is the way to protect jobs, provide security, and strengthen the UK's economy for every family in this country – a clear path into the future, in contrast to the uncertainty of leaving.' The Leave Campaign wished to leave the European Union and one of its prominent supporters was the former Mayor of London, Boris Johnson. The Leave Campaign won the referendum and the following day Cameron resigned. His successor was Theresa May who attempted to reconcile remain and leave supporters within the Cabinet and wider parliamentary party. After triggering Article 50 of the Treaty on European Union, which announced that the United Kingdom would be leaving in two years' time, May negotiated a withdrawal agreement with the European Union's negotiating team. This agreement was rejected on a number of occasions by the House of Commons and eventually after facing a vote in the House of Commons on whether she continued to have the confidence of the House, as well as a confidence vote within her own party, Theresa May was forced to resign. Her successor, Boris Johnson, inherited a very small majority that was dependent on the supply and confidence agreement with the Democratic Unionist Party. Before Johnson became Prime Minister in July 2019, the Foreign Office Minister, Sir Alan Duncan, resigned from the government and unsuccessfully attempted to get the House of Commons to vote on whether it had confidence in May's successor as leader of the Conservative Party, before he could then be appointed as Prime Minister.[48]

8.3.2 The Cabinet

The Cabinet takes the important decisions and it is chaired by the Prime Minister. The Cabinet must take decisions collectively. The Prime Minister can determine the membership of the Cabinet. The role of the Cabinet is to direct government policy. Bagehot described it as 'a board of control chosen by the legislature, out of persons whom it trusts and knows, to rule the nation.'[49] The Cabinet comprises the most senior members of the government and there will be between 22 and 24 members. The Cabinet takes important decisions and the Prime Minister should consider the views of his colleagues. Recently Prime Ministers have been accused of becoming presidential and ruling through an inner-circle of advisors and not involving the entire Cabinet with making important decisions. Tony Blair (who was Prime Minister between 1997 and 2007) was accused of having a kitchen Cabinet, which meant that the Prime Minister would rely on a small circle of advisors rather than his Cabinet. Many of his decisions, including to invade Iraq in 2003, were discussed outside of Cabinet which was informed once the decision had effectively been taken. This led some members of the Cabinet to resign about the lead-up to the invasion.[50]

Cabinet government has developed from the days when the monarch would chair the meetings of his ministers, to a meeting chaired by the Prime Minister. The name Prime Minister became the term used to describe by the most important person in the Cabinet. The Prime Minister is responsible for deciding whom to promote to a ministerial position and the monarch traditionally consents to the Prime Minister's request to use the prerogative to make the appointments.[51]

The most senior members of the government serve in the Cabinet. There can be up to 22 members of Cabinet, 21 of whom can draw a salary under Schedule 1 of the Ministerial and other Salaries Act 1975. The salary of a Secretary of State is £68,827.[52] There are four great offices of State – that is senior government departments – and these are headed by the Home Secretary, the Foreign Secretary, Chancellor of the Exchequer and Secretary of State for Defence. The most important of these is the Treasury which is responsible for government spending, and the Chancellor of the Exchequer and the Prime Minister need to have a good working relationship in order for the Prime Minister to have the support of the Treasury. An example of this is the good relationship between David Cameron and his Chancellor, George Osborne, which can be compared to the bad working relationship between Tony Blair and Gordon Brown.[53]

Some important members of the government are not members of Cabinet. The Attorney-General, chief government lawyer, is not a member of Cabinet, but can attend meetings to give advice to his colleagues. The Chief Secretary to the Treasury, who is the second highest minister at the Treasury, is a member of Cabinet. The Cabinet is assisted by the Cabinet Office, which is headed by the Cabinet Secretary, and run by civil servants. The Cabinet Office is responsible for the publication of the Cabinet Manual.

The Cabinet meets each week to discuss important government business and to decide important policy decisions. It is the Prime Minister who chairs the meetings and notes are taken by the civil servants in attendance. The proceedings of Cabinet should be confidential and members free to speak their mind in the knowledge that what they say will remain private, even if they are opponents of the policy that is eventually agreed upon. The Cabinet takes decisions collectively; that is even if a majority of members agree, the decision must be presented as a decision endorsed by the entire Cabinet. The Cabinet Manual describes the Cabinet as

> the ultimate decision-making body of government. The purpose of Cabinet and its committees is to provide a framework for ministers to consider and make collective decisions on policy issues. Cabinet and its committees are established by convention but it is a matter for the incumbent government to determine the specific arrangements for collective decision-making.[54]

Collective decision-making is important as the Cabinet must present a united front to the public, even if a particular policy, such as the Poll Tax introduced by the Thatcher government, is deeply unpopular. This is not to say that leaks do not take place and Cabinet discussions made public, as ministers are frequently accused of leaking information to the press. Jennings observed that:

> The Cabinet deliberates in secret; its proceedings are confidential. The Privy Councillor's oath imposes an obligation not to disclose information; and the Official Secrets Acts forbid the publication of Cabinet as well as other official documents. But the effective sanction is neither of these. The rule is, primarily, one of practice. Its theoretical basis is that a Cabinet decision is advice to the Queen, whose consent is necessary to its publication. Its practical foundation is the necessity of securing free discussion by which a compromise can be reached, without the risk of publicity for every statement made and every point given away.[55]

However, the importance of this constitutional convention of collective responsibility for decision making was summed up by Viscount Melbourne, a Prime Minister during the reigns of William IV and Victoria. In 1841 during a discussion on repealing the Corn Laws, Melbourne made it clear to his Cabinet that: 'Bye the bye, there is one thing we haven't agreed upon, which is, what are we to say? Is it better to make our corn dearer, or cheaper, or to make the price steady? I don't care which: but we had better all tell the same story.'[56] A later prime minister, the Marquis of Salisbury, informed the House of Lords, that:

> *[A]ll that passes in a Cabinet, each Member of it who does not resign is absolutely and irretrievably responsible, and that he has no right afterwards to say that he agreed in one case to a compromise, while in another he was persuaded by one of his Colleagues.* Consider the inconvenience which will arise if such a great Constitutional law is not respected. Supposing all the Members of Cabinets were to rip up the history of their proceedings, and to ask who was responsible for this inaction or that neglect – a question which it might be impossible to answer – what, I should like to know, would be the result? *It is, I maintain, only on the principle that absolute responsibility is undertaken by every Member of a Cabinet who, after a decision is arrived at, remains a Member of it, that the joint responsibility of Ministers to Parliament can be upheld, and one of the most essential conditions of Parliamentary responsibility established.*[57]

Therefore all those in Cabinet must take a decision and in public support the government, and if they cannot (then as happened with Boris Johnson in 2018, when as Foreign Secretary he could not accept the Prime Minister's plan on how to leave the European Union), they should resign from Cabinet and become a backbench MP.[58]

8.3.2.1 The convention of collective ministerial responsibility

The government makes its decisions through Cabinet and these are made collectively by all senior ministers. The Ministerial Code states that 'Decisions reached by the Cabinet or Ministerial Committees are binding on all members of the Government.'[59] In order for the Cabinet to function its proceedings must be secret. A minister cannot speak freely if there is a risk that his opinions will be reported to the press by his colleagues. In order to avoid such publicity, the convention of collective ministerial responsibility operates to ensure that what is said during Cabinet meetings is not revealed by those who attend. Ministers must not criticise decisions reached on a particular matter by the Cabinet. It is essential that the Cabinet speaks with one voice and there is no dissent. The Ministerial Code outlines the general principle:

> collective responsibility requires that Ministers should be able to express their views frankly in the expectation that they can argue freely in private while maintaining a united front when decisions have been reached. This in turn requires that the privacy of opinions expressed in Cabinet and Ministerial Committees, including in correspondence, should be maintained.[60]

PUBLIC LAW IN CONTEXT

Occasionally, Cabinet ministers will be allowed to take different public positions on policies that are controversial. This occurred during the referendum on whether the United Kingdom should continue its membership of the then European Union in 1975, and the referendum on changing the voting system in 2011. More recently the convention was waived during the referendum campaign on the United Kingdom's continued membership of the European Union. This campaign saw the government campaign to remain, with literature sent to UK households on behalf of the government, and some ministers deciding to publicly campaign to leave the European Union.

Often there will be a leak, which is when a Cabinet member will reveal what has been said to the press. In these circumstances the press will not reveal the name of their source. The decisions of the Cabinet are binding on all ministers and if a minister cannot agree, then they ultimately must tender their resignation, as occurred when Michael Heseltine resigned in 1986 over the Westland affair. However, there may be times when a minister appears to disagree with a decision made collectively by the Cabinet and will say so publicly. In 2017, the then Foreign Secretary, Boris Johnson, was accused of breaching the convention by setting out his own view on Brexit.[61] This happened again in 2018.[62] Ultimately, Mr Johnson resigned as Foreign Secretary.

Even where there is a coalition government it is important that the convention still applies. The 2010 Coalition Agreement explicitly stated that the convention still applies unless exceptions are made.

The convention of collective ministerial responsibility is important as this convention enables the Cabinet to act as a whole and appear undivided when they make an important decision. In *Attorney-General v Jonathan Cape Ltd*[63] one of the issues to be determined was whether the convention of the collective ministerial had been breached. Richard Crossman had been a member of the Labour government and had served in the Cabinet. Crossman had written a series of diaries known as the Crossman Diaries. Upon his death his estate and a publisher planned to publish his diaries and to serialise them in a national newspaper (*The Sunday Times*). The Attorney-General, who is a law officer of the Crown and a member of the government, sought to prevent publication and argued that the diaries revealed what had been discussed at Cabinet meetings and that publication was not in the public interest. The court held that it was in the public interest that collective ministerial responsibility was protected; however they would only prevent publication for ten years after the events described. This meant that since the first volume of the diaries covered events that had occurred more than ten years previously, the court was not willing to prevent publication. The court refused to hold that there was a legal obligation to comply with the convention of collective ministerial responsibility; rather the court had relied on the tort of confidentiality to prevent publication before ten years had expired. The importance of the convention would demonstrate that a duty of confidentiality existed, however the convention was not in itself legally enforceable. Lord Widgery CJ held that the Cabinet discussions were only protected by the confidential character of the information discussed. Lord Widgery CJ noted that the information would be unprotected once it lost its confidential character:

It may, of course, be intensely difficult in a particular case, to say at what point the material loses its confidential character, on the ground that publication will no longer undermine the doctrine of joint Cabinet responsibility. It is this difficulty which prompts some to argue that Cabinet discussions should retain their confidential character for a longer and arbitrary period such as 30 years, or even for all time, but this seems to me to be excessively restrictive. The court should intervene only in the clearest of cases where the continuing confidentiality of the material can be demonstrated. In less clear cases – and this, in my view, is certainly one – reliance must be placed on the good sense and good taste of the Minister or ex-Minister concerned.[64]

It is clear that whilst not being legally binding the convention of collective ministerial responsibility was important to the court finding that the information had the necessary quality of confidentiality. Joseph Jaconelli considered the question of whether constitutional conventions bind:

> Was this additional element [the convention], which was decided in favour of the Attorney-General ('I find overwhelming evidence that the doctrine of joint responsibility is generally understood and practised and equally strong evidence that it is on occasion ignored') decisive in awarding him judgment on the general point? If the constitutional element were to be subtracted from the case – if the author of the diaries, say, was the director of a leading public company who had kept a record of discussions at board meetings which he now proposed to publish – would the result of the case have been the same? It is possible that the factor of collective responsibility had a critical impact on the result. What is clear is that the 'enforcement' of the constitutional convention in such cases is parasitic on the ascription of rights and duties of hitherto uncertain extent. It is inconceivable that the breach of a constitutional convention could furnish a free-standing cause of action.[65]

8.3.3 Junior ministers

There are 50 junior ministers who are entitled to draw a salary under Schedule 1 of the Ministerial and other Salaries Act 1975. There are also up to 83 Parliamentary Secretaries who also draw a salary because they help ministers with their executive duties.

8.3.4 A government department

A government department such as the Ministry of Justice will employ thousands of civil servants and will be responsible for many important aspects of running the country. The Ministry of Justice has responsibilities for running the courts and the justice system. The department is headed by the Lord Chancellor who is the Secretary of State for Justice. To assist the Secretary of State there are a number of junior Ministers of State and Parliamentary Under Secretaries of State. They are all politicians and are members of either the House of Commons or the House of Lords. Alongside the politicians, the civil servants run the Ministry of Justice and will try and fulfil the ministerial objectives. The Civil Service is headed by the Permanent Secretary, who is not a politician and will remain in office despite a change in government. The Civil Service has an important role, as it is rare that a minister will be in charge of a department long enough to really understand how it works.

8.3.5 Training for Cabinet ministers?

One example of a minister who moved from one department to another over a short period of time is John Reid MP, who from 1999 to 2007 was responsible for several government departments:

- Secretary of State for Scotland
- Secretary of State for Northern Ireland
- Leader of the House of Commons and Lord President of the Council
- Secretary of State for Health
- Secretary of State for Defence
- Secretary of State for the Home Department

How qualified are ministers to run a government department? Jacqui Smith has admitted that when she was Home Secretary she lacked the experience to run such a large department. During an interview with Total Politics, Jacqui Smith was asked, 'Do you think it's a weakness of our political system that there is no kind of career path planning at all and that people are plonked into jobs, sometimes for absolutely no reason?' Smith responded:

> Yes, if I ever describe the process of becoming a minister – moving from one ministerial job to another – to somebody in almost any other job outside they think it is, frankly, pretty dysfunctional in the way that it works. That's not just this government. . . . To be fair, Gordon had talked to me about whether or not I wanted to do a different job but you have to get to a pretty senior position in government – and you have to be pretty powerful as hell – before you can even express a view, let alone expect to influence where you go. I think we should have been better trained. I think there should be more induction. There's more now than when I started as a minister but it's still not enough. I think there should be more emphasis given to supporting ministers more generally in terms of developing the skills needed to lead big departments, for example. When I became Home Secretary, I'd never run a major organisation. I hope I did a good job but if I did it was more by luck than by any kind of development of those skills.[66]

The Institute of Government has advised that ministers should receive training and that the Prime Minister should not appoint individuals to key positions without proper consideration. One Cabinet minister was quoted as saying, '[t]he largest thing I'd run before this was my constituency office of four people – now I have a department of tens of thousands and a budget of billions.'[67] This means that the minister will be dependent upon the Civil Service, which will run a department and will attempt to give effect to the minister's agenda.

The classic BBC comedy series *Yes, Minister* explored the relationship between Jim Hacker, a minister, and his permanent private secretary, Sir Humphrey Appleby. The fictional Sir Humphrey was a senior civil servant who pursued his own policy in defiance of the views of the minister, Jim Hacker MP. The series parodied the Civil Service's relationship with ministers and in one famous scene, in the episode 'Economy Drive,' Sir Humphrey explained that the civil service did not have to do everything that a minister demanded because of the fact that they were chosen by the electorate. The reasoning adopted by Sir Humphrey was that as there were some 300 MPs from the governing party and about 100 ministerial positions to fill, once those MPs who were not suitable were removed from the equation this left 100 MPs. This meant that a minister owed his office to the fact that everyone else was unsuitable. The BBC comedy *Yes, Minister* highlighted the belief (which still exists) that the civil service really ran the government.

Sir Humphrey Appleby to Jim Hacker MP:

> The argument that we must do everything a Minister demands because he has been 'democratically chosen' does not stand up to close inspection. MPs are not chosen by 'the people' – they are chosen by their local constituency parties: thirty-five men in grubby raincoats or thirty-five women in silly hats. The further 'selection' process is equally a nonsense: there are only 630 MPs and a party with just over 300 MPs forms a government and of these 300, 100 are too old and too silly to be ministers and 100 too young and too callow. Therefore there are about 100 MPs to fill 100 government posts. Effectively no choice at all.[68]

8.3.6 Accountability

A minister will hold considerable power and will be responsible for a large government department. The Secretary of State for Defence will be responsible for the armed forces and the on-going conduct of any oversees military action.

The minister will be responsible to his own political party, the Prime Minister, his colleagues in Cabinet, Parliament, the public, his own constituents and the press. What exactly is the minister responsible for? The minister is responsible for his department, the policy and any failures for which his department is responsible. Finally, a minister is responsible for his own personal life, i.e. sexual affairs, financial irregularities and inappropriate friendships.

Professor Dawn Oliver looked at the parameters of ministerial accountability and identified the following areas of accountability:

- 'to the Prime Minister';
- to the House of Commons and the House of Lords;
- 'to the Parliamentary Commissioner for Administration and the Select Committee on the PCA';

- 'to the Comptroller and Auditor General, National Audit Office and Committee for Public Accounts';
- to the 'Parliamentary Party';
- to the 'National Party';
- to the 'General Public';
- to the press;
- to clients, who are those with whom the minister has links; and
- to the courts.[69]

We will look at some important forms of ministerial accountability and consider their effectiveness.

8.3.7 The Ministerial Code

The Ministerial Code was first established in 1948 and sets out the standards expected of ministers. Ministers are obliged to follow the code, although it is not legally binding. The code was first made public in 1992.

Importantly, ministers must reveal all private interests to the Civil Service in order to avoid a conflict of interest between a minister's private interests and his role as a minister. If a minister breaches the code, then the available sanction is that minister's resignation or the risk of being dismissed by the Prime Minister. For example, the Secretary of State for Defence, Dr Liam Fox MP, breached the Ministerial Code in 2011 and was compelled (by the reaction of the press) to resign.[70] The code promotes ministerial accountability and a duty not to mislead Parliament. Patricia Leopold notes that ministers upon leaving office are required not to lobby the government for two years (i.e. act on behalf of an interest group or business);[71] if they do lobby within this time, there are no penalties that can be imposed (see also the Transparency of Lobbying, Non-Party Campaigning and Trade Union Administration Act 2014).

Lobbying means that you advocate the views of a particular organisation and attempt to influence policy on its behalf. Organisations will employ lobbyists to work on their behalf. In 2010 several senior former ministers were caught offering to lobby on behalf of organisations and in 2013 journalists uncovered lobbying by parliamentarians.[72]

8.3.8 Public accountability: freedom of information

The Freedom of Information Act 2000 imposes a legal obligation on public authorities to disclose information when requested by members of the public. A public authority must consider these requests and determine whether it is justified in withholding the material. The Act was intended to increase the transparency of government.

The executive exercises considerable power and it is important that we are able to have access to what happens. If the executive's actions were secret then how could we ensure that that the executive was truly accountable? Gavin

Dewry wrote that '[t]he biggest single obstacle to effective public accountability is lack of transparency. It is quite impossible for Parliament, the public and, for that matter, the media, to hold public authorities to account if their actions are shrouded in secrecy.'[73] Therefore, freedom of information is extremely important to hold the government to account. Dewry notes that the Freedom of Information Act 2000 has proved controversial, because the executive can rely on loopholes and exemptions to prevent the revelation of certain information. *The Guardian* in February 2012 reported that the Ministry of Justice has revealed that the Freedom of Information Act 2000 has not improved accountably, nor has it improved governmental decision-making.[74] There was a concern that the Act was being used by journalists who were fishing for a story. The Freedom of Information Act 2000 covers 100,000 public authorities and imposes obligations for these authorities to consider and process requests made by members of the public. There are a considerable number of requests made each year, with some 200,000 requests being made in 2010. Rodney Austin criticised the Freedom of Information Act by calling it,

> a sheep in wolf's clothing . . . [as the Act] purports to provide a legally enforceable individual right to access governmental information subject only to specified and justifiable exemptions. It purports also to provide general publication duties in respect of governmental information. But in reality it does neither of these.[75]

Patrick Birkinshaw noted that whilst 'FOI was accompanied by grand claims . . . in his autobiography, Blair wrote off the FOIA as "so utterly undermining of sensible government."'[76] Birkinshaw observed that the United Kingdom has areas of strengths and weaknesses regarding its implementation of freedom of information: 'The FOIA 2000 assist[s] in meeting its identified objectives – openness, transparency, accountability, and access to information – but other procedures and opportunities need to be developed.'[77]

8.3.9 The convention of individual ministerial responsibility

The convention of individual ministerial responsibility is an important method of executive accountability. According to Diana Woodhouse, '[t]he description of individual ministerial responsibility as a single convention is convenient, but perhaps misleading.'[78] This is because what is expected from a minister will depend on the context. Ministers are expected as a matter of convention to act responsibly, and to ultimately resign in the event of failures in their departments or their own personal lives. Gay and Powell provided a succinct account as to the origin of this constitution convention:

> It must be borne in mind that the development of the modern conception of ministerial responsibility arose in the so-called Bagehotian/Victorian

'golden age' of Parliamentary government at a time when Cabinets and governments were much smaller and the business of government much less than nowadays. This made it potentially easier in the last century for an administration to be composed of like-minded people around the Cabinet table. Westminster politics and Whitehall government were much more localised and personal affairs in which many of the participants would be known, to some degree, to each other, and were sometimes even related. Ministerial confidentiality and an outward appearance of unanimity helped to prevent or at least minimise political and social embarrassment for the monarch's ministers.[79]

Woodhouse has provided a detailed account of how the convention worked and its limitations, which included the dominance of the executive and Parliament losing its reputation.[80]

Ministers have the freedom to ignore this convention as a convention is not legally binding and cannot be enforced in a court; however, it must be stressed that a minister may be forced to resign depending on the amount of public, press and political support they receive. Ultimately, a minister who loses the confidence of the Prime Minister will be forced to resign or risk being dismissed. The Defence Select Committee which was investigating the Westland affair in the mid-1980s observed that ministerial responsibility was not as straightforward as a minister resigning" '[a] Minister does not discharge his accountability to Parliament merely by acknowledging a general responsibility and, if the circumstances warrant it, by resigning. Accountability involves accounting in detail for actions as a Minister.'[81]

Gay and Powell observed that the convention of ministerial responsibility requires that:

1   the minister informs and explains their actions to Parliament;
2   the minister apologises to Parliament;
3   the minister takes steps to remedy the problem; and
4   the minister, if necessary, tenders his resignation.[82]

It is important to note that the person who determines whether a minister must resign is the Prime Minister. Even if a minister breaches the Ministerial Code and misleads Parliament, then it will be the Prime Minister who must decide whether to ask for and accept the minister's resignation. The Ministerial Code is explicit as to this:

> Ministers are personally responsible for deciding how to act and conduct themselves in the light of the Code and for justifying their actions and conduct to Parliament and the public. However, Ministers only remain in office for so long as they retain the confidence of the Prime Minister. He is the ultimate judge of the standards of behaviour expected of a Minister and the appropriate consequences of a breach of those standards.[83]

8.3.9.1 Departmental failures: when must a minister resign?

At the outset it is important to note that there have been calls to distinguish between a failure of policy and administrative failure. If it were a failure of a policy that was under the minister's control, then the minister should take responsibility and ultimately resign, whereas the Civil Service is responsible for administrative failings and civil servants should take responsibility where there have been failures. This distinction has modified the traditional approach to individual ministerial responsibility.

In looking at when ministers are expected to resign for failings in their departments, it is important to look at the Crichel Down affair and the guidance that emerged as a consequence of this scandal. The Crichel Down affair involved the sale of land which had been compulsorily purchased by the government in 1938. The family who owned the land had been promised in Parliament that they could repurchase the land at a later date. The promise was not kept and the family fought to be able to repurchase the land. The Crichel Down affair provided an opportunity for Parliament and the then government in 1954 to address ministerial responsibility. According to Griffiths, '[c]onstitutionally, one of the most important questions raised was that of Ministerial responsibility.'[84] The minister whose department was involved, Sir Thomas Dugdale, resigned. The Parliamentary debate in the aftermath of the Crichel Down affair looked at ministerial responsibility and whether the minister should protect the civil servants involved. During that debate, the most famous contribution was from Sir David Maxwell Fyfe who stated that:

> I, as Minister, must accept full responsibility to Parliament for any mistakes and inefficiency of officials in my Department, just as, when my officials bring off any successes on my behalf, I take full credit for them.
>
> Any departure from this long-established rule is bound to bring the Civil Service right into the political arena, and that we should all, on both sides of the House, deprecate most vigorously. I shall have something more to say about Ministerial responsibility before I sit down; I would only add, at this stage, that it should not be thought that this means that I am bound to endorse the actions of officials, whatever they may be, or that I or any other Minister must shield those who make errors against proper consequences.[85]

Sir David Maxwell Fyfe laid down four circumstances and looked at whether the minister should resign in each of these

A minister should resign or defend the actions of the civil servant:

- where a minister orders a civil servant to act; or
- where a civil servant who acts in accordance with a policy established by the minister; or
- where a civil servant makes a mistake or causes a delay. If this is unimportant, the minister should take responsibility.

A minister should not resign or take responsibility:

- if the civil servant takes action without the approval of the minister, then the minister is not responsible and does not have to defend the civil servant.[86]

It is interesting to consider the reason in full for the final point made by Sir David Maxwell Fyfe:

> But when one comes to the fourth category, where action has been taken by a civil servant of which the Minister disapproves and has no prior knowledge, and the conduct of the official is reprehensible, then there is no obligation on the part of the Minister to endorse what he believes to be wrong, or to defend what are clearly shown to be errors of his officers. The Minister is not bound to defend action of which he did not know, or of which he disapproves. But, of course, he remains constitutionally responsible to Parliament for the fact that something has gone wrong, and he alone can tell Parliament what has occurred and render an account of his stewardship.[87]

Geoffrey Marshall observed that the resignation of Dugdale in 1954 and that of Lord Carrington in 1982 were 'precedents and with a dash of principle may be treated as evidence of a convention.'[88] A constitutional convention only exists if it is actually followed. We shall see that not all ministers feel obliged to resign in the event of a departmental failing.

PUBLIC LAW IN CONTEXT

In 2013, Lord Carrington, the former Foreign Secretary, was interviewed by Jonathan Powell for the BBC.[89] When asked about his resignation in 1982 over the Falklands War, Lord Carrington agreed that his decision was influenced by his experiences during the Crichel Down affair.

Carrington: 'Yes, I tried to resign because I was parliamentary secretary to Tommy Dugdale who was the minister who resigned (in Crichel Down). But I was sent for by Churchill (the then Prime Minister), who looked at me and said "do you want to go?", and I said, "no, no, I don't", and he said, "you'd better not". I probably should have gone, but it is quite difficult when the Prime Minister tells you not to be so silly.'

Powell: 'But most people think that you probably shouldn't have gone over the Falklands, and yet you did insist on resigning that time.'

Carrington: 'I should, it was absolutely right ... even if it is a small war like the Falklands you do not want to go to war with people having a row about who was responsible. . . . [Y]ou have got to be united in it and so I think it cleared the air.'

David Laws who was the Chief Secretary to the Treasury in the coalition government, has recounted the reason for why he resigned in 2010 over issues relating to his parliamentary expenses:

Nick Clegg[90], Paddy Ashdown[91], and the Prime Minister[92] were all very supportive and tried to persuade me to stay. But you expect that from friends and colleagues. When you are a politician in this type of circumstances, you owe it to everyone else to accept the responsibility to determine, yourself, whether to stay or go.

I was sure that it was in my personal and family interest for me to resign, and I never doubted that this was in the government's best interest too.

By the end of Friday, I was determined on resignation. On Saturday, Nick Clegg and Paddy Ashdown made further attempts to change my mind, but my view was now settled.[93]

The fact that many other ministers do not offer to resign should not be taken as evidence that the convention of individual ministerial responsibility does not exist. Diana Woodhouse has observed that

[b]y the time the Conservative government left office in 1997, the convention of individual ministerial responsibility had been distorted to the point where evasion and half-truths had replaced any notion of giving an account and the acceptance of responsibility for political errors or misjudgements were seldom.[94]

The government had witnessed a number of scandals. Powell and Gay observed that the convention was fluid as it is unwritten and that '[i]n practice, few senior politicians are likely to base decisions affecting their political careers solely, or even mainly, on some uncertain constitutional convention, the exact details of which they may not be fully aware of.'[95] Rhodes, Wanna and Weller observed that

[the convention] is often said to be honoured only in breach. Ministers often seek to evade responsibilities and not 'answer' for actions taken in their name. They rarely resign or stand aside unless the prime minister feels it expedient for them to depart than remain. Politics, not ethics, governs the convention. There may be a 'smoking gun', it may be in the minister's hand, but that does not mean he or she will resign.

We will look at some key examples of when ministers have or have not resigned because of departmental failings.

So when will a minister resign? Diana Woodhouse noted that '[m]inisterial responsibility will always depend on the integrity of the ministers concerned,' whilst Geoffrey Marshall stated that the existence of conventions required 'a dash of principle.'[96]

Table 8.1

Minister	Grounds	Resigned?
George Brown	As Foreign Secretary refused to take the blame for a failure to properly handle compensation for former prisoners of war in the 1960s.	No
Lord Carrington and two ministerial colleagues	Failed to foresee the Argentinean invasion of the Falklands in 1982.	Yes
Sir Thomas Dugdale and Sir David Maxwell-Fyfe	Involved in the Crichel Down affair in 1954.	Yes
Theresa May	Border checks not carried out in 2011. Claimed that it was not government policy but the initiative of civil servants. Refused responsibility and the civil servant at fault was dismissed.	No
Amber Rudd	Resigned over the Windrush scandal that saw individuals deported from the UK back to the Caribbean. Rudd was accused of misleading the House of Commons.	Yes
William Whitelaw	Home Secretary in 1982 when an intruder avoided the police and entered the Queen's bedroom. The Queen had to talk to the intruder until the police arrived.	No

8.3.9.2 Personal scandal: when must a minister resign?

The convention of individual ministerial responsibility also covers personal scandals. In the event of scandal a minister is often expected to resign; otherwise this will bring his position and department into disrepute. There are some key examples below of ministers who have refused or have resigned.

So why did Robin Cook refuse to resign? The answer is that Cook had the support of the Prime Minister and that there were no other circumstances which would have forced him to resign. Woodhouse notes that Mellor's and Profumo's resignations were because of other circumstances rather than just their adultery.[99] Mellor's resignation is attributable to mishandling the press, whilst Profumo's mistress was sleeping with a Russian spy. Profumo never returned to politics and spent the rest of his life undertaking charitable work. Woodhouse notes that Cook's refusal to resign 'does not therefore indicate a change in the requirement of ministerial responsibility,' just that there 'was neither a constitutional nor a political requirement for resignation.'[100]

8.3.9.3 Does the convention of individual ministerial responsibility exist?

We have seen above that ministers cannot always be expected to resign for departmental failings or failures in their personal life. Academics have argued

Table 8.2

Minister	Grounds	Resigned?
Gavin Williamson	Accused of leaking discussions from a meeting of the National Security Council to a journalist from *The Daily Telegraph*. The then Secretary of State for Defence admitted speaking to the journalist after the meeting, but denied leaking the information in question (2019). A civil service investigation had found that this was a breach of the Ministerial Code.[97]	Dismissed by the Prime Minister.
Damien Green	He was found to have breached the Ministerial Code over misleading statements concerning the discovery by police of pornography on his House of Commons computer.[98]	Effectively sacked. Asked to resign by the Prime Minister.
Priti Patel	Allegations that the International Development Secretary had met with senior Israeli diplomats during her holiday in Israel and had conducted unofficial diplomacy without the knowledge of the Foreign and Commonwealth Office (2017).	Effectively sacked. Asked to resign by the Prime Minister.
Sir Michael Fallon	Allegations of sexual misconduct were made against the Secretary of State for Defence (2017).	Resigned.
Liam Fox	Allowed his friend to have access to the Ministry of Defence and to attend foreign trips and meetings (2011).	Resigned.
Robin Cook	Had an affair and divorced his wife, whilst serving as Foreign Secretary (late 1990s/early 2000).	Did not resign.
Ron Davies	Sexual relations with a male stranger on Clapham common (1998).	Resigned.
Geoffrey Robinson	Failure to disclose all financial interests, as he was a discretionary beneficiary of an offshore trust, whilst looking into the law in this area (1998).	Resigned.
David Mellor	Had an affair (1992).	Resigned.
Tim Smith	Accepted payments to ask questions in Parliament (1994).	Resigned.
John Profumo	Minister of War, who had an affair with a prostitute, who was also the lover of a Russian spy (1963)	Resigned.

that the failure to resign should not negate the existence of the convention. Munro (concluded that 'it seem preferable to say that there is a rule of some sort here, even if it cannot be stated with precision and is not invariably obeyed.'[101] We can see that Munro's conclusion is a valid one.

PUBLIC LAW IN PRACTICE

A newspaper has uncovered that a minister has been having an affair. In which circumstances would you expect the minister to resign?

The minister has been spearheading a morality campaign []
The minister's mistress had access to government information []
The minister was having a homosexual affair and lied to the press []
The minister has the support of the Prime Minister and is doing a good job []

8.3.9.4 Parliamentary resolution on ministerial accountability 1997

In 1997 the House of Commons and House of Lords passed a resolution that called for greater ministerial accountability to Parliament. The resolution was the result of the recommendations of the Public Service Select Committee. There was a concern that ministers and civil servants were not sufficiently accountable to Parliament. The Resolution on Ministerial Accountability established that the following principles should govern the conduct of Ministers of the Crown in relation to Parliament:

1   Ministers have a duty to Parliament to account and to be held to account for the policies, decisions and actions of their departments and Next Steps Agencies.
2   It is of paramount importance that Ministers give accurate and truthful information to Parliament, correcting any inadvertent error at the earliest opportunity. Ministers who knowingly mislead Parliament will be expected to offer their resignation to the Prime Minister.
3   Ministers should be as open as possible with Parliament, refusing to provide information only when disclosure would not be in the public interest, which should be decided in accordance with relevant statutes and the Government's Code of Practice on Access to Government Information.
4   Similarly, Ministers should require civil servants who give evidence before Parliamentary Committees on their behalf and under their directions to be as helpful as possible in providing accurate and truthful and full information in accordance with the duties and responsibilities of civil servants as set out in the Civil Service Code.[102]

The rest of the resolution is clear that ministers are under an obligation to account to Parliament and to ensure that they and their civil servants give accurate information and sufficient help to parliamentary committees. This will be discussed below.

8.4 Executive accountability to Parliament

One of Parliament's most important functions is to hold the executive to account. The executive cannot act illegally and will rely on statutory powers from Parliament, in the form of delegated legislation. In addition to statutory powers, the executive can rely upon the prerogative powers.

The executive is accountable to Parliament and the House of Commons can bring down a government through a vote of no confidence under the Fixed-term Parliaments Act 2011. Under section 2(3) of the Act an early general election will be called when the House of Commons passes a motion of no confidence under subsection (4) 'That this House has no confidence in Her Majesty's Government' and within 14 days it does not pass a subsequent motion to state 'That this House has confidence in Her Majesty's Government.'

The House of Commons can also bring down a government, but not trigger an early general election, using the convention that a government must resign if it no longer has the confidence of the House of Commons. According to the House of Commons Public Administration and Constitutional Affairs Committee:

> There is no reason why the principle that the government of the day must retain the confidence of the House of Commons should have altered. It continues to operate through convention, as it has for a long time. The Cabinet Manual reflects the established consensus and makes clear that this relationship remains central to our system of parliamentary democracy. The principle, if not the mechanics, of establishing authority to govern, which underpins this relationship, is unchanged by the Fixed-term Parliaments Act 2011.[103]
>
> . . .
>
> The Fixed-term Parliaments Act 2011 provides the only means of bringing about an early general election. Outside the terms of the Act, if the House were to express no confidence in the Government, unless that authority could be restored, the Prime Minister would be expected to give notice that he or she will resign, but only when he or she is in a position to recommend to the Sovereign an alternative person to form a new administration. In the event that no alternative person can be found, it remains available to the House to bring about an early general election under section 2(1) of the Act.[104]

In the United Kingdom there is considerable debate as to whether it is the executive that dominates Parliament.[105] Historically a government will usually command the support of a majority of the House of Commons. If this is the case, then the ability of Parliament to hold the executive to account is significantly reduced and, importantly, the government enjoys the freedom to make whatever law it wishes. However, in recent years the government has not had an outright majority:

- David Cameron had to form a coalition government in 2010 in order to have a majority.

- David Cameron won an outright majority in 2015.
- Theresa May had to form a supply and confidence agreement in 2017 in order to have a majority.
- Theresa May's attempts to get the House of Commons to vote to support her withdrawal agreement with the European Union was defeated in the House of Commons, as even members of her government voted against it.
- In 2019, when MPs successfully sought to pass an amendment preventing the government from proroguing Parliament (in order to prevent the House of Commons from preventing a no-deal Brexit), the government sought to defeat this and even its own ministers decided not to support the government.
- Boris Johnson had a majority of one (including the supply and confidence agreement) when he became Prime Minister in July 2019. He subsequently lost his majority on 3 September 2019 when a Conservative MP joined the Liberal Democrats. On 4 September 2019 the whip was withdrawn (no longer allowed to represent the party) from 21 Conservative MPs in response to their voting against the government. Later that week Amber Rudd, a member of the Cabinet resigned as a Conservative MP. This meant that Johnson's was a minority government.
- Boris Johnson gained a large majority as a result of the 2019 general election.

We have seen in **Chapter 7** just how effective Parliament is in holding the executive to account. Importantly, we have noted the limited ability of Parliament to review the executive's use of the prerogative powers.

8.5 Executive accountability to the judiciary

The judiciary provides an important check and balance on the powers of the executive. The courts can judicially review executive decision-making using statutory and prerogative powers. Arguably, it is the courts rather than Parliament which controls executive use of the prerogative.

The courts can quash executive decisions, where for example a minister has acted *ultra vires*, which is when a minister acts outside of the powers conferred by Parliament in the form of delegated legislation. The courts can also question whether a minister has acted unreasonably, and can quash a decision that it deems to be unreasonable.

The courts are aware that it is the role of the executive to take important decisions which are needed to govern the country, and so are often unwilling to decide matters of policy. The former Supreme Court justice Lord Sumption had written extra-judicially about the limits of judicial review, when he argued that the courts should avoid making policy decisions.[106] We will look at the role of the courts in the constitution in **Chapter 9**.

The judiciary is independent of the executive and judges are no longer appointed by the Lord Chancellor, but instead through the independent

Judicial Appointment Commission (see the Act of Settlement 1701 and the Constitutional Reform Act 2005). Ministers and civil servants who disregard court orders can be prosecuted for contempt of court (see for example *M v. Home Office*[107] where the Home Secretary was threatened with contempt of court). This is unlike the Crown, which has immunity from being prosecuted for disobeying court orders.

8.6 The press and the electorate

Politicians need to be re-elected and so public opinion is important. The executive is held accountable by the public. A government that is seen as out of touch and unpopular will be voted out of office. Politicians have courted the press and the Prime Ministers have needed to have a close relationship with the owners of the leading newspapers. This close relationship between politicians and the press led in part to the Leveson Inquiry in 2012.

PUBLIC LAW IN CONTEXT

This close relationship has proved embarrassing for politicians as the phone-hacking scandal has revealed just how close politicians and the press have been. An example of the influence the press have had in the United Kingdom is that some at the time believed that John Major owed his victory in the 1992 General Election to *The Sun* endorsing the Conservative Party.[108] The Leveson Inquiry revealed the close relationship between a senior journalist, Rebekah Brooks, and the former Prime Minister Gordon Brown (whose wife Sarah Brown invited the journalist to a sleepover party)[109] and the current Prime Minister, David Cameron (who went horse riding with her). Texts between Mr Cameron and Brooks revealed her having to explain what 'lol' meant to the Prime Minister.[110] Brooks and another former editor of the *News of the World*, Andy Coulson, were prosecuted for their alleged involvement with phone hacking at the paper. After a lengthy trial Brooks was acquitted by a jury. Coulson, who had subsequently been the Prime Minister's director of communications, was found guilty of conspiracy to unlawfully intercept communications.[111]

8.7 Official loyal opposition

The opposition in Parliament is known as Her Majesty's Most Loyal Opposition.[112] The party which controls the second highest number of seats in the House of Commons is the official opposition. The leader of the opposition will ask the Prime Minister questions at Prime Minister's Question Time, and each government minister will be shadowed by a member of the opposition. The shadow Cabinet is headed by the leader of the opposition. The opposition receives assistance from the Civil Service to help shadow ministers to prepare for government and to formulate alternative policies. This is outlined in the

Cabinet Manual and was established as a matter of convention.[113] The Prime Minister must give her permission for these meetings to take place and such permission had been granted by Tony Blair before the 2005 election and Gordon Brown before the 2010 election.[114] The contact between civil servants and the opposition parties is crucial to allow the opposition to prepare for the possibility of forming a government. The Leader of the Opposition receives a salary (£63,098)[115] under section 1(1)(b) and section 2 of the Ministerial and other Salaries Act 1975. The opposition's chief whip and assistant whips also receive a salary under the Act.[116]

There are more than two political parties, so now more than one opposition party, such as the Scottish National Party and the Liberal Democratic Party.

In order to assist an opposition party to conduct itself and carry out its business, Short Money is provided.[117] In 2018/19 the Labour Party received £7,879,789.73 in Short Money, which included £823,420.19 to fund the office of Jeremy Corbyn, the Leader of the Opposition.[118] All political parties that meet a two seat requirement or one seat and 150,000 votes are entitled to Short Money.[119] For example, Plaid Cymru received £101,920.04 in Short Money during 2018/19.[120]

PUBLIC LAW IN PRACTICE

Last week *The Daily Trumpet*, a national newspaper, published the following story:

'NEW KING CLASHES WITH THE PRIME MINISTER'

King George VII began his reign last year somewhat controversially by insisting that he attend the start of every other Cabinet meeting. The Prime Minister has publicly supported the move and has repeatedly told the press that the King left each Cabinet meeting prior to policy decisions being taken. However, a secret memo has been leaked to *The Daily Trumpet*, which threatens to shake the monarchy to its very core. The memo reveals that:

(i)   The king has threatened to veto any bill that does not meet his approval.
(ii) The king's public interventions in the National Nuclear Workers strike have infuriated the Secretary of State for Energy.
(iii) The king has indicated that the Prime Minister's likely successor as leader of party, Teddy Delaware MP is a poor choice for Prime Minister. The king has also indicated that if the current governing party wins an early general election, that he will ask the Home Secretary, Lord Robin Jones of Wellington to form the next government.
(iv) The Prime Minster is considering asking Parliament to present the king with a bill, which will ask His Majesty George VII to abdicate, in favour of his son, the Prince of Wales.
(v) The Memo contains a transcript of three Cabinet meetings, and it is likely, that the Secretary of State for Energy is the author of the memo.'

The above scenario is based on a monarch who does not act constitutionally. In (i) the king is threatening to use his prerogative power to withhold royal assent. Legally speaking the king can do this. However, as a matter of constitutional principle it would be improper for the king to refuse royal assent, as there is a constitutional convention that assent will be given. In (ii) the king is intervening in political events and this is not what a monarch should do, as it is the government which governs, and the king should be above politics. In (iii) the issue concerns the appointment of the next Prime Minister. The monarch has the prerogative power to appoint whomever he chooses to this position. However, there is a constitutional convention that the person appointed must command the confidence of the House of Commons and must be a MP rather than a member of the House of Lords.

In (iv) the Prime Minister is clearly reacting to the king's unconstitutional use of his prerogative powers. As discussed in (i) the monarch is expected as a matter of constitutional convention to give his royal assent and therefore abdicate. The last time a monarch disagreed with his Prime Minister over what he should do, which was Edward VIII and his wish to marry his mistress, Wallace Simpson, the monarch abdicated in order to avoid a constitutional crisis. As a matter of constitutional principle the king should abdicate. This reinforces the position that it is Parliament that ultimately determines royal succession (see His Majesty's Declaration of Abdication Act 1936).

Finally, in (v) there appears to be a breach of the convention of collective ministerial responsibility. Whilst notes are taken by the Cabinet Office of Cabinet meetings, ministers must not disseminate what is said outside of the meeting, as it is of utmost important that the proceedings are confidential and only the agreed position is made public. The government may wish to bring legal proceedings, as in *Attorney-General v Jonathan Cape* to prevent the publication of the memo based on the tort of confidentiality, and not based on the existence of a convention.

8.8 Delegated legislation and the prerogative powers

Ministers derive their power from delegated legislation and the prerogative powers. A minister's use of these powers can be judicially reviewed by the courts. A minister cannot act illegally.

8.9 The Civil Service

There are hundreds of thousands of civil servants employed throughout the United Kingdom, from staff who manage Job Centres, work for Her Majesty's Revenue and Customs, and those civil servants working at the heart of British government in 10 Downing Street. The Civil Service was traditionally not organised on a statutory basis and was instead organised under the prerogative. The Constitutional Reform and Governance Act 2010 finally placed the Civil Service on a statutory footing, long after it was first recommended in

1854. Section 2 of the Act established a Civil Service Commission to determine appointments to the Civil Service. The head of the Civil Service is the Cabinet Secretary, and he is responsible for 500,000 civil servants. However, section 3 of the Constitutional Reform and Governance Act 2010 states that it is the Minister for the Civil Service who manages all non-diplomatic civil servants, and this post holder is the Prime Minister. The Cabinet Secretary is a high-profile figure who will look to protect the interests of the civil servants and will at times disagree with the Prime Minister.

Civil servants work in the government departments and are not political appointees. The Liberal Prime Minister William Gladstone in 1853 sought to reform the Civil Service and asked Sir Stafford Northcote and Charles Trevelyan to make recommendations in their report. Their subsequent report recommended the creation of a professional and independent Civil Service. The reforms prevented the Civil Service from being used as political patronage, i.e. preventing posts in the Civil Service from being awarded to supporters of the government. The report called for promotion on merit and the requirement that anyone could apply to become a civil servant so long as they were able to pass an examination. In 1870, the Civil Service Commission (which was created in 1855) introduced examinations for junior members of the Civil Service and this ensured that the Civil Service was competent and professional.[121] This has meant that the key feature of the British Civil Service is neutrality and not loyalty to one particular political party. Nonetheless, it has become usual for governments to employ political advisors to give advice on policy issues.

There is a Civil Service Code and the civil servants.[122] The Code is established by section 5 of the Constitutional Reform and Governance Act 2010. Section 8 of the Act also states that the Minister for the Civil Service must publish a code of conduct for special advisors; these are people who work in government alongside ministers, but are not civil servants, who keep their job regardless of which political party is in power, but are political appointees. The Civil Service Code states that: [a]s a civil servant, you are appointed on merit on the basis of fair and open competition and are expected to carry out your role with dedication and a commitment to the Civil Service and its core values: integrity, honesty, objectivity and impartiality.' The Code reinforces the idea that civil servants must be politically impartial (in their job, as they can still join a political party in their personal capacity). Civil servants are warned that they 'must not act in a way that is determined by party political considerations, or use official resources for party political purposes [or] allow your personal political views to determine any advice you give or your actions.' The Code is more extensive than the discussion above; however, the key principles around which the duties are established are integrity, honesty, objectivity and impartiality.

The Code of Conduct for special advisors states that 'Special advisors are a critical part of the team supporting Ministers.[123] They add a political dimension to the advice and assistance available to Ministers while reinforcing the political impartiality of the permanent Civil Service by distinguishing the source of political advice and support' and

> [s]pecial advisers should be fully integrated into the functioning of government. They are part of the team working closely alongside civil servants to deliver Ministers' priorities. They can help Ministers on matters where the work of government and the work of the government party overlap and where it would be inappropriate for permanent civil servants to become involved.

It is clear that special advisors are intended to have a political role and although they will work alongside civil servants, there is an important distinction. This is not to say that the obligations upon special advisors are too dissimilar to civil servants, as the Code of Conduct for special advisors states that

> [s]pecial advisers are bound by the standards of integrity and honesty required of all civil servants as set out in the *Civil Service Code*. However, they are exempt from the general requirement that civil servants should be appointed on merit and behave with impartiality and objectivity, or that they need to retain the confidence of future governments of a different political complexion. They are otherwise required to conduct themselves in accordance with the *Civil Service Code*.[124]

Civil servants can take decisions using the discretionary powers delegated to a minister by Parliament under the Carltona principle (*Carltona Ltd v. Commissioners of Works*[125]). There are restrictions on the decisions which civil servants may take using these delegated powers (see *R v. Secretary of State of the Home Department ex p. Doody*).[126] Where there has been unauthorised delegation to a civil servant, then the decision made by the civil servant can be judicially reviewed. Civil servants should be protected under the guidance laid down by Sir David Maxwell Fyfe following the Crichel Down affair. Despite this ministers have continued to blame civil servants for their department's failings.

The original Osmotherly Rules date back to 1980 and are guidance for civil servants for when they give evidence to Parliamentary Select Committees. The current guidance published by the Cabinet Office in 2014 is clear that

> '[t]he Civil Service Code makes clear that civil servants are accountable to Ministers who in turn are accountable to Parliament. It therefore follows that when civil servants give evidence to a Select Committee they are doing so, not in a personal capacity, but as representatives of their Ministers[127]

and

> '[t]his does not mean that officials may not be called upon to give a full account of government policies, or the justification, objectives and effects

of these policies, but their purpose in doing so is to contribute to the process of ministerial accountability not to offer personal views or judgements on matters of government policy – to do so could undermine their political impartiality.'[128]

8.10 Local authorities and agencies

Local authorities are responsible for running their communities. Local authorities are, amongst other things, responsible for waste management, schools and planning permission. The actions of a local authority can be judicially reviewed by the courts.

8.11 Devolution and the executive

Powers have been devolved under Tony Blair's Labour government. In London there is an elected mayor, and in Scotland, Wales and Northern Ireland there are First Ministers who are responsible for their respective governments. Devolution affects approximately 19,200,000 people, with London's population of 8,787,892, Scotland's population of 5,425,000, Wales' population of 3,125,000 and Northern Ireland's population of 1,871,000.

8.11.1 Mayor of London

The mayor of London is directly elected and is responsible for setting policies and a budget to govern the capital. A directly elected mayor came about as a consequence of a referendum that took place in May 1998.[129] The mayor is held

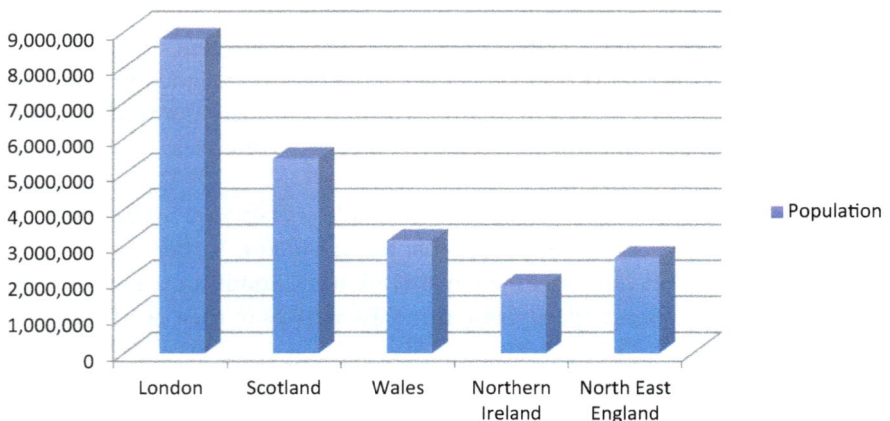

Figure 8.5
The respective population of devolved areas (or in the case of North East England what would have been devolved)

to account by the London Assembly, which was voted for as part of the referendum. As a consequence of the support for creating a directly elected mayor and the London Assembly, the Greater London Authority Act 1999 was enacted to create these institutions. The Mayor of London governs more people than live in Scotland or Wales. The mayor is assisted by a large team of advisors and his offices are in City Hall, London. The office of mayor is important and the post holders have attracted international attention. The current Prime Minister Boris Johnson was Mayor of London from 2008 to 2016 and Sadiq Khan, the current mayor had a high-profile disagreement with the President of the United States. The mayor is responsible for areas such as policing, transport, planning, regeneration and health. There is a considerable budget, £17 billion, which the mayor is responsible for.

8.11.2 Welsh Assembly

Post devolution the leader of the largest party in the National Assembly of Wales is the First Minister. The First Minister of Wales is responsible for chairing Welsh Cabinet meetings and governing Wales using the powers devolved by the Westminster Parliament. The Welsh government is responsible for the legislative programme of the National Assembly of Wales, Cabinet meetings and Cabinet statements.[130] The Welsh government is held to account by the National Assembly for Wales. It was as a result of the Labour government's policy of devolution for Wales that a referendum was held in 1997 to ask the people of Wales whether they would support the creation of a single assembly and government. As a result of the outcome of the referendum the Government of Wales Act 1998 created the new devolved institution, which was treated as a single legal entity, despite having legislative and executive responsibility.[131] It was not until the Government of Wales Act 2006 that the government and assembly were divided into two separate institutions. The 2006 Act devolved more powers to the Welsh government, with further powers devolved by the Wales Act 2014, the Tax Collection and Management (Wales) Act 2016 and the Wales Act 2017.[132] In 2019, the First Minister of Wales, Mark Drakeford, was reported as supporting possible Welsh independence from the rest of the United Kingdom, as he said Wales remaining as part of the United Kingdom was conditional.[133] However, the First Minister denied supporting independence.[134]

8.11.3 Scottish government

Prior to the creation of Great Britain in 1707 Scotland was a separate country and had its own monarch, the King of Scots, and government based in Edinburgh. The Act of Union with England 1707 created the way for a union with England, and the government of the new territory took place in London. It was not until the attempt by the then Labour government in 1979 to devolve power to Scotland, that Scotland would have had its own distinct governing institutions. The Scottish electorate rejected the proposals for devolution in 1979. However, the Labour government that came to power in 1997 had as one of its policies devolution for Scotland. A referendum was held in 1997 and a majority of the Scottish electorate supported devolution. The Scotland Act 1998 created the Scottish Parliament and the Scottish government. The Scottish government is responsible for those areas that have been devolved, as opposed to those areas reserved by the central United Kingdom government. These areas include education, justice, housing and taxation. Additional powers were devolved by the Scotland Act 2012 and the Scotland Act 2016.

Following devolution the first Scottish governments were coalition governments, whereby the Scottish Labour and Scottish Liberal Democrats parties shared power. Since 2007, there has been a single party government, with the Scottish National Party holding power at Holyrood, where the Parliament is based. The current First Minister of Scotland is Nicola Sturgeon and she heads the Scottish government and chairs Cabinet meetings. The current Scottish government supports Scottish independence from the United Kingdom. In 2014, the Scottish government supported the Yes campaign during the referendum on Scottish independence, which narrowly saw the No remain campaign win. In the event that Scotland was to become independent from the rest of the United Kingdom, the current monarch would become head of state of the newly independent country. In 2019, the First Minister of Scotland announced that it was the policy of the Scottish government that there would be a second referendum on Scottish independence before 2021.[135] The Scottish government published a bill to lay out the legal framework for this referendum.

8.11.4 Northern Ireland

As a result of the Good Friday Agreement in 1998 and the Northern Ireland Act 1998 the Northern Ireland Assembly was created and the North Ireland Executive carries out the executive functions. The Northern Ireland Assembly does not work on the Westminster model and all parties must share power, whereas at Westminster the largest party controls power. Since 2017, Northern Ireland has been without a government as the political parties have been unable to power share.[136]

8.11.5 North East England

The then Labour government also wanted to devolve powers to the English regions. The first and only referendum on regional devolution was held in North East England in 2004, which saw the electorate reject the proposals. The North East Assembly, had it been created, would have been responsible for a population almost the same size of Wales.

8.11.6 Directly elected mayors

There are 15 directly-elected Mayors in England and Wales, excluding the Mayor of London; the statutory framework is set out by the Local Government Act 2000, the Localism Act 2011 and the Cities as Local Government Devolution Act 2016.[137]

8.12 Practical application

Last week *The Daily Trumpet*, a national newspaper, published the following story:

'MINISTER CAUGHT IN SEXTING SCANDAL'

Angela Griffin, the Secretary of State for Defence, was caught sexting Lilly Smith, who is a junior colleague in her department during a meeting with fellow EU defence ministers in Brussels. Ms Griffin has refused to respond to the allegations and claims that this is classic press intrusion. Ms Griffin is married to Susana Bedford, a leading human rights lawyer and childhood friend of the Prime Minister. Ms Griffin is a keen user of social media, and last week she secretly live tweeted during a Cabinet meeting with the #Number10Live. Her tweets revealed what happened during the meeting. During her latest trip to Brussels, Ms Griffin had apparently informed the French Defence Minister that the Prime Minister will refuse to give the House of Commons any say over the forthcoming decision to invade the Republic of Utopia.

Ms Griffin has also indicated on twitter that Lord Mitchell, a member of the House of Lords, is likely to succeed the Prime Minister when she resigns next year. Ms Griffin in a series of tweets named and shamed several civil servants, who had overseen the construction of Ms Griffin's legacy project, HMS Flawed, a billion pound warship. However, because it violated many EU environmental laws, HMS Flawed had to be scrapped halfway through its construction.

The UK Constitution Hub, a charity that aims to safeguard the constitution, has contacted you to advise on whether the issues raised in the above story involve any constitutional conventions. If they do, have there been, or is there likely to be, any possible breaches of a convention, and what are the possible political or legal consequences of such a breach?

In your answer you will be expected to make reference to relevant case law, factual examples and academic opinion.

8.13 Key points to take away from this chapter

- The position of Prime Minister has developed since the 18th century. Prime Ministers have been accused of becoming too presidential and relying on a small circle of advisors, as opposed to their Cabinet colleagues.
- The convention of collective ministerial responsibility ensures the secrecy of Cabinet deliberations.
- The convention of individual ministerial responsibility holds a minister accountable for their department's failings and their own personal affairs.
- The executive is held to account by the courts and Parliament.

Notes

1   Reigned 1509–1547.

2   Reigned 1952–present.

3   F Maitland, *The Constitutional History of England* (CUP 1965) 418.

4   R Blackburn, 'Queen Elizabeth II and the Evolution of Monarchy' in M Qvortrup (ed), *The British Constitution: Continuity and Change: A Festschrif for Veron Bogdanor* (Hart Publishing 2013) 167.

5   See section 2 of the Act of Settlement 1700 and section 2 of the Succession to the Crown Act 2013.

6   V Bogdanor, *The Monarchy and the Constitution* (OUP 1995) 302.

7   ibid 307.

8   W Bagehot, *The English Constitution* (Fontana 1867) 85.

9   R Ekins and S Laws, 'Stop This Power Grab by MPs or Chaos Governs' *The Sunday Times* (31 March 2019).

10 T Poole, 'The Executive Power Project' (*London Review of Books Blog*, 2 April 2019) <www.lrb.co.uk/blog/2019/april/the-executive-power-project>.

11 J King, 'Can Royal Assent to a Bill Be Withheld if so Advised by Ministers?' (*UK Constitutional Law Blog*, 5th April 2019) <https://ukconstitutionallaw.org/>.

12 DR Thorpe, 'Queen Elizabeth and Her 12 Prime Ministers' (*The History of Government Blog*, 1 September 2012) <https://history.blog.gov.uk/2012/09/01/queen-elizabeth-and-her-twelve-prime-ministers/>.

13 Cabinet Manual [2.12] 15.

14 Bagehot (n 8) 98–99.

15 ibid 111.

16 S Bradford, 'Meeting the Monarch, the Private Ritual Shared with Her Prime Ministers' *The Telegraph* (28 June 2007).

17 R Booth, 'Secret Papers Show Extent of Senior Royal's Veto Over Bills' *The Guardian* (15 January 2013) <www.theguardian.com/uk/2013/jan/14/secret-papers-royals-veto-bills>.

18 'Queen's or Prince's Consent' Office of the Parliamentary Counsel, September 2018, [7.12] <https://assets.publishing.service.gov.uk/government/uploads/system/uploads/attachment_data/file/742221/Queen_s_and_prince_s_consent_pamphlet__September_2018___accessible_.pdf>.

19 'Magic or Not, Let in the Daylight: We Need a Level and Sober Debate' *The Guardian* (6 December 2000) <www.theguardian.com/uk/2000/dec/06/monarchy.guardianleaders>.

20 E Webber, 'Scottish Independence: What Will Happen to the Queen?' *BBC News* (11 September 2014) <www.bbc.co.uk/news/uk-29126569>.

21 See N Wildash, 'The Monarchy: Popular Across Society and "Here to Stay"' *YouGov* (8 September 2015) <https://yougov.co.uk/topics/politics/articles-reports/2015/09/08/monarchy-here-stay>. See also L Elliot, 'How the British Royal Family Killed Off Republicanism' *The Guardian* (13 June 2019) <www.theguardian.com/commentisfree/2019/jun/13/how-the-british-royal-family-killed-off-republicanism>.

22 See R Blackburn, *King and Country: Monarchy and the Future King Charles III* (Politico 2006).

23 The judgment of the Supreme Court in *R (on the application of Evans) v Attorney General* [2015] UKSC 21 enabled the publication of the letters.

24 'Read the Prince Charles "Black Spider" Memos in Full' *The Guardian* (13 May 2015) <www.theguardian.com/uk-news/ng-interactive/2015/may/13/read-the-prince-charles-black-spider-memos-in-full>.

25 *Cabinet Manual* [2.12] 15.

26 P Schleiter and V Belu, 'Avoiding Another "Squatter in Downing Street" Controversy: The Need to Improve the Caretaker Convention Before the 2015 General Election' (2014) 85(4) *The Political Quarterly* 454.

27 P Schleiter and V Belu, 'Why the UK Needs Improved Caretaker Conventions Before the May 2015 General Election' (*The Oxford University Politics Blog*, 26 January 2015) <https://blog.politics.ox.ac.uk/uk-needs-improved-caretaker-conventions-may-2015-general-election/>.

28 Leader of the Liberal Democrats.

29 A Adonis, *5 Days in May: The Coalition and Beyond* (Biteback Publishing Ltd 2013) 130.

30 ibid 131.

31 ibid.

32 This sometimes does not happen as a person who is not a member of either Houses of Parliament could be appointed to serve in the government. This happened during the First World War when the South African military leader and politician Jan Smuts was appointed to the Imperial War Cabinet in 1917. Smuts was not a UK parliamentarian. During the Second World War there were plans in the event that the Prime Minister, Winston Churchill, was killed to appoint Smuts as his successor.

33 For an interesting account of the role of the whips and how they operate see 'Power of the Whips: The Silent Enforcers' *BBC Radio 4* (24 July 2016) <www.bbc.co.uk/programmes/b07lfrjz>.

34 J McTernan, 'Chief Whips: They're Not as Nice as They Look' *The Telegraph* (17 July 2014) <www.telegraph.co.uk/news/politics/conservative/10972784/Chief-Whips-theyre-not-as-nice-as-they-look.html>.

35 A Asthana, 'Dark Rumours in Westminster Over Tory Whips' Behaviour' *The Guardian* (15 December 2017) <www.theguardian.com/politics/2017/dec/15/rumours-of-government-whipping-operation-abound-in-westminster>.

36 V Bogdanor, 'Introduction' in V Bogdanor (ed), *From New Jerusalem to New Labour: British Prime Ministers from Atlee to Blair* (Palgrave Macmillan) 7. Bogdanor was quoting The Earl of Oxford and Asquith, *Fifty Years of Parliament* (Cassell 1926) 184–85.

37 A Blick and G Jones, 'The Institution of Prime Minister' (2012) <www.number10.gov.uk/history-and-tour/the-institution-of-prime-minister/>.

38 P Hennessy, *The Prime Minister: The Office and its Holders Since 1945* (Penguin 2001) 56.

39 ibid 56.

40 ibid 516.

41 ibid 519. Interview by Michael Cockerell, Blair's Thousand Days, BBC 2.

42 ibid 520.

43 Quoted in Hennessy (n 40) 525. See the original article for a full account of the interview, A Applebaum, 'I am Still Normal' *The Sunday Telegraph* (19 March 2001) <www.telegraph.co.uk/news/uknews/4722273/I-am-still-normal.html>.

44 Bogdanor, 'Introduction' (n 38) 6.

45 A Giddens, 'Tony Blair, 1997–2007' in V Bogdanor (ed), *From New Jerusalem to New Labour: British Prime Ministers from Atlee to Blair* (Palgrave Macmillan) 188.

46 ibid 188.

47 J Forsyth, 'Will "Chairman Boris" Revive Cabinet Government?' *The Spectator* (20 July 2019) <www.spectator.co.uk/2019/07/will-chairman-boris-revive-cabinet-government/>.

48 The motion read 'That this house has considered the merits of the newly chosen leader of the Conservative party, and supports his wish to form a government' see P Walker and R Mason, 'Alan Duncan Quit to Test of Boris Johnson Has Confidence of MPs' *The Guardian* (22 July 2019) <www.theguardian.com/politics/2019/jul/22/alan-duncan-quits-as-minister-before-boris-johnson-arrival-at-no-10>.

49 Bagehot (n 8) 67.

50 See 'Clare Short's Resignation Letter' *The Guardian*, 12 May 2003 <www.theguardian.com/politics/2003/may/12/labour.voluntarysector>; 'Robin Cook's Resignation Letter' *The Guardian* (17 March 2003) <www.theguardian.com/politics/2003/mar/17/labour.iraq1>.

51 Interestingly the 2010 Coalition Agreement stated that the Prime Minister would not remove a Liberal Democrat minister without consulting the Deputy Prime Minister.

52 Schedule 1 of the Ministerial and other Salaries Act 1975.

53 J Rentoul, 'Did the Blair-Brown Relationship Contain the Seeds of Labour's Destruction' *The Independent* (30 October 2016) <www.independent.co.uk/voices/alastair-campbell-new-labour-tony-blair-gordon-brown-relationship-contain-the-seeds-of-labours-a7383746.html>.

54 [4.1].

55 I Jennings, *Cabinet Government* (3rd edn, CUP 1969) 267.

56 Spencer Walpole, *The Life of Lord John Russell* (Volume 1, 1889) 369, quoted in O Gay and T Powell, 'The Collective Responsibility of Ministers – an Outline of the Issues' Parliament and Constitution Centre, Research Paper 4/82, 15 November 2004.

57 HL Deb 8 April 1878, Volume 239 cc 833–35. Please note that Salisbury was not prime minister at the time (emphasis added).

58 Boris Johnson's resignation letter was clear on why he had to resign: 'On Friday I acknowledged that my side of the argument were too few to prevail, and congratulated you on at least reaching a cabinet decision on the way forward. *As I said then, the government now has a song to sing*. The trouble is that I have practised the words over the weekend and find that they stick in the throat. *We must have collective responsibility*. Since I cannot in all conscience champion these proposals, I have sadly concluded that I must go' (emphasis added). The Prime Minister' response was that: 'As I outlined at Chequers, *the agreement we reached requires the full, collective support of Her Majesty's Government*. During the EU referendum campaign, collective responsibility on EU policy was temporarily suspended. As we developed our policy on Brexit, I have allowed Cabinet colleagues considerable latitude to express their individual views. But the agreement we reached on Friday marks the point where that is no longer the case, and if you are not able to provide the support we need to secure this deal in the interests of the United Kingdom, it is right that you should step down' (emphasis added). The two letters are available at 'Boris Johnson's Resignation Letter and May's Reply in Full' *BBC News* (9 July 2018) <www.bbc.co.uk/news/uk-politics-44772804>.

59   Ministerial Code 2018, 4.

60   ibid.

61   R Mason, 'Theresa May Defends Decision Not to Sack Boris Johnson' *The Guardian* (3 October 2017) <www.theguardian.com/politics/2017/oct/03/theresa-may-defends-decision-not-to-sack-boris-johnson>.

62   O Wright, 'Resign Now, Boris Johnson Told in Row Over Sabotaging Theresa May' *The Times* (12 May 2018) <www.theguardian.com/politics/2017/oct/03/theresa-may-defends-decision-not-to-sack-boris-johnson>.

63   [1976] QB 752.

64   (at 771).

65   J Jaconelli, 'Do Constitutional Conventions Bind?' [2005] CLJ 149, 160.

66   I Dale, 'In Conversation with . . . Jacqui Smith' (*Total Politics*, 17 July 2009) <www.totalpolitics.com/articles/interview/conversation-jacqui-smith>.

67   'Lack of Training for New Ministers Is Madness' The Institute for Government (6 May 2010) <www.instituteforgovernment.org.uk/news/latest/lack-training-new-ministers-madness>.

68   Further information about *Yes, Minister* can be found at <www.bbc.co.uk/comedy/yesminister/ and details about this episode at www.bbc.co.uk/programmes/b007jlbc>.

69   D Oliver, 'Ministerial Accountability' in D Butler et al (eds), *The Law, Politics and the Constitution: Essays in Honour of Geoffrey Marshall* (OUP 1999).

70   G Cordon, 'Liam Fox Breached Ministerial Code' *The Independent* (18 October 2011) <www.independent.co.uk/news/uk/home-news/liam-fox-breached-ministerial-code-2372167.html>.

71   P Leopold, 'Standards of Public Life' in J Jowell and D Oliver (eds), *The Changing Constitution* (7th edn, OUP 2011).

72   See P Wintour and A Stratton, 'Ex-Ministers Suspended from Labour Party Over Lobbying Allegations' *The Guardian* (23 March 2010) <www.theguardian.com/politics/2010/mar/23/ex-ministers-suspended-lobbying-allegations>. See also R Syal, 'Lobbying: Ministers Race to Change Rules as Scandals Hit Home' *The Guardian* (2 June 2013) <www.theguardian.com/politics/2013/jun/02/lobbying-ministers-scandals>.

73   Freedom of Information Act 2000, 2011.

74   P Wintour, 'Freedom of Information Act Has Not Improved Government, Says MoJ' *The Guardian* (13 February 2012) <www.guardian.co.uk/politics/2012/feb/13/freedom-of-information-ministry-justice?INTCMP=SRCH>.

75   R Austin, 'Freedom of Information Act 2000 – A Sheep in Wolf's Clothing' in J Jowell and D Oliver (eds), *The Changing Constitution* (6th edn, OUP 2007) 397.

76   P Birkinshaw, 'Regulating Information' in J Jowell, D Oliver and C O'Cinneide (eds), *The Changing Constitution* (8th edn, OUP 2015) 390.

77   ibid 406–9.

78   D Woodhouse, *Ministers and Parliament: Accountability in Theory and Practice* (Clarendon Press 1994) 27.

79   O Gay and T Powell, 'The Collective Responsibility of Ministers – an Outline of the Issues' Parliament and Constitution Centre, Research Paper 4/82, 15 November 2004, 8–9.

80   Chapter One, 'Accountability of Ministers to Parliament' in D Woodhouse, *Ministers and Parliament: Accountability in Theory and Practice* (Clarendon Press 1994).

81   (HC 519, 1985–86 para 235).

82 O Gay and T Powell, 'Individual Ministerial Responsibility – Issues and Examples' House of Commons Research Paper 4/31, 5 April 2004 <https://research briefings.parliament.uk/ResearchBriefing/Summary/RP04-31>.

83 [1.5].

84 J Griffith, 'The Crichel Down Affair' (1955) 18(6) MLR 556.

85 HC Deb, 20 July 1954, col 1186.

86 ibid cols 1285–87.

87 ibid.

88 G Marshall (ed), *Oxford Readings in Politics and Government – Ministerial Responsibility* (OUP 1989) 131.

89 The Art of the Foreign Minister, BBC Radio 4, broadcast on 19 May 2013.

90 The Deputy Prime Minister and leader of the Liberal Democrats.

91 A member of the House of Lords and the former leader of the Liberal Democrats.

92 David Cameron.

93 David Laws, *Coalition: The Inside Story of the Conservative-Liberal Democrat Coalition Government* (Biteback Publishing 2016) 40–41.

94 [1999] 127.

95 [2004].

96 See D Woodhouse, 'Individual Ministerial Responsibility and a "Dash of Principle" ' in D Butler et al (eds) *The Law, Politics and the Constitution: Essays in Honour of Geoffrey Marshall* (OUP 1999) 130.

97 'Gavin Williamson Sacking: Former Deference Secretary Denies Huawei Leak' *BBC News* (2 May 2019) <www.bbc.co.uk/news/uk-politics-48129280>.

98 'Damian Green Sacked After "Misleading Statements" on Porn Claims' *BBC News* (21 December 2017) <www.bbc.co.uk/news/uk-politics-42434802>.

99 ibid 110.

100 ibid 111–12.

101 Munro (n 47) 86.

102 The Resolution on Ministerial Accountability (1997).

103 House of Commons Public Administration and Constitutional Affairs Committee, 'The Role of Parliament in the UK Constitution Interim Report: The Status and Effect of Confidence Motions and the Fixed-Term Parliaments Act 2011' Fourteenth Report of Session 2017–18, HC 1813 [57].

104 ibid 60.

105 See A King and I Crewe, *The Blunders of Our Governments* (Oneworld 2013) 361, 'As a legislative assembly, the parliament of the United Kingdom is, much of the time, either peripheral or totally irrelevant. It might as well not exist.' For a contrary view see M Russell and P Cowley, 'The Policy Power of the Westminster Parliament: The "Parliamentary State" and the Empirical Evidence' (2015) 29(1) Governance: An International Journal of Policy, Administration and Institutions 121.

106 J Sumption, 'Judicial and Political Decision-Making: The Uncertain Boundary' The FA Mann Lecture 2011.

107 [1994] 1 AC 377.

108 For an interesting commentary see P Worrall, 'Fact Check: Does the Sun Win Elections' *Channel 4 News* (30 April 2015) <www.channel4.com/news/factcheck/factcheck-sun-win-elections>.

109 'Sun Source Comes Forward to Question Brown's Claims' *The Times*, 13 July 2011, <www.thetimes.co.uk/article/sun-source-comes-forward-to-question-browns-claims-pchsgw2wg37>.

110 L O'Carrol, 'Rebekah Brooks: David Cameron signed off texts "LOL"' *The Guardian*, 11 May 2012, <www.theguardian.com/media/2012/may/11/rebekah-brooks-david-cameron-texts-lol>.

111 L O'Carrol, 'Andy Coulson Jailed for 18 Months for Conspiracy to Hack Phones' *The Guardian* (4 July 2014) <www.theguardian.com/uk-news/2014/jul/04/andy-coulson-jailed-phone-hacking>.

112 For information about the support provided to the opposition see M Sandford, 'Opposition Parties in the House of Commons' Parliament and Constitution Centre, SN/PC/06057, 2 August 2013.

113 O Gay, 'Pre-Election Contacts Between Civil Servants and Opposition Parties' Parliament and Constitution Centre, SN/PC/03318, 22 May 2014.

114 ibid.

115 Figure correct as of 2019. Note that this salary is in addition to the salary as an MP.

116 Section 1(1)(b) and section 2.

117 See R Kelly, 'Short Money' House of Commons Library, No 01663, 4 October 2018 <https://researchbriefings.parliament.uk/ResearchBriefing/Summary/SN01663>.

118 ibid.

119 ibid.

120 ibid.

121 I Jennings, *The Queen's Government* (Pelican 1960) 106.

122 See <www.gov.uk/government/publications/civil-service-code/the-civil-service-code>.

123 See [1]-[2] <https://assets.publishing.service.gov.uk/government/uploads/system/uploads/attachment_data/file/579768/code-of-conduct-special-advisers-dec-2016.pdf>.

124 ibid 8.

125 [1943] 2 All ER 560.

126 [1994] 1 AC 531.

127 See [4] <https://assets.publishing.service.gov.uk/government/uploads/system/uploads/attachment_data/file/364600/Osmotherly_Rules_October_2014.pdf>.

128 ibid 5.

129 The legal basis for the referendum was the Greater London Authority (Referendum) Act 1998.

130 For more information see <https://gov.wales/about-us>.

131 For more information see <www.assembly.wales/en/abthome/role-of-assembly-how-it-works/Pages/history-welsh-devolution.aspx>.

132 ibid.

133 'Independence: Mark Drakeford Rejects Plaid Cymru Claim He's "Indy-Curious"' *BBC News* (9 July 2019) <www.bbc.co.uk/news/uk-wales-politics-48923999>.

134 ibid.

135 L Brooks, 'Scottish Government Publishes Independence Referendum Bill' *The Guardian* (29 May 2019) <www.theguardian.com/uk-news/2019/may/29/scotland-publishes-second-independence-referendum-bill>.

136 B Kelly, 'Why Is There No Government in Northern Ireland and How Dis Power-Sharing Collapse' *The Independent* (30 April 2019) <www.independent.co.uk/news/uk/politics/northern-ireland-talks-latest-power-sharing-deal-stormont-sinn-fein-dup-a8893096.html>.

137 M Sanford, 'Directly-Elected Mayors' House of Commons Library Briefing Paper, No 05000, 7 May 2019 <https://researchbriefings.parliament.uk/ResearchBriefing/Summary/SN05000>.

Further reading

Austin R, 'Freedom of Information Act 2000 – A Sheep in Wolf's Clothing' in J Jowell and D Oliver (eds), *The Changing Constitution* (6th edn, OUP 2007)

Bagehot W, *The English Constitution* (Fontana 1983)

Birkinshaw P, 'Regulating Information' in J Jowell, D Oliver and C O'Cinneide (eds), *The Changing Constitution* (8th edn, OUP 2015)

Blackburn, R, 'Queen Elizabeth II and the Evolution of Monarchy' in M Qvortrup (ed), *The British Constitution: Continuity and Change: A Festschrif for Veron Bogdanor* (Hart Publishing 2013) 167

Blick A and G Jones, 'The Institution of Prime Minister' (2012) <www.number10.gov.uk/history-and-tour/the-institution-of-prime-minister/>

Bogdanor V, *The Monarchy and the Constitution* (OUP 1995)

—— (ed), *From New Jerusalem to New Labour: British Prime Ministers from Atlee to Blair* (Palgrave Macmillan 2010)

Dewry G, 'The Executive: Towards Accountable Government and Effective Governance?' in J Jowell and D Oliver (eds), *The Changing Constitution* (7th edn, OUP 2011)

Ekins R and S Laws, 'Stop This Power Grab by MPs or Chaos Governs' *The Sunday Times* (31 March 2019)

Griffith J, 'The Crichel Down Affair' (1955) 18(6) MLR 556

Hennessy P, *The Prime Minister: The Office and Its Holders Since 1945* (Penguin 2001)

Jaconelli J, 'Do Constitutional Conventions Bind?' [2005] CLJ 149

Leopold P, 'Standards of Public Life' in J Jowell and D Oliver (eds), *The Changing Constitution* (7th edn, OUP 2011)

King A and I Crewe, *The Blunders of Our Governments* (Oneworld 2013)

Maitland F, *The Constitutional History of England* (CUP 1965)

Munro C, *Studies in Constitutional Law* (2nd edn, OUP 2005)

Oliver D, 'Ministerial Accountability' in D Butler et al (eds), *The Law, Politics and the Constitution: Essays in Honour of Geoffrey Marshall* (OUP 1999)

Poole T, 'The Executive Power Project' (*London Review of Books Blog*, 2 April 2019) <www.lrb.co.uk/blog/2019/april/the-executive-power-project>

Rhodes RAW, J Wanna and P Weller, *Comparing Westminster* (OUP 2009)

Woodhouse D, 'Individual Ministerial Responsibility and a "Dash of Principle"' in D Butler et al (eds), *The Law, Politics and the Constitution: Essays in Honour of Geoffrey Marshall* (OUP 1999)

9 The Courts and the Judiciary

This chapter will

- consider the role played by the judiciary in England and Wales;
- reflect upon the creation of the UK Supreme Court and its predecessor, the Appellate Committee of the House of Lords;
- discuss the role played by the judiciary and address themes such as judicial law-making and judicial review; and
- explore what is meant by judicial independence, judicial power, judicial activism and judicial deference.

9.1 Introduction

The judiciary plays an important role in our constitutional system, as the courts are tasked with applying the law and interpreting Acts of Parliament. Members of the judiciary have traditionally observed the separation of powers and the doctrine of Parliamentary Sovereignty. But what does this actually mean? We will see how the courts, by observing the separation of powers, have sometimes shown deference to the executive and have avoided making decisions that should only be made by elected officials. However, a counter argument is that the courts have become too activist and are taking decisions on topics where it could be inappropriate to do so, given political considerations and questions of institutional competence (i.e., the executive's expertise to take high policy decisions and resource allocation decisions). In recent years the Policy Exchange, a non-governmental UK Think Tank, has established the Judicial Power Project, to look at the use of powers by judges and raise concerns over judicial overreach. We will see that the courts and judges, their decisions and use of power, is controversial and academics and legal practitioners often take different views. This chapter will consider these arguments and the variety of different opinion.

We shall also see how the courts have acknowledged that Parliament is legally sovereign and consequently the courts cannot question or set aside an Act of Parliament. However, as you will have seen in **Chapter 6** there has been

371

DOI: 10.4324/9780429293498-11

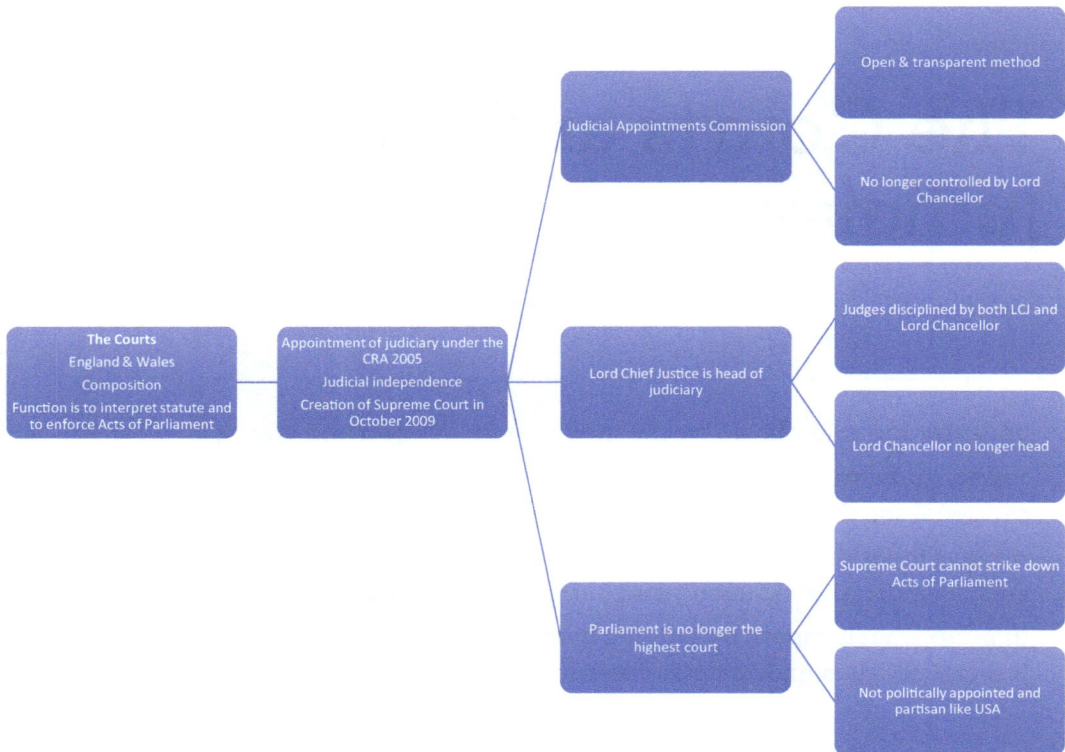

Figure 9.1
Chapter overview

judicial disagreement (albeit in *obiter*) about whether the courts can impose qualifications on parliamentary sovereignty. We will look at the function of the courts, how judges are appointed and whether they have adequate independence from the executive.

Before reading this chapter, it is important to reflect on a number of key points:

- The separation of powers: in **Chapter 3** we saw the importance of having the three branches of government distinguished from each other, in terms of making laws, using the law to govern the country and finally enforcing the law. It is important that each branch of government is composed of different people. The judiciary have traditionally supported the notion that the United Kingdom's constitution observes the separation of powers, whereas it has been academics that have dismissed the notion that the separation of powers is part of the United Kingdom's constitution. In this chapter we will look at whether the separation of powers exists with regards to the judiciary and the legal system. This will involve looking at the importance of judicial independence, as first stated in the Act of Settlement 1701 and then reiterated in the Senior Courts Act 1981 and the

Constitutional Reform Act 2005. We will also look at judicial law-making and the role of senior members of the judiciary in overseeing governmental bodies and chairing public inquiries.

- Accountability of the executive: in **Chapter 8** we looked at the executive and the considerable power which the government has. Since 1979–2010 most governments had enjoyed a majority in the House of Commons and this control of Parliament permitted the government to introduce any legislation that it wished. Since 2010 there has been a coalition government (2010–15), a Conservative majority government (2015–17), and a Conservative government with a supply and confidence agreement with the Democratic Unionist Party (2017–19). The present Conservative government (2019-present) under Prime Minister Boris Johnson has a large majority in the House of Commons.

- We will look at how the judiciary has held the executive to account by upholding the rule of law. The courts have held that the executive cannot act unless there is lawful authority for its actions (see *Entick v. Carrington*[1]), or it is not illegal for the executive to act in a certain way (see *Malone v. Metropolitan Police Commissioner [No.2]*[2]). The courts have developed judicial review through a series of important common law decisions as an effective way of holding the executive to account. The importance of judicial review cannot be overstated; given the executive's historic (if now disputed) dominance of Parliament; it is the courts which have questioned the legality of detaining suspected terrorists indefinitely (see *A v. Secretary of State for the Home Department*[3]) and this led to the introduction of the Prevention of Terrorism Act 2005 and the use of control orders. The use of control orders and the use of closed material by the government (i.e. evidence not revealed to the person subject to the order) was considered by the House of Lords in *Secretary of State for the Home Department v. MB*.[4]

- Judicial activism is controversial as according to the theory of the separation of powers it should be the executive and not the courts that make policy decisions. Equally, the courts should not intervene and question policy decisions if these are made lawfully using the powers given by Parliament to a local authority, health authority or indeed the government. However, the courts have been criticised for making policy decisions and for violating the separation of powers.

- In **Chapter 5** and **Chapter 6** we saw that Parliamentary Sovereignty is the key feature of the United Kingdom's constitution. The courts must give effect to an Act of Parliament. Under no circumstances can the courts refuse to give effect to an Act of Parliament, the only exception being where there was (prior to the United Kingdom leaving the European Union) a conflict between an Act of Parliament and the law of the European Union (see the European Communities Act 1972). However, the courts cannot declare an Act of Parliament void, even where it violates human rights or the rule of law. The courts can declare an Act of Parliament to be incompatible with rights protected under the European Convention on Human Rights. This power was given to the courts by Parliament and is contained in section 4 of the Human Rights Act 1998. It is important to note that a declaration of incompatibility does not affect the continuing validity of the Act of Parliament. The courts' role is to interpret an Act of Parliament; however, the courts have been accused of creative interpretation to avoid the effect of an Act of Parliament (see *Anisminic Ltd v. Foreign Compensation Commission*[5]). This means that Parliament's intentions can potentially be ignored, but judicial interpretation in defiance of plain meaning would be unjust.

9.2 The courts and judiciary

In the United Kingdom the Queen is the fount of justice and the courts carry out the administration of justice in her name. We shall begin by exploring the Supreme Court and the impact of the Constitutional Reform Act 2005. See Figure 9.2 for a diagram of the court structure in England and Wales. We will not be considering the court structure in Northern Ireland or Scotland, as these are different legal systems.

9.3 The United Kingdom's Supreme Court

The Constitutional Reform Act 2005 has had a significant impact on the judiciary. The Act changed the way judges were appointed, reformed the role of the Lord Chancellor and created a new Supreme Court. The United Kingdom's

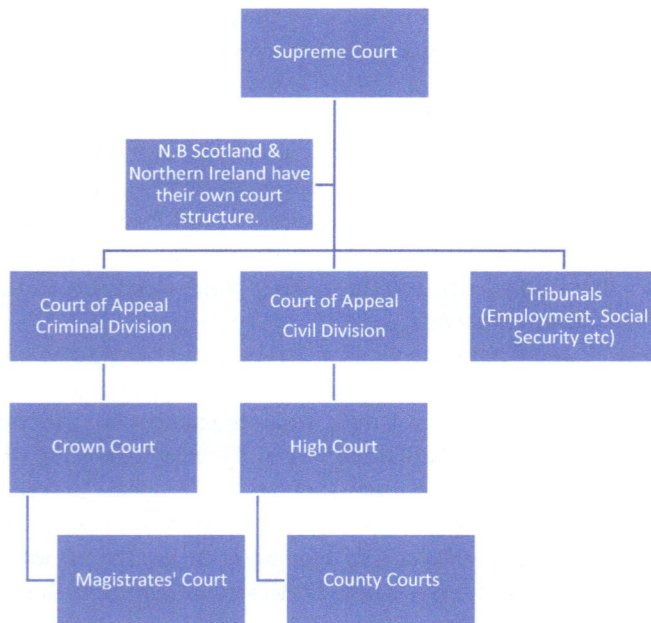

Figure 9.2
Basic court structure in England and Wales

Supreme Court came into existence in October 2009, having been created by the Constitutional Reform Act 2005. As we have seen in **Chapter 3**, the creation of the Supreme Court was intended to reinforce the perception that the judicial branch of the state was independent from both the government and the legislature. The theory of the separation of powers requires the three branches of government to each be separate in terms of function (i.e. their role) and personnel (i.e. membership).

Prior to the Constitutional Reform Act 2005, the position of the United Kingdom's highest court did not conform to the doctrine of the separation of powers (see Figure 9.3). As we shall see it was Parliament that was the highest court, and the judicial function of Parliament was carried out by specially appointed members of the House of Lords, known as Lords of Appeal in Ordinary (commonly referred to as the Law Lords and who were appointed from judiciary, former Lord Chancellors and occasionally from the bar). These Law Lords sat in Parliament and could take part in parliamentary debates. Did this actually matter? In order to answer this question, it is necessary to consider the position prior to the Constitutional Reform Act 2005.

9.3.1 The position before the Constitutional Reform Act 2005

9.3.1.1 Parliament was the highest court

Historically Parliament was the highest court in the United Kingdom (see Figure 9.4). The judicial function of Parliament was carried out by specially

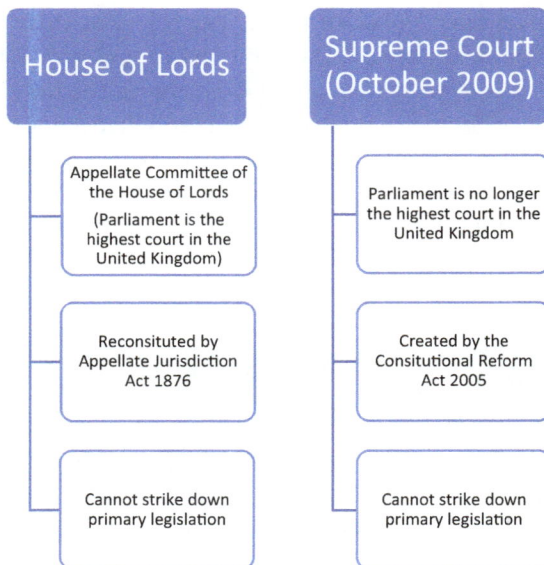

Figure 9.3
The House of Lords and the Supreme Court

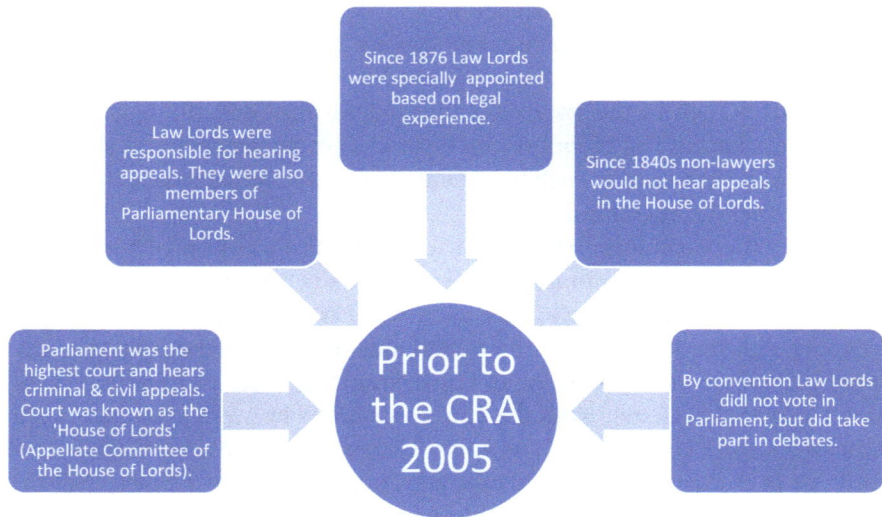

Figure 9.4
Position of the House of Lords before the Constitutional Reform Act 2005

appointed Lords who, as Lords of Appeal in Ordinary, were members of the Appellate Committee of the House of Lords (see the Appellate Jurisdiction Act 1876). The court was known as the House of Lords, and its members the Law Lords, which caused confusion to the public because the judges were members of the legislative chamber of the House of Lords.

Since the 1840s non-legally trained members of the House of Lords have not exercised its judicial function. Prior to this anyone who was a member of the parliamentary House of Lords, regardless of their legal training, was entitled to hear an appeal. As Lord Bingham observed, some cases were tried solely by non-lawyers, whilst on other occasions the non-lawyers would ignore directions on how to vote from the Lord Chancellor.[6] The Appellate Jurisdiction Act 1876 appointed lawyers to the House of Lords in order to carry out the judicial function of Parliament. However, even as late as 1883 a lay peer had attempted to vote on an appeal and was refused permission to do so.

PUBLIC LAW IN PRACTICE

The Duke of Thames (fictitious) is a non-lawyer member of the parliamentary House of Lords. Could he hear an appeal in 2008?

The Duke's great-great-great-great grandfather, the Earl of Thames (fictitious), was a member of the parliamentary House of Lords. Could the Earl of Thames hear an appeal in 1808?

9.3.1.2 The Law Lords as members of the parliamentary House of Lords

By convention the Law Lords (Lords of Appeal in Ordinary) most often refrained from voting and did take part in parliamentary debates in the legislative chamber of the House of Lords.

PUBLIC LAW IN CONTEXT
THE LAW LORDS TOOK PART IN PARLIAMENTARY DEBATES

In 2019, Lady Hale, the then President of the United Kingdom Supreme Court, and a former Lady in Appeal in Ordinary, observed, 'But the Law Lords remained full members of the House and were entitled to play a full part in Parliamentary business if they so chose. They did so increasingly rarely and usually on issues of legal or constitutional significance. Some, like me, did not even make a maiden speech. The position was summed up in a statement read in the House by the Senior Law Lord, Lord Bingham of Cornhill, in June 2000 (HL Hansard, 22 June 2000, cols 418–20). In deciding whether to participate or vote in a matter, the Law Lords considered themselves bound by two principles:

> First, the Lords of Appeal in Ordinary do not think it appropriate to engage in matters where there is a strong element of party political controversy; and secondly the Lords of Appeal in Ordinary bear in mind that they might render themselves ineligible to sit judicially if they were to express an opinion on a matter which might later be relevant to an appeal in the House.[7]

This is really interesting and demonstrated the considerations that a Law Lord would need to take in account, when deciding whether to participate in the parliamentary business of the House of Lords. It might appear more straightforward to have avoided such need for consideration and caution, by removing the Law Lords from the House of Lords or by way of statutory amendment to the Appellate Jurisdiction Act 1876 removing the ability to do anything other than perform the judicial function of the House of Lords.

An example of judges taking part in parliamentary debates was Lord Browne-Wilkinson, who took part in the debate over the Human Rights Act 1998. His Lordship argued against making the jurisprudence (case law) of the European Court of Humans Rights binding on the House of Lords:

> Perhaps I may be heard briefly on this point because soon it will concern me intimately. I am not a great supporter of the amendment . . . the doctrine of precedent, whereby we manage to tie ourselves up in knots for ever bound by an earlier decision of an English court, does not find much favour north of the Border, finds no favour across the Channel and is an indigenous growth of dubious merit. It would be unhappy if in dealing with the

convention law we enacted that an English court, unlike any other court subject to the convention, was bound to follow an earlier decision of the European Court at Strasbourg.[8]

Lord Nicholls of Birkenhead took part in the parliamentary debate surrounding the Constitutional Reform Bill (later the CRA 2005) and observed that:

> I regret to have to say that the proposal, put forward with the best of intentions, is misguided. It is unnecessary and would do more harm than good. It is unnecessary because it would achieve nothing of real value. Under the present arrangements the Law Lords do not lack independence from government – no one suggests that they do. Nor do they lack independence from the legislature. By convention of this House, our Law Lords participate in its judicial business, as all your Lordships know. No one could suggest the Law Lords' membership in itself of your Lordships' House compromises our judicial independence in some way.[9]

Lord Nicholl's comments illustrate the working relationship between the Law Lords and their fellow peers in the House of Lords.

The Law Lords would often deliver their judgments in the legislative chamber of the House of Lords, although they heard the appeal elsewhere in the Palace of Westminster. Lord Steyn noted that as the Law Lords delivered their judgments in the legislative chamber, this often led to confusion as it appeared to some members of the public that the non-lawyers in the House of Lords could vote.[10] By tradition the Law Lords heard one short appeal in the Chamber each year in order to maintain tradition. Otherwise they heard appeals in the more workmanlike surroundings of a Committee Room.

This overlap of function and personnel, with the Law Lords sitting in Parliament and exercising the judicial function of Parliament, led to the creation of an independent Supreme Court. Some interesting comments were made by a leading human rights lawyer, Baroness Kennedy QC, who was critical of the position prior to the creation of the Supreme Court:

> [The creation of a Supreme Court] will be a great moment in our transition to a modern constitutional state and would reinvigorate public confidence. The Law Lords, who by self-denying ordinance now rarely speak or vote in the House of Lords, should have their right to do so removed altogether. Just as it is inappropriate for a Cabinet minister to sit as a judge, it is not acceptable for judges to sit in the legislature.[11]

Kennedy argued that the Law Lords should have no place in the legislative House of Lords, even though she noted that one Law Lord 'even claimed in a debate that being in the House kept him in touch with public concerns.'[12] Lady Hale, a member of the Appellate Committee of the House of Lords, noted the increasing case for a separate Supreme Court, when Her Ladyship made reference to the litigation in *R (on the application of Jackson) v Attorney-General*[13]:

> Two Law Lords 'rendered themselves ineligible' to sit on the three fascinating cases we had about the Hunting Act 2004 because they had voted against it. This functional separation made it easier to contemplate the transfer of the Lords' jurisdiction to a new Supreme Court. It was also beginning to become apparent that there might be cases which it was quite inappropriate to resolve in a court consisting of a committee of the upper House of Parliament. The great case of R (Jackson) v Attorney General [2005] UKHL 56, [2006] 1 AC 262 challenged the Hunting Act 2004 on the ground that it was not a valid Act of Parliament.[14]

It is interesting to note the Law Lords' response to the government's proposed creation of a Supreme Court.[15] Whilst the majority of the Law Lords supported the creation of the Supreme Court, there were those Law Lords who did not:

> [I]t should not be thought that the Law Lords as a body support the proposal to establish a new Supreme Court of the United Kingdom. A number of serving Law Lords believe that, on pragmatic grounds, the proposed change is unnecessary and will be harmful. The present arrangements work well. They believe that the Law Lords' presence in the House is of benefit to the Law Lords, to the House, and to others including the litigants. Appeals are heard in a unique, suitably prestigious, setting for this country's court of final appeal.

A supporter of a new Supreme Court was Lady Hale, who was clear that she agreed with her former colleague, Lord Bingham of Cornhill, that it was not ideal for the Law Lords to be in the House of Lords, as 'The institutional structure should reflect the practical reality. We were a court and should be seen to be such. The public and people from overseas should not be misled into thinking that we are also legislators.'[16] Lady Hale took the view that the move to the Supreme Court was the right thing to do and one that had the support of non-judges in the House of Lords, 'As Lord Wallace of Saltaire put it in the short farewell debate, "we don't want to lose you, but we think you ought to go." ' However, Lady Hale observed that, 'Of course, our leaving was not uncontroversial. There was a strong element of "if it ain't broke, don't fix it." ' Prior to the Constitutional Reform Act 2005, Lord Woolf LCJ and the Lord Chancellor had reached a Concordat about the relationship between the judiciary and the executive.

9.3.2 The position after the Constitutional Reform Act 2005

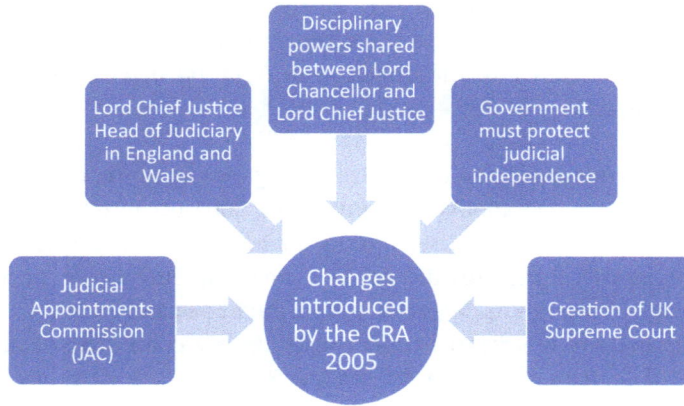

Figure 9.5
Changes introduced by the Constitutional Reform Act 2005

9.3.2.1 The United Kingdom Supreme Court

The Constitutional Reform Act 2005 created a new Supreme Court for the United Kingdom. The Supreme Court and the Judicial Committee of the Privy Council are based in the former Middlesex Guildhall. The Supreme Court is accessible to members of the public who can visit the court, browse the court's website, follow the court on Twitter, and watch hearings on livestream on the Supreme Court's website.

The reforms have reinforced public perception that the Supreme Court is independent from Parliament. Importantly, under section 137 of the Constitutional Reform Act 2005 its members are disqualified from sitting or voting in Parliament whilst they serve as Justices of the Supreme Court.

9.3.2.2 Control and membership of the Supreme Court

The Supreme Court is outside the control of the Lord Chief Justice, who, as a result of the Constitutional Reform Act 2005, is the head of the judiciary in England and Wales. The head of the Supreme Court is the President, who is assisted by a Deputy President.

Justices of the Supreme Court are not appointed because of their political views. Appointment to the Supreme Court should depend on merit and experience. This is important as the executive cannot control who will become a member of the Supreme Court, and subsequently ensures that the court will be deferential towards the current government. In total there are 12 Justices of the Supreme Court. Presently there are only two members of the Supreme Court and these are Lady Arden and Lady Rose. There were once three female Justices, when Lady Hale of Richmond was the President of the Supreme Court and Lady

Black served alongside Lady Arden. The Queen appoints Justices of the Supreme Court on the advice of the Prime Minister. A suitable candidate is presented to the Lord Chancellor by the Judicial Appointments Commission. The commission that recommends members of the Supreme Court will consist of President and Deputy President of the Supreme Court, and one member from the Judicial Appointment Commission and its counterparts from Scotland and Northern Ireland (Schedule 8).

Members of the Supreme Court will be appointed by a commission which will present its chosen candidate for approval. The Crime and Courts Act 2013 has amended the Constitutional Reform Act 2005 (s.27A) and will permit the Lord Chancellor and the President of the Supreme Court to make regulations concerning the commission and these could permit the Lord Chancellor to have the power to ask the commission to reconsider its selection or to reject the commission's selection.

9.3.2.3 A comparison with the United States Supreme Court

We will briefly compare the Supreme Courts of the United Kingdom and the United States.

Table 9.1 Comparing Supreme Courts

Key facts	UK Supreme Court	US Supreme Court
Date of creation?	October 2009.	February 1790.
Created by ?	Constitutional Reform Act 2005.	United States constitution and the Judiciary Act 1789.
How are justices appointed?	The Judicial Appointments Commission (JAC) appoints each new member. The JAC is independent from the executive.	Each new member is chosen by the President. However, the President's candidate must be approved during confirmation hearings in the Senate. The Senate could reject the President's choice.
Politically partisan?	The UK Supreme Court is not accused of being politically partisan. It is independent from the politics of whatever political party is in government.	The US Supreme Court is often regarded as being politically partisan, with justices being appointed because of their political views. There is a divide between justices who are Democratic and Republican appointments.
Power to veto primary legislation on the grounds that it is unconstitutional?	There is no power to do this. Although see the *obiter* comments in *R (on the application of Jackson) v. Attorney-General* [2005].	The Supreme Court in *Marbury v. Madison* [1803] gave itself the power to veto primary legislation. The US Supreme Court will challenge President Obama's Health Care legislation as to whether it is unconstitutional.

PUBLIC LAW IN CONTEXT
JUDICIAL APPOINTMENTS AND PERCEPTIONS OF BIAS

The method of appointing members to the United Kingdom's Supreme Court is different to the most famous Supreme Court in the world, the United States Supreme Court. The United States Supreme Court was established by the United States Constitution and has played an important part in the constitutional development of the country. In the United States the Justices of the Supreme Court are political appointments by the President. The President's choice must be confirmed by Congress and his nominee is essentially a political appointment. This means that the US Supreme Court is often divided along party lines and thus partisan as its members will vote according to their own partisan views. Controversially in 2000, the US Supreme Court effectively had to decide who would become the next President of the United States after there was a problem with counting votes in Florida. If more votes were permitted to be counted then there was a good chance that Al Gore would become President, whereas if no more counting was permitted, George W. Bush would become President. In *Bush v. Gore*[17] the United States Supreme Court found in favour of Bush and he was declared President of the United States. The decision of the Supreme Court was controversial. According to Nicholson and Howard:

> The fallout was immediate. Democrats accused the Court of engaging in partisan politics and handing the election to Republican presidential candidate George W. Bush. Republicans, on the other hand, spoke of the Court's courage in following the rule of law (and the Constitution) amidst great pressure. . . . The [Supreme Court's] decision fell along ideological, and to some degree, partisan lines. The five most conservative justices formed the majority, while the four most liberal justices, including the two Democrats . . . dissented.[18]

It should be noted that *Bush v. Gore* was an exceptional case, and when in 2020 President Donald Trump sought the Supreme Court to overturn some of the results in the November 2020 General Election, the Republican majority Supreme Court rejected the President's lawsuit.[19]

In the United Kingdom it is important that the Supreme Court is not perceived as reaching a decision due to the judges' own political bias.

9.3.2.4 Making difficult decisions

Judges do have to make some difficult decisions and the Supreme Court will have the final say in all civil matters in the United Kingdom and all criminal matters in England and Wales. Over the past decade the courts have had to decide some controversial issues. Below are some important cases, involving issues that most people will have a view on (either one way or the other). These include cases from the House of Lords (the Appellate Committee) and the Court

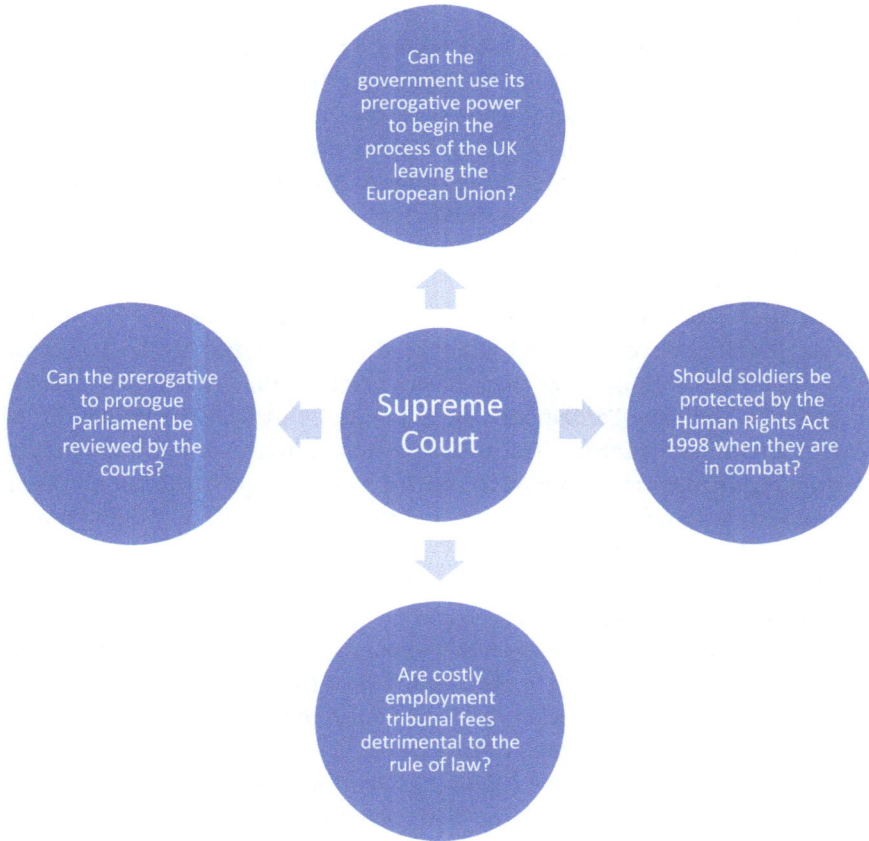

Figure 9.6
Importance of the Supreme Court

of Appeal, which have been included as they were significant and controversial decisions at the time:

- In *Smith v Ministry of Defence*[20] the Supreme Court had to decide whether to extend the protection accorded by the Human Rights Act 1998 and the European Convention on Human Rights to British military personnel who had either been killed or injured whilst on active duty in Afghanistan and Iraq. The Supreme Court held that the soldiers were protected by human rights and that a duty was owed to protect their right to life under Article 2 of the European Convention on Human Rights. The decision proved controversial as critics were quick to point out the problem of protecting soldiers' right to life in active combat and saw it is a judicialization of warfare. However, the Supreme Court was clear that it would apply in certain circumstances and made a distinction between decisions taken away from the battlefield (such as whether to equip the soldiers in protective equipment) and those taken in the heat of combat.

- In *R (on the application of Miller) v Secretary of State for Exiting the European Union (No.1)*[21] the Supreme Court held the government could not use its prerogative power to trigger Article 50 of the Treaty of Lisbon. This meant that if the UK government wanted to give the European Union notice that the United Kingdom would be leaving the European Union, then an Act of Parliament was required in order to give notice. The decision was highly controversial and as we have seen in **Chapter 3** the judges in the earlier High Court decision were called 'the enemies of the people' by *The Daily Mail*.

- The Supreme Court's decision in *R (on the application of Miller) v Prime Minister (No.2)*[22] concerned the legality of the advice given to the monarch by the Prime Minister, so that the monarch would use her prerogative power to prorogue Parliament. The Supreme Court held the Prime Minister's advice was unlawful. This was a controversial decision and the judges were regarded by some as having reached an inappropriate decision, which entailed deciding political matters and that the court should have treated the issue as non-justiciable.

- In *(R on the application of Unison) v Lord Chancellor*[23] the Supreme Court had to consider the issue of costly employment tribunal fees, which made it expensive for an employee or worker to pursue a claim against an employer. The Supreme Court quashed the fees and held that it went against the rule of law as it prevented access to justice and the courts. We discuss this landmark decision in more detail in **Chapter 3**.

- The Court of Appeal in *Re A (Children) (Conjoined Twins: Medical Treatment) (No.2)*[24] had to decide whether a doctor could save one conjoined twin, if saving that twin would inevitably kill the other twin. The Court of Appeal held that the doctor could operate.

- In *R (on the application of Purdy) v. DPP*[25] the House of Lords had to decide whether the Director of Public Prosecutions was required to indicate what factors he would consider when deciding whether to prosecute anyone who assisted someone with a debilitating illness to travel abroad for the purpose of committing suicide. The House of Lords found in favour of Mrs Purdy's appeal and held that the DPP would need to issue offence-specific policy on the facts and circumstances which would be taken into account, when the DPP decided whether to prosecute.

- In *Airedale NHS Trust v. Bland*[26] the House of Lords had to decide whether withdrawing medical treatment from someone who was in a persistent vegetative state amounted to a violation of the sanctity of life. The House of Lords decided that since the patient could not consent, the task of deciding what was in the patient's best interest fell to the doctors. The court distinguished between taking active steps to end a life, which were not lawful, and withholding treatment which was lawful.

Do you think that if MPs had a say over who became a member of the Supreme Court, the candidates' views on divorce, religion, politics and abortion might influence their decision? Kenneth Clarke MP, a previous Lord Chancellor, when appearing before the House of Lords Constitutional Reform Committee was critical of introducing confirmation hearings for the appointment of members of the Supreme Court:

> I think there's a danger that they would become political. . . . The US experience is just shocking. Some US confirmation hearings are just consumed by the social attitudes of the judge and his sexual history. . . . Anything that got near that would be deplorable. Sooner or later you would have some stray MP asking what a judge's views are on this or that. A certain partisanship could creep in.[27]

ACADEMIC DEBATE
A ROLE FOR PARLIAMENT IN THE APPOINTMENT OF SENIOR JUDGES?

In the aftermath of the Supreme Court's decision in *Miller (No. 2)* there was talk of reforming the way that senior judges were appointed to permit parliamentary involvement with the process.[28] This was due to the concern from some Conservative politicians that the Supreme Court had reached a political decision, and that it would have been better to have declined to decide whether the Prime Minister's advice to the monarch to prorogue Parliament was unlawful. At the time it was reported that: 'Government insiders have suggested that the idea of a US-style appointed supreme court is not being considered. However, Johnson has previously warned that "some form of accountability" may be needed if judges interfere in political decisions, while the attorney general, Geoffrey Cox, has raised the idea of parliamentary scrutiny of judicial appointments.' This is not say the proposed solution would be based on the United States: 'the attorney general Geoffrey Cox said it could be time for "parliamentary scrutiny" of judicial appointments. He later said the government had no "current plans" to do so, and insisted US-style hearings "would be a regrettable step for us in our constitutional arrangements."'[29] This met with pushback from those who opposed giving Parliament a role in the appointment of judges. An example of this included Lady Hale, who was clear that political neutrality of the Supreme Court should not be comprised. Shortly before retiring Lady Hale observed, 'We don't want to be politicised. . . . We don't decide political questions, we decide legal questions. And in any event, parliament always has the last word.'[30] Furthermore, Lady Hale remarked, 'Judges have not been appointed for party political reasons in this country since at least the Second World War. . . . We do not want to turn into the Supreme Court of the United States, whether in powers, or in process of appointments. . . . We [Justices of the court] do not know one another's political opinions, although occasionally we may have a good guess and long may that remain so.'[31]

Richard Ekins and Graham Gee have recently recommended reforms to how senior judges (which would include the Supreme Court) are appointed.[32] Ekins and Gee proposed giving the Lord Chancellor a greater role in selecting judges and were critical of the current system under the Constitutional Reform Act 2005.

> In a constitutional democracy, it is entirely proper for the responsible minister to decline to appoint to high office a person whose commitment to constitutional fundamentals, including the rule of law, is reasonably in doubt. In the constitution as it stood before the CRA, the Lord Chancellor routinely and rightly appointed, or promoted, judges who were in no sense unduly deferential to the executive. The Lord Chancellor likely also passed over appointees who seemed unwilling or unable to recognise the constitutional limits of judicial power. This would have been a responsible exercise of the appointments power. Similarly, it is entirely appropriate for a Lord Chancellor to decline to appoint some-one to a senior leadership role where there are well-founded doubts about whether they have the requisite administrative skills. It would be a mistake to politicise judicial appointments, attempting to misuse the power for partisan advantage or as a means of patronage. Increasing ministerial involvement in appointments, in concert with a con-tinuing role for the relevant selection bodies, is not to politicise judicial appointments. It is to restore a much-needed measure of political responsibility for senior appointments, the exercise of which is likely to help support judicial independence, encourage judicial diversity and to support the constitution, avoiding its transformation by stealth. Judges should not be free to choose their colleagues or successors.

What do you think about Ekins and Gee's proposals; should the Lord Chancellor have a greater say in senior judicial appointments and the judiciary less of a role in determining who becomes a senior judge? It is an interesting report and useful to read. You might find it helpful to look below at the discussion on the reforms to the role to the position of the Lord Chancellor under the Constitutional Reform Act 2005.

It is interesting to note the emphasis on political responsibility for judicial appointments and the warning about politically motivated appointments.

Ekins and Gee are clear that giving the Lord Chancellor a greater role would avoid unsuitable appointments, where a candidate who does not respect the rule of law would not be appointed. This raises the question of whether under the system created by the Constitutional Reform Act 2005 unsuitable candidates have been appointed.

9.3.2.5 Jurisdiction of the Supreme Court

The United Kingdom's Supreme Court is the court of final appeal for civil cases in the United Kingdom. It must be remembered that the United Kingdom is comprised of nation-states which have their own independent legal systems:

- England and Wales
- Northern Ireland
- Scotland

The Supreme Court is also the final court of appeal for criminal cases from the English and Welsh Court of Appeal, and the Northern Ireland Court of Appeal. The Scotland Act 1998 states that the United Kingdom Supreme Court does not have the jurisdiction to hear criminal appeals from Scotland unless there is a devolution issue for the court to resolve, which has been determined by two or more justices of the High Court of Justiciary. Scotland's final court of criminal appeal is the High Court of Justiciary.

When does the Supreme Court have jurisdiction to hear criminal appeals from Scotland?

In *Fraser (Nat Gordon) v. HM Advocate*[33] the Supreme Court held that it had jurisdiction to hear a criminal appeal from Scotland. The appellant had been convicted of arranging the murder of his wife. Subsequently, he had argued that there had been a miscarriage of justice. He appealed on the basis that the prosecution had failed to disclose relevant evidence during the trial. He also wished to include a devolution minute that would state that his case involved a human rights issue. The appellant had argued that the non-disclosure had violated the right to a fair trial, which was guaranteed by Article 6(1) of the European Convention on Human Rights. In *Fraser (Nat Gordon) v. HM Advocate*[34] the High Court of Justiciary rejected both the appeal and the inclusion of the devolution minute. The court also refused the appellant's appeal to the Supreme Court. However, the Supreme Court held that under the Scotland Act 1998 it had the jurisdiction to hear the appeal. This was because the High Court of Justiciary had determined a devolution issue and it was arguable that the non-disclosure of evidence in the original trial had breached Article 6. The test used by the High Court of Justiciary to determine whether the evidence should have been disclosed was held to be incompatible with the appellant's human rights. A retrial was ordered and subsequently, the appellant was convicted by a jury in 2012. In 2013, Channel 4 televised the retrial, and this was the first time that television cameras were allowed to film a criminal trial.

9.3.2.6 How the Supreme Court works

Appeals are heard by between five and seven Justices of the Supreme Court. In exceptionally important cases there may be up to 11 Justices of the Supreme Court hearing an appeal. Each judge hearing the appeal will give reasons for her decision and often the judges will reach the same decision, but based on different reasons. Occasionally a judge will disagree and will dissent from the majority. The dissenting judgment will be technically *obiter* and not carry precedential value as it is not law. Justices of the Supreme Court are encouraged to work together on judgments and where possible to give a single judgment (a move supported by Lord Phillips when he was the President of the Supreme Court), rather than several individual judgments that all agree on the main points. The judgments are all made available on the Supreme Court's website, alongside press summaries, that highlight the main reasons for the decision.

9.3.2.7 Importance of the Supreme Court in the United Kingdom's constitutional system

This section will consider the importance of the Supreme Court in the United Kingdom's constitutional system. The United Kingdom does not have a written constitution, although it is possible to say that it does have a constitution, one that comprises a variety of written and unwritten sources. This is significant as the constitution is not the highest legal order and the Supreme Court is not required to protect the constitution from Parliament. Unlike the US Supreme Court, the UK Supreme Court does not have the power to strike down an Act of Parliament. Its powers of reviewing the validity of an Act are limited to those conferred by Parliament by the European Communities Act 1972 (prior to the United Kingdom leaving the European Union) and the Human Rights Act 1998. We have seen above that the United States Supreme Court gave itself the power to declare an Act of Congress to be unconstitutional. The United States Supreme Court can judicially review primary legislation. This is something that the United Kingdom's Supreme Court cannot do, as its powers under the European Communities Act 1972 and Human Rights Act 1998 are given by Parliament and could be revoked in the case that the Human Rights Act 1998 and the European Communities Act 1972 were repealed. The landmark cases of *Miller (No.1)* and *Miller (No.2)* have proved controversial as the Supreme Court has enforced the constitution as understood by the court and consequentially restricted the executive.

PUBLIC LAW IN CONTEXT
STRIKING DOWN LEGISLATION

Could the United Kingdom's Supreme Court gain the power to judicially review primary legislation? In order to answer this, we must appreciate that such a power conflicts with Parliamentary Sovereignty. It is worth considering the *obiter* in *R (Jackson) v. Attorney General* and the fact that both the United States and Israeli Supreme Courts gave themselves the power to judicially review primary legislation. We know from Chapter 1 that the United Kingdom along with New Zealand and Israel does not have a written constitution. In Israel the Supreme Court gave itself the power to review primary legislation. The Israeli cases of *Bergman v. Minister of Finance*[35] and *United Mizrahi Bank v. Migdal – Cooperative Village*[36] have been described by Eli Salzberger 'as equivalents of the famous American case of Marbury v. Madison.' In *Mizrahi* the Supreme Court (in *obiter*) 'acknowledged the power of any court (not only the Supreme Court) to conduct judicial review of legislation against the two basic laws enacted by the Knesset in its capacity as a constituent assembly.'[37]

9.3.2.8 The Supreme Court, a success or failure?

Has the Supreme Court been a success or a failure? Lady Hale had this to say about the Supreme Court:

> The Supreme Court has brought, not only the negative benefits of taking us out of Parliament, but the positive benefits of having our own premises, our own staff and our own facilities for doing our own thing. . . . We are also a great deal more open and accessible than we used to be. It is much easier to get into our building than it is to the Houses of Parliament. We are not guarded by armed police officers. We try to be friendly and accessible to students and interested visitors of all kinds. People just pop in to see what we are about. We have an exhibition space and a café on the lower ground floor.[38]

These are practical benefits for those working in the court, but also in making the work of the court more accessible. The court proceedings are televised, and visitors to the court are actively encouraged.

In July 2020 Derrick Wyatt QC and Richard Ekins produced a paper titled 'Reforming the Supreme Court,[39] where in his essay, Wyatt put forward a suggestion of the abolition of the Supreme Court and replacing it with a UK Final Court of Appeal. It is interesting to note the criticism of the court:

> I agree with Professor Ekins that if there is a problem with the judicial approach of the UK Supreme Court, it may in part be attributed to the fact that it sees itself as a constitutional court, and as guardian of the Constitution, but I would add that it is part of the judicial responsibility of every court in the United Kingdom to uphold our Constitution, and the role of all superior courts to make an appropriate contribution to the evolution of that Constitution. If there is a problem with the judicial approach of the UK Supreme Court, I think it is its willingness on occasion to decide cases on policy grounds, without disclosing an adequate or convincing legal basis. In this respect, I do not believe that the approach of the Supreme Court differs significantly from that of the Judicial Committee of the House of Lords before it.
>
> I also believe that any excessive judicial activism on the part of the Supreme Court is linked to the fact that it comprises a relatively small elite corps of judges distinguished by title and by composition from the rest of the UK judiciary. If I am right in my analysis, and if it is sought to reduce the risk and incidence of excessive judicial activism, then renaming the Supreme Court as the Upper Court of Appeal, or something similar, would be unlikely of itself to make any significant change in the judicial approach of our final court of appeal.

In the report Ekins' view on Wyatt's proposal was that 'Professor Wyatt's proposal to abolish the Supreme Court is a bold institutional reform. It would be more constitutionally significant and therefore more politically challenging than my modest proposal to rename the Court.'

Sir Patrick Elias, a retired Court of Appeal judge, responded to Wyatt's proposal to abolish the Supreme Court and observed:

> Nor do I see why the proposals would necessarily achieve the objective of making judges less activist. The premise of this argument is that unaccountable judges are more likely to be activist than accountable ones. I am not convinced that this is so. I suspect that a judge's perception of his or her own role is determined principally by temperament and political and social outlook. Indeed, it may be argued that in so far as it can be said that there is a culture of activism in the Supreme Court, it would be exacerbated if the Justices – who would no doubt retain considerable influence in the final appeal tribunal – were to swim in the same pool as the current Court of Appeal judges.[40]

We can see that concerns about judicial activism in the Supreme Court were not entirely dismissed by Sir Patrick Elias. Are Justices of the Supreme Court too active? This will depend on your views as to whether the political constitution needs to be augmented by increasing reference to a legal constitution, and the role of judges within the constitution.

9.4 Constitutional Reform Act 2005: guaranteeing independence of the judiciary?

The Constitutional Reform Act 2005 did much to improve the separation of functions and personnel between the judicial and the executive and legislative branches of state (see Figure 9.5).

9.4.1 The Lord Chief Justice replaces the Lord Chancellor as the head of the judiciary of England and Wales

The Lord Chief Justice was made the head of the judiciary of England and Wales. In this capacity he replaces the Lord Chancellor. According to section 7(2) of the Constitutional Reform Act 2005 the Lord Chief Justice is tasked with representing the views of the judiciary to Parliament, the Lord Chancellor and the government. Lord Hailsham, who served as Lord Chancellor, had justified the many roles carried out by the Lord Chancellor by arguing that the Lord Chancellor was in the best place to represent the view of judges to Parliament and the government. Section 7(2) gives the Lord Chief Justice the right to represent the views of judges. Section 5(1) permits the Lord Chief Justice to make representations to Parliament. A previous Lord Chief Justice has described section 5(1) as the 'nuclear option' (see **Chapter 3**).[41] However, more recent Lord Chief Justices have not seen it this way.

PUBLIC LAW IN CONTEXT
SECTION 5 OF THE CONSTITUTIONAL REFORM ACT 2005

Section 5 CRA 2005 representations to Parliament:

'(1) The chief justice of any part of the United Kingdom may lay before Parliament written representations on matters that appear to him to be matters of importance relating to the judiciary, or otherwise to the administration of justice, in that part of the United Kingdom.'

The Lord Chief Justice is responsible for training, offering guidance and the deployment of the judiciary. The Lord Chief Justice has no responsibility towards the running of the Supreme Court.

9.4.2 *The Judicial Appointments Commission*

Section 61 creates the Judicial Appointments Commission. This was established in March 2006. Under section 64 the commission must have regard to encouraging diversity, and must select candidates based on merit and then only if they have good character. The commission consists of 14 commissioners and a chairman, which consist of judges, practitioners and non-lawyers. In order to fill the posts of Lord Chief Justice and other senior members of the judiciary, the Lord Chancellor under section 69 may ask the commission to recommend a candidate. Under section 73 the Lord Chancellor can accept, reject or ask the commission to reconsider its recommendation. Similar provisions cover the appointment of Lord Justices of Appeal. If the Lord Chancellor rejects the commission's candidate or asks it to reconsider its selection, the Lord Chancellor is required to explain in his opinion why the person chosen was not a suitable candidate. This decision must be based on evidence and this helps to improve the transparency of judicial appointments. Sections 25 to 31 cover the appointment of judges to the Supreme Court. It is important to note that the Crime and Courts Act 2013 will transfer the Lord Chancellor's role in the appointment process for a large number of judges to the Lord Chief Justice (s.20).

9.4.3 *Are judges representative of the population?*

Many people often regard judges as being out of touch, and the average judge tends to be privately educated, middle-aged, white and male.

This is a common perception that judges are out of touch with members of the public. Professor Penny Darbyshire has observed that in comedy sketches judges are portrayed as:

[S]tern, old buffoons, ignorant of modern life. . . . When judges are retired judges make radio comments, their accents and vocabulary betray their years at independent school and/or the Bar. They sound condescending. . . . Famously, Harman J asked who "Gazza" was, when Paul Gascoigne played for England, and denied knowing who Kevin Keegan, or Bruce Springsteen, or Oasis were. . . . Because journalists are vigilant for evidence of judges' ignorance, language can be misinterpreted. . . . Judges commonly ask questions to which they know the answer, for the jury's sake.[42]

It is clear that this can do lasting damage to their reputations.

Lady Hale had this observation to make about how the judiciary should reflect wider society:

> In a democracy governed by the people and not by an absolute monarch or even an aristocratic ruling class, the judiciary should reflect the whole community, not just a small section of it. The public should be able to feel that the courts are their courts; that their cases are being decided and the law is being made by people like them, and not by some alien beings from another planet. In the modern world, where social deference has largely disappeared, this should enhance rather than undermine the public's confidence in the law and the legal system.[43]

This is important as society must have confidence in the judiciary and there are dangers where judges are seen as distinct from society and those using the courts.

Figure 9.7 shows a statistical breakdown of the composition of the judiciary. We can see from Figure 9.7 that women and ethnic minorities are underrepresented in the judiciary. In 2019, 68 per cent of judges were men and 32 per cent were women.[44] The percentage of women judges was even fewer in the High

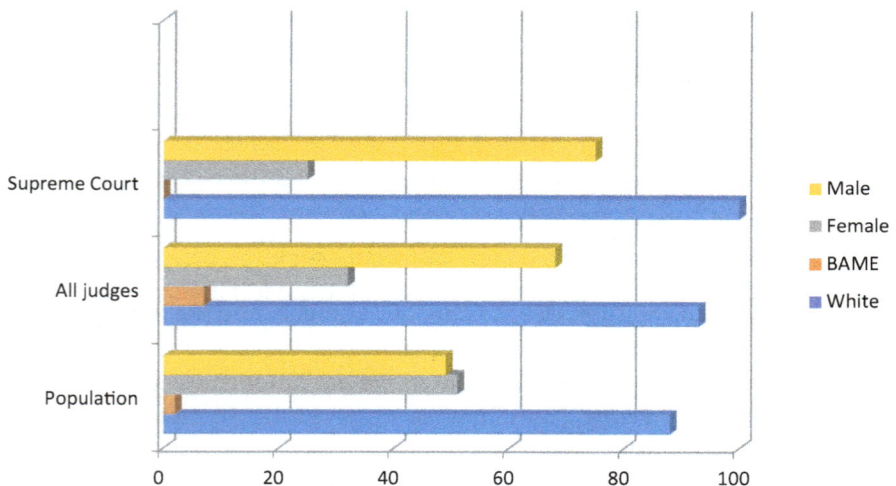

Figure 9.7
Judicial diversity statistics 2019

Court (27 per cent) and the Court of Appeal of England and Wales (23 per cent). Twenty-five per cent of the Supreme Court judges were women. Until recently Baroness Hale was the first and only female member of the Supreme Court (and its predecessor, the House of Lords), and there have been no non-white members of either court. In 2017, Lady Black was appointed and in 2018, Lady Arden was appointed to the Supreme Court. Only 7 per cent of all judges were from a BAME background. where are only two BAME Court of Appeal judges and three BAME High Court judges in England and Wales.

The Crime and Courts Act 2013 has inserted section 27(5A) into the CRA 2005. This allows the commission, when appointing a Justice to the Supreme Court, to favour one candidate over another, where both candidates are of equal merit, on the grounds that it will improve diversity.

PUBLIC LAW IN CONTEXT
DIVERSITY, THE SUPREME COURT AND THE WIDER JUDICIARY

In 2017, the then President of the Supreme Court of the United Kingdom, Lord Neuberger of Abbotsbury, was keen to improve the diversity within the judiciary: 'The higher echelons of the judiciary in the United Kingdom suffer from a marked lack of diversity and here I must admit the supreme court does not score at all well. We have one white woman and 10 white men, and, although two of the 11 were not privately educated, none of us come from disadvantaged backgrounds.'[45] This was within the context of his own retirement from the Supreme Court and the fact there would be a number of vacancies to be filled.

Lord Sumption, a former Justice of the Supreme Court of the United Kingdom, gave an interview to the *Evening Standard* newspaper and warned against attempt to seek equal gender representation too quickly:

'His most striking comments, however, were on diversity as he warned that equal representation for women in the judiciary would take decades to achieve. "These things simply can't be transformed overnight, not without appalling consequence in other directions," he said.

'"It takes time. You've got to be patient. The change in the status and achievements of women in our society, not just in the law but generally, is an enormous cultural change that has happened over the last 50 years or so. It has to happen naturally. It will happen naturally. But in the history of a society like ours, 50 years is a very short time."'

'Warning that the judiciary and the quality of British justice was "a terribly delicate organism", Lord Sumption added: "We have got to be very careful not to do things at a speed which will make male candidates feel that the cards are stacked against them."'[46]

Lord Sumption had given an earlier extra-judicial lecture in 2012 along the same theme and he observed that '[i]n modern Britain, the fastest way to make enemies is to deliver a public lecture about judicial diversity. Unless you confine yourself to worthy platitudes, you are almost bound to cause offence to some one. It is of course quite possible to live a reasonably fulfilled life without thinking seriously about the subject at all.'[47] Sumption had noted that '[w]ithout some kind of positive discrimination, the judiciary is never going to be significantly more diverse than the pool from which it is drawn' and that '[w]e need, as a society, to have an honest public debate about the hitherto unmentionable subject of positive discrimination. We have to decide whether we want to accept a measure of positive discrimination in the selection of judges, as the price of making faster progress towards judicial diversity. There are arguments both for and against it. But the real problem is that the debate has not happened.' Sumption warned '[i]n any honest debate about positive discrimination, we would need to measure the advantages of a more representative judiciary against a realistic assessment of the cost of achieving it. In particular, we need to make some assessment of the impact on the quality of the bench which would result from qualifying the principle of selection "solely on merit."' Sumption took the view that 'Positive discrimination is patronising. Those women and ethnic minority candidates who have been appointed under the current system are justifiably proud of having achieved this under a system based exclusively on individual merit. Many, probably most of those who are not judges but aspire to be appointed, do so because the principle of selection on individual merit makes it an ambition worth achieving. A partial abandonment of that principle would therefore be likely to make judicial office a great deal less attractive to the very people that its proponents are trying to help.'

Lady Hale disagreed with Lord Sumption's two arguments against positive discrimination. Lady Hale noted that 'His second reason is that he does not agree that diverse courts are better courts, because they are able to draw upon a diversity of experience in reaching their decisions. He thinks that this overstates the importance of personal as opposed to vicarious experience.' Lady Hale argued against this view: 'So this brings me to the business case for diversity – that diverse courts are better courts. I too used to be sceptical about the argument that women judges were bound to make a difference, because women are as different from one another as men, and we should not be expected to look at things from a particularly female point of view, whatever that might be. But I have come to agree with those great women judges who think that sometimes, on occasions, we may make a difference.'[48]

However, Lord Hodge disagreed that it would take that long to achieve a gender balance within the judiciary:

> 'The balance is shifting faster than some people think,' Lord Hodge said. The justice said he would be 'quite astonished' if, by the time he retired in eight years' time, there was not a significant number of women at the Supreme Court.
>
> 'I would be very surprised if, even at Supreme Court level, the picture was not radically different from today. I don't think Lord Sumption was right to say it would take 50 years, but I don't think he is against diversity.'
>
> . . .
>
> Lord Hodge said the solution to the problem of lack of diversity at the Supreme Court would have to come from the legal profession, and the task of the judiciary was to 'express our intention in having a broad and diverse judiciary at all levels.'[49]

The then Lord Chief Justice of England and Wales, Lord Thomas was reported in *The Times* as saying: '"I simply do not accept that this is an issue where we should be content to sit back and just wait for things to happen." In a key intervention he urged "robust judicial activism" to achieve a diverse judiciary, saying that it was important both to public confidence and fairness.'[50]

The problem is that the legal profession which the judges come from is predominately white and male. In January 2012, the Bar Council of England and Wales revealed that in 2010 only 34.8 per cent of barristers were female, and that 77.2 per cent of barristers were white, 10.2 per cent were from minority backgrounds and for 12.6 per cent of barristers there was no data. Barmes and Malleson have carried out research into the composition of the judiciary and have looked at potential reforms.[51] They have noted that whilst most lawyers are solicitors (85%), the Bar dominates when it comes to judicial appointment. This means that the composition of the Bar will reflect the composition of the judiciary. They note that 'any changes that occur are more likely to be driven by developments in the legal profession . . . than by calls for greater judicial diversity.'[52] The 2019 judicial diversity statistics for England and Wales revealed that 67 per cent of all judges had been barristers, and the vast majority of judges from other professional backgrounds had been solicitors. In fact only 3 per cent of Court of Appeal and 4 per cent of High Court judges had been solicitors. To date the only Justice of the Supreme Court of the United Kingdom to have been a solicitor, rather than a barrister, has been Lord Collins of Mapesbury. In addition, some Scottish Law Lords and JSCs had started their careers by qualifying and practising for a while as solicitors in Scotland, as that has for long been and remains a preferred route to qualification for the Scots Bar. The first member of the Supreme Court to join straight from academia was Lord Andrew Burrows, who had been a professor at the University of Oxford.

PUBLIC LAW IN PRACTICE

Do you think that where a male and female candidate are evenly matched for a judicial role, that the female candidate should be given the job? Could this be justified on the ground of attempting to make the judiciary more representative of the population?

9.4.4 Judicial discipline

Section 108 of the Constitutional Reform Act 2005 covers the disciplinary powers of the Lord Chancellor and the Lord Chief Justice of England and Wales.[53] The Lord Chancellor ultimately has the power to remove a judge below the level of a High Court judge; however, there is a prescribed procedure in order to do this. The Lord Chief Justice's disciplinary powers can only be exercised in agreement with the Lord Chancellor, and include giving a judge a formal reprimand or suspending him from office. Importantly under section 110 of the CRA 2005, a judge who has been disciplined can apply to the Ombudsman to review the exercise of the powers contained in section 108 of the CRA 2005.

9.4.5 Judicial independence

It is important that judges are independent of both the government and Parliament. If judges owed their positions and salaries to either of these branches of state, then there would be a real risk that the judiciary would cease to be truly independent. Judicial independence was enshrined in the Act of Settlement 1700, which stated that judicial office holders (High Court and above) held their offices subject to their good behaviour, and could only be removed by a resolution from both Houses of Parliament. This took away the ability of the executive to remove judges, and limited the ability of either House of Parliament to remove a judge for political reasons.

Why is judicial independence important? Prior to the Act of Settlement 1701 judges could be removed by the executive if a judge disagreed with the executive and found against them. In the early 17th century, Coke CJ defended the independence of the Bench against the Crown. In the *Case of Prohibitions*[54] Coke advised the King that he could not intervene and determine cases, and in *Peacham's Case*[55], Coke refused to permit the King to force judges to deliberate individually rather than collectively. This was because Coke feared that this would undermine the judicial independence. Coke, according to JR Tanner, believed that the judges 'should be independent of the Crown and should act as arbiter of the Constitution to decide all disputed questions.'[56] Unsurprisingly, the King dismissed Coke for his attempts to limit the Crown's prerogative and views on the constitution.

Ann Lyon noted that James II[57] had 'taken care to appoint judges who accepted his policies and was prepared to use his powers of dismissal against those who showed too great a degree of independence.'[58] In total James II had dismissed 12 judges and his predecessor, Charles II, had likewise suspended judges. The Act of Settlement protects judges from being removed whilst they behave in office, i.e. subject to their good behaviour. According to Ann Lyon, the effect of the Act of Settlement must be appreciated:

> [t]he importance of these developments cannot be overstated. For much of the 17th century, the judges had tended to interpret the law on the basis of what was good for the Crown. Very few were prepared to risk dismissal by incurring the king's wrath. From the early 18th century, the judiciary increasingly applied and developed the law without fear or favour.[59]

Ann Lyon observed that ' "[g]ood behaviour" was a vague phrase and has yet to be judicially defined' and that only one judge has been removed by an address of both Houses of Parliament, that being the Irish judge Sir Jonah Barrington in 1830. There was discussion in the House of Lords in 1805 about removing another senior Irish judge, Luke Fox, either through the mechanism provided by the Act of Settlement 1701 or through the use of impeachment. In the end Fox was neither removed under the Act of Settlement 1701 nor was he impeached. The removal mechanism for judges is now found in section 11 of the Senior Courts Act 1981:

(3) A person appointed to an office to which this section applies shall hold that office during good behaviour, subject to a power of removal by Her Majesty on an address presented to Her by both Houses of Parliament.

(3A) It is for the Lord Chancellor to recommend to Her Majesty the exercise of the power of removal under subsection (3).

Judges who are not protected by this provision of the Senior Courts Act 1981 (circuit judges, etc.) can be disciplined by the Lord Chief Justice and Lord Chancellor.

Judicial independence has been reinforced by section 3 of the Constitutional Reform Act 2005, which places a duty on the executive to uphold judicial independence:

(1) The Lord Chancellor, other Ministers of the Crown and all with responsibility for matters relating to the judiciary or otherwise to the administration of justice must uphold the continued independence of the judiciary.

In **Chapter 4** (section 4.4.5) we have looked at the issue of judicial independence in the aftermath of the press' reaction to *Miller (No.1)* litigation and the perceived failure of the then Lord Chancellor to uphold judicial independence.

PUBLIC LAW IN CONTEXT
JUDICIAL INDEPENDENCE AND THE RULE OF LAW

Lord Phillips, in a speech delivered to the UCL Constitution Unit in February 2011, had observed:

> If the rule of law is to be upheld it is essential that there should be an independent judiciary. The rule of law requires that the courts have jurisdiction to scrutinise the actions of government to ensure that they are lawful. In modern society the individual citizen is subject to controls imposed by the executive in respect of almost every aspect of life. The authority to impose most of those controls comes, directly or indirectly, from the legislature. The citizen must be able to challenge the legitimacy of executive action before an independent judiciary. Because it is the executive that exercises the power of the State and because it is the executive, in one form or another, that is the most frequent litigator

in the courts, it is from executive pressure or influence that judges require particularly to be protected.[60]

Lord Phillips is quite clear that the courts must be able to protect citizens by providing a sufficient check on executive action. Without an independent judiciary, free from executive influence, the courts could not carry out this role effectively. An independent judiciary does not exist in countries such as China, where one political party controls the state, and this has an impact on the rule of law and preventing violations of human rights.

9.4.5.1 Does the United Kingdom have judicial independence?

Munro has noted that 'Parliamentary motions (under the Act of Settlement 1701) for the removal of judges have been unsuccessful on a few occasions.'[61] One example of this is Sir John Donaldson, when as a High Court Judge and President of the National Industrial Relations Court (NIRC) in the early 1970s some 200 Labour MPs sought his dismissal, by a motion in the House of Commons, in relation to his controversial work as President of the NIR. The motion failed and Donaldson went on to become Master of the Rolls.

Even if politicians cannot easily remove judges, the judiciary needs protection from being criticised in Parliament and by politicians in the press. The sub judice rule prevents parliamentarians from commenting on current cases in Parliament, although they can properly criticise sentencing policy. Convention prevents judges speaking out of court, while still working as judges, to explain their judgments.

PUBLIC LAW IN CONTEXT
DEBATING THE SUB JUDICE RULE

The sub judice rule serves an important purpose. This debate from 2019 illustrates why the rule is so important. During the debate Lord Brown of Eaton-under-Heywood stated:

> Essentially the rule requires Members in most proceedings before the House not to refer to active court proceedings, except where the Lord Speaker, in his discretion, allows it, and the Lord Speaker must be given at least 24 hours' notice of any proposal to refer to a matter which is sub judice. Civil proceedings cease to be 'active' on judgment.[62]

Lord Norton of Lough observed:

> The sub judice . . . is a self-imposed rule. Its embodiment in the rules of both Houses has developed over time, with some uniformity now between the two. The first edition

of *Erskine May* made no reference to it.... The rule has been developed and reported on by Joint Committees and the Commons Procedure Committee. There is a recognition of its importance, not just for comity between the legislature and the courts; as Lord Nicholls said, it 'goes much deeper than that, because it is inherent in the proper discharge by the courts and Parliament of their separate constitutional roles. It is vital that both Houses retain freedom of speech to carry out their functions, but it is essential to the courts in fulfilling theirs that the rule is observed. The courts must operate free of parliamentary interference and must be seen to do so. Judges may well be able to ignore or resist MPs or Peers making comments about live cases, but they need to be seen to be free of such interference.'[63]

9.4.5.2 Did the role of the Lord Chancellor undermine judicial independence?

The role of the Lord Chancellor prior to the Constitutional Reform Act 2005

Prior to the Constitutional Reform Act 2005 the Lord Chancellor was the head of the judiciary, which meant that he was responsible for appointing judges, for representing the views of the judiciary to the government, and for the discipline and training of judges. Additionally, the Lord Chancellor was able to sit as a judge in the House of Lords.

The Constitutional Reform Act 2005 has significantly transformed the role of the Lord Chancellor and has notably transferred responsibility as head of the judiciary in England and Wales to the Lord Chief Justice, established a Judicial Appointment Commission and removed the right of the Lord Chancellor to sit as a judge (see Figure 8.8). Importantly, the Lord Chancellor is still a member of the executive, and his main title is now the Secretary of State for Justice and he is responsible for the Ministry of Justice. The Ministry of Justice is responsible for the running of the courts and the provision of legal aid. The recent reforms to legal aid have proved controversial.

As we have seen above, the Lord Chancellor can still veto a judicial appointment and is jointly responsible for judicial discipline. However, there is now a degree of openness and, with regards to judicial appointments, the Lord Chancellor must give reasons and must be able to justify his decision.

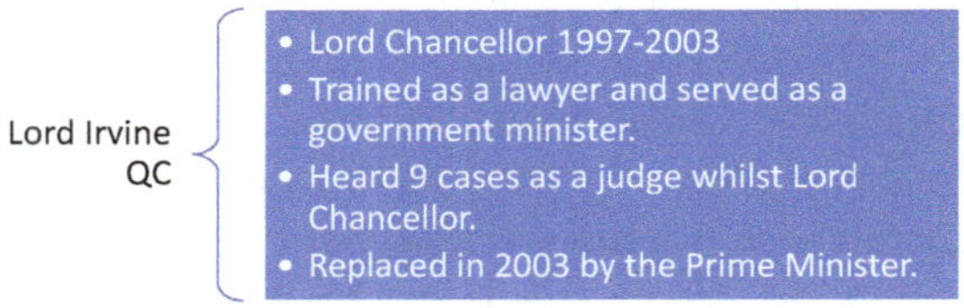

Lord Irvine QC
- Lord Chancellor 1997-2003
- Trained as a lawyer and served as a government minister.
- Heard 9 cases as a judge whilst Lord Chancellor.
- Replaced in 2003 by the Prime Minister.

Figure 9.8
Lord Irvine, Lord Chancellor, 1997–2003

ACADEMIC DEBATE

Baroness Kennedy QC was critical that the Lord Chancellor (prior to the Constitutional Reform Act 2005) was able to sit as a judge, arguing that this served no purpose, as Lord Irvine, the last Lord Chancellor to sit as a judge, was only able to do this on a few occasions.[64] Lord Bingham noted that until Lord Falconer announced in 2003 that he would no longer sit as a judge, the number of days that Lord Chancellors had sat in court had declined and that Lord Irvine as Lord Chancellor, had only sat as a judge in nine cases.[65] Lord Bingham observed that the Lord Chancellor sitting as a judge in a court, which had to decide whether the government (of which he was a senior member) had acted illegally, raised questions of judicial impartiality: 'Lord Irvine himself accepted that he could not properly sit in cases of judicial review involving the government or its agencies, or devolution, or human rights, or any cases raising issues in which the government might reasonably be thought to have an interest. In the view of many, this would include crime.'[66]

Diana Woodhouse has written that for most of the 20th century Lord Chancellors had avoided sitting in cases where the government had a direct interest.[67] However, Woodhouse observed that Lord Mackay, the then Lord Chancellor, had sat in the important appeal in *Pepper v. Hart*,[68] which was a case that involved taxation. Lord Mackay, according to Woodhouse, took the view 'that the government had no direct interest in Revenue cases [but this] . . . was disputed by, amongst others, Lords Lester and Goodhart, who believed that Lord Mackay was wrong to sit in the case.'[69]

It was important that the Lord Chancellor should not sit as a judge where the government has either a direct or an indirect interest. The principles of natural justice require that no man can be a judge in his own court. Clearly in a wide number of areas there was a risk that the Lord Chancellor would have to determine an issue in which he and his ministerial colleagues had an interest. This arguably could give rise to accusations of judicial bias and a violation of Article 6 of the European Convention on Human Rights (ECHR), which guarantees the right to a fair trial.

In *McGonnell v. United Kingdom*[70] the European Court of Human Rights held that the situation in Guernsey, where the Bailiff of Guernsey was President of the Court of Appeal and also served in the legislature and the executive, violated Article 6 of the ECHR, which protects the right to a fair trial. The case involved an application for planning permission, which was rejected. The European Court of Human Rights considered the UK government's argument that there was no violation of Article 6. The government's position was as follows:

> They maintained that whilst the Bailiff has a number of positions on the island, they cannot give rise to any legitimate fear in a reasonably well-informed inhabitant of Guernsey of a lack of independence or impartiality because the positions do not involve any real participation in legislative or executive functions. In particular, they underlined that when the Bailiff presides over the States of Deliberation or one of the four States committees

in which he is involved, his participation is not that of an active member, but rather he is an independent umpire, who ensures that the proceedings run smoothly without taking part in or expressing approval or disapproval of the matters under discussion.[71]

Lord Bingham had observed that the Lord Chancellor in his judicial capacity did not enjoy security of tenure and judicial independence as he could be removed from office by the Prime Minister.[72] Thus the most senior judge in the country could be removed and therefore owed his position to the Prime Minister.

PUBLIC LAW IN PRACTICE

The Home Secretary has been accused of acting illegally when using his statutory powers under the New Terrorism Act 1999 (fictitious), by ordering the detention of 200 suspected terrorists. The people arrested are British citizens. They are alleging that their detention violates Article 5 of the ECHR (the right to liberty).

Prior to the Constitutional Reform Act 2005 could the Lord Chancellor have heard their appeal in a judicial capacity?

If the government believed that the detained individuals posed a threat to national security, could it be presumed that the Lord Chancellor (as a member of government and privy to Cabinet discussion) would be biased against the suspected terrorists?

We have seen that the role of the Lord Chancellor has been transformed by the Constitutional Reform Act 2005. However, in order to appreciate the significance of the changes you must be able to understand the position prior to the Constitutional Reform Act 2005.

9.5 Role of the judiciary

We have seen in **Chapter 3** that the courts and the judiciary have a number of functions (see Figure 9.9) We shall briefly look at these.

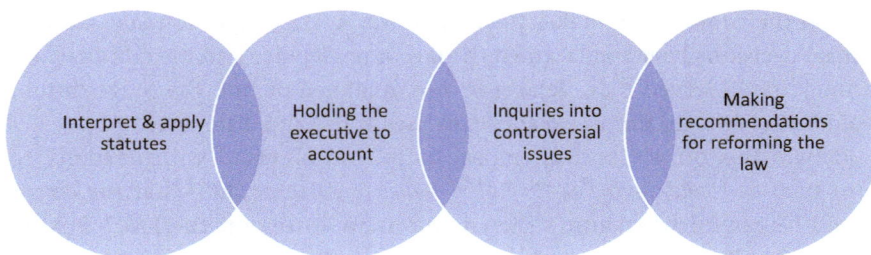

Interpret & apply statutes

Holding the executive to account

Inquiries into controversial issues

Making recommendations for reforming the law

Figure 9.9
The role of the judiciary

9.5.1 Judges as lawmakers

Do judges make law? Cases such as *Shaw v. DPP*[73] and *R v. R (Rape: Marital Exemption)*[74] clearly demonstrate that the courts do in fact make law. In *Shaw v. DPP* the appellant had published a magazine containing advertisements by prostitutes. The court held that his conduct amounted to the common law offence of conspiracy to corrupt morals. In effect the court had made his conduct a criminal offence and therefore, in the absence of legislation criminalising his conduct, the appellant's conduct did not escape sanction. It had been argued by the appellant that as Parliament had created legislation in this area, the court could not use the common law to criminalise his actions. However, this argument was rejected as the court held that it still had a residual power to use the law to defend public morality. The court distinguished this from creating law, which only Parliament could do.

In *Shaw v. DPP* Viscount Simmonds held that the courts, in the absence of an applicable statute, would need to act in some circumstances to criminalise a novel form of obscenity, as otherwise the common law would be powerless to prevent the obscenity:

> In the sphere of criminal law I entertain no doubt that there remains in the courts of law a residual power to enforce the supreme and fundamental purpose of the law, to conserve not only the safety and order but also the moral welfare of the State, and that it is their duty to guard it against attacks which may be the more insidious because they are novel and unprepared for. That is the broad head (call it public policy if you wish) within which the present indictment falls. . . .
>
> I now assert, that there is in that court a residual power, where no statute has yet intervened to supersede the common law, to superintend those offences which are prejudicial to the public welfare. Such occasions will be rare, for Parliament has not been slow to legislate when attention has been sufficiently aroused. But gaps remain and will always remain since no one can foresee every way in which the wickedness of man may disrupt the order of society.[75]

In fact, vast amounts of the law of contract, tort and restitution have been created by the courts. According to the separation of powers it is Parliament and not the court which makes the law. However, the courts do make law and judicial decisions have transformed the law of negligence and the criminal law. Pannick has observed that, '[e]ager or not, qualified or not, the judge cannot avoid acting as legislator in exceptional cases at the appellate level.'[76]

Richard Buxton, a Court of Appeal judge, has observed with reference to cases such as *Hedley Byrne & Co Ltd v. Heller & Partners Ltd*[77], that the courts should be careful when using the common law to reform the law.[78] Buxton notes that '[t]he particular weaknesses of case law as an instrument of reform [include that] . . . [t]he purpose of any case is to decide the issue between the parties, and not to reform the law.' It is a moot point whether in the context of any particular case judges make new law, or apply existing principles of law which no previous case has invoked. For more detail on judges as lawmakers please see **Chapter 3**.

9.5.2 Interpret statutes

The courts interpret and give effect to Acts of Parliament. The courts use a number of rules to do this. Judges have been accused of interpreting statutes in such a way to ignore the intentions of Parliament. This is contrary to Parliamentary Sovereignty. For example, see the controversial approach of Lord Steyn in *R v. A (Complainant's Sexual History)*[79] in **Chapter 6** where we consider the limitations on Parliamentary Sovereignty.

According to Lord Hoffmann in *R v. Secretary of State for the Home Department ex p. Simms*[80], when interpreting an Act of Parliament the courts in the absence of express words to the contrary should presume that Parliament had the best intentions and did not intend to violate fundamental rights: '[i]n the absence of express language or necessary implication to the contrary, the courts therefore presume that even the most general words were intended to be subject to the basic rights of the individual.' Lord Hoffmann had stated that the courts could not prevent Parliament from legislating contrary to an individual's fundamental rights.

In his 2011 FA Mann Lecture Jonathan Sumption, prior to joining the Supreme Court, noted that the courts have made unrealistic assessments of what Parliament intended.[81] Sumption referred to the decision in *R v. Secretary of State for Social Security ex p. Joint Council for the Welfare of Immigrants*[82], where the Secretary of State had introduced regulations under powers given to him by the Social Security Contributions and Benefits Act 1992, which prevented asylum seekers who had not claimed benefits upon their arrival and also those whose application for asylum had been refused from claiming cash payments or seekers from claiming benefits. The majority of the Court of Appeal, aware of the consequences for the asylum seekers, had refused to believe that Parliament intended to give the executive such powers, and therefore held that the regulations were illegal (ultra vires).[83] According to Simon Brown LJ in *ex p. Joint Council for the Welfare of Immigrants*:

> Parliament cannot have intended a significant number of genuine asylum seekers to be impaled on the horns of so intolerable a dilemma: the need either to abandon their claims to refugee status or alternatively to maintain them as best they can but in a state of utter destitution. Primary legislation alone could in my judgment achieve that sorry state of affairs.[84]

Sumption observed that judicial policy-making occurred where the courts took what are essentially political decisions, which are decisions that according to the separation powers, only are to be made by the executive. This means that the court will look at how a minister has used the discretionary decision-making power which Parliament has given him, and when deciding whether the decision is illegal or not, might look at 'what it is thought right for Parliament to wish to do.' These are judgments which 'are by their nature political.' Referring to the decision in *Ex p. Joint Council for the Welfare of Immigrants*, Sumption commented that the courts' assessment as to what Parliament had intended, when giving the Secretary of State powers to make the regulations, was unrealistic. It is important to appreciate that the courts cannot review an Act of Parliament and they can only judicially review secondary or delegated legislation. The Social Security Contributions and Benefits Act 1992 had given the Secretary of State the power to make regulations (which were delegated legislation) and the courts could judicially review these. Depriving asylum seekers from financial assistance is a politically sensitive and controversial decision, and whether to restrict benefits is a political decision which ought to have been made by elected politicians.

Sir Stephen Sedley, then a Court of Appeal judge, was critical of Sumption's argument. Sedley was unconvinced by Sumption's examples of the court's ignoring Parliament's intention when interpreting legislation. Sedley made reference to the *Ex p. Joint Council for the Welfare of Immigrants* decision:

> Mr Justice Collins, a conscientious and experienced High Court judge, who tried to take a principled approach to the problem of hungry and ill asylum seekers on our streets, was rewarded with public abuse by a home secretary who appeared to have a shaky grasp of the separation of powers; but he was vindicated by both the Court of Appeal and the House of Lords which, duly applying Parliament's own legislation, held that it did not authorise executive action that would render the treatment of the already destitute inhuman or degrading. One might have considered this something to be proud of; but Sumption considers it to be evidence of judges failing to read Parliament's intentions accurately – in this case an intention contained in an Act of 1993 which neither expressly nor implicitly conferred any such extreme power.[85]

PUBLIC LAW IN PRACTICE

One of the ways that the courts can quash the regulation would be to find that the Secretary of State had acted illegally, i.e. that Parliament had not intended to give him powers to do X. Therefore, the regulations enabling him to do X were illegal as the Secretary of State had no legal authority to do X.

Returning to Sumption's observations on the decision, the courts must have regard to what Parliament intended when enacting the legislation. In his 2011 FA Mann Lecture Jonathan Sumption QC considered the decision in *Ex p. Council for the Welfare of Immigrants* and observed that:

> [The courts] therefore quashed regulations which had that effect. Parliament evidently did not agree. It immediately passed fresh legislation

authorising such regulations in terms. Some might say that this was a vindication of the proper role of the Courts. They were not prepared to allow a harsh policy to be followed by the executive on such an issue until Parliament had authorised it in unmistakable terms. But another possible conclusion is that the Court of Appeal's view that Parliament could not have intended such a thing always was unrealistic. It ignored the political background to the legislation and underrated the level of Parliamentary concern about the effect of the UK's relatively generous level of social provision in drawing asylum-seekers across Europe to our shores.[86]

We have seen above that the House of Lords in *Anisminic*[87] had interpreted a statutory attempt to exclude judicial review of an executive decision in such a way that ignored Parliament's intention. These are not isolated examples. However, Sumption's lecture was criticised by Sir Stephen Sedley LJ, who disagreed with much of his argument. Sedley commented that 'there is a repeated insinuation that judicial interference in the political process regularly occurs: "The judicial resolution of inherently political issues is difficult to defend." It is not only difficult to defend; it does not happen.'[88] Sedley rejected the view that judges 'routinely cross the boundary separating law from politics.'[89]

9.5.3 Holding the executive to account

Chapter 8 explored the composition and functions of the executive and saw how the executive is held to account under the United Kingdom's constitution. We have seen that the executive is powerful, and governments have historically enjoyed a majority in Parliament. There is concern that Parliament does not effectively hold the executive to account and that this is detrimental to individual rights.

The judiciary serves as an important check on the power of the executive by ensuring that the government and public bodies are accountable. This accountability is crucial both at a national and local level as those affected by a decision of a local council or government department can ask the courts to review the validity of the decision.

The separation of powers requires that each branch of government is checked and balanced by the others. Given that the executive dominates Parliament, the role of the courts to hold the executive to account is important.

Baroness Kennedy has observed that by reviewing the validity of the executive's actions the courts are upholding Parliamentary Sovereignty. Kennedy notes that judicial independence is important because if the executive controlled judicial appointments and tenure, there is a risk that the courts would be unable to carry out this role effectively:

[I]t is not MPs who decide on whether a minister's actions are legal or illegal. Since 1688 our constitution has made it clear that the only way ministers can ultimately be rendered answerable to parliament is through judges in courts ensuring that they do not deploy powers that parliament has not given them. The judges are in fact asserting the supremacy of parliament rather than their own and they need to do so from a position of independence.[90]

This statement is controversial as it ignores the role of Parliament in holding the executive to account.[91] However, it is arguable that the courts are often in a stronger position than Parliament to review and hold the executive to account.

9.5.3.1 Judicial review

Judicial review is an important way of holding the executive to account, whether at a national or local level. The decisions of a local authority often have an important impact on citizens' daily lives, such as a decision to grant or refuse planning permission and the decision to cut funding for local educational services.

Judicial review permits someone affected by the decision of a public body to have the decision reviewed by the court.

A decision can be reviewed on the following grounds:

- The decision was unreasonable or irrational.
- The decision was illegal.
- The decision was not proportionate (where the decision violates the Convention rights).
- The decision lacked procedural fairness, or the decision-maker was biased.
- The decision-maker has given a legitimate expectation and the decision would breach this.

It is important to note that the courts cannot judicially review an Act of Parliament. The courts can judicially review both delegated legislation and the prerogative (see the *decision in Council of Civil Service Unions v. Minister for the Civil Service*[92]). Parliament has given the senior courts the power to issues a declaration of incompatibility under section 4 of the Human Rights Act 1998.

There are limits on judicial review. Certain prerogative powers are considered to be non-justiciable and the courts are reluctant to question the decisions of the executive in areas such as foreign affairs and defence. The courts are aware that they lack the expertise and that it is the executive's role and not theirs to make these types of decisions. In *Rehman v. Secretary of State for the Home Department*[93] Lord Hoffmann had observed that:

> [T]he question of whether something is 'in the interests' of national security is not a question of law. It is a matter of judgment and policy. Under the constitution of the United Kingdom and most other countries, decisions as to whether something is or is not in the interests of national security are not a matter for judicial decision. They are entrusted to the executive.[94]

His Lordship's postscript to his judgment in *Rehman* is interesting, as it was delivered in the aftermath of the 9/11 terrorist attacks in the United States.

In *Rehman*, Lord Hoffmann stated in the postscript to his judgment that decisions of a national security nature should be taken by the executive and not usurped by the courts:

> It is not only that the executive has access to special information and expertise in these matters. It is also that such decisions, with serious potential results for the community, require a legitimacy which can be conferred only by entrusting them to persons responsible to the community through the democratic process. If the people are to accept the consequences of such decisions, they must be made by persons whom the people have elected and whom they can remove.[95]

Such an approach is based in institutional competence, i.e. ministers are much better placed than judges to reach such a determination and that they are accountable to Parliament and the electorate.

PUBLIC LAW IN CONTEXT
WEIGHING UP INSTITUTIONAL COMPETENCE

In *R (on the application of Lord Carlile of Berriew QC) v Secretary of State for the Home Department*[96] the Supreme Court considered whether the Home Secretary's refusal to allow an Iranian dissident politician to visit the United Kingdom in order for her to speak to parliamentarians amounted to a violation of the ECHR. The Home Secretary was of the view that it was not in the public good and would harm the United Kingdom's relationship with Iran, which could put British interests and lives at risk.

In his judgment Lord Sumption considered how the court should approach the question of institutional competence and gave a useful review:

> [A]lthough a recognition of the relative institutional competence of the executive and the courts in this field is a pragmatic judgment and not a constitutional limitation, it is consistent with the democratic values which are at the heart of the Convention, because it reflects an expectation that in a democracy a person charged with making assessments of this kind should be politically responsible for them. Ministers are politically responsible for the consequences of their decision. Judges are not. These considerations are particularly important in the context of decisions about national security on which, as Lord Hoffmann pointed out in Rehman, 'the cost of failure can be high.' It is pre-eminently an area in which the responsibility for a judgment that proves to be wrong should go hand in hand with political removability.[97]

In *Lord Carlile* the majority of the Supreme Court decided in favour of the government. However, Lord Kerr dissented and His Lordship's assessment of institutional competence and how much weight the courts should give the executive to such decisions is interesting:

It is also plainly wrong to suppose that, because the Home Secretary enjoys particular expertise in assessing the risk to British interests, this places an inhibition on the court's performance of the balancing exercise. The first factor is one on which the Home Secretary can claim expertise and knowledge which put her in a better position than the court to make a judgment; it follows that the court must either accept that judgment or accord it considerable weight. But that is not an end of the court's role and function. On the second part of the balancing exercise, the court is entirely competent – and duty bound – to reach its own independent judgment.[98]

Put simply, it is perfectly feasible for courts to accord considerable respect to the political reasons underlying a particular ministerial decision but to conclude that that decision has a disproportionate effect on the Convention rights at stake. Such a conclusion should not be portrayed as government by the courts. It is simply an instance of the courts looking at the basis on which intrusion on a person's Convention right has been sought to be justified, examining and assessing the nature of the right and finding that, given the importance of that right in the particular circumstances of the case, justification for the interference has not been established.[99]

Lord Kerr's dissent was in a human rights context and the infringement of the applicant's rights under the ECHR. It is interesting and stresses that the courts should accord weight to the Home Secretary's judgment, but it should not abdicate applying its own judgment on the matter. We will look below at what is meant by judicial deference, that it is where the judiciary defer to the executive when reviewing governmental decisions and give greater weight to the executive's reasons based in part on institutional competence and the separation of powers. What Lord Kerr is saying here is that the courts should not within the particular decision retreat from being critical of the executive's reasons and forming their own view as to the legality of the decision. This approach is not deferential; however, it would be wrong to regard it as overly active, rather rooted in the need for healthy judicial oversight and tangible checks and balances on the use of executive power.

More recently in *R (on the application of Begum) v Special Immigration Appeals Commission*[100] the Supreme Court considered the legality of the Home Secretary's decision to strip of the applicant under the British Nationality Act 1981. The applicant had travelled when she was 15 years old to live in the Islamic State in Syria and had married one of their fighters. The applicant wished to return to the United Kingdom and sought to challenge the executive's decision. Giving judgment for the court, Lord Reed, the President of the Supreme Court, was critical of the Court of Appeal's decision to discount to reasons provided by the Home Secretary. Importantly, Lord Reed gave reasons for his decision to find the decision lawful. One of these reasons was that:

[T]he Court of Appeal erred in its approach to the appeal against the dismissal of Ms Begum's application for judicial review of the Home Secretary's refusal of leave to enter the United Kingdom. It made its own assessment of the requirements of national security, and preferred it to that of the Home Secretary, despite the absence of any relevant evidence before it, or any relevant findings of fact by the court below. Its approach did not give the Home Secretary's assessment the respect which it should have received, given that it is the Home Secretary who has been charged by Parliament with responsibility for making such assessments, and who is democratically accountable to Parliament for the discharge of that responsibility.[101]

This approach could be criticised as being detrimental to the executive, whereby the court should disregard its assessment for that of the Home Secretary's. However, equally it could be regarded as giving sufficient recognition to institutional competence and the need for the branches of government to accord each other respect for one another.

Writing extra-judicially, Lord Hodge observed how the courts and the executive recognise their respective roles:

> There is . . . what I call 'role recognition'. It is incumbent on judges to see with clarity the limits of the judicial role. . . . I [have previously] discussed judgments in which judges have recognised the constraints on their ability to change the law and I suggested that this was not a matter of deference or restraint but one of role recognition . . . in short, there are decisions of policy, which involve social, economic or political preferences that are properly the domain of the elected branches of government. Not only do the courts lack the resources to formulate policy and assess the practical consequences of decisions in such matters, but also the courts cannot be politically accountable for them in a democracy. Because the boundaries of judicial activity are a question of law for the courts to determine, it can be argued that words such as 'deference' or 'restraint' are appropriate descriptors of the judges' recognition of the constraints on judicial activity. But, where the primary decision-maker is afforded a discretionary area of judgement, I wonder if it is really a selfdenying ordinance? Might it not better be seen as role-recognition? The executive makes policy, governs and preserves the security of the country. Parliament legislates and scrutinises the activities of the executive. And the courts preserve the rule of law, including the enforcement of constitutional or human rights against public authorities.[102]

After reading this final quote you might find it useful to consider the following questions: What do you think Lord Hodge is saying here? Do you agree with his comments about role recognition and the respective competences and resource allocations of the executive and the courts? In what sense does Lord Hodge refer to judicial discretion and his doubts of the term self-denying ordinance?

It not just decisions concerning national security which are considered non-justiciable. In **Chapter 11** we will look at judicial review of the prerogative powers and how some subject-matter is considered inappropriate for the courts to review. Paul Daly has explored justiciability of certain types of decisions and has observed that whilst some decisions are considered non-reviewable, i.e.

that they are primary non-justiciable, there are two different meanings. On the one hand the courts will not review a decision, whilst on the other the courts review the decision and have 'found judicial intervention to be inappropriate.'[103] The decision in *Miller (No.2)* is an example of a controversial area where the laws have reviewed the lawfulness of government decisions, in finding that the advice to the monarch to prorogue Parliament was unlawful as it restricted parliamentary accountability of the executive and Parliament's ability to exercise its legislative sovereignty.

This means that the courts should avoid making policy decisions when carrying out judicial review. The court must review the decision under one of the judicial review grounds. As we shall see in **Chapter 16** the courts when questioning whether a decision was unreasonable or disproportionate risk making a policy decision, which is a decision that according to the separation of powers must only be taken by the executive. This is because the courts are attempting to review whether the decision is a reasonable one, or whether it was proportionate and such decisions pose a risk that the court might attempt to substitute their own decision for that of the minister or local authority. It is worth considering the judgment of Lord Scarman in *R v. Secretary of State for the Environment ex p. Nottinghamshire CC*,[104] where His Lordship stated that, 'Judicial review is a great weapon in the hands of the judges: but the judges must observe the constitutional limits set by our parliamentary system upon their exercise of this beneficent power.'[105]

9.5.3.2 Dangers of judicial policy-making

Lord Sumption has warned that if the judiciary makes political decisions then it risks an introduction of 'democratic influence over their selection,' i.e. a political nomination system.[106] Sumption has warned that this would politicise the judiciary as has occurred in the United States:

> The attraction of judicial decision-making is that it is animated by a combination of abstract reasoning and moral value-judgment, and the decision imposed by the judiciary's plenitude of power to declare and enforce law. To some, this will seem more straightforward than the messy compromises required to build a political consensus. However, for those who are concerned with the proper functioning of our democratic institutions, the judicial resolution of inherently political issues is difficult to defend. It has no legitimate basis in public consent, because judges are quite rightly not accountable to the public for their decisions.[107]

If judges use judicial review to make decisions as to the merits of a minister's or a local authority's actions, then there is a danger that the judges will cross the boundary between judicial review and making essentially political decisions. It is the executive that must take political decisions, as they have democratic legitimacy and are accountable to the electorate in a way that judges are not. By deferring to the executive over inherently political decisions or ones that involve matters of defence, national security and foreign policy the courts uphold the theory of the separation of powers. That is not to say that the courts should not review executive action just because it is linked with defence or foreign affairs, as the courts have demonstrated that there are few areas of executive decision-making which the courts will refuse to review.

PUBLIC LAW IN CONTEXT
JUSTICIABILITY

We can see the changing judicial approach to non-justiciability of foreign policy decisions in *Marchiori v. Environment Agency*[108], where Laws LJ observed that '[i]t seems to me, first, to be plain that the law of England will not contemplate what may be called a merits review of any honest decision of government upon matters of national defence policy.' However, His Lordship held that, '[d]emocracy itself requires that all public power be lawfully conferred and exercised, and of this the courts are the surety. No matter how grave the policy issues involved, the courts will be alert to see that no use of power exceeds its proper constitutional bounds.'[109] This is important as the courts will not refuse to review a decision where there has been a misuse of power.

Lord Sumption explored the judicial approach to foreign policy in a lecture at the LSE's Department of Government where he was of the opinion that '[t]he last decade has witnessed the progressive retreat of the non-justiciability theory and the advance of the qualified division of powers theory, which as I have suggested is simply a rather grand way of emphasising the breadth of the government's discretion.'[110] The courts will look at the actual decision in order to see whether it is amenable to review.

Lord Sumption viewed the judicial retreat from holding that foreign policy decisions were non-justiciable to be based on the 'growing emphasis on the protection of human rights and the barely concealed revulsion of English judges against the conduct of the United States.'[111] His Lordship cited *Al Rawi v. Secretary of State for Foreign and Commonwealth Affairs*[112] and *Binyam Mohammed v. Secretary of State for Foreign and Commonwealth Affairs*[113] as examples of a changing judicial attitude. In *Al Rawi* the Court of Appeal reviewed the Foreign Secretary's decision not to intervene in Mr Al Rawi's detention in Guantanamo Bay. The decision was reviewed like any other public law decision would be, albeit the subject-matter warranting a wider margin of appreciation. In *Binyam Mohammed* the Court of Appeal allowed the publication of material, which was embarrassing to the UK and US governments, and doubted the Foreign Secretary's assessment that publication would harm the United Kingdom's future cooperation with the United States. For more examples of the courts' willingness to review previously non-justiciable areas of the prerogative please refer to **Chapter 11**.

In 2019 Lord Sumption delivered BBC Radio 4's Reith Lectures and his discussion of law, politics and judicialization of politics was brought to a large audience. Sumption's lectures were published as a book, *Trials of State*, and Sumption inter alia argued that: 'As politics have lost their prestige, judges have been only too ready to fill the gap. The catch-phrase that justifies this is the "rule of law". But in the last half century the courts have developed a broader concept of the rule of law, which penetrates well beyond their traditional role of deciding legal disputes and into the realms of legislative and ministerial policy.'[114] Sumption acknowledged that as part of the common law the judges always made law. He however, raised his concern about a change in approach: 'Judges have done this within an existing framework of legal principle, and without trespassing on the functions of Parliament and the executive. In the last three decades, however, there has been a change of judicial mood. The courts have come to share the general suspicion of the political process and of political reasoning as an element in public decision-making.'[115] According to Sumption the result of this change in mood was that, '[the judges] have developed a broader concept of the rule of law which greatly enlarges their constitutional role. Thy have claimed a wider supervisory authority over other organs of the state. They have inched their way towards a notion of fundamental law overriding ordinary processes of political decision-making.'[116]

Sumption's account generated considerable controversy and some took exception with the arguments put forward. Patrick O'Connor QC reviewed Lord Sumption's 2019 Reith Lectures and was highly critical of Sumption's arguments:

> Sumption suggests that an 'empire of the law' has expanded to fill a void left by the 'decline of politics.' This 'empire' represents a threat to democracy, and he concludes the series with a portentous warning about the imperceptible draining of democracy from our institutions. He attributes much of the responsibility to 'judicial overreach': a term which he does not use, but which is an accurate and common shorthand. The accusation is that the courts exceed the proper scope of their powers, by taking over issues which are 'political' and better decided by the messy compromises of politics. This is the third time that Sumption has attempted to advance this argument, and we can examine its progression. As we shall see, this issue is the subject of an ongoing political campaign, to which his approach clearly belongs. . . . What can explain Sumption's persistence and vehemence on 'judicial overreach'? Without any explanatory theory or principle, he presents himself as free of any 'agenda,' and even of personal views. . . . His accusation that our judiciary has weakened democracy is politically motivated and absurd.[117]

In an extra-judicial lecture Lady Hale rejected Sumption's argument of judicial overreach as being demonstrated by the cases chosen by Sumption (such as *Charlie Gard* and *Evans*).[118] Her Ladyship observed:

> [I]t is on the development of public law principles and practice that Lord Sumption con-centrates most of his fire. He comments that judges have traditionally developed the law

'within an existing framework of legal principle and without trespassing on the functions of Parliament and the executive' (p 34). He identifies a change in 'judicial mood' in last three decades (but might it not go further back than that?). The judges have developed a broader concept of the rule of law which greatly enlarges their role; they have claimed wider supervisory authority over other organs of the state; they have inched their way towards a notion of fundamental law overriding the ordinary processes of political decision making. He puts this down to the use of the principle of legality which he calls legitimacy. . . . We can all agree that there are many big picture decisions for which political processes are much more suitable than judicial ones. But . . . I reject the suggestion that judicial processes are not also democratic processes. They are a necessary part of the checks and balances in any democratic Constitution. . . . We in the courts will always ultimately do Parliament's bidding. Forgive me if I don't quite understand what the problem is with that. Is there a moral for judges in all of this? The courts have to go on doing their job – the job which Parliament has given them or which the common law has expected of them for centuries.

Lady Hale's observations are sound and see the proper role of the judiciary as upholding the constitution. However, it depends on a person's viewpoint as to whether the increased exercise of purported power by the judiciary within the constitution is something to be concerned about, or whether the courts are to be regarded as fulfilling their proper constitutional role in ensuring appropriate checks and balances regulate the use of executive power.[119]

9.5.3.3 Judicial activism

The role of the judiciary in holding the executive to account is of upmost importance in ensuring that the United Kingdom has executive accountability. Judges are often criticised for deferring to the executive on grounds such as relative institutional expertise or national security considerations, or on the other hand for being too active in terms of reviewing decisions made by the executive.

As we have seen, the judiciary must uphold Parliamentary Sovereignty and the separation of powers and as a consequence:

• The judiciary cannot review primary legislation and must give effect to Parliament's intention when interpreting an Act of Parliament.
• When judicially reviewing secondary legislation, the courts must avoid making political decisions or decisions which are those that the executive is best placed to make.

Nonetheless judges have challenged the executive over policy decisions and have not always given effect to what Parliament intended. For more detail see **Chapter 6** which looks at judicial use of section 3 of the HRA 1998.

Firstly, what is meant by judicial activism? Dame Elisabeth Laing has observed that: 'Judicial activism' is a phrase which people use when they feel judges have made dodgy law, or have made law (dodgy or otherwise) in a dodgy way.' Laing continued,

> It is easy to dismiss this criticism, when it is made, as ignorant, or politically motivated. But I think it should be taken seriously unless it can be shown to be unfounded. If people think judges are not following the rules, or are colouring too far outside the lines, or are making the rules up as they go along, they will ask themselves why.

To Laing the risk was that

> They may conclude that it is because judges are trying to bring their own moral, social or political values to the party. Whether or not that conclusion is justified, generally, or in a specific case, its existence is may undermine the independence and authority of the judiciary, and, in that way, undermine the rule of law. There is an obvious irony in this, as some of the judges who are accused of activism claim that they are doing what they are doing in order to uphold the rule of law.[120]

Sir John Laws, a former Lord Justice of Appeal, delivered a paper on the theme of judicial activism.[121] According to Laws

> Judicial activism is an ambiguous phrase. It may mean lawmaking by judges. Or it may mean judicial decision-making in areas of policy. Though the distinction between these two has fuzzy edges, it is a real distinction. I think it is both inevitable and desirable that the judges should make law. But in policy areas, where they have to some extent been invited to tread by the Human Rights Act, I think the judges need to show a good deal of restraint.[122]

Furthermore, Laws observed:

> Now I will turn to judicial decision-making in areas of policy, where, as I said at the beginning, I think the judges need to show a good deal of restraint. The danger is that the judges may step too far, or be thought to step too far, onto territory that properly belongs to the elected arms of government.[123]

It is interesting to consider Lord Lloyd Jones' views on the role of judges and the dangers posed by judicial activism:

> Some academic critics complain of 'judicial overreach' which 'increasingly threatens the rule of law and effective, democratic government.' There are, no doubt, limits to the judicial function in this regard, although they are

difficult to formulate with any precision. It does seem to me, however, that recent criticism in this regard of the conduct of the judiciary in our jurisdiction has been considerably overblown and the dangers of judicial activism greatly exaggerated.[124]

This appears to be a sound conclusion to draw, and we consider below the Judicial Power Project, which was established to investigate the use of judicial power. Lord Neuberger's observation on the balance judges need to strike when fulfilling their duties is important note: 'The line between judicial over-activism and judicial timidity is sometimes a little hard to tread with confidence, but it is worth remembering that, while judicial bravery and independence are essential, the rule of law is not served by judges failing to accord appropriate respect to the primary policy-making and decision-making powers of the executive.'[125]

ACADEMIC DEBATE
THE JUDICIAL POWER PROJECT

The Judicial Power Project was established by the think tank Policy Exchange to look at the use of judicial power and the role of judges within the constitution.[126] It is intended to debate judicial power and '[t]he project's concern is with how and by whom public power is exercised.' The Judicial Power Project identified 50 problematic cases that illustrated misuse of judicial power.[127] These included the decision in *R (on the application of Jackson) v Attorney General*[128] and *R (on the application of Purdy) v Director of Public Prosecutions*.[129] This has led to significant academic debate about judicial power and the aims of the Judicial Power Project. Professor Paul Craig is of the view that 'I do not, for the reasons set out above, believe that there is a crisis of judicial legitimacy in the UK, nor do I believe that the courts have in some systemic and unwarranted manner encroached on terrain that is beyond their remit. There are perforce legal decisions that are open to criticism, but this does not constitute a legitimacy crisis, any more than instances in which Parliament strays from a deliberative ideal, or the executive constrains the opportunity for legislative input, betokens a deep crisis in the functioning of our political institutions.'[130] Craig was critical of the 50 problematic cases assembled by the project.[131] Lord Hodge observed the role played by the Judicial Power Project and the need for judges to use their power responsibly: 'Some of the criticism is strongly worded in its attacks on "judicial overreach" and has been judged by other commentators to be overstated. But judges should be aware that all power requires justification and we should be alive to and reflect upon the arguments of those who are concerned about the enhancement of the judicial role in the common law world.'[132]

9.5.3.4 Judicial deference

The courts have been accused of deferring to the executive on occasions and not adequately holding the executive to account. Professor TRS Allan criticised judicial deference to the executive where it meant that individual rights were not protected. Allan reviewed the consequences of judges deferring to the executive because of the presumed view that the executive had more expertise in that area. He argued that it is dangerous for judges to hold certain areas non-reviewable:

> A doctrine of justiciability seeks to insulate certain types of governmental action from judicial review without regard to their effect on the rights or interests of the persons involved. Invoking general notions of governmental expertise or superior democratic credentials, such a doctrine effectively places administrative discretion beyond the purview of the rule of law. The courts abandon their ordinary function of ensuring legality, within the relevant fields, leaving protection of the rights of those affected to the operations of the political process, which may or may not in time provide a remedy.[133]

Allan does not support a doctrine of judicial deference to the executive and argues that deference can actually harm the separation of powers. Within the context of human rights, Allan notes that the 'surrender of judgment is inconsistent with the rigorous scrutiny of governmental action that the protection of human rights requires.' If we look at Allan's arguments it is clear that that if the courts defer to the executive and do not review the legality or reasonableness of an executive decision, then in that instance there is no accountability. The problem which has been identified is that some areas may appear to be far too sensitive politically, or diplomatically, for the courts to review executive action.

Aileen Kavanagh has written on judicial deference and has noted that in some circumstances it can be defended:

> However, a defence of the judicial duty to exercise a constitutionally appropriate degree of restraint when the context demands it, does not necessarily rest on a conservative view of the judicial role. The analysis provided here is compatible with an interventionist role for judges. It simply denies that judicial intervention is appropriate in every case and every context. Sometimes judges should recognise that they are not well-suited or well-placed to pass judgment on, or oppose, decisions of the elected branches of government. But when they are well-placed to do so, there is no justification for them to shy away from fulfilling their constitutional duty to the full. Giving deference when it is due is very different from kow-towing to the elected branches of government simply because they are elected.[134]

We can see that the courts might be reluctant to review executive action where the decisions are deemed to be ill-suited for judicial review. An example of judicial deference is the Court of Appeal's decision in *R (on the application of Lord Carlile of Berriew & others) v. Secretary of State for the Home Department*[135]. The court was reluctant to be seen as usurping the executive's role in making decisions of this nature. The Supreme Court in *R (on the application of Lord Carlile of Berriew QC) v Secretary of State for the Home Department*[136] upheld the decision.

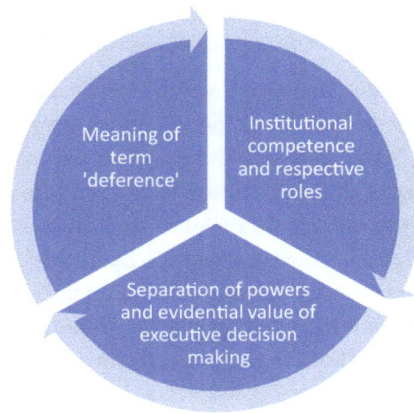

Figure 9.10
Lord Sumption and judicial deference

We have looked at the decision above within the context of institutional competences. In his judgment Lord Sumption considered what was meant by judicial deference:

> As a tool for assessing the practice by which the courts accord greater weight to the executive's judgment in some cases than in others, the whole concept of 'deference' has been subjected to powerful academic criticism: see, notably, TSR Allan, 'Human Rights and Judicial Review: a Critique of "Due Deference"' [2006] CLJ 671; J. Jowell, 'Judicial Deference: Servility, Civility or Institutional Capacity?' [2003] PL 592. At least part of the difficulty arises from the word, with its overtones of cringing abstention in the face of superior status. In some circumstances, 'deference' is no more than a recognition that a court of review does not usurp the function of the decision-maker, even when Convention rights are engaged. Beyond that elementary principle, the assignment of weight to the decision-maker's judgment has nothing to do with deference in the ordinary sense of the term. It has two distinct sources. The first is the constitutional principle of the separation of powers. The second is no more than a pragmatic view about the evidential value of certain judgments of the executive, whose force will vary according to the subject-matter.'[137]

PUBLIC LAW IN CONTEXT
A DEFERENTIAL DECISION?

Perhaps one of the most striking examples of judicial deference to the executive is the House of Lords' decision in *R (Bancoult) v. Secretary of State for the Foreign and Commonwealth Affairs (No.2)*[138]. Bancoult is a controversial decision and illustrates the differing views as to the extent (or limitations) of judicial review. The case involved the Chagos Islands which are administered as the British Indian Ocean Territory. The islanders were removed from the islands in the 1970s after the United States requested the use of the largest island, Diego Garcia, as a military base. The treatment of the islanders was acknowledged as appalling. The islanders attempted to return to the unoccupied islands and after the Divisional Court finding in favour of Mr Bancoult (an islander), the then Foreign Secretary announced that the government would permit the islanders to return. However, in 2004 the government through an Order in Council (as the prerogative was used to legislate for British Overseas Territories) prevented the islanders from returning without the express permission of the government. The government had argued that Orders in Council could not be judicially reviewed. However, the House of Lords unanimously rejected this argument. Where their Lordships could not all agree was with the legality of exiling and preventing the return of the islanders.

The majority held that there was prerogative power to do this and consequentially the executive had not acted illegally. This was disputed by Lords Bingham and Mance who rejected the view that such a prerogative power existed (the government could provide no precedent of its existence), and that despite the subject-matter of the decision (it involved foreign policy and national security) the courts could still question its legality and whether the executive had acted reasonably. Lord Hoffmann had observed that the rationality of the decision could not be reviewed by the courts as national security and diplomatic decisions are matters for the executive and not for the courts. Bridget Hadfield observed that the majority decision in Bancoult was 'a sad concluding note to the House of Lords' constitutional jurisprudence.'[139] Bancoult is interesting because we have the majority deferring to the executive in a case which involved the forced expulsion of a people from their homeland. The minority argued that this was exile and was a violation of the islanders' basic rights.

9.6 Judge-led inquiries

Judges are asked by the executive to chair public inquiries to review major events and to propose recommendations. The most famous recent example of a judge chairing an inquiry is Lord Justice Leveson who looked at the culture, practice and ethics of the press. The inquiry has seen the Prime Minister David Cameron and former Prime Ministers Tony Blair and Gordon Brown give evidence. The inquiry was prompted by allegations of illegal phone-hacking at a newspaper owned by News International.[140] The publication of the Leveson report resulted in considerable political debate in the House of Commons. Eventually, the main political parties reached a consensus and they sought to introduce a royal charter to regulate the press. This cross-party royal charter had a rival proposal, which was supported by newspaper publishers who wished to block the government from preventing the charter to the monarch for her approval. In October 2013, the Press Standards Board of Finance Ltd attempted to get an injunction to prevent the cross-party royal charter from being approved.

The court rejected their application for an injunction and judicial review (*R [Press Standards Board of Finance Ltd] v. The Secretary of State for Culture, Media and Sport*[141]). The monarch approved the royal charter. In May 2014, the Press Standards Board of Finance Ltd were unsuccessful in their attempt to judicially review the royal charter.

The Hutton Inquiry chaired by Lord Hutton was tasked with carrying out an investigation into the death of Dr David Kelly, who had been involved with the claims that Iraq had weapons of mass destruction in the build-up to the 2003 invasion.[142] The inquiry and the subsequent report were regarded by some commentators as flawed.

9.7 Law reform

The executive asks senior judges to review the law and to propose reform. Lord Roskill chaired the Roskill Committee which was tasked with proposing reforms for fraud trials. Lord Roskill's report in 1986 controversially proposed that serious fraud cases should be heard by specialist fraud tribunals consisting of a judge and two lay experts rather than a jury. The government ignored this recommendation. Lord Justice Auld carried out a review into criminal procedure and His Lordship's report contained numerous recommendations, many of which were enacted into law by the Criminal Justice Act 2003.

Baroness Kennedy QC criticised the use of judges by the government to carry out reviews of the law, because some areas of the report had constitutional significance and were political. Kennedy QC was critical, observing that the government 'cherry-picked' the least expensive reforms and could point to judicial approval for their reforms.[143]

9.8 Practical application

Question One

Last month *The Daily Gossip* (fictitious) published pictures of a senior judge at a music festival. One of the pictures appears to show the judge smoking cannabis. In the same picture, a Circuit Judge is also shown rolling a joint.

Yesterday, the Supreme Court delivered a judgment that found against the government's policy on motorway expansion. One of the judges declared in his judgment that 'the Prime Minister has demonstrated the same ineptitude that one has grown accustomed to.' There have been rumours that the judge is suffering from dementia.

Are there any grounds for dismissing any of the three judges? Who could dismiss these judges and how could it be achieved?

Question Two

In 2017, the government has announced plans to reform the Constitutional Reform Act 2005. The government plan to amend the way that judges to the Supreme Court and the Court of Appeal are appointed (please note that these changes are fictitious).

The planned changes are:

- The Judicial Appointments Commission (or special Commission for UK where this the Supreme Court) will nominate two candidates where there is a vacancy on the Court of Appeal or the Supreme Court.
- The nominations will go the Prime Minister, Lord Chancellor and Lord Chief Justice of England and Wales who will then, subject to having consulted with the Law Society, the Bar Council and any other relevant professional body, select one candidate. No reasons will be given for their selection. They may reject both candidates and do not have to give reasons.
- The successful candidate will then appear before a special House of Commons Select Committee and will be asked questions about their political views, previous judgments and anything that they have previously written.
- The Select Committee may consent to the appointment unconditionally, conditionally (whereupon the judge serves five years' probation and does not enjoy security of tenure during this time) or reject the appointment.

You will need to consider whether these proposals impact upon:

1 **Judicial Independence**
2 **The Rule of Law**
3 **Differ from the current way that judges are appointed to the Court of Appeal and the Supreme Court**
4. **Democracy or accountability**

Would you support these proposed changes?

9.9 Key points to take away from this chapter

- The Constitutional Reform Act 2005 has had a significant impact on the judiciary and the office of Lord Chancellor.
- The Lord Chief Justice is now the head of the judiciary in England and Wales, and the Judicial Appointments Commission is responsible for judicial appointments.
- The Appellate Committee of the House of Lords was replaced with the United Kingdom Supreme Court.
- Judicial independence is important and is secured through the Act of Settlement 1701 and the Constitutional Reform Act 2005.

- The judiciary serves an important role in holding the executive to account.
- Some decisions are considered unsuitable for merits-based judicial review. However, the types of decisions which are considered non-justiciable have been reduced, as the courts are more ready to review executive decisions.

Notes

1   (1765) 19 State Tr 1029.
2   [1979] 2 All ER 620.
3   [2004] UKHL 56.
4   [2007] UKHL 46.
5   [1969] 2 AC 147.
6   Lord Bingham, *The Lives of the Law: Selected Essays and Speeches 2000–2010* (OUP 2011) 159.
7   Lady Hale, 'What Is the United Kingdom Supreme Court For?' Macfadyen Lecture 2019, Edinburg, 28 March 2019, 6, <www.supremecourt.uk/docs/speech-190328.pdf>.
8   Hansard, HL, vol. 583, cols 490–527 (18 November 1997).
9   Hansard, HL, vol. 657, col 1228 (12 February 2004).
10 Lord Steyn, 'The Case for a Supreme Court' [2002] LQR 382.
11 Baroness Kennedy, *Just Law: The Changing Face of Justice and Why It Matters to Us All* (Vintage 2005) 151.
12 ibid.
13 [2005] UKHL 56.
14 Hale (n 7).
15 House of Lords, 'The Law Lords' Response to the Government's Consultation Paper on Constitutional Reform: A Supreme Court for the United Kingdom (CP 11/03 July 2003), <www.parliament.uk/globalassets/documents/judicial-office/judicialscr071103.pdf>.
16 Lady Hale, 'Should the Law Lords Have Left the House of Lords' Michael Ryle Lecture 2019, 14 November 2018 <www.supremecourt.uk/docs/speech-181114.pdf>.
17 531 U.S. 98 (2000).
18 SP Nicholson and RM Howard, 'Framing Support for the Supreme Court in the Aftermath of Bush v Gore' (2003) 65(3) Journal of Politics 676.
19 'US Supreme Court Rejects Trump-Backed Bid to Overturn Election' *BBC News* (12 December 2020) <www.bbc.co.uk/news/world-us-canada-55283024>.
20 [2003] UKSC 41.
21 [2017] UKSC 5.
22 [2019] UKSC 41.
23 [2017] UKSC 51.
24 [2001] 1 FLR 267.
25 [2009] UKHL 45.
26 [1993] AC 789.
27 House of Lords Constitutional Reform Committee.
28 M Savage, 'Top Lawyers Warn Johnson Over Role of Judges as Constitution Fears Grow' *The Guardian* (21 December 2019) <www.theguardian.com/politics/2019/dec/21/law-society-warns-boris-johnson-on-independent-judiciary>,

29 A Forrest, 'Lady Hale Warns Government Against US-Style "Politicisation" of Court Appointments' *The Independent* (27 December 2019) <www.independent. co.uk/news/uk/politics/lady-hale-boris-johnson-supreme-court-appointments-conservatives-a9261131.html>.

30 ibid.

31 A Cowburn, 'Lady Hale Warns Boris Johnson Against Political Appointees to Supreme Court: "We Do Not Want to Turn into the US"' *The Independent* (18 December 2019) <www.independent.co.uk/news/uk/politics/lady-hale-boris-johnson-supreme-court-us-appointments-a9252146.html>.

32 R Ekins and G Gee, 'Reforming the Lord Chancellor's Role in Senior Judicial Appointments' *Policy Exchange* (February 2021) <https://policyexchange.org. uk/wp-content/uploads/Reforming-the-Lord-Chancellor%E2%80%99s-Role-in-Senior-Judicial-Appointments.pdf>.

33 [2011] UKSC 24.

34 [2009] HCJAC 27.

35 (HCJ 98/69) [1969] IsrSC 23(1) 693.

36 (CA 6821/93) [1995] IsrSC 49(4) 221.

37 E Salzberger, 'Judicial Activism in Israel' in B Dickson (eds), *Judicial Activism in Common Law Supreme Courts* (OUP 2007).

38 Lady Hale, 'Should the Law Lords Have Left the House of Lords' Michael Ryle Lecture 2019, 14 November 2018 <www.supremecourt.uk/docs/speech-181114. pdf>.

39 Policy Exchange <https://policyexchange.org.uk/publication/reforming-the-supreme-court/>.

40 <http://judicialpowerproject.org.uk/professor-wyatts-proposal-a-response/>.

41 See Chapter 3 for recent comments by Lord Judge CJ on the limitations of using section 5 of the Constitutional Reform Act 2005 and the lack of dialogue between the judiciary and the other branches of the state.

42 P Darbyshire, *Sitting in Judgment: The Working Lives of Judges* (Hart Publishing 2011) 23.

43 Lady Hale, 'Women in the Judiciary' Fiona Woolf Lecture for the Women Lawyers' Division of the Law Society' 27 June 2014 <www.supremecourt.uk/docs/speech-140627.pdf>.

44 For the 2019 statistics see <www.judiciary.uk/about-the-judiciary/who-are-the-judiciary/diversity/judicial-diversity-statistics-2019/>.

45 O Bowcott, 'UK' Stop Judge Unveils Plan to Make Supreme Court More Diverse' *The Guardian* (21 November 2016) <www.theguardian.com/law/2016/ nov/21/lord-neuberger-uks-top-judge-unveils-supreme-court-diversity-plan-retirement>.

46 M Bentham, 'Rush for Gender Equality with Top Judges "Could Have Appalling Consequences for Justice"' *Evening Standard* (21 September 2015) <www. standard.co.uk/news/uk/rush-for-gender-equality-with-top-judges-could-have-appalling-consequences-for-justice-a2952331.html>.

47 'Home Truths About Judicial Diversity' Bar Council Law Reform Lecture, 15 November 2012 <www.supremecourt.uk/docs/speech-121115-lord-sumption.pdf>.

48 Hale, 'Women in the Judiciary' (n 44).

49 'Lord Hodge: I Don't Agree with Sumption About Women Judges' *Legal Futures* (3 November 2015) <www.legalfutures.co.uk/latest-news/lord-hodge-i-dont-agree-with-sumption-about-women-judges>.

50 F Gibb, 'Lord Chief Justice Intervention After Sumption Comments About Women Judges' *The Times* (22 October 2015) <www.thetimes.co.uk/article/lord-chief-justice-intervention-after-sumption-comments-about-women-judges-znxfjxpc7px>.

51 L Barmes and K Malleson, 'The Legal Profession as Gatekeeper to the Judiciary' (2011) 74(2) MLR 245.

52 ibid.

53 We are only discussing this in relation to the arrangements for England and Wales.

54 (1607) Twelfth Coke Reports.

55 (1615) State Trials, ii, 869–80.

56 JR Tanner, *Constitutional Documents in the Reign of James I 1603–1625* (CUP 1961) 176.

57 (1685–88).

58 A Lyon, *Constitutional History of the United Kingdom* (Cavendish 2003) 243.

59 ibid 263.

60 Lord Phillips, 'Judicial Independence and Accountability: A View from the Supreme Court' Lecture delivered to the UCL Constitution Unit, February 2011.

61 C Munro, *Studies in Constitutional Law* (OUP 2005) 314.

62 HL Deb 23 May 2019, vol 797, col 2083.

63 ibid col 2097.

64 Kennedy (n 12).

65 ibid.

66 Bingham (n 7) 84.

67 D Woodhouse, 'The Office of Lord Chancellor – Time to Abandon the Judicial Role – the Rest Will Follow' (2002) 22(1) Legal Studies 128.

68 [1993] AC 593.

69 ibid 128.

70 No 28488/95 (2000) 30 EHRR 289.

71 ibid 47.

72 Bingham (n 7).

73 [1962] AC 220.

74 [1992] 1 AC 599 (HL).

75 ibid.

76 D Pannick, *Judges* (OUP 1987) 4.

77 [1964] AC 465.

78 R Buxton, 'How the Common Law Gets Made: Hedley Byrne and Other Cautionary Takes' [2009] LQR 60.

79 [2001] UKHL 25.

80 [2000] 2 AC 115.

81 Lord Sumption, 'Judicial and Political Decision-Making the Uncertain Boundary' The FA Mann Lecture, 2011.

82 [1997] 1 WLR 275.

83 [1997] 1 WLR 275 at 293.

84 ibid 293.

85 S Sedley, 'Judicial Politics' (2012) 34(4) LRB <www.lrb.co.uk/the-paper/v34/n04/stephen-sedley/judicial-politics?hq_e=el&hq_l=13&hq_m=1520086&hq_v=37e11ac692&utm_campaign=3404&utm_medium=email&utm_source=newsletter>.

86 Sumption, 'Judicial and Political Decision-Making the Uncertain Boundary' (n 81).

87 [1969] 2 AC 147.

88 Sedley (n 86).

89 ibid.

90 Kennedy (n 12) 127.

91 Please refer to Chapter 7 to see how Parliament holds the executive to account.

92 [1985] (*GCHQ*).

93 [2001] UKHL 47.

94 ibid 50.

95 ibid 62.

96 [2014] UKSC 60.

97 ibid 32.

98 ibid 156.

99 ibid 157.

100 [2021] UKSC 7.

101 ibid 134.

102 PS Hodge, 'Judicial Law-Making in a Changing Constitution' (2015) 26(3) Stell LR 471, 484.

103 P Daly, 'Justiciability and the "Political Question" Doctrine' [2010] PL 160.

104 [1986] AC 240.

105 ibid 250–51.

106 Sumption, 'Judicial and Political Decision-Making the Uncertain Boundary' (n 82).

107 ibid.

108 [2002] EU LR 225.

109 ibid [38].

110 Lord Sumption, 'Foreign Affairs in the English Courts Since 9/11' Lecture at the Department of Government, London School of Economics, 14 May 2012.

111 ibid.

112 [2008] QB 289.

113 [2011] QB 218.

114 J Sumption, *Trials of the State: Law and the Decline of Politics* (Profile Books 2019) 34.

115 ibid 34.

116 ibid 34–35.

117 P O'Connor QC, ' "Judicial Overreach": A Response to Sumption' *Counsel Magazine* (19 July 2019) <www.counselmagazine.co.uk/articles/judicial-overreach-a-response-to-sumption>.

118 Lady Hale, 'Law. and Politics: A Reply to Reith' Dame Frances Patterson Memorial Lecture, 8 October 2019 <www.supremecourt.uk/docs/speech-191008.pdf>.

119 For a consideration of the political constitution see M Loughlin, 'What Would Have John Griffith Made of Jonathan Sumption's Reith Lectures?' (2019) 90(4) The Political Quarterly 785.

120 E Laing, 'Two Cheers for Judicial Activism' Debating Judicial Power: Papers from the ALBA Summer Conference <http://judicialpowerproject.org.uk/wp-content/uploads/2016/11/DameElisabethLaing.pdf>, [7] (emphasis added).

121 J Laws, 'Judicial Activism' Debating Judicial Power: Papers from the ALBA Summer Conference <http://judicialpowerproject.org.uk/wp-content/uploads/2016/12/Laws-text-final.pdf>.

122 ibid 1.

123 ibid 30.

124 Lord Lloyd-Jones, 'General Principles of Law in International Law and Common Law' Conseil d'Etat, Paris, 16 February 2018 <www.supremecourt.uk/docs/speech-180216.pdf>.

125 *R (on the application of Rotherham Metropolitan Borough Council) v Secretary of State for Business, Innovation and Skills* [2015] UKSC 6, [65].

126 See <https://judicialpowerproject.org.uk>.

127 See <http://judicialpowerproject.org.uk/50-problematic-cases/>.

128 [2005] UKHL 56.

129 [2009] UKHL 45.

130 P Craig, 'Judicial Power, the Judicial Power Project and the UK' (2017) UQLR 355, 374.

131 ibid 357–60.

132 Lord Hodge, 'Preserving Judicial Independence in an Age of Populism' North Strathclyde Sheriffdom Conference, Paisley, 23 November 2018 <www.supremecourt.uk/docs/speech-181123.pdf>, [47].

133 TRS Allan, 'Human Rights and Judicial Review: A Critique of "Due Deference"' (2006) 65(3) CLJ 671.

134 A Kavanagh, 'Defending Deference in Public Law and Constitutional Theory' (2010) 126 LQR 22.

135 [2013] EWCA Civ 199.

136 [2014] UKSC 60.

137 ibid 22.

138 [2008] UKHL 61.

139 B Hadfield, 'Constitutional Law' in L Blom-Cooper et al (eds), *The Judicial House of Lords: 1876–2009* (OUP 2009) 522.

140 See <www.levesoninquiry.org.uk/>.

141 [2013] EWHC 3824 (Admin).

142 See <www.the-hutton-inquiry.org.uk>.

143 Kennedy (n 12) 151–52.

Further reading

Allan TRS, 'Human Rights and Judicial Review: A Critique of "Due Deference"' (2006) 65(3) CLJ 671

Bingham, Lord, *The Lives of the Law: Selected Essays and Speeches 2000–2010* (OUP 2011)

Blom-Cooper L, B Dickson and G Drewry (eds), *The Judicial House of Lords 1876–2009* (OUP 2009)

Buxton R, 'How the Common Law Gets Made: Hedley Byrne and Other Cautionary Takes' [2009] LQR 60

Craig P, 'Judicial Power, the Judicial Power Project and the UK' [2017] UQLJ 355

Darbyshire P, *Sitting in Judgment: The Working Lives of Judges* (Hart Publishing 2011)

Dickson B, 'Judicial Activism in the House of Lords 1995–2007' in B Dickson (ed), *Judicial Activism in Common Law Supreme Courts* (OUP 2007)

———, 'Activism and Restraint Within the UK Supreme Court' (2015) 21(1) EJCLI

Ekins R and G Gee, 'Reforming the Lord Chancellor's Role in Senior Judicial Appointments' *Policy Exchange* (February 2021)

Hale L, 'Women in the Judiciary' Fiona Woolf Lecture for the Women Lawyers' Division of the Law Society, 27 June 2014

———, 'Should the Law Lords Have Left the House of Lords' Michael Ryle Lecture 2019, 14 November 2018

———, 'Law and Politics: A Reply to Reith' Dame Frances Patterson Memorial Lecture, 8 October 2019

Hodge PS, 'Judicial Law-Making in a Changing Constitution' (2015) 26(3) SLR 471

Kavanagh A, 'Defending Deference in Public Law and Constitutional Theory' (2010) 126 LQR 222

Kennedy B, *Just Law: The Changing Face of Justice and Why It Matters to Us All* (Vintage 2005)

Malleson K, 'Safeguarding Judicial Impartiality' (2002) 22(1) Legal Studies 53

Mance J, 'The Frontiers of Executive and Judicial Power: Differences in Common Law Constitutional Traditions' (2018) 26(2) APLR 109

Nicholson SP and RM Howard, 'Framing Support or the Supreme Court in the Aftermath of "Bush v Gore"' (2003) 65(3) JP 676

Pannick D, *Judges* (OUP 1987)

Phillips, Lord, 'Judicial Independence and Accountability: A View from the Supreme Court' Lecture delivered to the UCL Constitution Unit, February 2011

O'Connor P, ' "Judicial Overreach": A Response to Sumption' *Counsel Magazine* (19 July 2019)

Sedley S, 'Judicial Politics' (2012) 34(4) LRB 15

Sumption, Lord, 'Judicial and Political Decision-Making the Uncertain Boundary' The FA Mann Lecture, 2011

———, 'Foreign Affairs in the English Courts Since 9/11' Lecture at the Department of Government, London School of Economics, 14 May 2012

———, *Trials of the State: Law and the Decline of Politics* (Profile Books 2019)

Woodhouse D, 'The Office of Lord Chancellor – Time to Abandon the Judicial Role – the Rest Will Follow' (2002) 22(1) Legal Studies 128

Wyatt D and R Ekins, 'Reforming the Supreme Court' *Policy Exchange* (July 2020)

The prerogative I

Foundations, powers and parliamentary control

This chapter will

- define the prerogative and provide an outline of why it exists today and explore its origins;

- review how the prerogative is exercised by the government and the monarch;

- evaluate the use of constitutional conventions in regulating how the prerogative is used; and

- consider whether parliamentary control of the prerogative is effective and what could be done to improve this.

10.1 Introduction

The prerogative is an important source of power for the Crown. Despite its historical origins it remains an important part of the constitution. The decision to launch airstrikes against the Syrian government in April 2018, the attempt to trigger Article 50 of the Lisbon Treaty[1] before it was prevented from doing so by the Supreme Court's decision in *R (on the application of Miller) v Secretary of State for Exiting the European Union (No.1)*[2], and the appointment of Theresa May as Prime Minister in July 2016 all took place using the prerogative. It is an important power and today it confers considerable discretion on the government to act independently of Parliament. The term 'prerogative' is confusing as it is often used, but is seldom explained and therefore this chapter will begin by defining what is meant by the term *prerogative*. The chapter will then proceed to see how the prerogative is used today. It is important to appreciate that the prerogative is an important part of the constitution. This chapter will consider how the government uses the prerogative and why it is significant that this important source of executive power is not conferred by, or always effectively held to account by, Parliament. An example of this is the deployment and use of United Kingdom armed forces and whether when exercising the 'war

DOI: 10.4324/9780429293498-13

prerogative' the Prime Minister must as a matter of constitutional convention obtain the consent of the House of Commons.

It is important to appreciate that the prerogative and the royal prerogative are the same; the use of the word *royal* simply acknowledges that historically these powers were exercised by the monarch. The reason for this is that before the evolution of Cabinet government in the 18th century and the emergence of the office of Prime Minister, the monarch governed the country, and the prerogative powers were an importance source of royal power that was independent of Parliament. In the 17th century it was the monarchy's perceived misuse of its prerogative powers that led to the English Civil Wars, the abolition of the monarchy in 1649, and the overthrow of James II in 1688.

The present monarch, Her Majesty Queen Elizabeth II, still retains her personal prerogative powers and these have not been effectively transferred to her government. It is important to appreciate that the monarch cannot use these personal prerogative powers in any manner that she wishes. In matters relating to the exercise of her personal prerogative powers, the monarch will act under the advice of Prime Minister and only in exceptional circumstances will she have to take a decision without such advice.[3] Walter Bagehot, a leading constitutional writer in the mid-19th century, observed that the monarch had 'three rights – the right to be consulted, the right to encourage, the right to warn'[4] and that 'The Queen is only at the head of the dignified part of the constitution. The prime minister is at the head of the efficient part. The Crown is according to the saying, the "fountain of honour;" but the Treasury is the spring of business.'[5] This chapter will consider the most important personal prerogative powers of the monarch, which include the ability to refuse royal assent to proposed legislation, the choice of Prime Minister and the status of the prerogative power to dissolve Parliament, in light of the Fixed-term Parliaments Act 2011 and the subsequent academic debate surrounding the status of this particular prerogative power.

This chapter will consider why the United Kingdom still has prerogative powers and why Parliament has not just simply abolished these by introducing legislation to replicate each power. It is important to appreciate that Parliament can do, and has done, this for certain prerogative powers, such as the Bill of Rights in 1689 that abolished the monarch's power to dispense with an Act of Parliament, or the Constitutional Reform and Governance Act 2010 which placed the civil service on a statutory footing. This chapter will consider how these powers are used in a manner that is arguable often unaccountable to Parliament.

10.2 Defining the prerogative

This section will define what is meant by the prerogative. The prerogative is the power of the Crown. It is a power that is recognised by the common law and is a relic from the time when England was ruled exclusively by the monarch. It is because of this inherent royal connection that writers refer to the prerogative

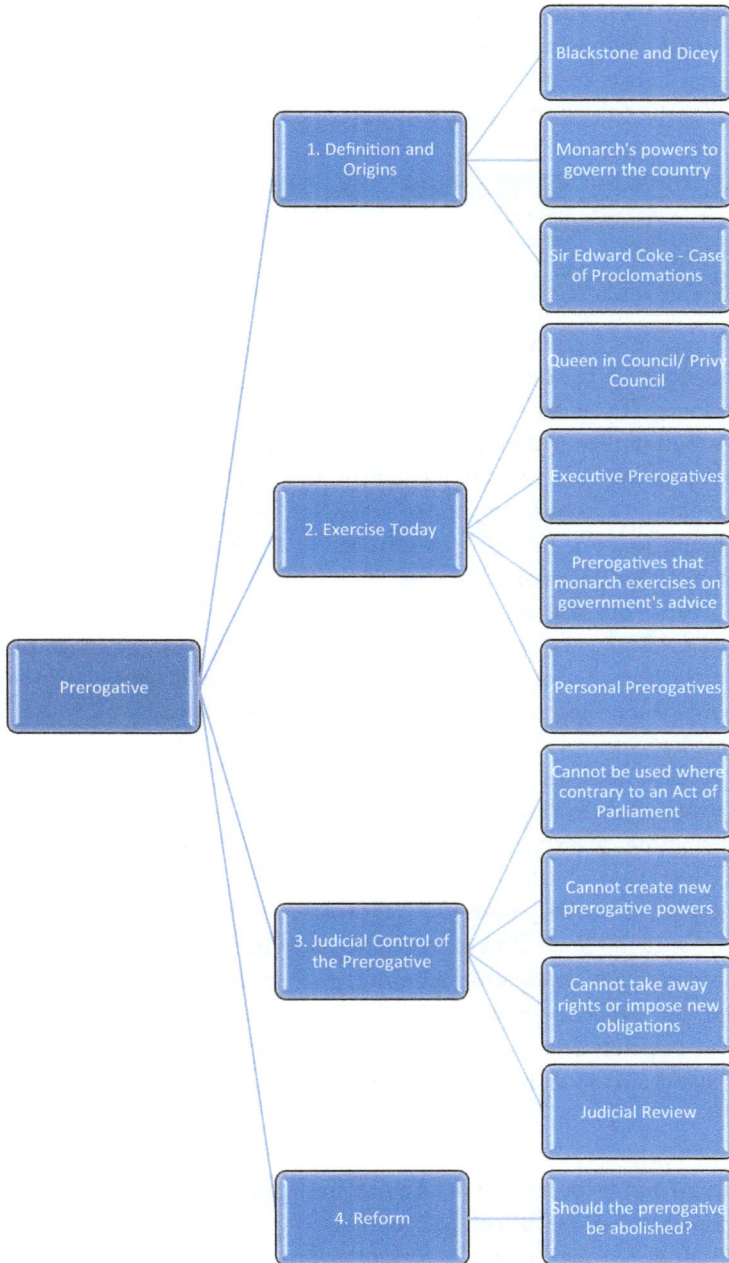

Figure 10.1
Chapter overview (**Chapters 10** and **11**)

powers as the royal prerogative, although the majority of these powers are not exercised by the monarch personally, but rather by her ministers. It might be useful to think of the prerogative as one of the sources of power that authorises the Crown to act in a certain way. There are two other sources of power.

The first is an Act of Parliament, and the second stems from the idea that a government (just like an individual) is able to do anything that is not prohibited from doing. This is known as the Ram Doctrine.[6]

Consider the following example:

PUBLIC LAW IN PRACTICE
THE PREROGATIVE AS A SOURCE OF POWER

At the next General Election Ms Smith's political party wins a majority of the seats in the House of Commons. The monarch has the power by virtue of the prerogative to decide who will form her next government. However, as we shall see below, the use of the prerogative by the monarch is largely a matter of constitutional convention, which are non-legal rules of the constitution that regulate how the actors within the constitution use their powers. Therefore, the monarch has no real choice and based upon the advice of her outgoing Prime Minister, she must appoint Ms Smith to form her next government,[7] as Ms Smith's political party commands the confidence of the House of Commons.[8]

Ms Smith and her government will exercise the prerogative powers on the monarch's behalf.[9] In addition to the prerogative powers the government will firstly be given the power to act by Parliament through an Act of Parliament and can be given the power to enact delegated legislation. Unlike the prerogative, this type of power is voted on by Parliament and therefore if the government requests the power to do X, then they will need Parliament's approval. This means that there were will be scrutiny in the House of Commons and the House of Lords. Secondly, the government will have powers derived from the common law and these inherent powers will permit the government to do anything that is not limited by an Act of Parliament.[10]

However, in exercising any of these powers the government is 'subject to an overriding duty to act in accordance with the law.'[11] This means that if Ms Smith's government uses the prerogative powers in a way that is considered unlawful, then an individual or organisation can bring an application for the court to judicially review the use of the prerogative. The courts can then quash the decision if the government does not have such a power, or if it has been used in a manner that is unreasonable or fails to give effect to a legitimate expectation.

It is important to be able to define the prerogative and to look at the particular emphasis placed by different academics.

The Cabinet Manual, which is a non-legally binding document created by the Cabinet Office, provides the following definition:

> The scope of the Royal the Royal Prerogative power, which is the residual power inherent in the Sovereign, has evolved over time. Originally the Royal Prerogative would only have been exercised by the reigning Sovereign. However, ministers now exercise the bulk of the prerogative powers, either in their own right or through the advice that they provide to the Sovereign, which he or she is constitutionally bound to follow. The Sovereign

is, however, entitled to be informed and consulted, and to advise, encourage and warn ministers.[12]

. . .

The Sovereign retains prerogative powers but, by constitutional convention, the majority of these powers are exercised by, or on the advice of, his or her responsible ministers, save in a few exceptional instances (the 'reserve powers').[13]

In the late-19th century AV Dicey stated that the prerogative was 'the residue of discretionary power or arbitrary authority which at any one time is legally left in the hands of the crown.'[14] This meant that the prerogative was the remainder of the monarch's discretionary powers, i.e. these powers had not been conferred by Parliament. By what 'is legally left' in the hands of the Crown (meaning the monarch and her ministers), Dicey meant that certain prerogative powers have been abolished by Acts of Parliament, limited by the courts, or surrendered over time. An example of the Crown surrendering prerogative powers is the fact Henry III[15] sought the consent of Parliament to enact taxation and this relationship was cemented during the reign of his successor Edward I,[16] who required Parliament to finance his wars. The right of Parliament to give its consent to both taxation and legislation was confirmed during the reign of Edward III.[17] This is significant as from then onwards a monarch could not effectively rule a country without summoning a Parliament to authorise new laws or to approve the monarch's request for taxation. This meant that Parliament could effectively challenge the policies of a weak monarch (such as Henry VI), or even question and hold the Crown to account over how it spent the tax revenue (such as Edward III over the Hundred Years War).

Sir William Blackstone, in his *Commentaries on the Law of England*, defined the prerogatives the powers that 'the King enjoys alone, in contradistinction to others, and not to those he enjoys in common with any of his subjects.'[18] The monarch enjoys immunity from prosecution and from civil suit as by virtue of her prerogative power is in effect above the law. This immunity from being sued was enjoyed by the government and executive departments before the Crown Proceedings Act 1947 was enacted to permit claims in contract and tort. More recently, Professor Robert Blackburn offered the following definition,

[t]he Crown 'prerogative' is a concept well known to lawyers, though others often have difficulty grasping its nature and character. It is the term used to describe the network of inherent common law powers, privileges and immunities of the Crown which have existed since time immemorial and exist by virtue of past *de facto* judicial recognition.[19]

Blackburn's definition is interesting as the continued existence of the prerogative is dependent on the courts being willing to recognise the validity of the Crown's claim to possess such powers. We will consider below the role of the courts in setting limits on the prerogative and in particular the judgments and legal commentary of Sir Edward Coke in the beginning of the 17th century.

Another definition is provided by the constitutional historian, JR Tanner, who observed that:

> It has been the fashion with some writers to regard prerogative as if it were something illegitimate and tyrannical; but, strictly speaking, the royal prerogative is neither more nor less than the legal exercise of the royal authority. . . . This doctrine of prerogative was essential to the existence of a civilised State; and it came to the Crown by right of inheritance, for in early days, when the State was as yet imperfectly developed and the province of law small, it was to the right 'of *kings* to rule and *princes* to decree justice' that the country owed internal security as well as military glory.[20]

This definition is interesting as Tanner was clearly making the point that the Crown's exercise of the prerogative cannot be viewed as illegal, as the law recognises the legality of the Crown using such powers. The simple rationale for accepting that the Crown has certain prerogative powers is that in order for a country to operate these powers were needed. In other words, when William, Duke of Normandy, had himself crowned King of England on 25 December 1066, he needed to do certain things to ensure that his new kingdom functioned: raise taxation, enact laws, make treaties with foreign powers, create new nobility to subjugate the local population and reward his followers, built fortifications and raise soldiers. These are things that were all done under the prerogative and if a monarch could not do any of these, then the country would be in chaos and the monarch disposed.

To conclude it is important to appreciate that the courts play an important role in limiting ministerial use of the prerogative by preventing the creation of new prerogative powers. The courts will not allow prerogative powers to be used where these are inconsistent with an Act of Parliament. Parliament can ultimately control the prerogative by abolishing a particular power or by introducing statutory powers that overlap with the prerogative. An example of how this can occur is the decision of the House of Lords in *Attorney-General* v. *De Keyser's Royal Hotel Ltd*[21] where the government sought to rely on the prerogative to pay less compensation than what was owed under an Act of Parliament. Unsurprisingly, the House of Lords ruled that the compensation payable was under the Act of Parliament and the prerogative would no longer apply whilst the Act was in force (i.e. the prerogative power was said to have gone into abeyance).

Key points:
1   Can you define the prerogative in your own words?
2   Why is the history of the prerogative so important in understanding its extent today?
3   What is the rationale for the prerogative?

10.3 History and evolution of the prerogative

This section will consider the history of the prerogative and how it has evolved over time. It is important to appreciate that the prerogative is a product of

```
┌─────────────────┐    ┌─────────────────┐    ┌─────────────────┐    ┌─────────────────┐
│ Rule by monarch │    │ Tudor Monarchs  │    │ Stuart Monarchs │    │   Hannovarian   │
│     alone       │    │                 │    │                 │    │    Monarchs     │
│                 │    │  (1485-1603)    │    │  (1603-1714)    │    │                 │
│                 │    │                 │    │                 │    │  (1714-1901)    │
└─────────────────┘    └─────────────────┘    └─────────────────┘    └─────────────────┘
```

Rule by monarch alone	Tudor Monarchs (1485-1603)	Stuart Monarchs (1603-1714)	Hannovarian Monarchs (1714-1901)
Henry I's coronation oath to uphold the law	King Henry VIII given powers to make legislation using prerogative	Sir Edward Coke - setting limits on king's prerogative	Development of constitutional monarchy and cabinet government
Magna Carta 1215 (limiting royal power)		Charles I uses the prerogative to rule without Parliament	Prerogative largely exercised by government
Establishment of Parliament (and surrender of power to make legislation & raise taxes)		James II uses the prerogative to dispense with Acts of Parliament	Monarch's personal prerogative powers are regulated by constitutional convention
		Glorious Revolution & Bill of Rights 1688 - abolishes certain prerogative powers	

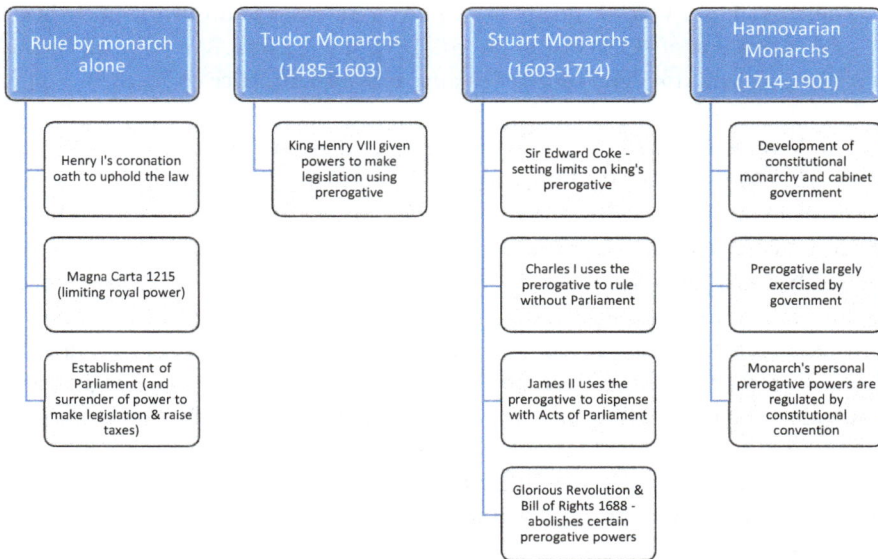

Figure 10.2
The history and evolution of the prerogative

history and that when a dispute concerning the exercise of a particular power reaches the Court of Appeal or the Supreme Court, the judges will consider the origins of this power and whether the government does have the legal authority to act under a particular prerogative.[22]

10.3.1 The historical role of the monarch

Before the development of Cabinet government in the 18th century, the monarch was responsible for running the executive branch of government. This is not say that the monarch acted alone or took all decisions; rather the monarch was served by advisors and other royal officials who would govern the country. The monarch would raise taxes, raise armies, dispense justice and oversee the administration of the kingdom. The monarch ruled through the Privy Council and was assisted by privy councillors who would act as his advisors. The powers of the monarch were not granted by Parliament (as until the 13th century it did not exist); instead the monarch exercised the power that was necessary to govern the country.

The monarch was restricted from abusing his power by the nobility and William the Conqueror's son, Henry I, promised upon becoming king to uphold the law. The Baron's revolt against King John was an example of the monarch agreeing to have his power limited by the Magna Carta in 1215.[23] Whilst there has been a risk of overplaying the actual significance of Magna Carta,[24] the language used conferred a clear check on the power of the monarch over his nobles. An example of this is Chapter 29, which is still in force:

> NO Freeman shall be taken or imprisoned, or be disseised of his Freehold, or Liberties, or free Customs, or be outlawed, or exiled, or any other wise

destroyed; nor will We not pass upon him, nor condemn him, but by lawful judgment of his Peers, or by the Law of the Land. We will sell to no man, we will not deny or defer to any man either Justice or Right.[25]

The Magna Carta and the need for an eventual establishment of a Parliament in 1258 by Henry III demonstrated that aristocracy could, and did, rebel against the monarch and so the fear of rebellion prevented the monarch from abusing his power. Parliament became an important institution in England the monarch could not effectively rule without summoning the Lords and representatives of the Commons. During the 13th and 14th centuries the prerogative powers to enact legislation and levy taxation were surrendered to Parliament. This is extremely important as firstly Parliament would be seen as the legitimate institution for making law and imposing obligations, and this would lead to conflict where the monarch should to rule through the prerogative.

It is important to appreciate that a royal proclamation cannot create new legal obligations and can only enforce existing legal obligations. Writing in 1820, Joseph Chitty observed that '[p]roclamations have been frequently made the tools of tyranny and oppression' and that Parliament gave Henry VIII the power under statute to make laws using royal proclamations and that this power was repealed after the King's death.[26] The power was granted by Parliament under the Statute of Proclamations 1539. Such was the constitutional impropriety of the king being able to make law outside of Parliament, that the power was abolished upon his death. The notoriety of the power granted by Parliament to Henry VIII lives on, in 'Henry VIII clauses,' which are clauses in a bill (or eventually a section in an Act) that enables the government to repeal or amend primary legislation without asking Parliament to do this.

CURRENT DEVELOPMENTS
HENRY VIII POWERS AND THE EUROPEAN UNION (WITHDRAWAL) ACT 2018

The European Union (Withdrawal) Act 2018 has proved controversial because of the Henry VIII powers granted to the government. The government can make regulations in areas that an Act of Parliament covers, without the need to seek Parliament's approval. Section 9 concerns dealing with deficiencies arising from withdrawal and states that:

(1) A Minister of the Crown may by regulations make such provision as the Minister considers appropriate for the purposes of implementing the withdrawal agreement if the Minister considers that such provision should be in force on or before exit day, subject to the prior enactment of a statute by Parliament approving the final terms of withdrawal of the United Kingdom from the EU.
(2) Regulations under this section may make any provision that could be made by an Act of Parliament.

(3) But regulations under this section may not –

    (a) impose or increase taxation or fees,

    (b) make retrospective provision,

    (c) create a relevant criminal offence,

    (d) establish a public authority, or

    (e) amend, repeal or revoke the Human Rights Act 1998 or any subordinate legislation made under it.

(4) No regulations may be made under this section after exit day.

Before we proceed to consider the relationship between Sir Edward Coke and the prerogative it is important to appreciate that:

- The prerogative powers had a common law origin as a record of their existence was recorded in the case law and histories of the period. The power was recognised by the common law.
- The role of the monarch was gradually restricted by Parliament. For example, the ability to raise taxation was controlled by the need for parliamentary approval; and that
- This led to a conflict with the Stuart kings who believed that their prerogative power were absolute.

10.3.2 Sir Edward Coke CJ on the prerogative

Sir Edward Coke CJ was an important judge at the beginning of the 17th century and is still regarded as a leading judge. According to Roland Usher, '[I]f an assemblage of lawyers were asked to name the greatest English lawyer, the great majority would nominate unhesitatingly Sir Edward Coke.'[27] Sir Stephen Sedley observed '[I]n tracking the history of English public law it is difficult not to be struck by modernity of the later Elizabethan and the early Jacobean judges, Edward Coke prominent amongst them.'[28]

Coke had served as Elizabeth I's attorney-general and had been seen as a defender of the monarch's prerogative powers. As attorney-general he had prosecuted Robert Devereux, the Earl of Essex, who had attempted to overthrow the Queen in 1601. He continued as attorney-general when James I became King in 1603 and prosecuted the gunpowder plotters and Sir Walter Raleigh. When James appointed Coke as Chief Justice of the Court of Common Pleas in 1606 he might have expected Coke to continue to defend the King's prerogative powers; however, this was not the case, and Coke shocked contemporaries be his transformation to a leading critic of the misuse of the prerogative.[29] It is important to note the Coke was not a critic of the prerogative per se, rather just the misuse of this power and the impact this would have on the common law and its jurisdiction (as at this time there was a fierce rivalry between the rights of the King's subjects).

The concept of the courts imposing limits upon the prerogative had existed prior to Coke becoming a judge. In the *Case of Monopolies*[30] Coke acted as the attorney-general in a challenge against the Crown's right to grant a monopoly under the prerogative, which would give Ralph Bowes the sole right to produce and sell playing cards. Popham CJ held in the Court of King's Bench that the monopoly was void as an Act of Parliament prohibited the importation of playing cards and the common law which was opposed to the granting of monopolies as these would restrict the public's right to engage in trade. Coke had argued unsuccessfully that, 'the Queen hath Prerogative *given by the Law* to take such order for such moderate use of them as shall seem good to her.'[31] In the case of *Penal Statutes*[32] the judges of England were asked to determine the validity of the monarch using her prerogative powers to dispense with a statute. In his reports, Coke recorded that the judges held '[t]hat the grant was utterly against Law . . . . [as] when a Statute is made by Parliament for the good of the Commonwealth the King cannot give the penalty, benefit, and dispensation of such Act to any subject.'[33]

As Chief Justice of the Court of Common Pleas Coke would find himself in conflict with the king. In *Bates's Case*[34] Coke and Chief Justice Popham of the King's Bench held that the common law prevented the king from using his prerogative to impose tariffs and customs 'unlesse it be for the advancement of Trade and Traffic, which is the life of very Island, *Pro bono publico.*'[35]

In *Prohibitions Del Roy*[36] Coke rejected the king's right to sit as a judge. It is important to appreciate that at this time judges were seen as servants of the crown part of the government. Equally important was that under the prerogative the king was the fount of justice and was responsible for dispensing it. The view put forwarded by Coke placed a clear limit on his this power could and could not be exercised. Coke argued that, '[t]he King may sit in the King's Bench, but the Court gives the judgment. No King after the conquest assumed to himself to give any judgment in any cause whatsoever which concerned the administration of justice, within the realm; but these causes were solely determined in the Courts of Justice.'[37] Coke reported that 'the King was greatly offended, and said, that then he should be under the Law, which was Treason to affirm; To which I said . . . The King ought not to be under any man, but under God and the Law.'[38] However, according to Sir Rafe Bowswell, who had witnessed Coke informing the king that he could not sit as judge,

'his Majesty fell into that high indignation as the like was never known in him, looking and speaking fiercely with bended fist, offering to strike him etc., which the Lord [Coke] perceauing fell flat on all fours; humbly beseeching his Majesty to take compassion on him and to pardon him, if he thought zeal had gone beyond his duty and allegiance.'[39]

The *Case of Proclamations*[40] concerned a question by King James I to his judges concerning his use of proclamations. It must be appreciated that the

House of Commons was concerned about the use of proclamations to impose new legal obligations, as according to JR Tanner, James I in the first years of his reign had issued proclamations more than Elizabeth I.[41] Coke and the other judges held that:

1   The king 'by his Proclamation . . . cannot change any part of the Common Law, or Statute Law, or the Customs of the Realm.'[42]
2   Proclamations could not be used to create new offences.[43]
3   The king could not use the prerogative to increase the jurisdiction of the Star Chamber, which was a prerogative court.[44]

According to Coke, 'it was resolved, that the king hath no prerogative but that which the law of the land allows him.'[45] JR Tanner summed up the significance of this decision: '[t]he reply of the judges is one of the minor Charters of English liberty.'[46] Sheppard observed that '[i]t was one of Coke's most significant attacks on the royal prerogative.'[47]

In his extra-judicial writings Coke reiterated the maxim '[t]hat the Common Law hath so admeasured the Prerogatives of the King, that they should neither take away nor prejudice the inheritance of any.'[48] This meant that that the prerogative could not be used to take away a common law right and so the prerogative was restricted by judicial decisions. Coke's judgments and extra-judicial writing show the development of the idea that the king was not above the law and that the courts would control the king's use of the prerogative. Coke demonstrates that the claim for royal absolutism (i.e. that the king was above the law and was not bound by the common law or an Act of Parliament) was rejected before the English Civil Wars. He upheld the supremacy of an Act of Parliament and would not allow the prerogative to take away fundamental common law rights. Guy Burgess summed up the changes in Coke's views on the prerogative:

> [Coke] always believed that the operation of the royal prerogative was bounded and restricted by the common law, but in his later writings and speeches the implications deduced from this proposition became more stringent. Not only did his later writings show no signs of a belief that certain royal powers were immune from legal limitation even with the king's consent in parliament, but on many specific points too he seems to have changed his mind. The general trend is towards binding ever more tightly the scope for royal discretion.[49]

It is unsurprising that Coke was dismissed by the king in 1616 and ordered to edit his writings. When he eventually died in 1634 the new king, Charles I, ordered his agents to seize Coke's writings due to a concern that they would argue for further limitations upon the prerogative.

In *R (on the application of Miller) v Secretary of State for Exiting the European Union*[50] the issue was whether the UK government could use the prerogative to trigger Article 50 of the Lisbon Treaty, which would start the process for the

UK leaving the European Union. The claimants argued that because the European Union Communities Act 1972 (which had been required to give effect to the UK's membership of the European Communities in 1973) conferred legal rights, the prerogative could not be used to take away these rights. This argument drew upon the Coke's judgment in the *Case of Proclamations* and was accepted by the High Court and the Supreme Court.

PUBLIC LAW IN CONTEXT
SIR EDWARD COKE AND *R (ON THE APPLICATION OF MILLER) V SECRETARY OF STATE FOR EXITING THE EUROPEAN UNION*

In *Miller* the Supreme Court referred to Sir Edward Coke's decision in the *Case of Proclamations*. It is important to appreciate that Coke's position as to the limits that the court should impose on the prerogative were eventually accepted and enacted by the English and Scottish Parliaments in the Bill of Rights 1688 and the Claim of Right 1689. The relevant passages of the Supreme Court's judgment are:

In the early 17th century *Case of Proclamations* (1610) 12 Co Rep 74, Sir Edward Coke CJ said that 'the King by his proclamation or other ways cannot change any part of the common law, or statute law, or the customs of the realm'. Although this statement may have been controversial at the time, it had become firmly established by the end of that century. In England and Wales, the Bill of Rights 1688 confirmed that 'the pretended power of suspending of laws or the execution of laws by regall authority without consent of Parlyament is illegall' and that 'the pretended power of dispensing with laws or the execution of laws by regall authoritie as it hath beene assumed and exercised of late is illegall.'[51]

...

Exercise of ministers' prerogative powers must therefore be consistent both with the common law as laid down by the courts and with statutes as enacted by Parliament.[52]

...

The Miller claimants, on the other hand, rely on decided cases concerned with the use of prerogative powers in other situations. They argue that those cases establish the existence of legal constraints on the exercise of those powers, and that those constraints are applicable in the admittedly different situation with which we are now concerned. They argue that the effect of those constraints is that Ministers cannot lawfully give notification under article 50(2) unless an Act of Parliament authorises them to do so.[53]

The starting point of this argument is the *Case of Proclamations* (1611) 12 Co Rep 74, which concerned the question whether James I could, by proclamation, prohibit the construction of new buildings in and around London, and prohibit the manufacture of starch from wheat. Coke CJ stated that 'the King by his proclamation or other ways cannot change any part of the common law, or statute law, or the customs of the realm' (p 75). Those three categories were exhaustive of English law: 'the law of England is divided into three parts, common law, statute law, and custom; but the King's proclamation is none of them' (ibid). It followed that 'the King cannot create any offence by his prohibition or proclamation, which was not an offence before, for that was to change the law' (ibid).'[54]

10.3.3 Conflict between the monarch and Parliament (pre-Civil War)

The Stuart kings had an uneasy relationship with Parliament. In 1626, Charles I sought to raise money through the use of forced loans. Henry VII[55] had used this practice to gain independence from Parliament. The use of forced loans would give Charles independence from Parliament as he could raise revenue without having to gain Parliament's approval for taxation. However, the imposition of forced loans and the arrest of those who refused to pay led to concerns about the legality of the king's policy. The arbiters of legality were the judges who could give an opinion which the king could use to defend his policy. However, Sir Ranulph Crewe, the Chief Justice of the King's Bench, was dismissed when he refused to say that the forced loans were lawful.[56] Those who had refused to pay were arrested and were denied bail. In the *Five Knights' Case*[57] the court held that despite the writ of Habeas Corpus, that the men should not be released.[58] The Petition of Right of 1628, which was forced upon Charles I by his next Parliament, was a response to the king's policy, as it outlawed imprisonment without trial (which had been the issue in the *Five Knights' Case*) and prevented the king from raising money outside of Parliament. Ann Lyon observed that, '[t]he Petition of Right required the king to endorse the proposition that he could not by the prerogative alone levy taxation, imprison with trial, billet troops or impose martial law . . . Though it has gone down as a key element of constitutional mythology, its immediate significance was small.'[59]

In response to the Petition of Right Charles I ruled from 1629 to 1640 without calling a Parliament. However, the king needed to raise money to finance his wars and to govern the country. Charles I used his prerogative powers to levy taxation through the payment of Ship money, which had been used in the past to raise money from coastal communities to pay for their defence. However, Ship money was now being raised all across the country and not just in coastal areas, in order to fund the government. This attempt to raise revenue using the prerogative was contrary to the Petition of Right. The consequence was that 'Ship money bound together strands of objection and exposed the weakness of Charles's hold over the country.'[60] In the *Case of Ship Money*, otherwise known as *Hampden's Case*[61], the majority of the court ruled that the king could levy such a tax on his subjects in order to fund the navy. Five judges had found in Hampden's favour, with Croke J holding that there needed to be parliamentary approval for this tax. The consequence was that Charles I's rule was regarded as unpopular and the judges were seen as collaborators.[62] Jones wrote that:

> [i]n the 1630s, devices which aroused most opposition were not over-thrown in the courts. The King's Bench, wrote Gardiner, was the 'great prop' of Charles's government. . . . It was as though men had come to fear that a novel concept, that of King and judiciary, was on the threshold of replacing that older understanding of King and Parliament.'[63]

In 1640 Charles I was forced to recall Parliament and Parliament introduced an Act Declaring the Illegality of Ship-Money in 1641. The judges who had found in the king's favour were impeached. This Parliament was known as the Long Parliament and it attempted to punish the king's key advisors. Parliament forced the king to consent to the execution of Archbishop Laud and the Earl of Stafford. Soon afterwards the king declared war on Parliament and started the First English Civil War. By 1649, Parliament had defeated the king in two civil wars and the king was tried at Westminster Hall and executed at Whitehall.

10.3.4 Conflict between the monarch and Parliament (post-Restoration, 1660–88)

Eventually in 1660 the Stuart monarchy was restored under Charles II[64] and this period is known as the Restoration. Charles II's successor, James II[65], clashed with Parliament and claimed that his prerogative permitted him to dispense with Acts of Parliament, as illustrated by the events surrounding *Godden* v *Hales*.[66] In the case of *Godden* v *Hales* the king promoted a Catholic friend, Sir Edward Hales, to the rank of colonel without the undertaking an oath to the Anglican Church, as was required by the Test Act 1673. The king used his dispensing power to remove this statutory obligation from Sir Edward Hales. Dixon noted the controversial use of the prerogative dispensing power by James II:

> 'he used it to systematically dispense with a vast array of religious legisla-tion and rules governing the universities. The was no 'emergency incon-venience' to justify the use of the power other than that there was now a Catholic king who wished to pursue pro-Catholic policies and needed to be rid of the laws that upheld the Protestant Ascendancy.[67]

In *Godden* v *Hales* Herbert CJ gave judgment and upheld the use of the prerog-ative. The decision was not unanimous, as some of the judges doubted the use of the prerogative powers. However, the majority held that king's use of the pre-rogative was not restricted by an Act of Parliament. The judgment was recorded that, 'the Kings of England were absolute Sovereigns; that the laws were the King's laws; that the King had a power to dispense with any of the laws of Gov-ernment as he saw necessity for it; that he was sole judge of that necessity; that no Act of Parliament could take away that power.'

It is interesting to note the reasoning of Herbert CJ:

> To say the King cannot dispense with a law that is made *pro bono publico*, is to say, that he can dispense with no law at all; for all laws are supposed to be *pro bono publico*, when they are first made.
>
> To say that the dispensing with the law may be of dangerous consequence, is no argument at all, for that may be said of the exercise of the King's prerogative in many cases, supposing that he would abuse the exercise of it; none will deny but that the King hath power to proclaim war when he pleaseth, and yet it may be said that he may keep us always in war, and so ruin his subjects.

Herbert CJ did not believe that there were *no* restrictions on the prerogative, but rather that an Act of Parliament was not one of them.

What we can see is that the Stuart monarchs, most notably Charles I and James II, clashed with Parliament when they attempted to use their prerogative powers to govern in defiance of an Act of Parliament. According to Professor GR Elton, the Stuarts, unlike the Tudors, who avoided controversy in their use of the prerogative as a flexible source of non-statutory powers, spoilt the prerogative by treating it as a source of absolutism.[68] This is interesting as this was the last attempt by the monarch to usurp the supremacy of Parliament.

10.3.5 The Glorious Revolution, the Bill of Rights and the Survival of the Prerogative (1688–)

James II was overthrown in 1688 as he had managed to alienate his subjects and therefore former parliamentarians[69] invited Prince William of Orange and his wife Princess Mary, James II's eldest daughter, to become joint monarchs and invade England. This is known as the Glorious Revolution, as James II fled to France and Parliament now asserted its supremacy. The English and Scottish thrones were offered to William and Mary on the condition that they accepted the English Bill of Rights 1688[70] and the Scottish Claim of Right 1689. The Bill of Rights expressly abolished the following purported prerogative powers:

Dispensing Power.

That the pretended Power of Suspending of Laws or the Execution of Laws by Regal Authority without Consent of Parliament is illegal.

Late dispensing Power.

That the pretended Power of Dispensing with Laws or the Execution of Laws by Regal Authority as it hath been assumed and exercised of late is illegal.

Levying Money.

That levying Money for or to the Use of the Crown by pretence of Prerogative without Grant of Parliament for longer time or in other manner then the same is or shall be granted is Illegal.

The Bill of Rights reversed the decision in *Godden v Hales* as the prerogative could not dispense with Acts of Parliament. This meant that the prerogative could not used to dissapply an Act of Parliament if the king disagreed with it. The prerogative could not be used to raise money and this removed the monarch's power to try to rule without Parliament, as the monarch would be solely reliant on Parliament to fund td government. The Bill of Rights also made it a legal requirement for the regular summoning of Parliament:

Frequent Parliaments.

And that for Redress of all Grievances and for the amending strengthening and preserving of the Laws Parliaments ought to be held frequently.

This limited the prerogative power to decide whether or not to summon a Parliament. The Triennial Act 1694 established that Parliament must meet every year and that the lifetime of each Parliament was limited to three years. This removed the power of the monarch to refuse to summon a Parliament. Today the power of the monarch over Parliament has been further reduced by the Fixed-term Parliaments Act 2011, which removes the ability of the monarch to dissolve Parliament using her prerogative powers. The lifetime of Parliament is fixed at five years and at the expiry of this period it will be dissolved.

The new Parliament abolished some of the prerogative powers and replaced others with Acts of Parliament. The monarchy was preserved because the rule of Parliament and the Lord Protector (exercising both the legislature and executive functions during the Commonwealth) had been unpopular. There were many who favoured the return of a monarch as head of the executive, who would have responsibility for diplomacy and war. One such supporter of this separation of powers was John Locke, who argued that '[w]here the legislative and executive power are in distinct hands (as they are in all moderated monarchies and well-framed governments) there the good of the society requires that several things should be left to the discretion of him that has the executive power.'[71] Locke defended the use of discretionary powers by noting that the legislature could not predict what laws would be needed in the future for the good of the population. This discretionary power to act 'for the public good' was defined by Locke as the prerogative.

As the prerogative powers are used at the discretion of the executive without parliamentary approval and accountability, why did Parliament simply not abolish all the prerogative powers? The answer is that the executive needed discretionary powers to act, and that soon parliamentarians would form part of the executive. This was because the monarchs soon stopped making day-to-day decisions concerning the running of the country and surrendered their day-to-day powers to the Cabinet. This means that the government had little to gain from surrendering the prerogative powers and Parliament little choice, given the dominance of the legislative branch by the executive, in legislating to abolish them. According to Professor Munro, '[i]t is not surprising that modern governments have found it useful to retain such broad discretionary powers to act, which enable action to be taken without the necessity of prior parliamentary approval.'[72] The prerogative ceased to become contentious as the remaining prerogative powers of the monarch were controlled by convention, and the majority of the powers were exercised by the government, which itself had to command the confidence of the House of Commons.

10.4 The prerogative today

We will now look at how the prerogative is exercised today. This will involve looking at the composition and function of the Privy Council. We will then look at who exercises the prerogative and the different categories of prerogative powers.

10.5 The Queen in Council or Privy Council

The Privy Council was the mechanism that was used by the monarch to govern the country. Prior to the creation of Cabinet government, the business of government would be conducted by the Privy Council. Today, whilst the Privy Council still exists, it is through the Cabinet and government departments that

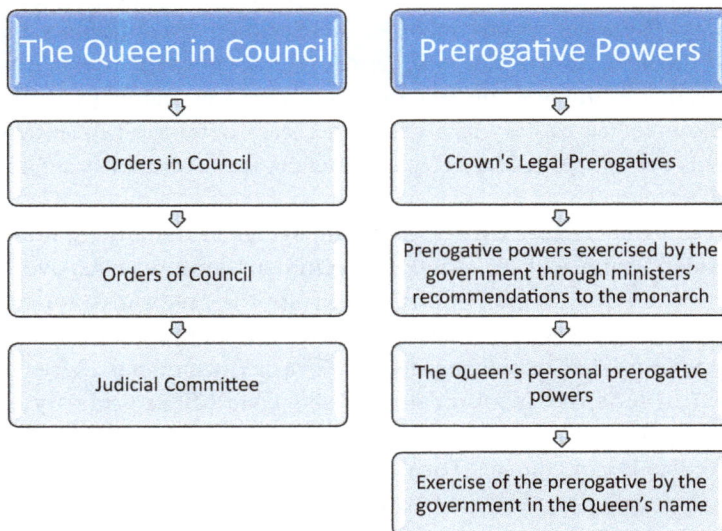

Figure 10.3
Who exercises the prerogative powers today?

the executive runs the country and consequentially the bulk of government business is done outside of the Privy Council. However, some governmental business is still conducted through the Privy Council and this means that those Privy Counsellors, who are members of the government, will advise the monarch on how to use her prerogative powers. The Lord President who is a member of the Cabinet heads the Privy Council. So, for example in the case of the prerogative power to enact colonial legislation, this means that the ministers within the Foreign and Commonwealth Office will approve an Order in Council for a particular British Overseas Territory, and then present the Order for the monarch's approval. It is important to appreciate that the monarch's approval is a formality. During Privy Council meetings everyone including the Queen will stand. This practice originated during the reign of Queen Victoria.[73]

Today membership of the Privy Council includes senior politicians from the government and the opposition and members of the Royal Family.[74] Although members will be drawn from the opposition, it is only those members who are members of the government that will advise the monarch. The Privy Council still serves an important role. Firstly, the Privy Council has a judicial function; secondly, Orders in Council can be made during meetings of the Privy Council; and thirdly important information can be shared with non-governmental members of Privy Council terms. This occurred in response to the government's decision to launch airstrikes against the Syrian state in April 2018.

If the government wishes to hold a public inquiry to look into the events that led up to a controversial event or disaster, then the government could decide to ask a Committee of Privy Counsellors to lead an inquiry. These inquires are *ad hoc* and are not regulated by the Inquiries Act 2005. An example of such an inquiry is the Iraq Inquiry, otherwise known as the Chilcot Inquiry, which was held to look at the decision to invade Iraq in 2003. Sir John Chilcott, who was a retired civil servant and member of the Privy Council, chaired the Iraq Inquiry. The other inquiry members were also Privy Counsellors, but who were also members of the House of Lords, retired civil servants or from academia. Another example is the Falkland Islands Review chaired by Lord Franks which conducted an inquiry into the events leading up the Falklands War in 1982.[75] This review was led by Privy Counsellors and operated as a committee of the Privy Council.

Orders in Council can be made during meetings of the Privy Council. The Lord President, who will be a senior government minister, will oversee the meeting of the Privy Council. Ministers can use the prerogative (or statutory powers) to make Orders in Council. Such orders do not require parliamentary sanction, as Orders in Council require the assent of the monarch. Recent Orders in Council include the appointment of Sajid Javid MP as Secretary of State for the Home Department[76] and the making of three proclamations relating to the specification of coinage. The proclamations were 'three Orders directing the Lord Chancellor to affix the Great Seal to the Proclamations.'[77] Orders in Council are used by the government to legislate for British Overseas Territories as the power to enact legislation for a colonial territory is a prerogative power. The power to determine which laws to introduce to introduce is broad and is said to be for peace, order and good governance.[78] The most controversial use of this power was in 2004 in connection to the British Indian Ocean Territory, whereby the Secretary of State for Foreign and Commonwealth Affairs was able to prevent the exiled Chagossian Islanders from returning home by presenting two Orders in Council for the monarch's approval.[79] The two Orders in Council were unsuccessfully challenged before the House of Lords in *R (on the application of Bancoult) v Secretary of State for Foreign and Commonwealth Affairs (No.2)*.[80] Finally, Orders of Council differ as these do not require the monarch's personal approval and just require the approval of a minimum number of Privy Counsellors.

The Privy Council was used in 2014 to create the Press Recognition Panel by Royal Charter. The panel regulates the press and was a result of the Leveson Report in 2012. All legislation from Crown Dependencies, such as Guernsey and Jersey, must be referred to the Privy Council for approval. This is only a formality as assent will be given by the monarch.

We know that an Order in Council can be judicially reviewed. However, could an Order in Council giving assent to legislation from a Crown Dependency be reviewed by the courts? The Supreme Court in *R (on the application of Barclay) v Secretary of State for Justice and Lord Chancellor*[81] held that the Administrative Court should not have reviewed an Order in Council giving assent to legislation from Sark and Guernsey. However, in certain circumstances an Order in Council could be judicially reviewed and ultimately quashed: Lady Hale observed that there is

> 'indeed a very powerful reason why the courts of England and Wales should not interfere in something which is no business of theirs but is very much the business of the people of Sark and the Bailiwick of Guernsey. But it does not follow that there is no jurisdiction to entertain a challenge in a more appropriate case.'[82]

This followed on from the House of Lords' decision in *Bancoult (No.2)* where the House rejected the argument that an Order in Council enacting colonial legislation could not be reviewed.

ACADEMIC DEBATE
THE CONTROVERSIAL STATUS OF THE PRIVY COUNCIL

The existence of the Privy Council has been criticised. In 2004, when giving evidence to the Public Administration Select Committee, William Hague MP, described the Privy Council as 'the cloak that covers' a number of important activities.[83] Hague argued that the prerogative powers exercised through the Privy Council ought to be made subject to parliamentary control.

Patrick O'Connor QC regarded the Privy Council as 'a dysfunctional body' and there is ambiguity on its own website about what it actually does: '[t]he repeated reference to an "advisory" role, and the absence of any acknowledgment that the [Privy Council] is a vehicle for the direct exercise of constitutional powers is less than transparent.'[84] O'Conner argued that there was no need for Orders in Council to be used, when Parliament could provide an alternative statutory framework to achieve the outcome that the minister wanted: '[i]s there any need for a law-making power by [Order in Council] under the Royal Prerogative? Surely not. Any such law could be passed or approved by Parliament. . . . There is a fundamental question about why government ministers need to have recourse to any prerogative [Order in Council] at all. . . . Why cannot all the powers of ministers to make law be defined by statute, a many now are?'[85]

This is an attractive argument given the problems of ensuring accountability in how the prerogative is used by ministers. An example is the introduction in 2004 of two Orders in Council removing the Chagos Islander's right of abode from the British Indian Ocean Territory. Sir Stephen Sedley noted that this was achieved by presenting the draft Orders to the monarch before Parliament was aware of what was happening.[86] This is a controversial point, especially as the Foreign and Commonwealth Office failed to consult Parliament on the grounds that the Chagos Islanders might seek to frustrate the attempt to prevent them from returning home. There have been calls to list all prerogative powers and to consider placing certain prerogative powers on a statutory footing.[87] The author has argued the power to enact colonial legislation through Orders in Council should be replaced by an Act of Parliament.[88] Sedley has also criticised the fact that the only those members of the Privy Council who advise the monarch on decisions are ministers and everyone is excluded from offering advice, arguing that making 'legally binding enactments behind closed doors without public notice or debate [is] an affront to the rule of law.'[89]

Finally, Ronan Cormacain has criticised the poor drafting and accessibility of older Orders in Council.[90] Cormacain observed that if 'law libraries, on the FCO distribution list, do not have the legislation, how can anyone be expected to access it? . . . There are few non-governmental sources of BIOT Orders. Westlaw has none of the key BIOT Orders. LexisNexis is only marginally better. . . . The top ranked Google search result for the 2004 Order gives a text which has spelling and grammatical mistakes as well as missing out a section. It has only been through making personal contact with the legal team for the Chagossians that I was eventually able to get a full list of the statutes.'[91] The Privy Council's website only contains copies of Orders in Council from 2010[92] onwards and it is clear that there is merit in Cormacain's argument that the inaccessibility of such orders goes against the rule of law.

10.5.1 *The judicial function of the Privy Council*

The Privy Council also has a judicial function which is performed by the Judicial Committee of the Privy Council. As result of the Constitutional Reform Act 2005 the Privy Council is now based in the new Supreme Court building, rather than at 9 Downing Street. The Justices of the Supreme Court hear the cases that are appealed to the Privy Council. Some countries within the Commonwealth still use the Judicial Committee of the Privy Council as their highest appeal court. In these countries the Privy Council will be the highest court and its decision will be legally binding. The role of the Privy Council has diminished over time as many Commonwealth countries now have their own appeal courts. For example, New Zealand created a Supreme Court in 2004 and no longer refers cases to the Privy Council.

There are many practical considerations in having a country's final court of appeal in another continent. In 2012, Jamaica had announced that it is considering no longer sending cases to the Privy Council. One of the reasons for this was that the Judicial Committee, when hearing an appeal from Jamaica, would often have to decide whether to permit an execution. However, whilst the death penalty is 'widely supported' in the Caribbean, 'the privy council has been viewed as the court that prevents the execution of the death penalty.'[93] In 2014, the Jamaican Minister of Industry, Investment and Commerce, the Hon Anthony Hylton, outlined the practical problems of having his country's final court of appeal in in London:

> It cannot be acceptable that I, as a Jamaican citizen, am forced to obtain a visa to visit my constitutionally mandated final court of appeal. . . . The result is that there is no guarantee that a Jamaican citizen appealing to the Privy Council will be able to participate in their appeal by being present at the hearing of the matter. This is unacceptable and inappropriate.[94]

To date the Judicial Committee is still Jamaican final court of appeal. The Judicial Committee is also the highest court for Crown Dependencies, such as the Jersey and Guernsey, which are collectively known as the Channel Islands and a located of the coast of Normandy in France.

10.6 Who exercises the prerogative powers?

We will look now at the types of prerogative power exercised today:

- exercise of the prerogative by the government in the Queen's name
- exercise of the prerogative by the monarch and where the monarch has actual choice
- exercise of the prerogative by the monarch where the monarch has very little choice, as the use of the prerogative is regulated by constitutional convention

10.6.1 The Crown's legal prerogatives

The Queen is the fount of justice and is responsible for the administration of law and justice in the United Kingdom. The monarch has prerogative powers to create courts and appoint judges and prior to the Constitutional Reform Act 2005 this power was exercised on behalf of the monarch by the Lord Chancellor. The

Crown no longer has immunity from being sued in contract and tort although the monarch is personally immune from prosecution.[95]

10.6.2 Exercise of the prerogative by the government in the Queen's name

Due to the United Kingdom's system of Cabinet government most prerogative powers are now exercised by Her Majesty's government. These powers are known as executive powers to distinguish them from those powers that require the monarch's approval or personal use. Therefore a minister will have at her disposal powers which are conferred by an Act of Power, which are statutory powers, and the prerogative, which is a non-statutory power. Powers conferred by Parliament may give a minister the power to create secondary legislation that is known as delegated legislation. A minister can create legislation or use the power provided under the Act to do certain things. The prerogative powers are not conferred by Parliament and the existence and extent of the precise prerogative powers will be found by looking back at the common law. According to Dicey, the retention of the prerogative powers by each successive government, 'leaves in the hands of the Premier and his colleagues, large powers which can be exercised, and constantly are exercised, free from Parliamentary control.'[96] This is a major criticism of the prerogative. Academics, lawyers and politicians have called for reform and we shall look at this below. We will now look at the main prerogative powers which are exercised by the government. As we explore these below, it might be worthwhile to consider the impact that these prerogative powers have on people's lives both within, and outside of, the United Kingdom.

10.6.2.1 The deployment and use of the armed forces overseas

This section will consider how the government uses the prerogative to deploy UK armed forces and to send armed personnel into combat. The deployment of UK armed forces overseas and the declaration of war is a prerogative power. This is an important power and its use could result in civilian and military fatalities. Although there has been no formal declaration of war since the decision to declare war on Nazi Germany in 1939, since 1945 UK forces have been involved in military action in countries including:

- Korea (as part of the United Nations during the Korean War)
- Egypt (during the Suez Crisis)
- Malaysia (fighting a communist insurgency)
- Kenya (fighting a rebellion)
- The Falklands (in response to Argentina's invasion of a British Overseas Territory)
- Iraq (in response to the Iraqi invasion of Kuwait)

- Sierra Leone (to restore order on behalf of the United Nations during the civil war)
- Afghanistan (in response to the Al Qaeda attacks on the United States in 2001)
- Iraq (concerns that Iraq had weapons of mass destruction)
- Libya (to protect the inhabitants of Benghazi from harm)

The legality of United Kingdom involvement in each conflict is often questionable.[97] Because the deployment and use of military personnel and using military force is a prerogative power, then government does not require parliamentary approval for military action, although an Act of Parliament is required to maintain the armed forces. This requirement was a result of the monarch's use of a standing army against Parliament in the 1640s and King James II's attempt to consolidate power in the 1680s. The legal status of the UK armed

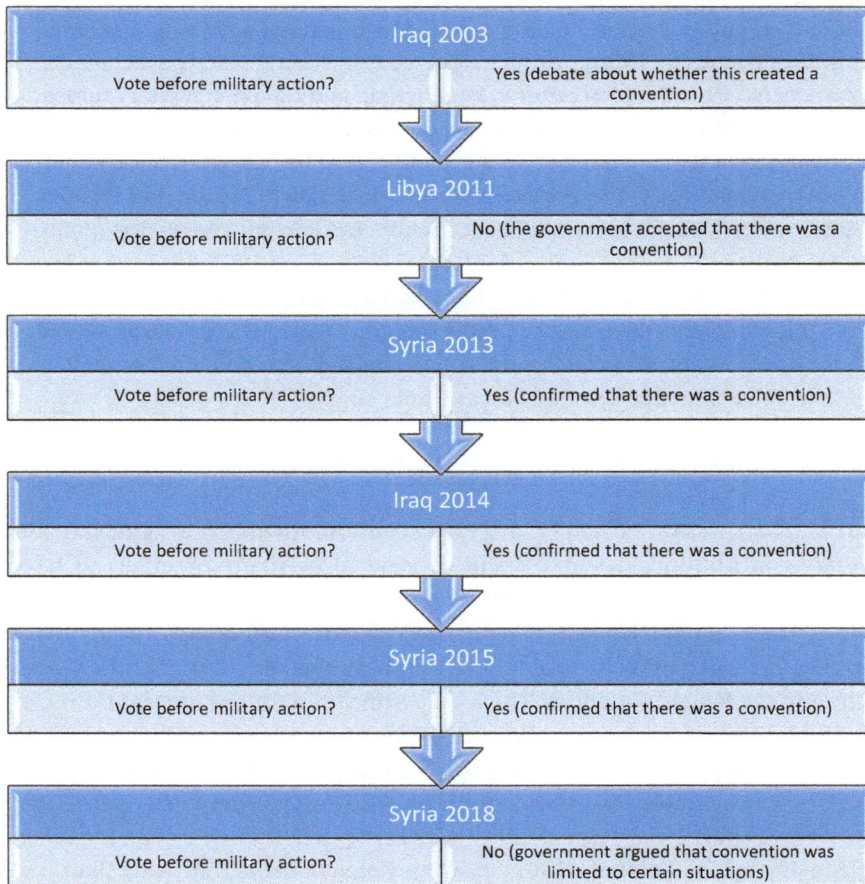

Figure 10.4
Votes in the House of Commons prior to military action taking place

forces is dependent on Parliament enacting an Armed Forces Act. Such an Act must be enacted every five years. The current Act is the Armed Forces Act 2016 which has amended the Armed Forces Act 2006. This is required by the Bill of Rights 1688 which states '[t]hat the raising or keeping a standing Army within the Kingdome in time of Peace unlesse it be with Consent of Parlyament is against Law.'

PUBLIC LAW IN CONTEXT
THE SUEZ CRISIS AND LYING TO THE HOUSE OF COMMONS

Prior to the invasion of Iraq in 2003, the most controversial deployment of United Kingdom military forces was in Egypt during in 1956 during the Suez Crisis. The then Prime Minister, Anthony Eden, had in conjunction with the French, sent United Kingdom military forces to occupy the Suez Canal zone in Egypt. Until the Egyptian government had nationalised the Suez Canal it had been owed by an Anglo-French company. The invasion was in response to an Israeli invasion of the Sinai Peninsular in Egypt, which gave the British and French governments an opportunity to occupy the Suez Canal in order to keep Israeli and Egyptian military forces apart. The government had relied on legal advice from the Lord Chancellor, rather than the attorney-general, as they knew that the advice 'would say that what he proposed to do could not be justified in international law.'[98] The problem was that the British, French and Israelis had orchestrated the invasion and the subsequent occupation. By denying knowledge of the planned Israeli attack, Anthony Eden had lied to the House of Commons.[99] Unfortunately for Eden, the United States of America, whose President Eden had mislead, refused to support the United Kingdom, and this meant that the occupation was brought to an end. Eden resigned on health grounds (as his predecessor, Winston Churchill, had advised him) and the Chancellor of the Exchequer, Harold MacMillan, succeeded him as Prime Minister.

The 2003 invasion of Iraq by a US led coalition, including a significant UK military contribution, has and is still considered by many observers to have been a breach of international law. The invasion was in a response to allegations that Saddam Hussein, the then President of Iraq, had 'weapons of mass destruction' and was capable of using these against other countries, even including the United Kingdom. The legal justification for the invasion was earlier Resolutions of the Security Council of the United Nations.[100] The decision of then Prime Minister, Tony Blair, to join the United States led invasion of Iraq is of considerable importance from a constitutional perspective. The first is collective ministerial responsibility which requires that decisions are taken collectively by the Cabinet. However, there were concerns that Tony Blair had not allowed the Cabinet to have a full role in the decision making process and had taken the decision to assist the United States outside of Cabinet. This includes the use of the attorney-general's legal advice and the non-disclosure of opinion that was contrary to Lord Goldsmith's opinion.[101] The second is that many commentators had argued that the decision to permit the House of Commons to vote prior to military action taking place created a new constitutional convention.

Did the House of Commons' vote in 2003 over Iraq create a constitutional convention?

A constitutional convention is a non-legal rule of the constitution and the only consequences for breaching a constitutional convention would be political as opposed to legal.[102] Two of his key Cabinet colleagues, Robin Cook MP and Jack Straw MP, persuaded Tony Blair to hold the vote. It is important to appreciate that there was no lawful or constitutional reason to hold the vote, as the prerogative power to go to war can be exercised independently of Parliament. The government won the vote and UK forces took part in the invasion of Iraq. Although the House of Commons voted in support of military action it did so at a time when UK troops were already deployed in Kuwait and posed to invade. This led to suggestions that MPs might have felt pressured to vote to support the government, despite the significant amount of opposition to the invasion amongst the UK population. As there was no legal requirement for the vote, at the time some observers believed that the vote might have created a new constitutional convention.[103] If this was the case, then it meant that in the future, a government would be *obliged* to seek the support of the House of Commons before formally engaging in military action.

The Arab Spring and the emergence of an accepted constitutional convention

In 2011, the Arab Spring began in Tunisia and quickly led to popular uprisings in many countries in the Middle East and North Africa. In Libya there was an uprising against the Libyan regime which attempted to use military force to crush the rebels. In response to the likelihood of a humanitarian disaster should the Libyan regime's forces capture the rebel stronghold of Benghazi, countries including the US, France and the UK used military force to halt the advance of the regime's military forces. The then UK Prime Minister, David Cameron, held a vote in the House of Commons *after* UK forces had been deployed in Libya to gain parliamentary support. The government won the motion. The Cabinet Manual confirmed that there was now such a convention: '[i]n 2011, the Government acknowledged that a convention had developed in Parliament that before troops were committed the House of Commons should have an opportunity to debate the matter and said that it proposed to observe that convention except when there was an emergency and such action would not be appropriate.'

As a consequence of the Arab Spring there had been an uprising in Syria and by 2013 the country was in a state of civil war. The Syrian regime were accused of breaking international law by using chemical weapons against its own population. The US, France and the UK intended to launch airstrikes against the Syrian regime in response to this breach of international law. The House of Commons was given the opportunity to vote on whether to support military involvement in Syria. The vote took place before military action had commenced. The government lost the vote and David Cameron announced that he respected the decision. The decision to permit the House of Commons to vote in 2013 reinforced the view that there is now a clearly established constitutional convention requiring the House of Commons to vote before committing British forces to military action. Gavin Phillipson has set out a persuasive argument for the clear existence of a convention and used Sir Ivor Jennings' three-stage test to establish that there was now an established rule that the government must hold a vote in the House of Commons.[104] It is important to appreciate that the convention does not apply to emergency situations where it is necessary to use military force before consulting the House of Commons, nor does it cover the deployment of special forces. Finally, there were subsequent votes in the House of Commons to authorise taking military action in Iraq against the Islamic State in 2014 and Syria in 2015. It would appear that the prerogative power of the use of military force had been made more accountable by the development of an accepted constitutional convention.

The decision in 2018 to not to seek the House of Commons' approval before taking military action in Syria

In April 2018 chemical weapons were used against Syria citizens by the Syrian government. In response, Donald Trump, the President of the United States, together with the UK and France, used military force to destroy facilities in Syria that were connected to chemical weapons. The use of force was restricted to missiles and airstrikes. Theresa May, the UK Prime Minister, did not summon the House of Commons to vote on whether to authorise the use of military force. This was a departure from the approach of her predecessor, David Cameron, who as Prime Minister had sought the approval of the House of Commons on four occasions, albeit unsuccessfully in 2013. Until 2018, it appeared that there was an established convention that would require a vote prior to military action taking place. In 2018, the military action had been in response to the use of chemical weapons, and the use of such weapons breached international law. It is important to appreciate that based on the convention as it was understood after the government lost the vote on launching similar airstrikes in 2013 that a vote should have been held prior to the airstrikes. In both instances the airstrikes were in response to the use of chemical weapons.

CURRENT DEVELOPMENTS
THE DEBATE SURROUNDING THE WAR PREROGATIVE AFTER SYRIA

Prior to the UK taking part in military action against the Syrian regime in 2018, the former Prime Minister, Tony Blair, drew a distinction between ground forces and airstrikes being used:

Interviewer: 'Would Theresa May have to ask Parliament if she were to take military action to support the United States in its military action?'

Tony Blair: 'I think in circumstances where the action would be a form of air action rather than ground force action. I don't think, strictly, it is necessary.'

Interviewer: 'Why should there be a difference between dropping a bomb and firing a shell?'

Tony Blair: 'Just because in practical terms, about the degree of commitment, most people feel that there is. I think this is something she can consider. I think if the Americans are prepared to act and are going to act fast, I think ourselves and probably the French Government would be in the same position. We should be supportive because it is important that when chemical weapons are used in this way and the international community has taken a firm position against it, that you have to enforce it.'[105]

Following the decision not to seek the House of Commons' approval prior to taking military action, the Cabinet sought to defend the decision. When asked in an interview, Penny Mordaunt MP, the Secretary of State for International Development, was of the opinion that the decision to take military action belonged to the government and not to the House of Commons: 'Outsourcing that decision to people who do not have the full picture is quite wrong and the convention that was established I think is very wrong.'[106] In a debate following the airstrikes, the Prime Minister informed the House of Commons that:

> Our ability to exploit uncertainty was a critical part of the operation, and that uncertainty was also a critical part of its success. We know the Syrian regime was not aware in advance of our detailed plans. And yet if I had come here to this House to make the case for action in advance, I could not have concealed our plans and retained that uncertainty. . . . I would have faced questions about what aircraft and weapons we were planning to use, when the operation was going to take place. . . . All of this would have provided invaluable information that would have put our armed forces at greater risk and greatly increased the likelihood of the regime being able to shoot down our missiles and get their chemical weapons away from our targets.[107]

The Prime Minister appeared to suggest that the convention should only apply to full-scale military deployments, such as occurred in Iraq in 2003. The Prime Minister stated that

> [t]here are situations, not least major deployments like the Iraq War, where the scale of the military build-up requires the movement of military assets over weeks and where it is absolutely right and appropriate for parliament to debate military action in advance But that does not mean it is always appropriate. It therefore cannot and should not be codified into parliamentary right to debate every possible overseas mission in advance.[108]

The Prime Minister pointed to an exception that had been outlined in 2016 by the then Secretary of State for Defence:

> The exception to the convention is important to ensure that this and future Governments can use their judgment about how best to protect the security and interests of the UK.

In observing the convention, we must ensure that the ability of our armed forces to act quickly and decisively, and to maintain the security of their operations, is not compromised. . . . If we were to attempt to clarify more precisely circumstances in which we would consult Parliament before taking military action, we would constrain the operational flexibility of the armed forces and prejudice the capability, effectiveness or security of those forces.[109]

The Leader of the Opposition, Jeremy Corbyn MP, argued that:

It seems the convention established in 2003 and that is in the Cabinet manual is being tossed aside as simply inconvenient. It is necessary and urgent that the House has the opportunity to discuss its rights and responsibilities in respect of decisions on UK military intervention. . . . Those rights and responsibilities are not currently codified by law and which, as we have discovered in recent days, cannot be guaranteed by conventions alone.[110]

Mr Corbyn had argued that there should be a War Powers Act to ensure that the House of Commons is legally entitled to vote.[111] However, the Prime Minister rejected such a reform: 'a war powers act would remove that capability from a prime minister and remove the vital flexibility from the convention that has been established, for it would not be possible to enshrine a convention in a way that is strong and meaningful but nonetheless flexible enough to deal with what are by definition unpredictable circumstances.'[112]

The debate in the House of Commons demonstrates just how controversial the exercise of this prerogative power is. The Prime Minister was clearly of the opinion that the circumstances necessitated an immediate response and that the element of surprise would be lost if the House of Commons were to vote on the matter, whereas the Leader of the Opposition interpreted this as a breach of the constitution and ignoring a well established constitutional convention. The Prime Minister argued that the convention should be confined to certain situations such as Iraq in 2003, and rejected the need for a War Powers Act.

Academics have previously debated the need for a War Powers Act. Rosara Joseph argued that such an Act was needed due to the uncertainty surrounding the convention.[113] The proposed War Powers Act would retain the prerogative power but require that a vote would be held in the House of Commons.[114] Whether there will ever be a War Powers Act in the UK s a moot point. Gavin Phillipson has noted that as the government is unlikely to make it a legal requirement that the House of Commons would be given a vote.[115]

The government's ability to respond to global events without the approval of the House of Commons is an important reason for keeping this power as part of the prerogative. Although in the case of Afghanistan, Iraq and arguably Libya (from a defence, if not a humanitarian perspective), there was no immediate need to act and therefore there was sufficient time to hold such a vote. Even in the United States of America where it is Congress and not the

President which has the power to declare war, the President still has extensive power to deploy US armed forces around the world and engage in hostilities without seeking prior approval. This allows the President to deploy forces without Congress having first declared war. The War Powers Act 1973 delegates the power to declare war to the President. The President has 60 days to seek Congress' authorisation. In 2004 the House of Commons Public Administration Select Committee issued a report, *Taming the Prerogative: strengthening ministerial accountability to Parliament*, which included a proposed statute, the Ministers of the Crown (Executive Powers) Bill, that would place statutory limitations on the use of this prerogative power.[116] Clauses 5 and 6 of the bill would restrict the use of British forces in armed conflict and the declaration of war with a resolution from both Houses of Parliament. However, no resolution was needed if the deployment of armed force was in self-defence. When giving evidence to the committee in 2004, William Hague MP stated that 'I think that actually should be laid down in an Act of Parliament or in the Standing Orders of the House . . . the power to commit troops to action needs codifying, so that parliamentary approval is required before it takes place or as soon as possible thereafter if the circumstances do not permit such a vote to be taken beforehand.'[117]

10.6.2.2 Making and ratifying treaties

The United Kingdom has a dualist as opposed to monist legal system. This means that in English law there is a distinction between domestic and international law. Because of the UK's dualist legal system once a treaty has been ratified by the executive, it must then be enacted into English law by an Act of Parliament, in order for the provisions of the treaty to become part of domestic law. An example is the Hague-Visby Rules 1968 which were enacted into domestic law by the Carriage of Goods by Sea Act 1971. Foreign policy and the making and ratifying of treaties are the functions of the executive and the government uses the prerogative to undertake these.

However, it had been accepted that Parliament should be allowed to debate a treaty before it came into force. This was known as the Ponsonby Convention and it required that the government lay a new treaty before Parliament. This would give Parliament 21 days to debate the treaty. This, according to the Ponsonby Convention, must happen before the treaty can be ratified. There is now a legal requirement to do this under section 20 of the Constitutional Reform and Governance Act 2010. This has limited the use of the prerogative as there is a legal requirement for this happen.[118] In *R (on the application of Miller) v Secretary of State for Exiting the European Union*, the government had sought to rely on its prerogative power to enter into a treaty, in order to leave the European Union. This is a prerogative power, albeit the ratification of a treaty is regulated by the Constitutional Reform and Governance Act 2010. However, whilst the government does have the prerogative power to withdraw the UK from a treaty and this is a non-justiciable matter and could not be reviewed by the courts, in *Miller* the courts could restrict the use of the prerogative as it would impact on existing legal rights. In an extra-judicial speech, Lord Mance observed that:

> [t]he *Miller* case was not about abuse of the prerogative power. Had it been, then Lord Roskill's dictum that the making (and so presumably unmaking) of treaties remains immune from review would have been relevant. The *Miller* case was about whether the prerogative power existed or survived at all, to enable the executive to alter the processes or sources of law-making, as well as potentially the content of domestic law, in the UK.[119]

10.6.2.3 The power to issue, refuse, impound and revoke passports

The government has the prerogative power to issue, refuse, impound and revoke passports. This is an important power as it restricts travel from the United Kingdom. A citizen can be effectively prevented from ever leaving the United Kingdom. The use of the prerogative to issue passports has been controversial. One example is the refusal to grant the Egyptian national Mr Mohammed Al Fayed, the then owner of Harrods in London, a British passport, which resulted in allegations of MPs being paid cash to ask questions in Parliament about this. According to Lord Lester, in his evidence to the 2004 Public Administration Select Committee, 'it seems to me entirely anomalous that the right to freedom of movement, which is a fundamental right, should be subject, at least in theory, entirely to the prerogative, unregulated by Parliament.'[120]

10.6.2.4 Acquiring and ceding territory

The government can use the prerogative to acquire and cede British territory. An example of this is the Heligoland islands which are just off the north-eastern coast of Germany. These islands were part of the British Empire until 1890 when the government under the Heligoland–Zanzibar Treaty exchanged the islands for the German territory of Zanzibar. The decision to exchange these territories was unpopular with the then monarch, Queen Victoria. The decision was made for strategic reasons. Another example occurred in 1965, when the UK government used the prerogative to transfer territory from Mauritius and the Seychelles to create a new British Overseas Territory, the British Indian Ocean Territory.

10.6.2.5 The conduct of diplomacy

The government has the prerogative power to conduct foreign policy and can send and receive ambassadors. Foreign policy is the responsibility of the Secretary of State for the Foreign and Commonwealth Affairs, although the Prime Minister will dominate foreign policy by her dealings with foreign leaders (e.g. Tony Blair and Presidents Bill Clinton and George W. Bush, or Margaret Thatcher and President Ronald Reagan).

10.6.2.6 The organisation of the civil service

The Civil Service has now been placed on a statutory basis by the Constitutional Reform and Governance Act 2010 and is no longer organised under the prerogative powers. Previously this meant that the creation of government departments such as the Ministry of Justice in 2007 did not require parliamentary approval. In the United States and Canada the approval of the legislature is required before the creation of government departments.

10.6.2.7 Colonial legislation

The creation of colonial legislation is a prerogative power. This is an important power and is used to make laws for the UK's remaining colonies, otherwise known as British Overseas Territories. The Foreign and Commonwealth Office is responsible for drafting such legislation and the monarch will give formal approval to the Order in Council during a Privy Council meeting.

10.6.7 Prerogative powers that are exercised by the government through ministers' recommendations to the monarch

In reality the monarch has surrendered certain prerogative powers to the government. The government will make recommendations to the monarch and the monarch will agree to these. These powers have been gradually relinquished by the monarch.

10.6.7.1 The granting of honours or decorations

The honour system in the United Kingdom has been controversial as the choice of which individuals would receive honours was made by the government. The honour system is contentious as it was seen as a way to reward political allies. Recently, there has been an attempt to open up the honour system by allowing individuals to recommend local people who have served their community. The Honours and Appointments Secretariat was established in 2008 and it recommends the granting of honours to the Prime Minister, who will then make a recommendation to the monarch. Some honours are at the personal gift of the monarch and are not granted on the advice of ministers; these include the Order of the Garter.

10.6.7.2 The prerogative of mercy

The prerogative of mercy is used to grant pardons to those who have been convicted of criminal offences. In December 2013, Alan Turing, an important mathematician during the 1940s and 1950s who is most famously credited with breaking the Enigma code in the Second World War, was pardoned for a criminal conviction in the 1950s. Turing had been chemically castrated after choosing to undergo this medical procedure as an alternative to a custodial sentence. The conviction related to homosexual activity and the offence under which Turing was convicted is now obsolete.

10.6.7.3 The granting of peerages

The granting of peerages is distinct from the honours system. A hereditary peerage, prior to the House of Lords Act 1999, would entitle an individual to sit in the legislative chamber of the House of Lords. Today a life peerage entitles the recipient to become a member of the House of Lords. There have been accusations that peerages have been granted in return for donations to political parties. In 2006, the police interviewed the then Prime Minister, Tony Blair, over allegations that large sums had been given to the Labour Party in exchange for peerages. The House of Lords Appointments Commission will vet the nominations for peerages and ultimately a recommendation will be made to the monarch. Nonetheless, the granting of peerages is very political as a newly elected government will wish to create enough peers to ensure that their legislation is not defeated in the House of Lords. A recent example includes controversy surrounding the Prime Minister's nomination of ten new Conservative peers to ensure that the government's Brexit policy can be approved by the House of Lords.[121] This type of appointment is designed to top up the number of peers representing one of main political parties. An outgoing Prime Minister can choose to put forward a resignation honours list to reward those individuals who have served him or her during their time in 10 Downing Street. However, resignation honours have proved controversial, such as David Cameron's nominations in 2016.

10.6.7.4 The appointment of ministers

In the United Kingdom the Prime Minister has developed from being the first among equals to exercising virtual control over the Cabinet. The Prime Minister will make decisions as to the appointment of ministers. The monarch will authorise the appointments made by the Prime Minister. Since the late 19th century the monarch can no longer attempt to block ministerial appointments. Whilst the Prime Minister could choose any member of either House of Parliament to be a minister, section 2 of the Constitutional Reform Act 2005 places a limited restriction on who can become the Lord Chancellor: 'A person may not be recommended for appointment as Lord Chancellor unless he appears to the Prime Minister to be qualified by experience.'[122]

10.6.8 Personal prerogatives of the monarch that are regulated by constitutional conventions

As a matter of law, if not as a matter of constitutional reality, the monarch still has considerable powers at her disposal. The ability of the monarch to use these powers is now restricted by the political changes which have occurred over the last three centuries: the most important of these being the development of Cabinet government and the constitutional monarchy, and universal male and female suffrage. The survival of the monarchy is based on the constitutional restrictions which have been placed upon the monarch's use of the prerogative. It is important that the monarch must remain neutral and not be seen to endorse or disagree with the policies of a particular political party and that she must use her prerogative powers in a manner that avoids controversy. For example, Queen Victoria's close friendship with Viscount Melbourne, who had been her first Prime Minister, and her subsequent disagreements with her other Prime Ministers was at the time controversial, as it risked the neutrality of the monarchy. The monarch could not afford to be seen to prefer one political party over another, as this would risk the monarchy becoming political partisan.

10.6.8.1 The choice of government and Prime Minister

It is Her Majesty's government that exercises many of the key executive powers in the United Kingdom. However, under the prerogative the monarch technically has the power to choose her own government. Often when people vote they may take the view that they are really voting for the person who becomes Prime Minister, rather than their preferred particular constituency candidate. Thus there is a strong degree of personality politics, as we might vote for a political party based upon the personality and attributes of the party leader. In the 2010, General Election, the party leaders agreed to take part in televised debates and thus reinforced this misconception. However, in the 2016 General Election, the Prime Minister, Theresa May, refused to take part in a televised debate and instead the other party leaders debated without the Prime Minister being preset. In reality at the General Election voters will vote for the person who will become their local Member of Parliament. The Member of Parliament will most likely belong to a political party and the party which can command the confidence of the House of Commons will form the new government. According to convention, it is the leader of that political party who will be asked to form the next government:

- In the 1997, 2001 and 2005 General Elections the Labour Party enjoyed a majority in the House of Commons.
- In 2010, the Conservatives won more seats than the other parties but did not enjoy an overall majority. Consequentially the Conservatives formed a coalition government with the Liberal Democrats.
- In 2015, the Conservatives won the majority of seats in the House of Commons and David Cameron was invited to form a single party government.
- In 2017, the Conservatives had the most seats in the House of Commons, but did not have a majority of Members of Parliament. The government remained in office as the Prime Minister was able to secure a supply and confidence arrangement with the Democratic Unionist Party.

The Cabinet Manual outlines the role of the monarch in determining who becomes Prime Minister. It is clear that save in exceptional circumstances the monarch has no real choice. The key requirement as that the government needs the confidence of the House of Commons. In the event that a Prime Minister resigns the monarch 'will invite the person who appears most likely to be able to command the confidence of the House to serve as Prime Minister and to form a government.' The obligation to advise the monarch is wider than just the Prime Minister as the political parties should communicate to the monarch 'who is best placed to be able to command the confidence of the House of Commons.'[123] However, the Prime Minister has a key role in the process,

> [a]s the Crown's principal advisor this responsibility falls especially on the incumbent Prime Minister, who at the time of his or her resignation may also be asked by the Sovereign for a recommendation on who can best command the confidence of the House of Commons in his or her place.[124]

Therefore if a Prime Minister resigns after failing to secure enough seats in the House of Commons to ensure that her government commands the confidence of the House, then they will advise the monarch as to who should succeed them. In the case of a Prime Minister resigning before a General Election (as was the case of Tony Blair in 2007 and David Cameron in 2016), they would be succeeded by whoever became the new leader of their political party.[125]

PUBLIC LAW IN PRACTICE
HOW MUCH CHOICE DOES THE MONARCH HAVE IN WHO BECOMES PRIME MINISTER?

Imagine in 2017 that the monarch decided that because the Conservative party had lost its majority in the House of Commons, that she would instead ask the Labour party to form a government. As a matter of convention the monarch would be advised by her current Prime Minister about whether to ask the Leader of the Opposition to form a new government. For example, in 2010, the Prime Minister, Gordon Brown, had advised the monarch that he no longer commanded the confidence of the House of Commons and that the monarch should call for David Cameron to form the next government. However, in 2017 the monarch had the prerogative power to appoint Jeremy Corbyn as her next Prime Minister. It would be extremely unlikely that the Leader of the Opposition would accept in those circumstances. However, had this occurred then the Labour government would have been unable to govern the United Kingdom, as they could not command a majority in the House of Commons. The government would have been unable to pass any laws, it would have been accused of being undemocratic, it would have been viewed as unpopular in the press and with the electorate, and finally it would have risked being destroyed by a vote of no confidence that would trigger a fresh General Election. The monarch would have faced considerable controversy and risked becoming very unpopular (indeed this might have prompted calls for a republic).

The last monarch to seriously challenge the House of Commons over his right to choose his own government was George III in 1783. George III eventually backed down and allowed the parliamentary grouping that enjoyed a majority to form a government. The king was forced to do this as no one else would form a government. Even then there was a risk of unrest caused by the monarch's unconstitutional use of his prerogative powers.[126] Traditionally, the monarch had to choose between leader figures in a party that had a majority in the House of Commons. This happened in 1963 when the Prime Minister Harold Macmillan resigned due to ill health. The monarch had to make a choice between two senior Conservative politicians. Such a choice was controversial. The need to make this choice has been largely removed by internal party rules. The Labour Party had always had internal leadership rules, but in 1965 the Conservative Party introduced leadership rules. As a consequence the monarch has not had to make a choice since 1963. However, in our system there is always a risk that the monarch could still be involved in political controversy where there is a hung Parliament (that is, when no one party enjoys a majority in the House of Commons). The monarch might be forced to make a choice between different political parties. In 1931 as result of the Great Depression, George V responded to the collapse of the Labour government by asking the other parties to form a national government. This was very controversial and the king was criticised by the Labour Party. Finally, once appointed, the monarch has the prerogative power to dismiss the Prime Minister. The last Prime Minister to be dismissed was Lord Melbourne in 1834 by William IV. Even then the dismissal proved ineffective, as Lord Melbourne commanded the majority of the House of Commons and was quickly reinstated.[127]

10.6.8.2 The dissolution of Parliament

Traditionally the monarch had the prerogative power to dissolve Parliament. The dissolution of Parliament would result in a general election and the monarch

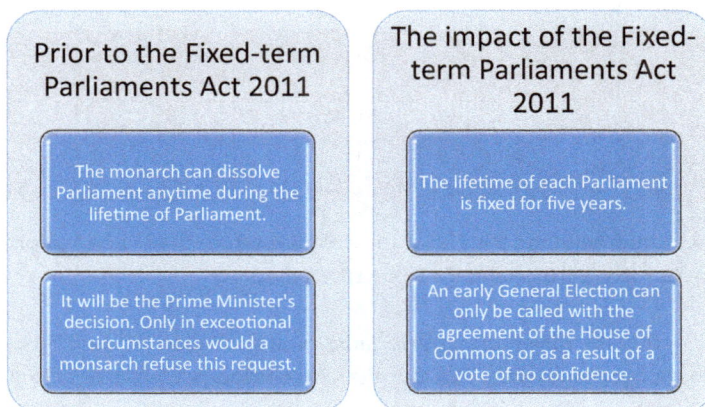

Figure 10.5
Dissolution of Parliament

would then by Proclamation summon the new Parliament. The Parliament Act 1911 stated that the maximum lifetime of Parliament was five years. This meant that the Prime Minister could request that the monarch dissolve Parliament anytime during those five years in order to trigger a General Election. The Prime Minister would request a dissolution where he believed that his party could secure more seats in the House of Commons. It is important to note that the right to dissolve parliament was one of the monarch's prerogative powers and the monarch could refuse such a request. Once again, convention regulates the monarch's ability to refuse such a request. The monarch would by convention grant the Prime Minister his request to dissolve Parliament apart from in exceptional circumstances. The monarch's actual dissolution was regarded as a formality. For example, in 1905 Edward VII was shocked that the Prime Minister, Arthur Balfour, had informed the House of Commons that Parliament would be dissolved because the Cabinet had decided to do this.[128]

The Fixed-term Parliaments Act 2011 has thoroughly reformed how Parliament can be dissolved. The impetus for this statutory reform was the Coalition government that was created in 2010. There was a concern that the Prime Minister could decide during the course of the Parliament to dissolve Parliament to the detriment of the Liberal Democrats. The Act fixes the lifetime of Parliament to five years. The Prime Minister can no longer request that the monarch dissolves Parliament. Instead, if the Prime Minister wishes to call an early General Election, then she must under section 2 of the Fixed-term Parliaments Act 2011 obtain the support of two-thirds of all Members of Parliament. This is how Theresa May was able to call an early General Election in 2017. Section 2 of the Fixed-term Parliaments Act has also changed how votes of no confidence will operate. It is still possible to have an early General Election if the government loses a vote of no confidence, but on if the motion is worded as 'That this House has no confidence in Her Majesty's Government.'[129]

The Fixed-term Parliaments Act 2011 will be repealed during the lifetime of this Parliament. See **Chapter 7** for details of how this will happen.

ACADEMIC DEBATE
DID THE FIXED-TERM PARLIAMENT ACT 2011 ABOLISH THE PREROGATIVE POWER TO DISSOLVE PARLIAMENT?

Robert Craig has considered whether the Fixed-term Parliament Act 2011 has abolished the prerogative power to dissolve Parliament. He has written that:

It is arguable therefore that the dissolution prerogative was abolished by the FTPA.
    On the 'underground' analogy, the FTPA put the dissolution prerogative into abeyance – as a matter of *construction* – but the prerogative would remain fixed underneath the FTPA. 'Abolishing' the prerogative would be like trying to get rid of the ground

underneath Parliament (this is admittedly controversial and is addressed further below). An Act that repeals the FTPA, if correctly worded, would restore the status quo ante by simply removing the layers of law sitting above the prerogative and the prerogative would be 'reinstated' by default.

The vast majority of the time, none of this matters because when a statute is passed, it sits on top of the prerogative, and that is the end of the issue. This time, however, it matters because, on the 'underground' analogy, repeal of the FTPA, using the correct form of words, would result in the dissolution prerogative being expressly reinstated, whatever the FTPA says.[130]

It has been argued that reviving the dissolution prerogative, while entirely legally possible, is not appropriate for democratic and other reasons. This post has suggested that a Bill will anyway be necessary to repeal the FTPA.[131]

Craig's commentary is interesting as it demonstrates that there is uncertainty amongst constitutional scholars as to the legal affect of the Fixed-term Parliaments Act 2011 on the prerogative power. This is not just academic debate, as if a future Parliament wished to repeal the Act, in order to reinstate the discretion once enjoyed by the Prime Minister, then it would entail serious consideration as to whether the prerogative power has been abolished, or whether it is an abeyance and can be used again, or even if it is in abeyance, whether it would be appropriate to return to the situation pre-2011.

The planned repeal of the Fixed-term Parliaments Act 2011 has seen the government propose that the prerogative should be revived within a statutory framework. See **Chapter 7** for more details ('**7.8 The lifetime of each Parliament and the Fixed-term Parliament Act 2011.**'

10.6.8.3 Royal Assent

An Act of Parliament is legally sovereign and is the highest form of law within the UK. However, before a bill becomes law the monarch must give royal assent. Unless this is given the bill is not law and the courts will not enforce it. The monarch has the prerogative power to give or refuse her assent. The Royal Assent Act 1967 prescribes how assent can be granted and there is no requirement that the monarch gives assent in person. According to section 1(1) of the Royal Assent Act 1967,

An Act of Parliament is duly enacted if Her Majesty's Assent thereto, being signified by Letters Patent under the Great Seal signed with Her Majesty's own hand, – (a) is pronounced in the presence of both Houses in the House of Lords in the form and manner customary before the passing of this Act; or (b) is notified to each House of Parliament, sitting separately, by the Speaker of that House or in the case of his absence by the person acting as such Speaker'

In the United States the President can also refuse his assent to bills passed by Congress. Whilst Congress can override the President's refusal where a two-thirds majority in both Houses of Congress votes to do this, there is no legal device available to do this in the United Kingdom. The last monarch to refuse royal assent was Queen Anne in 1707. Previously monarchs including William III had refused their assent to bills. The bill in question was the Scottish Militia Bill 1707 and it was intended to regulate the militia across the newly created United Kingdom by including Scotland in these arrangements. The Queen acting upon the advice of her ministers refused her assent. This is the last time that a monarch has refused her assent to a bill and has given rise to a convention that royal assent should not be refused. Despite the existence of the convention, the monarch has the prerogative power to refuse royal assent. This convention has survived the conflicts between monarch and the House of Commons since 1708.

It is interesting to consider whether a monarch would ever refuse royal assent and if so in what circumstances this would be, and what the resulting consequences would be. The monarch legally could refuse her assent despite the existence of the convention. Equally, an Act of Parliament could not abolish the requirement that the monarch must give assent, unless the monarch gave her assent to a bill abolishing this prerogative power. Writing in the mid-19th century, Walter Bagehot regarded the monarch as lacking the ability to veto legislation and he observed that if Parliament presented her with a bill for her own death warrant, then the monarch must sign it.[132] A striking example of the convention binding a monarch's prerogative power was the controversial Fox's India Bill in 1783. George III detested his government and the bill, but nonetheless accepted that his power to veto legislation had gone into abeyance and was forced to rely on his supporters to defeat the controversial bill in the House of Lords. However, as recently as 1913, George V believed that he could refuse royal assent to the Irish Home Rule Bill. Whether George V would have vetoed the bill is now redundant, as the outbreak of the First World War and the Easter Rising in 1916 made Irish independence inevitable.

PUBLIC LAW IN CONTEXT
WHAT WOULD HAPPEN IF A MONARCH REFUSED ROYAL ASSENT?

Professor Rodney Brazier has considered the circumstances in which assent might be refused and the dialogue between the monarch and Prime Minister beforehand:

We know that the last Sovereign seriously to consider a possible veto was George V in 1913–1914 over the Home Rule Bill, but in the event he fell in with his Government's wishes. What needs to be kept in mind is that no veto would come out of the blue. As part of a Sovereign's famous conventional rights to be consulted, to encourage, and to warn (which might be dubbed the tripartite convention), any objections or misgivings about proposed legislation could be passed from Buckingham Palace to Downing Street, perhaps months before any question of royal assent could arise, and ministerial answers could be given – perhaps allaying royal uncertainties, perhaps leading to changes, perhaps not.[133]

Professor Robert Blackburn has questioned what would happen where the monarch faced an ethical dilemma over proposed legislation:

> What if, after the future accession of Charles III, the new King is given a Bill to sign by the government that he finds fundamentally at odds with his own personal conscience and core beliefs? Such a situation arose in Belgium in 1990, where King Baudouin did believe there was a personal element in the Royal Assent, which as a result caused him to refuse to sign a Bill legalising abortion, on the grounds that he was a devout Catholic. . . . [I]is not difficult to imagine the philosophically inquiring and soul-searching personality of Prince Charles having similar difficulties in reconciling his private beliefs with his public duties if and when he were ever confronted by such a dilemma as monarch.[134]

There has been speculation on this point in popular entertainment. In 2017 the BBC televised a programme based on a play, *King Charles III*, whereby the fictional Charles is encouraged to refuse royal assent to a bill and this results in popular unrest and his abdication in favour of Prince William. If in the event a monarch did refuse royal assent then this prerogative power (subject to assent being granted) could be abolished by statute.

10.7 Parliamentary control of the prerogative

As we have seen above the prerogative is largely exercised by the government. The government will have at their disposal a considerable amount of power which has not been conferred on them by Parliament. When statutory powers are conferred on a minister there is a debate as to whether these powers are needed, the extent of the powers and clear limitations are imposed. It is possible to find the statutory power and see if the minister has exceeded his power. This is not the case with prerogative powers. These powers are outside the control of Parliament. These powers are not consolidated and written down, but exist through precedents from case law and history. The prerogative powers permit ministers to act without parliamentary approval. The House of Commons Public Administration Select Committee observed that:

> These powers are among the most significant that governments possess, yet Ministers regularly use them without any parliamentary approval or scrutiny. . . . We recognise that Parliament is not powerless in the face of

these weighty prerogatives. In the past, it has limited or abolished individual prerogative powers, and has also put some prerogatives on a statutory footing. But these restrictions on Ministers' prerogative powers are inevitably limited. Ministers still have very wide scope to act without Parliamentary approval. Perhaps more surprisingly in an era of increasing freedom of information, Parliament does not even have the right to know what these powers are. Ministers have repeatedly answered parliamentary questions about Ministers' prerogative powers by saying that records are not kept of the individual occasions on which those powers are used, and that it would not be practicable to do so. Ministers have also said that it would be impossible to produce a precise list of these powers, and have asserted that, as Rt Hon John Major put it when he was Prime Minister 'It is for individual Ministers to decide on a particular occasion whether and how to report to Parliament on the exercise of prerogative powers.[135]

The flexibility that the prerogative gives a minister is the reason why the request for a complete list was rejected. However, this means that ministerial use of the prerogative is uncertain. It could be argued that all ministers are accountable to Parliament, but as the government is likely to enjoy a majority in the House of Commons there is little that will be done to hold a minister to account. Parliament could abolish or restrict the use of the prerogative. This is problematic as the government has no incentive to see its own powers reduced.

Furthermore the government is deemed to have the power to do anything that is not prohibited by law. This concept is known as the Ram Doctrine and therefore increases the powers that the government has at its disposal. Ministerial use of the Ram Doctrine is also problematic, as the doctrine states that a minister can do anything so long as he is not prevented from doing so by the law. The use of the Ram Doctrine has been criticised as unconstitutional as it permits arbitrary use of discretionary powers.[136]

Parliament's control of the executive is an important check and balance and the absence of effective accountability over the use of the prerogative is a problem. According to Colin Munro 'the exercise of prerogative powers is imperfectly subject to parliamentary control, and in many – perhaps most – instances removed from the purview of the Parliamentary Ombudsman.'[137] The ultimate parliamentary control is legislation to abolish the prerogative; however, this would not happen unless initiated by the government. Select committees do provide a review of ministerial use of the prerogative, but this can be ineffective as ministers do not have to provide a complete list of their powers. The Governance of Britain White Paper[138] did consider the prerogative powers and provided the groundwork for reforming certain powers. An example of weak parliamentary control of the prerogative is *R (Bancoult) v Secretary of State for Foreign and Commonwealth Affairs (No.2)*[139], where the issue concerned colonial legislation made under the prerogative. The Foreign Affairs Committee should have reviewed the colonial legislation before it came into effect. But the committee was bypassed on grounds of secrecy and the colonial legislation was brought into force without any parliamentary scrutiny.

10.8 Reforming the prerogative

The prerogative powers have been restricted by the growth of legislation. However, the remaining powers are imprecise and unaccountable to Parliament. It is arguable that the courts provide the only effective review of ministerial use of the prerogative. The problem as identified above is that the government finds the prerogative useful and however keen politicians are to reform the prerogative, this enthusiasm does not extend to their time in government. An example is the Labour Party before winning the 1997 General Election which was concerned about the prerogative power to go to war. Jack Straw had argued that, '[t]he royal prerogative has no place in a modern western democracy. [The prerogative] has been used as a smoke-screen by Ministers to obfuscate the use of power for which they are insufficiently accountable.'[140]

In 2004 the House of Commons Public Administration Select Committee report identified the need for reform.[141] The chief problem identified with ministerial use of the prerogative was the lack of accountability to Parliament. Professor Brazier proposed the solution that was supported by the Select Committee. Professor Rodney Brazier recommended the passing of legislation that would require the government to compile a complete list of all their prerogatives within six months. These prerogative powers would then be restricted by legislation and this would increase the accountability of ministers to Parliament. The enhanced accountability would mean that Parliament would have a right to know about ministerial action before the minister acted, as opposed to the current situation where Parliament would be informed afterwards. Some key prerogative powers could only be used with the consent of Parliament, such as the decision to deploy the armed forces and enter into treaties. The power to dissolve Parliament would be made under statutory rules and this would restrict the use of the prerogative. The draft bill that was annexed to the 2004 report presents a major restriction on ministerial non-statutory powers. The government did not adopt the draft bill.

The government responded in 2007 by launching *The Governance of Britain* Green Paper to look into reforming the prerogative powers. This was followed by the *Governance of Britain* White Paper in 2008. In *The Governance of Britain Review of the Executive Prerogative Powers: Final Report*[142] the Ministry of Justice outlined the steps being taken to review ministerial use of the prerogative. The report rejected the introduction of a statutory footing for all of these powers and stated that there was sufficient parliamentary control of the prerogative. The report noted that many of the prerogative powers have been replaced with statutory powers and that they offered much needed flexibility. In this final report it was stated that:

> Parliament already exerts considerable oversight in the areas covered by these powers, for example through the Foreign Affairs Committee, the Intelligence and Security Committee and through calling Ministers to account. Change could only be contemplated after a lengthy and thorough

review, which the Government does not believe to be an effective use of resources at present, given the extensive oversight of these powers already in place.[143]

Professor Tomkins argued that the reforms proposed do not go far enough and that the government cannot be relied upon to reform the prerogative. Tomkins criticised the report by the select committee as ineffective and argues that Parliament needs to act, rather than rely on the government of the day to reform the prerogative. It can be observed that independent Parliamentary action is very unlikely to happen as

[n]o government can realistically be expected to volunteer to surrender (their prerogative) powers: this is not the way politics works. The Stuart kings . . . did not volunteer to surrender power. They were forced into it . . . if the prerogative is going to be wrested away from the government it is going to be as a result of parliamentary insistence, not government self-sacrifice.[144]

10.9 Practical application

Question One

Earlier this year the Prime Minister, Ms Smith, using her prerogative powers invoked Article 2 of the Free Trade Treaty with South Utopia. This triggered the United Kingdom's withdrawal from the Free Trade Partnership with South Utopia. Helene and Sam are legal academics who believe that the prerogative powers cannot be used to do this due to the Free Trade Partnership Act 1994 which conferred rights on UK citizens as a consequence of the UK's membership of the Free Trade Partnership.

Helene and Sam publish a number of articles in which they argue that the Prime Minister had acted illegally.

On 1 July, the Prime Minister invokes the prerogative and signs a warrant authorising the police to search Helene and Sam's homes and seize their computers and any material relating to Article 50.

On 2 July, the Home Office rejects Sam's passport application.

On 4 July, the Prime Minister dispatches *HMS Warship* and 1,200 Royal Marines to Dystopia, a country that is suspected of harbouring several terrorist training camps. Only once the Royal Marines have gained control of Dystopia's main port did the Prime Minister inform the House of Commons about the military action.

On 8 July the Prime Minister travels to Buckingham Place and requests that the Queen dissolves Parliament. The Queen uses her prerogative powers to do this and the Prime Minister subsequently tweets that there will be a general election next month.

On 11 July, Helene visits Mumbai for a conference and is seized by a third country's secret service operatives. Helene's family believe that she was secretly rendered to a remote

British Overseas Territory. The Foreign and Commonwealth Office have refused to offer any diplomatic assistance to either Helene or her family.

Please identify the issues relating to the prerogative in the above question.

An outline answer is available on the companion website.

Question Two

Prime Minister Scott Roland has won a majority in the 2019 General Election and has formed a new government. You have been asked by legal a campaigner to advise on the following five scenarios:

1   Last week, the Prime Minister announced that he will use his prerogative power to repeal the Fixed-term Parliaments Act 2011.
2   Earlier this week, during an audience at Buckingham Palace, the Prime Minister instructed the monarch that she has no power to refuse her assent to legislation, and that if she were to do so, then she would be breaking the law.
3   Four days ago, the Prime Minister authorised the invasion of Blue Island by 500 UK Royal Marines. He later announced the invasion to the House of Commons.
4   Two days ago, the Secretary of State for Defence decided to live-tweet a Cabinet meeting to her followers on social media. The Prime Minister has announced that he is furious as the tweets have revealed discussions in Cabinet. The Prime Minister has made it known that he wishes to appoint General Bob, a retired general, to become the new Secretary of State for Defence.
5   This morning, the Prime Minister announced that Parliament would be prorogued for ten weeks. The opposition parties are furious as they will be unable to hold the government to account.

10.10 Key points to take away from this chapter

- The prerogative has been defined by academics such as Dicey and Blackstone.
- Despite being known as the 'royal' prerogative, most prerogative powers are exercised by the government.
- The monarch still has personal prerogative powers that are regulated by constitutional conventions.
- The prerogative plays an important role in the governance of the United Kingdom.
- Key powers such as the ability to conduct foreign policy and go to war are prerogative powers.

Notes

1 Article 50 of the Lisbon Treaty.

2 [2017] UKSC 5, following an appeal of the High Court's decision in *R (on the application of Miller) v Secretary of State for Exiting the European Union* [2016] EWHC 2768 (Admin).

3 This would only be in the most exceptional of circumstances.

4 W Bagehot, *The English Constitution* (Fontana 1963) 111.

5 ibid 66.

6 The Ram Doctrine will be explored below.

7 See the Cabinet Manual, 'The Principles of Government Formation' [2.9] 14.

8 ibid 2.7.

9 ibid 'The Sovereign' [6] 3.

10 This known as the Ram Doctrine. See the decision in *Malone v Commissioner of Police of the Metropolis (No. 2)* [1979] Ch 344; [1979] 2 WLR 700 where Sir Robert Megarry VC held that the state could do anything, so long as it was not prohibited by law. In this case the Post Office had tapped Malone's telephone: 'England, it may be said, is not a country where everything is forbidden except what is expressly permitted: it is a country where everything is permitted except what is expressly forbidden' 357.

11 The Cabinet Manual, 'The Prime Minister and Ministers' [12] 3.

12 ibid 'The Royal Prerogative' [1.5].

13 ibid [6] 3.

14 AV Dicey, *Introduction to the Study of the Law of the Constitution* (reprint edn, Liberty Fund 1915) 282.

15 Reigned 1216–72.

16 Reigned 1272–1307.

17 Reigned 1327–77.

18 W Blackstone, *Commentaries on the Laws of England* (1st edn, 1765–69) 111.

19 R Blackburn, 'Monarchy and the Personal Prerogatives' [2004] PL 546–48.

20 JR Tanner, *Constitutional Documents of the Reign of James I 1603–1625* (CUP 1961) 5.

21 [1920] AC 508.

22 Examples include the House of Lords in *R (on the application of Bancoult) v Secretary of State for Foreign and Commonwealth Affairs (No 2)* [2008] UKHL 61 and *Miller* (n 2).

23 The origins of baronial discontent were the reforms introduced by John's father, Henry II, to centralise royal control following the civil war between his mother, Matilda. and King Stephen. According to JC Holt Henry II's reign was regarded as giving rise to evil government and 'unlawful arbitrary innovation' (p. 98) and 'he, perhaps even as much as John, was the real object of attack in the Charter' (p. 34). JC Holt, *Magna Carta* (CUP 1965).

24 See Lord Sumption, 'Magna Carta Then and Now' *Address to the Friends of the British Library* (9 March 2015). Lord Sumption was critical of those who placed too much constitutional significance on the Magna Carta. Sumption's account of the limits on royal government provides context: '[t]he first thing that we need to do, if we are to appreciate the historical significance of Magna Carta, is to understand the world in which it was created. Contrary to common belief, the middle ages was not an age of absolute monarchy, either before or after

Magna Carta. It never could have been. . . . Governments had limited resources of money and manpower. They could not govern without the tacit support of their subjects, and the active support of at least the most powerful of them. . . . This meant that kings could not afford to act in a way that defied the contemporary consensus about how a king should behave. One of the key elements of that consensus was that the King should act in accordance with law' (p. 4). Sumption was also dismissive of the view that the Magna Carta was the origins of the rule of law: '[s]o, it is true that Magna Carta stands for the rule of law. But it is not true that Magna Carta was the origin of the principle' (p. 6). Sir Edward Coke took a contrary view and wrote that '[i]t is called *Magna Charta*, not that it is great in quantity . . . but in respect of the great importance and weightinesse of the matter' (Sir Edward Coke, *The Second Part of the Institutes of the Laws of England* [1642]).

25 The Magna Carta was reissued by King Henry III in 1224 and by Edward I in 1297. The original number for Chapter 29 was Chapter 39.

26 J Chitty, *A Treaties on the Law of the Prerogatives of the Crown* (Joseph Butterworth and Son 1820) 104.

27 R Usher, 'Sir Edward Coke' (1930) 15 St Louis LR 325.

28 S Sedley, *Lions Under the Throne: Essays on the History of English Public Law* (CUP 2015) 2–3.

29 According to TFT Plucknett Coke had a medieval mind and changed his outlook when appointed as the Chief Justice of the Court of Common Pleas, which amounted to a 'complete revision of his attitude towards the Crown' (*A Concise History of the Common Law* [5th edn, Butterworths 1956] 243). Coke is often viewed as pro-prerogative during time as a law officer and anti-prerogative as a judge. However, David Chan Smith has put forward a more nuanced analysis of Coke's treatment of the prerogative (*Sir Edward Coke and the Reformation of the Laws: Religion, Politics and Jurisprudence, 1578–1616* [CUP 2014]).

30 (1602) Trinity Term, 44 Elizabeth I; 11 Co Rep 84b. See S Sheppard (ed), *The Selected Writings of Sir Edward Coke* (Volume I, Liberty Fund 2003) 394. For commentary on this decision see D Seaborne Davies, 'Further Light on the Case of Monopolies' (1932) 48 LQR 391.

31 ibid 85b (emphasis added) 398.

32 (1605) Hilary Term, 2 James I; 7 Co Rep 36b. See Sheppard (n 30) 241.

33 ibid.

34 12 Co Rep 33.

35 ibid.

36 (1607) 12 Co Rep 63.

37 ibid 64.

38 ibid 65.

39 R Usher, 'James I and Sir Edward Coke' (1903) English Historical Review 665, 670. The quotation if from a letter from Sir Rafe Boswell to Dr Milborne. The original language has been up-dated for readability.

40 (1611) 12 Co Rep 74.

41 Tanner (n 20) X.

42 (1611) 12 Co Rep 74, 75.

43 The king 'by Proclamation cannot make a thing unlawful, which was permitted by the Law before' ([1611] 12 Co Rep 74, 75).

44 (1611) 12 Co Rep 74, 76.

45   ibid.

46   Tanner (n 20) 174.

47   Sheppard (n 30) 486.

48   Coke, 3 Inst, 84. It is important to appreciate that the famous maxim that 'altho by the Common Law the King has many Prerogations touching his Person, his Goods, his Debts and Duties, and other personal Things, yet the Common Law has so admeasured his Prerogatives, that they shall not take away nor prejudice the Inheritance' was from *Cavendish's Case* (1587) Anderson Rep 152. For commentary see WS Holdsworth, 'The Prerogative in the Sixteenth Centurt' (1921) 21(6) Col LR 554. Holdsworth noted that'[t]he supremacy of the law was a theme on which Coke was never tired of dilating. In fact, it would not be going too far to say that it was of all the leading lawyers and statesmen and publicists of the Tudor period (556).

49   G Burgess, *Absolute Monarchy and the Stuart Constitution* (Yale Press 1996) 200.

50   [2017] UKSC 5.

51   ibid 44.

52   ibid 50.

53   ibid 164.

54   ibid 165.

55   Reigned 1485–1509.

56   WJ Jones, *Politics and the Bench: The Judges and the Origins of the English Civil War* (Allen and Unwin 1971) 70.

57   (1627) 15–28 November 1627. State Trials, iii. 114–39.

58   For commentary see M Kishlansky, 'Tyranny Denied: Charles I, Attorney General Heath, and the Five Knights' Case (1999) 42(1) The Historical Journal 53; S Willms, 'The Five Knights' Case and Debates in the Parliament of 1628: Division and Suspicion Under King Charles I' (2006) 7(1) Constructing the Past 92.

59   A Loyn, *Constitutional History of the United Kingdom* (Cavendish 2003) 208.

60   Jones (n 56) 123.

61   *R v Hampden* (1637) 3 State Tr 826. For commentary see D Keir, 'The Case of Ship-Money' [1936] LQR 546.

62   See Jones (n 56) 129.

63   ibid 19–20.

64   Reigned 1660–85.

65   Reigned 1685–88.

66   (1686) 2 Shower KB 475.

67   D Dixon, 'Godden v Hales Revisited – James II and the Dispensing Power' (2006) 27(2) The Journal of Legal History 129, 136.

68   GR Elton, *The Tudor Constitution: Documents and Commentary* (2nd edn, CUP 1982).

69   James II had dissolved Parliament. The legality of Glorious Revolution is questionable as James was declared to have abdicated when in fact he had not and he subsequently sought to regain his throne by military force.

70   Please note that although the Act received royal assent in 1689, it was assigned to the parliamentary period of 1688.

71   J Locke, *The Second Treaties on Civil Government* (Basil Blackwell 1946) 80.

72   C Munro, *Studies in Constitutional Law* (2nd edn, OUP 2005) 271.

73   Reigned 1837–1901.

74   The monarch's right to appoint individuals to the Privy Council is justiciable and can be challenged in court: *R v Speyer; R v Cassel* [1916] 1 KB 595 and *R v*

Speyer; R v Cassel [1916] 2 KB 858. The reasoning was that section 3 of the Act of Settlement curtailed the prerogative power to anyone to the Privy Council. See Sedley (n 28) 229–31.

75 Falkland Islands Review, Report of a Committee of Privy Counsellors.

76 'This Day the Right Honourable Sajid Javid Did, by Her Majesty's Command, Make Solemn Affirmation as Secretary of State for the Home Department' (2 May 2018).

77 24 April 2018.

78 A restriction was accepted by Laws LJ in Bancoult (No. 1).

79 The British Indian Ocean Territory (Constitution Order) 2004 and the British Indian Ocean Territory (Immigration Order) 2004.

80 For commentary see C Monaghan, 'Show Me the Precedent! Prerogative Powers and the Protection of the Fundamental Right Not to Be Exiled: Lord Mance in *R (Bancoult) v. Secretary of State for Foreign and Commonwealth Affairs (No.2) [2007] UKHL 61*' in N Geach and C Monaghan (eds), *Dissenting Judgments in the Law* (Wildy, Simmonds & Hill 2012).

81 [2014] UKSC 54.

82 ibid 47.

83 Taming the Prerogative: Strengthening Ministerial Accountability to Parliament: Fourth Report of Session 2003–4, HC 422, 12.

84 P O'Conner QC, 'The Constitutional Role of the Privy Council and the Prerogative' A Justice Report, 2009, 36. <https://justice.org.uk/the-constitutional-role-of-the-privy-council-and-the-prerogative/>.

85 ibid 29.

86 Sedley (n 28) 134.

87 See Taming the Prerogative (n 84) 3: 'While recognising that such powers are necessary for effective administration, especially in times of national emergency, the Report considers whether they should be subject to more systematic parliamentary oversight. . . . The Report concludes . . . comprehensive legislation should be drawn up which would require government within six months to list the prerogative powers exercised by Ministers. The list would then be considered by a parliamentary committee and appropriate legislation would be framed to put in place statutory safeguards where necessary.' The Constitutional Reform and Governance Act 2010 did place certain prerogative powers on a statutory footing.

88 C Monaghan, 'An Imperfect Legacy: The Significance of the *Bancoult* Litigation on the Development of Domestic Constitutional Jurisprudence' in S Allen and C Monaghan (eds), *Fifty Years of the British Indian Ocean Territory: Legal Perspectives* (Springer 2018).

89 Sedley (n 28) 134.

90 R Cormacain, 'Prerogative Legislation as the Paradigm of Bad Law-Making: The Chagos Islands' (2013) 39(3) Commonwealth Law Bulletin 487.

91 ibid 504.

92 21 May 2018.

93 P Dayle, 'Casting Away the Colonial Privy Council Is a Fitting Gesture for Jamaica' *The Guardian* (6 January 2012).

94 L Linton, 'Time for Jamaica to Replace Privy Council – Hylton' *Jamaica Social Investment Fund* (4 December 2014).

95 See the Crown Proceedings Act 1947.

96 Dicey (n 14) 465.

97 See Lord Alexander of Weedon QC, 'Iraq: The Pax Americana and the Law' (2004) 36 BLJ 6; Lord Steyn, 'The Legality of the Invasion of Iraq' (2010) EHRLR 1.

98 Lord Owen, 'The Effect of Prime Minister Anthony Eden's Illness on His Decision-Making During the Suez Crisis' (2005) 98 QJ Med 387, 395.

99 J Bingham, 'Sir Anthony Eden's Cabinet Discussed Concealing Suez "Collusion", Records Show' *Telegraph* (2 October 2008).

100 See Attorney-General's Legal Advice (7 March 2003) <www.theguardian.com/politics/2005/apr/28/election2005.uk>.

101 See the findings of the Chilcot Report, which states *inter alia*: 'Cabinet was not provided with written advice which set out, as the advice of 7 March had done, the conflicting arguments regarding the legal effect of resolution 1441 and whether, in particular, it authorised military action without a further resolution of the Security Council. The advice should have been provided to Ministers and senior officials whose responsibilities were directly engaged and should have been made available to Cabinet' (The Report of the Iraq Inquiry, Volume V, July 2016).

102 *Attorney General v Jonathan Cape Ltd* [1975] 3 All ER 484.

103 See V Bogdanor, *The New British Constitution* (Hart Publishing 2009). Bogdanor considered whether following 2003 there was a constitutional convention: '[i]t is perfectly possible for a single instance, in this case the House of Commons vote on the Iraq war on 18 March 2003, to create a precedent' (225).

104 For an interesting discussion on this see G. Phillipson, 'Historic Commons' Syria Vote: The Constitutional Significance (Part I)' (*UK Constitutional Law Blog*, 19 September 2013).

105 BBC Today Programme, Radio 4, 10 April 2018.

106 ibid 16 April 2018. Reported in A Perkins, 'Cabinet Member Says MPs Should Not Be Able to Veto Military Action' *The Guardian* (16 April 2018).

107 HC vol 639 Col 205, 17 April 2018.

108 ibid Col 204.

109 ibid Col 200, referring to HC Vol 606 Col 10WS, 18 April 2016.

110 HC Vol 639 Col 195, 17 April 2018.

111 ibid Col 196.

112 ibid Col 208.

113 R Joseph, *The War Prerogative: History, Reform, and Constitutional Design* (OUP 2013).

114 ibid 186–87.

115 G. Phillipson, 'Historic Commons' Syria Vote: The Constitutional Significance. Part II – the Way Forward' (*UK Constitutional Law Blog*, 29 November 2013).

116 Taming the Prerogative (n 84), HC 422.

117 ibid 9.

118 For commentary see J Barrett, 'The United Kingdom and Parliamentary Scrutiny of Treaties: Recent Reforms' [2011] ICLQ 225.

119 Lord Mance, *International Law in the UK Supreme Court* (King's College London, 13 February 2017) [33].

120 Taming the Prerogative (n 84) 11–12.

121 D Sabbagh and L O'Carroll, 'PM Set to Nominate 10 Tory Peers After String of Brexit Defeats' *The Guardian* (18 May 2018).

122 Section 2(1) of the Constitutional Reform Act 2005.

123 Cabinet Manual (n 7).

124 ibid.

125 This might not always be the case. For example when Neville Chamberlain resigned as Prime Minister in 1940 he remained the leader of the Conservative party.

126 See J Cannon, *The Fox-North Coalition: Crisis of the Constitution 1782–1784* (CUP 1969).

127 S Heffer, *Power and Place: The Political Consequences of King Edward VIII* (Phoenix 1999) 296–97.

128 ibid 113–14.

129 Section 2(4) of the Fixed-term Parliaments Act 2011.

130 R Craig, 'Zombie Prerogatives Should Remain Decently Buried: Replacing the Fixed-term Parliaments Act 2011 (Part 1)' (*UK Constitutional Law Blog*, 24 May 2017).

131 R Craig, 'Zombie Prerogatives Should Remain Decently Buried: Replacing the Fixed-term Parliaments Act 2011 (Part 2)' (*UK Constitutional Law Blog*, 25 May 2017).

132 Bagehot (n 4) 98.

133 R Brazier, 'Royal Assent to Legislation' [2013] LQR 184, 200.

134 Blackburn (n 19) 546.

135 The House of Commons Public Administration Select Committee's Fourth Report, *Taming the Prerogative: Strengthening Ministerial Accountability to Parliament* (House of Commons 2004).

136 For criticism of the Ram Doctrine see Lord Lester and M Weait, 'The Use of Ministerial Powers Within Parliamentary Authority: The Ram Doctrine' [2003] PL 415.

137 Munro (n 72) 278.

138 'The Governance of Britain – Constitutional Renewal' CM 7342 – I.

139 [2008] UKHL 61.

140 J Straw, 'Abolish the Royal Prerogative' in A Barnett (ed), *Power and the Throne: The Monarchy Debate* (Vintage 1994) 125, 129.

141 See Taming the Prerogative: Strengthening Ministerial Accountability to Parliament.

142 (2009).

143 Taming the Prerogative: Strengthening Ministerial Accountability to Parliament, 24.

144 A Tomkins, *Our Republic Constitution* (Hart Publishing 2005) 134.

Further reading

Allott P, 'The Courts and the Executive: Four House of Lords Decisions' [1977] CLJ 255

Barrett J, 'The United Kingdom and Parliamentary Scrutiny of Treaties: Recent Reforms' [2011] ICLQ 225

Blackburn R, 'Monarchy and the Personal Prerogatives' [2004] PL 546

Blake R, 'Constitutional Monarchy: The Prerogative Powers' in D Butler et al (eds), *The Law Politics and the Constitution: Essays in Honour of Geoffrey Marshall* (OUP 1999)

Brazier R, 'Royal Assent to Legislation' [2013] LQR 184

Burgess G, *Absolute Monarchy and the Stuart Constitution* (Yale Press 1996)

Cormacain R, 'Prerogative Legislation as the Paradigm of Bad Law-Making: The Chagos Islands' (2013) 39(3) CLB 487

Craig R, 'Zombie Prerogatives Should Remain Decently Buried: Replacing the Fixed-term Parliaments Act 2011 (Part 1)' (*UK Constitutional Law Blog*, 24 May 2017)

———, 'Zombie Prerogatives Should Remain Decently Buried: Replacing the Fixed-term Parliaments Act 2011 (Part 2)' (*UK Constitutional Law Blog*, 25 May 2017)

Dicey AV, *Introduction to the Study of the Law of the Constitution* (Liberty Fund 1982)

House of Commons Public Administration Select Committee's Fourth Report, *Taming the Prerogative: Strengthening Ministerial Accountability to Parliament* (House of Commons 2004)

Joseph R, *The War Prerogative: History, Reform, and Constitutional Design* (OUP 2013)

Ministry of Justice, *The Governance of Britain Review of the Executive Prerogative Powers: Final Report* (Ministry of Justice 2009)

Munro C, *Studies in Constitutional Law* (2nd edn, OUP 2005)

O'Conner QC P, 'The Constitutional Role of the Privy Council and the Prerogative' A Justice Report <https://justice.org.uk/the-constitutional-role-of-the-privy-council-and-the-prerogative/>

Phillipson G, '"Historic" Commons' Syria Vote: The Constitutional Significance. Part II – the Way Forward' (*UK Constitutional Law Blog*, 29 November 2013)

Sedley S, *Lions Under the Throne: Essays on the History of English Public Law* (CUP 2015)

Sumption L, 'Foreign Affairs in the English Courts Since 9/11' Lecture at the Department of Government, London School of Economics, 14 May 2012

Tomkins A, *Our Republican Constitution* (Hart Publishing 2005)

Walker C, 'Review of the Prerogative: The Remaining Issues' [1987] PL 62

The prerogative II

Judicial control of the prerogative powers

This chapter will

- consider how the courts have traditionally placed controls on the executive's use of prerogative powers;

- appreciate the prerogatives relationship with an Act of Parliament and how the courts give effect to Parliamentary Sovereignty;

- discuss the importance of the litigation in *Miller (No.1)* and *Miller (No.2)*; and

- explore the importance of judicial review as a way to regulate the executive's use of its prerogative powers.

11.1 Introduction

The role of the judiciary in controlling the use of the prerogative power will be explored in this chapter. For over 400 years the courts have questioned the monarch's and the government's claim to have certain prerogative powers, or to be able to use the powers that they do have in a certain way. The Supreme Court's landmark decision in *Miller* could be described as the court following the approach of Sir Edward Coke in the beginning of the seventeenth century, who declared in the *Case of Proclamations*[1] that the prerogative could not be used to impose new obligations or to take away existing rights. The courts have also had to manage conflict between a sovereign Parliament and the prerogative, and have done this by holding that an Act of Parliament takes precedent over the prerogative. However, the courts have only been able to judicially review the use of the prerogative since 1985, after the House of Lords in *Council of Civil Service Unions v Minister for the Civil Service (GCHQ)*[2] ruled that the prerogative should be reviewed. The consequences of the *GCHQ* decision are important and whilst the courts could review the exercise of all prerogative powers, such as going to war, the choice of Prime Minister, and whether to enter into a treaty,

DOI: 10.4324/9780429293498-13

they will not do so – firstly, because certain prerogative powers are not suitable for judicial review and the courts will regard these as non-justiciable; secondly, the court may prefer to defer to the government concerning its use of certain powers, and this may lead to criticisms of undue judicial deference, or in the alternative judicial activism.

In light of the limitations of effective parliamentary control of the prerogative the courts have limited the extent of the prerogative since the *Case of Proclamations*. Effective judicial control of the prerogative ensures that the executive is held to account, but only if individuals are willing to bring an application for judicial review. This accountability is crucial to ensure that executive prerogative powers are not abused. In Chapters 15 and 16 we shall see that the courts, through judicial review, can prevent the executive from abusing its statutory powers. Traditionally, the prerogative could not be judicially reviewed, but as we shall see the courts are now able to judicially review the prerogative. Judicial control is an important check and balance on executive accountability.

The courts have held the executive's use of the prerogative to account. This has been achieved in a number of ways:

- firstly, the courts have upheld the supremacy of Parliament by preventing the prerogative from being used in a way that was either expressly contrary or went against the intention of an Act of Parliament;
- secondly, the courts have restricted the creation of new prerogative powers and have prevented any prerogative powers that no longer exist from being used; and
- finally, the courts can judicially review ministerial use of the prerogative.

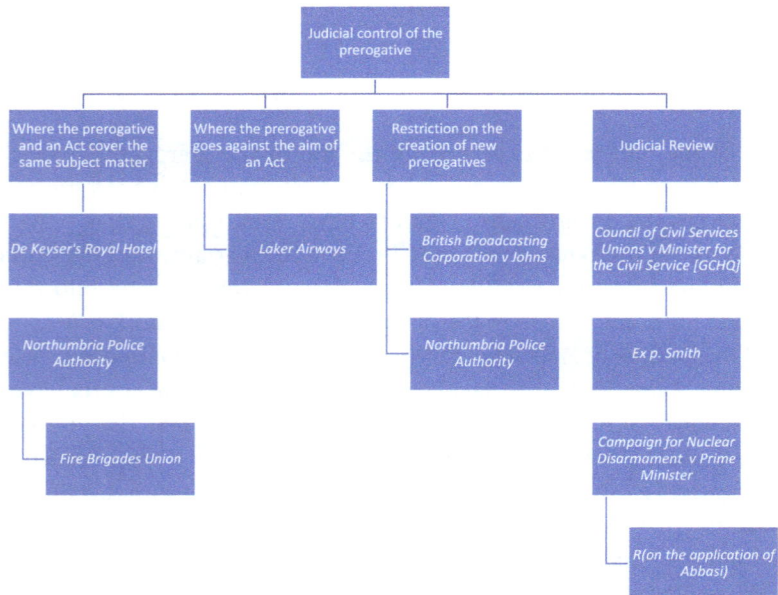

Figure 11.1
Judicial control of the prerogative

11.2 Inconsistency with or covering the same subject matter as an Act of Parliament

An Act of Parliament is legally sovereign. The courts will not allow a minister to use his prerogative power where an Act of Parliament covers the same subject-matter. The courts are giving effect to Parliamentary Sovereignty. Parliament is the highest law-maker and since the 17 century the prerogative can no longer be used to disregard the intention of a statute Where an Act of Parliament covers the same subject matter as a prerogative power, then the prerogative goes into abeyance and therefore so long as the Act remains on the statute book the prerogative cannot be used. The leading case is *Attorney-General v De Keyser's Royal Hotel Ltd.*[3] In this case the government requisitioned a hotel to house the headquarters of the newly formed Royal Flying Corps. This occurred during the First World War. The government sought to rely on the prerogative to take possession of land and buildings for the defence of the realm. The hotel owner argued that they were entitled to compensation under the Defence Act 1842. The Defence of the Realm Consolidation Act 1914 did not affect the ability to recover compensation under the early Act. The House of Lords held that compensation was payable. The government could not seek to rely on the prerogative where an Act of Parliament existed covering the same subject-matter. The prerogative power would go into abeyance, which meant that it could not be used unless the inconsistent Act was amended or repealed. This judgment gave effect to Parliamentary Sovereignty.

Figure 11.2
The issue in *De Keyser's Royal Hotel Ltd*

PUBLIC LAW IN CONTEXT
JUDICIAL REASONING IN *DE KEYSER'S ROYAL HOTEL LTD*

The opinion of Lord Atkinson addressed a number of issues. First, His Lordship raised the fact that the Act imposes restrictions on the executive and that the court must not allow the prerogative to be used to avoid these. Secondly, if the prerogative and an Act covered the same subject-matter the prerogative did not disappear altogether, rather it went into abeyance.

This means that the executive must use its statutory power rather than its prerogative power. Lord Atkinson stated that:

> It is quite obvious that it would be useless and meaningless for the Legislature to impose restrictions and limitations upon, and to attach conditions to, the exercise by the Crown of the powers conferred by a statute, if the Crown were free at its pleasure to disregard these provisions, and by virtue of its prerogative do the very thing the statutes empowered it to do. One cannot in the construction of a statute attribute to the Legislature (in the absence of compelling words) an intention so absurd. It was suggested that when a statute is passed empowering the Crown to do a certain thing which it might theretofore have done by virtue of its prerogative, the prerogative is merged in the statute. I confess I do not think the word 'merged' is happily chosen. I should prefer to say that when such a statute, expressing the will and intention of the King and of the three estates of the realm, is passed, it abridges the Royal Prerogative while it is in force to this extent: that the Crown can only do the particular thing under and in accordance with the statutory provisions, and that its prerogative power to do that thing is in abeyance. Whichever mode of expression be used, the result intended to be indicated is, I think, the same – namely, that after the statute has been passed, and while it is in force, the thing it empowers the Crown to do can thenceforth only be done by and under the statute, and subject to all the limitations, restrictions and conditions by it imposed, however unrestricted the Royal Prerogative may theretofore have been.[4]

Lord Parmoor stated that the court could challenge the executive's assertion as to the extent of their prerogative powers. Lord Parmoor rejected the view that the prerogative could be used to take possession of or occupy land and buildings without paying compensation. As we shall see below, the court's task is one of conducting a historical enquiry to see whether there exists such a prerogative power and how it can be used. Lord Parmoor observed that 'If no precedents can be found prior to the year 1688 of a claim to use and occupy the land of the subject for an indefinite time without the payment of compensation, it would be improbable that such precedents would be found at a later date.'[5]

Lord Parmoor identified the important role the courts played in protecting citizens from the executive's use of the prerogative. His Lordship stated:

> The growth of constitutional liberties has largely consisted in the reduction of the discretionary power of the executive, and in the extension of Parliamentary protection in favour of the subject, under a series of statutory enactments. The result is that, whereas at one time the Royal Prerogative gave legal sanction to a large majority of the executive functions of the Government, it is now restricted within comparatively narrow limits.[6]

This process is important in order for the rule of law to operate as by relying on statute as opposed to the prerogative, there is a consistency of application. Lord Parmoor's argument supports the view that an unrestrained approach to the prerogative will harm civil liberties.

The key point to take away from *De Keyser's Royal Hotel Ltd* are:

- the government wished to use the prerogative to pay lower compensation on an ex gratia basis;
- an Act of Parliament provided for higher compensation under a statutory scheme where land had been requisitioned;
- the court held that compensation was payable under the Act; and
- the prerogative went into abeyance

Not every Act of Parliament that covers the same subject-matter as the prerogative will result in the prerogative powers going into abeyance. An example of this is *R (on the application of XH) v Secretary of State for the Home Department*[7] where it was argued that the Terrorism Prevention and Investigation Measures Act 2011 placed the prerogative power to issue or revoke a passport in abeyance. The court held that the Act inferred no implication that this would happen and to do so was unreasonable and unnecessary. The court held that the Act did not cover such powers and it could not be inferred that it meant to remove the prerogative power to do so. Interestingly, the court considered whether abeyance required an actual overlap between the prerogative and statute, and held that this was not the case:

> A number of other points were made by Mr James Eadie QC, for the Secretary of State, but we are not satisfied they carry the matter any further. He emphasised the extent to which the TPIM Act and the royal prerogative to cancel passports do not overlap, both within and outside the area of terrorism-related activity. He went so far as to submit that there has to be a precise overlap for a necessary implication of abridgment of the royal prerogative. We do not agree. While the extent of overlap is always relevant and important, the question at the end of the day (as he accepted) is always one of statutory interpretation.[8]

It is not just where the prerogative is inconsistent with an Act of Parliament that the court will restrict its use. If Parliament has intended to achieve X by passing an Act and the government's use of the prerogative would undermine X, then the courts may restrain the use of the prerogative. This occurred in *Laker Airways Ltd v Department of Trade*[9]. In *Laker Airways* Mr Laker had set up an airline and wished to challenge British Airways by running a transatlantic service between London and the United States. Laker Airways would require a licence from both the United States and United Kingdom's aviation authorities. The UK Civil Aviation Authority granted a licence which was then revoked by the UK government. The government wished to protect the monopoly of the state-owned British Airways. Air travel between the US and UK was governed by the Bermuda Treaty which stated that each state would appoint designated carriers to carry passengers on each route. The decision to make Laker Airways a designated carrier (and to grant a licence) was made by the Civil Aviation Authority subject to the Civil Aviation Act 1971. Section 3(1) of the Act set out

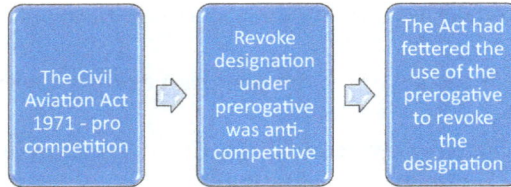

Figure 11.3
The issue in *Laker Airways*

four objectives that had to be satisfied when granting licences; the second of these was to prevent British Airways having a monopoly. Laker Airways was approved as a designated carrier. The government then announced that there would only be one designated carrier for each route and this would prevent Laker Airways from running a transatlantic service. This governmental guidance on the issuing of licences was regarded as unlawful by Laker Airways. It was argued by the government that the power to withdraw a designation was a prerogative power and that the court could not investigate how it was used.

The Court of Appeal in *Laker Airways* had to consider whether the prerogative could be used to withdraw the designation. Lord Denning MR acknowledged that that Secretary of State could have used his statutory powers under section 4 of the Civil Aviation Act 1971 to withdraw the designation. Therefore, the Secretary of State could not use the prerogative here and had exceeded his discretionary powers, which meant that the guidance given to the Civil Aviation Authority was illegal and could not override the statutory criteria that the Civil Aviation Authority should follow.

Roskill LJ considered the question of whether the government could use the prerogative to revoke the designation. The government had argued that there were no restrictions on using the prerogative, as designations were made under the Treaty of Bermuda. Roskill LJ referred to *De Keyser's Royal Hotel Ltd* and looked at whether the Civil Aviation Act 1971 had fettered the prerogative from being used. His Lordship took the view that the Civil Aviation Act 1971 imposed a restriction on the prerogative. This was because Parliament must have intended the process of granting licences to have restricted the ability of the prerogative to revoke them outside of the statutory framework. Roskill LJ stated that:

> The two powers are inextricably interwoven. Where a right to fly is granted by the Authority under the statute by the grant of an air transport licence which has not been lawfully revoked and cannot be lawfully revoked in the manner thus far contemplated by the Secretary of State, I do not see why we should hold that Parliament in 1971 must be taken to have intended that a prerogative power to achieve what is in effect the same result as lawful revocation would achieve, should have survived the passing of the statute unfettered so as to enable the Crown to achieve by what I have called the back door that which cannot lawfully be achieved by entry through

the front. I think Parliament must be taken to have intended to fetter the prerogative of the Crown in this relevant respect. I would therefore dismiss this appeal.[10]

Lawton LJ observed that the prerogative if unfettered could be used to go against the statutory framework:

the Attorney-General was submitting that a licence to operate a scheduled route, which had been granted under statute and after full inquiry by the Authority and which had been made effective internationally by designation, could be rendered useless by a decision of the Secretary of State made without the holder being given any opportunity of being heard or appealing to the courts.[11]

It is clear that the prerogative could be restricted by implication if it was inconsistent with the intention of Parliament. Put simply, the statute was pro-competition whereas the prerogative was used to create a monopoly.

In *R v Secretary of State for the Home Department ex p. Fire Brigades Union and Others*[12] the case concerned the executive's use of the prerogative power and was held to conflict with an Act of Parliament. What was interesting here was that the prerogative was found to be incompatible with a yet to be introduced statutory provision. The issue concerned criminal injuries compensation. The statutory scheme under the Appropriation Act 1994 would be more favourable to those injured than the prerogative scheme. The Secretary of State had declared that the statutory provisions would not be brought into force. The House of Lords ruled that the Secretary of State could not validly refuse ever to introduce the statutory provisions, just to ensure that the prerogative scheme remained valid. Lord Browne-Wilkinson's judgment discussed the approach of the courts where an Act of Parliament and the prerogative are inconsistent. His Lordship stated, 'My Lords, it would be most surprising if, at the present day, prerogative powers could be validly exercised by the executive so as to frustrate the will of Parliament expressed in a statute and, to an extent, to pre-empt the decision of Parliament whether or not to continue with the statutory scheme even though the old scheme has been abandoned.'[13] His Lordship acknowledged that following *De Keyser's Royal Hotel* there would only be inconsistency once the provisions were introduced, as only then would rights be conferred on the victims of crime. What was different here was that the decision of the Secretary of State to not introduce the provisions, which the House of Lords held to be invalid. This was because the Secretary of State had illegally used his powers as conferred by Parliament.

In *R v. Secretary of State for the Home Department ex p. Northumbria Police Authority*[14] there were two powers that covered the same subject matter: an Act of Parliament and the prerogative. The Court of Appeal held that the prerogative could be used to equip the police, even though an Act of Parliament provided the power to do this. The issue that will be discussed below concerned whether such a prerogative power existed, and the Court of Appeal was willing to assume that it did. The fact that there were two powers did not mean that the prerogative went into abeyance and could not be used. The reasoning of the CA will be explored below.

In *R (on the application of Miller) v Prime Minister (No.2)*[15] the Supreme Court had to decide whether the Prime Minister's advice to the monarch to use her prerogative to prorogue Parliament for five weeks was lawful. The Supreme Court held that it was unlawful, and the prorogation was treated as void. This meant that Parliament was still in session and could conduct its business. The prorogation took place at a time when the government were keen to move ahead with exiting the European Union and it could have been seen as a tactic to avoid parliamentary scrutiny. The Supreme Court was clear that the use of the prerogative was unlawful because it prevented Parliament from exercising its legal sovereignty, which meant that as Parliament was not in session, then it could make law. It was also unlawful as the excessive length of the prorogation frustrated the ability of Parliament to hold the government to account. This meant that the government could exercise its statutory and non-statutory powers without being accountable to Parliament for how they used these powers. We must appreciate that the Supreme Court by holding the prerogative power to prorogue Parliament was justiciable meant it fell within the scope of review by the courts. However, the Supreme Court did not reach a conclusion as to what the Prime Minister's motives were for prorogation. The Supreme Court's reasoning is clear:

> That principle is not placed in jeopardy if Parliament stands prorogued for the short period which is customary, and as we have explained, Parliament does not in any event expect to be in permanent session. But the longer that Parliament stands prorogued, the greater the risk that responsible government may be replaced by unaccountable government: the antithesis of the democratic model. So the same question arises as in relation to Parliamentary sovereignty: what is the legal limit upon the power to prorogue which makes it compatible with the ability of Parliament to carry out its constitutional functions?[16]

How significant was the judgment in *Miller (No.2)*? One view is that 'The Supreme Court's acceptance of this expanded concept of what was meant by Parliamentary Sovereignty is certainly a bold step, in so much that it is determining precisely what is meant by, and needed for, Parliament's legislative role within the constitution to be protected.'[17]

11.3 Restrict the abuse of discretionary powers

The prerogative is a discretionary power and traditionally could not be judicially reviewed, although this changed as a result of the House of Lords' decision in *Council of Civil Service Unions* v. *Minister for the Civil Service*.[18] According to Blackstone the prerogative could exist where there were no conflicting laws, but it could not be exercised in a manner that was unconstitutional. Sir William Blackstone stated that '[f]or prerogative consisting in the discretionary power of acting for the public good, where the positive laws are silent, if that discretionary power be abused to the public detriment, such prerogative is exerted in an unconstitutional manner.'[19]

In *Laker Airways* Lord Denning MR had stated that:

> It is a serious matter for the courts to declare that a minister of the Crown has exceeded his powers. So serious that we think hard before doing it. But there comes a point when it has to be done. These courts have the authority – and I would add, the duty – in a proper case, when called upon to inquire into the exercise of a discretionary power by a minister or his department. If it is found that the power has been exercised improperly or mistakenly so as to impinge unjustly on the legitimate rights or interests of the subject, then these courts must so declare.'[20]

Today it would be possible to judicially review the Secretary of State's use of the prerogative in these circumstances, and to apply the same grounds which are used when reviewing the use of statutory powers.

11.4 Decide upon the existence and impose limitations on the extent and use of the prerogative

The role of the court is very important in deciding the limitations on executive discretionary power. In *De Keyser's Royal Hotel* the House of Lords accepted that there existed a prerogative to requisition property and goods in times of war, but rejected the argument put forward by the government that there was no obligation to pay compensation. Lord Aitkens stated that 'it does not appear that the Crown has ever taken for these purposes the land of the subject without paying for it, and that there is no trace of the Crown having, even in the times of the Stuarts, exercised or asserted the power or right to do so by virtue of the Royal Prerogative.'[21]

It is important to appreciate the prerogative, unlike an Act of Parliament, cannot be found easily by reference to Westlaw or LexisNexis. The court when looking at, first, whether a prerogative power exists and, second, whether it can be used in the way argued by the government, must embark on a search for legal and historical precedents. We must rely on non-legal accounts of how the constitution operates, governmental reports and leading textbooks for a description of these powers. In *Burmah Oil Company Ltd* v. *Lord Advocate*[22] the House of Lords had to decide whether the prerogative could be used to destroy property during war, without the requirement that compensation would be paid. During the Second World War the British Commander in Burma ordered that the company's oil wells were to be destroyed to prevent them falling into the hands of the Japanese. The House of Lords held that there existed a prerogative power to order the destruction of private property in times of war, but as a general rule there was no right to deny compensation. The court drew a distinction between military operations (where compensation was not payable) and preventative measures (where it was payable). This was an important limitation on the use of the prerogative, as the House of Lords held that it could not be used to deny compensation. The government responded to the decision by introducing a bill to Parliament, which as the War Damages Act 1965 retrospectively reversed the House of Lords' decision. Lord Reid considered the approach that the court should adopt. His Lordship stated: 'The prerogative is really a relic of a past age, not lost by disuse, but only available for a case not covered by statute. So I would think the proper approach is a historical one: how was it used in former times and how has it been used in modern times?'[23] The approach of Lord Reid in *Burmah Oil* was to view the judge as a historian. This is critical. The prerogative is the remnants of the monarch's discretionary powers and must be restricted to how it is actually used. If the court permitted the prerogative powers to be extended by novel uses unsupported by precedent, then the executive could be seen as creating new prerogative powers or resurrecting long since abandoned powers.

Controversially, in *Ex p. Northumbria Police Authority* the Court of Appeal permitted the prerogative to be used despite the existence of an Act of Parliament that covered the same subject-matter. The prerogative in question was that of maintaining the peace. The Secretary of State wished to supply riot equipment to chief constables without the permission of the local police authority. However, the Northumbria Police Authority contested this. They argued that they had a monopoly under the Police Act 1964 to supply their police force and that section 41 did not give the Secretary of State the power to do this. Section 4 of the Act established the role of the police authority to equip the police force in their area. They also argued that there was no prerogative power to do this. It would appear that Parliament intended for the police authority to supply and equip the police under the Act. However, the Secretary of State argued that he had prerogative power to do this, and the use of the prerogative power was not inconsistent with the Act.

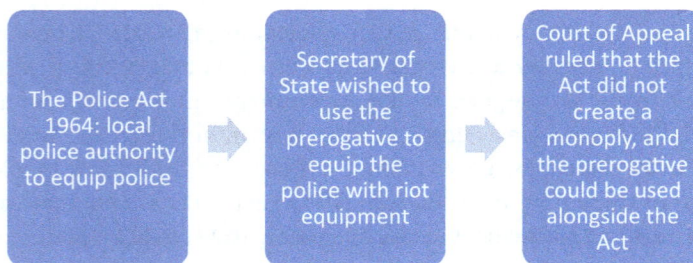

Figure 11.4
The issue in *Ex Parte Northumbria Police Authority*

PUBLIC LAW IN CONTEXT
THE JUDICIAL REASONING IN *EX P. NORTHUMBRIA POLICE AUTHORITY*

In delivering his opinion Crome-Johnson LJ dismissed the argument that section 41 of the Police Act 1964 did not give the Secretary of State the authority to supply the police with riot equipment. His Lordship then proceeded to discuss whether in the absence of such a power in section 41, the Secretary of State could use the prerogative to do this. Counsel for the police authority had argued that there was no prerogative power enabling the Secretary of State to equip the police. His Lordship dismissed this argument and stated that such a prerogative did exist.

Crome-Johnson LJ continued to discuss the argument that the prerogative, if it existed, would be incompatible with the Police Act. His Lordship found that there would be no inconsistency as 'section 4 does not expressly grant a monopoly, and that granted the possibility of an authority which declines to provide equipment required by the chief constable there is every reason not to imply a Parliamentary intent to create one.'[24] Therefore the prerogative power to equip the police would not go into abeyance, as there was no parliamentary intention that the Act would confer the only method to equip the police. The prerogative was not attempting to deprive someone of their statutory rights (*De Keyser's* the right to compensation, and *Ex p. Fire Brigades Union* the right to higher compensation); rather it provided an additional method to supply the police. However, there was clearly a statute to govern the equipping of the police and surely it is arguable that any such prerogative power ought to go into abeyance. Crome-Johnson LJ readily accepted the existence of the prerogative without evidence of a clear precedent.

Interestingly, Nourse LJ rejected the need for a complete list of the prerogative powers and argued that the absence of a precedent should not be fatal. Nourse LJ seemingly rejected a restrictive approach to the prerogative and instead accepted that such a prerogative ought to have existed, despite the lack of evidence as to its existence. His Lordship's assumption that it does exist is supported by Lord Campbell CJ in *Harrison* v. *Bush*[25] and Hood Phillips in his textbook. Nourse LJ observed:

> References in reported cases and authoritative texts to a prerogative of keeping the peace within the realm are admittedly scarce. The police authority relied especially on Chitty's silence as to that matter in his Prerogatives of the Crown (1820). I do not think that the scarcity is of any real significance. It has not at any stage in our history been practicable to identify all the prerogative powers of the Crown. It is only by a process of piecemeal decision over a period of centuries that particular powers are seen to exist or not to exist, as the case may be. From time to time a need for more exact definition arises. The present need arises from a difference of view between the Secretary of State and a police authority over what is necessary to maintain public order, a phenomenon which has been observed only in recent times. There has probably never been a comparable occasion for investigating a prerogative of keeping the peace within the realm.[26]

...

I have already expressed the view that the scarcity of references in the books to the prerogative of keeping the peace within the realm does not disprove that it exists. Rather it may point to an unspoken assumption that it does. That assumption is, I think, made in the judgment of Lord Campbell C.J. in *Harrison* v. *Bush* (1855) 5 E. & B. 344, 353. Professor Hood Phillips has taken it for granted in Constitutional and Administrative Law, pp. 272–81, and so may other learned authors whose works do not specifically refer to it.[27]

...

For these reasons I am of the opinion that a prerogative of keeping the peace within the realm existed in mediaeval times, probably since the Conquest and, particular statutory provision apart, that it has not been surrendered by the Crown in the process of giving its express or implied assent to the modern system of keeping the peace through the agency of independent police forces.[28]

The assumption that such a prerogative power must exist is controversial. Given that the prerogative is used by the executive without the need to be accountable to Parliament, it is only the courts that can constitutionally hold ministerial use of the prerogative to account. Tomkins referred to *Ex p. Northumbria Police Authority* and stated that 'ministers do from time to time claim new prerogative powers for themselves and when they do the courts have not demonstrated great eagerness to stop them.'[29]

The British Indian Ocean Territory (BIOT) is a British Overseas Territory and was created in November 1965 by the prerogative. Prior to then the territory that encompassed the BIOT, the Chagos Archipelago was part of the then British colony of Mauritius. The Chagos Archipelago is located to the south of the Maldives. As a result of the Lancaster House Conference in 1965 the Mauritian Premier had agreed to cede the Chagos Archipelago to the United Kingdom. The islanders had been removed (in an underhanded manner, often arranging on false pretenses visits to Mauritius) in order for the United States to build a military base. The largest island Diego Garcia has since the early 1970s been home to an American military base. There have been accusations that the airbase has been used for the secret rendition of suspected terrorists and that there has been a floating prison. In 2008, a majority of the House of Lords in *R (on the application of Bancoult) v Secretary of State for Foreign and Commonwealth Affairs (No.2)*[30] had accepted that the prerogative power to legislate for British colonial territories could extend to exiling the entire population of the BIOT and subsequently preventing their return. The prerogative power in question was the power to create laws for the peace, order and good government of British colonies. The islanders had been expelled in the 1970s and wished to return. It was argued that there was no prerogative power to exile the islanders. However, the majority of the House of Lords rejected this argument.

It is important to consider the background to this decision. In an earlier decision in 2001, the Divisional Court had held the decision to expel the islanders to be invalid.[31] Laws LJ had noted that the prerogative power to legislate for the BIOT was not unrestrained and there was a limit to the extent of the prerogative power claimed, as 'the colonial legislature's authority is not wholly unrestrained. Peace, order and good government may be a very large tapestry, but every tapestry has a border.'[32] The Divisional Court's decision had placed a limit on the power to enact colonial legislation and had declared the Order in Council to be unlawful. The Foreign Secretary had accepted the decision and the Chagos Islanders could return to the outer islands. However, in 2004, the Foreign and Commonwealth Office had introduced two new Orders in Council which removed the right of abode and prevented the Chagos Islanders' right of return. It was the legality of these two Orders in Council that was being challenged in *Bancoult (No.2)*.[33] Whilst the majority accepted the legality of the two Orders in Council, two judges disagreed and delivered dissenting judgments. Lord Bingham and Lord Mance held that there was no precedent of such a power existing, the power being the exile of an entire population from their homeland. Lord Bingham stated that in the absence of evidence that such a prerogative existed, then 'authority negates the existence of such a power.'[34] His Lordship referred to Sir William Holdsworth who had written that '[t]he Crown has never had a prerogative power to prevent its subjects from entering the kingdom, or to expel them from it.'[35] Lord Mance noted that '[i]t would be surprising if any precedent could be found for such a provision, and none has been shown.'[36] It would appear the absence of a precedent will not be fatal to ministerial use of the prerogative, however important the rights that are deprived by its use.

11.5 The Supreme Court's decision in *R (on the application of Miller) v Secretary of State for Exiting the European Union*

In *R (on the application of Miller) v Secretary of State for Exiting the European Union*[37] the Supreme Court held that the prerogative could not be used to trigger Article 50 of the Lisbon Treaty. Instead, an Act of Parliament would be required to give the Prime Minister the authority to trigger the two year period before the UK left the European Union. The issue was that the European Communities Act 1972 gave effect to the UK's membership of the European Union, and this entailed the automatic extension of EU rights to UK law. Once the UK left the European Union these rights would be terminated and thus, rights granted to UK citizens via the European Communities Act 1972 would no longer apply. If the prerogative could be used to withdraw the UK from the European Union then it would take away rights. The Supreme Court held that because of this the prerogative could not be used:

> We accept, of course, that it would have been open to Parliament to provide expressly that the constitutional arrangements and the EU rights introduced

by the 1972 Act should themselves only prevail from time to time and for so long as the UK government did not decide otherwise, and in particular did not decide to withdraw from the EU Treaties. But we cannot accept that the 1972 Act did so provide. . . . Had the Bill which became the 1972 Act spelled out that ministers would be free to withdraw the United Kingdom from the EU Treaties, the implications of what Parliament was being asked to endorse would have been clear, and the courts would have so decided.[38]

. . .

In our judgment, far from indicating that ministers had the power to withdraw from the EU Treaties, the provisions of the 1972 Act, particularly when considered in the light of the unusual nature of those Treaties and the Act's unusual legislative history, support the contrary view. . . . It would scarcely be compatible with those provisions if, in reliance on prerogative powers, ministers could unilaterally withdraw from the EU Treaties, thereby reducing the volume and extent of EU law which takes effect domestically to nil without the need for Parliamentary approval.[39]

11.6 To prevent the creation of new prerogative powers

The courts will not allow the executive to create new prerogative powers. In *British Broadcasting Corporation v Johns*[40] Diplock LJ stated that:

it is 350 years and a civil war too late for the Queen's courts to broaden the prerogative. The limits within which the executive government may impose obligations or restraints upon citizens of the United Kingdom without any statutory authority are now well settled and incapable of extension.

This is an important check on the executive's use of the prerogative. The prevention on the creation of new prerogatives has been undermined by judicial assumptions about the existence of prerogatives.[41] In 2009 the Ministry of Justice observed in its report *The Governance of Britain, Review of the Executive Royal Prerogative Powers: Final Report*: 'the ban on creating new prerogatives can be undermined by courts recognising prerogatives which were previously of doubtful provenance, or adapting old prerogatives to modern circumstances.'

11.7 Judicial review of the prerogative

Traditionally it was thought that the prerogative was immune from judicial review.[42] This meant that the courts could not review whether the use of the prerogative was procedurally unfair or unreasonable. In *R v Criminal Injuries Board Ex parte Lain*[43] the High Court held that a decision of a tribunal established under the prerogative could be reviewed, as according to Lord Parker CJ it should make no difference as to whether a board was established by way of statute or the prerogative as '[o]nce the jurisdiction is extended, as it clearly has been, to tribunals as opposed to courts, there is no reason why the remedy by way of certiorari.'[44] The prerogative was held to be judicially reviewable by the House of Lords in *Council of Civil Service Unions* v. *Minister for the Civil Service*[45].

11.7.1 Council of Civil Service Unions v Minister for the Civil Service *(the* GCHQ *case)*

The Government Communications Headquarters (GCHQ) is the intelligence hub of British security and is responsible for intelligence gathering and intercepting information. It is based in Cheltenham in Gloucestershire, England. The *Council of Civil Service Unions v Minister for the Civil Service* is known in shorthand as *GCHQ*. It is important to appreciate the facts of the case. The staff at GCHQ had been allowed to join trade unions since 1947. The management had always consulted with the trade union officials when the terms of employment were to be varied. The Civil Service was not regulated by statute, but by the prerogative and the Prime Minister is minister responsible for the Civil Service. The Prime Minister, Margaret Thatcher, wished to prevent employees at GCHQ from belonging to trade unions. Rather than consult with the trade union officials as had happened previously, the Prime Minister in 1982 unilaterally varied the contracts of employment through an Order in Council. In response the trade unions attempted to judicially review the decision, arguing that the unilateral variation was unfair as there was a legitimate expectation that the employees and officials would have been consulted. Counsel for the government argued that whilst the courts could enquire as to the existence and extent of the prerogative, it could not review the exercise of valid prerogative powers. This argument drew a distinction between statutory powers conferred on a minister by Parliament whose exercise could be reviewed, and non-statutory prerogative powers that could not be reviewed.

The government argued that the Order in Council was immune from review because they were exercised at the monarch's discretion, albeit upon the advice of the government, and the use of power delegated under the prerogative, such still be regarded as an exercise of the monarch's prerogative power.[46] The House of Lords rejected the argument that there was a distinction between statutory and non-statutory powers for the purpose of judicial review.

PUBLIC LAW IN CONTEXT
THE JUDICIAL REASONING IN *GCHQ*

Lord Fraser held that, 'I am unable to see why the words conferring the same powers should be construed differently merely because their source was an Order in Council made under the prerogative.'[47] The concluding paragraphs of Lord Scarman's judgment succinctly sum up the importance of the House of Lords' decision in the evolution of judicial control and now review of the prerogative:

> I believe that the law relating to judicial review has now reached the stage where it can be said with confidence that, if the subject matter in respect of which prerogative power is exercised is justiciable, that is to say if it is a matter upon which the court can adjudicate, the exercise of the power is subject to review in accordance with the principles developed in respect of the review of the exercise of statutory power. Without usurping the role of legal historian, for which I claim no special qualification, *I would observe that the royal prerogative has always been regarded as part of the common law,* and that Sir Edward Coke had no doubt that it was subject to the common law. . . . It is, of course, beyond doubt that in Coke's time and thereafter *judicial review of the exercise of prerogative power was limited to inquiring into whether a particular power existed and, if it did, into its extent. . . . But this limitation has now gone,* overwhelmed by the developing modern law of judicial review. . . . Just as ancient restrictions in the law relating to the prerogative writs and orders have not prevented the courts from extending the requirement of natural justice, namely the duty to act fairly, so that it is required of a purely administrative act, so also has the modern law, a vivid sketch of which my noble and learned friend Lord Diplock has included in his speech, extended the range of judicial review in respect of the exercise of prerogative power. *Today, therefore, the controlling factor in determining whether the exercise of prerogative power is subject to judicial review is not its source but its subject matter.*[48]

Lord Diplock acknowledged that the prerogative powers could be quite mundane and yet so important as 'they extend to matters so vital to the survival and welfare of the nation as the conduct of relations with foreign states and – what lies at the heart of the present case – the defence of the realm against potential enemies.'[49] His Lordship stated that he could 'see no reason why simply because a decision-making power is derived from a common law and not a statutory source, it should *for that reason only* be immune from judicial review.'[50]

Lord Roskill held certain prerogative powers to be non-justiciable. These included defence, foreign policy, ministerial appointments and the dissolution of Parliament. Lord Roskill had stated:

> *I do not think that that right of challenge can be unqualified.* It must, I think, depend upon the subject matter of the prerogative power which is exercised. Many examples were given during the argument of prerogative powers which as at present advised I do not think could properly be made the subject of judicial review. *Prerogative powers such as those relating to the making of treaties, the defence of the realm, the prerogative of mercy, the grant of honours, the dissolution of Parliament and the appointment of ministers as well as others are not, I think, susceptible to judicial review because their nature and subject matter are such as not to be amenable to the judicial process.* The courts are not the place wherein to determine whether a treaty should be concluded or the armed forces disposed in a particular manner or Parliament dissolved on one date rather than another.[51]

It is important to appreciate that as a result of the landmark decision in *GCHQ* the prerogative was held to be reviewable, certain prerogative powers were considered by Lord Roskill to be non-justiciable (i.e. non-reviewable). The reason is that the courts did regard themselves as being able to review decisions such as national security. These decisions were best taken by the executive and not the courts. This meant that the decision in *GCHQ* still demonstrated that the judges were deferential to the executive. This self-imposed restriction demonstrates that Lord Roskill was aware that the courts lacked the expertise and the constitutional position to review whether Ms X was a suitable choice of minister. The monarch when acting on the Prime Minister's recommendation is best placed to decide this sort of decision. The decision to enter into a treaty with country Y is also arguably best decided by the Foreign Secretary and not by the courts. The decision to go to war or deploy forces abroad would be difficult for the courts to review. The theory of the separation of powers is based on the executive taking such decisions and not the judiciary. The ministerial use of the prerogative could be reviewed to see whether its exercise was unfair. On the facts the House of Lords held that breach of the legitimate expectation of the employees at GCHQ could be justified because of national security considerations.

The idea that certain prerogative powers should not be reviewed on the basis of institutional competence is important. This is a point addressed extra-judicially by Lord Mance:

> [t]he courts have an important role in ensuring the legality and propriety of executive action, at home and abroad. They can never be primary decision-makers. It is the function of the executive to decide and to administer, and the executive is in many respects much better placed to judge on the necessity or appropriateness of action at the international level.[52]

11.7.2 *Post* GCHQ

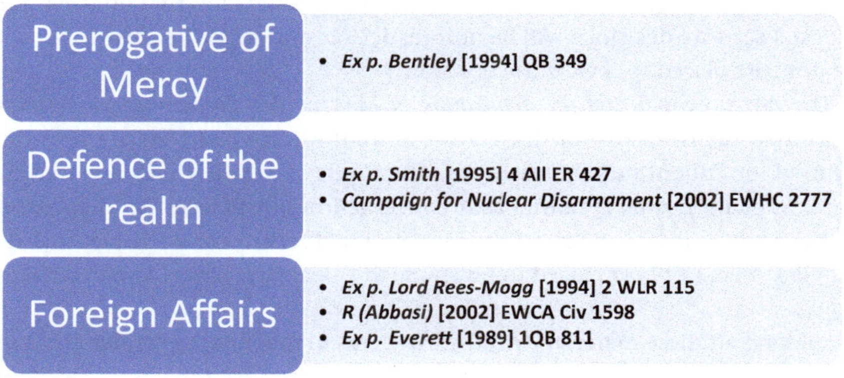

Prerogative of Mercy	• *Ex p. Bentley* [1994] QB 349
Defence of the realm	• *Ex p. Smith* [1995] 4 All ER 427 • *Campaign for Nuclear Disarmament* [2002] EWHC 2777
Foreign Affairs	• *Ex p. Lord Rees-Mogg* [1994] 2 WLR 115 • *R (Abbasi)* [2002] EWCA Civ 1598 • *Ex p. Everett* [1989] 1QB 811

Figure 11.5
The review of the prerogative post *GCHQ*

Commenting shortly after the decision Clive Walker observed,

> [t]hus, on the one hand, their Lordships readily concluded that the exercise of prerogative powers is now subject to review, but, on the other hand, their judgments went to equal pains to cordon off from review many of the important and frequent usages of those powers. The most explicit champion of the cause of judicial self-abnegation was Lord Roskill.[53]

Whilst *GCHQ* is an important case in terms of making the executive accountable, judicial decisions since then have encroached upon Lord Roskill's reserved list of non-justiciable prerogative powers.

11.7.2.1 Prerogative of mercy

In *GCHQ* the prerogative of mercy was held to be non-justiciable. In *R v. Secretary of State for the Home Department ex p. Bentley*[54] the Divisional Court held that the prerogative of mercy was justiciable (i.e. reviewable). This case concerned the refusal of the Secretary of State to grant a posthumous pardon to the Mr Bentley, who had been executed after being convicted of murdering a police officer in 1952. Watkins LJ held that the prerogative of mercy could be reviewed as Lord Roskill's list of non-justiciable prerogatives was only *obiter*.

11.7.2.2 Defence of the realm

In *R v. Ministry of Defence ex p. Smith*[55] the Ministry of Defence dismissed members of the armed forces because they were homosexual. This dismissal had occurred under a policy made under the prerogative. The Ministry of Defence had argued that the policy was non-justiciable because it was connected to the defence of the realm. This argument was rejected by the Divisional Court which reviewed the policy. Simon Brown LJ held that 'only cases involving national security properly so called and where in addition the courts really do lack the expertise or material to form a judgment on the point at issue' would be non-justiciable.[56] The decision in *Ex p. Smith* demonstrates that only genuine national security decisions will be non-justiciable and this is because the courts are not best placed to review the decision.

The decision in *R (on the application of Marchiori) v Environmental Agency*[57] concerned the discharge of nuclear waste from Ministry of Defence sites that are used for Trident nuclear warheads. The Court of Appeal were clear that the decision could not be reviewed as it concerned national security. The reasons for this were based on the importance of national security and the fact that the judiciary were not best placed to review such a decision. Laws LJ argued that:

> Taking all these materials together, it seems to me, first, to be plain that *the law of England will not contemplate what may be called a merits review of any honest decision of government upon matters of national defence policy.* Without going into other cases which a full discussion might require, I consider

that there is more than one reason for this. The first, and most obvious, is that *the court is unequipped to judge such merits or demerits*. The second touches more closely the relationship between the elected and unelected arms of government. The graver a matter of State and the more widespread its possible effects, the more respect will be given, within the framework of the constitution, to the democracy to decide its outcome. *The defence of the realm, which is the Crown's first duty, is the paradigm of so grave a matter. Potentially such a thing touches the security of everyone; and everyone will look to the government they have elected for wise and effective decisions.* Of course they may or may not be satisfied, and their satisfaction or otherwise will sound in the ballot-box. There is not, and cannot be, any expectation that the unelected judiciary play any role in such questions, remotely comparable to that of government.[58]

The decision demonstrates the limitations on judicial review regarding national security matters. A similar outcome was reached when the decision to invade Iraq in 2003 was challenged by the Campaign for Nuclear Disarmament pressure group, who sought judicial review as to whether the UN Resolution 1441 permitted military invasion. In *Campaign for Nuclear Disarmament v Prime Minister of the United Kingdom*[59] the court held that foreign affairs and the deployment of British forces were non-justiciable. The court stated that these were forbidden areas (although whether they were justiciable was based on the subject-matter) and the government had the expertise in taking the decision to deploy British forces.

11.7.2.3 Colonial legislation

In *Bancoult (No.2)*[60] the government had argued that colonial legislation made through an Order in Council was not reviewable as it had equivalence to primary legislation. The House of Lords dismissed the government's argument and held that it could be reviewed by the courts; however, the court was not best placed to decide the issue, due to national security and foreign policy considerations.

11.7.2.4 Foreign affairs

PUBLIC LAW IN CONTEXT
LORD SUMPTION ON THE COURT'S RELUCTANCE TO REVIEW UK FOREIGN POLICY

In 2012, Lord Sumption gave a lecture in which His Lordship considered the historic unwillingness of the courts to review foreign policy.[61] Lord Sumption noted the impact of the House of Lords' decision in *GCHQ* and the fact that Lord Roskill had held that certain prerogative powers were non-justiciable. Lord Sumption stated:

> Until recently, foreign policy was one area in which government did indeed pass unscathed through Balzac's spider's web.[62]
>
> . . .
>
> The truth is that *the principle of non-justiciability has never been a very satisfactory explanation of the reluctance of the courts to interfere with the conduct of foreign relations.* The Foreign Act of State doctrine is not based on non-justiciability, and has no bearing on acts of the United Kingdom executive. The acts of the executive are by definition justiciable in its own courts. The powers of the Crown in the conduct of foreign relations, save in the few areas which are governed by statute, are discretionary powers. There are principles of public law governing the exercise of discretionary powers which are perfectly capable of being applied to the conduct of foreign policy as they are in any other area of executive action. If in practice the courts intervene very rarely in these matters, *it cannot be on the ground that there are no relevant juridical standards or that the issue is incapable of being resolved judicially. It must be on the ground that the constitutional distribution of powers among the organs of the state makes foreign policy the peculiar province of the executive.* But so what? All executive discretions are assigned by the constitution to the executive.[63]

His Lordship presented an in interesting analysis of why the courts had been reluctant to review matters concerning foreign policy and why this particular prerogative power was treated differently from other such powers.

The decision to ratify the Treaty on European Union (Maastricht) 1992 was held to be non-justiciable in *R* v. *Secretary of State for Foreign and Commonwealth Affairs ex p. Lord Rees-Mogg*.[64] Lord Rees-Mogg had attempted to review the legality of transferring increased powers to the new European Union. The Foreign and Commonwealth Office is responsible for relations with foreign states. The diplomatic dealings with other countries concerning British nationals were held to be non-justiciable in *GCHQ*. This was reiterated in *R* v. *Secretary of State for Foreign and Commonwealth Affairs ex p. Ferhut Butt*[65] where Lightman J had stated that

> [t]he general rule is well established that the courts should not interfere in the conduct of foreign relations by the Executive, most particularly where such interference is likely to have foreign policy repercussions. . . . This extends to decisions whether or not to seek to persuade a foreign government of any international obligation (e.g. to respect human rights) which it has assumed. What (if any) approach should be made to the Yemeni authorities in regard to the conduct of the trial of these terrorist charges

must be a matter for delicate diplomacy and the considered and informed judgment of the FCO. In such matters the courts have no supervisory role.[66] Lightman J was of the opinion that the courts had no role to play concerning that representations which were made to a foreign power on behalf of a British national.

In *R (Abbasi)* v. *Secretary of State for Foreign and Commonwealth Affairs*[67] the court refused to judicially review the decision of the Foreign Office's refusal to make representations to the United States regarding the internment of a British National in Guantanamo Bay, which is a US military base in Cuba. Mr Abbasi was detained indefinitely without trial after being captured in Afghanistan. The Secretary of State had argued that the decisions of the executive in its dealings with other countries which concerned the treatment of British nationals was non-justiciable. The court rejected the argument that there could never be scope for judicial review of the executive's refusal to offer diplomatic assistance to a British national in Mr Abbasi's circumstances. A British national would have a legitimate expectation that the Secretary of State would consider making representations. This meant that so long as the Secretary of State had considered whether to make representations to the United States government concerning Mr Abbasi, then the actual decision of whether to make a representation and the actual diplomacy deployed was non-justiciable. Lord Phillips MR gave the judgment of the court and held that had the Secretary of State refused outright to consider making a representation, then his decision would have been reviewable. This was regarded as an extreme case and unlikely to occur. What was clear is that the court refused to allow the Secretary of State to invoke foreign affairs to prevent any review. Whether the courts could review the prerogative power of foreign affairs would depend on the subject matter. Lord Phillips MR stated:

> Whether to make any representations in a particular case, and if so in what form, is left entirely to the discretion of the Secretary of State. That gives free play to the 'balance' to which Lord Diplock referred in GCHQ. The Secretary of State must be free to give full weight to foreign policy considerations, which are not justiciable. However, that does not mean the whole process is immune from judicial scrutiny. The citizen's legitimate expectation is that his request will be 'considered, and that in that consideration all relevant factors will be thrown into the balance. . . . [68]
>
> It is not an answer to a claim for judicial review to say that the source of the power of the Foreign Office is the prerogative. It is the subject matter that is determinative.[69]

The reluctance to review foreign policy was confirmed by Lord Bingham in *R v Jones*[70]. His Lordship held that the court could not decide that a crime of aggression had taken place in respect of the invasion of Iraq. The reason was that it would result in finding that officials in the UK or the US had acted illegally. Lord Bingham observed there are well-established rules that the courts will be very slow to review the exercise of prerogative powers in relation to the conduct of foreign affairs and the deployment of the armed services, and very slow to adjudicate upon rights arising out of transactions entered into between sovereign states on the plane of international law.[71]

The Court of Appeal's decision in *Al Rawi v Secretary of State for Foreign and Commonwealth Affairs*[72] concerned Guantanamo Bay and the detainees held there by the United States. The challenge related to the Foreign Secretary's use of her prerogative power not to treat UK nationals and non-UK nationals the same, where exerting diplomatic pressure on the US to release detainees. The applicants had either lived in the UK with indefinite leave to remain or as asylum seekers. Trey argued that the difference in treatment, in terms of the diplomatic pressure used by the Foreign Secretary, was unlawful as it made a distinction between nationals and non-nationals. The Court of Appeal refused their appeal for a number of reasons. The court found that was no discrimination, as the Foreign Secretary was not obliged by international law to exert such pressure. The court was clear that this was usually a non-justiciable area and the court could not order the Foreign Secretary to reach a different decision as to how she should use her prerogative power: 'In our judgment the claimants' submissions on this part of the case fall foul of two principles. First, they invite the court to enter into what in *Abbasi's case [2003] UKHRR 76* was described as a "forbidden area."'[73] However, what was interesting from a constitutional position was the fact the court acknowledge that the previous reluctance to review foreign policy was no longer absolute and that it would depend on the facts:

> The conduct of foreign relations by the executive government of the United Kingdom would have been regarded as beyond the scope of judicial review. A generation or more ago the courts would, we think, have said there was no jurisdiction to conduct such a review. More recently the line would have been – has been – that the conduct of foreign relations is so particularly the responsibility of government that it would be wrong for the courts to tread such ground; and aside from the division of constitutional territory, the courts have not the competence to pass objective judgment, hardening into law, in so intricate an area of state practice. . . . [74]
>
> . . .
>
> What has been the engine of so painstaking a review in an area which in recent years was thought barely apt for judicial review at all? The prisoners at Guantanamo Bay, some of them at least, have suffered grave privations. . . .[75]
>
> . . .
>
> The case is thus acute on its facts. The force which seeks to press the courts into this area, and within it to exercise a robust independent judgment, is the legal and ethical muscle of human rights and refugee status.[76]
>
> . . .
>
> [T]o our mind, the centre of the case consists in appeals to the claimants' human rights and, in the case of Mr El Banna and Mr Deghayes,

refugee status. We have to decide how far such appeals should rightly press the courts into territory they do not generally occupy or have not so far occupied.[77]

The UK's foreign policy towards another state might be controversial, such as the UK's relationship with Israel. In *R (on the application of Al-Haq) v Secretary of State for Foreign and Commonwealth Affairs*[78] the claimant wanted the court to declare that the UK had breached international law by not denouncing and stating that Israel's action towards Gaza were unlawful. The court held that the court did not have the competence to determine the matter.

In *R (on the application of Sandiford) v Secretary of State for Foreign and Commonwealth Affairs*[79] the Supreme Court reviewed the decision of the Foreign and Commonwealth Office to refuse to fund Mrs Sandiford's defence costs. The Foreign and Commonwealth Office had a policy that it would not provide financial assistance to UK nationals who were facing criminal prosecution in other countries. The policy was based on the prerogative powers. Mrs Sandiford had been convicted of drug offences in Indonesia and had been sentenced to death. From a prerogative viewpoint, the decision is important as the Supreme Court were willing to review a policy created under the prerogative. However, the Supreme Court distinguished between policies stemming from powers derived from an Act of Parliament and those created under the prerogative:

> But prerogative powers do not stem from any legislative source, nor therefore from any such legislative decision, and there is no external originator who could have imposed any obligation to exercise them in one sense, rather than another. They are intrinsic to the Crown and it is for the Crown to determine whether and how to exercise them in its discretion.[80]
>
> In our opinion, in agreement with the Court of Appeal, this does have the consequence that prerogative powers have to be approached on a different basis from statutory powers. There is no necessary implication, from their mere existence, that the State as their holder must keep open the possibility of their exercise in more than one sense. There is no necessary implication that a blanket policy is inappropriate, or that there must always be room for exceptions, when a policy is formulated for the exercise of a prerogative power. In so far as reliance is placed on legitimate expectation derived from established published policy or established practice, it is to the policy or practice that one must look for the limits, rigid or flexible, of the commitment so made, and of any enforceable rights derived from it.[81]

This was significant as with the prerogative there was no implication that there would be an implication that the policy maker would keep an open mind and be expected to be willing to make exceptions to their policy. To date Mrs Sandiford faces execution by firing squad.

The concept of an Act of State was considered in *Rahmatullah (No.2) v Ministry of Defence*[82], which concerned legal action by individuals who had been detained and alleged mistreatment by UK and US armed forces following the invasions of Afghanistan in 2001 and Iraq in 2003. The case concerned liability for an Act of State, which when the state uses the prerogative power in international affairs. The Supreme Court held that the government could rely on the Act of Stare as a defence against liability in tort for the alleged mistreatment of the claimants. This was because the acts where 'by their nature sovereign acts, acts which are inherently governmental, committed in the conduct of the foreign relations of the Crown'.[83] However, there were limits on what could be regarded as an Act of State. Lady Hale observed that '[t]he Government accepts that it cannot apply to acts of torture, even supposing that the Government of the United Kingdom would ever authorise or ratify such acts.'[84] In his judgment Lord Sumption observed,

> a decision by the United Kingdom government to authorise or ratify torture or maltreatment would not as a matter of domestic English law be a lawful exercise of the royal prerogative. It could not therefore be an act of state. Nor would there be any inconsistency with the proper functions of the executive in treating it as giving rise to civil liability.[85]

More recently in *R (on the application of Youssef) v Secretary of State for Foreign and Commonwealth Affairs*[86] the Supreme Court observe that although the 'source of [the Foreign Secretary's] powers under domestic law lay not in any statute but in the exercise of prerogative powers for the conduct of foreign relations. That did not make it immune from judicial review, but it is an area in which the courts proceed with caution.'[87]

11.7.2.6 Granting passports

The granting of passports was found to be justiciable in *R v. Foreign Secretary ex p. Everett*[88] after the government introduced a policy which stated that new passports would not be issued for British subjects who had a warrant outstanding for their arrest. Mr Everett lived in Spain and was refused a passport. He sought to judicially review the decision. Taylor LJ contrasted the non-justiciable matters of high policy, such as the making of treaties, and those prerogative powers which were essentially administrative and were therefore justiciable, namely the decision to grant a passport.

11.8 Practical application

Earlier this year the Prime Minister, Ms Smith, using her prerogative powers invoked Article 2 of the Free Trade Treaty with South Utopia. This triggered the United Kingdom's withdrawal from the Free Trade Partnership with South Utopia. Helene and Sam are legal academics who believe that the prerogative powers cannot be used to do this due to the Free Trade

Partnership Act 1994 which conferred rights on UK citizens as a consequence of the UK's membership of the Free Trade Partnership.

Helene and Sam publish a number of articles in which they argued that the Prime Minister had acted illegally.

On 1 July, the Prime Minister invokes the prerogative and signs a warrant authorising the police to search Helene and Sam's homes and seize their computers and any material relating to Article 50.

On 2 July, the Home Office rejects Sam's passport application.

On 4 July, the Prime Minister dispatches *HMS Warship* and 1,200 Royal Marines to Dystopia, a country that is suspected of harbouring several terrorist training camps. Only once the Royal Marines have gained control of Dystopia's main port did the Prime Minister inform the House of Commons about the military action.

On 8 July the Prime Minister travels to Buckingham Place and requests that the Queen dissolves Parliament. The Queen uses her prerogative powers to do this and the Prime Minister subsequently tweets that there will be a general election next month.

On 11 July, Helene visits Mumbai for a conference and is seized by a third country's secret service operatives. Helene's family believe that she was secretly rendered to a remote British Overseas Territory. The Foreign and Commonwealth Office have refused to offer any diplomatic assistance to either Helene or her family.

Please identify the issues relating to the prerogative in the above question.

An outline answer is available on the companion website.

11.9 Key points to take away from this chapter

- The courts have traditionally placed limits on the exercise of the prerogative powers.
- The courts have not permitted the executive to create new prerogative powers.
- The decision in *Miller (No.2)* is a significant development in terms of the judicial protection of parliamentary accountability and a widening out the scope of Parliamentary Sovereignty.
- The *GCHQ* decision permits the courts to judicially review the exercise of prerogative powers, although certain powers are still considered by the courts to be non-justiciable.

Notes

1   (1611) 12 Co. Rep 74.
2   [1985] AC 374. This case is also referred to by some academics as the CCSU case.
3   [1920] AC 508.
4   ibid 539.
5   ibid 573.

6   ibid 568.
7   [2017] WLR 1437.
8   ibid 102.
9   [1977] QB 643.
10 ibid 722.
11 ibid 726.
12 [1995] 2 WLR 464.
13 ibid 552.
14 [1988] 2 WLR 590.
15 [2019] UKSC 41.
16 ibid 48.
17 C Monaghan, 'The Prorogation Litigation: "Which Was as if the Commissioners Had Walked into Parliament with a Blank Piece of Paper"' (2019) 24(2) Cov LJ 7, 22.
18 [1985] AC 374.
19 W Blackstone, *Commentaries on the Laws of England* (1st edn, 1765–69) 252.
20 *Laker Airways Ltd* (n 9) 707–8.
21 *De Keyser's Royal Hotel* (n 3) 539.
22 [1965] AC 75.
23 ibid 101.
24 *Ex p Northumbria Police Authority* (n 14) 44–45.
25 (1855) 5 E&B 344.
26 *Ex p Northumbria Police Authority* (n 14) 56.
27 ibid 58.
28 ibid 58–59.
29 A Tomkins, *Our Republican Constitution* (Hart Publishing 2005) 133.
30 [2008] UKHL 61.
31 *R (on the application of Bancoult) v Secretary of State for Foreign and Commonwealth Office (No.1)* [2001] QB 1067.
32 ibid 1103.
33 *Bancoult (No.2)* (n 30).
34 ibid 70.
35 W Holdsworth, *A History of English Law* (vol X, 7th edn, Sweet & Maxwell 1938) 393.
36 *Bancoult (No.2)* (n 166) [150].
37 [2017] UKSC 5.
38 ibid 87.
39 ibid 88.
40 [1964] WLR 1071.
41 *Ex p Northumbria Police Authority* (n 14).
42 *de Freitas v Benny* [1976] AC 239.
43 [1967] 2 QB 864.
44 ibid 881.
45 [1985] AC 374.
46 ibid 397–98.
47 ibid 399.
48 ibid 407 (emphasis added).
49 ibid 410.
50 ibid 410.

51   ibid 418 (emphasis added).
52   Lord Mance, *International Law in the UK Supreme Court* (King's College London, 13 February 2017) 33.
53   C Walker, 'Review of the Prerogative: The Remaining Issues' [1987] PL 62.
54   [1994] QB 349.
55   [1995] 4 All ER 427.
56   ibid.
57   [2002] EWCA Civ 3.
58   ibid 38.
59   [2002] EWHC 2777.
60   [2008] UKHL 61.
61   Lord Sumption, 'Foreign Affairs in the English Courts Since 9/11' Lecture at the Department of Government, London School of Economics, 14 May 2012.
62   ibid 3.
63   ibid 6–7.
64   [1994] 2 WLR 115.
65   [1999] EWHC Admin 624.
66   ibid 11.
67   [2002] EWCA Civ 1598.
68   ibid 99.
69   ibid 106.
70   [2005] 2 WLR 772.
71   [30].
72   [2008] QB 289.
73   ibid 131.
74   ibid 2.
75   ibid 3.
76   ibid 4.
77   ibid 5.
78   [2009] EWHC 1910 (Admin); [2009] ACD 76.
79   [2014] UKSC 44; [2014] 1WLR 2697.
80   ibid 61.
81   ibid 62.
82   [2017] UKSC 1.
83   ibid 36.
84   ibid.
85   ibid 96.
86   [2016] UKSC 3.
87   ibid 24.
88   [1989] 1 QB 811.

Further reading

Allott P, 'The Courts and the Executive: Four House of Lords Decisions' [1977] CLJ 255

Cohn M, 'Medieval Chains, Invisible Inks: On Non-Statutory Powers of the Executive' [2005] OJLS 97

Cormacain R, 'Prerogative Legislation as the Paradigm of Bad Law-Making: The Chagos Islands' (2013) 39(3) CLB 487

Monaghan C, 'An Imperfect Legacy: The Significance of the *Bancoult* Litigation on the Development of Domestic Constitutional Jurisprudence' in S Allen and C Monaghan (eds), *Fifty Years of the British Indian Ocean Territory: Legal Perspectives* (Springer 2018)

———, 'The Prorogation Litigation: "Which Was as if the Commissioners Had Walked into Parliament with a Blank Piece of Paper"' (2019) 24(2) Cov LJ 7

O'Conner QC P, 'The Constitutional Role of the Privy Council and the Prerogative' A Justice Report <https://justice.org.uk/the-constitutional-role-of-the-privy-council-and-the-prerogative/>

Sedley S, *Lions Under the Throne: Essays on the History of English Public Law* (CUP 2015)

Sumption L, 'Foreign Affairs in the English Courts Since 9/11' Lecture at the Department of Government, London School of Economics, 14 May 2012

Walker C, 'Review of the Prerogative: The Remaining Issues' [1987] PL 62

Human Rights I

Foundations and rights

This chapter will:

- consider what is meant by human rights and civil liberties;

- appreciate the important role served by both the European Convention on Human Rights and the European Court of Human Rights;

- evaluate the protection of rights under the Human Rights Act 1998; and

- debate why the issue of human rights has proved just so controversial in the United Kingdom.

12.1 Introduction

Human rights, the European Convention on Human Rights, the European Court of Human Rights, the Human Rights Act 1998 and a British Bill of Rights have been written about by national newspapers for the past decade, often quite negatively.[1] The concept that we all have human rights, from the person protected from being discriminated against because of their gender or sexuality, to the newspaper columnist who enjoys freedom of expression, is not controversial.[2] What, however, is controversial is the protection afforded under the European Convention on Human Rights to people who are deemed by some elements of the media to be 'undeserving' of having their human rights protected. The concept of people who are underserving of rights is very subjective, as some people may believe that prisoners are underserving of having their human rights protected, whereas other people may see prisoners, having a significantly higher rate of mental health problems and suicides than the general population, as being acutely vulnerable as a group and therefore it is important that their rights are protected.[3] The campaign group Liberty makes this point about the universality of human rights which is not dependent on whether a particular group of individuals, are, or are not, deemed worthy of having their rights protected: 'They apply to all people simply on the basis of being human. . . . They cannot be taken away simply because we do not like the

DOI: 10.4324/9780429293498-15

Figure 12.1
Chapter overview

person seeking to exercise their rights. . . . You cannot pick and choose which rights you want to honour.'[4] Human rights can be the subject of an entire module on an LLB degree and so here we will only look briefly at the individual Convention rights. We will look at what is meant by human rights, the European Convention on Human Rights, the European Court of Human Rights and the Human Rights Act 1998.

We have used the term 'human rights,' but what exactly is meant by human rights? According to Griffin, human rights are 'a right that a person has, not in virtue of any special status or relation to others, but simply in virtue of being human.'[5] This definition sees rights afforded to all humans and there is no distinction as to who they apply to. Many people will disagree as to what will and will not amount to a human right. We shall see that the proponents of a British Bill of Rights want to broaden the rights which are already given a special status.

12.2 What are human rights?

The rights that are classified as fundamental human rights will often depend on who is drafting a statement of rights. The drafters of the United States Bill of Rights and the French Declaration of the Rights of Man had incorporated rights such as the freedom of expression and personal liberty. We shall see the development of fundamental rights, which cumulated in the Universal Declaration of Human Rights and the European Convention on Human Rights. Human rights can mean equal treatment, the ending of restrictions on civil rights, equal political rights and the ability to live one's life being able to practice a religion openly without fear of persecution, or sexuality without fear of societal and social repercussions. Human rights should be regarded as very much a work in progress, in the sense that it has unfortunately taken a very long time to achieve many basic rights within democracies such as the United Kingdom and the United States of America. For example, it has only been comparatively recently that same-sex couples have been able to marry, that schools can teach about same-sex relationships, that the age of consent mirrors that of opposite-sex individuals, and that homosexuality is decriminalised. There can be a risk when discussing human rights to focus on how an individual or a group of people's rights have been restricted, rather than to celebrate the rights that are enjoyed. Professor Conor Gearty observed that:

> This negative side of human rights, the version of the subject that is all about bad news, human horrors and how to prevent them, is an important strand to our subject, but it is not the only one. . . . Human rights has an upbeat dimension as well, one that stresses positive human potentialities rather than our dismally ineradicable inclination to harm each other. This part of our subject speaks to our right to thrive, not only as individuals but also through those associations and connections – with family, community, culture, national identity and so on- by which our humanity is further enriched.[6]

PRACTICAL APPLICATION

You have been asked to draft a new declaration of rights for a country that has just gained its independence after leaving a union with another country.

- What rights which you would protect? Could there be any restriction on these rights? If there was to be a restriction, why and in which circumstances could a right be restricted?

The chances are that your list of protected rights would be broadly similar to the European Convention on Human Rights.

What would be interesting is the relative importance that you might choose to give each right.

- Would the rights be absolute and thus impossible for a state to restrict, or would they be qualified, meaning that a state could justify restricting a right?

It might be worth considering freedom of expression and whether the press should be subject to any degree of state control.

12.2.1 Covid-19 and infringement of civil liberties – the lawful action of the state

The year 2020–21 saw arguably the largest limitation of our civil liberties and human rights in history, with a lockdown introduced to prevent people from leaving their homes except in prescribed circumstances.

When the lockdown was first introduced in March there was questions over whether people were legally required to comply, as no new law had been introduced. The legislation that followed, the Coronavirus Act 2020, gave legal effect to lockdown. The media has highlighted stories of the powers given to the police to enforce lockdown being used in questionable circumstances, for example see the case of two women fined in January 2021: 'Two women have described how they were surrounded by police, read their rights and fined £200 each after driving five miles to take a walk. The women were also told the hot drinks they had brought along were not allowed as they were "classed as a picnic."'[7] The police have been given the power to issue fixed penalty notices to people who do not follow the lockdown rules. In England the maximum fine is £10,000. In terms of the number of fines issued in England, some 15,659 were issued between 27 March 2020 and 19 June 2020, 6,843 between 5 November 2020 and 2 December 2020, and so far, 26,911 since 6 January 2021.[8] In terms of actual criminal charges, 987 people have been charged in England and Wales with 14 per cent of those charged, being charged incorrectly.[9]

The Joint Committee on Human Rights considered the government's response to Covid-19 and the impact that this had had on peoples' human rights:

> The central aim of the Government's response to the Covid-19 outbreak in the UK has been to protect lives. The right to life is protected in law in Article 2 of the European Convention on Human Rights. This requires the state to take appropriate steps to safeguard lives. However, inevitably, attempts to save lives through government actions including the restriction of movements, gatherings, and school closures have engaged numerous other rights. Many have experienced the widest and deepest set of government interferences with their rights in their lifetimes.
>
> . . . .
>
> The lockdown regulations have had a huge impact on the rights of millions of people across the country. There has been confusion over the status and interpretation of guidance, and the relationship between guidance and the law. There have been additional questions about the type of policing that is most appropriate in a health crisis, and the disproportionate impact of policing decisions on young men from black, Asian and minority ethnic backgrounds. Lessons must be learnt urgently from this period of lockdown in order to avoid the worst elements of confusion and disproportionality before any second wave and any further lockdowns either at a local or national level. This is all the more important given the speed and frequency with which national and local lockdown laws change and the consequent difficulty for people to keep on top of what is legally required and what is reasonably expected of them.[10]

The Joint Committee on Human Rights were clear that whilst the lockdown restrictions were intended to save lives, these have had significant impact on peoples' rights under the European Convention on Human Rights. The challenges discussed by the Joint Committee on Human Rights include the uncertainty surrounding the restrictions and the difficulties that people may have in keeping up to date and understanding restrictions in their geographic area. Furthermore, particular groups in society are being disproportionality affected by how the police enforce the restrictions.

PUBLIC LAW IN PRACTICE

You might want to take this opportunity to think about how your own human rights may have been restricted during the national and local lockdowns. You might want to discuss this with friends and family members and hear their experiences.

12.3 Protection of liberty

Until the Human Rights Act 1998 took effect in October 2000 there was nothing on the statute book resembling a modern Bill of Rights in the United Kingdom. Yes, there was the Bill of Rights 1689 and the Claim of Right 1689 in Scotland, yet these were not intended to set out the rights to be enjoyed by the subject in the then independent and separate kingdoms. The Bill of Rights was intended to address grievances against the deposed king, James II, who many believed had misused his prerogative powers at the expense of Parliament, the law, and the rights of the subject. That is not to say that fundamental liberties such as a fair trial and freedom from arbitrary government action have not been considered important in terms of the development of English and Welsh law.

The United Kingdom was not unique in not having a Bill of Rights (or now Human Rights Act 1998). For example, Australia's federal constitution does not have any legislative bill of rights, because the drafters of its constitution could not see 'any particular connection between rights protection and federation.'[11] Some Australian states such as Victoria have, however, introduced a bill of rights at a state level.[12] In Australia it is the Australian Parliament that is entrusted to protect human rights and not the courts. We shall see below how the courts protect human rights in the United Kingdom, having been given increased powers to do so under the Human Rights Act 1998. In Australia '[g]iving Parliament the primary, if not sole, responsibility for this task is said to be democratically sound because it ensures that contentious and value-laden decisions about rights are made by elected representatives rather than unelected judges.'[13] However, entrusting the protection of human rights to parliamentarians and not the courts can prove problematic, as '[t]his can mean that Parliament is unlikely or unwilling to protect the rights of unpopular minorities or those who lack political power.'[14] The legitimacy of human rights, questions of not only who should have rights but also who should determine the extent of rights protection and should be responsible for protecting rights in a democratic society are pertinent to appreciating the controversies that are integral to human rights.

12.3.1 Why Dicey did not believe that the United Kingdom needed a Bill of Rights

AV Dicey was a leading academic and writer on the United Kingdom's constitution. He took the view that the United Kingdom did not require a fundamental bill of rights, as citizens' rights were protected by the common law. Dicey argued that the common law was more effective than a statement of fundamental rights:

> The Habeas Corpus Acts have achieved this end, and have therefore done for the liberty of Englishmen more than could have been achieved by any declaration of rights. One may even venture to say that these Acts are of really more importance not only than the general proclamations of the Rights of Man which have often been put forward in foreign countries, but even than such very lawyer-like documents as the Petition of Right or the Bill of Rights, though these celebrated enactments show almost equally with the Habeas Corpus Act that the law of the English constitution is at bottom judge-made law.[15]
>
> Lustgarten and Leigh observed that 'Dicey's hostility to the idea of fundamental rights, as embodied in the French Declaration of the Rights of Man of 1789, was as much empirical as philosophical: he doubted their effective worth. Hence his famous assertion that 'the Habeas Corpus Acts declare no principle and define no rights, but they are for practical purposes worth a hundred constitutional articles guaranteeing individual liberty.'[16]

This was a view shared by the former Conservative Prime Minister John Major, who rejected the need for a British Bill of Rights, arguing that civil liberties were adequately protected by the law.[17] We will have a look at the major developments in the protection of liberties and 'rights' in the United Kingdom and the rest of the world (see Figure 12.2).

12.3.2 Magna Carta 1215

The English monarchs had their power to rule challenged by the nobility. King John was forced to sign the Magna Carta in 1215. The barons were attempting to check the king's arbitrary power and were intending to protect their own interests against the Crown. The original charter was annulled by Pope Innocent III shortly afterwards, but it was reissued by Edward I and the most important provision, Chapter 29, states that:

> No Freeman shall be taken or imprisoned, or be disseised of his Freehold, or Liberties, or free Customs, or be outlawed, or exiled, or any other wise destroyed; nor will We not pass upon him, nor [condemn him] but by

lawful judgment of his Peers, or by the Law of the Land. We will sell to no man, we will not deny or defer to any man either Justice or Right.

Chapter 29 is still in force today. It was concerned with safeguarding the liberty of the Crown's subjects from arbitrary punishment without first having been tried by a jury of their peers. In English legal tradition trial by jury has been strongly regarded as an important right, and any attempt to restrict trial by jury has been met with hostility.[18]

12.3.3 Dr Bonham's Case *(1609) 8 Coke Reports 113b*

Sir Edward Coke CJ regarded the common law as safeguarding the important rights and liberties of the Crown's subjects. Coke famously stated in *Dr Bonham's Case* that

> the common law will controul Acts of Parliament, and sometimes adjudge them to be utterly void: for when an Act of Parliament is against common right and reason, or repugnant, or impossible to be performed, the common law will controul it, and adjudge such Act to be void.[19]

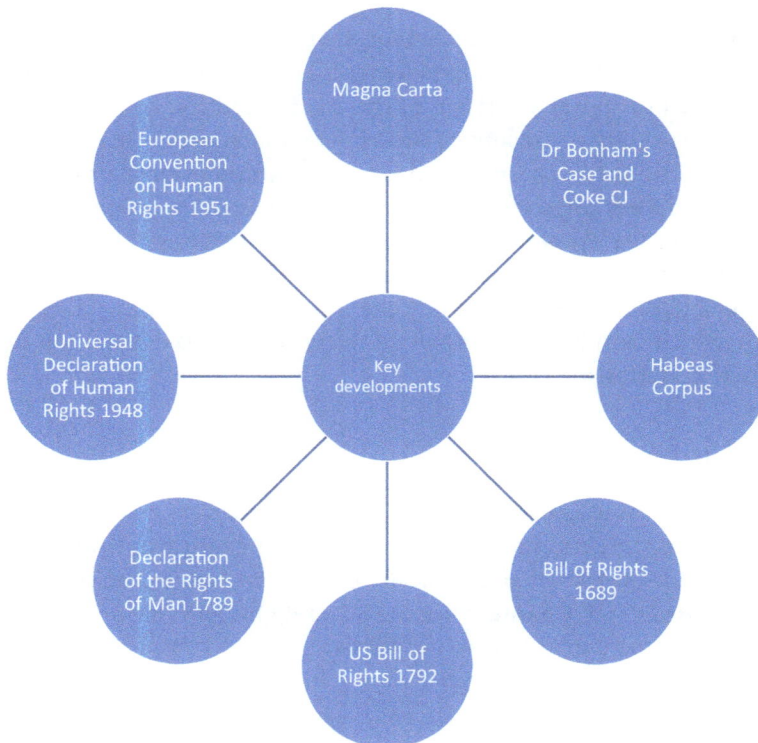

Figure 12.2
Key developments in the protection of civil liberties and fundamental rights

Coke CJ observed that the common law would not let Parliament legislate against important rights that were protected by the common law. Dicey dismissed the idea that the courts would have the ability to declare Acts of Parliament void because they are immoral as '[a] modern judge would never listen to a barrister who argued that an Act of Parliament was invalid because it was immoral.'[20]

12.3.4 Petition of Right 1628

The Petition of Right 1628 restricted the power of King Charles I to use his prerogative powers to undermine the rights of his subjects. Sir Edward Coke played an important role in drafting the petition and it stated that only Parliament could authorise taxes and that people could only be imprisoned in accordance with English law. Charles I was forced to accept the petition.

12.3.5 Habeas corpus

Habeas corpus is a prerogative writ and gives you the right to prevent yourself from being unlawfully detained. If you are detained, you have the right to be brought before a court or magistrate to determine whether there is evidence to detain you.

The first Act to reinforce the prerogative writ was the Habeas Corpus Act 1679 which stated that it was '[a]n act for the better securing the liberty of the subject, and for prevention of imprisonments beyond the seas.' Habeas corpus cannot be used to appeal a decision of the court, and is primarily intended to challenge the validity of executive action in areas such as immigration and the criminal law. The Act has been suspended at various times since its enactment. For example, habeas corpus was suspended by Parliament during the 1790s on the initiative of the Prime Minister, William Pitt the Younger, because of the fear of civil disorder during the French Revolution.[21] Parliament has allowed for indefinite detention without trial; see the Anti-Terrorism, Crime and Security Act 2001 which permitted the Home Secretary to order the detention of suspected foreign terrorists.

12.3.6 Bill of Rights 1689

The Bill of Rights was enacted after the Glorious Revolution and protected parliamentary freedoms and limited the power of the executive. It included the freedom not to suffer cruel and unusual punishment, and not to be set excessive bail. Please refer to **Chapter 2** for the Bill of Rights and the protections that were afforded to parliamentarians and citizens.

12.3.7 Empire and the slave trade

Edmund Burke was a famous politician and philosopher and was dismissive of the formal protection offered by the French Declaration of the Rights of Man (see below). Burke observed the English constitution protected the liberties of Englishmen: '[y]ou will observe, that from the Magna Charta to the Declaration of Right, it has been the uniform policy of our constitution to claim and assert our liberties, as an entailed inheritance derived to us from our forefathers . . . without any reference whatever to any other more general or prior right.'[22] Burke was critical of the French Revolution and the rights conferred by the new constitution. We can see that Burke believed that the rights were enjoyed without the need to be conferred by the state.[23]

In 1787, Edmund Burke led the impeachment of Warren Hastings, the former governor-general of Bengal, for his conduct whilst ruling much of modern-day India and Bangladesh. At this time the English East India Company effectively owned its own territory in India and enjoyed an exclusive monopoly over trade between the Cape of Good Hope and Cape Horn. Hastings was a company servant but had also been appointed by the government under the Regulating Act 1773. Burke and others including Charles James Fox, Philip Francis and Richard Sheridan accused Hastings of arbitrary rule, violating the rights of the people he ruled and acting immorally. It is important to appreciate that Hastings had been tasked with ending corruption amongst the East India Company's servants in India and was regarded as permitting the practice of servants making a large personal fortune to continue. Hastings, in his defence, had attempted to justify his behaviour by making a distinction between the conditions in Britain and those in India. This defence was rejected by Burke:

> these gentlemen have formed a plan of geographical morality, by which the duties of men, in public and private situations, are not be governed by their relative relation to the great Governor of the universe, or by their relation to mankind, but by climates, degrees of longitude, parallels not of life but of latitudes; as if, when you have crossed the equinoctial, all the virtues die. . . . This geographical morality we do protest against. Mr Hastings shall not screen himself under it. . . . the laws of morality are the same everywhere.[24]

The prosecution of Hastings by Parliament is important, and it demonstrated that it was not acceptable in the 18th century to abuse the rights of people ruled by the Britain.[25] Hastings was impeached by the House of Commons in 1787 and tried before the House of Lords. Hastings' trial lasted from 1788 to 1795 and he was eventually acquitted. However, Hastings no longer held any public offices, although he was later made a Privy Councillor.

Slavery was a large part of the British economy and enabled British subjects to become rich at the expense of Africans who were forced to work on their property. Slavery as an institution treats people as personal property which can be bought and sold like any other chattel. Slaves are deprived of rights and legal protections as they are the personal property of their owners. The Atlantic slave trade saw slaves being purchased in Africa and sold to plantation owners in the Americas, with large plantations across the Caribbean and in the North

American colonies. Slave owners had also kept slaves in metropolitan Britain and the question arose as to whether slavery could exist in Britain itself. In *R v Knowles Ex p. Somersett*[26] Lord Mansfield ruled that a slave owner could not force a slave to leave Britain. His Lordship had stated that

> [t]he state of slavery is of such a nature that it is incapable of being introduced on any reasons, moral or political, but only by positive law, which preserves its force long after the reasons, occasions, and time itself from whence it was created, is erased from memory. It is so odious, that nothing can be suffered to support it, but positive law.[27]

However this case must not be viewed in isolation. In *The Zong* slave traders had sought to recover payment from their insurers after 132 slaves had died at sea. This is an odious case, as the slave traders had deliberately thrown men, women and children overboard after getting lost and running low on supplies. It might surprise you that this was not a decision concerned with whether the slaver traders were guilty of murder, as no, the question was whether they could recover for the loss of their property. Lord Mansfield ruled that although the slaves were to be treated as mere chattels, that there needed to be a retrial in order to determine whether the insurers were liable to pay out in the circumstances.[28]

PUBLIC LAW IN CONTEXT
THE ZONG

Jane Webster has written an engaging article on the *Zong* litigation. She commented upon how Lord Mansfield prepared the jury to treat the case on the basis of whether the slavers could recover upon their insurance policy:

> Murder had been on no one's mind at the Guildhall sessions two months before, but that word was used nine times in the King's Bench, and this despite Mansfield having taken pains to assert at the opening of the proceedings that:
> The Matter left to the Jury [at Guildhall] was, whether it [the jettison] was from necessity for they had no doubt (tho' it shocks one very much) the Case of Slaves was the same as if Horses had been thrown over board it is a very shocking Case.

Much of what was said in court rehearsed the arguments of two months before, but this time the three judges concluded that the case for necessity in jettisoning the slaves was not proven. A retrial was ordered, and it is interesting to speculate what would have happened if the case had come back to court, but speculate is all we can do. There is no record of a further trial, and it would appear that none ever took place.'[29]

James Walvin has written that: 'What happened on the *Zong* was an exceptional story of mass murder, but those killings have come to be seen not merely as a single event (the story of one ship among thousands) but as a representation of the wider story of the slave trade.'[30]

In 1807, Parliament abolished the slave trade by enacting the Slave Trade Act 1807. The campaign was led by individuals including William Wilberforce and supported by millions of British people. Given the financial benefits of the trade to British merchants it was a key achievement, and the Royal Navy freed many slaves who were being exported from Africa on ships. This did not change the fact that Britain has profited enormously from the slave trade and that many families had built significant fortunes from the fact that they had bought and sold fellow humans and profited from their forced labour, in what were appalling conditions.[31] Britain encouraged other countries to end the slave trade. The 1807 Act did not free existing slaves and this was only achieved by the Slavery Abolition Act 1833. This meant that until 1833 slavery still existed as an institution within Britain's colonies, the only restriction being that it was no longer possible to purchase slaves from Africa. Somewhat controversially, the abolition of slavery was accompanied by a large amount of compensation for slave owners. In Britain there is still controversy over how institutions still benefit from the profits of slavery, as the slave owners and traders often left considerable amounts of money to institutions and had buildings named after them, such as Colston Hall in Bristol. In 2019, the University of Cambridge announced that it was carrying out a review over how the university had benefitted from slavery.[32] Slavery continued in the United States of America until the defeat of the Confederacy in 1865, and in Brazil until 1880.

In 2020, the statue of Edward Colston, a slave trader, was toppled by a crowd in Bristol and thrown into the nearby water.[33] This had been the culmination of a very lengthy campaign through legal means to try to get the controversial statue removed. The non-legal removal of the statue was highly controversial; however, the key question was whether it is appropriate in the contemporary United Kingdom to commemorate those involved with the slave trade and profiting from the suffering of others and gross abuses of their human rights. The removal of the statue was in the wider context of the Black Lives Matter movement that was protesting against racial injustice in the aftermath of the killing of George Floyd in the United States of America.

Human rights abuses took place during the course of the British rule across a quarter of the world. Notable incidents include the repression of the Indian War of Independence in the 1850s (otherwise known as the Indian Mutiny), the Amritsar Massacre in 1919, the treatment of Irish subjects following the Easter Sunday Uprising in 1916, the repression of the Mau Uprising in Kenya in the 1950s and the response to a communist insurgency in Malaysia during the 1950s.

It is important to note that the British Empire continued until the mid-20th century, with India and Pakistan only becoming independent in 1947. Many African countries only gained their independence in the 1960s and 1970s. Today the United Kingdom still possess the remnants of empire, which exist in the form of British Overseas Territories. The most controversial issue that has arisen in modern times is the treatment of the inhabitants of the Chagos Islands, otherwise known as the British Indian Ocean Territory, who were expelled from their homeland in the early 1970s in order to accommodate a United States military base on Diego Garcia, the largest of the islands in the Chagos Archipelago. The abuses committed by British authorities during the course of British imperial rule continue to remain controversial, and movements such 'Rhodes Must Fall' are leading the way in forcing the modern United Kingdom to reconsider its assumptions about the inherent good of the British Empire.

12.3.8 United States Declaration of Independence and Bill of Rights

In 1776, the 13 British North American colonies declared their independence from Great Britain and with this rejected being ruled from Westminster. American colonists accused Britain of violating their rights, such as Parliament imposing taxation on the colonies without the assent of the colonial assemblies.

The Continental Congress, in its Declaration of Independence, on 4 July 1776 stated:

> We hold these truths to be self-evident, that all men are created equal, that they are endowed by their Creator with certain unalienable Rights, that among these are Life, Liberty, and the pursuit of Happiness. That to secure these rights, Governments are instituted among Men, deriving their just powers from the consent of the governed. That whenever any Form of Government becomes destructive of these ends, it is the Right of the People to alter or to abolish it, and to institute new Government, laying its foundation on such principles and organizing its powers in such form, as to them shall seem most likely to effect their Safety and Happiness.

What did the American colonists mean? The Declaration of Independence held that all men are born equal and that people automatically have certain rights. These rights do not have to be given by the state in order to exist. However, at the time that the Declaration of Independence was written, slavery existed in the American colonies and it would continue for almost another 90 years. Therefore, these rights did not extend to African American slaves or Native Americans. Even after the end of the American Civil War, which saw the emancipation of the slaves by President Abraham Lincoln in 1865, African Americans were treated as second-class citizens and in many states the law enforced segregation, which meant that people were denied goods or services on the basis of their race. This led to the Civil Rights Movement in the 1960s that was notably led by Dr Martin Luther King Jr. Native Americans were forced off their land

and sent to live in reservations. The attitude that many white Americans had towards Native Americans was summed up by General Philip Sheridan, when he was alleged to said in the 1870s, that 'the only good Indian is a dead Indian.'[34]

In response to the abolition of slavery in 1865 former Confederate soldiers formed the Ku Klux Klan, an organisation of white supremists that terrorised and often killed African Americans. The Ku Klux Klan is still in existence today.

The United States Constitution has a special legal status and is protected from repeal by the legislature or the executive. To amend the constitution, it is necessary to go through a lengthy and complex procedure. The constitution was amended (the first amendment) to incorporate a Bill of Rights which was ratified in 1791. The rights protected included freedom of speech, press freedom and freedom of assembly. The state was not allowed in peacetime to force citizens to house soldiers and the power of the state to search private premises was restricted. Trial by jury in civil cases was protected, as was the right of citizens to carry arms. The constitution and the Bill of Rights are protected by the Supreme Court which has the power to strike down any statute which it considers to be unconstitutional.

12.3.9 Declaration of the Rights of Man 1789

The French Revolution occurred in 1789 and would eventually see the monarchy abolished and the king executed in 1793. In 1789 the National Assembly of France issued the Declaration of the Rights of Man. This was intended to protect individual rights from intrusion by the legislature or the executive. However, the revolution would result in the reign of terror and mass executions, before Napoleon reintroduced a monarchy in 1804.

PUBLIC LAW IN CONTEXT
DECLARATION OF THE RIGHTS OF MAN 1789

The following are some of the most important provisions of the Declaration of the Rights of Man 1789:

Article 1: Men are born and remain free and equal in rights. Social distinctions may be founded only upon the general good.

Article 4: Liberty consists in the freedom to do everything which injures no one else; hence the exercise of the natural rights of each man has no limits except those which assure to the other members of the society the enjoyment of the same rights. These limits can only be determined by law.

It is clear that the exercise of rights in France in 1789 would only be limited where they would injure others. The only restrictions would be legal restrictions. Freedom of expression and religion would be permitted, subject to the condition that it did not disturb the public good or break the law. Property rights would be protected and property would only be confiscated by the state in circumstances proscribed by law.

12.3.10 *The Universal Declaration of Human Rights 1948*

The United Nations was established by the allied powers during the Second World War and it adopted the Universal Declaration of Human Rights in 1948. Article 1 states that, 'All human beings are born free and equal in dignity and rights. They are endowed with reason and conscience and should act towards one another in a spirit of brotherhood.' Article 2 is clear that human beings enjoy these rights regardless of race, religion or sexuality.

12.4 Council of Europe

The Council of Europe was established in 1949 after the Second World War. It is based in Strasbourg and was established to prevent future human rights abuses. It is important not to confuse the Council of Europe with the European Union and its institutions (see Figure 12.2). Both were established for different reasons and in consequence of the Second World War. Membership of the Council of Europe is wider than the European Union, with 47 member states, opposed to the European Union's 27. For example, Turkey is applying to become a member of the European Union but is already a member of the Council of Europe. Also the United Kingdom is no longer a member of the European Union, but is a member of the Council of Europe.

The Second World War had been preceded by fascist governments in Germany and Italy (amongst others), where human rights had been violated. The Second World War saw the Holocaust and wholesale murder of Jews, homosexuals, gypsies, political opponents of the Nazi party and many other groups. One of the powerful advocates for setting up the Council of Europe was the former British Prime Minister, Sir Winston Churchill. Churchill, who had been an opponent of appeasing Hitler in the 1930s, stated in Strasbourg on 12 August 1949 that:

> The dangers threatening us are great but great too is our strength, and there is no reason why we should not succeed in achieving our aims and

Figure 12.3
The Council of Europe and the European Union

establishing the structure of this united Europe whose moral concepts will be able to win the respect and recognition of mankind, and whose physical strength will be such that no one will dare to hold up its peaceful journey towards the future.[35]

The Council of Europe promotes human rights, democracy and the rule of law. It actively pursues these objectives and it should be remembered that the Council of Europe is far more than just the European Convention on Human Rights.

12.4.1 Institutions of the Council of Europe

We will now look at the institutions of the Council of Europe.

12.4.1.1 Parliamentary Assembly and the Committee of Ministers

The Parliamentary Assembly has 318 representatives from each of its member states' national parliaments. They meet four times a year and propose initiatives. The Parliamentary Assembly elects the judges of the European Court of Human Rights and the Commissioner for Human Rights. The Parliamentary Assembly has the power to suspend a member state's membership of the Council of Europe if that state has repeatedly breached its obligations.

The Committee of Ministers is the body responsible for making decisions in the Council of Europe. Its members are the representatives or foreign ministers of the contracting states to the Council. The committee is intended to set out the aims to be pursued by the Council of Europe and as its members represent each contracting state, this ensures that the national interest is protected.

12.4.1.2 Commissioner for Human Rights

The Commissioner for Human Rights is tasked with promoting respect for human rights within the 47 member states.

12.4.1.3 European Court of Human Rights

The European Court of Human Rights (ECtHR) is based in Strasbourg and it hears petitions from individuals and states concerning alleged violations of human rights. It was established in 1959. The first case heard by the ECtHR was *Lawless v. Ireland*[36] which concerned an allegation that Mr Lawless has been detained in a military detention camp without trial. Ireland claimed that his detention was authorised by section 4 of the Offences against the State (Amendment) Act 1940

The ECtHR can fine states which have violated Convention rights. The ECtHR recognises that each member state is different, in terms of culture, politics, society and legal system, and therefore applies the margin of appreciation.

| UK nominates 3 judges | Elected by Parliamentary Assembly | Could be non-UK nationals |

Figure 12.4
Appointment and election of judges

The margin of appreciation means that '[The ECtHR] case law lays down a minimum "floor" of human rights protection, not an optional "ceiling."'[37] Therefore, the court acknowledges that contracting states such as Russia, Turkey, Switzerland and Spain are not the same and a uniform approach in terms of the precise protection of human rights is not helpful.

Decisions are delivered by a Chamber Judgment, although the parties can request a referral to the Grand Chamber, where 17 judges will hear the case. The ECtHR was reformed in 1998 and now sits as a full-time court. In 2012 a conference in Brighton (which was arranged through the Committee of Ministers) considered ways to reform the ECtHR.[38]

Judges are appointed to the European Court of Human Rights in accordance with Article 22 of the European Convention on Human Rights, which states, 'The judges shall be elected by the Parliamentary Assembly with respect to each High Contracting Party by a majority of votes cast from a list of three candidates nominated by the High Contracting Party.' Article 21 establishes the criteria for office and Article 23 the judges' term of office and how they can be dismissed.

PUBLIC LAW IN CONTEXT

In the United Kingdom the ECtHR has received controversial press coverage. The United Kingdom does not allow prisoners to vote and this blanket ban (i.e., no permitted exceptions) was successfully challenged in *Hirst v. United Kingdom*.[39] Prisoner voting is a contentious issue and the role of the ECtHR has proved controversial as many people regard Parliament as the body that should decide this issue (see Chapter 7 for more details).

Another controversial issue was the initial inability of the United Kingdom to deport the radical Muslim cleric Abu Qatada to Jordan, because of the risk that the Jordanian authorities would use evidence obtained by torture against him, which would violate Article 6 (*Othman v. United Kingdom*[40]). The consequence of the decision was that there was talk of the United Kingdom temporarily leaving the European Convention in order to deport him. The United Kingdom then sought assurances from Jordan that evidence obtained by torture would not be used against him. Having received this assurance, the Home Secretary decided to resume the deportation. The Home Secretary's decision was successfully challenged by Abu Qatada (see *Othman v. Secretary of State for the Home Department*[41]). This decision led the United Kingdom to have to enter into a treaty with Jordan to guarantee that such evidence would not be used against Abu Qatada. Some elements of the press have been highly critical of the protection afforded to Abu Qatada. For example, see 'Qatada "to be booted out by Sunday": At last! Britain deals with hate preacher as farcical bid to deport him finally nears its conclusion.'[42]

Speaking in 2009, Lord Hoffmann, then a Lord of Appeal in Ordinary, made this observation about the way that the European Court of Human Rights was regarded in the United Kingdom:

> [I]t lacks constitutional legitimacy. The court now has 47 judges, one for each member state of the Council of Europe. One country, one judge; so that Liechtenstein, San Marino, Monaco and Andorra, which have a combined population slightly less than that of the London Borough of Islington, have four judges and Russia, with a population of 140 million, has one judge. The judges are elected by a sub-Committee of the Council of Europe's Parliamentary Assembly, which consists of 18 members chaired by a Latvian politician, on which the UK representatives are a Labour politician with a trade union background and no legal qualifications and a Conservative politician who was called to the Bar in 1972 but so far as I know has never practised. They choose from lists of 3 drawn by the governments of the 47 members in a manner which is totally opaque. It is therefore hardly surprising that to the people of the United Kingdom, this judicial body does not enjoy the constitutional legitimacy which the people of the United States accord to their Supreme Court. This is not an expression of populist Euroscepticism.[43]

What do you think Lord Hoffmann was saying here? Do you think countries should be accorded more judges if they have a larger population?

12.4.2 European Convention on Human Rights

The European Convention on Human Rights (ECHR or the Convention) is central to the Council of Europe. The members who have signed the treaty have agreed to respect fundamental freedoms and rights. It was adopted in 1950 and ratified in 1951 by member states. In 1953 the ECHR came into force. Given the key role of British lawyers in drafting the ECHR, it is somewhat ironic that it the United Kingdom has been extremely slow in incorporating the ECHR into domestic law.

12.5 The United Kingdom and the ECHR

12.5.1 The long road to Strasbourg

Despite the prominent role of British lawyers, it was not until 1966 that Harold Wilson's Labour government allowed individuals to bring petitions to the

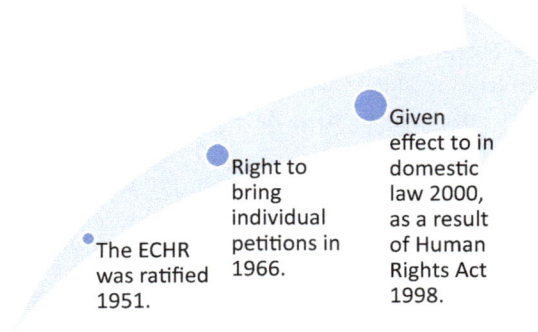

Given effect to in domestic law 2000, as a result of Human Rights Act 1998.

Right to bring individual petitions in 1966.

The ECHR was ratified 1951.

Figure 12.5
The United Kingdom's relationship with the ECHR and ECtHR

ECtHR at Strasbourg. This permitted individuals to sue the United Kingdom's government for alleged violations of Convention rights. British citizens were faced with having to bring their cases to Strasbourg, which became known as the 'long road to Strasbourg.' Bringing a case to the ECtHR proved expensive and was a lengthy process. This meant that Convention rights could not be protected by domestic courts, and only a very small fraction of those whose rights were violated would be able get redress for this.

The Labour government wished to incorporate the Convention rights into domestic law (see Figure 12.5). The intention of the new government was clear in 1997:

> It takes on average five years to get an action into the European Court of Human Rights once all domestic remedies have been exhausted; and it costs an average of £30,000. Bringing these rights home will mean that the British people will be able to argue for their rights in the British courts – without this inordinate delay and cost.[44]

Findings against the United Kingdom did sometimes lead to changes in the law. For example, the decision in *Malone v. United Kingdom*[45] resulted in the Interception of Communications Act 1985. What happened in this decision was that the police tapped an individual's phone without lawful authority, and the English courts had held that the police had such a power despite having no specific statutory power to do so.

PUBLIC LAW IN CONTEXT

An example of the differences between the protection of individuals' rights before a domestic court and the ECtHR was demonstrated in *R v. Secretary of State for Defence ex p. Smith*[46]. In *Ex p. Smith* the United Kingdom had dismissed homosexual military personnel. The Court of Appeal held that this did not violate administrative law, as it was not unreasonable to dismiss the personnel. We shall see in **Chapter 13** that the decision was challenged as being unreasonable. The ECtHR in *Smith v. United Kingdom*[47] held that the decision violated Article 8 of the ECHR as dismissing the personnel was not proportionate. Because English judges were not able to rely on the jurisprudence of the ECtHR and the ECHR in protecting the rights of citizens, it is hardly surprising that many people were forced to bring their cases to Strasbourg.

12.5.2 Judges could not apply the ECHR domestically – did the existing common law adequately protect human rights?

Sir Leslie Scarman took the view that the common law did not adequately protect human rights.[48] His Lordship favoured limiting the ability of Parliament to legislate contrary to fundamental rights. His Lordship noted Coke CJ's classic quote from Dr Bonham's case, which stated that the common law would not apply an Act of Parliament that violated an important common law right. Scarman observed:

> There are many who believe that the response of the common law to pressure for the incorporation of a declaration of human rights into English law should be, quite simply, that it is unnecessary. The point is a fair one and deserves to be taken seriously. When times are normal and fear is not stalking the land, English law sturdily protects the freedom of the individual and respects human personality. But when times are abnormally alive with fear and prejudice, the common law is at a disadvantage: it cannot resist the will, however frightened and prejudiced it may be, of Parliament.[49]

Sir Leslie Scarman warned that the courts are powerless against an Act of Parliament and stated that:

> It is the helplessness of the law in face of the legislative sovereignty of Parliament which makes it difficult for the legal system to accommodate the concept of fundamental and inviolable human rights. Means therefore have to be found whereby (1) there is incorporated into English law a declaration of such rights, (2) these rights are protected against all encroachment, including the power of the state, even when that power is exerted by a representative legislative institution such as Parliament.[50]

It is clear that Parliamentary Sovereignty prevents the courts from challenging an Act of Parliament. However, many lawyers argued that the common law did adequately protect fundamental rights.

Of course, many important rights had been developed in English law, and these included:

- habeas corpus
- the Magna Carta
- Petition of Right
- Bill of Rights
- natural justice and procedural fairness

Lustgarten and Leigh refer to the opinion of Simon Brown LJ in *Ex p. Smith*[51], who stated that the courts could be less deferential to the executive,

> if the Convention . . . were part of our law and we were accordingly entitled to ask whether the policy answers a pressing social need and whether the restriction on human rights involved can be shown to be proportionate to its benefits, then clearly the primary judgment (subject only to a limited 'margin of appreciation') would be for us and not others: the constitutional balance would shift.[52]

Prior to 2000, judges could not develop English law in conformity with the jurisprudence of the ECtHR; neither could they give effect to the ECHR. Simon Brown LJ's comments are indicative of the gulf between what the court was able to do before and after the enactment of the HRA 1998. Examples of the fact that the ECHR could not be used in domestic courts include *R v Morrisey*[53] where the evidence used to convict the defendant would have breached Article 6 of the ECHR 'the right to a fair trial' and had the ECHR been enforceable in domestic courts, then the evidence would not have been admissible. The court was clear that:

> We are in agreement with [counsel] on one point, namely that the present position is very unsatisfactory. It would appear that the appellants have or certainly may have grounds for complaining in Strasbourg and, if the penalty is enforced and they incur costs in seeking relief, they may have claims to compensation against Her Majesty's Government. That is not, however, something which the courts can remedy. Our domestic law remains as declared by this Court in *Saunders*. The United Kingdom is subject to a Treaty obligation to give effect to the European Convention of Human Rights as interpreted by the Court of Human Rights, but that again is not something which this Court can enforce. We conceive that we have no choice but to dismiss these appeals on that ground as on others.'[54]

12.5.3 New Labour: bringing rights home

The Labour Party was determined to incorporate the ECHR into domestic law. This would allow individuals the right to enforce the Convention rights in domestic courts against the state, without having the delay and the expense of going to Strasbourg. As part of the Labour manifesto, Jack Straw and Paul Boateng wrote 'Bringing Rights Home' in 1996, which led to Rights Brought Home: The Human Rights Bill 1997.

12.6 Human Rights Act 1998

In October 2000, the Human Rights Act 1998 (HRA 1998) came into force and has proven to be a very controversial statute. It has significant constitutional importance, as for the first time everyone has been given rights by Parliament that could be enforced in a domestic court. The impact of the HRA 1998 is not just confined to constitutional and administrative law, but also extends to every other area of law. The HRA 1998 is an ordinary statute and can be both expressly and impliedly repealed by another Act of Parliament. In *Thoburn v. Sunderland City Council*[55] Laws LJ suggested in *obiter* that there was a special status of constitutional statutes in the United Kingdom, which included the HRA 1998. According to Laws, again in *obiter*, these constitutional statures could not be impliedly repealed. This is only *obiter* and the HRA 1998 could be both expressly and impliedly repealed. The idea of constitutional statutes has gained traction and the Supreme Court accepted that certain statutes had a 'constitutional character' in *R (on the application of Miller) v Secretary of State for Exiting the European Union*[56] and *R (on the application of HS2 Action Alliance Limited) v Secretary of State for Transport*[57]. The principle of legality, as expressed by Lord Hoffmann in *R v Secretary of State for the Home Department ex p. Simms*[58], acknowledges that Parliament could, if it chose to do so, legislate contrary to fundamental rights, but the courts would presume that without clear words to that effect, that Parliament did not intend to legislate contrary to fundamental rights.

We can see that the Human Rights Act 1998 is an important constitutional statute. The HRA 1998, in the absence of a British Bill of Rights, confers free-standing rights that can be enforced in a domestic court. These rights are those parts of the European Convention on Human Rights that are given effect by the HRA 1998. These rights are constitutionally significant, as no one would deny that the rights to a fair trial or freedom of assembly and association are important in a 21st-century democracy.

12.6.1 The need for precision

It is important that you are precise when you talk about human rights. You should not confuse the ECHR with the HRA 1998. Article 6 of the ECHR (the right to a fair trial) has been given effect in domestic law by section 1 of the HRA 1998. Therefore, you should not say that it is 'Article 6 of the HRA 1998' or that 'section 6 of the HRA 1998 protects the right to a fair trial.' Your lecturers and the examiners will expect you to be precise.

12.6.2 Section 1 HRA gives effect to the European Convention on Human Rights

The HRA 1998 has given effect to much of the ECHR into domestic law. Section 1 gives effect to the following rights and fundamental freedoms:

- Articles 2 to 12 and 14 of the ECHR
- Articles 1 to 3 of the First Protocol
- Article 1 of the Thirteenth Protocol

12.6.3 The relationship between the domestic courts and the European Court of Human Rights

Section 2 of the HRA 1998 is concerned with the court's interpretation of the Convention rights. Subsection (1) instructs the court that:

> A court or tribunal determining a question which has arisen in connection with a Convention right must take into account any –
>
> (a) judgment, decision, declaration or advisory opinion of the European Court of Human Rights,
> (b) opinion of the Commission given in a report adopted under Article 31 of the Convention,
> (c) decision of the Commission in connection with Article 26 or 27(2) of the Convention, or
> (d) decision of the Committee of Ministers taken under Article 46 of the Convention,
>
> whenever made or given, so far as, in the opinion of the court or tribunal, it is relevant to the proceedings in which that question has arisen.

Importantly section 2(1) does not make the jurisprudence of the European Court of Human Rights binding on English courts. Instead, the court must take the decisions of the ECtHR into account. As we have seen earlier in Chapter 3, Lord Browne-Wilkinson, during the parliamentary debate on the Human Rights Bill, opposed the attempt to make the decisions binding.

The relationship between Strasbourg and domestic courts has given rise to the mirror principle, where British courts will develop domestic law in line with Strasbourg's jurisprudence. The domestic court will only depart from the jurisprudence of Strasbourg in exceptional circumstances.

In *R (Ullah) v. Special Adjudicator*[59] Lord Bingham observed:

> While such case law is not strictly binding, it has been held that courts should, in the absence of some special circumstances, follow any clear and constant jurisprudence of the Strasbourg court. . . . This reflects the fact that the Convention is an international instrument, the correct interpretation of which can be authoritatively expounded only by the Strasbourg

court. From this it follows that a national court subject to a duty such as that imposed by section 2 should not without strong reason dilute or weaken the effect of the Strasbourg case law. It is indeed unlawful under section 6 of the 1998 Act for a public authority, including a court, to act in a way which is incompatible with a Convention right. It is of course open to member states to provide for rights more generous than those guaranteed by the Convention, but such provision should not be the product of interpretation of the Convention by national courts, since the meaning of the Convention should be uniform throughout the states party to it. The duty of national courts is to keep pace with the Strasbourg jurisprudence as it evolves over time: no more, but certainly no less.[60]

We can see that Lord Bingham emphasised the importance of the uniformity of interpretation of the ECHR. The final say as to how the ECHR was to be interpreted was given to Strasbourg. The domestic court should avoid adopting a more generous interpretation of the ECHR. An exception to applying the principles established by Strasbourg was held to apply in *R v. Horncastle*[61], where the Supreme Court refused to apply the jurisprudence of the ECtHR because the fine balance contained in domestic law was not sufficiently accommodated by Strasbourg. The Supreme Court believed that the rules contained under the Police and Criminal Evidence Act 1984 still permitted the defendant to have a fair trial. The Supreme Court was clear that

> the requirement to 'take into account' the Strasbourg jurisprudence will normally result in this Court applying principles that are clearly established by the Strasbourg Court. There will, however, be rare occasions where this court has concerns as to whether a decision of the Strasbourg Court sufficiently appreciates or accommodates particular aspects of our domestic process. In such circumstances it is open to this court to decline to follow the Strasbourg decision, giving reasons for adopting this course.[62]

In *Manchester City Council v Pinnock*[63] the Supreme Court was clear that there were circumstances when the court would not follow the ECtHR. Lord Neuberger held that:

> This Court is not bound to follow every decision of the EurCtHR. Not only would it be impractical to do so: it would sometimes be inappropriate, as it would destroy the ability of the Court to engage in the constructive dialogue with the EurCtHR which is of value to the development of Convention law. . . . Of course, we should usually follow a clear and constant line of decisions by the EurCtHR. . . . But we are not actually bound to do so or (in theory, at least) to follow a decision of the Grand Chamber. As Lord Mance pointed out in *Doherty v Birmingham* [2009] 1 AC 367, para 126, section 2 of the HRA requires our courts to 'take into account' EurCtHR decisions, not necessarily to follow them. Where, however, there is a clear and constant line of decisions whose effect is not inconsistent with some

fundamental substantive or procedural aspect of our law, and whose reasoning does not appear to overlook or misunderstand some argument or point of principle, we consider that it would be wrong for this Court not to follow that line.[64]

In *Secretary of State for the Home Department v. AF*[65] Lord Rodger commented that, '[e]ven though we are dealing with rights under a United Kingdom statute, in reality, we have no choice: Argentoratum locutum, iudicium finitum – Strasbourg has spoken, the case is closed.' In *Moohan v Lord Advocate*[66] Lord Wilson was clear that the domestic courts had the ability to go beyond the ECtHR and offer greater protection of human rights: 'where there is no directly relevant decision of the ECtHR with which it would be possible (even if appropriate) to keep pace, we can and must do more. We must determine for ourselves the existence or otherwise of an alleged Convention right.'[67] In *Commissioner of Police of the Metropolis v DSD*[68] Lord Kerr supported this view, when His Lordship made clear that

Reticence by the courts of the UK to decide whether a Convention right has been violated would be an abnegation of our statutory obligation under section 6 of HRA. . . . I would firmly reject the suggestion that the decision of this court on whether the respondents enjoy a right under the HRA to claim compensation against the appellant should be influenced, much less inhibited, by any perceived absence of authoritative guidance from ECtHR.[69]

ACADEMIC DEBATE
THE MEANING OF SECTION 2 OF THE HUMAN RIGHTS ACT 1998

In an article in 2012 Lord Irvine, the former Lord Chancellor, disagreed that the domestic courts did not have a choice.

I beg to differ. Section 2 of the HRA means that the domestic court always has a choice. Further, not only is the domestic court entitled to make the choice, its statutory duty under s.2 obliges it to confront the question whether or not the relevant decision of the ECHR is sound in principle and should be given effect domestically. Simply put, the domestic court must decide the case for itself.[70]

Lord Irvine believed that the domestic courts are under a constitutional duty to say when Strasbourg has made a mistake. When this occurs, the courts should not apply Strasbourg's jurisprudence. Irvine was critical of the domestic courts' approach to section 2:

I can understand this temptation. For a judge faced with an unprincipled or aberrant decision (or line of decisions) of the ECHR, *Ullah* is the path of least resistance. It is only too easy to shelter behind *Ullah* rather than to confront the issue head on and make the case explaining why the Strasbourg Court's decision is flawed and should not be followed.[71]

Sir Philip Sales QC responded to Lord Irvine's article, which had called for domestic courts to develop their own interpretation of the Convention rights.[72] Sales argued that the domestic courts in mirroring Strasbourg's jurisprudence were adopting the preferred approach and is justified by the reason for passing the Human Rights Act 1998.

The mirror principle means that the Supreme Court takes into account the interpretation given by Strasbourg of the Convention rights. Baroness Hale has observed extra-judicially,

> [i]f you come and listen to a human rights case being argued in the Supreme Court, you will be struck by the amount of time counsel spend referring to and discussing the Strasbourg case law. They treat it as if it were the case law of our domestic courts. This is odd, because the Strasbourg case law is not like ours. It is not binding upon anyone, even upon them.[73]

Baroness Hale commented that many people had criticised the court for not developing domestic human rights jurisprudence independently of Strasbourg, and argued that that there were cases 'where we have definitely gone further than Strasbourg had gone at the time and probably further than Strasbourg would still go.'[74]

However, Lord Justice Laws in his 2013 Hamlyn Lecture disagreed with Lord Bingham's approach to section 2 and held that the domestic should develop and interpret the ECHR without feeling obliged to follow Strasbourg:

> Essentially (1) s.2 of the 1998 Act enjoins no subservience to the Strasbourg jurisprudence: it is to be '[taken] into account.' (2) Lord Bingham's reference to 'the correct interpretation' of the Convention, and his statement that it is in the hands of the Strasbourg court implies that there is such a thing: a single correct interpretation, a universal jurisprudence, across the boundaries of the signatory States. I think that is a mistake. (3) So close an adherence to Strasbourg gravely undermines the autonomous development of human rights law by the common law courts.[75]

Lord Judge CJ takes a similar view:

> Personally, I have never doubted, and have spoken publicly to the effect that the words mean what they say. To take account of the decisions of the European Court does not mean that you are required to apply or follow them. If that was the statutory intention, that would be the language used in the statute. . . . In my view, the Strasbourg Court is not superior to our Supreme Court.[76]

Jack Straw, the former Lord Chancellor, took a similar view in 2013:

> That the Human Rights Act has been a resounding success. It is here to stay. It is not the problem, rather part of the solution to a fundamental impediment to the operation of

democratic politics across Europe: namely, the ever-widening jurisdiction of the European Court in Strasbourg, for which there is neither authority in the treaties, nor popular consent. . . . That our higher courts should have the confidence to come to their own interpretations of rights under the European Convention on Human Rights, without having automatically to follow Strasbourg's jurisprudence. Here I come down strongly on the side of those such as Lord Irvine of Lairg, former Lord Chancellor, and Baroness Hale, Justice of the UK Supreme Court, in their rejection of the 'mirror' principle set out in a series of leading cases, starting with Alconbury and Ullah.[77]

12.6.4 The interpretation of Acts of Parliament

We shall see that section 6(1) makes it unlawful for a public authority to act in a manner which is incompatible with Convention rights (see Figure 12.6). However, it is not unlawful under section 6(2) for a public authority to apply the provisions of an Act of Parliament which is incompatible with Convention rights. This is hugely significant for the person who has been directly affected by the public authorities' actions.

12.6.4.1 Section 3: Interpretation of legislation to ensure ECHR compliance

Section 3(1) instructs the courts (High Court and above) to interpret primary and secondary legislation to make them compatible with the Convention rights: 'So far as it is possible to do so, primary legislation and subordinate legislation must be read and given effect in a way which is compatible with the Convention rights.'

You should note that the courts can only interpret legislation so far as it is possible to do so, which means that the courts cannot ignore Parliament's intention. This means that if an Act of Parliament is incompatible with Convention

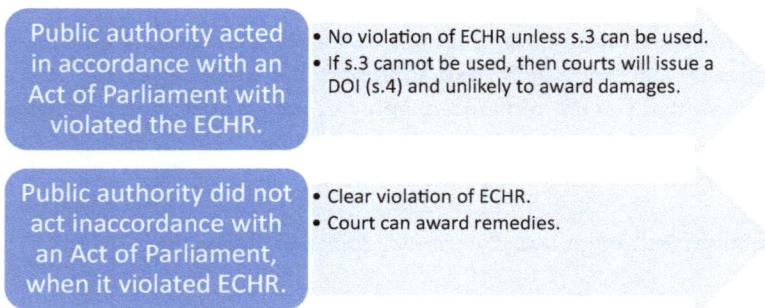

Public authority acted in accordance with an Act of Parliament with violated the ECHR.	• No violation of ECHR unless s.3 can be used. • If s.3 cannot be used, then courts will issue a DOI (s.4) and unlikely to award damages.
Public authority did not act inaccordance with an Act of Parliament, when it violated ECHR.	• Clear violation of ECHR. • Court can award remedies.

Figure 12.6
Did the public authority act in accordance to the law?

rights that the courts can read down words in the Act to make the Act compatible – however, they cannot do this, if doing so, would ignore Parliament's intention (see Figure 12.6). Importantly, section 3(2)(c) states that if the courts are unable to interpret the legislation to give effect to Convention rights, then it 'does not affect the validity, continuing operation or enforcement of any incompatible subordinate legislation.'[78]

Section 3 gives the court an important power to interpret an Act of Parliament to prevent it from being incompatible with the ECHR. We must remember that the court cannot ignore Parliament's intention, as this would offend Parliamentary Sovereignty. Nonetheless, the courts have considerable freedom to interpret legislation to protect Convention rights. Controversially in *R v. A*[79] Lord Steyn relied on section 3 to permit a rape victim's previous sexual history to be adduced as evidence by the defence, whereas Parliament had expressly legislated to prevent this.

Where primary legislation can be interpreted to give effect to the Convention rights, the victim is entitled to a remedy under section 8 of the HRA 1998. This is because in retrospect the public authority (although acting legally at the time) has now violated the victim's Convention rights and the violation is now no longer in accordance with the law. Section 8(1) permits the court to 'grant such relief or remedy, or make such order, within its powers as it considers just and appropriate.' Crucially, the public authority must be acting illegally (see Figure 12.8).

If the public authority acted without legal authority to detain someone for an invalid reason, then as there was no Act of Parliament which authorised the public authority's action, there would no need to consider the use of section 3 as the public authority's actions were illegal and the court could award a remedy under section 8.

The House of Lords in *R v. Lambert*[80] used section 3 to protect the defendant's right to a fair trial under Article 6 ECHR. This case involved the burden of proof

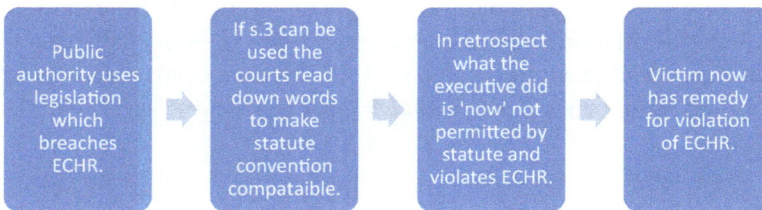

Figure 12.7
The use of s.3 HRA 1998

Figure 12.8
Public authority acts without lawful authority

being placed on a defendant accused of being in possession of illegal drugs under section 28 of the Misuse of Drugs Act 1971.

12.6.4.2 Declaration of incompatibility

Section 4 of the HRA 1998 permits the High Court or any more senior court to make a declaration of incompatibility. Under section 4(2) the declaration of incompatibility can be made where 'the court is satisfied that the provision is incompatible with a Convention right, it may make a declaration of that incompatibility.' Section 4 is used where the court is unable using section 3 to interpret the legislation to give effect to the Convention rights.

What must be remembered is that section 4 does not give the court the power to strike down offending Acts of Parliament or secondary legislation made in accordance with the powers delegated by Parliament (see Figure 12.9). Subsection (6) is clear that the making of a declaration of incompatibility, (a) 'does not affect the validity, continuing operation or enforcement of the provision in respect of which it is given; and (b) 'is not binding on the parties to the proceedings in which it is made.'

Section 4 of the HRA 1998 does not permit the courts to strike down an Act of Parliament (even if it did then this would be incompatible with Parliamentary Sovereignty). Instead, the courts can make a declaration of incompatibility, which does not affect the validity of legislation. Conor Gearty is in favour of the position in the United Kingdom where the courts are unable to strike down legislation, as this system, unlike the United States' system, does not remove the ability of Parliament to legislate contrary to human rights. Gearty observed that, '[t]here is something inherently distasteful about elected representatives waiting to see whether their judgments about the public interest, made on a bona fide basis with the interests of the community genuinely at heart, meet with the approval of a bench of unelected and unaccountable lawyers.'[81] Gearty was of the opinion that 'declarations of incompatibility are courteous requests for a conversation, not pronouncements of truth from high.'[82]. In the United States, legislation which affects human rights is often challenged in the Supreme Court and examples include the US Defence of Marriage Act which had a key provision struck down in *United States v Windsor*[83], as it discriminated

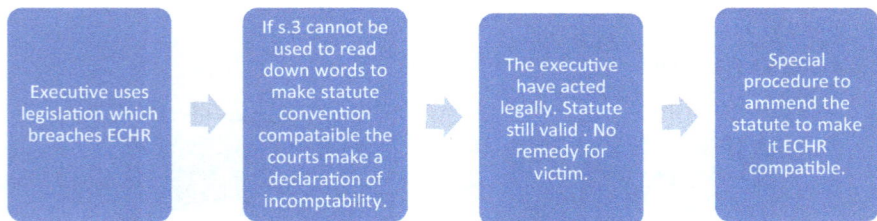

Figure 12.9
The use of s.4 HRA 1998 to issue a declaration of incompatibility

against same-sex couples who did not qualify for the benefits afforded to married heterosexual couples.[84]

The effect of a declaration of incompatibility does not affect the validity of the Act of Parliament, which through the judicial observance of Parliamentary Sovereignty remains good law and the public authority is not prevented from breaching the victim's Convention rights. The consequence of the courts issuing a declaration of incompatibility, rather than interpreting the statute under section 3 to give effect to Convention rights, is that the victim is unable to enforce their Convention rights.

Lord Steyn has argued in favour of judicial use of section 3 as opposed to section 4. His Lordship explained his reasons for this in *Ghaidan v. Godin-Mendoza*[85].

PUBLIC LAW IN CONTEXT
WHY LORD STEYN PREFERRED USING SECTION 3 RATHER THAN SECTION 4 HRA 1998

The decision in *Ghaidan v. Godin-Mendoza* concerned a same-sex relationship and whether the surviving partner could be protected under the Rent Act 1977. His Lordship stated that, '[t]he linch-pin of the legislative scheme to achieve (bringing rights home) . . . was section 3(1). Rights could only be effectively brought home if section 3(1) was the prime remedial measure, and section 4 a measure of last resort.'[86] Lord Steyn observed that, '[w]hat is necessary, however, is to emphasise that interpretation under section 3(1) is the prime remedial remedy and that resort to section 4 must always be an exceptional course. In practical effect there is a strong rebuttable presumption in favour of an interpretation consistent with Convention rights.' His Lordship is stating that section 3 ought to be the preferred remedy, and section 4 only should be used where the court cannot rely upon section 3.[87]

In *Re S (Children) (Care Order: Implementation of Care Plan), Re W (Children) (Care Order: Adequacy of Care Plan)*[88] Lord Nicholls of Birkenhead stated that section 3 cannot be used to permit the court to interpret the statute to have 'a meaning which departs substantially from a fundamental feature of an Act of Parliament (and therefore the court) . . . is likely to have crossed the boundary between interpretation and amendment.'[89] Lord Nicholls was adamant that the courts must not be tempted to use section 3 as a way to amend legislation (to change the meaning), rather that is the job for Parliament and the court's role was to interpret the statute before it.[90]

An example of where the court has used section 4 rather than section 3 is the decision in *R (on the application of Anderson) v. Secretary of State for the Home Department*[91]. The Home Secretary's power to fix sentencing tariffs (a minimum sentence) was found to be incompatible with Article 6, which guarantees the right to a fair trial. This was because the sentence was a judicial matter, and it should not be made by the executive. The House of Lords refused to use section 3 to interpret section 29 of the Crime (Sentences) Act 1997 in a way that protected the victim's right under Article 6 ECHR, but instead issued a declaration of incompatibility. Lord Bingham in his judgment observed that Parliament gave the Home Secretary discretionary powers to fix tariffs, therefore, to use section 3 to restrict his discretion would go against Parliament's intention:

> Since, therefore, the section leaves it to the Home Secretary to decide whether or when to refer a case to the board, and he is free to ignore its recommendation if it is favourable to the prisoner, the decision on how long the convicted murderer should remain in prison for punitive purposes is his alone. It cannot be doubted that Parliament intended this result when enacting section 29 and its predecessor sections. . . . To read section 29 as precluding participation by the Home Secretary, if it were possible to do so, would not be judicial interpretation but judicial vandalism: it would give the section an effect quite different from that which Parliament intended and would go well beyond any interpretative process sanctioned by section 3 of the 1998 Act.[92]

Lord Steyn agreed with Lord Bingham:

> Counsel for the appellant invited the House to use the interpretative obligation under section 3 to read into section 29 alleged Convention rights, viz to provide that the tariff set by the Home Secretary may not exceed the judicial recommendation. It is impossible to follow this course. It would not be interpretation but interpolation inconsistent with the plain legislative intent to entrust the decision to the Home Secretary, who was intended to be free to follow or reject judicial advice. Section 3(1) is not available where the suggested interpretation is contrary to express statutory words or is by implication necessarily contradicted by the statute. It is therefore impossible to imply the suggested words into the statute or to secure the same result by a process of construction.[93]

12.6.5 Remedial action

Section 10 permits the government to amend legislation which violates the ECHR. Schedule 2 establishes the procedure for ministers to use remedial orders to amend offending legislation. The procedure states that the draft order must be approved by a resolution of both Houses of Parliament, unless the matter is considered urgent. Constitutionally there is no requirement that the government takes remedial action; however, the effect of a declaration of incompatibility most often will compel remedial action to be taken. Returning to *R (on the application of Anderson) v. Secretary of State for the Home Department*, the government responded by repealing the offending legislation by introducing the provisions in the Criminal Justice Act 2003. In *A v. Secretary of State for the Home*

Department[94] the House of Lords held that the Home Secretary's decision to detain suspected foreign terrorist suspects indefinitely without trial amounted to a violation of Articles 5 and 14 ECHR. The House of Lords made a declaration of incompatibility and the government responded by eventually replacing indefinite detention with control orders. Control orders place restrictions on when an individual can leave their house.

12.6.6 Section 19 HRA 1998

Section 19 of the HRA 1998 has imposed an obligation on the minister in charge of a bill to inform Parliament upon introducing the bill, whether the bill is compatible with Convention rights. This is important as compatibility with the Convention rights will be an important consideration during the drafting and parliamentary debates on the bill.

12.6.7 What is a public authority?

Section 19 does not prevent incompatibility; rather it imposes a duty to expressly state whether there will be incompatibility with the ECHR.

12.6.7.1 Vertical and horizontal effect of the HRA 1998

The Human Rights Act 1998 was only intended to have a vertical effect. That is Convention rights were only intended to be enforced against public authorities which have breached a Convention right. The Act was not intended to have a horizontal effect, which means that the Convention rights were not meant to be enforceable against private parties, such as individuals and companies.

12.6.7.2 Section 6 – what is a public authority under the HRA 1998?

So, what then is a public authority for the purposes of the HRA 1998? Section 6(1) makes it 'unlawful for a public authority to act in a way which is incompatible with a Convention right.' Subsection (3) states that ' "public authority" includes – (a) a court or tribunal, and (b) any person certain of whose functions are functions of a public nature, but does not include either House of Parliament or a person exercising functions in connection with proceedings in Parliament.' In reality the Convention rights can have a horizontal effect, which means that an individual can enforce their right to respect for a private and family life under Article 8 ECHR against a private party, such as a tabloid newspaper. This is due to the court's status as a public authority under section 6(3) (see Figure 10.8). The courts must act in a way that is not incompatible with the ECHR and this means that the court must give effect to the Convention rights.

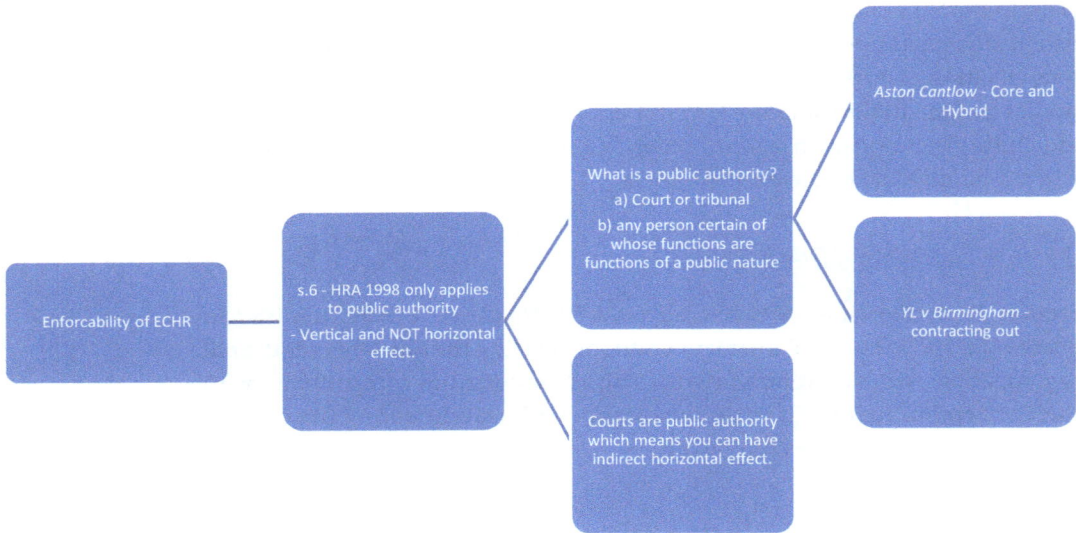

Figure 12.10
What is a public authority for the purposes of the HRA 1998?

PUBLIC LAW IN PRACTICE

How can the Convention rights have a horizontal effect? Imagine that Victor, a famous politician, has been photographed leaving his mistress's house and wishes to prevent publication of the pictures in a national newspaper. Because the HRA 1998 does not permit the Convention rights to be enforced horizontally against private parties, Victor would need to bring an action against the newspaper in private law. The particulars of claim would be for breach of the tort of confidence. Once in court Victor could then argue that his right under Article 8, which protects his right to respect for his private and family life, has been breached. The court, as a public authority, must give effect to the ECHR and this is known as indirect horizontal effect. The court will read the jurisprudence of Strasbourg into the domestic tort of confidence and in the absence of a domestic tort of privacy it could prevent the publication of the photographs.

'[A]ny person certain of whose functions are functions of a public nature'

In *Aston Cantlow and Wilmcote with Billesley Parochial Church Council v. Wall-bank*[95] the question was whether a parochial church council was a public authority within the meaning of section 6(3) HRA 1998. The case involved the Wallbank's obligation to pay towards the upkeep of the church or more precisely, to contribute towards the upkeep of the church's chancel. Liability towards the repair of a church is a risk for those people buying property in villages, and surprisingly in towns and cities as well. When buying a property, it is advisable to carry out a chancel repair search to ensure that you are not going to end up paying for the upkeep of a local church. In *Aston Cantlow* the House of Lords distinguished between two types of public authorities: a core public authority and a hybrid public authority. The House of Lords held that the parochial church council was neither a core nor hybrid public authority and that the enforcement of the defendant's contribution towards the upkeep of the church was a private law matter. Lord Nicholls' judgment in *Aston Cantlow* is very important. His Lordship noted that the HRA 1998 does not define what is meant by a public authority. His Lordship stated that examples of what is a public authority include 'government departments, local authorities, the police and the armed forces.'[96] However, '[I]n the interests of efficiency and economy, and for other reasons, functions of a governmental nature are frequently discharged by non-governmental bodies. Sometimes this will be a consequence of privatisation, sometimes not.'[97] Lord Nicholls emphasised that it was important was whether the functions carried out were of a public nature. It did not mean that the functions had to be of a governmental nature.[98] These private enterprises carrying out these functions could be a public authority, where the act is a public function rather than a private act. A hybrid public authority will carry out 'both public and non-public functions.'

Lord Nicholls questioned when a function carried out by a body is a public function for the purposes of section 6 HRA 1998. His Lordship stated:

> What, then, is the touchstone to be used in deciding whether a function is public for this purpose? Clearly there is no single test of universal application. There cannot be, given the diverse nature of governmental functions and the variety of means by which these functions are discharged today. Factors to be taken into account include the extent to which in carrying out the relevant function the body is publicly funded, or is exercising statutory powers, or is taking the place of central government or local authorities, or is providing a public service.[99]

His Lordship did not regard the parochial church council as a core public authority, since the Church of England promoted its own interests and '[t]his is far removed from the type of body whose acts engage the responsibility of the state under the European Convention.'[100] Lord Nicholls then considered whether it was a hybrid public authority and stated that 'it is not necessary to analyse each of the functions of a parochial church council and see if any of them is a public function. What matters is whether the particular act done by the plaintiff council of which complaint is made is a private act as contrasted with the discharge of a public function.'[101]

It is therefore important to appreciate that:

A core public authority is a body whose functions are effectively governmental and all of which are of a pubic nature.

A hybrid public authority is a body which carries out functions, some of which are of a public nature.

We can see that:

- A private company could be a public authority if it is carrying out public functions.
- To determine whether a body is a core public authority it is necessary to look at its funding, statutory powers and whether it is acting in the place of national or local government.

12.6.7.3 Contracting out

In *YL v. Birmingham City Council*[102] the House of Lords held that a private care home that provided care and accommodation was not exercising functions of a public nature. The majority held that the relationship between the residents and the care home was of a private law nature and was on a commercial basis.

Lord Scott held that the care home was not a public authority because it:

> is a company carrying on a socially useful business for profit. It is neither a charity nor a philanthropist. It enters into private law contracts with the residents in its care homes and with the local authorities with whom it does business. It receives no public funding, enjoys no special statutory powers, and is at liberty to accept or reject residents as it chooses . . . and to charge whatever fees in its commercial judgment it thinks suitable. It is operating in a commercial market with commercial competitors.[103]

Lord Scott warned that if every time a local authority contracted out a function to a private company, it made that company a hybrid public authority, then

> where does this end? Is a contractor engaged by a local authority to provide lifeguard personnel at the municipal swimming pool a section 6 (3)(b) public authority? If so, would a local authority employee engaged by the local authority as a lifeguard at the pool become a public authority?[104]

Furthermore, His Lordship likened a care home to a private school or hospital and dismissed the argument that residents required special protection. Lords Neuberger and Mance concurred with Lord Scott and rejected the view that a company carrying out a function for a local authority would be a hybrid public authority. Parliament reversed the effect of decision by introducing section 145 of the Health and Social Care Act 2008.[105]

12.6.8 Only a victim can bring proceedings under the HRA 1998

It is important to note that only a victim can bring proceedings under the HRA 1998. Section 7(3) states that '[i]f the proceedings are brought on an application for judicial review, the applicant is to be taken to have a sufficient interest in relation to the unlawful act only if he is, or would be, a victim of that act.' Subsection (7) makes reference to Article 34 ECHR, stating that 'a person is a victim of an unlawful act only if he would be a victim for the purposes of Article 34 of the Convention.' Article 34 of the European Convention on Human Rights concerns individual applications and states that

> [t]he Court may receive applications from any person, non-governmental organisation or group of individuals claiming to be the victim of a violation by one of the High Contracting Parties of the rights set forth in the Convention or the Protocols thereto. The High Contracting Parties undertake not to hinder in any way the effective exercise of this right.

12.6.9 Time limit

Section 7(5) states that proceedings against a public authority under the HRA 1998 must be brought 'before the end of – (a) the period of one year beginning with the date on which the act complained of took place; or (b) such longer period as the court or tribunal considers equitable having regard to all the circumstances.'

12.6.10 Violating convention rights is not a criminal offence

Section 7(8) states that '[n]othing in this Act creates a criminal offence.' This is important as a violation of Convention rights is not a criminal matter.

12.6.11 Jurisdictional issues – when and where do the Convention rights apply?

The Convention rights will only apply where a violation falls within the jurisdiction of a contracting state. This means that if there is an allegation there has been a violation of a Convention right in Bordeaux, the domestic French courts and ultimately Strasbourg will have jurisdiction to decide whether there has been a breach. For the purposes of the HRA 1998 domestic courts will not be able to give effect to the ECHR unless:

- the court has jurisdiction under Article 1, which states that '[t]he High Contracting Parties shall secure to everyone within their jurisdiction the rights and freedoms defined in Section I of this Convention'; or
- the court has jurisdiction under Article 56, where the contracting state has extended the application of the ECHR to a colonial territory under its control.

Article 1

The Grand Chamber in *Al-Skeini v. United Kingdom*[106] held that the court had jurisdiction to hold that there had been a breach of Article 2, where Iraqi nationals had died whilst being detained by the British Army in Basra. The court held that there was a jurisdictional link between the United Kingdom and the deaths, because whilst the general rule was that jurisdiction was territorial and did not extend beyond a contracting state's own territory, where a contracting state exercised effective control there could be a jurisdictional link. The court stated: 'It is a question of fact whether a Contracting State exercises effective control over an area outside its own territory. In determining whether effective control exists, the Court will primarily have reference to the strength of the State's military presence in the area. Other indicators may also be relevant, such as the extent to which its military, economic and political support for the local subordinate administration provides it with influence and control over the region.'[107] Prior to *Al-Skeini*, the Grand Chamber's decision in *Bankovic v. Belguim*[108] had held that jurisdiction was territorial and was concerned with whether the breach occurred in the contracting state's territory, rather than whether the breach occurred whilst the state had control.

In *Issa v Turkey*[109] there was an application relating to the murder of Iraqi nationals in Iraq by Turkish soldiers, which had occurred during the course of Turkish military action. However, the application was unsuccessful:

> The Court does not exclude the possibility that, as a consequence of this military action, the respondent State could be considered to have exercised, temporarily, effective overall control of a particular portion of the territory of northern Iraq. Accordingly, if there is a sufficient factual basis for holding that, at the relevant time, the victims were within that specific area, it would follow logically that they were within the jurisdiction of Turkey (and not that of Iraq, which is not a Contracting State and clearly does not fall within the legal space (*espace juridique*) of the Contracting States. However, notwithstanding the large number of troops involved in the aforementioned military operations, it does not appear that Turkey exercised effective overall control of the entire area of northern Iraq.'[110]

In *Medvedyev and Others v. France*[111] the Grand Chamber held that the ECHR applied where the French military had intercepted a vessel suspected of carrying drugs. This had occurred outside of French territory and the applicants, who were onboard the vessel, which was registered in Cambodia, complained that their human rights had been violated because they had not been brought promptly before a judge by the French authorities. The court held that the ECHR applied: 'France having exercised full and exclusive control over the *Winner* and its crew, at least *de facto*, from the time of its interception, in a continuous and uninterrupted manner until they were tried in France, the applicants were effectively within France's jurisdiction for the purposes of Article 1.'[112] See also *Hirsi Jamaa v Italy*[113] where ships carrying 200 people were intercepted by the Italian authorities. The court held that because 'the events took place entirely on board ships of the Italian armed forces, the crews of which were composed exclusively of Italian military personnel' Article 1 ECHR applied.[114]

PUBLIC LAW IN CONTEXT
SMITH V. MINISTRY OF DEFENCE

The Supreme Court in *Smith v. Ministry of Defence*[115] held that the United Kingdom's jurisdiction under Article 1 covered military personnel who were killed on active service outside of military bases in Iraq. The government had previously accepted that soldiers on military bases were within the United Kingdom's jurisdiction. Therefore, the soldiers enjoyed the right to life under Article 2. This overruled the earlier decision in *R (Smith) v. Oxfordshire Assistant Deputy Coroner*[116], which held that the soldiers on active duty were not within the United Kingdom's jurisdiction for the purposes of Article 1. The decision *in Smith v. Ministry of Defence* has been criticised by retired military leaders, such as Lord West, for interfering in military operations. Giving judgment Lord Hope had warned that the courts should proceed carefully and should draw a distinction between battlefield decisions and decisions taken off the battlefield (such as the supply of military equipment and the amount of training given to soldiers).[117]

Article 56

Article 56 gives the contracting state the decision of whether to extend the Convention rights to its overseas territories. This opt-in under Article 56 reflects the time that the Convention was drafted, when the signatories had colonial empires and did not wish to automatically extend the rights beyond their own metropolitan territories. In *Chagos Islanders v. United Kingdom*[118] the ECtHR rejected an application by the Chagossians, as it was held that the alleged violations did not fall within the jurisdiction of the United Kingdom. This was because the United Kingdom had not extended its jurisdiction under Article 56, nor did the alleged violations fall within the United Kingdom's jurisdiction for the purposes of Article 1. It was argued that the court should have jurisdiction because the decision to remove the islanders and prevent their return was taken in the United Kingdom and the United Kingdom exercised complete control of the territory. This decision followed the court's earlier decision in *Quark Fishing Ltd v. United Kingdom*.[119]

12.7 What is it exactly that the HRA 1998 gives effect to?

Section 1 of the HRA 1998 gives effect to the European Convention on Human Rights. It only gives effect to:

- Articles 2 to 12 and 14 of the Convention
- Articles 1 to 3 of the First Protocol
- Article 1 of the Thirteenth Protocol.

12.8 The Convention rights

The Convention rights can be divided between those rights which are absolute, limited and qualified (see Figure 10.9). Articles 2 (apart from lawful acts of war), 3, 4 and 7 are absolute rights and member states are not permitted to derogate from these. This means that the member state cannot justify violating any of these rights, whereas member states are permitted in certain circumstances to derogate from limited rights (Articles 5, 6, 12 and 14). Articles 8, 9, 10 and 11 are qualified rights and restrictions on these rights can be justified by the member state.

The Convention rights are set out in schedule 1. The core Convention rights are set out in the following:

12.8.1 Article 2: right to life

Article 2(1) states that, '[e]veryone's right to life shall be protected by law. No one shall be deprived of his life intentionally save in the execution of a sentence of a court following his conviction of a crime for which this penalty is provided by law.' The state is permitted to take life where it uses force 'which is no more than absolutely necessary' to defend others, to arrest a suspect or prevent escape, or to quell a riot or insurrection.

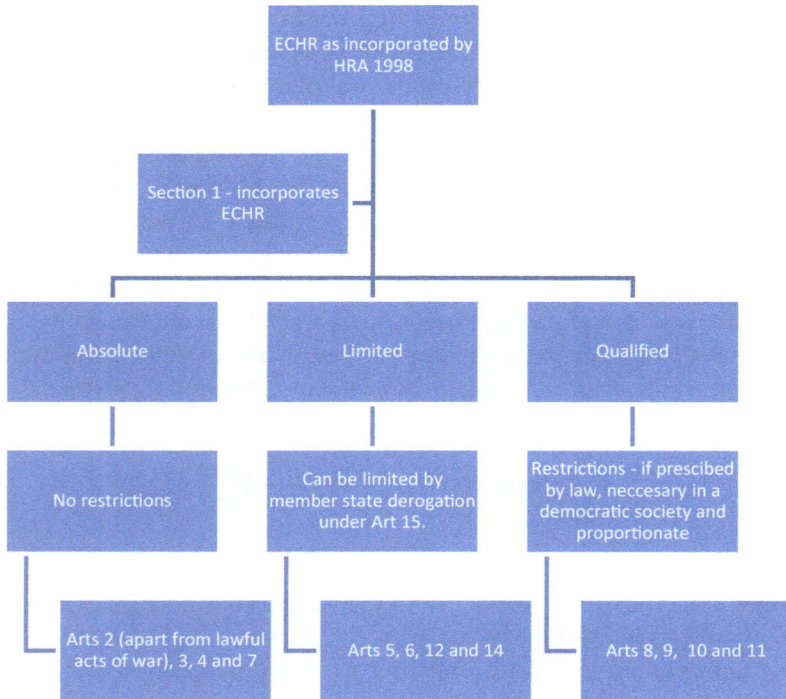

Figure 12.11
Overview of the Convention rights

In *McCann v United Kingdom*[120] several members of the IRA were shot and killed by British security forces. This raised questions of whether the UK government had a policy of killing active members of the IRA. The ECtHR held that there had been a breach of Article 2 ECHR. The UK authorities had evidence to believe that the individuals would be involved in carrying out a terrorist attack on British military personnel stationed in Gibraltar.

12.8.2 Article 3: prohibition of torture

Article 3 states that, '[n]o one shall be subjected to torture or to inhuman or degrading treatment or punishment.' Article 3 can be breached where there has either been (a) torture, or (b) inhuman or (c) degrading treatment. Even severe interrogation techniques by the security services will not necessarily amount to torture, unless they are considered to have reached the required level of intensity of suffering.

In *Ireland v. United Kingdom*[121] the security service had used five techniques during interrogations of suspects in Northern Ireland and whilst Strasbourg considered there to

> exist . . . violence which is to be condemned both on moral grounds and also in most cases under the domestic law of the Contracting States, there needed to be a 'distinction between "torture" and "inhuman or degrading treatment", should by the first of these terms attach a special stigma to deliberate inhuman treatment causing very serious and cruel suffering.'

We can see that for torture to exist the suffering must be very serious and cruel. Ireland was unsuccessful in trying to get case reopened.[122] In *Maslova v. Russia*[123] the repeated rape of a suspect by two police officers amounted to torture, as it was an especially cruel act.

PUBLIC LAW IN CONTEXT
HUMAN RIGHTS AND THE 'WAR ON TERROR'

The United States' response to the terrorist attack on 11 September 2001, in which the Twin Towers were destroyed in New York City as was part of the Pentagon (the headquarters of the US military) in Washington DC, has led to allegations that the human rights of those individuals captured or abducted by the United States have been tortured. Where this torture takes place in Europe it will mean that the Contacting State in which this has occurred could be found by the European Court of Human Rights to have breached Article 3 ECHR. In *Al Nashiri v Poland*[124] there had been a violation of Article 3 because Poland had been complicit in the CIA's secret detention centre in Poland and had not addressed allegations of torture. This all had happened in Poland. In *El-Masri v The Former Yugoslav Republic of Macedonia*[125] the applicant was tortured in Macedonia by the CIA. The ECtHR subsequently held that there was a violation of Article 3.

There can also be a violation of Article 3 where an individual will be deported from one country to another, where it is likely that they will suffer inhuman or degrading treatment, or torture. In *Soering v United Kingdom*[126] the applicant was successful in arguing that his deportation would violate Article 3 because he would be placed on Death Row when extradited to the United States. In *Othman v United Kingdom*[127] it was argued that the applicant would inter alia be tortured upon his extradition to Jordan. The ECtHR held that the reassurances that the UK had received from Jordan that the applicant would not be tortured were sufficient, which meant that the extradition would not violate Article 3. The court held:

> Moreover, the Court does not consider that the general human rights situation in Jordan excludes accepting any assurances whatsoever from the Jordanian Government. Instead, the Court considers the United Kingdom and Jordanian Governments have made genuine efforts to obtain and provide transparent and detailed assurances to ensure that the applicant will not be ill-treated upon return to Jordan.[128]

12.8.3 Article 4: prohibition of slavery and forced labour

Article 4 prevents slavery, servitude or compulsory labour. The member state will not be in breach where the labour is a condition of the sentence (community service), it is military service, it is imposed on individuals during a calamity or an emergency, or it is part of normal civic obligations. Some European countries still require military service and so this would not amount to a breach of Article 4. According to Article 4(3) forced or compulsory labour does not relate to prisoners who are required to work as part of their detention. Equally, normal civic obligations, such as jury duty in the United Kingdom, will not violate Article 4 ECHR. The domestic law needs to protect people from being forced to provide involuntary labour and suffering servitude. In *Siliadin v France*[129] a young girl was forced to provide work for a family who exploited her position as an illegal immigrant. The French courts had acquitted the family who had been charged with mistreating the girl. The European Court of Human Rights held that there had been a violation of Article 4 ECHR as she was living in servitude, and because she was an illegal immigrant, she was unable to access resources or to leave. The fact that someone performs unpaid work does not necessarily amount to a breach of Article 4 ECHR, even where there was an entitlement to pay.[130] In *Chowdury v Greece*[131] there was no violation of Article 4 ECHR even when the applicant was working with pay but under the watch of armed guards, who had opened fired when the workers went on strike.

PUBLIC LAW IN CONTEXT

Several years ago, in England and Wales a jobseeker who was forced to undergo unpaid work in a shop in order to keep her entitlement to benefits took the government to court. In

R (Reilly) v. Secretary of State for Work and Pensions[132] the court rejected the argument that this amounted to a breach of Article 4. Although the regulations requiring unpaid work were quashed on appeal as they did not comply with the section 17A of the Jobseekers Act 1995, the Court of Appeal held that there had not been a breach of Article 4.[133] Upon appeal the Supreme Court held that this did not amount to a breach.[134]

12.8.4 Article 5: right to liberty and security

Article 5 states that, '[e]veryone has the right to liberty and security of person.' The member state cannot deprive anyone of their liberty unless the reason for the detention falls within the circumstances in paragraph (1)(a)–(f), and it is in accordance with a procedure prescribed by law. These circumstances include 'the lawful arrest or detention of a person effected for the purpose of bringing him before the competent legal authority on reasonable suspicion of having committed an offence or when it is reasonably considered necessary to prevent his committing an offence or fleeing after having done so.' Paragraphs [2]–[4] outline the requirements which must be met when a person is deprived of their liberty. Article 5(2) states that '[e]veryone who is arrested shall be informed promptly, in a language which he understands, of the reasons for his arrest and of any charge against him.' Article 5(3) requires that anyone detained under Article 5(1)(c) must be 'brought promptly before a judge or other officer authorised by law to exercise judicial power and shall be entitled to trial within a reasonable time or to release pending trial. Release may be conditioned by guarantees to appear for trial.' The European Court of Human Rights was clear in *Khlafia v Italy*[135] that it was the classification of the confinement under the ECHR and not in domestic law that mattered: 'the Court finds that the classification of the applicants' confinement in domestic law cannot alter the nature of the constraining measures imposed on them.'[136]

12.8.5 Article 6: right to a fair trial

Article 6 establishes the right to a fair trial. This applies to both criminal and civil proceedings. Paragraph 2 establishes the presumption of innocence and paragraph (3) sets down the minimum rights of a person accused of committing a criminal offence. Article 6(3) states that everyone charged with a criminal offence must have access to legal assistance and the deprivation of legal advice has been found to amount to a breach.[137]

12.8.6 Article 7: no punishment without law

Article 7 prevents retrospective criminalisation of any act or omission which was not a criminal offence at the time it originally took place. It also prevents a higher penalty from being imposed than the penalty that existed when the criminal offence took place. This is why those who are accused of committing a criminal offence before the law has been reformed will be charged and prosecuted under the old rather than the new law.

12.8.7 Article 8: right to respect for private and family life

We will consider the right to a respect for a private and family life in **Chapter 13**.

12.8.8 Article 9: freedom of thought, conscience and religion

Article 9 protects the freedom of thought, conscience and religion of those living in a member state. This is an important Article as the 20th century saw mass killings of Jews during the Second World War and Muslims during the Balkans War. People are permitted to have and to change religious beliefs and to manifest these in public. The rights under Article 8 have been given indirect horizontal effect by the courts. This is because there is no right to privacy in domestic law.

In *Eweida v. United Kingdom*[138] the United Kingdom was taken to the ECtHR by a number of parties who have been prevented from manifesting their religious belief. It was alleged that there was a violation of the four applicants' rights under Articles 9 and 14 ECHR. We will look at the decision of the court in relation to two of the applicants:

- Eweida was a former British Airways employee who was prevented from wearing a cross at work. Eweida was successful at the ECtHR, which held that the domestic courts had not struck the correct balance between permitting Eweida to manifest her religious belief at work and British Airways' desire to maintain a corporate image. The United Kingdom had breached the positive obligation under Article 9, which required that the domestic law protected individuals' rights under Article 9.
- Ladele worked as a registrar for a local authority and because of her Christian faith refused to be designated as a registrar for same-sex civil partnerships. This resulted in her losing her job. The court held that there had not been a breach as the balance struck by the domestic authorities fell within the United Kingdom's margin of appreciation.

12.8.9 Article 10: freedom of expression

This is an important right as free speech is essential in a democracy and permits different political views to be represented. There needs to be a free press which is not censured by the state and can hold the executive to account. Freedom of expression is important for the spoken word, traditional print media and the internet. The use of social media proved important in the Arab Spring that toppled dictators, and Twitter allows issues to trend within this country and raise debate. Article 10 is a qualified right and can be restricted under Article 10(2). However, any restrictions must be prescribed by law and be necessary in a democratic society. Furthermore, any restrictions must be proportionate. The law must protect individuals' rights to express political opinion and be members of non-prescribed political parties. In *Redfearn v United Kingdom*[139] a bus driver was dismissed by his employer. He had been nominated for an award for his service and had worked with passengers who were mainly of an Asian origin. He stood as a candidate for the British National Party who only permitted white members to join and its constitution stated that the party was

> wholly opposed to any form of integration between British and non-European peoples. It is therefore committed to stemming and reversing the tide of non-white immigration and to restoring, by legal changes, negotiation and consent, the overwhelmingly white makeup of the British population that existed in Britain prior to 1948.[140]

The applicant was elected and was consequently dismissed by his employer. He sought to bring a claim for discrimination through the Employment Tribunal and was unsuccessful. The decision of the Employment Tribunal was upheld by the Court of Appeal. The European Court of Human Rights held that the domestic law in not offering him protection violated his rights under Article 10 and Article 11 (see below).

PUBLIC LAW IN CONTEXT
THE LEVESON REPORT

The British press has exposed many important scandals such as the abuse of parliamentary expenses, which has led to the prosecution of many parliamentarians. However, the press has been accused of many negative practices such as phone-hacking and making false accusations about individuals. A public inquiry was chaired by Lord Justice Leveson and investigated the culture, practice and ethics of the press. The report called for press regulation that would be underpinned by statute. Only the first part of the initially planned two-part public inquiry was ever undertaken.

The recommendation in the Leveson Report for press regulation has proved controversial. The report's recommendations have been challenged by some politicians and elements of the press. They argue that regulation would restrict the freedom of expression by the press and harm free speech. The three main political parties agreed that the press would be regulated by a royal charter, rather than by statute. However, the press had submitted to the Privy Council their own proposals for an alternative royal charter. The rival proposals differed from the one put forward by the three main political parties, as future regulation would have to be agreed by the bodies including trade bodies. Former editors would be allowed to sit on the panel regulating the press, and the readers of the publication would have a say over how the press was regulated. In October 2013, the *Press Standards Board of Finance Ltd* applied to the court to get an injunction to prevent the government from presenting the cross-party royal charter to the Queen. However, in *R (Press Standards Board of Finance Ltd) v. The Secretary of State for Culture, Media and Sport*[141] the court rejected the application for an injunction and to judicially review the proposed royal charter. The Press Standards Board of Finance Ltd were unsuccessful in their appeal to the Court Appeal in May 2014.

12.8.10 Article 11: freedom of assembly and association

Article 11 states that, '[e]veryone has the right to freedom of peaceful assembly and to freedom of association with others, including the right to form and to join trade unions for the protection of his interests.' This is important as peaceful assembly and the right to associate with others is important in a democracy. Trade union membership is vital to protect workers' rights and was only decriminalised in the 19th century. We will look at this in more detail in Chapter 14.

12.8.11 Article 12: right to marry

The right to marry and to establish a family is an important right. A man and a woman in the United Kingdom may marry upon reaching the age of sixteen. There are limitations on this right, which include the criminalisation of bigamy and incest. In *B v. United Kingdom*[142] the ECtHR held that there had been a breach of Article 12, where a father-in-law and daughter-in-law were prevented from marrying whilst their respective spouses were still alive.

12.8.13 Article 14: prohibition of discrimination

Article 14 prevents people from being denied the Convention rights by reasons including race, religion, sexuality and colour.

12.8.14 Restricting the Convention rights

In *A v. Secretary of State for the Home Department*[143] the circumstances for a derogation to be used was accepted by the majority of the House of Lords (with only Lord Hoffmann dissenting as to whether there was an emergency threatening the life of the nation – see Chapter 4 on the Rule of Law). However, the House of Lords found the Home Secretary's decision to be disproportionate and discriminatory and violated Article 14. This was because it was discriminatory in permitting the detention solely on the grounds of nationality or immigration status.

There is no definition of when the state can interfere and restrict the rights under the ECHR. Where the right is limited it may only be restricted where the member state derogates under Article 15. In order to derogate from the ECHR any restriction on the Convention rights will need to be proportionate.

It is important to consider what Article 15 actually says:

Derogations under Article 15 ECHR

1   In time of war or other public emergency threatening the life of the nation any High Contracting Party may take measures derogating from its obligations under this Convention to the extent strictly required by the exigencies of the situation, provided that such measures are not inconsistent with its other obligations under international law.

2   No derogation from Article 2, except in respect of deaths resulting from lawful acts of war, or from Articles 3, 4 (paragraph 1) and 7 shall be made under this provision.

3   Any High Contracting Party availing itself of this right of derogation shall keep the Secretary-General of the Council of Europe fully informed of the measures which it has taken and the reasons therefor. It shall also inform the Secretary-General of the Council of Europe when such measures have ceased to operate and the provisions of the Convention are again being fully executed.

Where the right is qualified the member state may restrict it but must do so in circumstances where the restriction is prescribed by law and proportionate. In *A v. Secretary of State for the Home Department* Lord Bingham stated that, 'Article 15 requires that any measures taken by a member state in derogation of its obligations under the Convention should not go beyond what is "strictly required by the exigencies of the situation". Thus, the Convention imposes a test of strict necessity or, in Convention terminology, proportionality.'[144]

12.9 Proportionality

If there is a violation of a Convention right, then the court must adopt the test of proportionality (see Figure 12.12). The court must ask whether the public authority's actions were proportionate to the violation.

In no circumstances can a public authority restrict a Convention right without lawful authority. If the public authority is not pursuing a legislative objective, then it is acting illegally. The qualified rights, e.g. Articles 8, 10 and 11, can be restricted where the restriction is either:

- in accordance with the law or prescribed by law;
- necessary in a democratic society. It is here that the question of proportionality would be key.

We will look in more detail at proportionality as a ground for judicial review in Chapter 16. Since the decision in *R (on the application of Daly) v. Secretary of State for the Home Department*[145] the domestic courts can ask whether the

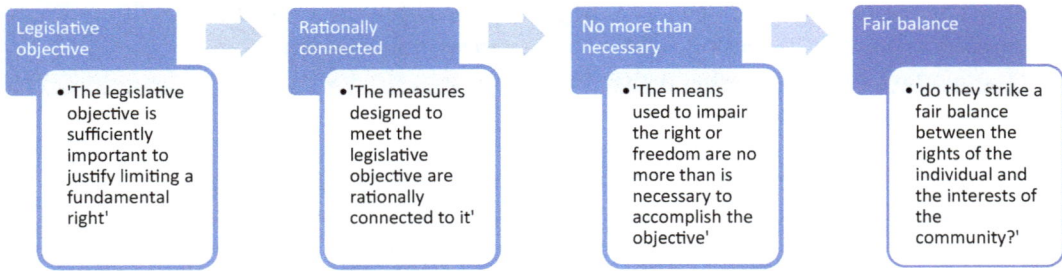

Legislative objective		Rationally connected		No more than necessary		Fair balance
• 'The legislative objective is sufficiently important to justify limiting a fundamental right'	⇒	• 'The measures designed to meet the legislative objective are rationally connected to it'	⇒	• 'The means used to impair the right or freedom are no more than is necessary to accomplish the objective'	⇒	• 'do they strike a fair balance between the rights of the individual and the interests of the community?'

Figure 12.12
The test for proportionality

decision was proportionate, rather than whether it was unreasonable. This will necessarily involve a higher standard of review. We will see that the classic limb test for proportionality was formulated by Lord Clyde in *De Freitas v. Permanent Secretary of Ministry of Agriculture, Fisheries, Land and Housing*[146]. However, Lord Reed's judgment in *Bank Mellat v. Her Majesty's Treasury (No.2)*[147] endorsed the use of a fourth limb. It is important to note, as Lord Reed reiterated in *Bank Mellat* that

> [a]n assessment of proportionality inevitably involves a value judgment at the stage at which a balance has to be struck between the importance of the objective pursued and the value of the right intruded upon. The principle does not however entitle the courts simply to substitute their own assessment for that of the decision-maker.[148]

In *R (on the application of Steinfeld and Keidan) v Secretary of State for International Development*[149] Lord Kerr laid out the accepted test for proportionality:

> The four-stage test designed to establish whether an interference with a qualified Convention right can be justified is now well-established. . . . They are (a) is the legislative objective (legitimate aim) sufficiently important to justify limiting a fundamental right; (b) are the measures which have been designed to meet it rationally connected to it; (c) are they no more than are necessary to accomplish it; and (d) do they strike a fair balance between the rights of the individual and the interests of the community?[150]

12.10 Margin of appreciation

Because of the large number of political and cultural differences between the member states, the ECtHR has developed a margin of appreciation, which essentially gives each state discretionary scope and avoids setting uniform standards for strict observance of each Article.

Helen Fenwick has argued that the margin of appreciation was not suitable for domestic courts when applying the ECHR:

The doctrine of the margin of appreciation is a distinctively international law doctrine, based on the need to respect the decision-making of nation states within defined limits. Therefore it would not appear to have any application in national law. As Sir John Laws puts it:

'The margin of appreciation doctrine as it has been developed at Strasbourg will necessarily be inapt to the administration of the Convention in the domestic courts for the very reason that they are domestic; they will not be subject to an objective inhibition generated by any cultural distance between themselves and the state organs whose decisions are impleaded before them.' However, under section 2 of the Human Rights Act the domestic judiciary 'must take into account' any relevant Strasbourg jurisprudence, although they are not bound by it.'[151]

Lord Hope in *A v. Secretary of State for the Home Department* was clear that the large margin of appreciation given by the ECtHR on derogations 'cannot be taken as the last word on the matter so far as the domestic courts are concerned. That is especially so in this case, as section 30 of the 2001 Act itself recognises that the derogation may be reviewed by the judiciary.'[152] This is a clear statement that the domestic courts should not follow the approach of the ECtHR. Lord Bingham in *A v. Secretary of State for the Home Department* drew an analogy between the margin of appreciation and judicial deference to the executive on political matters:

These were matters of a political character calling for an exercise of political and not judicial judgment. Just as the European court allowed a generous margin of appreciation to member states, recognising that they were better placed to understand and address local problems, so should national courts recognise, for the same reason, that matters of the kind in issue here fall within the discretionary area of judgment properly belonging to the democratic organs of the state. It was not for the courts to usurp authority properly belonging elsewhere.[153]

Lord Reed reiterated this in in *Bank Mellat v. Her Majesty's Treasury (No.2)*[154], where His Lordship noted that the test for proportionality as applied by Strasbourg afforded contracting states a margin of appreciation, and thus 'the approach adopted to proportionality at the national level cannot simply mirror that of the Strasbourg court.'[155]

12.11 The Conservative Party and the Human Rights Act 1998

The Human Rights Act 1998 is a controversial statute. In September 2014, the then Prime Minister, David Cameron, announced that a future Conservative government would repeal the Human Rights Act 1998 and replace it with a

British Bill of Rights. The Coalition government established a Commission on a Bill of Rights to look at whether a British Bill of Rights was needed. The commission's final report was not unanimous, but overall, it generally supported the introduction of a Bill of Rights (see below).

The Conservative Party has criticised Strasbourg and the perceived interferences of that court into issues such as prisoner voting rights. The Conservative Party has often been portrayed as wishing to abolish the HRA 1998:

> Two years ago David Cameron, said he would abolish the Act after it emerged that the killer of London headmaster Philip Lawrence could not be extradited because of human rights considerations.
>
> Last night, the Conservatives reasserted their policy. Dominic Grieve, the Shadow justice secretary, said: 'The Human Rights Act is not the only way to implement human rights in Britain.'
>
> David Davies, the Welsh Conservative MP, a member of the Home Affairs select committee, said: 'We should tear up the Human Rights Act and replace it with something that protects law abiding citizens from violent criminals. . . . The Human Rights Act has given drug addicts in jail the right to sue for the inconvenience of not having heroin.'[156]

We can see that if the HRA 1998 was repealed by a future Conservative government then it could be replaced by a British Bill of Rights which would continue to incorporate the ECHR into domestic law. We can also see that the current government and previous governments have encountered problems with the judiciary which has restricted government action using the powers afforded by the HRA 1998. The Conservatives were seeking to change Britain's relationship with the ECtHR.

In 2011, Dominic Grieve QC MP, the then Attorney-General in the Coalition government, set out why the government believed that the Human Rights Act 1998 needed to be reformed.[157] Grieve was clear that

> We also need to be clear about what abolishing the Human Rights Act means. The Human Rights Act is not synonymous with the Convention. Nor is it some sacred tablet of stone. It is simply the means by which – in our dualist system of law – the United Kingdom has chosen to incorporate the Convention into domestic law.[158]

This meant that the UK, regardless of whether the Act was repealed, would remain a signatory to the ECHR. Furthermore, 'British politicians from Winston Churchill to David Maxwell Fyfe were instrumental in the development of the Convention.'[159] What was significant, was Grieve's observation that

> There has been a failure in the past to explain how the operation of the Convention affects the lives of all of us in a significant and positive manner – and how it is not just for the benefit of those sections of society for whom the public has little sympathy, such as criminals, illegal immigrants and suspected terrorists.[160]

12.12 United Kingdom Bill of Rights

The Coalition government established a Commission on a Bill of Rights in March 2011. It had been tasked with investigating ways to create a UK Bill of Rights to replace the HRA 1998, by incorporating the Convention rights. Its term of reference states that the Commission 'will examine the operation and implementation of these obligations, and consider ways to promote a better understanding of the true scope of these obligations and liberties.'[161]

This is quite telling, as the Conservative Party had been critical of judicial use of the Convention rights. The commission's second consultation paper was published in July 2012 detailing the responses to its first consultation paper.[162] Interesting points to note include:

- Opponents of a Bill of Rights point out that the HRA 1998 is effective.
- Supporters argue that the word UK would distance the association with Europe, allow other rights to be given the same status as the Convention rights, and perhaps become entrenched (cannot be repealed by Parliament) as part of a UK written constitution. Such new rights could include a right to equality and extend the private law protection in the Equality Act 2010.
- Some of the respondents called for the right to trial by jury to be included, and for a greater level of protection for criminal and civil justice than what currently exists under Article 5–7.
- Some of the respondents called for guidance to be given to courts on how to balance the competing qualified rights of Articles 8 and 10 ECHR (see **Chapter 13**).
- The definition of public authority (or lack of it) under the HRA 1998 has been criticised and better guidance is needed.

The Commission published its final report in December 2012, 'A UK Bill of Rights? The Choice Before Us.' The report concluded that there was a strong argument in favour of a Bill of Rights, but said that this was a matter for Parliament. The report's conclusion was far from unanimous as it was supported by only seven out of the nine commissioners. The two dissenters, Baroness Kennedy QC and Philippe Sands QC, were critical of the commission's findings.

ACADEMIC DEBATE
A UK BILL OF RIGHTS

Mark Elliot was critical of the commission's report and observed that, '[t]he bizarre collection of individually and co-authored papers appended to the main Report demonstrates that the majority itself is united by an agreement so formal as to be largely meaningless.'[163] Elliot notes that the commission did not provide a definitive list of the rights which should be included, and that there is no clear conscious of whether the right to trial by jury would be included. Elliot observed that:

> If the Report is tentative about what rights should be upheld by a domestic Bill of Rights, it is even more circumspect when it comes to how those rights should be protected. The mechanisms for protecting rights 'should be broadly similar' to those found in the HRA, according to the Report, there is particular – but not uniform – enthusiasm for retaining declarations of incompatibility. However, no clear position is adopted on whether – and, if so, to what extent – the interpretative and obligation under section 3 of the HRA should survive.[164]

Elliot was critical that the majority's position 'is inspired by little more than gut feelings generated by anecdotal evidence' and seemed to think that a British Bill of Rights which was broadly similar to the HRA 1998 would avoid the perceived unpopularity of the HRA 1998. Elliot referred to the high level of support for the ECHR's incorporation in domestic law in the consultations and stated that, 'it is quite extraordinary that the findings of the Commission's own consultations appear to have played such a marginal role in informing the majority's conclusions.'[165]

According to Klug and Williams:

> The quest to rebrand the existing human rights framework to make it more popular is clearly at variance with the objective of substantively changing it [and the Commission] fails to identify a reliable evidence base for its claimed 'ownership' problem. Having dismissed polling as 'notoriously unreliable' (para. 80), the majority Commissioners virtually discount the 96 per cent of responses to the Commission's consultation exercises expressing support for retaining the HRA.[166]

This is critical, as the commission proceeded on a basis that the HRA 1998 was unpopular and in need of a makeover. The report was criticised as not indicating in which direction the majority wished to go. The main utility of the report according to Klug and Williams, 'is to illuminate the contours of the "British" Bill of Rights debate and the likely direction of travel if there is a Conservative Government following the next general election.'[167]

12.13 Reforming the Human Rights Act

There have continued to be calls to repeal or reform the Human Rights Act 1998. In their submission to the Joint Committee on Human Rights: 20 Years of the Human Rights Act in 2018, Ekins and Gee argued that 'In our view, the HRA should never have been enacted – it threatened to compromise the rule of law, to politicise the courts, and to distort democratic deliberations, and each of these threats has been realized.'[168] Ekins and Gee called for the HRA 1998 to be repealed, or if it was not to be repealed, that it should be amended inter alia by changing section 3 to limit interpretation of legislation to the original ECHR, change section 4 to reiterate that legislation subject to a declaration of incompatibility is not unlawful, and to limit the application of the HRA 1998 to the UK and not overseas.[169] Chakrabarti was critical of those who criticized the Human Rights Act.[170] She was skeptical of the argument that the Act was too European, or it had given away British sovereignty: 'The Human Rights Act is the law that gives our judiciary the power to referee on Convention rights here at home. . . . So the Act does the very opposite of ceding power to Europe.'[171] The argument that there needed to be a Bill of Rights to replaced the Act was also greeted with skepticism: 'they promise new mythical and magical bills of rights that would protect the worthy and never the wicked.'[172]

In its 2019 election manifesto the Conservative Party said that

> We will update the Human Rights Act and administrative law to ensure that there is a proper balance between the rights of individuals, our vital national security and effective government. . . . In our first year we will set up a Constitution, Democracy & Rights Commission that will examine these issues in depth, and come up with proposals to restore trust in our institutions and in how our democracy operates.

The Labour Party stated in its manifesto that 'We are guided by our firm commitment to the Human Rights Act and Convention on Human Rights that have been consistently attacked by the Conservatives.'

RECENT DEVELOPMENT
INDEPENDENT HUMAN RIGHTS ACT REVIEW

In 2020 the Conservative government established the Independent Human Rights Act Review. Its term of reference was 'limited to consideration of the HRA, which is a protected enactment under the devolution settlements. Issues falling outside the domestic HRA framework, including consideration of potential changes to the operation of the Convention or European Court of Human Rights, are not within the scope of this Review.'[173] The Review was asked to consider the operation of section 2 of the HRA and the relationship between domestic courts and the European Court of Human Rights. It was also asked to consider the relationship between the three branches of government (judiciary, legislature and executive) and whether the HRA 1998 had impacted upon this. The Review will report back to the government in 2021.

12.14 Practical application

Tim and John are out shopping with their three children in Bedfordshire, when John is detained by a privately operated police force, Rent a Bobbie Ltd. John is arrested and detained in a cell for five weeks. The conditions that he is kept in are bad. It is arguable that there has been a breach of John's rights under the ECHR. Rent a Bobbie Ltd argue that their powers are outlined in the Bedfordshire Police Act (fictitious) and that they have followed 'the letter of the law.'

Advise John as to whether he can bring a claim under the HRA 1998 and any issues relating to the HRA 1998 that are raised in the above scenario.

12.15 Key points to take away from this chapter

- The European Convention on Human Rights was given effect to in domestic law by the Human Rights Act 1998.
- The European Court of Human Rights is based in Strasbourg and oversees the interpretation of the ECHR. The domestic courts will mirror the principles established in Strasbourg's jurisprudence.
- The Conservative Party had supported the creation of a British Bill of Rights which would have replace the Human Rights Act 1998 and the Act is currently under review by the Independent Human Rights Act Review.
- The Human Rights Act 1998 was not intended to restrict Parliamentary Sovereignty. However, section 3 permits the court considerable interpretive powers and section 4 allows the court to make a declaration of incapability.
- The Human Rights Act 1998 was intended to have a vertical effect and can be enforced against public authorities. However, Convention rights can be enforced against private parties via indirect horizontal effect.

Notes

1 See for example 'A Nation Imperilled by the Human Rights Act' *The Daily Mail* (1 August 2015) <www.dailymail.co.uk/debate/article-3181945/DAILY-MAIL-COMMENT-nation-imperilled-Human-Rights-Act.html>. The opening paragraph of this article was clearly hostile to the Act: 'Another day, another insult to common sense courtesy of the Human Rights Act and the lawyers enriched by this toxic piece of legislation, which allows them so profitably to ride roughshod over the wishes of Parliament and the British public.' See also; 'Sorry, Human Rights Do Shield Terrorists' *Daily Mail* (8 June 2017) <www.dailymail.co.uk/debate/article-4583006/DAILY-MAIL-COMMENT-Human-rights-shield-terrorists.html>; 'Human Rights Laws Are a Charter for Criminals, Sat 75% of Britons' *Daily Mail* (16 April 2012) <www.dailymail.co.uk/news/article-2130224/Human-rights-laws-charter-criminals-say-75-Britons.html>.

2 For an interesting critique of some newspapers approach to the Human Rights Act 1998, see B Cathcart, 'Comment' *Press Gazette* (4 June 2015). Professor Catchcart argued that 'Getting rid of the HRA has been a Mail cause for several years. The paper accuses the Act of "undermining the sovereignty of Parliament and our judicial system". It also denounces the European Convention on

Human Rights, which the HRA incorporates into British law, as "a charter for criminals and politically-correct interest groups." . . . And not only does the Mail not hesitate to seek the benefits of the HRA, but it is also happy sometimes to see those benefits bestowed on others. A conspicuous example was the case of Gary McKinnon, the hacker whose extradition to the United States the Mail campaigned to prevent.'

3   'Mental Health Care in Prisons' *Prison Reform Trust* <www.prisonreformtrust.org.uk/WhatWeDo/Projectsresearch/Mentalhealth>.

4   'What Are Human Rights?' *Liberty* <www.libertyhumanrights.org.uk/human-rights/what-are-human-rights>.

5   J Griffin, 'First Steps in an Account of Human Rights' [2001] EJP 306.

6   C Geaty, *Can Human Rights Survive? The Hamlyn Lectures 2005* (CUP 2006), 6.

7   C Lowbridge, 'Covid: Women on Exercise Trip "Surrounded by Police"' *BBC News* (8 January 2021) <www.bbc.co.uk/news/uk-england-derbyshire-55560814>.

8   J Brown, 'Coronavirus: Enforcing Restrictions' House of Commons Briefing Paper, No 9024, 26 February 2021.

9   ibid.

10 Joint Committee on Human Rights, 'The Government's Response to Covid-19: Human Rights Implications' Seventh Report (2019–21 HC 265, HL 125).

11 C Saunders, *The Constitution of Australia* (Hart Publishing 2011) 16–17.

12 ibid 285–86.

13 G Williams and L Burton, 'Australia's Exclusive Parliamentary Model of Rights Protection' (2013) 34(1) SLR 58–59.

14 ibid 93.

15 AV Dicey, *Introduction to the Study of the Law of the Constitution* (8th edn, Palgrave Macmillan 1915) 134.

16 L Lustgarten and I Leigh, 'Making Rights Real: The Courts, Remedies, and the Human Rights Act' [1999] CLJ 509.

17 ibid.

18 See the Auld Report, Mode of Trial Bills 1999 and 2000, and sections 43–44 of the Criminal Justice Act 2003.

19 91609) 8 Coke Reports 113b at 118a.

20 Dicey (n 15) 20.

21 For a detailed account of habeas corpus see PD Halliday, *Habeas Corpus: From England to Empire* (Belknap Press 2010).

22 E Burke, *Reflections on the Revolution in France* (Pelican Classics 1978) 119.

23 ibid.

24 Edmund Burke's speech during the trial of Warren Hastings.

25 See PJ Marshall, *The Impeachment of Warren Hastings* (OUP 1965); NB Dirks, *The Scandal of Empire: India and the Creation of Imperial Britain* (Belknap Press 2008).

26 (1772) 20 State Tr 1.

27 ibid.

28 For commentary of the legal reasoning see TT Arvind, ' "Though It Shocks One Very Much": Formalism and Pragmatism in the *Zong* and *Bancoult*' (2012) 32(1) OJLS 113.

29 J Webster, 'The Zong in the Context of the Eighteenth-Century Slave Trade' (2007) 28(3) The Journal of Legal History 285, 295

30 J Walvin, *The Zong: A Massacre, the Law and the End of Slavery* (Yale Press 2011) 206.

31 See 'The National Trust's Colonial Countryside Project That Is Led by Dr Corinne Fowler' <www.nationaltrust.org.uk/features/colonial-countryside-project>.

32   S Weale, 'Cambridge University to Study How It Profited from Colonial Slavery' *The Guardian* (30 April 2019) <www.theguardian.com/education/2019/apr/30/cambridge-university-study-how-it-profited-colonial-slavery>.

33   T Wall, 'The Day Bristol Dumped Its Hated Slave Trader in the Docks and a Nation Began to Search Its Soul' *The Guardian* (14 June 2020) <www.theguardian.com/uk-news/2020/jun/14/the-day-bristol-dumped-its-hated-slave-trader-in-the-docks-and-a-nation-began-to-search-its-soul>.

34   See 'Philip Henry Sheridan (1831–1888)' *PBS* <www.pbs.org/weta/thewest/people/s_z/sheridan.htm>.

35   See <www.coe.int/en/web/about-us/founding-fathers#{"7040945":[0]}>.

36   (1961) (Application No. 332/57).

37   J Wadham, H Mountfield and A Edmundosn, *Blackstone's Guide to the Human Rights Act 1998* (3rd edn, OUP 2003) 44.

38   See <https://www.echr.coe.int/Documents/2012_Brighton_FinalDeclaration_ENG.pdf>

39   (No.2) (Application 74025/01).

40   (2012) 55 EHRR 1.

41   [2013] EWCA Civ 277.

42   *The Daily Mail* (2 July 2013).

43   Lord Hoffmann, 'The Universality of Human Rights' Judicial Studies Board Annual Lecture, 19 March 2009 <www.judiciary.uk/wp-content/uploads/2014/12/Hoffmann_2009_JSB_Annual_Lecture_Universality_of_Human_Rights.pdf>, [38]–[39].

44   'Rights Brought Home: The Human Rights Bill 1997' [1.14].

45   (1985) 7 EHRR 14.

46   [1996] QB 517.

47   (2000) 29 EHRR 493.

48   Sir Leslie Scarman, *English Law – The New Dimension, The Hamlyn Lectures* (Stevens & Sons 1974).

49   ibid 16–17.

50   ibid 14–15.

51   [1995] 4 All ER 427.

52   Lustgarten and Leigh (n 16) 509.

53   [1997] 2 Cr App Rep 426.

54   ibid 443–44.

55   [2002] EWHC 195 (Admin).

56   [2017] UKSC 5.

57   [2014] UKSC 3.

58   [2000] 2 AC 115.

59   [2004] UKHL 26.

60   ibid 20.

61   [2009] UKSC 14.

62   ibid 11.

63   [2010] UKSC 45.

64   ibid 48.

65   (No.3) [2009] UKHL 28.

66   [2014] UKSC 67.

67   [105].

68   [2018] UKSC 11.

69 [78]–[79]. See also *P v Cheshire West and Chester Council, P and Q v Surrey County Council* [2014] UKSC 19 [86] per Lord Kerr.

70 Lord Irvine, 'A British Interpretation of Convention Rights' [2012] PL 237, 241.

71 ibid 252.

72 P Sales, 'Strasbourg Jurisprudence and the Human Rights Act: A Response to Lord Irvine' [2012] PL 253.

73 B Hale, '*Argentoratum Locutum*: Is Strasbourg or the Supreme Court Supreme?' (2012) 12(1) HRLR 65.

74 ibid.

75 Sir John Laws, 'Lecture III: The Common Law and Europe' The Hamlyn Lecture 2013 [25].

76 Lord Judge, *Constitutional Change: Unfinished Business* (King's College London, 4 December 2013) [41]–[42].

77 J Straw, *Aspects of Law Reform: An Insider's Perspective* (CUP 2013) 25.

78 For more detailed coverage on how the courts use section 3 HRA 1998 please refer to Chapter 6 where we look at the impact of section 3 on Parliamentary Sovereignty.

79 (No.2) [2002] 1 AC 45.

80 [2002] 2 AC 545.

81 C Gearty, *Can Human Rights Survive – Hamlyn Lectures 2005* (CUP 2006) 92.

82 ibid 96.

83 570 US 744 (2013).

84 R Jalabi, 'Defense of Marriage Act: Highlights from the Supreme Court Ruling' *The Guardian* (26 June 2013) <www.theguardian.com/world/2013/jun/26/doma-highlights-supreme-court>.

85 [2004] UKHL 30.

86 ibid 46.

87 ibid 50.

88 [2002] UKHL 10.

89 ibid 40.

90 ibid 39.

91 [2002] UKHL 46.

92 ibid 31.

93 ibid 59.

94 [2004] UKHL 56.

95 [2003] UKHL 37.

96 ibid 7.

97 ibid 9.

98 ibid 10.

99 ibid 12.

100 ibid 14.

101 ibid 16.

102 [2007] UKHL 27.

103 ibid.

104 ibid 30.

105 C Costigan, 'Contracting Out of the Human Rights Act 1998' in N Geach and C Monaghan (eds), *Dissenting Judgments in Law* (Wildy, Simmonds & Hill 2012).

106 (2011) 53 EHRR 18.

107 [139].

108 (Admissibility) (52207/99).

109 (2005) 41 EHRR 27.

110 [74]–[75].

111 (2010) Application No. 3394/03.

112 [67].

113 (2009) Application No. 27765/09.

114 [81].

115 [2013] UKSC 41.

116 [2010] UKSC 29.

117 [2013] UKSC 41.

118 (App. No. 35622/04) (2013) 56 EHRR SE15. For more detail see C Monaghan, 'The Chagossians Go to Strasbourg: Convention Rights and the Chagos Islands' [2013] EHRLR 309.

119 (2007) 44 EHRR SE4.

120 (1995) 21 EHRR 97.

121 (1979–80) 2 EHRR 25.

122 *Ireland v United Kingdom* (5310/71) (2018) 67 EHRR SE1.

123 (2009) 48 EHRR 37.

124 (2015) 60 EHRR 16.

125 Application No. 39630/09.

126 (1989) 11 EHRR 439.

127 (2012) 55 EHRR 1.

128 ibid 194.

129 (Application no. 73316/01).

130 *Sokur v Ukraine* (Application no. 29439/02).

131 (Application no. 21884/15).

132 [2012] EWHC 2292 (Admin).

133 *R (Reilly) v. Secretary of State for Work and Pensions* [2013] EWCA Civ 66.

134 *R (Reilly) v. Secretary of State for Work and Pensions* [2013] UKSC 68.

135 (Application no. 16483/12).

136 ibid 71.

137 *Magee v. United Kingdom* (2000) (28135/95) (2001) 31 EHRR 35.

138 (2013) 57 EHRR 8.

139 (Application no. 47355/06).

140 ibid 9.

141 [2013] EWHC 3824 (Admin).

142 (2006) 42 EHRR 11.

143 [2004] UKHL 56.

144 ibid 30.

145 [2001] 2 AC 532.

146 [1999] 1 AC 69.

147 [2013] UKSC 39.

148 ibid 71.

149 [2018] UKSC 32.

150 ibid 41.

151 H Fenwick, 'The Right to Protest, the Human Rights Act and the Margin of Appreciation' (1999) 62(4) MLR 491.

152 [2004] UKHL 56, [131].

153 ibid 37.

154 [2013] UKSC 39.

155 ibid 71.

156 'Keir Starmer under attack after human rights broadside' *The Times* (22 October 2009).

157 D Grieve QC MP, 'European Convention on Human Rights: Current Challenges' (24 October 2011) <www.gov.uk/government/speeches/european-convention-on-human-rights-current-challenges>.

158 ibid.

159 ibid.

160 ibid.

161 See <www.justice.gov.uk/about/cbr>.

162 See <www.justice.gov.uk/downloads/about/cbr/second-consultation/cbr-second-consultation.pdf>.

163 M Elliot, 'A Damp Squid in the Long Grass: The Report of the Commission on a Bill of Rights' [2013] EHRLR 137.

164 ibid.

165 ibid.

166 F Klug and A Williams, 'The Choice Before Us? The Report of the Commission on a Bill of Rights' (2013) PL 460.

167 ibid.

168 See <https://policyexchange.org.uk/wp-content/uploads/2018/10/JPP-submission-to-the-JCHR-inquiry-18-September-2018.pdf>.

169 ibid.

170 S Chakrabarti, *On Liberty* (Penguin 2015).

171 ibid 143.

172 ibid.

173 See <https://assets.publishing.service.gov.uk/government/uploads/system/uploads/attachment_data/file/953347/human-rights-review-tor.pdf>.

Further reading

Chakrabarti S, *On Liberty* (Penguin 2015)

Costigan C, 'Contracting Out of the Human Rights Act 1998' in N Geach and C Monaghan (eds), *Dissenting Judgments in Law* (Wildy, Simmonds & Hill 2012)

Dicey AV, *Introduction to the Study of the Law of the Constitution* (Liberty Fund 1982)

Elliot M, 'A Damp Squid in the Long Grass: The Report of the Commission on a Bill of Rights' [2013] EHRLR 137

Fenwick H, 'The Right to Protest, the Human Rights Act and the Margin of Appreciation' (1999) 62(4) MLR 491

Gearty C, *Can Human Rights Survive – Hamlyn Lectures 2005* (CUP 2006)

Hale B, 'Argentoratum Locutum: Is Strasbourg or the Supreme Court Supreme?' (2012) 12(1) HRLR 65

Irvine, Lord, 'A British Interpretation of Convention Rights' [2012] PL 237

Klug F and A Williams, 'The Choice Before Us? The Report of the Commission on a Bill of Rights' [2013] PL 460

Lustgarten L and I Leigh, 'Making Rights Real: The Courts, Remedies, and the Human Rights Act' [1999] CLJ 509

Oliver D, 'The Frontiers of the State: Public Authorities and Public Functions Under the Human Rights Act' [2000] PL 476

Straw J, *Aspects of Law Reform: An Insider's Perspective* (CUP 2013)

Human Rights II

Two competing rights?
Articles 8 and 10 ECHR

This chapter will

- consider the right to respect for private and life under Article 8 of the European Convention on Human Rights
- discuss the protection accorded to freedom of expression under Article 10 of the European Convention on Human Rights
- explore the interaction between the two rights and consider the degree to which it can be said that these rights are competing
- evaluate the extent to which a right to privacy is protected in England and Wales

13.1 Introduction

The phone hacking of celebrities and members of the public's voicemails, the false accusations made by newspapers against members of the public, the pictures of members of the Royal Family ending up on the front pages of national and international publications – these were just some of the notorious incidents which have appeared in newspaper headlines. In 2012, the Leveson Inquiry on the culture, practice and ethics of the press delivered its report which criticised the press and called for reforms. Elements of the press and some politicians proceeded to criticise the report and warned that any statutory reforms would restrict the freedom of the press. The recent accusations made by Their Royal Highnesses the Duke and Duchess of Sussex that their privacy had been infringed by the press and the that the coverage has had racist overtones, demonstrates the power of the media in the United Kingdom and the impact that it can have on individuals' lives.

At the centre of press freedom and individuals' rights to privacy are two very important rights, which have been incorporated into domestic law by the Human Rights Act 1998 (HRA 1998). Article 8 of the European Convention on Human Rights (ECHR) protects the right to respect for a private and

DOI: 10.4324/9780429293498-15

No freestanding
right to privacy

HRA 1998 - incorporates
ECHR (Articles 8 and 10 ECHR)

Reliance on breach of
confidence

Reasonable expectation
of privacy in *Campbell*.

Does Article 8 have horizontal effect?

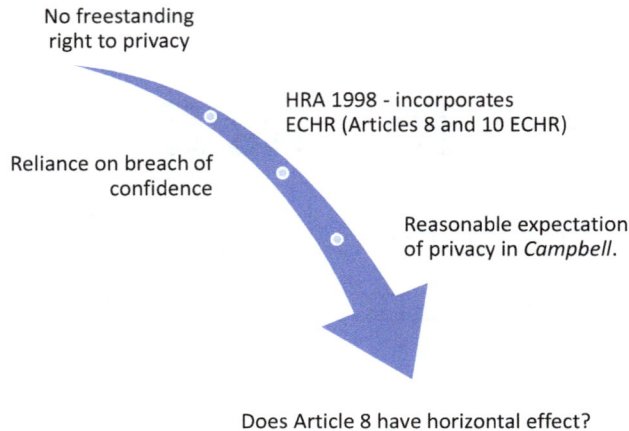

Figure 13.1
Introduction

family life and Article 10 of the ECHR protects freedom of expression. We shall look at the extent of the rights afforded by these Articles and how they conflict. This is because the right to publish material about an individual will have a negative impact on that individual's private life. These two articles are very controversial, and the press often negatively report judicial decisions. Newspapers often argue that they should be able to publish stories about politicians and celebrities, whilst those individuals wish to keep their private lives private.

13.2 Article 8 ECHR

Before we begin it is important to consider which rights are protected by Article 8.

Article 8 – the right to respect for private and family life

1. Everyone has the right to respect for his private and family life, his home and his correspondence.
2. There shall be no interference by a public authority with the exercise of this right except such as is in accordance with the law and is necessary in a democratic society in the interests of national security, public safety or the economic well-being of the country, for the prevention of disorder or crime, for the protection of health or morals, or for the protection of the rights and freedoms of others.

13.2.1 Everyone has the right to respect for his private and family life, his home and his correspondence

Under Article 8 ECHR everyone has the right to respect for their private and family life, their home and their correspondence. This means that our private lives are protected from intrusion from the state and private parties. Equally, our right to a family life is protected, which could extend to allowing parents contact with their children and permitting asylum seekers to remain in the United Kingdom. Our right to a private home life and the right not to have our correspondence (such as post, direct messages on social media, emails, text messages and phone calls) interfered with is protected under Article 8.

13.2.2 The right to respect for private and family life is a qualified right

Article 8 is a qualified right. A public authority is permitted to restrict the right where the conditions under Article 8(2) are satisfied. Article 8(2) outlines where a restriction could be permitted and could be for reasons such as national security. Interference by a public authority is permitted where all three of the following bullet points are satisfied:

- The reasons for interference are, 'national security, public safety or the economic well-being of the country, for the prevention of disorder or crime, for the protection of health or morals, or for the protection of the rights and freedoms of others.'
- The interference is 'in accordance with the law,' which means that the right to interfere is permitted by the law. The rule of law states that the government cannot act unless it is authorised by law.[1] But note the approach in *Malone v Metropolitan Police Commissioner*[2] where the court said that the government could phone tap without requiring lawful authority to do so, as long as there was no law against this. This approach was rejected by the ECtHR in *Malone v United Kingdom*[3] where the court held that 'the phrase "in accordance with the law" does not merely refer back to domestic law but also relates to the quality of the law, requiring it to be compatible with the rule of law. . . . the law must be sufficiently clear in its terms to give citizens an adequate indication' on when the state will interfere with their Article 8 rights.'[4]
- The interference 'is necessary in a democratic society.' The public authority must show that it the interference is required, and that any interference must be proportionate. The test which the domestic courts use to determine whether a decision is proportionate can be found in Chapter 12. You must make sure that you consider how the courts apply the test.

The following information gives an overview of some ways that the courts have protected Article 8 ECHR.

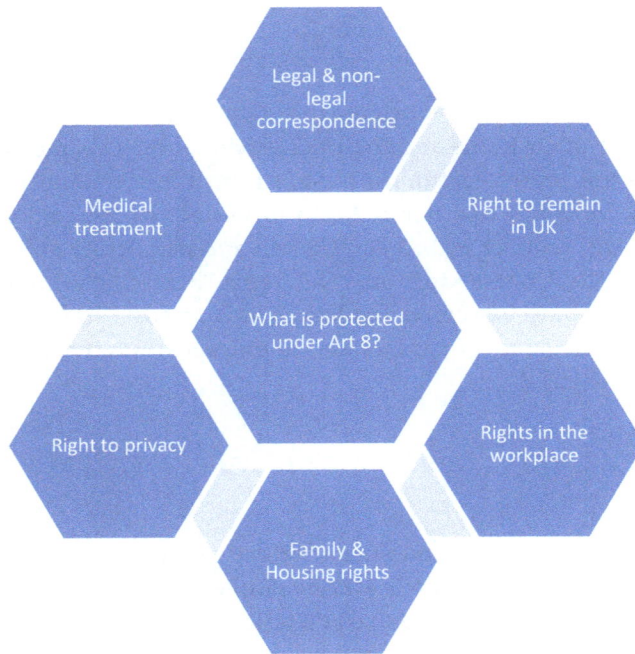

Figure 13.2
The extent of Article 8 ECHR

13.2.2.1 Legal correspondence

The House of Lords in *R (Daly) v Secretary of State for the Home Department*[5] held that Article 8 had been violated where a prisoner's correspondence with his solicitor was examined by prison officers without him being present. This had been authorised by the Home Secretary. The House of Lords held that this was not permitted under the Prison Act 1952 and consequentially, as the search was not in accordance to the law, Article 8 had been violated.

As we saw in Chapter 12, the House of Lords in *Daly* held that where there was an alleged breach of Convention rights, the court would have to ask whether the public authority's infringement was proportionate.

13.2.2.2 Right to remain in the United Kingdom

Article 8 has had a considerable significance on the right not to be deported from the United Kingdom. In *Machado v Secretary of State for the Home Department*[6] the Court of Appeal held that when reviewing the decision to deport a failed asylum seeker who was married to an EU national living in the United Kingdom, the Immigration Appeal Tribunal needed to protect the asylum seeker's right to a family life by asking whether it was proportionate to deport him. This means that Article 8 requires the tribunal to consider whether the infringement of Article 8, in the present case deportation, is proportionate.

The Asylum and Immigration Tribunal[7] permitted a Bolivian national the right to remain in the United Kingdom. The Home Secretary had appealed against the decision to let the respondent remain. The tribunal held that 'the grant of reconsideration refers to the inappropriate weight placed on the appellant having to leave behind not only his partner but also their joint cat.' The tribunal held that 'The Immigration Judge's determination is upheld and the cat . . . need no longer fear having to adapt to Bolivian mice.' Unfortunately, the newspapers seized upon this decision as being based on the fact that he owned that cat with his partner. The story had been reported in *The Telegraph* as 'Immigrant allowed to stay because of pet cat,' although the subtitle said that it only part of the reason.[8]

The human rights lawyer Adam Wagner was critical of the way the case had been reported: 'So had the policy been properly applied, the immigration judge would have had to allow the appeal anyway, cat or no cat. And not only did the decision have nothing to do with a cat, it also had nothing to do with human rights either.'[9]

13.2.2.3 Rights in the workplace

The right to a private life at work is protected by Article 8. In *Halford v United Kingdom*[10] the ECtHR held that intercepting phone calls of a senior police officer at home and work, where there had been no prior warning would amount to a breach of Article 8. This was because the employee had a reasonable expectation of privacy. There was a breach of Article 8 in *Copland v United Kingdom*[11] where a college had monitored an employee's phone calls, internet and email usage. We will discuss below whether there is a right to privacy in English law. However, Article 8 will be violated where there is a reasonable expectation of privacy. In *Halford* the college had no policy in place to permit this and had not informed the employee. Therefore, the employee had a reasonable expectation of privacy. Of course, the employer could have informed the employee that all communications and internet usage would be monitored and this would not have amounted to a breach.

In *Barbulescu v Romania*[12] the Grand Chamber of the European Court of Human Rights held that a company which monitored an employee's work email and messaging account would be violating the employee's rights under Article 8 ECHR, where the employer had not properly warned the employer that not only was using it for personal reasons prohibited, but of the nature and the extent of the employer's monitoring. The notice of monitoring needs to take place before the actual monitoring begins: 'As to whether the applicant had received prior notification from his employer, the Court observes that it has already concluded that he did not appear to have been informed in advance of the extent and nature of his employer's monitoring activities, or of the possibility that the employer might have access to the actual content of his messages.'[13] For recent commentary on this decision and the protection of employee's privacy whilst working from home, see Eleni Frantziou, 'The Right to Privacy While Working From Home ("WFH"): Why Employee Monitoring Infringes Art 8 ECHR.'[14]

13.2.2.4 Housing

Article 8 has had an impact in housing law and planning law. In *Buckley v United Kingdom*[15] the ECtHR ruled that the refusal of planning permission did not breach Article 8. Whilst Article 8 covered the right to respect the landowner's right to live on the land, the infringement of refusing planning permission was in accordance to the law, it was necessary and proportionate. The decision in *Buckley* was applied in *Harrow LBC v Quazi*[16], where the right to evict a tenant who had no legal or equitable rights to remain was found not to infringe Article 8. The decision in *Quazi* was doubted in *Manchester City Council v Pinnock*[17], where Article 8 was held to protect anyone who was going to be disposed from their home by a local authority. In all situations, the court would have to apply the test of proportionality to assess whether the infringement was lawful.

13.2.2.5 Family life

In *MAK v United Kingdom*[18] a child was admitted to hospital with bruises, which were signs of suspected abuse. The father was separated from the child for ten days, before being allowed to make supervised visits. It was later established that the bruises were caused by a rare condition. The ECtHR ruled that this separation was not permitted by law and breached Article 8. Permitting the father to visit whilst supervised at all times was also a breach, because the delay in finding out what had caused the bruises had meant that it was not proportionate. The ECtHR in *K v United Kingdom*[19] ruled that there had been no breach of Article 8 where a child had been placed into care after a medical misdiagnosis. The decision to place the child in care was lawful and was necessary in a democratic society and proportionate, since there had been unexplained fractures.

13.2.2.6 Medical treatment

Taking blood samples from a child without the parents' consent amounted to a breach of Article 8 in *MAK v United Kingdom*[20].

13.2.2 How does the domestic law protect the rights under Article 8?

Many people refer to Article 8 as the right to privacy. As we shall see below when we consider the relationship between Articles 8 and 10, there is no domestic freestanding right to privacy. The common law has not recognised a tort of privacy and instead English judges rely on the equitable doctrine of confidence and the tort of misuse of private information.[21] This gives individuals a degree of protection.

The Data Protection Act 2018 (DPA 2018) regulates the collection and use of personal information and stipulates the safeguards required for protecting information from abuse. The DPA 2018 requires that there is a data controller to ensure that the Act is complied with.

13.2.2 Interferences with Article 8

We will now look at interferences with Article 8 ECHR. It is interesting to consider state interference with citizens' private lives, as this is highly controversial. The Regulation of Investigatory Powers Act 2000 is a controversial Act which criminalises unlawful interception of public and private communications. The Investigatory Powers Act 2016 is also a controversial piece of legislation and empowers and regulates how the state uses its investigatory powers. The power to carry out covert investigations is not limited to the security services and there have been instances where local authorities have been recording what items an individual puts into their bins, or whether a family lives in a school's catchment area. According to the Home Office, the Protection of Freedoms Act 2012 was intended to prevent frivolous intrusions:

> Unwarranted state intrusion into private lives will be brought to an end after the Protection of Freedoms Bill became law today. It will curb local authority snooping, see the destruction of DNA samples and profiles given by innocent people and radically scale back the employment vetting process which would have routinely monitored 9.3m people. Millions more people will be protected from state intrusion into their lives through a sweeping range of policies which will restore common sense to government.

There is also considerable overt surveillance which is carried out by public authorities and private organisations. An example of this are the millions of CCTV cameras in use in the United Kingdom which track an individual's journey to work, which shops they go into and who they socialise with. Finally, our emails can be monitored, our phone calls tapped, and internet usage monitored by the state.

PUBLIC LAW IN CONTEXT
AN EXAMPLE OF VIOLATING ARTICLE 8, THE DECISION IN *WAINWRIGHT V HOME OFFICE*

In *Wainwright v Home Office*[22] the House of Lords held that a strip-search carried out on a mother and son at a prison whilst amounting to a battery regarding the son, did not give rise to any liability for a new tort of privacy. The strip-search was required before they were allowed to visit a prisoner. It had occurred prior to the HRA 1998 being enacted.

Upon appeal the ECtHR in *Wainwright v United Kingdom*[23] held that there had been a violation of Article 8. The room in which they had been searched had a window and this meant that the strip-search could have been observed. There was intimate inspection of the genitalia of both visitors. The search could be justified where there was suspicion that they were supplying drugs. However, the prison officers had failed to follow the proper procedure as they had failed to ask for their formal consent before the search and there was no suspicion that they were carrying drugs. This meant that the search had been intended to humiliate and was not lawful and nor was it proportionate.

The government had argued that there had been no interference with their Article 8 rights because they had agreed to be strip-searched and even if there had been an interference, that the strip-search had been in accordance to the law. Crucially, the government argued that the search was proportionate as it was needed to prevent drugs from entering the prison and protect prisoners. The ECtHR observed that:

> It has accepted above that the search pursued the aim of fighting the drugs problem in the prison, namely the prevention of crime and disorder.
>
> On the other hand, it is not satisfied that the searches were proportionate to that legitimate aim in the manner in which they were carried out. Where procedures are laid down for the proper conduct of searches on outsiders to the prison who may very well be innocent of any wrongdoing, it behoves the prison authorities to comply strictly with those safeguards and by rigorous precautions protect the dignity of those being searched from being assailed any further than is necessary. They did not do so in this case.
>
> Consequently, the Court finds that the searches carried out on the applicants cannot be regarded as 'necessary in a democratic society' within the meaning of Art.8(2) of the Convention. There has been, accordingly, a breach of Art.8 of the Convention in that regard.'[24] It is worth considering whether thee outcome in the domestic courts would be substantially different today, or whether the case would still have to be resolved by Strasbourg.

Alongside the state's negative obligation to refrain from breaching Article 8 through interfering with the right to respect for a private and family life, the state also has a positive obligation to protect individuals from having their rights under Article 8 violated by private parties. In *X and Y v The Netherlands*[25] the European Court of Human Rights recognised the positive obligations under Article 8:

> The Court recalls that although the object of Article 8 (art. 8) is essentially that of protecting the individual against arbitrary interference by the public authorities, it does not merely compel the State to abstain from such interference: in addition to this primarily negative undertaking, there may be positive obligations inherent in an effective respect for private or family life.[26]

Guidance on how the court would approach the question of the state's positive obligations were considered by the Grand Chamber in *Hamalainen v Finland*.[27] The Grand Chamber observed:

> While the essential object of Article 8 is to protect individuals against arbitrary interference by public authorities, it may also impose on a State certain positive obligations to ensure effective respect for the rights protected by Article 8. . . . The principles applicable to assessing a State's positive and negative obligations under the Convention are similar. Regard must be had to the fair balance that has to be struck between the competing interests of the individual and of the community as a whole, the aims in the second paragraph of Article 8 being of a certain relevance. . . . In implementing their positive obligations under Article 8, the States enjoy a certain margin of appreciation. A number of factors must be taken into account when determining the breadth of that margin. Where a particularly important facet of an individual's existence or identity is at stake, the margin allowed to the State will be restricted. . . . Where, however, there is no consensus within the member States of the Council of Europe, either as to the relative importance of the interest at stake or as to the best means of protecting it, particularly where the case raises sensitive moral or ethical issues, the margin will be wider. . . . There will also usually be a wide margin of appreciation if the State is required to strike a balance between competing private and public interests or Convention rights.[28]

13.3 Article 10 ECHR

Article 10 protects the right to freedom of expression:

1   Everyone has the right to freedom of expression. This right shall include freedom to hold opinions and to receive and impart information and ideas without interference by public authority and regardless of frontiers. This Article shall not prevent States from requiring the licensing of broadcasting, television or cinema enterprises.
2   The exercise of these freedoms, since it carries with it duties and responsibilities, may be subject to such formalities, conditions, restrictions or penalties as are prescribed by law and are necessary in a democratic society, in the interests of national security, territorial integrity or public safety, for the prevention of disorder or crime, for the protection of health or morals, for the protection of the reputation or rights of others, for preventing the disclosure of information received in confidence, or for maintaining the authority and impartiality of the judiciary.

Article 10 is an important right as free speech is essential in a democracy to permit different political views to be represented, and there needs to be a free press which is not censured by the state and can hold the executive to account.[29]

Freedom of expression is important for the spoken word, traditional print media, social media and the internet. The use of social media proved important in the Arab Spring which toppled dictators, and Twitter allows issues to trend within this country and raise debate.

It is important to note that there is interplay between Article 10 and Article 11, which protects the right to freedom of peaceful assembly and to freedom of association with others. Under Articles 10 and 11 the state has a positive obligation to not only allow people to express themselves freely but also to allow them to do so whilst taking part in a peaceful assembly or associating with others. This exists alongside the state's negative obligations not to restrict the rights under Article 10 or 11, unless there are valid reasons to restrict these. We will look at Article 11 in more detail in Chapter 14.

13.3.1 Restrictions on Article 10

Article 10 is a qualified right and can be restricted under Article 10(2). However, any restrictions must be prescribed by law and necessary in a democratic society. Furthermore, any restrictions must be proportionate. We will now look at some of the restrictions on Article 10.

13.3.2 Contempt of Court Act 1981

The Contempt of Court Act 1981 (CCA 1981) imposes restrictions on court reporting and prevents members of a jury from publicly speaking about their deliberations during or after the conclusion of the trial. The Act is intended to prevent publication of information from interfering with the course of justice. An offence can be committed where information is published which might prejudice a fair trial, or jurors use social media to tell others about the trial and the jury's deliberations. Under the CCA 1981 there is a strict liability offence where information is published before or during a trial, and this information 'creates a substantial risk that the course of justice in the proceedings in question will be seriously impeded or prejudiced.' This has an impact on the freedom of expression, as a newspaper which publishes material which could undermine the trial might face prosecution. Whilst the CCA 1981 creates a strict liability offence there are a number of defences which are available. In addition, there is a common law offence which is not a strict liability offence. An example of when a prosecution might be brought is *Attorney General v MGN Ltd*[30]. Here a newspaper was prosecuted for publishing articles which vilified a suspect in a murder investigation. The case concerned the murder of a young woman and the vilification of her landlord. Eventually, another neighbour was convicted of murdering the victim. It was contended that the publication would have prevented the landlord from having a fair trial. The court held that an offence had been committed. We can see that the CCA 1981 imposes a restriction on the media's freedom of expression under Article 10 in order to protect the integrity of the legal system and ensure that people have a fair trial. It must be noted that where the CCA 1981 restricts freedom of expression the requirements under Article 10(2) must be met and the restriction must be proportionate.

PUBLIC LAW IN CONTEXT
LAW COMMISSION CONSULTATION PAPER NO. 209, *CONTEMPT OF COURT*

The Law Commission has looked at reforming the law around contempt of court (Law Commission Consultation Paper No. 209, *Contempt of Court*). The Law Commission was conscious that social media is leading to increased potential for people being in contempt of court, as we all have the ability to publish information concerning court cases and jurors have used social media to carry out their own research and contact the defendant or their lawyers, contrary to the CCA 1981 and the Juries Act 1974. An example of a juror being prosecuted for contempt of court is Joanne Fraill, who was convicted for contempt of court after communicating with a defendant's boyfriend on Facebook and causing the trial to collapse (see *Attorney General v Fraill and Others*)[31]. The recommendations put forward by the Law Commission have become law in the Criminal Justice and Courts Act 2015.

13.3.3 The use of 'super-injunctions'

An injunction will prevent someone from revealing information, whilst a so-called 'super-injunction' will prevent the fact that there is an injunction from being made initially public. The uses of 'super-injunction' by wealthy and private companies has led to criticism by the press and politicians. Thomas Bennett observed that:

> There have been suggestions that the development of privacy protection encourages claimants to exaggerate trivial claims by asserting violations of their human rights. Even the [then Prime Minister David Cameron] has entered this debate, publicly stating his unease at recent judicial develop-ment of a 'backdoor' privacy law.[32]

Anyone who reveals the identities of those protected by the injunction can be prosecuted under the CCA 1981. This led to one MP revealing the name of a person who had successfully sought an injunction in the House of Commons, and thus was immune from prosecution as he enjoyed Parliamentary Privilege. The courts have defended their use of these types of injunctions. Eady J, who has been criticised by the press for bringing in a privacy law through the 'back door,' has defended the use of injunctions. Eady J has spoken extra-judicially on the balancing act the court has to strike between Articles 8 and 10 ECHR. Eady J describes the use of 'super-injunctions':

> The classic example of this is of a threatening blackmailer, which is sur-prisingly common: I'm dealing with one at the moment and I can think

of three or four this year. People who know somebody who's in the public eye and know something that they think is discreditable see the opportunity for making money. They're in touch with journalists who are ready to pay it.[33]

We shall see below that injunctions are used as a way to protect peoples' rights under Article 8.

13.3.4 Confidentiality clauses, non-disclosure agreements

In *ABC & Ors v Telegraph Media Group Ltd*[34] the Court of Appeal had to consider issue of an interim injunction to prevent the publication of information relating to allegations by former employees of a senior executive. The employees had all signed settlement agreements with their employer, which the court referred to as non-disclosure agreement. The agreements were in exchange for financial consideration and related to the complaints made against the executive. The Court of Appeal observed that 'The Agreements safeguarded the complainants' rights to make legitimate disclosures (including reporting any criminal offences) if they chose.'[35] The Court of Appeal held that the employer could receive an interim injunction that would enforce the non-disclosure agreements, which would apply until the full trial took place. The court observed:

> The importance of the role of the media is not in issue or in doubt. It is, however, only one side of the scales in determining where the balance of the public interest lies on the particular facts of the present case. As we have said, on the very limited information currently before the court, it is likely that the Claimants will establish at trial both that the relevant information was acquired by the Telegraph with knowledge of the NDAs and of the general obligation of confidentiality owed by the employees of the Claimant companies, and also that the information was imparted to the Telegraph in breach of either the NDAs or by employees who were aware of the NDAs and that, in either case, there was a breach of the duty of confidentiality to the Claimants.[36]

In 2018, the Labour Peer, Lord Hain, relied upon parliamentary privilege to reveal that the executive was Sir Philip Green. The decision to reveal the identify the person who had been accused of misconduct was criticised. Paul Wragg argued that:

> [Hain's] words prevent justice being done. Matters would be different if the decision in *ABC v Telegraph Group* concerned a permanent injunction or if the resolution of the full trial had raised serious matters of legal principle. But the Court of Appeal had done no such thing. It had issued an interim injunction to retain the integrity of the judicial process (since they recognised that revealing ABC's identity would destroy the subject matter

of the claim). It had also indicated to the defendants that the claim would succeed if they could not demonstrate the non-disclosure agreements had been obtained through something like coercion. And, most gallingly of all, it had recognised the need to deal with these matters expeditiously. This is why Hain's behaviour is so frustrating. He knew that the judicial process was ongoing, but he decided that he was above the law. He knew that his actions would destroy the parties' rights to justice, but he did it anyway.[37]

13.3.5 Pornography restrictions

Television and films are censured by the British Board of Film Classification and they can prevent the showing of pornography and other offensive material. The Obscene Publications Act 1958 was unsuccessfully used to prosecute Penguin Books in *R v Penguin Books Ltd*[38], when Penguin Books sought to publish DH Lawrence's *Lady Chatterley's Lover*. The book used sexual swear words that were deemed offensive at the time and the prosecution was brought by the Lord Chamberlain's department.

PUBLIC LAW IN CONTEXT
LADY CHATTERLEY'S LOVER

Lady Chatterley's Lover was written by DH Lawrence and is now considered a classic work of fiction. However, at the time of publication it was controversial as it contained description of sexual acts and used an offensive swear word. The leading human rights lawyer Geoffrey Robertson QC has written on the legacy of the decision to prosecute Penguin Books. Robertson observed that:

The choice of *Lady Chatterley* as a test-case was inept, but it suited the anti-intellectual temper of the legal establishment and it would mean the defeat of an impeccably liberal cause. Besides, DH Lawrence had form. Back in 1915 all copies of *The Rainbow* had been seized by police and burned (as much for its anti-war message as for its openness about sex). . . . With parochial arrogance, the prosecuting authorities ignored the New York court of appeal, which in 1959 had overturned a ban on *Lady Chatterley* because it was written with "a power and tenderness which was compelling" and which justified its use of four-letter Anglo-Saxon words. Those words were a red rag to Manningham-Buller and the "grey elderly ones" (as Lawrence had described his censors), a breach of the etiquette and decorum relied on to cover up unpleasant truths. In 1960, in the interests of keeping wives dutiful and servants touching their forelocks, Lady Constance Chatterley's affair with a gamekeeper was unmentionable. The prosecutors were complacent: they would have the judge on their side, and a jury comprised of people of property, predominantly male, middle aged, middle minded and middle class. And they had four-letter words galore: the prosecuting counsel's first request was that a clerk in the DPP's office should count them carefully. In his opening speech to the jury, he played them as if they were trump cards: "The word 'fuck' or 'fucking' appears no less than 30 times. . . . 'Cunt' 14 times; 'balls' 13 times; 'shit' and 'arse' six times apiece; 'cock' four times; 'piss' three times, and so on."[139]

It might appear strange today, when the words used by DH Lawrence appear on television and in films, that the decision was taken to prosecute the publishers. However, the 1960s were a radically different time than today and the establishment were keen to police public morality and prevent the publication of what some regarded not so much as a work of outstanding literature, but rather a novel reliant on filth and obscenity.

In decision in *Handyside v United Kingdom*[40] concerned a book which was published in Europe, was published in the United Kingdom for distribution to schools. The book was intended to teach teenagers about sexual intercourse and health information. The publisher was prosecuted under the Obscene Publications Act 1958 and found guilty. The European Court of Human Rights found that there had been no breach of Article 10 in this case. The court ruled that it was within the state's margin of appreciation to determine what could or could not be published for being considered obscene. The court gave its reasons, noting that the fact that in parts of Europe this book could be distributed was not a reason to find that there was a breach of Article 10 in the present case:

> The applicant and the minority of the Commission laid stress on the further point that, in addition to the original Danish edition, translations of the 'Little Book' appeared and circulated freely in the majority of the member States of the Council of Europe. Here again, the national margin of appreciation and the optional nature of the 'restrictions' and 'penalties' referred to in Article 10 para. 2 (art. 10–2) prevent the Court from accepting the argument. The Contracting States have each fashioned their approach in the light of the situation obtaining in their respective territories; they have had regard, inter alia, to the different views prevailing there about the demands of the protection of morals in a democratic society. The fact that most of them decided to allow the work to be distributed does not mean that the contrary decision of the Inner London Quarter Sessions was a breach of Article 10 (art. 10). Besides, some of the editions published outside the United Kingdom do not include the passages, or at least not all the passages, cited in the judgment of 29 October 1971 as striking examples of a tendency to 'deprave and corrupt.'[41]

13.3.6 Blasphemy

The common law offence of blasphemy was used to prosecute those accused of insulting Christianity. The most famous successful prosecution was *Whitehouse v Lemon* [1979] 2 WLR 281, where Jesus was portrayed as a homosexual. The offence was abolished by the Criminal Justice and Immigration Act 2008. It is still an offence to incite hatred on grounds such as sexual orientation, religion or race.

13.3.7 Harassment and malicious communications

The internet and social networking sites such as Facebook and Twitter are now used by some people as forums to abuse others. For example, during the 2012 London Olympics, Tom Daley the diver was abused on Twitter after he missed out on securing a medal. The perpetrator was arrested under the Malicious Communications Act 1998. The Protection from Harassment Act 1997 also makes it a criminal offence to harass someone by any means, whether it is online or face to face. The Protection from Harassment Act 1997 made it an offence to send a message of a menacing character by a public electronic communication. For more information on these statutory offences see N Geach and N Haralambous, 'Regulating Harassment: Is The Law Fit for the Social Networking Age?'[42]

PUBLIC LAW IN CONTEXT
'I AM BLOWING THE AIRPORT SKY HIGH!!'

In 2012, Paul Chambers' conviction for uploading a joke about blowing up Nottingham airport was quashed. Mr Chambers had tweeted, 'Crap! Robin Hood Airport is closed. You've got a week and a bit to get your shit together otherwise I am blowing the airport sky high!!' He had been prosecuted under the Communications Act 2003. The High Court in *Chambers v DPP*[43] quashed the conviction as the tweet had been clearly intended as a joke and would be understood as such. In his judgment Lord Judge, the then Lord Chief Justice of England and Wales, was clear than a criminal offence had not been committed. It is interesting to note what Lord Judge had to say about the reasons for this decision:

> So, if the person or persons who receive or read it, or may reasonably be expected to receive, or read it, would brush it aside as a silly joke, or a joke in bad taste, or empty bombastic or ridiculous banter, then it would be a contradiction in terms to describe it as a message of a menacing character. In short, a message which does not create fear or apprehension in those to whom it is communicated, or who may reasonably be expected to see it, falls outside this provision, for the very simple reason that the message lacks menace.[44]

The lack of menace was important, as the tweet was obviously meant as a joke and would be understood that way. The lack of intention to tweet something of a menacing character, as required by the Communications Act 2003, was central to the court's decision. Lord Judge was clear that,

> the mental element of the offence is directed exclusively to the state of the mind of the offender, and that if he may have intended the message as a joke, even if a poor joke in bad taste, it is unlikely that the mens rea required before conviction for the offence of sending a message of a menacing character will be established.[45]

When is a joke not a joke? Do you agree with the decision to prosecute Mr Chambers? Mr Chamber had been supported by high profile comedians who had argued that the prosecution should not have gone ahead. The problem is that today many people use social media sites such as Twitter to make public statements and these could be deemed to be offensive or indeed amounting to a criminal offence.

13.3.8 Racial and religious hatred

It is an offence under Criminal Justice and Public Order Act 1994 (amended by the Racial and Religious Hatred Act 2006) to stir up religious or racial hatred. There is also an offence under s.18 of the Public Order Act 1986. A person accused does not have to intend to stir up religious or racial hatred but can be guilty where 'having regard to all the circumstances racial hatred is likely to be stirred up thereby.' Therefore, someone putting on a play which involves abusive words or behaviour could be liable for conviction.

13.3.9 Sexual orientation

Section 74 of the Criminal Justice and Immigration Act 2008 criminalises inciting hatred based on sexual orientation.

13.3.10 Defamation

Defamation is a tort and anyone who makes an untrue statement in print or by spoken word could be sued. It is possible to defame both individuals and private companies. However, the government cannot sue for defamation.[46] Publishers and authors must take great care not to publish material which is deemed defamatory. Prior to its abolition by section 4 of the Defamation Act 2013 the press could rely on the *Reynolds* defence from *Reynolds v Times Newspapers Ltd*.[47] The case concerned a libellous statement of fact which had been made in the course of political discussion. The former Irish Prime Minister could only recover £1 in damages for libel. *The Times* argued that they should not be liable as the statement had been published in good faith. Lord Nicholls in his judgment stated that there could be a defence of qualified privilege where publication was in the public interest. His Lordship listed the factors that the court should consider and stated that,

> The court should be slow to conclude that a publication was not in the public interest and, therefore, the public had no right to know, especially when the information is in the field of political discussion. Any lingering doubts should be resolved in favour of publication.[48]

The decision in *Reynolds* was reconsidered by the Supreme Court in *Flood v Times Newspapers Ltd*.[49] The Defamation Act 2013 establishes the requirements for defamation, as there needs to be serious harm and also outlines the defences that are available. Section 4 permits a defence where publication is a matter of public interest. Professor Ewing has contrasted *Reynolds* with the position in the United States. Making reference to the Supreme Court's decision in *New York Times v Sullivan*,[50] Ewing states that

> there is a much greater emphasis on 'a profound national commitment to the principal that debate on public issues should be uninhibited, robust, and wide-open, and that it may well include vehement, caustic, and sometimes unpleasantly sharp attacks on government and public officials.'[51]

For further commentary on Canada, the United States, and England and Wales see Richard Mullender, 'Defamation and Responsible Communication.'[52]

13.3.11 The tort of Wilkinson v Downton [1897] 2 QB 57

In *James Rhodes v OPO*[53] the issue was whether the publication of a memoir could be prevented as it would cause harm to the author's son under the tort of *Wilkinson v Downton*.[54] The Supreme Court referred to the tort as 'liability in tort for wilful infringement of another's right to personal safety.'[55] The memoir depicted childhood abuse suffered by the author. His former wife (and the mother of their son) argued that reading the book would cause distress to the boy. The Supreme Court found in favour of publication. In his judgment Lord Neuberger was of the view that:

> it would, I think, be an inappropriate restriction on freedom of expression, an unacceptable form of judicial censorship, if a court could restrain publication of a book written by a defendant, whose contents could otherwise be freely promulgated, only refer in general and unobjectionable terms to the claimant, and are neither intended nor expected by the defendant to harm the claimant, simply because the claimant might suffer psychological harm if he got to read it (or extracts from it).[56]

13.3.12 The Leveson inquiry and press regulation

The British press has exposed many important scandals such as the abuse of parliamentary expenses, which has led to the prosecution of many parliamentarians. However, the press has been accused of many negative practices such as phone hacking and making false accusations about individuals. A public inquiry was chaired by Lord Justice Leveson and investigated the culture, practice and ethics of the press called for press regulation that would be underpinned by statute.

The recommendation by the Leveson report for press regulation has proved controversial. The report's recommendations have been challenged by some politicians and elements of the press.[57] The opponents to the recommendations argued that regulation would restrict the press' freedom of expression and harm free speech. The three main political parties agreed that the press would be regulated by a Royal Charter rather than by statute. However, the press then submitted their own proposals for an alternative Royal Charter to the Privy Council. The rival proposals differed from the one put forward by the three main political parties, as future regulation would have to be agreed by the bodies including trade bodies. Former editors would have been allowed to sit on the panel regulating the press, and the readers of publications would have an input on regulation.

13.4 Privacy and English Law

Privacy is a very important restriction on the freedom of expression. This will be main focus of the rest of this chapter.

13.4.1 Shortcomings in the protection of privacy before the HRA 1998

Confidential information has been protected by the equity. The duty of confidence if breached offers the claimant the right to claim damages and to seek an injunction to prevent publication of confidential material, or to stop on-going publication. Breach of confidence is used to protect business interests, such as trade secrets and intellectual property. The decision in *Coco v AN Clark (Engineers) Limited*[58] established the requirements need for breach of confidence. The three requirements were

1   that the information was of a confidential nature,
2   that it was communicated in circumstances importing an obligation of confidence and
3   that there was an unauthorised use of the information.

We can see that breach of confidence had been used as a cause of action in non-business cases:

*   In *Duke of Argyll v Duchess of Argyll*[59] the parties were getting divorced and there was an allegation that the duchess had committed adultery. It was argued that the duchess's diary would provide evidence of this. The duchess

argued that her diary was confidential. The House of Lords held that a diary was confidential and that it did not lose its confidentiality unless it was published or abandoned. The fact that the duchess had made some admissions about certain entries did not waive confidentiality for the whole diary. It is important to note that the diary could lose its confidentiality and at that point to disclose its content would not amount to a breach.

- In *Prince Albert v Strange*[60] the court held that there had been a breach of confidence when the defendant obtained copies of Prince Albert's private etchings and had attempted to publish these.
- Confidentiality prevented the publication of Richard Crossman's diaries in *Attorney-General v Jonathan Cape Ltd*[61] until ten years after the events described. This was because Crossman had written about Cabinet discussions which attracted the necessary quality of confidence.
- In *Attorney-General v Guardian Newspapers Ltd (No. 2)*[62] the House of Lords considered the *Spycatcher* book written by a former member of MI5, Peter Wright, whether extracts could be published in the United Kingdom. The House of Lords held that a duty of confidence was owed by Wright to his employers on the basis of the contract between them and in equity. This was a lifelong duty to not breach confidence. However, in light of the worldwide publication of the book, the House of Lords would not permit further injunctions. The material published in the *Sunday Times* breached the newspaper's duty of confidence and the Crown could claim its profits for publishing this material. However, the *Guardian* and *Observer* articles published information that did not harm the public interest and did not breach a duty of confidentiality. For a consideration of whether the injunctions preventing publication breached Article 10 ECHR, see the decision of the European Court of Human Rights in *Observer v United Kingdom*[63]).

In *Kaye v Roberston*[64] Gordon Kaye who was the star of a popular television show was injured in an accident and recovering in hospital. Kaye was in a private hospital room and in order to help him recover the number of visitors he could receive were limited. There were notices asking all visitors to report to the reception. The journalists ignored these and carried out an unauthorised interview during which they took photographs of Kaye's injuries. Kaye's representatives argued that given his medical condition he could not have consented. The interview was going to be published and the newspaper would claim that the interview was authorised. In the Court of Appeal Glidewell LJ stated that in English law there was no tort of privacy and that there could be no action for breach of privacy. The only action was in existing common law torts. Glidewell LJ observed:

> It is well-known that in English law there is no right to privacy, and accordingly there is no right of action for breach of a person's privacy. The facts of the present case are a graphic illustration of the desirability of Parliament considering whether and in what circumstances statutory provision can be made to protect the privacy of individuals.

Bingham LJ was critical of the common law and its failure to protect Kaye's personal privacy: 'This case nonetheless highlights, yet again, the failure of both the common law of England and statute to protect in an effective way the personal privacy of individual citizens.' Bingham LJ noted that despite a gross interference with his privacy there was no entitlement to relief. The protection that was needed was a tort of privacy, but this was problematic. Bingham LJ stated, 'We cannot give the plaintiff the breadth of protection which I would, for my part, wish. The problems of defining and limiting a tort of privacy are formidable, but the present case strengthens my hope that the review now in progress may prove fruitful.'

It was clear that claimants such as Kaye had to rely on other common law torts, but there was no tort that protected his right to privacy. Prior to the Human Rights Act 1998 the law did not recognise that there was a right to privacy. We shall see below that following the introduction of the HRA 1998 the courts have attempted to protect privacy through the use of the common law breach of confidence. We shall note though that the Convention rights incorporated into domestic law by the HRA 1998 were only intended to have a vertical effect, but that the courts have been able to give the Convention rights an indirect horizontal effect.

13.4.2 Was breach of confidence sufficient as a remedy for interferences with a person's private life?

The European Commission of Human Rights in *Earl Spencer and Countess Spencer v United Kingdom*[65] held that breach of confidence was an effective remedy. The Earl Spencer and his wife had their privacy violated by *The News of the World* when it made front page allegations about their private lives. The newspaper published a photograph of the Countess taken using a telescopic lens when she was walking in the private grounds of a medical clinic. The applicants argued that the United Kingdom had failed to respect their private lives as the common law had failed to prevent publication of the photograph. The applicants had argued that the United Kingdom had failed in its positive obligation to protect their private lives and there was no domestic remedy for violation of Article 8. The government argued that the articles published confidential information and that the applicants had a remedy under domestic law. However, the republication of the information would not be protected as the information was no longer confidential. The applicants argued that breach of confidence was an ineffectual remedy for an invasion of their private lives. This was problematic as it required that the newspaper would have to be put on notice that the information was confidential. The applicants' arguments were rejected as breach of confidence was considered to be a suitable remedy and one that was being expanded by the courts to protect privacy. The European Commission of Human Rights stated that:

Accordingly, the Commission considers that the parties' submissions indicate that the remedy of breach of confidence (against the newspapers and their sources) was available to the applicants and that the applicants have not demonstrated that it was insufficient or ineffective in the circumstances of their cases. It considers that, in so far as relevant doubts remain concerning the financial awards to be made following a finding of a breach of confidence, they are not such as to warrant a conclusion that the breach of confidence action is ineffective or insufficient but rather a conclusion that the matter should be put to the domestic courts for consideration in order to allow those courts, through the common law system in the United Kingdom, the opportunity to develop existing rights by way of interpretation.

The Commission were clearly of the view:

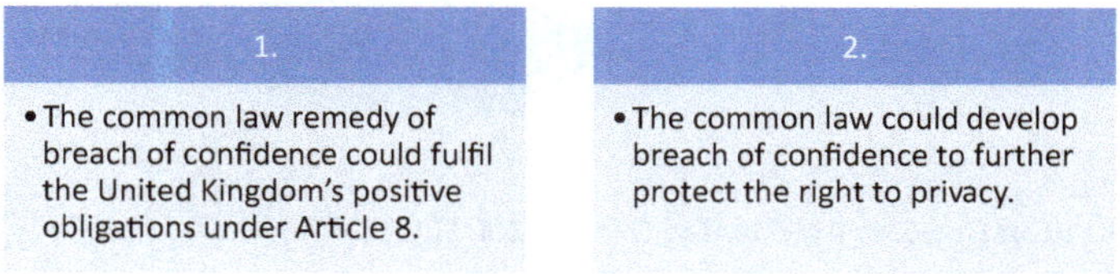

1.	2.
• The common law remedy of breach of confidence could fulfil the United Kingdom's positive obligations under Article 8.	• The common law could develop breach of confidence to further protect the right to privacy.

Figure 13.3
The decision in *Earl Spencer and Countess Spencer v United Kingdom* (1998) 25 EHRR CD 105

13.4.3 Celebrity wedding photographs are protected

In *Douglas v Hello! Ltd (No.1)*[66] the famous actors Michael Douglas and Catharine Zeta-Jones were getting married and had agreed an exclusive deal with *OK!* Magazine to publish pictures of their New York wedding in return for a considerable amount of money. As part of the agreement all guests at their wedding were searched for cameras. However, after the wedding *Hello!* Magazine announced that they planned to publish pictures of the wedding. It was not known how *Hello!* had acquired the photographs. The Douglases obtained an injunction at first instance on the grounds that publishing the photographs would amount to a breach of confidence, malicious falsehood and would interfere with their contract with *OK!* At first instance the trial judge accepted that the photographs were confidential and that publishing these would amount to a breach of confidence. The problem was that little reasoning was given for this decision. The defendant appealed to the Court of Appeal.

Brooke LJ in his judgment observed that that the case involved freedom of expression, which is protected by Article 10 ECHR:

'It goes without saying that this is a case concerned with freedom of expression. Although the right to freedom of expression is not in every case the ace of trumps, it is a powerful card to which the courts of this country must always pay appropriate respect.' His Lordship considered the fact that at the wedding there had been a concentrated effort to inform guests and staff about not taking pictures, and that in these circumstances the wedding had 'characteristics of confidentiality.' The guests and the staff knew that the wedding was confidential.

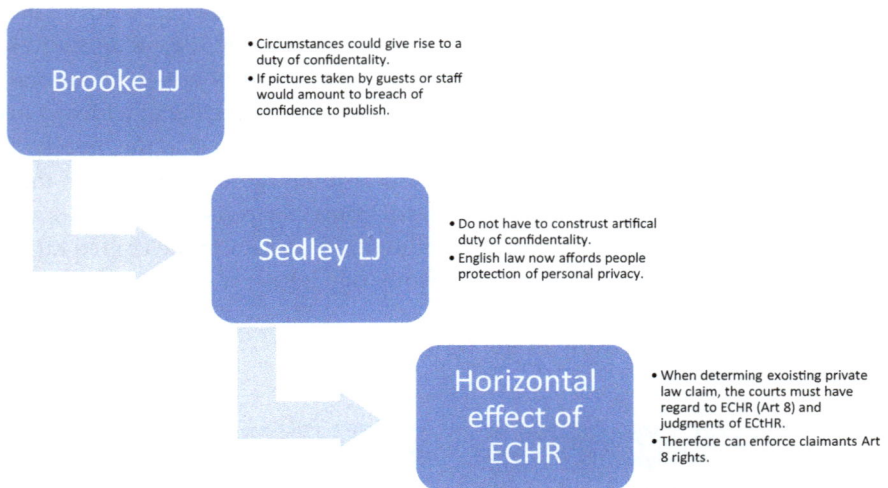

Figure 13.4
The reasoning in *Douglas v Hello! Ltd* (No.1) [2001] QB 967

Therefore, if someone in breach of their duty of confidentiality, which had been established by the Douglases' arrangements, took the pictures, then *Hello!* would be misusing confidential information. However, Article 8 would need to be balanced with Article 10 in order to protect *Hello!*'s right to freedom of expression. Restrictions on Article 10 can be justified under paragraph (2) which permits restrictions that are necessary for 'for preventing the disclosure of information received in confidence,' and also 'for the protection of the reputation or rights of others.' Brooke LJ held that there had been a breach of confidence, but discharged the injunction preventing *Hello!* from publishing the pictures.

In his judgment Sedley LJ observed whether there was a right to privacy in English law: 'we have reached a point at which it can be said with confidence that the law recognises and will appropriately protect a right of personal privacy.' Sedley LJ held that the reasons for the court recognising this right of privacy was the Human Rights Act which 'requires the courts of this country to give appropriate effect to the right to respect for private and family life set out in article 8 of the European Convention for the Protection of Human Rights and Fundamental Freedoms.' Section 2 of the HRA 1998 requires the court to have regard to the jurisprudence of the ECtHR and under s.6 of the HRA 1998 the courts must act in a way that is compatible with the ECHR. Sedley LJ went further than Brooke LJ, who had considered breach of confidence in relation to a picture taken by a guest or member of staff, who were subject to the Douglases' special arrangements. Sedley LJ observed that the law no longer needed to focus on constructing an artificial duty of confidentiality:

What a concept of privacy does, however, is accord recognition to the fact that the law has to protect not only those people whose trust has been abused but those who simply find themselves subjected to an unwanted intrusion into their personal lives. The law no longer needs to construct an artificial relationship of confidentiality between intruder and victim: it can recognise privacy itself as a legal principle drawn from the fundamental value of personal autonomy.

Sedley LJ held that Article 8 should have horizontal effect and the courts should give effect to Article 8 in a dispute between two private parties. This was because the courts are instructed to act in a manner compatible with the ECHR. The Douglases as a consequence of their private law claim for breach of confidence had a right to privacy under Article 8. Sedley LJ considered that because both Article 8 and 10 were qualified rights and not absolute, any interference with these rights must be proportionate. Sedley LJ agreed with Brooke LJ that the injunction should be discharged.

Therefore it is important to understand the judgment in *Douglas v Hello!*

- Brooke LJ held that there could exist a duty of confidentiality between the Douglases and the hotel employees and guests.
- Sedley LJ held that the Douglases had a right to privacy, which arose under Article 8 and the court when considering their private law claims had to have regarding to their rights under Article 8. Therefore Article 8 in this case was given a horizontal effect.
- However, there is no freestanding right of privacy in English law and the claimant must first bring an action in private law (i.e. breach of confidence). Article 8 is not an absolute right and is qualified; thus it can be restricted where it is proportionate to do so. This is best explained by the competing of demands of Article 8 and 10.

13.4.4 Pictures of a celebrity leaving Narcotics Anonymous cannot be published

The House of Lords in *Campbell v MGN Ltd*[67] extended breach of confidence to include taking a picture of a celebrity in public, where that the celebrity has a reasonable expectation of privacy.[68] Naomi Campbell is a famous model and had publicly stated that she did not take drugs. She was photographed leaving Narcotics Anonymous and sued for breach of confidence. The House of Lords discussed in detail the weighing up of the competing demands of Articles 8 and 10. We will consider the opinions of the Law Lords in this important case.

Lord Hope held that the detail of Naomi Campbell's attendance at Narcotics Anonymous was 'private information which imported a duty of confidence.'[69] His Lordship stated that the starting point should be assessing whether the claimant had a 'reasonable expectation of privacy' in order to determine whether the information was private. His Lordship stated that Article 8 and 10 were competing rights and that the court must undertake a balancing exercise:

> The effect of these provisions is that the right to privacy which lies at the heart of an action for breach of confidence has to be balanced against the

right of the media to impart information to the public. And the right of the media to impart information to the public has to be balanced in its turn against the respect that must be given to private life.[70]

According to Lord Hope any restriction on the newspaper's freedom of expression under Article 10, by not publishing the photographs must 'be subjected to very close scrutiny.'[71] This is crucial because freedom of the expression is so important in a democratic society.

Lord Hope identified a test[72] for publishing the photographs: 'whether publication of the material pursues a legitimate aim and whether the benefits that will be achieved by its publication are proportionate to the harm that may be done by the interference with the right to privacy.'[73] His Lordship noted that neither right was more important than the other. Lord Hope stated that the public benefit of publication needed to be weighed up against the harm caused to Naomi Campbell. His Lordship considered the fact that these pictures were taken in a public place but placed great weight on the fact that they had been obtained by stealth. His Lordship held that on the facts Naomi Campbell's right to privacy outweighed the newspaper's freedom of expression, because the infringement of privacy could not be justified by the publication of the photographs.

Baroness Hale considered when restrictions on both Article 8 and 10 could be justified. It is worthwhile considering Her Ladyship's approach.

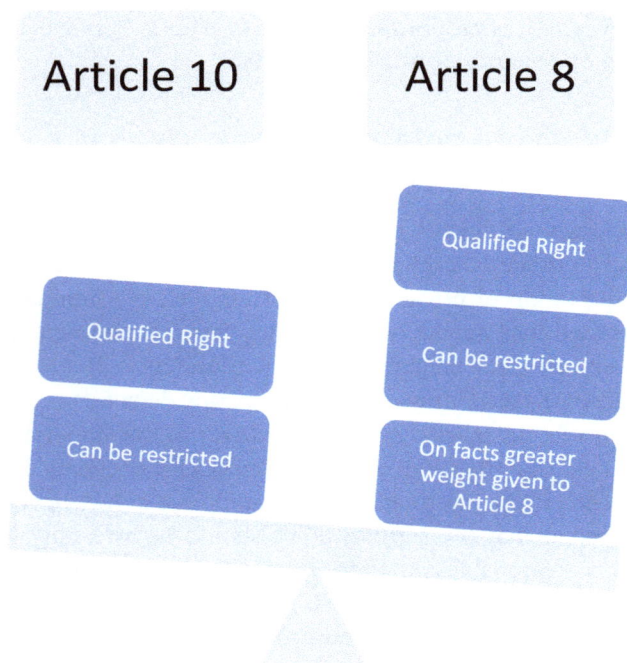

Figure 13.5
The approach of Baroness Hale in *Campbell v MGN Ltd* [2004] UKHL 22

Her Ladyship looked at Article 10 and the fact that as a qualified right it could be restricted under Article 10 (2):

- 'may be subject to such formalities, conditions, restrictions or penalties as are prescribed by law';
- which 'are necessary in a democratic society'; and
- 'in the interests of . . . the protection of the reputation or rights of others, for preventing the disclosure of information received in confidence.'

It is clear that any restrictions must be proportionate and necessary in a democratic society. Her Ladyship accepted that the photographs were confidential, because unlike other photographs taken, the accompanying text told the reader that she was attending the Narcotics Anonymous meeting. Lord Carswell accepted that the photographs had caused harm to Ms Campbell and that that the intrusion into her private affairs could not be justified and that he rejected the argument that 'publication was necessary to maintain the newspaper's credibility.'[74]

Lords Hoffmann and Nicholls dissented from the majority. Lord Nicholls rejected Naomi Campbell's claim that there had been a misuse of her private information, as the pictures taken by the reporter was not of a private nature. According to Lord Nicholls there could be a cause of action where there had been a misuse of private information. Lord Hoffmann was of the view that

> In the present case, the pictures were taken without Ms Campbell's consent. That in my opinion is not enough to amount to a wrongful invasion of privacy. The famous and even the not so famous who go out in public must accept that they may be photographed without their consent, just as they may be observed by others without their consent.

However, there is no right to publish every photograph. Lord Hoffmann stated that a mass publication of a picture which humiliated or embarrassed someone might amount to an infringement of someone's personal information. But on the present facts the photograph was neither embarrassing nor humiliating nor taken in a private place.

13.4.5 Von Hannover v Germany *(2005) 40 EHRR 1*

We will consider the decision of the European Court of Human Rights in *Von Hannover v Germany*[75]. Princess Caroline (Von Hannover) is a member of Monaco's Royal Family and apart from representing her family as charity events she did not carry out any official functions for Monaco. For years the applicant had been followed and photographed by the press and pictures of her shopping, walking, leaving restaurants and with her children were published in the German press. The applicant took Germany to the ECtHR arguing that German law did not adequately protect her right to respect for a private and family life under Article 8.

In in *Von Hannover v Germany* the court considered that there were two obligations under Article 8:

- a negative obligation – which was that the state should abstain from interfering in a person's private life
- A positive obligation – the state should have measures in place to 'ensure respect for private life even in the sphere of the relations of individuals between themselves'

The issue here was Germany's alleged breach of the positive obligation. The court held the competing right of freedom of expression under Article 10 had to be balance against Article 8. The ECtHR rejected the argument that tabloid photographs could be protected under freedom of expression, because of the harassment caused to the applicant and the fact that the photographs were intrusive into her private life. There was a fundamental distinction drawn between the reporting of facts which were: 'capable of contributing to a debate in a democratic society relating to politicians in the exercise of their functions, for example, and reporting details of the private life of an individual who did not exercise official functions.'

PUBLIC LAW IN CONTEXT
THE BALANCE THAT NEEDS TO BE STRUCK

The public in a democratic society has a right to be kept informed by the press. Whilst this could justify publication of photographs, here because the photographs were published out of curiosity they served no purpose in terms of genuine public debate. Just because Princess Caroline was famous it did not mean that there was sufficient justification to publish the photographs. On balance the press' freedom of expression was outweighed by her right to privacy. The court found that the German law was inadequate to protect the applicant's privacy as the courts had limited the protection afforded to public figures, which whilst it may have been appropriate for a politician, was not appropriate for someone who did not carry out official royal functions. The court held that there had been a breach of Article 8 as there was no justification in permitting the press to publish the pictures.

The court's observations serve as a useful summary on the court's reasoning:

As the Court has stated above, it considers that the decisive factor in balancing the protection of private life against freedom of expression should lie in the contribution that the published photos and articles make to a debate of general interest. It is clear in the instant case that they made no such contribution since the applicant exercises no official function and the photos and articles related exclusively to details of her private life.

Furthermore, the Court considers that the public does not have a legitimate interest in knowing where the applicant is and how she behaves generally in her private life even if she appears in places that cannot always be described as secluded and despite the fact that she is well known to the public.

Even if such a public interest exists, as does a commercial interest of the magazines in publishing these photos and these articles, in the instant case those interests must, in the Court's view, yield to the applicant's right to the effective protection of her private life.[76]

Von Hannover is an important decision as it demonstrates that whilst member states have a margin of appreciation, the ECtHR will still find that there has been a breach of Article 8 (or indeed 10), when the domestic courts or legislation has struck the wrong balance. However, this does not mean that the press will never be able to publish photographs of high-profile individuals.

The ECtHR in *Von Hannover v Germany*[77] rejected a subsequent claim by Princess Caroline of Monaco that the German courts, in permitting the publication of photographs of her and her husband on holiday in St Moritz, had violated her Article 8 rights. The ECtHR held that the publication of the photographs next to an article about Prince Rainier's illness was of public interest, as the photographs were of informational value and added to the public debate over the prince's illness, which was of interest to contemporary society. In the second *Von Hannover* case the ECtHR stated:

that irrespective of the question whether and to what extent the first applicant assumes official functions on behalf of the Principality of Monaco, it cannot be claimed that the applicants, who are undeniably very well known, are ordinary private individuals. They must, on the contrary, be regarded as public figures.[78]

The German courts had followed the approach established in the original *Von Hannover* decision and had correctly applied it. The ECtHR held that in light of the margin of appreciation afforded to the German court, the correct balance had been struck by the domestic court. The court set out how the balancing test should be approached and observed that the following criteria should be considered:

- contribution to a debate of general interest
- how well known the person concerned was and what the subject of the report was
- prior conduct of the person concerned
- content, form and consequences of the publication
- circumstances in which the photos were taken[79]

These criteria were applied and led to the court's decision.

13.4.6 Articles 8 and 10 'are the very content of the domestic tort that the English court has to enforce'

In *McKennitt v Ash*[80] the Court of Appeal had to consider whether there was a breach of confidence, where a former friend had written an unauthorised book about a famous singer-songwriter. The claimant objected to the book on the basis that it revealed personal information which she wanted to keep private. Buxton LJ noted that there 'is no English domestic law tort of invasion of privacy' and 'the English courts have to proceed through the tort of breach of confidence, into which the jurisprudence of articles 8 and 10 has to be "shoehorned."'[81] His Lordship acknowledged that there might be discomfort in using the tort of confidence where there was not a pre-existing confidential relationship. However, liability would arise from acquiring information which you knew that you were not permitted to use. It is important to note that the courts as a public authority under s.6 HRA 1998 must act in a way that is compatible with the ECHR. Buxton LJ stated that the correct approach was to:

> find the rules of the English law of breach of confidence we now have to look in the jurisprudence of articles 8 and 10. Those articles are now not merely of persuasive or parallel effect but . . . are the very content of the domestic tort that the English court has to enforce.[82]

13.4.7 The balancing act

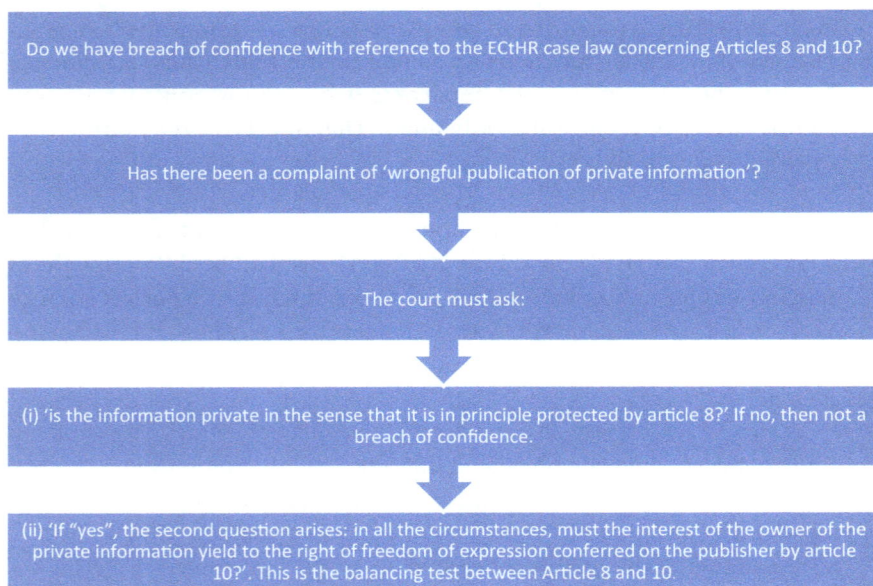

Figure 13.6
The approach that the court should take in balancing Articles 8 and 10

It is clear that the courts in determining whether there has been a breach of confidence must have regard to Article 8 and the jurisprudence of the ECtHR. This is very important as the courts will effectively read Strasbourg's jurisprudence into the equitable breach of confidence. We will consider the balancing act struck by the courts. However, there is some academic disagreement over the precise nature of this exercise and whether it is fact a balancing act undertaken by the courts.[83]

In *R (on the application of Khuja) v Times Newspapers Limited*[84] the Supreme Court considered the need for a balancing act between the rights protected under Article 8 and Article 10 of the ECHR. In this decision the applicant had been named by national newspapers in connection to child sex grooming allegations. He had been arrested and subsequently released without charge. The majority of the court found in favour of the newspaper's defence that naming the applicant was justified in the public interest. In his judgment on behalf of the majority, Lord Sumption had observed:

> The Convention right most often engaged in such cases is the right under article 8 to respect for private and family life. Article 8 rights are heavily qualified by the Convention itself, and even when they are made good they must be balanced in a publication case against the right to freedom of expression protected by article 10.[85]

Lord Sumption was clear that a balance needed to be struck:

> the principal English authorities [point to] an approach to the balancing exercise which is fact-specific rather than being dependent on any a priori hierarchy of rights. On some facts, the claimant's article 8 rights may be entitled to very little weight. On some facts, the public interest in the publication in the media may be slight or non-existent.[86]

The issue of whether the media could publish the names of those three individuals involved in sexual activity was considered by the Supreme Court in *PJS v News Group Newspapers*[87]. The media sought to publish the names and the individuals involved had obtained an injunction preventing their identities from being disclosed. Lord Mance considered the approach the court take including when initially deciding whether to grant an injunction, which was that '(i) neither article has preference over the other, (ii) where their values are in conflict, what is necessary is an intense focus on the comparative importance of the rights being claimed in the individual case, (iii) the justifications for interfering with or restricting each right must be taken into account and (iv) the proportionality test must be applied.'[88] The injunction was upheld by the Supreme Court, despite the fact that the identities of those involved being known by some of the public and published by the media outside of this jurisdiction.

13.4.8 The Prince of Wales' diary is protected by the duty of confidentiality

A further extension to breach of confidence occurred in *HRH Prince of Wales v Associated Newspapers Ltd*[89] where the diaries of the Prince of Wales were published by a national newspaper. The Prince of Wales had written his diaries to record his private opinions and the diaries contained some unflattering descriptions of members of the Chinese government which the Prince met in Hong Kong. It was clear that confidence no longer required a pre-existing confidential relationship. The Court of Appeal held that the Prince had the reasonable expectation that his diary was confidential. This was despite the fact that the Prince had distributed the diaries to a number of senior people, including current and former senior politicians. The employee who had leaked the diary owed the Prince a duty of confidentiality. The court had to weigh up the public interest in publication with the Prince's rights under Article 8.

13.4.9 Public figures

In *A v B Plc*[90] the Court of Appeal held that the trial judge should not have granted an injunction preventing a major newspaper from publishing details about a married footballer's affairs with two women. It was held that there was genuine public interest about every detail of his life and that given his position he could not claim to have more than a modest expectation of privacy. Lord Woolf CJ had stated:

> Where an individual is a public figure he is entitled to have his privacy respected in the appropriate circumstances. A public figure is entitled to a private life. The individual, however, should recognise that because of his public position he must expect and accept that his actions will be more closely scrutinised by the media. Even trivial facts relating to a public figure can be of great interest to readers and other observers of the media. Conduct which in the case of a private individual would not be the appropriate subject of comment can be the proper subject of comment in the case of a public figure. The public figure may hold a position where higher standards of conduct can be rightly expected by the public. . . . If you have courted public attention then you have less ground to object to the intrusion which follows. . . . It would be . . . accurate to say that the public have an understandable and so a legitimate interest in being told the information.[91]

It is clear that a celebrity who courts public attention and holds himself out as a role model cannot expect much protection from the courts.

In *Trimingham v Associated Newspapers Ltd*[92] the lover of a married MP became the focus of press attention. Journalists called her bisexual, a lesbian, published photographs of her and commented on her appearance. The court held that she did not have a reasonable expectation of privacy as she had become involved with a public figure who was a member of the government. Tugendhat J as the claimant had sold information about her lover's colleagues' sex lives to the press, giving the impression that 'she saw nothing wrong in disclosing to the newspapers information conveyed to her in or from a private conversation.'[93]

One of the most high-profile intrusions of a personal privacy was the secret recording of Max Mosley engaging to bondage and sexual acts with prostitutes. The recording was carried out on the mistaken premise that his activities were Nazi themed. In *Mosley v News Group Newspapers Ltd*[94] Eady J held that Mr Mosley had a reasonable expectation of privacy and that there was no public interest in publishing the recording, even if some people would disprove of his activities. Eady J was clear that it cannot be 'seriously . . . suggested that the case is likely to inhibit serious investigative journalism into crime or wrongdoing, where the public interest is more genuinely engaged.'[95]

Kirsty Hughes commenting on the decision in *Mosley v News Group Newspapers Ltd* has argued that the approach of Eady J in considering whether the claimant had a reasonable expectation of privacy, is to ask 'the question "was article 8 ECHR engaged" . . . Eady J uses the Convention right as the trigger for the cause of action.'[96] This is important, as the approach has been to protect the right under Article 8 through indirect horizontal effect. This means that there must a domestic cause of action, such as breach of confidence, before the court can address the question of whether the claimant's Convention rights are engaged. It must be remembered that the HRA 1998 was only intended to have a vertical effect. The effect of Article 8 has been very important in protecting people's rights to privacy against other private parties. Therefore, the Convention rights have been given indirect horizontal effect by the courts and people can seek protection where the press publishes information about them. It remains to be seen whether the courts will recognise the existence of a domestic tort of privacy, which would remove the need to artificially construe existing common law torts.

13.4.10 A reasonable expectation of privacy when under investigation for criminal offences

A reasonable expectation of privacy extends to those who are under investigation for criminal offences. Sir Cliff Richard had been under police investigation for a historic sexual offence since 2014 and the police had been in contact with the BBC. This meant that when the police made a search of Sir Cliff Richard's home, that the BBC were there to film the search. Sir Cliff Richard sued the BBC and sought damages. In *Cliff Richard v. The British Broadcasting Corporation*[97] Mann J found in favour of Sir Cliff and held that he had a reasonable expectation of privacy:

> It seems to me that on the authorities, and as a matter of general principle, a suspect has a reasonable expectation of privacy in relation to a police investigation, and I so rule. As a general rule it is understandable and justifiable (and reasonable) that a suspect would not wish others to know of the investigation because of the stigma attached. It is, as a general rule, not

necessary for anyone outside the investigating force to know, and the consequences of wider knowledge have been made apparent in many cases.[98]

Mann was clear though that 'whether or not there is a reasonable expectation of privacy in a police investigation is a fact-sensitive question and is not capable of a universal answer one way or the other.'[99]

13.4.11 The tort of misuse of personal information

The requirements for privacy to be protected under Article 8 have seen the gradual development of a new tort of misuse of private information, which has developed alongside the court's use of the equitable doctrine of breach of confidence to give effect to its obligations as a public authority for the purposes of section 6 of the Human Rights Act 1998. It is important to note the gradual acceptance of this new tort and the significance of this new way to protect privacy, especially in the absence of a freestanding tort of privacy.

ACADEMIC DEBATE

There is debate in the academic community over whether it is actually a new tort or whether it is a development of the existing law.[100] Thomas Bennett has criticised the development of misuse of personal information from the decision in Campbell:

> For rather than heralding the introduction of a distinct, novel cause of action apt to protect claimants' privacy interests, the *Campbell* decision moved the law only slightly beyond the position it had, by that time, already reached through the older, equitable doctrine of confidence. This was in preference to recognising a broad tort of 'invasion of privacy,' or even a number of discrete torts protecting distinct aspects of privacy. In making only relatively minor doctrinal changes to the position English law had already found itself in, the House of Lords threw its weight behind an unhelpful tendency to 'shoe-horn' all types of privacy interests into a legal mechanism suited only to dealing with the non-consensual publication of private facts. This has left English law with an inflexibility in respect of protecting individuals' privacy interests that has given rise to considerable uncertainty. In this essay, I evidence and critique one particular instance of this uncertainty: the confusion surrounding the very nature of the MPI doctrine. It is unclear whether the doctrine is part of tort law, or equity, or – perhaps – something else entirely. And whilst the courts have been forced recently to grapple with this conundrum, detailed analysis of their efforts reveals that the question has not been satisfactorily settled.[101]

In *Imerman v Tchenguiz*[102] Lord Neuberger MR considered the development of the tort of misuse of private information and accepted that it should be recognised.[103] In *Vidal Hall and Ors v Google Inc*[104] Tugendhat J confirmed that there was such a tort: 'there have since been a number of cases in which misuse of private information has been referred to as a tort consistently with *OBG* and these cannot be dismissed as all errors in the use of the words "tort." '[105] Tugendhat J concluded 'that the tort of misuse of private information is a tort within the meaning of ground 3.1(9).'[106]

ACADEMIC DEBATE

What was the significance of In *Vidal Hall and Ors v Google Inc*? Dominic Ruck Keene was clear that it was significant, not just in the explicit recognition that there was a tort of misuse of private information, but that this would have impact on the amount of damages that would be available.[107]

[I]t also represents a considered decision by the High Court <u>first</u> that there is a separate cause of action for misuse of such information, which should be protected solely on the basis of its personal nature, and <u>secondly</u> such an action is a tortious rather than an equitable cause of action. The bifurcation of the traditional action of breach of confidence into a redefined breach of confidence (excluding personal information) and breach of confidence i.e. privacy noted by Mr Justice Tugendhat is comparatively recent. . . . As Mr Justice Tugendhat noted, there is still also no tort of privacy per se. However, there has been a judge led creation of something approaching a privacy cause of action. This judgment therefore represents a further significant step towards the carving out of a legally distinct common law action for misuse of personal information. . . . Secondly, there had to date only been limited explicit judicial support for the recognition of the misuse of personal information as a tort, rather than a breach of the equitable principle of good faith. . . . Being a tort will also potentially open the door in this and other cases to damages, even exemplary damages, being awarded as of right, rather than remedies being equitable and therefore discretionary. . . . There is therefore more than just a name at stake.

Recently in *Duchess of Sussex v Associated Newspapers*[108] Warby J noted that

The tort of misuse of private information has grown out of the wrong of breach of confidence, and the argument for maintaining the privacy right even if future publication is in view cannot be weaker. Indeed, it seems to me it can only be stronger when the information is personal and private, and the law's objective is to protect the individual's Convention right to respect for her autonomy.[109]

13.5 Practical application

'There is no reason why the common law should not develop a freestanding tort of privacy.'

Discuss the above statement with reference to case law, academic opinion and legislation.

13.6 Key points to take away from this chapter

- Article 8 is a qualified right, which safeguards the right to respect for a private family life.
- Article 8 extends to protecting private correspondence, family life, access to housing and prevention from material being published about you.
- Article 8 must be balanced against Article 10, which protects the freedom of expression. Both Article 8 and 10 are qualified rights and the courts must weigh up whether the rights under Article 8 are more important than the freedom of expression.
- There are many restrictions on freedom of expression, such as liability for defamation in tort, contempt of court under the CCA 1981 and preventing persons from inciting racial or religious hatred.

Notes

1 See *Entick v Carrington* (1765) 19 St Tr 1030.
2 [1979] 2 All ER 620.
3 (1984) (App. 8691/79).
4 ibid 67.
5 [2001] UKHL 26.
6 [2005] EWCA Civ 597.
7 (IA/14578/2008).
8 D Barrett, 'Immigrant Allowed to Stay Because of Pet Cat' *The Telegraph* (17 October 2009) <www.telegraph.co.uk/news/newstopics/howaboutthat/6360116/Immigrant-allowed-to-stay-because-of-pet-cat.html>.
9 A Wagner, 'Catgate: Another Myth Used to Trash Human Rights' *The Guardian* (4 October 2011) <www.theguardian.com/law/2011/oct/04/theresa-may-wrong-cat-deportation>.
10 (20605/92) (1997) 24 EHRR 523.
11 (62617/00) (2007) 45 EHRR 37.
12 (61496/08) (2017).
13 ibid 133.
14 See <https://uklabourlawblog.com/2020/10/05/the-right-to-privacy-while-working-from-home-wfh-why-employee-monitoring-infringes-art-8-echr-by-eleni-frantziou/>.
15 (20348) (1997) 23 EHRR 101.
16 [2003] UKHL 43.
17 [2010] UKSC 45.
18 (45901/05) (2010) 51 EHRR.
19 (38000/05) (2009) 48 EHRR 29.
20 (45901/05) (2010) 51 EHRR.
21 There is some debate about where misuse of private information is a tort. For a contrary view see Thomas DC Bennett, 'Judicial Activism and the Nature of "Misuse of Private Information"' (2018) 23(2) CL 74.
22 [2003] UKHL 53.
23 (12350/04) (2007) 44 EHRR 40.

24 ibid 47–49.
25 (8978/80) (1985).
26 ibid 23.
27 (37359/09) (2014).
28 ibid 62–67.
29 For commentary see F Schauer, 'Free Speech and the Argument From Democ-racy' (1983) 25 Liberal Democracy 241; C Edwin Baker, 'Is Democracy a Sound Basis for a Free Speech Principle' (2011) 97(3) VLR 515; J Rowbottom, 'Laws, Miranda and the Democratic Justification for Expression' (*UK Constitutional Law Blog*, 22 February 2014) <https://ukconstitutionallaw.org/> and the classic text E Barendt, *Freedom of Speech* (2nd edn, OUP2005).
30 [2011] EWHC 2074 (Admin).
31 [2011] EWHC 1629 (Admin).
32 T Bennett, 'The Relevance and Importance of Third Party Interests in Privacy Cases' (2011) 127 LQR 531.
33 See D Eady and J Rozenberg, 'Mr Justice Eady on Balancing Acts' (2011) 40(2) Index on Censorship 47.
34 [2018] EWCA Civ 2329.
35 ibid 4.
36 ibid 66.
37 P Wragg, 'Lord Hain and Privilege: When Power, Wealth and Abuse Com-bine to Subvert the Rule of Law' *Inforrm* (27 October 2018) <https://inforrm. org/2018/10/27/lord-hain-and-privilege-when-power-wealth-and-abuse-combine-to-subvert-the-rule-of-law-paul-wragg/>.
38 [1961] Crim. L.R. 176.
39 G Robertson, 'The Trial of Lady Chatterley's Lover' *The Guardian* (22 October 2010) <www.theguardian.com/books/2010/oct/22/dh-lawrence-lady-chatterley-trial>.
40 (5493/72) (1976).
41 ibid 57.
42 [2009] JCL 241.
43 [2012] EWHC 2157 (Admin).
44 ibid 30.
45 ibid 39.
46 See *Derbyshire County Council v Times Newspapers Ltd* [1993] AC 534.
47 [2001] 2 AC 127.
48 ibid 205.
49 [2012] UKSC 11. For academic commentary see T Bennett, 'Flood v Times News-papers Ltd – Reynolds Privilege Returns to the UK's Highest Court' (2012) 23(5) ELR 134.
50 376 US 254 (1964), 270.
51 KD Ewing, *Bonfire of the Liberties: New Labour, Human Rights, and the Rule of Law* (OUP 2010) 153.
52 (2010) 126 LQR 368.
53 [2015] UKSC 32.
54 [1897] 2 QB 57.
55 [2015] UKSC 32 [77].
56 [2015] UKSC 32 [97].
57 For commentary see P Wragg, *A Free and Regulated Press: Defending Coercive Inde-pendent Press Regulation* (Hart Publishing 2020).

58 [1968] FSR 418.
59 [1962] S.C. (HL) 88.
60 (1849) 1 Hall & Twells 1.
61 [1976] QB 752.
62 [1988] UKHL 6.
63 (13585/88) (1991).
64 [1991] FSR 6.
65 (1998) 25 EHRR CD 105.
66 [2001] QB 967.
67 [2004] UKHL 22.
68 ibid.
69 ibid 95.
70 ibid 105.
71 ibid 113.
72 For commentary on the four tests advanced by the Law Lords see NA Moreham, 'Privacy in the Common Law: A Doctrinal and Theoretical Analysis' (2005) 121 LQR 628.
73 ibid 113.
74 ibid 170.
75 (2005) 40 EHRR 1.
76 ibid 76–77.
77 (40660/08 and 60641/08) [2012] EMLR 16.
78 ibid 120.
79 ibid 108–13.
80 [2006] EWCA Civ 1714.
81 ibid 8.
82 ibid 11.
83 See P Wragg, 'Protecting Private Information of Public Interest: Campbell's Great Promise, Unfulfilled' (2015) 7(2) Journal of Media Law 225.
84 [2017] UKSC 49.
85 ibid 15.
86 ibid 23.
87 [2016] UKSC 26.
88 ibid 20. This test was developed by Lord Steyn in *re S (FC) (a child)* [2004] UKHL 47, [17].
89 [2006] EWCA Civ 1776.
90 [2002] EWCA Civ 337.
91 ibid 208.
92 [2012] EWHC 1296 (QB).
93 ibid 153.
94 [2008] EWHC 1777.
95 ibid 234.
96 K Hughes, 'Horizontal Privacy' [2009] LQR 244.
97 [2018] EWHC 1837 (Ch).
98 ibid 248.
99 ibid 237.
100 See Bennett, 'Judicial Activism and the Nature of "Misuse of Private Information"' (n 21) 74.
101 ibid 74–75.

102 [2010] EWCA Civ 908.
103 ibid 65.
104 [2014] EWHC 13 (QB).
105 ibid 68.
106 ibid 70.
107 D Ruck Keene, 'New Year, New Tort of Misuse of Private Information' (*UK Human Rights Blog*, 23 January 2014) <https://ukhumanrightsblog.com/2014/01/23/new-year-new-tort-of-misuse-of-private-information/>.
108 [2021] EWCH 273 (Ch).
109 ibid 91.

Further reading

Barendt E, *Freedom of Speech* (2nd edn, OUP 2005)

Bennett T, 'The Relevance and Importance of Third Party Interests in Privacy Cases' (2011) 127 LQR 531

——, 'Flood v Times Newspapers Ltd – Reynolds Privilege Returns to the UK's Highest Court' [2012] ELR 134

——, 'Judicial Activism and the Nature of "Misuse of Private Information"' (2018) 23(2) CL 74

Bennett T and D Mac Síthigh, *The Campbell Legacy: Reflections on the Tort of Misuse of Private Information* (Routledge 2019)

Eady D and J Rozenberg, 'Mr Justice Eady on Balancing Acts' (2011) 40(2) Index on Censorship 47

Ewing KD, *Bonfire of the Liberties: New Labour, Human Rights, and the Rule of Law* (OUP 2010) – a very interesting critique of the law and recent developments between 1997–2007

Hughes K, 'Horizontal Privacy' [2009] LQR 244

Moosavian R, 'Charting the Journey from Confidence to the New Methodology' (2012) 34(5) EIPR 324

Moreham NA, 'Privacy in the Common Law: A Doctrinal and Theoretical Analysis' (2005) 121 LQR 628

Phillipson G, 'The Human Rights Act, "Horizontal Effect" and the Common Law: A Bang or a Whimper?' (1999) 62 MLR 824

——, 'Transforming Breach of Confidence? Towards a Common Law Right of Privacy Under the Human Rights Act' (2003) 66 MLR 726

Ruck Keene D, 'New Year, New Tort of Misuse of Private Information' (*UK Human Rights Blog*, 23 January 2014)

Schauer F, 'Free Speech and the Argument From Democracy' (1983) 25 Liberal Democracy 241

Wragg P, 'Protecting Private Information of Public Interest: Campbell's Great Promise, Unfulfilled' (2015) 7(2) JML 225

——, *A Free and Regulated Press: Defending Coercive Independent Press Regulation* (Hart Publishing 2020)

Human Rights III

Freedom of assembly and association

This chapter will

- consider what is meant by the freedom of assembly and association and how Articles 10 and 11 ECHR create the right to protest
- explore how domestic legislation restricts the rights under Article 11 ECHR
- debate whether an adequate balance has been struck by Parliament and the courts, in terms of how our rights to engage in peaceful protest have been restricted.

14.1 Introduction

Imagine that you are planning a protest against the government's decision to raise tuition fees. You decide that you will march through London and protest outside the Houses of Parliament. There will be over 50,000 protestors and you have no intention of being violent or disruptive, as all you wish to do is to protest. Are you permitted to protest without informing the police, will the police be able to prevent your protest from proceeding and could you be guilty of a criminal offence if you refuse to follow any conditions imposed by the police? We shall see that although Article 11 of the European Convention on Human Rights states that we have the right to freedom of assembly and association, the authorities can impose restrictions on this right. However, these restrictions must be necessary in a democratic society.

DOI: 10.4324/9780429293498-16

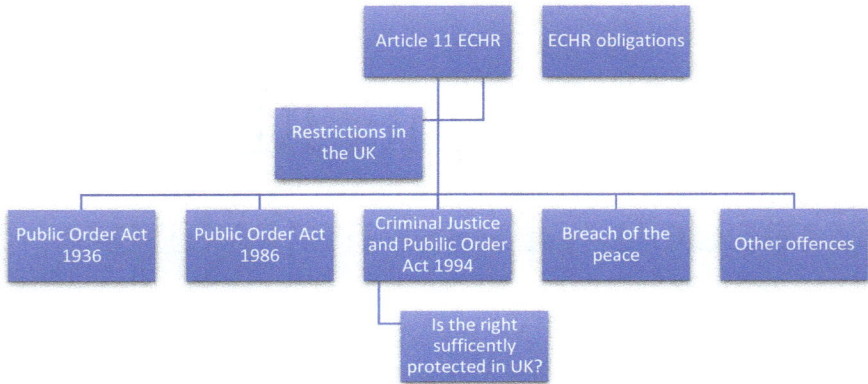

Figure 14.1
Article 11 Freedom of Assembly and Association

14.2 Public order and human rights

The key legislation in this area are the:

- Public Order Act 1936
- Public Order Act 1986
- Criminal Justice and Public Order Act 1994

These Acts of Parliament restrict the right to freedom of assembly and associ-ation. They are important in understanding how the police can control and regulate public protests and travellers and protect groups in society from the views and unwanted attention of others.

This chapter is concerned with the freedom of assembly and association. This means the right to associate with the people that you choose to and to assemble freely in public places. The right to do these is protected by Article 11 ECHR. However, we shall see that Parliament has restricted this freedom in the interest of public order and security. We shall focus on the Public Order Acts 1936 and 1986, as well as the Criminal Justice and Public Order Act 1994.

14.3 The Convention rights

Article 10 ECHR states that we have the right to freedom of expression and this right is relevant to any discussion on the freedom to have peaceful assemblies and associations. This is because the freedom of expression protects the wearing of slogans, the use of placards and signs, and above all free speech. These are elements of any protest and a restriction which limits Article 11 may also limit Article 10.

Article 11 ECHR protects the right to freedom of peaceful assembly and association. This is a qualified rather than an absolute right, meaning that restrictions can be imposed which restrict this right. Article 11(1) states that: 'Everyone has the right to freedom of peaceful assembly and to freedom of association with others, including the right to form and to join trade unions for the protection of his interests.' The right is for peaceful activity and does not protect activities which are violent. Article 11 specifically refers to trade union membership. Trade union membership is important as it enables workers to organise themselves to protect their rights and negotiate better working conditions.

PUBLIC LAW IN CONTEXT
TRADE UNIONS

Until the 1870s trade union membership was illegal as it amounted to conspiracy in criminal law. The Trade Union and Labour Relations (Consolidation) Act 1992 (TULR(C)A 1992) protects the rights of trade union members not to suffer detriment in the recruitment process and at work, as well as giving trade unions and their members the right to strike. The RMT trade union brought a case to the European Court of Human Rights (ECtHR) arguing that English law restricts the ability of trade unions to take industrial action. In *R.M.T. v. United Kingdom*[1], the ECtHR held that there had been violation of Article 11. The statutory protection under the TULR(C)A 1992 is narrow and contains a number of procedural requirements which make it difficult to take industrial action (see *British Airways Plc v. Unite the Union*[2]). The law has placed restrictions on picketing, which means that workers taking industrial action are restricted in their ability to demonstrate outside their own and associated workplaces. Trade unions have protection in law to prevent them from being sued by employers in the event of trade union members taking part in industrial action. An example of the limited protection afforded to trade unions is *Express Newspapers Ltd v. McShane*[3], where the Court of Appeal held that industrial action by the National Union of Journalists did not fall within the statutory protection and therefore the employers were able to obtain an injunction to prevent the industrial action. Lord Denning favoured a narrow interpretation of the statutory immunity and stated, 'I would also draw attention to the fact that, when Parliament granted immunities to the leaders of trade unions, it did not give them any rights. It did not give them a right to break the law or to do wrong by inducing people to break contracts. It only gave them immunity if they did' (at 395). The Court of Appeal's decision was reversed by the House of Lords in *Express Newspapers Ltd v. McShane*[4].

It is important to note that no restriction can be placed on the rights under Article 11 unless the restriction is:

* prescribed by law; and
* is necessary in a democratic society. Examples of when a restriction would be necessary include:

- in the interests of national security or public safety, or
- for the prevention of disorder or crime, or
- for the protection of health or morals, or
- for the protection of the rights and freedoms of others.

What does prescribed by law mean? It was defined by the ECtHR in *The Sunday Times v. The United Kingdom*[5]. The court identified two requirements which must be met:

> First, the law must be adequately accessible: the citizen must be able to have an indication that is adequate in the circumstances of the legal rules applicable to a given case. Secondly, a norm cannot be regarded as a 'law' unless it is formulated with sufficient precision to enable the citizen to regulate his conduct: he must be able – if need be with appropriate advice – to foresee, to a degree that is reasonable in the circumstances, the consequences which a given action may entail.[6]

There is no requirement that everyone must know the intricacies of the legal system, but rather that we should be capable, should we wish, of finding out what the law is and obtain advice to determine the legality of our actions.

The aim of the restriction must be necessary in a democratic society and the measure must be proportionate, i.e., it must go no further than what is necessary to achieving the legitimate aim which is being pursued. The test to determine whether a restriction is proportionate is outlined in Chapter 12. You should refer to the requirements which must be satisfied before a decision will be held to be proportionate. Crucially, Article 11(2) states that '[t]his Article shall not prevent the imposition of lawful restrictions on the exercise of these rights by members of the armed forces, of the police or of the administration of the State.'

In our daily lives we choose to associate with others whether they are friends, family or others who share the same political or religious views as ourselves.

In *Redfearn v. United Kingdom*[7] the ECtHR ruled that there had been a violation of Article 11 after an employee was dismissed for being a member of, and a political candidate for, the British National Party. The ECtHR held that there was insufficient protection in domestic law for an employee's political associations. The ECtHR observed that it was possible for employers to impose restrictions on employees' rights to safeguard the rights of others. However, the right to have the freedom to join political parties was a key requirement of a democracy and that 'the Court considers that in the absence of judicial safeguards a legal system which allows dismissal from employment solely on account of the employee's membership of a political party carries with it the potential for abuse.'[8] The lack of protection for employees dismissed by reason of their political beliefs amounted to a violation of Article 11. As a consequence, the Employment Rights Act 1996 was amended, and subsection section 108(4) was introduced. This demonstrated the impact that the ECtHR's decision had on domestic law.

14.4 The Public Order Act 1936

It is an offence under section 1(1) of the Public Order Act 1936 (POA 1936) to wear a uniform 'signifying his association with any political organisation or with the promotion of any political object' in a public place or at a public meeting. The purpose of section 1 was to prevent the political organisations in the United Kingdom from taking on quasi-military characteristics.

PUBLIC LAW IN CONTEXT
THE 1920S AND 1930S

In Germany during the 1920s and 1930s the Nazi party had a quasi-military branch known as the Brownshirts or SA, and in Italy Mussolini's fascists had a quasi-military branch known as the Blackshirts. In the 1930s, the former Labour minister, Sir Oswald Mosley, was the leader of the British Union of Fascists. His political supporters wore black shirts to signify their association to the party. Mosley's supporters clashed with rival communists in London's East End at the battle of Cable Street in 1936 and eventually Mosley was arrested at the start of the Second World War. The POA 1936 was designed to prevent the use of political uniforms.

Section 2 of the POA 1936 prevents the training and organisation of quasi-military organisations. The Act is designed to prevent the recruitment of political forces which could be used to usurp the functions of the state, such as the police. The Act also prohibits the wearing of uniform by supporters, which is to be used as 'signifying his association with any political organisation or with the promotion of any political object.' This is important as during the 1930s political quasi-military units were being used as a way of intimidating political opponents and undermining the state. A good example of this is how Hitler was invited to become Chancellor of Weimar Germany in 1933 because the authorities felt that they needed the support of his quasi-military SA (Brownshirts). Sections 1 and 2 of the POA 1936 have been used to outlaw paramilitary organisations in Northern Ireland, such as the Irish Republican Army (IRA).

PUBLIC LAW IN PRACTICE

Imagine that Go Green, a (fictitious) political party, decides that it needs to raise its public profile. The party decides to ask a famous fashion designer to create a uniform for party members to wear. Go Green plan to have all its 20,000 members wear this uniform at its conference in Swindon. The members will then proceed to an environmental rally in London. Go Green has been contacted by a party member who is concerned that if they do this, that they might be guilty of committing an offence under section 1 of the POA 1936. This is because the uniform signifies the members' association with Go Green.

Figure 14.2
Public Order Act 1986 key offences

14.5 The Public Order Act 1986

The Public Order Act 1986 (POA 1986) covers offences such as riot and affray, as well as the requirements for those organising public processions and assemblies. Finally, the POA 1986 covers the prohibition of racial hatred. We shall look at these in turn and see how the Act operates in practice.

ACADEMIC DEBATE

Peter Thornton QC has described the POA 1986 as

> an Act that strikes at the very heart of legitimate protest, particularly spontaneous protest. It extends existing police controls over processions and marches, it creates for the first time in the history of our law statutory controls over open-air meetings and picketing . . . (and) Above all it gives the police . . . an almost unchallengeable discretion, described by the Prime Minister . . . as a 'blank cheque'.[9]

We shall see that the POA 1986 severely restricts legitimate protest by restricting the ability to exercise our democratic rights. An example of spontaneous protest was in 2010 when members of the public gathered at the Liberal Democrats' head office and protested against their decision to enter into a coalition government with the Conservatives. Stone and Bonner (1987) commented that the changes introduced by the Act 'constitute steps down a route that is potentially damaging to police – community relations and to the expression of free speech by way of procession and assembly.' Therefore, we can see that there is a delicate balance between safeguarding public order and the right to freedom of expression and the right to freedom of assembly and association.

The POA 1986 creates several important offences (see Figure 14.2). It is important to note that the offences under sections 4 and 5 of the POA 1986 are used more often when charging defendants, than the offence of riot (s.1 of the POA 1986). We will look at these offences now.

14.5.1 Riot

Section 1 of the POA 1986 creates the offence of riot. Riot requires that '

> 12 or more persons who are present together use or threaten unlawful vio-
> lence for a common purpose and the conduct of them (taken together) is
> such as would cause a person of reasonable firmness present at the scene to
> fear for his personal safety.

The common purpose for why the people are present together can be inferred
from their conduct. Any of the 12 or more persons present 'using unlawful violence for the common purpose is guilty of riot.' Therefore, anyone present but
who does not use unlawful violence would not be guilty under section 1. Riot
carries a maximum custodial sentence of ten years. In order for an offence to
be committed a person of reasonable fitness must fear for their personal safety;
however, such a person need not be present and so this is a hypothetical test.
It is important to note that the consent of the Director of Public Prosecution is
required in order to bring a prosecution for the offence of riot.

14.5.2 Violent disorder

Section 2 of the POA 1986 concerns the offence of violent disorder. The crucial
difference between riot and violent disorder is that whereas riot requires 12 persons to be present and an offence to be committed by a person actually using
unlawful violence, violent disorder requires three persons to be present and a
person can be guilty if they either threaten or use unlawful violence. If tried
on indictment at the Crown Court, a person guilty of violent disorder could
receive a maximum five-year custodial sentence.

In *R v NW*[10] the Court of Appeal held that there was no requirement under
section 2 for people charged with violent disorder to share a common purpose,
just that they were present together. In this particular case a schoolgirl had been

Table 14.1 Riot	
Elements for section 1 Riot	**Satisfied?**
Do we have 12 or more persons present together?	Yes or no?
Do we have the use or threatening of unlawful violence?	Yes or no?
Is it for a common purpose?	Yes or no?
Would the conduct of them (taken together) cause a (hypothetical) person of reasonable fitness present at the scene to fear for his personal safety?	Yes or no?
Did the defendant accused of rioting actually use unlawful violence?	Yes or no?
Offence committed?	**If YES to all the above**

convicted of violent disorder after being present in a town centre and involved with an incident of violent disorder against the police.

Table 14.2 Violent Disorder

Elements for section 2 Violent Disorder	Satisfied?
Do we have three or more persons present together?	Yes or no?
Do we have the use or threatening of unlawful violence?	Yes or no?
Would the conduct of them (taken together) cause a (hypothetical) person of reasonable fitness present at the scene to fear for his personal safety?	Yes or no?
Did the defendant accused of violent disorder actually use or threaten unlawful violence?	Yes or no?
Offence committed?	**If YES to all the above**

PUBLIC LAW IN PRACTICE

Imagine that during a riot in London Hilda and her friends decided to target Enfield Town Centre. They use their phones to arrange to meet up. Having met up they start to swear and scream abuse at nearby shoppers and Hilda has a large cricket bat in her hands which she is waving at the shoppers. The police arrest Hilda and her friends. The police are unsure what offence to charge them with. PC Smith counts 11 people present and so realises that no offence under section 1 has been committed. However, there are sufficient people present for an offence under section 2 to have been committed. Based upon the circumstances Hilda could be guilty of the offence of violent disorder, as she is threatening unlawful violence and the conduct of her and her friends would cause a (hypothetical) person of reasonable fitness present at the scene to fear for his personal safety. Finally, Hilda herself is threatening unlawful violence.

14.5.3 Affray

Section 3 of the POA 1986 outlines the offence of affray. There needs to be only one person who has used or threatened unlawful violence towards another person. However, the threat cannot be by the use of words alone. In *R v Gnango*[11] the Supreme Court held that where several people were involved in an affray, that the threat of unlawful violence could be against each other and not a third party. Lord Phillips and Lord Judge CJ held to require the threat of violence to be against a third party, and not against the two men involved in a shoot-out, would not make sense. The Supreme Court also were of the opinion that there did not need to be any common purpose between the men, i.e. they were not involved in the threat of violence for a common purpose. This means that if A and B were to both hold guns and threaten to shoot each other, then they would be guilty of an offence under section 3. There would be no requirement that a third-party C was present, nor would there be a requirement that A and B had a common purpose, i.e. to threaten C. It is important to consider what Lord Phillips and Lord Judge CJ said on behalf of the Supreme Court:

> More significantly, if given their natural meaning, they would appear to suggest that two defendants can only be jointly liable on a single count of affray if they join in using violence towards another; if they fight each other each commits an individual offence of affray, but they are not guilty of a joint offence. This would be nonsensical. We do not consider that the Act has altered the common law offence of affray in this way. The joint offence of affray can be founded on the common product of individual conduct, viz violence capable of causing fear, and does not require any common intention or purpose on the part of the joint participants.[12]

Table 14.3 Affray

Elements for section 3 Affray	Satisfied?
Do we have one or more person?	Yes or no?
Do we have the use or threatening of unlawful violence towards another? (Note – threat cannot be by the use of words alone)	Yes or no?
Would the conduct of them (taken together) cause a (hypothetical) person of reasonable fitness present at the scene to fear for his personal safety?	Yes or no?
Offence committed?	**If YES to all the above**

14.5.4 Fear or provocation of violence

There are two ways to the commit the offence of fear or provocation of violence under section 4 of the POA 1986 (the *actus reus* of the offence):

1 section 4(1)(a) – using towards another person threatening, abusive or insulting words or behaviour; or
2 section 4(1)(b) – distributes or displays to another person any writing, sign or other visible representation which is threatening, abusive or insulting.

A person commits offences if he intends 'to cause that person to believe that immediate unlawful violence will be used against him or another by any person, or to provoke the immediate use of unlawful violence by that person or another, or whereby that person is likely to believe that such violence will be used or it is likely that such violence will be provoked.' This is the mens rea of the offence.

In *Horgle v DPP*[13] the High Court held that it was acceptable for a Magistrates Court to rule that an offence bad been committed where they had not found that the defendant had had to cause the victim fear of unlawful violence, but that based on the language used and the defendant's behaviour, the victim would probably have believed that the defendant would use violence.

There only needs to be one person involved for an offence to be committed. The threatening, abusive or insulting words or behaviour must be used towards another person. This means that the words are used 'in the presence of' and 'in the direction of another person directly.'[14] Whether the words used will qualify depends on their ordinary meaning. In *Brutus v. Cozens*[15] it was stated that 'an ordinary sensible man knows an insult when he sees or hears it.' Section 4(2) states that the offence can be committed in a public or private place, but that no offence will be committed if the victim was inside a private dwelling.

Although an offence under section 4 cannot be committed where the victim is in the private dwelling, an offence can be committed where the defendant shouts at the victim out of a window. It is important to note this distinction.

14.5.5 Intentional harassment, alarm or distress

The offence of intentional harassment, alarm or distress contrary to section 4A POA 1986 was introduced by the Criminal Justice and Public Order Act 1994.

The offence can be committed in two ways:

1   section 4A(1)(a) – where the defendant uses threatening, abusive or insulting words or behaviour, or disorderly behaviour; or
2   section 4A(1)(b) – where the defendant displays any writing, sign or other visible representation which is threatening, abusive or insulting, which causes that person or another person harassment, alarm or distress.

Section 4A is wider than section 4 because of the lower threshold of disorderly behaviour, which means that football hooligans or people who are drunk could fall within this provision. The behaviour must have the intention to cause the victim harassment, alarm or distress. Once again this is a lower threshold than section 4.

PUBLIC LAW IN CONTEXT
SHOULD A POLICE OFFICER BE HARASSED OR DISTRESSED BY RUDE WORDS WHILST IN THE LINE OF DUTY?

It is interest to consider whether a police officer could be harassed or distressed by rude words whilst in the line of duty. In *R (R) v. DPP*[16] the Divisional Court considered what was meant by 'distressed' for the purposes of section 4A. The defendant had been convicted by a youth court for calling a police officer a 'wanker' and making masturbatory gestures at the officer. At the time the incident had taken place the defendant was 12 years old and was less than five feet tall. The police officer was over six feet tall and weighed over 17 stone. The police officer claimed that he was distressed by the defendant's behaviour. The question for the court was whether the police officer had actually been distressed. The court stated: 'the word "distress" in this context requires emotional disturbance or upset. It does not have to be grave but nor should the requirement be trivialised. There has to be something which amounts to real emotional disturbance or upset.' The conviction was overturned.

Within the context of section 5 POA 1986 (see below) the court in *Harvey v. DPP*[17] commented that, '[a] number of cases establish that expletives such as "fuck" or "fucking" are potentially abusive words, whether the addressee is a police officer or a member of the public. But Parliament has not made it an offence to swear in public as such.'[18] However, it is clear that a rude word on its own does not constitute an offence, as the actual requirements of the offence must actually be satisfied. With this in mind it is worth considering the meaning of 'harassment,' which was considered in *Southard v. DPP*[19], where the defendant had told a police officer to 'fuck off.' The police officers had been carrying out a stop and search. The court stated that: 'Harassment, alarm and distress do not have the same meaning. One can be harassed, even seriously harassed, without experiencing emotional disturbance or upset at all. However, although the harassment does not have to be grave, it should not be trivial. The court has to find that the words or behaviour were likely to cause some real, as opposed to trivial, harassment.'

We need to remember that the defendant must intend to cause harassment, alarm or distress.

14.5.6 Harassment, alarm or distress

The offence of harassment, alarm or distress under section 5 POA 1986 can be committed in two ways:

1   section 5(1)(a) – using threatening or abusive words or behaviour, or disorderly behaviour; or
2   section 5(1)(b) – displays any writing, sign or other visible representation which is threatening, or abusive, within the hearing or sight of a person likely to be caused harassment, alarm or distress thereby.

The meaning of harassment and distress is the same for section 5 as it is for section 4A. Subsection (3) outlines the defences, which are that the defendant did not believe that there was someone likely to be caused harassment, alarm or distress within hearing, or that the words or behaviour were used in a dwelling and there was no reason to believe that it would be heard or seen by someone outside, or that the defendant's conduct was reasonable. In *DPP v D*[20] the High

Court held that a dwelling did not include someone's garden and therefore a person who had used racially aggravated language against a neighbour could be guilty of committing an offence contrary to section 5. The crucial difference between section 5 and section 4A is that under section 5 there is no need for the defendant to intend to cause harassment, alarm or distress. In DPP v Smith[21] the High Court held that a Magistrates Court had been wrong to acquit someone using threatening or abusive words because they lacked the intention to cause harassment, alarm or distress.

The word 'insulting' has been removed from section 5 POA 1986. The inclusion of the word 'insulting' had been controversial and there has been a long-standing campaign to amend section 5. People have been arrested for calling police horses gay, having religious discussions with guests staying at their hotel and for campaigning in support of or against particular religions. The changes were introduced by section 57 of the Crime and Courts Act 2013. The changes affect section 5 and 6 POA 1986.

14.5.7 Racial hatred and hatred on the grounds of religion or sexual orientation

The POA 1986 criminalises the use of words or behaviour that is likely to stir up racial, religious or sexual hatred. This prohibits the performances of plays and the publication of material. There are defences available.

14.6 The freedom to hold a procession or an assembly

We have already considered public order offences such as riot and affray, and now we will explore the freedom to hold a procession or an assembly (see Figure 14.3). This will entail looking at the right to protest, to march, gather and join together for a common cause. This is a fundamental requirement for a modern democratic state.

14.6.1 Advance notice of public processions

We will consider the need to give advance notice of public processions. The meaning of procession was defined by Lord Goddard CJ in *Flockhart v. Robinson*:

> A procession is not a mere body of persons: it is a body of persons moving along a route. Therefore the person who organises the route is the person who organises the procession. . . . [A person will be] organising the procession because, although he did not organise the body of people, he organised the route. There is no other way of organising a procession, because a procession is something which proceeds. By indicating or planning the route a person is in my opinion organising a procession.[22]

Group intends to hold a procession

- Are you demonstrating, promoting a cause or commenerating an event?
  - **Yes:** under s.11 POA 1986 you must give 6 clear days notice to police, unless exception applies.
    - Police can impose conditions on procession if requirements under s.12 POA 1986 are satisfied.
      - Conditions under s.12 can restrict route and prevent procession from entering a public place.
        - Breach of conditions will amount to a criminal offence.
    - If conditions in s.12 are considered inadequete ALL processions can be prohibited under s.13.
      - Prohibition can last up to 3 months. Must be approved by local authority.
        - Ignoring the prohibition will amount to a criminal offence.
  - **No:** requirement to give notice to police under s.11 POA 1986 is not required.
- Can the senior police officer on the scene of the procession/assembly impose conditions?
  - **Yes:** under s.14, where the requirements are satisfied. Can limit duration and numbers which can attend.
- Note restruictions on trespassory assembles under sections 14A, 14B and 14 C.

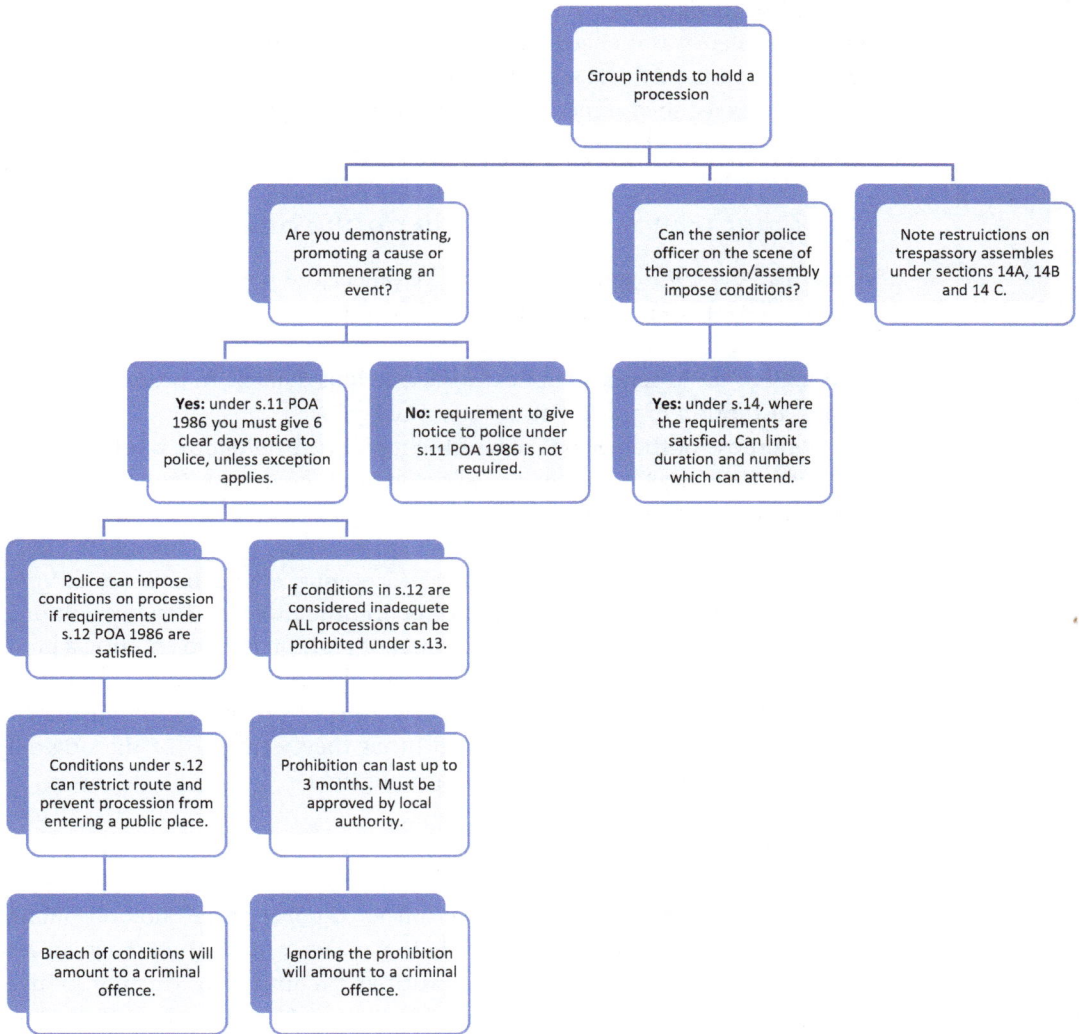

Figure 14.3
The requirements for holding a procession or an assembly

Section 11 POA 1986 states that if you intend to hold a public procession to demonstrate, publicise a cause or to commemorate an event, then you need to give written notice to the police, unless it is not reasonably practicable to do so. This requirement does not apply to funerals or processions which are customarily or commonly held. The notice must state the date, time, the intended route and the names of the organisers. It must be delivered six clear days before the procession. Failure to comply with the notice requirements under section 11 will amount to a criminal offence.

In *R (Kay) v. Commissioner of Police of the Metropolis*[23] an organised cycle ride had taken place each month over the period of 12 years. The cyclists followed no fixed route. The police informed the cyclists that they would need to inform them within six days of each cycle ride under section 11 POA 1986. The cyclists argued that there was no need to do this as this was a procession which was customarily or commonly held. The House of Lords allowed the appeal and held that no notice was required under section 11 because the procession could amount to one which was commonly or customarily held, despite having no fixed route.

14.6.2 Imposing conditions on public processions

Section 12 POA 1986 gives a senior police officer the power to impose conditions on a procession, where he reasonably believes:

- it may result in serious public disorder, serious damage to property or serious disruption to the life of the community; or
- the purpose of the persons organising it is the intimidation of others with a view to compelling them not to do an act they have a right to do, or to do an act they have a right not to do.

The directions given by the senior police officer must appear necessary to 'prevent such disorder, damage, disruption or intimidation' and the conditions imposed can alter the route of the procession or prohibit it from entering a public place. Failure to comply with the order will amount to a criminal offence.

In *Jukes v DPP*[24] protestors had breached section 12 when they left one march and then joined another. The court held that they were part of the original procession and were still subject to those conditions.

14.6.3 Prohibiting public processions

Section 13 POA 1986 permits the chief officer of police to prohibit all public processions for up to three months. Such a power will only exist where he 'reasonably believes that, because of particular circumstances existing in any district or part of a district, the powers under section 12 will not be sufficient to prevent the holding of public processions in that district or part from resulting in serious public disorder.' Therefore, the statute requires a reasonable belief that the powers under section 12 will prove insufficient to prevent serious public order. The application is made to the local authority.

14.6.4 Imposing conditions on public assemblies

Section 16 POA 1986 defines a public assembly as an assembly of two or more persons in a public place (somewhere the public has a right of access, i.e. the local town centre) which is wholly or partly open to the air. The senior police officer at a public assembly may under section 14 POA 1986 impose conditions, where he reasonably believes that:

- it may result in serious public disorder, serious damage to property or serious disruption to the life of the community; or

- the purpose of the persons organising it is the intimidation of others with a view to compelling them not to do an act they have a right to do, or to do an act they have a right not to do.

If either of the above are satisfied, then the conditions that the senior officer can impose can:

- limit its duration;
- limit the numbers of people who can attend.

So long as it appears necessary to impose these conditions in order 'to prevent such disorder, damage, disruption or intimidation.' Failure to comply with the conditions imposed will amount to a criminal offence.

According to section 14(2), the senior police officer for the purposes of section 14 means the most senior police officer present or at the assembly, or if the conditions are imposed before the assembly will take place the chief officer of police for that area. Furthermore, section 14A gives police the powers to prohibit trespassory assemblies. This applies to assemblies which will be held on land that the public has no right or a limited right to access. The police under section 14C have the power to stop people from proceeding to trespassory assemblies.

PUBLIC LAW IN PRACTICE

Action for Animals (fictitious) is an anti-vivisection organisation that plans to hold a procession to protest against animal testing. The organisers give notice to the police authority where the procession will take place, a full six days before the planned march. The route will go past Testing Incorporation's headquarters, which is an organisation that carries out animal testing. There will be 1,000 people at the protest and the police are concerned that some of the protestors will be violent. The police can impose conditions on the public procession under section 12 POA 1986, or ban it under section 13 POA 1986, but only if certain requirements are met.

RECENT DEVELOPMENT

The police will be given further powers to impose additional restrictions on processions and assemblies by the Police, Crime, Sentencing and Courts Bill. The bill inter alia plans to allow conditions to be imposed on single person protests and to place the tort of public nuisance on a statutory footing. The bill is extremely controversial.

14.7 Criminal Justice and Public Order Act 1994

The Criminal Justice and Public Order Act 1994 (CJPOA 1994) covers illegal raves and trespassers and gives the police powers to remove trespassers. It also covers travellers who are encamped on land without permission from the relevant authority. The Act is aimed at those exercising an alternative lifestyle such as New Age travellers and those who attend raves. Allen and Cooper were critical of the creation of ever more broad public order offences under the CJPOA 1994, and noted that the effect of the Act is that: '[p]ublic order is valued more than freedom of expression; the pressure to conform is greater than respect for non-conformity; the values of the majority justify the suppression of the values and lifestyles of minorities such as gypsies and other travellers.'[25]

14.8 Highways Act 1980

Section 137 of the Highways Act 1980 makes it an offence to 'wilfully obstruct the free passage along a highway' without lawful authority or excuse. The issue of whether the rights under Article 10 and Article 11 provided a lawful excuse for a demonstration that blocked the highway was considered in *DPP v Ziegler*.[26] According to Singh LJ and Farbey J,

> In other words, the fact that expression takes the form of obstruction of traffic does not mean that it falls outside the scope of protection of the Convention. However, it does mean that it is not at the core of the Convention rights in question and this may have implications for the question whether any interference with those rights is proportionate. One reason for this is that the essence of the rights in question is the opportunity to persuade others. In a democratic society it is important that there should be a free flow of ideas so that people can make their own minds up about which they accept and which they do not find persuasive. However, persuasion is very different from compulsion. Where people are physically prevented from doing what they could otherwise lawfully do, such as driving along a highway to reach their destination, that is not an exercise in persuasion but is an act of compulsion. This may not prevent what is being done falling within the concept of expression but it may be highly relevant when assessing proportionality under paragraph 2 of articles 10 and 11.[27]

This meant that there could be a lawful obstruction of the highway, unless it was found that the conviction of those protesting could be proportionate for the purposes of Articles 10 and 11.

14.9 Breach of the peace

This next section will consider breach of the peace as a restriction. The Court of Appeal in *R v. Howell (Errol)*[28] defined the circumstances when a breach of the peace would arise: 'there is a breach of the peace whenever harm is actually done or is likely to be done to a person or in his presence to his property or a person is in fear of being so harmed through an assault, an affray, a riot, unlawful assembly or other disturbance.' In English law a breach of the peace is not a criminal offence but is based on an application to bind over, i.e. an obligation not to breach the peace.

In *R (on the application of Laporte) v. Chief Constable of Gloucestershire*[29] the police had prevented three coaches from proceeding to Gloucestershire, where a protest was taking place. The police had taken action short of arrest because they believed that a breach of the peace would occur. The House of Lords held that there had been a violation of Article 11 because the interference with the right to peaceful assembly and association had not been prescribed by law, and even if it had been, the police's action had been a disproportionate restriction on the protestors' rights. In R *(on the application of Laporte) v. Chief Constable of* Gloucestershire the House of Lords held the following at common law:

- Police officers and members of the public have the power to take measures short of arrest, or to carry out an arrest, in order to prevent a breach of breach from occurring, or where they reasonably believed that a breach of the peace was to occur.
- However, if no breach of the peace had occurred there needed to be a reasonable apprehension of an imminent breach before action could be taken. According to Lord Mance, the question of when a breach of the peace would be imminent 'has to be judged in the context under consideration.'[30]

In *R (on the application of Hicks) v Commissioner of Police for the Metropolis*[31] the Supreme Court held that there was no violation of Article 5 of the ECHR, which protects the rights to liberty and security of the person where individuals were arrested to prevent an imminent breach of the peace. This was in the context of the police trying to pre-empt the protests that were due to take place around the Duke and Duchess of Cambridge's wedding in 2011. For academic commentary on this important decision see Richard Glover's article, 'Keeping the Peace and Preventive Justice – A New Test for Breach of the Peace?' [2018] *Public Law* 444.

14.10 The use of kettling by the police at demonstrations

Kettling is a tactic used by the police to control crowds during protests. The police will cordon protestors and will prevent the crowd from leaving until the

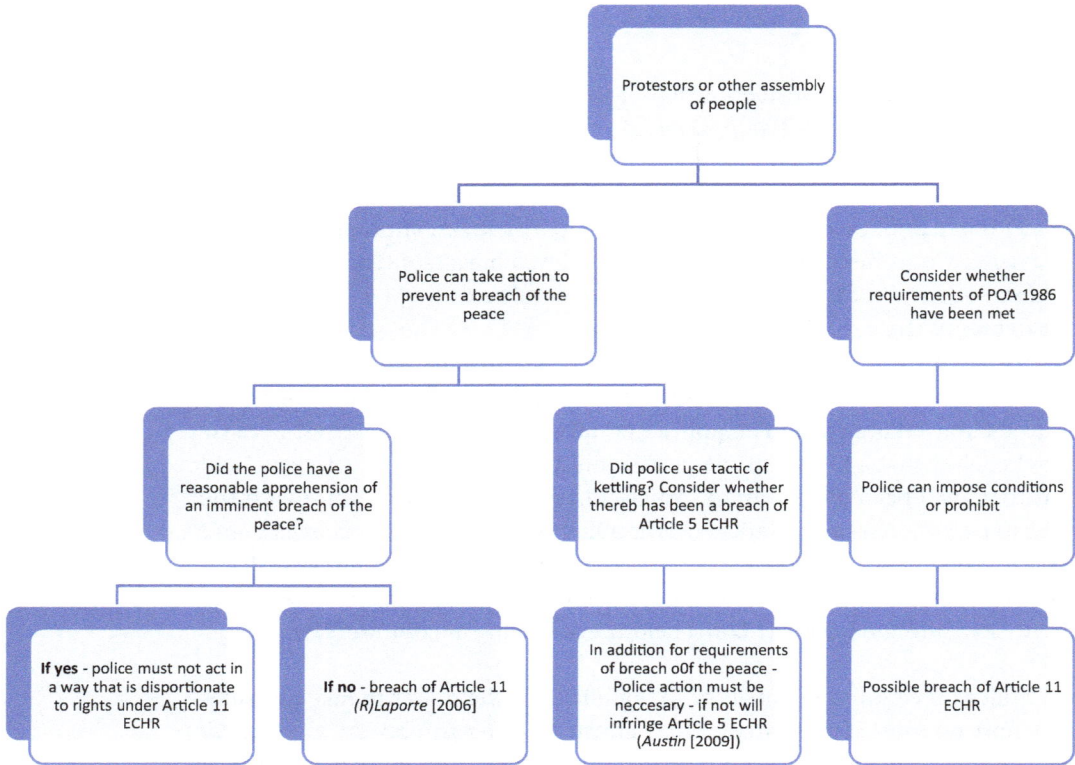

Figure 14.4
Diagram on restricting Article 5, false imprisonment, etc.

risk of violence or damage to property has been reduced. The case of *Austin v. Commissioner of the Police of the Metropolis*[32] concerned a protest in London and a very large group of protestors, some of whom were disorderly, who reached Oxford Circus and were placed in a cordon by the police. This tactic is known as kettling. People could not leave unless with the permission of the police. They were denied access to toilet facilities, food and drink. Austin had not been involved in the protest and asked permission to leave the police cordon and this was refused. Upon appeal the House of Lords held that the police had acted legally at common law as they had acted to prevent an imminent breach of the peace. The claimant had argued that their Article 5 ECHR right to liberty had been violated. The House of Lords held that Article 5 was a qualified right and could be restricted. The court held that the right balance had been struck by the police and therefore the restriction on the claimant's liberty was proportionate (see Figure 14.4 for Article 5 restrictions).

In *Austin v. United Kingdom*[33] the European Court of Human Rights held that the use of kettling did not violate Article 5 because the police had isolated the protestors to avoid a likely risk of damage and injury, and therefore the police action was necessary and proportionate.

14.11 Practical application

You work for a human rights organisation and have been asked to provide answers to a number of questions that will appear on its website. Please provide short answers to the following questions:

1. Should kettling be prohibited or is it a necessary method of controlling large crowds?
2. Do the Public Order Acts unnecessarily prevent peaceful protest? Should we have to notify the police in advance of peaceful demonstrations?
3. Do we have freedom of assembly and association in the United Kingdom?
4. What limitations are imposed on Article 11 ECHR by the Public Order Acts?

14.12 Key points to take away from this chapter

*   Article 11 ECHR protects the right to freedom of assembly and association.
*   The police can impose conditions and prohibit processions under the Public Order Act 1986.
*   Political uniforms and paramilitary training are illegal under the Public Order Act 1936.
*   Each public order offence requires slightly different elements in order to be committed.

Notes

1   [2014] ECHR 31045/10.
2   [2010] EWCA Civ 669.
3   [1979] 1 WLR 390.
4   [1980] AC 672.
5   (1979–80) 2 EHRR 245.
6   ibid 40.
7   (47335/06) [2013] IRLR 51.
8   ibid 55.
9   P Thornton, *Decade of Decline: Civil Liberties in the Thatcher Years* (National Council for Civil Liberties 1989) 35–36.
10 [2010] EWCA Crim 404.
11 [2011] UKSC 59.
12 ibid 36–37.
13 [2015] EWHC 856 (Admin).
14 *Atkin v. DPP* (1989) 89 Cr App R 199.
15 [1972] 2 All ER 1297.
16 [2006] EWHC 1375 (Admin).
17 [2011] EWHC 3992 (Admin).
18 ibid 6.

19 [2006] EWHC 3449 (Admin).
20 [2017] EWHC 2244 (Admin).
21 [2017] EWHC 3193 (Admin).
22 [1950] 2 KB 498 at 502.
23 [2008] UKHL 69.
24 [2013] EWHC 195 (Admin).
25 M Allen and S Cooper, 'Howard's Way: A Farewell to Freedom?' [1995] MLR 364.
26 [2020] QB 253.
27 ibid 52–53.
28 [1982] QB 416.
29 [2006] UKHL 55.
30 ibid 141.
31 [2017] UKSC 9.
32 [2009] UKHL 5.
33 (39692/09)(2012) 55 EHRR 14 ECtHR.

Further reading

Allen M and S Cooper, 'Howard's Way: A Farewell to Freedom?' [1995] MLR 364

Ewing KD, *Bonfire of the Liberties: New Labour, Human Rights, and the Rule of Law* (OUP 2010)

Glover R, 'Keeping the Peace and Preventive Justice – a New Test for Breach of the Peace?' [2018] PL 444

Mead D, 'Policing Protest in a Pandemic' (2021) 32(1) Kings LJ 96–108

———, 'Some Initial Thoughts on the Police, Crime, Sentencing and Courts Bill – the New Public Order Powers in Clauses 54–60' (*Protest Matters*, 2021) <https://protest-matters.wordpress.com/2021/03/12/some-initial-thoughts-on-the-police-crime-sentencing-courts-bill-the-new-public-order-powers-in-clauses-54-60/amp/?__twitter_impression=true>

Reid K, 'Letting Down the Drawbridge: Restoring the Right to Protest at Parliament' (2013) 3(1) LCH 16

Stone R and D Bonner, 'The Public Order Act 1986: Steps in the Wrong Direction?' [1987] PL 202

Judicial Review I

Foundations of judicial review

In this chapter we will look at

- what is meant by judicial review and what purpose does it serve;
- when can a decision be judicially reviewed;
- who can bring an application for judicial review; and
- what are the remedies that are available?

15.1 Introduction

The purpose of judicial review is to hold the executive at both a national and local level to account, which includes governmental agencies and anyone else who is responsible for making decisions of a public law nature. The courts play an important part in protecting the citizen's rights against the state. Examples of how judicial review can be used might include challenging the refusal of planning permission and elderly residents who have been told that they will move to another care home, despite being promised that they will not be moved. It has been noted in Chapters 7 and 8 that the parliamentary scrutiny of the executive is no longer always effective as a means to hold the executive to account. A government has not lost a vote of no confidence in the House of Commons since 1979, and even the current government which is without a comfortable majority in the House of Commons survived a vote of no confidence in 2019. Lord Steyn's comments at the beginning of his judgment in *R (on the application of Jackson) v Attorney-General*[1] are apt as His Lordship warned that every government since 1979 had enjoyed a majority and as a consequence it could dominate the House of Commons:

> My Lords, the power of a government with a large majority in the House of Commons is redoubtable. That has been the pattern for almost 25 years. In 1979, 1983 and 1987 Conservative Governments were elected

DOI: 10.4324/9780429293498-17

respectively with majorities of 43, 144 and 100. In 1997, 2001 and 2005 New Labour was elected with majorities of respectively 177, 165 and 67. As Lord Hailsham of St Marylebone explained in *The Dilemma of Democracy* (1978), p 126, the dominance of a government elected with a large majority over Parliament has progressively become greater. This process has continued and strengthened inexorably since Lord Hailsham warned of its dangers in 1978.[2]

Arguably, this means that the ability of Parliament to hold the government to account is limited. Therefore, the ability of the courts to review central government, local authorities and executive agencies is crucial to ensuring that we have an accountable government.

Judicial review is a check on the executive's discretionary decision-making powers and prevents the government from acting outside of its powers, either statutory or prerogative. We have seen in Chapter 4 the importance of the rule of law in English law. Neither the executive nor its agencies can act outside the powers given to it by Parliament, or the residual prerogative powers which are exercised by ministers.

Ministers are given the power to take decisions and make delegated legislation under statute. The courts must be able to prevent a minister, or indeed the local authority, from misusing this power; whether it is using this power for a purpose that Parliament did not intend or acting in a way that the court considers to be unreasonable. It is important to note that judicial review is not concerned with the validity of an Act of Parliament, nor whether the statute is unconstitutional. In Chapters 16 and 17 we shall look at the grounds under which a decision of a public body may be reviewed by the courts.

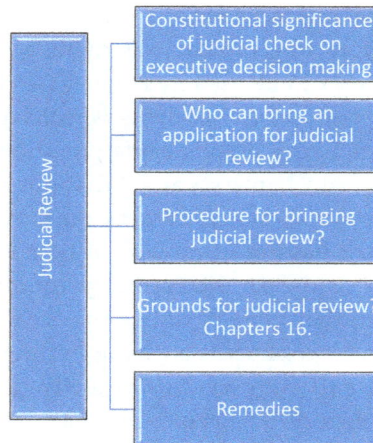

Figure 15.1
Overview of judicial review

15.2 The extent of judicial review

Only secondary legislation and prerogative powers exercised by ministers can be reviewed by the courts. The courts cannot review primary legislation. This is unlike the United States, where the United States Supreme Court can review primary legislation and if the legislation is held to be unconstitutional, the court can strike it down.

15.3 The importance of judicial review: it is not an appeal

It is important to note that judicial review is not an appeal. The court is not deciding whether it thinks that the actual decision was correct; rather the court is reviewing the decision and seeing if the decision is invalid because it is unreasonable, irrational, illegal, procedurally unfair or whether there has been a breach of legitimate expectation. Even if the court quashes the original decision and orders that the decision-maker remakes the decision, this does not mean that the applicant will get the outcome they want.

In *R (on the application of Hoareau and Bancoult) v Secretary of State for Foreign and Commonwealth Affairs*[3] Singh LJ and Carr J observed that:

> Judicial review is an important mechanism for the maintenance of the rule of law. It serves to correct unlawful conduct on the part of public authorities. However, judicial review is not an appeal against governmental decisions on their merits. The wisdom of governmental policy is not a matter for the courts and, in a democratic society, must be a matter for the elected government alone. . . . Judicial review is not, and should not be regarded as, politics by another means.[4]

Judicial review is concerned with how the decision was made and not the actual decision itself. However, it should be noted that the courts will look at whether a decision was unreasonable or irrational, a process which will look at the merits of the actual decision.

So why does this matter? Imagine that you have applied for a funding from your local council because you are looking after a disabled dependant. The funding is refused, but no reason is given for this. Understandably, you will be upset about this and would expect to have been told the reasons for this. Initially, you had been told to apply by the council and had been assured that you were eligible for funding. Someone else you know, whose circumstances are similar, has received funding and you cannot see why your application was refused. What can you do about this? The answer is that you can apply to judicially review the council's decision.

PUBLIC LAW IN CONTEXT
PRACTICAL AND CONSTITUTIONAL SIGNIFICANCE OF JUDICIAL REVIEW

Judicial review has both a practical and constitutional significance. In terms of how it can help individuals, organisations and communities in challenging decisions made by public bodies, there are many examples. The examples include the use of judicial review to successfully challenge the decision to cancel the refurbishment of schools by the Coalition government in 2010, unsuccessful challenge to the positioning of missile batteries on top of flats during the 2012 London Olympics[5], and the successful challenge to the Parole Board's controversial decision to release the serial rapist John Worboys from prison.[6]

In terms of the constitutional significance of judicial review it is important to note the role played by the courts in ensuring that public bodies make decisions that are not for example, illegal, unreasonable or biased. In Chapter 1 we saw that the United Kingdom does not have a codified constitution. The incorporation of the European Convention on Human Rights (ECHR) into domestic law by the Human Rights Act 1998 (HRA 1998), prevents a public authority (section 6[1] HRA 1998) from violating Convention rights. However, given the executive's dominance of Parliament, judicial review provides a method to scrutinise the use and interpretation of the statutory powers afforded to the executive. It must be emphasised that the validity of legislation cannot be reviewed, only the use of the legislation by the executive.

Executive accountability is an important aspect of any Constitutional and Administrative Law module and it is vital that you place judicial review within the broader context of how the government of the day is held to account. The executive's use of prerogative powers is inadequately subjected to Parliamentary scrutiny, as the powers are not derived from Parliament and therefore, there is little that Parliament can realistically do, short of abolishing or replacing it with legislation, to restrict the way a minister uses a certain prerogative power. We have seen this in Chapters 7, 8, 10 and 11 when we explored the role of Parliament, the executive and the extent of the prerogative powers.

Judicial review is important as it enables the courts to hold the executive to account, as ministerial use of both statutory and prerogative powers can be reviewed by the courts. However, judicial review raises some important constitutional problems. According to the theory of the separation of powers, it is the executive that is responsible for governing the country and developing policies; the powers needed to govern are given by Parliament or are the prerogative powers which Parliament has not abolished. There is a danger that if the courts subject the executive's decision-making process to too rigorous a scrutiny, then the courts might attempt to supplement their own decision for that of the executive. Therefore, judicial review must balance protecting citizens' rights with the need to avoid making policy decisions, when these decisions should only be made by the executive.

The importance of judicial review cannot be underestimated as a means to safeguard the rights of individuals and businesses. An example of this is Virgin Trains, which in 2012 judicially reviewed the decision to award the West Coast rail franchise to a rival company. Virgin Trains had argued that there were major flaws with the franchise bidding process.[7] Professor HWR Wade argued that the judicial review of the executive powers to prevent abuse had made an impact on everyone's lives, by preventing the government from creating a monopoly over air travel to the United States[8] and by preventing the government from cancelling 'our television licences[9] if we do something quite lawful but of which he disapproves.'[10]

15.4 Historical and recent development

The English courts have historically challenged the executive's misuse of power. In a famous example, Sir Edward Coke CJ prevented King James I from claiming more prerogative powers that what the law allowed the king to have.[11] The courts had restricted the monarch's powers to those recognised in law and prevented the monarch from claiming new powers. Decisions such as *Entick v Carrington*[12] demonstrate judicial willingness to prevent the government from acting illegally.

Historically the courts imposed limits on the power of the executive, namely that the government could not act outside the law (see Figure 15.2). This is essential for the rule of law. The case of *R v Cambridge University Ex p. Bentley*[13] demonstrated the importance of natural justice as a fundamental concept in English law. In *Ex p. Bentley* Eyre J observed that it was important that a person was able to defend himself: 'I remember to have heard it observed by a very learned man upon such an occasion, that even God himself did not pass

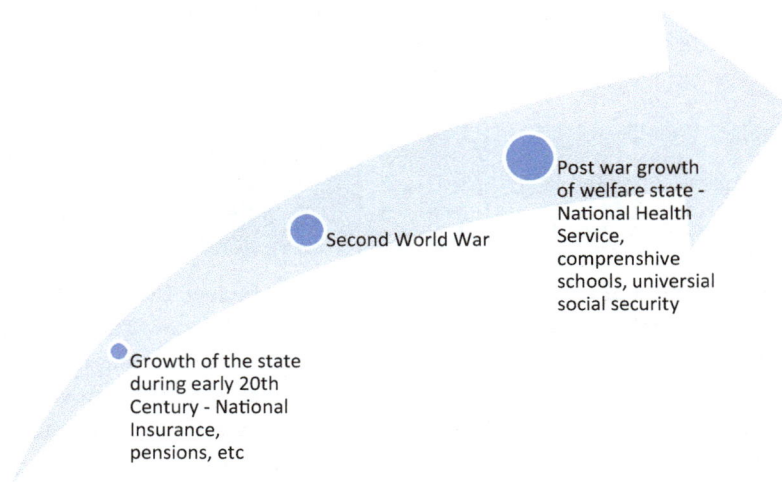

Figure 15.2
Key developments in the growth of the modern state

sentence upon Adam, before he was called upon to make his defence.'[14] The willingness of the courts to review executive action was considerably lower in *Local Government Board v Arlidge*.[15] In *Arlidge* the House of Lords held that a person affected by an administrative decision did not have a right to see the inspector's report which had led to the decision, neither did he have a right to make oral representations to the decision-maker. This case is viewed by many lawyers as undermining the concept of natural justice. The growing power of the modern state was met with increased judicial deference, which continued throughout the Second World War and 1950s post-war Britain. The House of Lords' decision in *Liversidge v Anderson*[16] is an extreme example of judicial deference to the executive. The case involved the detention of foreign nationals during the Second World War. A majority of the House of Lords held that the Home Secretary had the power to detain and the courts could not question the Home Secretary's decision. Lord Atkin dissented from the majority and observed,

> [t]he appellant's right to particulars, however, is based on a much broader ground, a principle which again is one of the pillars of liberty in that in English law every imprisonment is prima facie unlawful and that it is for a person directing imprisonment to justify his act.

This meant that the Home Secretary had to show that he was using his powers lawfully, by establishing that the conditions for imprisonment without charge were satisfied.

In the 1960s, the judiciary once again regained their constitutional role and started to effectively hold the executive to account. The House of Lords in *Ridge v Baldwin*[17] held that the requirements of natural justice applied to all administrative decisions. However, modern decisions such as *R (on the application of Bancoult) v Secretary of State for the Foreign and Commonwealth Office (No.2)*[18] demonstrate the continuing reluctance of the judiciary to review some areas of the executive's decision-making powers.

PUBLIC LAW IN CONTEXT
REFORMING JUDICIAL REVIEW

In 2012, the Coalition government proposed key reforms to judicial review. These proposed reforms were aimed at reducing the number of applications for judicial review. The Ministry of Justice intended to reduce the cost of judicial review and was of the view that unmeritorious claims were abusing the system. The reforms to judicial review are extremely controversial and have been criticised by senior members of the judiciary, practitioners and academics.

The then Secretary of State for Justice was critical of judicial review being used to challenge government policy, writing in *The Telegraph* (20 April 2014) that many decisions have been the subject of legal action, so-called judicial reviews, instigated by pressure groups, designed to force the Government to change its mind over properly taken decisions by democratically elected politicians. This includes using the legal system as a weapon to try to stop the difficult decisions we are taking to secure a better future for our country as part of our long-term economic plan.

The reforms to judicial review were linked to the reforms to legal aid.

Considering the fact that the applicant only has three months at present in which to submit his application, any reduction to the time limit could prove to be problematic. The time limit to judicially review a planning decision has now been changed and is six weeks. This change was introduced by the Civil Procedure (Amendments No.4) Rules 2013, which modified Part 54.5 of the Civil Procedure Rules 1998. You should note that this only applies to planning decisions.

Further reforms were introduced by the Criminal Justice and Courts Act 2015. Section 84 of the Criminal Justice and Courts Act 2015 amended section 31 of the Senior Courts Act 1981 (SCA 1981). In the government's response to the Ministry of Justice's reform proposals in 2014, Chris Grayling MP, the then Lord Chancellor, wrote,

> I believe in protecting judicial review as a check on unlawful executive action, but I am equally clear that it should not be abused, to act as a brake on growth. In my view judicial review has extended far beyond its original concept, and too often cases are pursued as a campaigning tool, or simply to delay legitimate proposals. That is bad for the economy and the taxpayer, and also bad for public confidence in the justice system.[19]

In terms of the impact of judicial review Tom Hickman and Maurice Sunkin wrote in response to the Ministry of Justice's report that only 1% of all judicial applications were unsuccessful.[20] They observed:

> Yet more significantly, of the 2014 cohort of 4062 cases lodged, the success rate for claimants at trial has actually been 36%. Of 144 final hearings so far 52 (36%) were won. And another 7 (2.7%) are recorded as having resulted in an outcome which is neither a win nor a loss. It is interesting that the MOJ chooses to highlight that only 1% of cases lodged have been won at a final hearing rather than that public authorities have prevailed at final hearings in only about 2% of cases lodged. The latter is perhaps the more revealing statistic given the very high number of cases that settle in favour of claimants before trial.

This demonstrates the problem of not addressing the wider context when looking at individual statistics and the use that unfavourable statistics, here the 1% success rate in 2014, could be put to show the perceived shortcomings with judicial review.[21]

Section 84 of the Criminal Justice and Courts Act 2015 inserted subsection (2A) into section 31, which states that

[t]he High Court – (a) must refuse to grant relief on an application for judicial review, and (b) may not make an award under subsection (4) on such an application, if it appears to the court to be highly likely that the outcome for the applicant would not have been substantially different if the conduct complained of had not occurred.

Subsection (2) inserted subsection (3B) into the SCA 1981. It informs the court that:

When considering whether to grant leave to make an application for judicial review, the High Court – (a) may of its own motion consider whether the outcome for the applicant would have been substantially different if the conduct complained of had not occurred, and (b) must consider that question if the defendant asks it to do so.

Subsection (3C) directed the High Court on this matter: '[i]f, on considering that question, it appears to the High Court to be highly likely that the outcome for the applicant would have been substantially different, the court must refuse to grant leave.'

Section 84 of the Criminal Justice and Courts Act 2015 reformed the ability of the court to grant relief. Subsection (1) inserted new subsection (2A) into the SCA 1981, which stated that: 'The High Court – (a) must refuse to grant relief on an application for judicial review, and (b) may not make an award under subsection (4) on such an application, if it appears to the court to be highly likely that the outcome for the applicant would not have been substantially different if the conduct complained of had not occurred.'

These reforms are designed to prevent unmeritorious claims from proceeding and have proved to be extremely controversial. The Criminal Justice and Courts Act 2015 restricted the award of protective costs orders which currently protect the applicant from excesses costs in the event that they are unsuccessful.

In July 2020 Conservative government established an independent panel to look at judicial review. The panel was chaired by Lord Faulks QC. On the launch of the review to look at judicial review, the Lord Chancellor was of opinion that 'This review will ensure this precious check on government power is maintained, while making sure the process is not abused or used to conduct politics by another means.'[22] This shows that there was a concern that in some instances judicial review was being abused. The panel was asked to look at:

- Whether the terms of Judicial Review should be written into law
- Whether certain executive decisions should be decided on by judges
- Which grounds and remedies should be available in claims brought against the government
- Any further procedural reforms to Judicial Review, such as timings and the appeal process[23]

The panel consisted of leading lawyers and legal academics including Professor Carol Harlow QC and Professor Alan Page.

15.5 No distinction between statutory and non-statutory powers

It is important to note that both statutory powers and the prerogative can be judicially reviewed

The landmark decision of the House of Lords in *Council for Civil Service Unions v. Minister of the Civil Service*[24] (*GCHQ*) held that there was no distinction between judicial review of prerogative and statutory powers. This is important given the considerable prerogative powers that the government has at its disposal. It should be remembered that Lord Roskill held that some areas of the prerogative were non-justiciable. This meant that they were not considered suitable for review by the courts. Recently, Prerogative Orders in Council were held by the House of Lords in *R (on the application of Bancoult) v Secretary of State for Foreign and Commonwealth Affairs (No.2)*[25] to be judicially reviewable.

15.6 Ousting judicial review

An ouster clause is an attempt by Parliament to restrict the courts from reviewing how a minister or local authority exercises their statutory power. It will prevent individuals from challenging a decision by seeking judicial review. According to the doctrine of Parliamentary Sovereignty the courts should follow Parliament's intention. However, the courts have interpreted such clauses in a way which permits judicial review. The most famous example is the decision in *Anisminic Ltd v. Foreign Compensation Commission*[26]. Is it possible for Parliament to prevent the courts from reviewing how a minister or local authority uses the powers which have been conferred on them by statute (ousting judicial review)? Section 4(4) of the Foreign Compensation Act 1950 stated that any determination of the Foreign Compensation Commission could not be questioned in court. Read literally this would have excluded the court from reviewing the decision. Such a clause in a statute is known as an ouster clause. The House of Lords in *Anisminic Ltd v. Foreign Compensation Commission*[27] were asked to review the decision that prevented Anisminic from recovering compensation for property that it had lost in Egypt in 1956. The House of Lords held that judicial review was not ousted by the use of an ouster clause in section 4(4) of the Foreign Compensation Act 1950, as the Foreign Compensation Commission had made a mistake as to their powers and therefore the decision was only a purported determination. Therefore, it was not a valid decision and was not protected by section 4(4). It is helpful to consider how the Law Lords regarded the attempt to oust the court's jurisdiction to review the decision. In *Anisminic*, Lord Reid provided context as to the use of such clauses:

> Statutory provisions which seek to limit the ordinary jurisdiction of the court have a long history. No case has been cited in which any other form

of words limiting the jurisdiction of the court has been held to protect a nullity. If the draftsman or Parliament had intended to introduce a new kind of ouster clause so as to prevent any inquiry even as to whether the document relied on was a forgery, I would have expected to find something much more specific than the bald statement that a determination shall not be called in question in any court of law. Undoubtedly such a provision protects every determination which is not a nullity. But I do not think that it is necessary or even reasonable to construe the word 'determination' as including everything which purports to be a determination but which is in fact no determination at all. And there are no degrees of nullity. There are a number of reasons why the law will hold a purported decision to be a nullity. I do not see how it could be said that such a provision protects some kinds of nullity but not others: if that were intended it would be easy to say so.[28]

In his opinion Lord Pearce gave reasons for why a determination should only include a proper decision and not one that was only a purported decision:

It has been argued that your Lordships should construe 'determination' as meaning anything which is on its face a determination of the commission including even a purported determination which has no jurisdiction. It would seem that on such an argument the court must accept and could not even inquire whether a purported determination was a forged or inaccurate order which did not represent that which the commission had really decided. Moreover, it would mean that however far the commission ranged outside its jurisdiction or that which it was required to do, or however far it departed from natural justice its determination could not be questioned. A more reasonable and logical construction is that by 'determination' Parliament meant a real determination, not a purported determination. On the assumption, however, that either meaning is a possible construction and that therefore the word 'determination' is ambiguous, the latter meaning would accord with a long-established line of cases which adopted that construction. One must assume that Parliament in 1950 had cognisance of these in adopting the words used in section 4 (4).[29]

Judicial review can be excluded by implication. An example of this is *R v. Secretary of State for the Environment ex p. Upton Brickworks*[30], where the court held that judicial review was excluded because the statute had stated that where an order was issued then only a statutory remedy could be applied for. However, the court stated that had there been an abuse of process in issuing the order, then judicial review would have been available. In *R (A) v. Director of Establishments of the Security Service*[31] the Supreme Court held that judicial review could not be brought by a former member of the UK security services. The reason why the Administrative Court did not have the jurisdiction to hear the application was that section 65(2)(a) of the Regulation of Investigatory Powers Act 2000 stated that the Investigatory Powers Tribunal was to have exclusive jurisdiction.

The Supreme Court distinguished this case from *Anisminic*, as their Lordships held that section 65(2)(a) was not attempting to oust judicial review; rather it outlined the source of judicial scrutiny. The difference in these two cases was that Parliament in the Foreign Compensation Act 1950 had intended to remove all judicial scrutiny.

PUBLIC LAW IN CONTEXT
R (ON THE APPLICATION OF PRIVACY INTERNATIONAL) V INVESTIGATORY POWERS TRIBUNAL[32] *(OUSTER CLAUSE)*

In *R (on the application of Privacy International) v Investigatory Powers Tribunal*[33] *(Ouster Clause)* the Supreme Court considered whether section 67(8) of the Regulation of Investigatory Powers Act 2000 ousted judicial review. This section attempted to prevent the decisions of the Investigatory Powers Tribunal from being judicially reviewed. This challenged Privacy International. Section 67(8) stated 'Except to such extent as the Secretary of State may by order otherwise provide, determinations, awards and other decisions of the Tribunal (including decisions as to whether they have jurisdiction) shall not be subject to appeal or be liable to be questioned in any court.' The Supreme Court disagreed as to whether the ouster clause was effective. The majority held that it did not oust the supervisory jurisdiction of the court. However, in their dissenting opinions Lord Wilson, Lord Reed and Lord Sumption disagreed. The majority applied the approach taken by the House of Lords in *Anisminic* and held that Parliament could not have intended section 67(8) to oust the review of all decisions, as otherwise purported decisions, where it was alleged that the decision was defective, could not be challenged.

Lord Carnwath in his majority judgment was clear that the wording of section 67(8) would not exclude purported determinations from judicial review: 'A determination vitiated by any error of law, jurisdictional or not, was to be treated as no determination at all. It therefore fell outside the reference in the ouster clause to a "determination of the commission". In other words, the reference to such a determination was to be read as a reference only to a legally valid determination.'[34] His Lordship was clear that

> Judicial review can only be excluded by 'the most clear and explicit words' (*Cart*, para 31). If Parliament has failed to make its intention sufficiently clear, it is not for us to stretch the words used beyond their natural meaning. It may well be that the promoters of the 1985 Act thought that their formula would be enough to provide comprehensive protection from jurisdictional review of any kind. (If so, as Lord Wilson observes, they would have gained support from the distinguished author of the notes to the 1985 Current Law Statutes.) But one is entitled to ask why they did not use more explicit wording.[35]

The decision has proved controversial for a number of reasons. The decision is said to have had significant implications for how the United Kingdom's constitution is to be understood and could be viewed as a challenge to parliamentary sovereignty. Mark Elliot and Alison Young observed:

[W]hat does the case tell us about parliamentary sovereignty? That (what might have been considered) a clearly worded ouster clause failed to exclude judicial review necessarily says something, if only obliquely, about Parliament's capacity to oust review. At the very least, it indicates that displacing the supervisory jurisdiction of the court cannot easily or casually be accomplished. But such a judicial interpretation might instead be understood more expansively, as evidence not of the linguistic difficulty of excluding review, but of the limits of Parliament's capacity to do so. *Anisminic* is open to being understood in either of those ways. There was certainly no explicit suggestion that Parliament, if only it had expressed itself more clearly, could not have ousted review. Yet it is arguably possible to infer that the velvet interpretive glove wielded by the House of Lords in *Anisminic* merely served to conceal an iron fist of irreducible constitutional principle.[36]

Mike Gordon argued that the decision had wider constitutional significance and questioned the extent to which this could be viewed as a challenge to parliamentary sovereignty:

The legacy of *Privacy International* is not, therefore, that it heralds the limitation of Parliament through the rule of law, and the abandonment of parliamentary sovereignty which would inevitably result. On the contrary, such speculation about this doctrine is not determinative of the scope of parliamentary legislative authority, for if Parliament truly is sovereign, this is not a matter the courts can decide. Yet the case is revealing in so far as it provides a clear insight into the constitutional framework within which many judges increasingly see ideas of legislative authority operating.[37]

15.7 Bringing an application for judicial review

The remainder of this chapter will focus on bringing an application for judicial review. In order to bring an application a number of criteria must be satisfied:

1   The decision is amenable to judicial review:

   a   if it was made by a public body and it is a public law decision;
   b   if the body was not established by statute or prerogative, then it can be amenable if its functions are of a public law nature.

2   The correct procedure has been used:

   a   it must be a public law rather than private law issue;
   b   the application must be brought within the three-month time limit.

3   The applicant has a sufficient interest in the decision:

   a   individual applicants;
   b   interest groups bringing the application on behalf of its members;
   c   pressure groups campaigning against a decision.

We shall look at each of these in turn. When approaching a question on judicial review the structure of your answer is very important, as your lecturer will expect you to deal with each issue in turn.

15.7.1 Which court to bring application

An application for judicial review must be made to the Queen's Bench Division of the High Court. This has been the case since 1977 as there is no longer a need to use different courts depending on the remedy which you are seeking. Unlike in many other European jurisdictions, there is no separate administrative court in England and Wales. This means that the High Court will hear both private law and public law claims. The Administrative Division of the High Court will hear the application.

15.7.2 Is the decision amenable to judicial review?

Only a public body can be judicially reviewed. This means that the decision being reviewed must have been made by a public body. It must be emphasised that judicial review concerns public law and not private law issues; therefore, judicial review cannot be brought against private parties. There are some exceptions to this, and we shall see below that a private party such as a business can be judicially reviewed, where they are carrying out functions of a public nature. In *R (on the application of Holmcroft Properties Ltd) v KPMG LLP*[38], Elias LJ and Mitting J observed,

> The question whether a body is susceptible to judicial review is not always easily answered. The principles are tolerably clear, albeit stated at a high level of abstraction, and they are not in dispute in this case. But their application in any particular case can be problematic and it is the application of the principles to the circumstances of this case which divides the parties.[39]

In *R v. Panel on Takeovers and Mergers ex p. Datafin Plc*[40] the court held that the decision of the panel was amenable to judicial review. This was because although the panel was not created either by statute or the prerogative, the functions it exercised in reviewing and regulating takeovers in the City of London were of a public law nature. The panel had liaised with the Treasury and therefore exercised quasi-governmental powers (see Figure 15.3).

The key test to determine whether a decision is amenable to judicial review is to ask whether the body exercises public law functions and not to rely solely on the source of its powers. The test was established in *Ex p. Datafin Plc*. This test requires the court to look at the functions carried out by the body and to ask whether these functions are of a public law nature.

Sir John Donaldson MR had outlined the circumstances in which a body would be amenable to judicial review. Donaldson MR had stated that:

> I do not agree that the source of the power is the sole test whether a body is subject to judicial review. . . . Of course the source of the power will often,

perhaps usually, be decisive. If the source of power is a statute, or subordinate legislation under a statute, then clearly the body in question will be subject to judicial review. If, at the other end of the scale, the source of power is contractual, as in the case of private arbitration, then clearly the arbitrator is not subject to judicial review. . . .

But in between these extremes there is an area in which it is helpful to look not just at the source of the power but at the nature of the power. If the body in question is exercising public law functions, or if the exercise of its functions have public law consequences, then that may . . . be sufficient to bring the body within the reach of judicial review.[41]

PUBLIC LAW IN PRACTICE

Bouncer & Parking Ltd (BPL) supplies security and event staff to nightclubs, festivals and pubs. BPL have acquired the right to run HMP Doverbury, which houses high-risk prisoners. Whilst BPL may be a private company for the purposes of running the prison, BPL would be considered a public body. This is because BPL is carrying out functions of a public nature. BPL could be judicially reviewed by the prisoners.

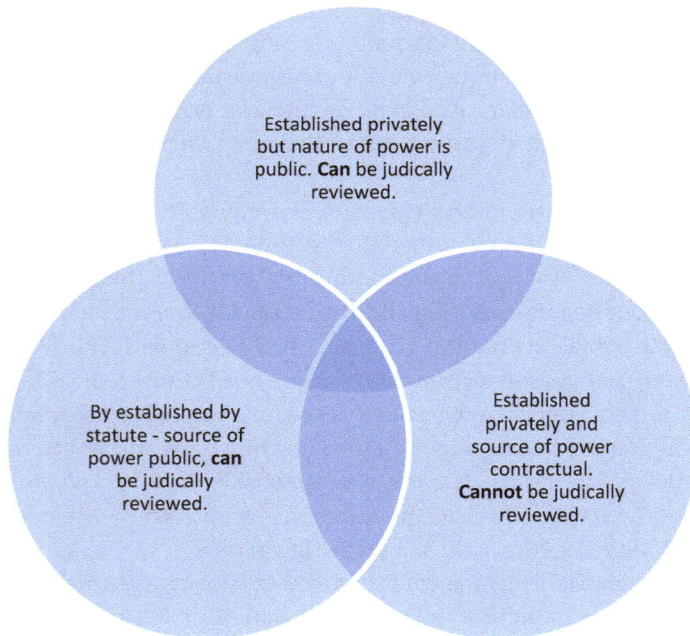

Figure 15.3
Nature and the source of the body's power

The Jockey Club and religious faiths

If there is a dispute, can the aggrieved party judicially review the decision of the organisation, or are they limited to private law remedies? One argument which has been used to argue that the decision is amenable to judicial review is the 'but for test.' The premise behind the 'but for test' can be best explained in *R v. Chief Rabbi of the United Hebrew Congregations of Great Britain and the Commonwealth, ex p. Wachman*[42], where Simon Brown J had stated the test as, '[w]ere there no self-regulatory body in existence, Parliament would almost inevitably intervene to control the activity in question.'

Does it always mean that where the government would have to intervene to create a regulating body, then such a body would be classed as a public body carrying out functions of a public law nature? The answer is no. The question is whether the functions carried out are governmental. Many professions and sports have formed organisations to govern their affairs and anyone wishing to operate in a profession or take part in a sport professionally must agree to the terms of that organisation's membership rules. This means that there often will be a contract between the members and the organisation which will mean that any dispute over that organisation's decision is likely to be a private law matter.

In *R v. Disciplinary Committee of the Jockey Club, ex p. Aga Khan*[43] the Aga Khan sought to judicially review the decision of the Jockey Club. The Court of Appeal held that the decision was not amenable to judicial review because it was not a public law decision. Although the Jockey Club had been established by the prerogative its functions were not governmental and it existed to regulate horse racing. The relationship between the Jockey Club and members such as the Aga Khan was contractual. Therefore, this was a private law matter. Sir Thomas Bingham MR had stated that even if the Jockey Club did not exist and Parliament had to legislate to create a new body, then that new body would still not be a public body as it did not exercise any public functions. It is clear that if the body is created by the prerogative or statute, but exists only to regulate the dealings of a certain sport and membership of the body is contractual, then that body's decision will not be amenable to judicial review.

In *R v Chief Rabbi of the United Hebrew Congregation of great. Britain and the Commonwealth Ex p. Wachman*[44] the court refused to judicially review the decision of the Chief Rabbi, who had decided that a Rabbi was unfit to hold office. The court held that religious rules and the regulation of the requirements to hold office was not governmental and was of no concern to the government.

The Football League sought to judicially review the Football Association's decision to create the Premier League in *R v. Football Association ex p. Football League*[45]. Permission was refused because the Football Association was not considered to be a public body. The reason was that the Football Association was a governing body whose powers came from private law. This was because its membership and governance were based on a contractual relationship between it and the clubs. The Football Association had not been set up by the state, indeed it was created by football teams to govern the sport and had it not existed, then the state would not have created it. Rather like other sports, private individuals

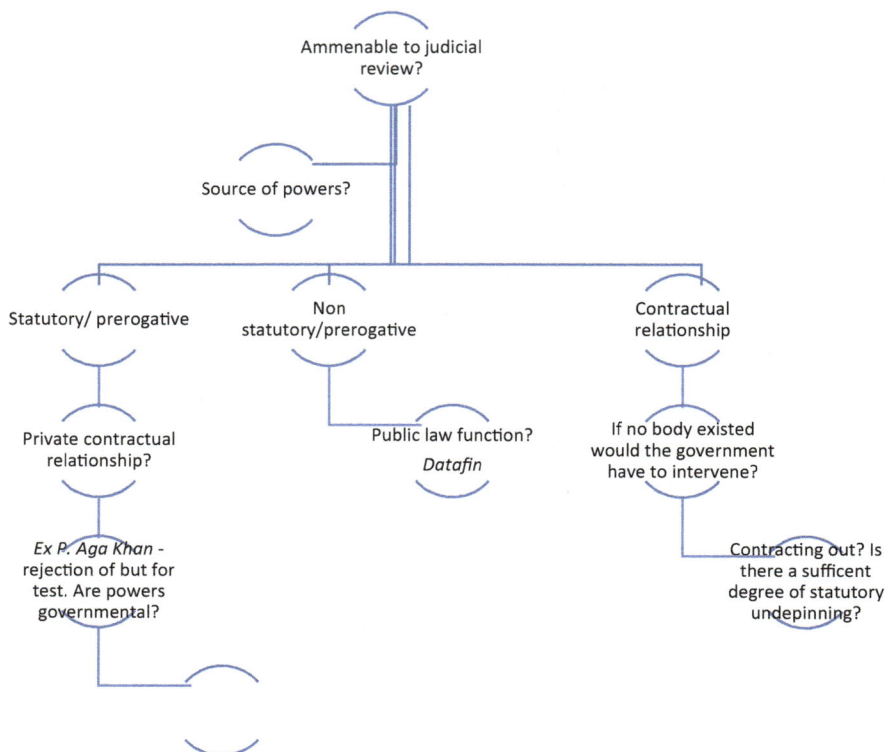

Figure 15.4
Is the body and decision amenable to judicial review?

and clubs would intervene and create such a body. The decision in *Ex p. Football League* was followed *in R v. Panel of the Federation of Communication Services Ltd ex p. Kubis*[46]. This case involved a trade association whose members had agreed contractually to be bound by its rules. When the association revoked a member's licence for breach of the rules, he sought to judicially review its decision. The court refused his application as the decision-making body was not created by statute and the relationship between the parties was contractual.

Contracting out by the local authority to a private care provider

In *R v. Servite Houses ex p. Goldsmith*[47] the local authority had a statutory duty to provide care for those groups in society who were in need of care and attention under the National Assistance Act 1948 (s.21[1][a]). The local authority was permitted to contract with other bodies to provide this service. This is known as contracting out. Today it is common for local authorities to contract out services to private bodies. This might include the provision of care for the elderly and the provision of social housing. Contracting out of services is encouraged as a way to save money. The problem is that the party responsible for carrying out this service is a private body and therefore the question is whether it is amenable to judicial review. The decision in *Ex p. Goldsmith* concerned an action for judicial review which had been brought by residents of a care home run by Servite Houses. Servite Houses was a private body which provided services for the local authority. Servite Houses decided to close the care home. The question was whether the decision was amenable to judicial review. Moses J stated:

> The court is concerned to decide where a case lies in the spectrum between, at one end, a body whose source of power is statutory and, at the other end, a body whose source of power is contractual. Thus, both ends of the spectrum require the courts to determine the issue of amenability by reference to the source of power, statutory on the one hand and contractual on the other. Between those two extremes lie many cases where the source of power test no longer provides an answer to the question of amenability.[48]

Reference was made to *Ex p. Datafin* where the amenability to judicial law was based on the public law nature of its function. However, if the powers are contractual then the body would not be amenable to judicial review (see *Ex p. Aga Khan*). The fact that government might have had to intervene and create such a body if none existed was irrelevant, because the body's powers would be based on the contract between it and its members. Therefore, such a body would have no special statutory powers. However, the court would have to draw a distinction between private bodies which had a statutory underpinning and were subject to government regulation. The court required more than just statutory regulation as to how the services were to be provided, as it 'must be able to identify sufficient statutory penetration which goes beyond the statutory regulation of the manner in which the service is provided.'[49]

The court in *R v. Servite Houses ex p. Goldsmith* held that the National Assistance Act did not create sufficient statutory underpinning as section 26, which permitted outsourcing, was silent as to how the accommodation was to be provided. The statutory duty was discharged by the local authority arranging accommodation. Moses J held:

> In my judgment that is a crucial distinction. It is the distinction between legislation which adds a public function to the private functions of a private body and legislation which permits a public law duty to be discharged by entry into private law arrangements. It does not seem to me that the applicants can successfully contend that because legislation permits a public authority to enter into arrangements with a private body, the functions of the private body are, by dint of that legislation, to be regarded as public functions.[50]

It would appear that, where services have been contracted out to a private company, judicial review could still be brought where there was a sufficient degree of statutory underpinning. So when will there be a sufficient degree of statutory underpinning? The decision in *Ex p. Goldsmith* can be contrasted with the decisions in *R v. Cobham Hall School ex p. G*[51], *R (A) v. Partnerships in Care Ltd*[52] and *R v. Advertising Standards Authority ex p. Insurance Services*[53], where there was a sufficient degree of statutory underpinning to make the decision in both cases amenable to judicial review. In *Ex p. G* an independent school was participating in a scheme to provide assisted places, which was regulated by the Education Act 1996. Therefore, the school was carrying out a public function and the decision to remove a child on the scheme was amenable to judicial review. In *Ex p. Insurance Services*, the decision of a private regulator was amenable to judicial review because had it not existed, then a governmental body would have to carry out its functions. The functions it carried out were held to be of a public law nature. In *Partnerships in Care Ltd* it was held that the treatment of mentally ill patients was a public law function and there was sufficient statutory underpinning which meant that the hospital had to follow statutory guidelines on treating patients. In *R (on the application of Unwritten Warranty Co Ltd [t/a Insurance Backed Guarantee Co]) v Fensa Ltd*[54] a scheme governed by Regulation 20 of the Building Regulations 2010 that provided for self-certification was governed by private law and therefore decisions made in the self-certification scheme could not be amenable for judicial review. Dove J was clear in his reasoning why the decision could be judicially reviewed:

> The question of whether or not the decision made by the defendant to remove the claimants from their list of approved IBGs in the present case has not been easy to resolve but, ultimately, I am satisfied that the decision is not one which is susceptible to judicial review and rather that it was a decision governed solely by the private law in relation to the contract which the first claimant had entered into with the defendant.[55]
>
> The starting point for the consideration of this issue must be the statutory scheme within which the defendant operates.[56]

The decision in *Ex p. Goldsmith* was followed in *R (Heather) v. Leonard Cheshire Foundation*[57]. The charity managed care homes and the local authority provided funding by paying to house those in need of care. It was argued that the charity was a public body for the purposes of judicial review and a public authority under the Human Rights Act 1998. Both these arguments were unsuccessful. Based on the public body argument the court held that there was insufficient statutory underpinning for the charity to be carrying out functions of a public law nature. A similar decision was reached in *YL v. Birmingham City Council*[58] where a care home was held not to be a public authority for the purposes of the HRA 1998.

15.8 Bringing a claim

Bringing judicial review involves two stages. The first is where the court determines whether to allow the application to proceed and the second is the full substantive hearing which will involve the actual grounds for judicial review. This chapter is concerned with the first stage. It must be remembered that the court will only grant an application for judicial review where there is a prima facie case to answer. Therefore, the claimant must adduce evidence to demonstrate that one of the grounds for judicial review exists.

15.8.1 Correct procedure

A decision by a public body can be judicially reviewed where it can be challenged under one of the grounds for review. The Human Rights Act 1998 permits actions against a public authority where it has been accused of breaching a Convention right. Whether a public authority is acting in contravention of a Convention right will depend on whether its division is held to be proportionate. This means that whilst there is legal authority for the public authority's actions, the question is whether the decision was necessary. Proportionality is a ground for judicial review (see **Chapter 16**) but is only available where that is a breach of a Convention right. Where a claim is brought for breach of a Convention right the requirements established under the HRA 1998 must be complied with (see **Chapter 12**). Only those who are regarded as a victim are able to bring a claim under the HRA 1998. The definition of victim for the purposes of HRA 1998 is narrower than the requirement for judicial review, which is that the applicant has a sufficient interest in the matter to which their application relates.

15.8.2 Part 54 of the Civil Procedure Rules and Section 31 of the Senior Courts Act 1981

In order to make an application for judicial review, section 31 of the Senior Courts Act 1981 requires that the correct rules have been followed. The rules governing judicial review can be found in Part 54 of the Civil Procedure Rules. Part 54.5 states that the deadline for submitting a claim form is three months after the events which gave rise to the claim occurred. Please note that a different time limit applies for planning application decisions. The time limit is strict as not even the parties themselves are able to agree to extend the time limit. Part 54.3 states the judicial review procedure applies where the claimant is seeking a declaration or an injunction. Part 54.2 states that judicial review must be used where the claimant is seeking a mandatory order, a prohibiting order or a quashing order. We shall look at the available remedies below. There are strict procedural rules which need to be complied with in order to bring judicial review. In practice you must advise your client of these and ensure that you file the claim in time and send copies to the relevant parties.

Please note that section 84 of the Criminal Justice and Courts Act 2015 inserted new subsections into section 31 of the Senior Courts 1981 which restricted the ability to bring judicial review where inter alia 'if it appears to the court to be highly likely that the outcome for the applicant would not have been substantially different if the conduct complained of had not occurred.'

15.8.3 Procedural exclusivity

We will consider what is meant by procedural exclusivity for the purposes of judicial review. The House of Lords in *O'Reilly v. Mackman*[59] held that where a person's public law rights had been breached, that person could only bring an application for judicial review. This was because judicial review was the exclusive procedure to be used in these circumstances. Therefore, you must determine whether the claim is a public law or a private law matter. In *O'Reilly v. Mackman* several prisoners had alleged that the Board of Visitors, when deciding to discipline them by forfeiting a remission of sentence, had breached their public law rights. However, as they were out of time for bringing judicial review, they sought a private law remedy. The House of Lords refused to permit this as judicial review would have provided a remedy. Lord Diplock held that because

> all remedies for infringements of rights protected by public law can be obtained upon an application for judicial review, as can also remedies for infringement of rights under private law if such infringements should also be involved [so to permit a person to sue a public body in private where there was protection afforded in public law would be] contrary to public policy and as such an abuse of process of the court.[60]

In *Roy v. Kensington and Chelsea and Westminster Family Practitioner Committee*[61] the House of Lords allowed a general practitioner to bring an action against the Family Practitioner Committee in private law, despite the action involving a public law decision. The decision in *O'Reilly* was doubted in *Clark v. University of Lincolnshire and Humberside*[62] where the Court of Appeal permitted a private law action for breach of contract, despite the case concerning both private law and public law issues. The case concerned a student whose work was marked at zero after she was accused of plagiarism. The student alleged that the university had breached their regulations. Therefore, it would appear that judicial review does not have procedural exclusivity where an action involves public law issues and private law issues. Given the strict three-month time limit for submitting an application for judicial review, this liberalisation of the approach of procedural exclusivity has meant that the longer time limit for bringing claims in private law is still available as an alternative remedy.

In *Richards v Worcestershire CC*[63] the claimant sued the defendant in private law, relying on section 117 of the Mental Health Act 1983. The defendant argued that this claim was an abuse of process as it was pursuing a private law claim for damages, when the correct procedure was to have used judicial review to challenge the decision. This was argued too contravene the exclusivity principle.

The Court of Appeal rejected this argument and held that the exclusivity principle should not be a barrier to the private law claim. Having considered the case law regarding the exclusivity principle, Rupert Jackson LJ was clear that it did not prevent the claim in the present case:

> From this review of the authorities I derive two general propositions:
>
> i)   The exclusivity principle applies where the claimant is challenging a public law decision or action and (a) his claim affects the public generally or (b) justice requires for some other reason that the claimant should proceed by way of judicial review.
> ii)   The exclusivity principle should be kept in its proper box. It should not become a general barrier to citizens bringing private law claims, in which the breach of a public law duty is one ingredient.'[64]

Rupert Jackson LJ observed that the exclusivity principle should not be used to create an injustice:

> This is a private law claim, even though based upon section 117 of the 1983 Act. It has no wider public impact. Justice does not require for any other reason that the claimant should proceed by way of judicial review. If the exclusivity principle is allowed to block this claim, it will become an instrument of injustice.[65]

15.8.4 Standing

In order to bring an applicant for judicial review the claimant must have standing, that is *locus standi*. Section 31(3) of the Senior Courts Act 1981 states that 'the court shall not grant leave to make such an application unless it considers that the applicant has a sufficient interest in the matter to which the application relates.' This means that unless a person (or a group) has sufficient interest, then they are unable to bring an application for judicial review.

The issue of sufficient interest was addressed in *R v. Inland Revenue Commissioners ex p. National Federation of Self Employed and Small Businesses Ltd*[66]. The case concerned an application brought by the National Federation who sought to challenge the decision of the Inland Revenue to grant casual workers in Fleet Street a tax amnesty. The House of Lords were critical of treating standing as always a preliminary issue as the factual and legal context, which would be explored at the hearing, should be discussed alongside the question of whether the applicant had sufficient interest. The issue of standing should be linked to the merits of the claim. The House of Lords ruled that the National Federation did not have sufficient interest in the matter. It was clear that none of the members of the National Federation were affected by the decision and the interests of one taxpayer should not concern another. The law draws a distinction between individuals bringing an application for judicial review and groups. The courts are far more willing to grant judicial review for an individual than

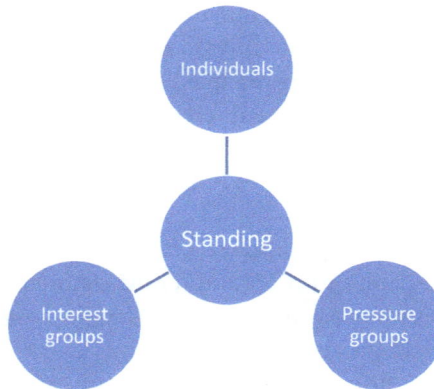

Figure 15.5
Standing

a group. However, we can see that an individual whose claim was frivolous or vexatious will not have standing. This is because the merits of the application are important.

15.8.4.1 An individual's standing

An individual who has sufficient interest in the matter will have standing to bring an application for judicial review. If the decision prejudicially affects your interests, then you are deemed to have standing. Indeed, the absence of personal interest will not be an impediment for standing. *In R (Kides) v. South Cambridgeshire DC*[67], Jonathan Parker LJ stated:

> I cannot see how it can be just to debar a litigant who has a real and genuine interest in obtaining the relief which he seeks from relying, in support of his claim for that relief, on grounds (which may be good grounds) in which he has no personal interest. It seems to me that a litigant who has a real and genuine interest in challenging an administrative decision must be entitled to present his challenge on all available grounds.[68]

This is narrower than the test for victim under section 7 HRA 1998, where the applicant must be directly affected. In *R v. Secretary of State for the Home Department ex p. Venables*[69] the killers of the Liverpool toddler Jamie Bulger were able to judicially review the Home Secretary's sentencing decision, which involved fixing a tariff period of 15 years. This was because the decision had prejudicially affected their interests

15.8.4.2 Challenging government policy

Individuals are able to challenge government policy and will be regarded as having sufficient interest. In *R v. HM Treasury ex p. Smedley*[70] a UK taxpayer was able to judicially review the government's undertaking to make payments to the European Community's Consolidated Fund. The court regarded standing and the seriousness of the issue as interlinked. Slade LJ stated that if the matter would have been 'of a frivolous nature' then the application could have been disposed of. The application was granted because '[i]t raises a serious question.' Regarding standing, Slade LJ stated that, 'I do not feel much doubt that Mr. Smedley, if only in his capacity as a taxpayer, has sufficient *locus standi* to raise this question by way of an application for judicial review.'[71] In *R (Wheeler) v. Office of the Prime Minister*[72] the claimant had standing to review the application of the Labour government's decision not to hold as promised a referendum on the ratification of the Lisbon Treaty. Finally, in *R v Secretary of State for Foreign and Commonwealth Affairs ex p. Rees-Mogg*[73], Lord Rees-Mogg, the former editor of *The Times*, was able to judicially review the ratification of the Maastricht Treaty because he was a UK citizen and had a genuine concern in the issues at stake. The Maastricht Treaty, which had created the European Union, had proved to be very controversial amongst members of the governing Conservative party and Lord Rees-Mogg, a Conservative member of the House of Lords, had sought to challenge the decision to ratify the treaty through the courts. In *ex p. Rees-Mogg* the court held that

> [t]here is no dispute as to the applicant's locus standi, and in the circumstances it is not appropriate to say any more about it. . . . It is suggested by Mr. Kentridge [the government's lawyer] that these proceedings are no more than a continuation by other means of arguments ventilated in Parliament. Be that as it may, *we accept without question that Lord Rees-Mogg brings the proceedings because of his sincere concern for constitutional issues.*[74]

Although the courts have held that individuals seeking to challenge government policy could have standing, it is clear that where the policy concerns foreign affairs (i.e., membership of the European Union) then the courts will hold that the issue is non-justiciable. We have seen in Chapters 10 and 11 that certain prerogative powers such as foreign affairs are considered to be non-justiciable. This was held to be the case in *Wheeler* and *Rees Mogg*.

15.8.4.3 Interest groups

An interest group will represent members and will often make representations to the government about their members' needs and, if necessary, will judicially review any decision which adversely affects their members. If an interest group, or an association, represents members who are prejudicially affected by a decision then they will be able to bring an application for judicial review on behalf of their members. In *R v. Liverpool Corporation ex p. Liverpool Taxi Fleet Operators Association*[75] the taxi owners' association was considered in order to have standing in order to bring judicial review. Lord Denning MR stated that the ability to bring judicial review 'does not include a mere busybody who is interfering in things which do not concern him; but it includes any person who has a genuine grievance because something has been done or may be done which affects him.' Therefore, as Liverpool council's decision to go back on its word regarding the issuing of new taxi licenses had prejudicially affected its members, the association had a sufficient interest. Similarly, in *Covent Garden Community Association v. Greater London Council*[76] an association was formed to protect the interests of residents and was deemed to have standing to bring judicial review. The case concerned an application to quash a decision of the council's planning committee.

15.8.4.4 Busybodies or concerned citizens

In *R v. Secretary of State for the Environment ex p. Rose Theatre Trust Co (No.2)*[77] members of the public, who wished to challenge a decision not to schedule the remains of a theatre as a monument, were held not to have sufficient interest in bringing judicial review. The court in *Ex p. Rose Theatre Trust Co (No.2)* was of the view that simply contacting the secretary of state about a decision was not enough to give concerned citizens sufficient interest. The court took the view that Parliament under section 31 of the Senior Courts Act 1981 only intended those with 'a sufficient interest in the matter to which the application relates' to bring a claim. Schiemann J stated '[m]erely to assert that one has an interest does not give one an interest. . . . The fact that some thousands of people join together and assert that they have an interest does not create an interest if the individuals did not have an interest.' However, this decision has not been applied rigidly in subsequent cases.

PUBLIC LAW IN CONTEXT

The courts have adopted a more liberal approach to standing for pressure groups, such as where none of the group members have a direct interest, but there is no one else who can realistically bring an application for judicial review.

In *R v Secretary of State for Foreign and Commonwealth Affairs Ex p. World Development Movement Ltd*[78] a pressure group, World Development Movement, was held to have sufficient interest to challenge a decision of the Secretary of State to fund the construction of a hydro-electric power station in Malaysia. The Secretary of State had relied upon the Overseas Development and Co-operation Act 1980 to help fund the project. World Development Movement was 'a non-partisan pressure group dedicated to improving the quantity and quality of British aid to other countries.'[79] World Development Movement had argued that the decision to finance the project was illegal and had initially sought assurances from the Secretary of State that he would not provide additional funding. These had been refused. World Development Movement had '7,000 full voting members throughout the United Kingdom with a total supporter base of some 13,000' and a national and international presence.[80]

The Court of Appeal held that the pressure group had sufficient interest.

Why was World Development Movement held to have standing? Rose LJ in *Ex p. World Development Movement Ltd* stated that:

- The courts have now taken a more liberal approach to standing. Standing should be addressed along with the far more important question of the substantial merits of the application. This means that the courts should not refuse an application based solely on whether an applicant has sufficient interest. Therefore standing could not be seen merely as a preliminary issue 'but must be taken in the legal and factual context of the whole case.'[81]

- Factors which were important in granting standing here were: 'the importance of vindicating the rule of law . . . the importance of the issue raised . . . the likely absence of any other responsible challenger . . . the nature of the breach of duty against which relief is sought . . . and the prominent role of these applicants in giving advice, guidance and assistance with regard to aid.'[82] These factors meant that the pressure group had sufficient interest.

- Rose LJ drew a comparison with the lenient approach to standing where the individual had a genuine interest in the matter, and stated: 'it seems to me that the present applicants, with the national and international expertise and interest in promoting and protecting aid to underdeveloped nations, should have standing in the present application.'[83]

In *R v Secretary of State for Social Services Ex p. Child Poverty Action Group*[84] the seriousness of the matter, and the fact that there were no other responsible challengers, permitted the Child Action Poverty Group to bring an application to judicially review delays in processing benefits. Importantly the Secretary of State had not contested the Child Action Poverty Group's standing.

In *R v Inspectorate of Pollution ex p. Greenpeace Ltd (No.2)*[85], Greenpeace sought to challenge permission which permitted radioactive waste to be discharged from a power station. Greenpeace was held to have sufficient interest because of its expertise in the area, its international reputation and the fact that it represented members who lived near the power plant, who otherwise would not have brought the application.

The liberal approach can also be seen in R v. *Somerset CC ex p. Dixon.*[86] The case involved an application for judicial review which sought to challenge the decision to allow a quarry to be extended. The county had argued that the applicant should not have standing, as they were not prejudicially affected by the decision. Sedley J stated that it was possible for concerned members of the public, who were neither busybodies nor troublemakers to alert the court to illegality:

> Public law is not at base about rights, even though abuses of power may and often do invade private rights; it is about wrongs – that is to say misuses of public power; and the courts have always been alive to the fact

that a person or organisation with no particular stake in the issue or the outcome may, without in any sense being a mere meddler, wish and be well placed to call the attention of the court to an apparent misuse of public power. If an arguable case of such misuse can be made out on an application for leave, the court's only concern is to ensure that it is not being done for an ill motive. . . . Mr Dixon is plainly neither a busybody nor a mere troublemaker, even if the implications of his application are troublesome for the intended respondents. He is, on the evidence before me, perfectly entitled as a citizen to be concerned about, and to draw the attention of the court to, what he contends is an illegality in the grant of a planning consent which is bound to have an impact on our natural environment.[87]

Having read Sedley J's comments above, it can be observed that a person who does not have sufficient interest in the traditional sense could still bring an application for judicial review.

In *R (on the application of Plantagenet Alliance Ltd) v Secretary of State for Justice*[88] the applicants were held to have sufficient interest and were held to have standing. The case related to the discovery of Richard III's remains in a car park in Leicester. The issue of standing was disputed. However, Haddon-Cave J was clear that:

A claimant seeking to bring judicial review proceedings must demonstrate that it has sufficient interest in the matter to which the 'application relates' (section 31(3) of the Senior Courts Act 1981). The phrase 'sufficient interest' is given a wide meaning. The Claimant is a campaigning organisation incorporated on 21st March 2013 by the 17th great-nephew of Richard III, Mr Stephen Nicolay. It represents a group of collateral descendants of Richard III who are aggrieved at the decisions taken regarding his re-interment without consultation. I am satisfied that the Claimant, and its subscribers, have sufficient interest and standing to bring these proceedings on all Grounds, both on conventional principles, and in the unusual circumstances of this case which involve the discovery of the proven remains of a former monarch.[89]

In *R (on the application of Jones) v Commissioner of Police for the Metropolis*[90], the Divisional Court held that where other applicants had standing, i.e. those individuals arrested during a protest, the other applicants, who were politicians, did not have standing as there were others who are 'better placed to bring the claim.'[91] Dingemans LJ and Chamberlain J were clear that

it is important to remind parties of the need to ensure that those who bring claims for additional review are limited to those best placed to bring the claim. This is because adding unnecessary claimant is likely to increase the costs of the litigation, if only by requiring solicitors to send out extra reports on the litigation.[92]

RECENT DEVELOPMENT

In *R (on the application of Good Law Project Ltd) v Secretary of State for Health and Social Care*[93] the pressure group, the Good Law Project Ltd, was held to have standing to judicially review the decision to award a procurement contract during the Covid-19 pandemic. Chamberlain J observed that, 'Since the early 1980s, the courts of England and Wales have generally adopted a liberal approach to the question of standing.'[94] Applying the decision in *World Development Movement*, the court held that the Good Law Project Ltd had standing:

> The position of the First Claimant in this regard is relevantly analogous to that of the World Development Movement. It has a sincere interest, and some expertise, in scrutinising government conduct in this area. There is no allegation (and no evidence) that it is seeking to use the public procurement regime as a tool for challenging decisions which it opposes for other reasons. There is no dispute about the importance of the transparency obligations it claims have been breached. As to the 'gravity' of the alleged breaches, they relate to contracts worth (at least) several billion pounds; and there is a pleaded allegation (in respect of which permission has been granted) that they result from a deliberate policy on the part of the Secretary of State. To my mind, there is a powerful public interest in the resolution, one way or the other, of the issues raised.[95]

However, the other applicants, who were MPs, were held by the court not to have standing:

> I have no doubt that they have a genuine and sincere interest in the issues the subject of this litigation. The fact that someone is a Member of Parliament does not, in and of itself, prevent her from having standing. But the availability of a better placed challenger remains an important – and often determinative – factor in considering whether it is necessary to accord standing to a person who is not herself directly affected by the decision challenged or the relief sought. Where there is already a claimant or claimants with standing, there is no reason to accord standing to additional parties.[96]

This is important as it could prevent the perception that politicians are using judicial review applications as a way to conduct politics through the courts. The approach taken by Chamberlain J appears to be sound, especially where it can be justified by the existence of an applicant who has the skills and expertise in bringing the claim.

PUBLIC LAW IN PRACTICE

Consider the two examples below. In what circumstances will a pressure group be held to have sufficient interest in a matter?

Example 1

The North London Football Supporters Guild (NFLSG) would like to challenge the decision of the Secretary of State to contribute £23,000,000 towards converting the Big Sports Stadium into a new football stadium, which will be used by East Ender United FC. The question here is whether NFLSG would have a sufficient interest in the decision. They appear to be a supporters' association and could represent their members. However, are the interests of their members affected by the decision of the Secretary of State? Or are they just interfering in a matter which they have no interest in? We would need to consider the decision *in Ex p. National Federation of Self Employed and Small Businesses Ltd.* NFLSG would be unlikely to have a sufficient interest and would be unable to judicially review the decision. This could be contrasted with a situation where a football club is denied funding from the Secretary of State, whereas another club receives funding.

Example 2

The Asylum Seekers Support Group (ASSG) is a charity that has been set up to look after the interests of asylum seekers in the United Kingdom. ASSG wishes to challenge the decision of the Secretary of State to reduce benefit payments to those asylum seekers whose application to remain in the United Kingdom has been rejected. We can presume that ASSG does not have members who are directly affected by the decision. However, as a charity they could have sufficient interest to bring judicial review, as shown by cases such as *Ex p. Child Poverty Action Group and Ex p. Greenpeace Ltd (No.2)*. We would need to consider ASSG's expertise, reputation and whether anyone else would realistically be able to bring an application for judicial review.

15.9 Remedies

The application may be awarded one or more of the following remedies (see Figure 12.5). It is important to note which remedy the applicant in any given circumstance will be seeking. We shall divide the remedies between non-prerogative and prerogative remedies.

15.9.1 Non-prerogative remedies

Since the Judicature Acts 1873–75 any court can award the equitable remedy of an injunction. An injunction will prevent a party from acting in a certain way or will force a party to act in a certain way. Breach of an injunction will result in contempt of court. The House of Lords in *M v. Home Office*[97] held that injunctions were available against ministers and government departments. Therefore, Crown immunity has been restricted with regards to liability for breach of an injunction. In *M v. Home Office* the Home Secretary had ordered the removal of a

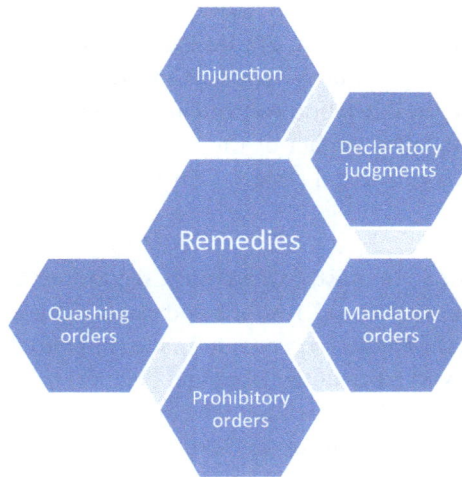

Figure 15.6
Remedies available for judicial review

political asylum seeker to Zaire. The court ordered the Home Secretary to return the asylum seeker to the United Kingdom, but the Home Secretary refused to comply with the injunction. The House of Lords held that injunctions could be used against officers of the Crown and they did not enjoy immunity.

The court can by way of a declaratory judgment state the parties' respective rights and, importantly for the purposes of judicial review, the applicant can ask the court to state whether the public body will be permitted by statute or the prerogative to act in a certain way. For example, an applicant may ask whether a planning committee can legally refuse to have a public hearing, and a declaratory judgment will merely state whether refusing to have a public hearing will be legal. It is also possible to recover damages where they would be available in private law.

15.9.2 Prerogative remedies

The court can award a number of prerogative remedies. A prohibitory order will stop a public body from acting in a certain way, a mandatory order will compel a public body to use its powers properly and to act in a certain way, whilst a quashing order will nullify the decision and the decision-maker will have to remake the decision. It must be noted that even if the original decision is quashed, the applicant may still not necessarily get the decision he wants when the public body makes a new decision. For example, when the Coalition government (2010–2015) came into power in 2010, Michael Gove, the Secretary of State for Education, decided to change the previous government's policy of rebuilding and refurbishing schools. It was decided that many schools would no longer be included in the list of those to be refurbished or rebuilt. However, the communication of this decision was rushed, and many schools were informed that they were still included, when in fact a decision had been taken to remove them from the list. The decision was challenged by many local authorities. In *R (on the application of Luton BC) v. Secretary of State for Education*[98] the Secretary of State for Education was ordered to reconsider his decision and have regard to the equality impact of the decision. This case is interesting as it illustrates the limits of judicial review. Consider the judgment of Holman J, who stated:

> [T]he Secretary of State must, I stress must, reconsider the position of each of the claimants with an open mind and paying due regard to whatever representations they may respectively make. But provided he discharges that duty and his equality duties, the final decision on any given school or project still rests with him. He may save all, some, a few, or none. No one should gain false hope from this decision.[99]

This was a clear warning that whilst a quashing order would lead to the new decision, it would not necessarily result in the applicant's preferred outcome.

15.10 Practical application

Please consider the following scenarios:

(1) Helen is a member of the Friends of the Soil, a group that is dedicated to protecting the environment. Last month, the Secretary of State announced the construction of a power station within a site of natural beauty. Helen lives within four miles of the proposed site of the power station. Helen and the Friends of the Soil both wish to judicially review the Secretary of State's decision.

(2) The Transport Act 2014 (fictitious) gives the Secretary of State for Transport the sole power to approve the construction of new motorways in England. Over the past 20 years, there has always been a public consultation before a decision about the construction of a new motorway has been taken. Last month, the Secretary of State for Business, Innovation and Skills announced that using the powers under the Transport Act 2014, a new motorway would be constructed between Birmingham and Swansea. The Secretary of State for Business, Innovation and Skills did not hold a consultation prior to making his decision. Several of the local authorities that will be affected by the construction of the motorway are aggrieved that there has been no consultation. In addition to the local authorities, two politicians, Lillian Nessa MP and Baroness Smithy, wish to be parties to the judicial review.

For each of the above scenarios (1)–(2), please advise as to the relevant issues in connection to judicial review. Where appropriate you must advise as to the preliminaries and the remedies. You must make reference to case law.

15.11 Key points to take away from this chapter

- Judicial review serves as an important check on the executive. It prevents the executive from abusing its powers.
- Judicial review is not an appeal of the substantive decision.
- Only the decisions of a public body are amenable to judicial review.
- You must have sufficient interest to bring an application for judicial review. It is possible for both individuals and groups to bring an application for judicial review.
- There is currently a three-month time limit (for non-planning application cases) for bringing an application for judicial review.
- There are a number of remedies available for judicial review, including a quashing order.

Notes

1 [2005] UKHL 56; [2006] 1 AC 262.
2 ibid 71.
3 [2019] EWHC 221 (Admin).
4 ibid 326.
5 *Harrow Community Support Limited v The Secretary of State for Defence* [2012] EWHC 1921 (Admin).
6 *R (on the application of DSD and another) v The Parole Board of England and Wales* [2018] EWHC 694 (Admin).
7 D Milmo and G Topham, 'How the West Coast Mainline Bid Process Was Derailed' *The Guardian* (3 October 2012).
8 *Laker Airways Ltd v Department of Trade* [1977] QB 643.
9 *Congreve v Home Office* [1976] QB 629.
10 see HWR Wade, *Constitutional Fundamentals, the Hamlyn Lectures* (Stevens 1980).
11 *Case of Proclamations* (1611) 12 Co. Rep 74.
12 [1765] 19 State Tr 1029.
13 (1724) 93 ER 698.
14 ibid 704.
15 [1915] AC 120.
16 [1942] AC 206.
17 [1964] AC 40 HL.
18 [2008] UKHL 61.
19 See <https://assets.publishing.service.gov.uk/government/uploads/system/uploads/attachment_data/file/761798/judicial-review-proposals-further-reform-government-response.pdf>.
20 See <https://assets.publishing.service.gov.uk/government/uploads/system/uploads/attachment_data/file/409386/civil-justice-statistics-october-december-2014.pdf>.
21 T Hickman and M Sunkin, 'Success in Judicial Review: The Current Position' (*UK Constitutional Law Blog*, 19 March 2014) <https://ukconstitutionallaw.org/>.
22 See <www.gov.uk/government/news/government-launches-independent-panel-to-look-at-judicial-review>.

23   ibid.
24   [1985] AC 374.
25   [2008] UKHL 61.
26   [1969] 2 AC 147.
27   [1969] 2 AC 147.
28   ibid 170.
29   ibid 199–200.
30   [1992] JPL 1044.
31   [2009] UKSC 12.
32   [2017] EWCA Civ 1868; [2018] 1 WLR 2572.
33   ibid.
34   ibid 105.
35   ibid 111.
36   M Elliot and AL Young, 'Privacy International in the Supreme Court: Jurisdiction, the Rule of Law and Parliamentary Sovereignty' (2019) 78(3) CLJ 490, 494.
37   M Gordon, 'Privacy International, Parliamentary Sovereignty and the Synthetic Constitution' (*UK Constitutional Law Blog*, 26 June 2019) <https://ukconstitutionallaw.org/>.
38   [2016] EWHC 323 (Admin).
39   ibid 23.
40   [1987] QB 815.
41   ibid 847.
42   [1993] 2 All ER 249.
43   [1993] 1 WLR 909.
44   [1992] 1 WLR 1036.
45   [1993] 2 All ER 833.
46   (1999) 11 Admin LR 43.
47   (2001) 33 HLR 35.
48   ibid 56.
49   ibid 76.
50   ibid 77.
51   [1998] ELR 389.
52   [2002] EWHC 529 (Admin).
53   (1990) 2 Admin LR 77.
54   [2017] EWHC 2308 (Admin).
55   ibid 42.
56   ibid 43.
57   [2001] EWHC Admin 429.
58   [2007] UKHL 27.
59   [1983] 2 AC 237.
60   ibid 10.
61   [1992] 1 AC 624.
62   [2000] 1 WLR 1988.
63   [2017] EWCA Civ 1998.
64   ibid 65.
65   ibid 67.
66   [1982] AC 617.
67   [2002] EWCA Civ 1370.
68   ibid 133–34.
69   [1998] AC 407.

70   [1985] QB 657.
71   *R (Wheeler) v. Office of the Prime Minister.*
72   [2008] EWHC 1409 (Admin).
73   [1994] QB 552; [1994] 2 WLR 115.
74   ibid 561–62.
75   [1972] 2 QB 299.
76   [1981] JPL 183.
77   [1990] 1 QB 504.
78   [1995] 1 WLR 386.
79   ibid.
80   ibid 393.
81   ibid 395.
82   ibid.
83   ibid 396.
84   [1990] 2 QB 540.
85   [1994] 4 All ER 329.
86   [1998] Env LR 111.
87   ibid 121.
88   [2013] EWHC B13 (Admin).
89   ibid 14–15.
90   [2019] EWHC 2957 (Admin).
91   ibid 61.
92   ibid 62.
93   [2021] EWHC 346 (Admin).
94   ibid 96.
95   ibid 104.
96   ibid 106.
97   [1994] 1 AC 377.
98   [2011] EWHC 217 (Admin).
99   ibid 126.

Further reading

Barnrett H, *Constitutional and Administrative Law* (13th edn, Routledge 2019)

Elliot M and AL Young, 'Privacy International in the Supreme Court: Jurisdiction, the Rule of Law and Parliamentary Sovereignty' (2019) 78(3) CLJ 490

Gordon M, 'Privacy International, Parliamentary Sovereignty and the Synthetic Constitution' (*UK Constitutional Law Blog*, 26 June 2019)

Ligere E, 'Locus Standi and the Public Interest: A Hotchpotch of Legal Principles' [2005] JPEL 292

Wade HWR, *Constitutional Fundamentals, the Hamlyn Lectures* (Stevens 1980)

Woolf H et al, *De Smith's Principles of Judicial Review* (2nd edn, Sweet & Maxwell 2020)

Judicial review II

The grounds

In this chapter we will

- consider the grounds that are available for judicial review
- explore the use of unreasonableness and irrationality as a ground for review
- discuss the purpose of illegality, procedural impropriety, bias and a breach of an illegitimate expectation
- evaluate the development of proportionality as a ground for review

16.1 Introduction

We have seen the procedure for bringing judicial review and now we will look at the grounds for bringing an application for judicial review. It is important to understand how these grounds arise and how they can be used to challenge the executive's decision. You should note that it is possible for more than one ground to be argued in an application for judicial review and so it is not possible to look at these grounds in isolation when considering the validity of a decision. The cases mentioned below involved challenges to decisions as diverse as banning hunting, selling off council homes and cancelling funding for a private education. These decisions impact the rights of citizens and therefore judicial review serves an important role in preventing abuse of power and protecting the rights of individuals.

Lord Diplock in *Council of Civil Service Unions and Others v. Minister for the Civil Service [GCHQ]*[1] identified the grounds which were available for judicial review:

> one can conveniently classify under three heads the grounds upon which administrative action is subject to control by judicial review. The first ground I would call 'illegality' the second 'irrationality' and the third 'procedural impropriety.' That is not to say that further development on a case by case basis may not in course of time add further ground.

DOI: 10.4324/9780429293498-18

Although Lord Diplock did suggest that in the future proportionality could become a ground for judicial review. We shall look at these grounds in detail below and see how they can arise.

The grounds on which an application for judicial review can be made are:

- unreasonableness or irrationality
- proportionality
- illegality
- legitimate expectation
- procedural impropriety and bias

Where the court finds that a ground for judicial review has been established, the court can award the claimant one or more of the remedies discussed previously in Chapter 15. These grounds are used to challenge the decision-maker's decision; thus in effect it permits the court to prevent the executive (or any other public body) from abusing its powers.

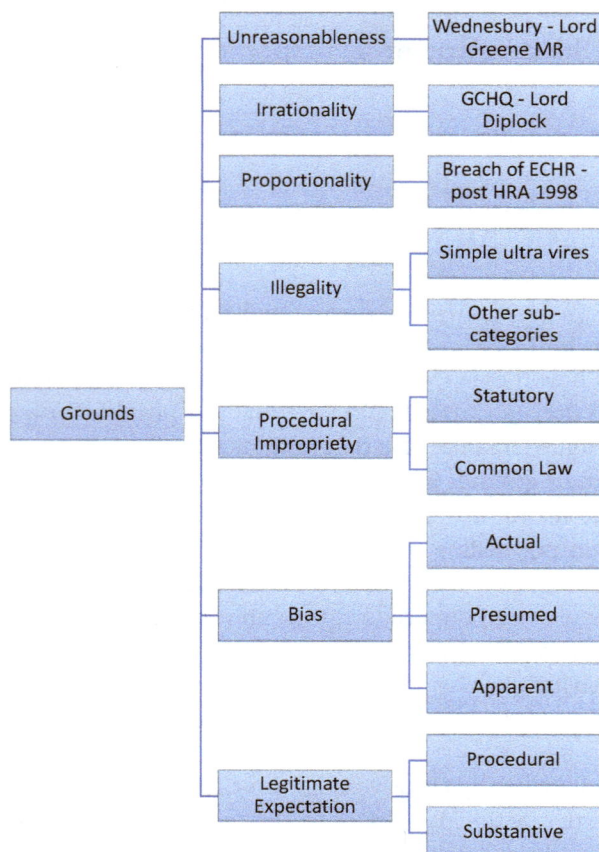

Figure 16.1
Chapter Overview

16.2 Unreasonableness or irrationality as a ground for judicial review

A decision can be challenged where the court is of the opinion that the decision-maker has acted unreasonably. This requires the court to assess whether the decision is one which no other reasonable decision-maker would make. It is important to appreciate that the decision-maker is not being challenged on the basis that he has exceeded his powers (acting illegally), but rather it is the substance of his actual decision that is being challenged. This raises important constitutional questions, as the courts are asking whether the decision is so unreasonable that no other decision-maker would reach the same decision.

The decision in *Associated Provincial Picture Houses Ltd v. Wednesbury Corporation*[2] established the unreasonableness test. It involved the decision to ban children from going to the cinema on a Sunday. Lord Greene MR considered what was meant by unreasonableness and held that:

> It is true to say that, if a decision on a competent matter is so unreasonable that no reasonable authority could ever have come to it, then the courts can interfere. That, I think, is quite right; but to prove a case of that kind would require something overwhelming, and, in this case, the facts do not come anywhere near anything of that kind. . . . It is not what the court considers unreasonable, a different thing altogether. If it is what the court considers unreasonable, the court may very well have different views to that of a local authority on matters of high public policy of this kind. Some courts might think that no children ought to be admitted on Sundays at all, some courts might think the reverse, and all over the country I have no doubt on a thing of that sort honest and sincere people hold different views.[3]

The decision in the present case was not held to be unreasonable. The case gave rise to the test known as *Wednesbury* unreasonableness.

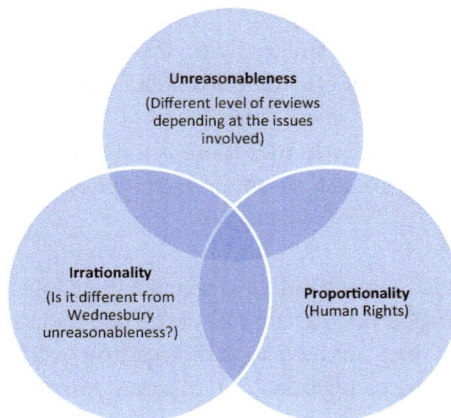

Figure 16.2
Unreasonableness, irrationality and proportionality

An example of when a decision would be unreasonable was given by War-
rington LJ in *Short v. Poole Corporation*:[4] if a teacher was dismissed 'because
she had red hair, or for some equally frivolous and foolish reason, the Court
would declare the attempted dismissal to be void.' In *R (on the application
of Clarke) v Birmingham City Council*[5] the council had spent £19,000,000 on
installing sprinklers in buildings that they owned in response to the Grenfell
Tower fire in London. This was challenged inter alia on the basis that the
decision was unreasonable. The Court of Appeal held that the decision was
reasonable. In *R (on the application of Veronika Kucherov) v Secretary of State
for the Home Department*[6] issue was whether an immigration officer had been
correct to refuse a foreign national entry to the United Kingdom. Nicol J was
clear as to the approach to be taken to determine whether the decision to
refuse entry was correct:

> Put shortly, my task then is to ask whether the Immigration Officer was
> entitled to come to the conclusion that she did. That requires a review
> according to the familiar decision in Associated Provincial Picture Houses
> Ltd v Wednesbury Corporation. In my judgment, the Immigration Officer
> was so entitled.[7]

We will now consider the development of the irrationality test. In *Council of
Civil Service Unions and Others v. Minister for the Civil Service [GCHQ]*[8] Lord Diplock offered a new formulation of the *Wednesbury* test, which asked whether the
decision-maker has acted irrationally. His Lordship stated that a decision would
be irrational if the decision was one 'which is so outrageous in its defiance of
logic or of accepted moral standards that no sensible person who had applied
his mind to the question to be decided could have arrived at it.'[9] Lord Diplock
held that judges would be able to distinguish between a rational and irrational
decision. Indeed, His Lordship stated that, '"Irrationality" by now can stand
upon its own feet as an accepted ground on which a decision may be attacked
by judicial review.'[10] Lord Diplock was of the view that it was the role of judges
to determine whether a decision was irrational: 'Whether a decision falls within
this category is a question that judges by their training and experience should
be well equipped to answer, or else there would be something badly wrong with
our judicial system.'[11]

It is important to consider whether there is a difference between unreasonableness and irrationality? In *A v. North Somerset Council*[12] Mr Justice Jarman QC
stated that:

- 'Unreasonableness is an objective concept which operates across a spectrum dependent upon the importance of the issues at stake. The test is high
. . . but a claimant does not have to demonstrate a decision that is so bizarre
that the author must be regarded as temporarily unhinged.'
- 'What the term "irrationality" generally means in this area of the law is a
decision which does not add up, in which in other words there is an error
of reasoning which robs the decision of its logic.'[13]

In *A v. North Somerset Council* the court held that whilst unreasonableness was 'an objective concept' and that '[t]he test is high' for establishing that a decision was unreasonable, 'a claimant does not have to demonstrate that 'a decision that is so bizarre that the author must be regarded as temporarily unhinged.' This narrows the potential interpretation of Lord Diplock's formulation of irrationality, where an irrational decision was one which is 'so outrageous in its defiance of logic or of accepted moral standards' meaning that no sensible decision-maker would reach such a decision.

In *Hayes v Willoughby*[14] Lord Sumption distinguished between rationality and reasonableness:

> 'Rationality is a familiar concept in public law . . . . Rationality is not the same as reasonableness. Reasonableness is an external, objective standard applied to the outcome of a person's thoughts or intentions. The question is whether a notional hypothetically reasonable person in his position would have engaged in the relevant conduct for the purpose of preventing or detecting crime. . . . A test of rationality, by comparison, applies a minimum objective standard to the relevant person's mental processes. It imports a requirement of good faith, a requirement that there should be some logical connection between the evidence and the ostensible reasons for the decision, and (which will usually amount to the same thing) an absence of arbitrariness, of capriciousness or of reasoning so outrageous in its defiance of logic as to be perverse.'[15]

Rationality meant more than whether the decision maker was reasonable based on an external standard and judged in terms of the outcome and not how the decision was actually made. Rationality required the court to look at the state of mind of the decision-maker and impose requirements that should not affect the decision-making process.

16.2.1 Constitutional problems

It is important that the courts must avoid misusing judicial review. As discussed in Chapter 15, the courts must be aware of the important constitutional principle of the separation of powers and thus must avoid restricting the discretionary powers of a minister or local authority, unless the decision is truly one which is unreasonable. As Lord Scarman stated in *R v. Secretary of State for the Environment ex p. Nottinghamshire County Council*[16], 'Judicial review is a great weapon in the hands of the judges: but the judges must observe the constitutional limits set by our parliamentary system upon their exercise of this beneficent power.'[17] Therefore, if Parliament has given discretionary power to a minister, then the courts can review the validity of the decision only where there has been an abuse of power and the decision exceeds the powers conferred by Parliament. However, the courts have recognised that where important rights are concerned then the court can exercise a heightened review. Conversely, the courts will be reluctant to review decisions which are of a political nature. In *Ex p. Nottinghamshire*

County Council the House of Lords was asked to review a financial decision by the Secretary of State. This according to Lord Scarman involved the exercise of discretion which 'inevitably requires a political judgment on his part.' Lord Scarman, because of the political nature of the decision, was of the opinion that:

> the courts below were absolutely right to decline the invitation to intervene. . . . But I cannot accept that it is constitutionally appropriate, save in very exceptional circumstances, for the courts to intervene on the ground of 'unreasonableness' to quash guidance framed by the Secretary of State and by necessary implication approved by the House of Commons, the guidance being concerned with the limits of public expenditure by local authorities and the incidence of the tax burden as between taxpayers and ratepayers. Unless and until a statute provides otherwise, or it is established that the Secretary of State has abused his power, these are matters of political judgment for him and for the House of Commons. They are not for the judges or your Lordships' House in its judicial capacity.[18]

Lord Templeman agreed with Lord Scarman's approach and held that whilst '[t]he courts will not be slow to exercise the powers of judicial review in order to strike down illegality or abuse of power,'[19] on the facts, however, the Secretary of State's action was lawful. It is apparent that where a political decision is being made by a minister, that the courts will not hold the decision to be unreasonable, unless there is evidence of abuse of power.

The courts' power to review administrative decisions was considered by Lord Bridge *in R v. Secretary of State for the Home Department ex p. Bugdaycay*[20]. The case concerned an application for asylum. The Home Secretary had refused the application and the asylum seeker brought an application for judicial review. The House of Lords held that the decision whether to grant asylum was one for the executive and therefore was valid, although the court held that the decision to remove one of the immigrants could be quashed. This was because the decision as to whether there was a danger in returning the applicant to his home country needed to be taken after considering the evidence provided. On the facts the evidence had not been considered. Giving judgment, Lord Bridge noted that, although the courts had limited powers of review, the courts are

> entitled to subject an administrative decision to the more rigorous examination, to ensure that it is in no way flawed, according to the gravity of the issue which the decision determines. The most fundamental of all human rights is the individual's right to life and when an administrative decision under challenge is said to be one which may put the applicant's life at risk, the basis of the decision must surely call for the most anxious scrutiny.[21]

We can see that depending on the type of decision, the courts will adopt a different level of review. Would a ban on homosexual military personnel be considered reasonable? This was a question which was addressed by the English courts in the 1990s. In *R v. Ministry of Defence ex p. Smith*[22] military personnel sought to challenge the decision of the Ministry of Defence, which had dismissed them from the armed forces. This occurred before the passing of the Human Rights Act 1998 and therefore, the domestic courts could not consider whether there had been a violation of Articles 8 and 14 ECHR. The court had to ask whether the decision was reasonable. Sir Thomas Bingham MR stated that the court should adopt a heightened review where there has been a substantial interference with human rights. This case is important as it demonstrates that the courts will adopt a sliding scale of review depending on the type of decision that they are reviewing. However, we should note that the heightened review may not be adequate to protect individual's rights. Sir Thomas Bingham MR had stated:

> The court may not interfere with the exercise of an administrative discretion on substantive grounds save where the court is satisfied that the decision is unreasonable in the sense that it is beyond the range of responses open to a reasonable decision-maker. But in judging whether the decision-maker has exceeded this margin of appreciation the human rights context is important. The more substantial the interference with human rights, the more the court will require by way of justification before it is satisfied that the decision is reasonable in the sense outlined above.[23]

Therefore, if a decision involves interference with human rights then the courts will more actively review the decision. It is important to note that the heightened review under the *Wednesbury* unreasonableness test was found to be inadequate to protect the military personnel's rights. The Court of Appeal found that the Ministry of Defence's decision to dismiss military personnel on the basis of their sexuality was not unreasonable. This was despite applying the heightened standard of review. Importantly, it could not be said that a reasonable decision-maker would not have reached this decision.

The appellants in *Ex p. Smith* subsequently brought their case to the European Court of Human Rights (ECtHR). In *Smith v. United Kingdom*[24] the ECtHR ruled that the military personnel's Convention rights had been violated, and that the violation could not be justified as it was not proportionate. The ECtHR acknowledged that the Court of Appeal was aware that there had been a violation of Article 8 ECHR and that the decision may not be proportionate; however, as the ECHR had yet to be incorporated into domestic law the domestic court had been unable to consider this. It is important to consider the different standards of review under the traditional unreasonableness test, the test for irrationality and that of proportionality.

16.3 Proportionality as a ground for judicial review

We shall now consider the development of proportionality as a ground for judicial review and look at whether it should replace unreasonableness.

Ex p. Smith
[1996]

R (Daly)
[2001]

Human
Rights Act
1998

Bank Mellat
[2013

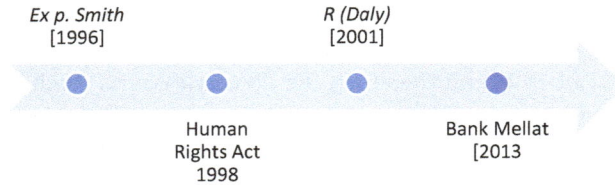

Figure 16.3
The development of proportionality

Before the Human Rights Act 1998 the test for proportionality could not be used in domestic law

The House of Lords in *R v. Secretary of State for the Home Department ex p. Brind*[25] held that the decision by the Home Secretary to ban direct speech from a proscribed terrorist organisation was not illegal, as the decision was not unreasonable. The case related to the fact that senior members of Sinn Fein during the 'Troubles' in Northern Ireland were banned from being able to directly broadcast in the United Kingdom. This meant that whenever Gerry Adams, the then leader of Sinn Fein, would deliver a speech, organisations like the BBC would have to dub his voice with that of an actor. This ban has since been lifted. The House of Lords considered the approach of the ECtHR when reviewing infringements of Convention rights. The ECtHR would ask whether the infringement was proportionate. The use of proportionality as a ground for review in domestic law was rejected, as Lord Ackner stated, '[u]nless and until Parliament incorporates the Convention into domestic law . . . there appears to me to be at present no basis upon which the proportionality doctrine applied by the European Court can be followed by the courts of this country.'[26]

16.3.1 The impact of the Human Rights Act 1998

The Human Rights Act 1998 gave effect to much of the ECHR in domestic law. This meant that Convention rights could be directly enforceable in domestic courts where there had been an infringement by a public authority. It is important to understand the effect of the Human Rights Act 1998 and the requirement under section 6(1) that '[i]t is unlawful for a public authority to act in a way which is incompatible with a Convention right.' We shall see that the HRA 1998 has provided for domestic enforcement of the European Convention on Human Rights. Chapter 12 outlines how the HRA 1998 works in practice and the meaning of public authority under section 6. In *R (on the application of Alconbury Developments Ltd) v. Secretary of State for the Environment, Transport and the Regions*[27] Lord Slynn thought the time had come to use proportionality where there were infringements of Convention rights. His Lordship observed that, '[t]rying to keep the Wednesbury principle and proportionality in separate compartments seems to me to be unnecessary and confusing.'[28] However, proportionality must not be used to 'provide for a complete rehearing on the merits of the decision. Judicial control does not need to go so far.' This is important as a merits-based review would risk violating the separation of powers.

The House of Lords in *R (Daly) v. Secretary of State for the Home Department*[29] considered the power of the prison authorities to search a prisoner's cell, without the prisoner being present, and to read his legal correspondence. According to Lord Bingham the decision was successfully challenged 'on an orthodox application of common law principles . . . and an orthodox domestic approach to judicial review.'[30] The House of Lords agreed that the same result would have been reached on the basis of Article 8 ECHR. Their Lordships were aware that relying on the common law and the ECHR might not always result in the same outcome. Reference was made to the decision in *R v. Ministry of Defence ex p. Smith*.[31]

Importantly, the House of Lords held that in the future where there were violations of Convention rights, it was no longer appropriate to ask whether a decision was unreasonable. Rather the correct question was whether the infringement was proportionate. English courts had experience of applying proportionality where there had an infringement of European Union Law. In *Daly*, Lord Steyn rejected the use of the heightened test for reasonableness which had been used by Sir Thomas Bingham MR in *Ex p. Smith*. His Lordship referred to the judgment of Lord Clyde in *De Freitas v. Permanent Secretary of Ministry of Agriculture, Fisheries, Lands and Housing*[32], where it was stated that the court should ask whether:

1 'the legislative objective is sufficiently important to justify limiting a fundamental right';
2 'the measures designed to meet the legislative objective are rationally connected to it'; and
3 'the means used to impair the right or freedom are no more than is necessary to accomplish the objective.'[33]

PUBLIC LAW IN CONTEXT
PROPORTIONALITY AND THE HUMAN RIGHTS ACT 1998

As a consequence of the Human Rights Act 1998, where there has been a violation of a Convention right, the courts will use proportionality as a ground for review. In order for a decision to be proportionate it needs to be shown that there is a legitimate objective which is sufficiently important to justify limiting a fundamental right, and that the measures used to achieve this objective are rationally connected to it. Consequentially, there needs to be a link between the measure and the objective. It is important to note that the test for proportionality requires a higher standard of review of executive decision-making. In *Daly* Lord Cooke had observed that whilst the application of the reasonableness test and that of proportionality may reach the same result, cases such as *Ex p. Smith* demonstrated the limitations of the former. Lord Cooke observed:

'The view that the standards are substantially the same appears to have received its quietus in Smith and Grady v. United Kingdom (1999) 29 EHRR 493.... And I think that the day will come when it will be more widely recognised that Associated Provincial Picture Houses Ltd v. Wednesbury Corpn [1948] 1 KB 223 was an unfortunately retrogressive decision in English administrative law, in so far as it suggested that there are degrees of unreasonableness and that only a very extreme degree can bring an administrative decision within the legitimate scope of judicial invalidation. The depth of judicial review and the deference due to administrative discretion vary with the subject matter. It may well be, however, that the law can never be satisfied in any administrative field merely by a finding that the decision under review is not capricious or absurd.'[34]

We can see above that Lord Cooke was critical of the unreasonableness test, namely that there needs to be unreasonableness of 'only a very extreme degree' before the courts will find the decision invalid. His Lordship implicitly questioned the survival of *Wednesbury* unreasonableness. This heightened review of proportionality has constitutional implications. The courts can question not just whether the decision is extreme, irrational or is one that no other reasonable decision would reach; as now the courts can ask whether the decision was more than was necessary to accomplish the executive's objective. Decisions which exceed what was required to meet this legitimate objective can be challenged by the courts.

In his judgment in *Daly* Lord Steyn observed that the Court of Appeal *in R v. Ministry of Defence ex p. Smith*[35] 'reluctantly felt compelled to reject a limitation on homosexuals in the army' which violated Articles 8 and 14, because the decision was found not to be unreasonable. However, the ECtHR found that it was not proportionate. His Lordship distinguished the two tests, because firstly 'the doctrine of proportionality may require the reviewing court to assess the balance which the decision-maker has struck, not merely whether it is within the range of rational or reasonable decisions,' and secondly 'the proportionality test may go further than the traditional grounds of review inasmuch as it may require attention to be directed to the relative weight accorded to interests and considerations.'[36]

16.3.2 The rediscovery of the fourth limb

In *Bank Mellat v. Her Majesty's Treasury (No.2)*[37] Lord Reed reconsidered the requirements of the proportionality test and approved the use of a fourth limb. His Lordship stated that the test adopted at Strasbourg was not the same as the test used domestically. This was because:

the Strasbourg court recognises that it may be less well placed than a national court to decide whether an appropriate balance has been struck in the particular national context. For that reason, in the Convention case law the principle of proportionality is indissolubly linked to the concept of the margin of appreciation. That concept does not apply in the same way at the national level, where the degree of restraint practised by courts in applying the principle of proportionality, and the extent to which they will respect the judgment of the primary decision-maker, will depend upon the context, and will in part reflect national traditions and institutional culture. For these reasons, the approach adopted to proportionality at the national level cannot simply mirror that of the Strasbourg court.[38]

Rather than mirroring Strasbourg, the domestic courts have been influenced by other common law jurisdictions. The test in *De Freitas* was based on South African, Zimbabwean and Canadian jurisprudence. Unlike Strasbourg, domestic courts should not adopt the margin of appreciation because this is an international concept which, whilst useful to the ECtHR, is not suitable for the domestic courts because they are much better placed to review a decision. This is because they understand the local political and social conditions.

Lord Reed accepted the inclusion of a fourth limb, which had been first used in *Huang v. Secretary of State for the Home Department*.[39] Lord Bingham had observed:

> This formulation [the three limb test] has been widely cited and applied. But counsel for the applicants (with the support of Liberty, in a valuable written intervention) suggested that the formulation was deficient in omitting reference to an overriding requirement which featured in the judgment of Dickson CJ in *R v Oakes [1986] 1 SCR 103*, from which this approach to proportionality derives. This feature is (p 139) the need to balance the interests of society with those of individuals and groups. This is indeed an aspect which should never be overlooked or discounted.[40]

There was an acceptance by the House of Lords that the fourth limb had originated along with the original test in *R v. Oakes*.[41]

According to Lord Reed in *Bank Mellat v. Her Majesty's Treasury (No.2)*[42] the fourth limb was 'whether, balancing the severity of the measure's effects on the rights of the persons to whom it applies against the importance of the objective, to the extent that the measure will contribute to its achievement, the former outweighs the latter.' His Lordship observed that, '[i]n essence, the question at step four is whether the impact of the rights infringement is disproportionate to the likely benefit of the impugned measure.'[43] It is not sufficient that the interference is the least drastic measure available to achieve the legislative aim, as the court must balance the importance of the measure against the impact on the individual whose rights have been breached.

Previously *in R (on the application of Aguilar Quila) v Secretary of State for the Home Department*[44] Lord Wilson had set out the four limbs in his judgment:

> (a) is the legislative objective sufficiently important to justify limiting a fundamental right?; (b) are the measures which have been designed to meet it rationally connected to it?; (c) are they no more than are necessary to accomplish it?; and (d) do they strike a fair balance between the rights of the individual and the interests of the community?[45]

RECENT DEVELOPMENT

In *R (on the application of Stenfield and Keidan) v Secretary of State for International Development*[46] the Supreme Court considered the government's refusal to extend civil partnerships to heterosexual couples. Lord Kerr in his judgment stated that, 'The four-stage test designed to establish whether an interference with a qualified Convention right can be justified is now well-established.'[47] The Supreme Court considered whether there was a legitimate aim which is sufficiently important to justify the limitation of a fundamental right. The decision presents an opportunity to see the test being applied. Lord Kerr noted, 'The legitimate aim articulated by the respondent in the present appeal is the need to have time to assemble sufficient information to allow a confident decision to be made about the future of civil partnerships.'[48] In terms of discrimination in the present case, Lord Kerr observed that

> The present case does not involve a form of discrimination that was historically justified but has gradually lost its justification. The exact reverse is the case here. A *new* form of discrimination was introduced by the coming into force of MSSCA. There was, therefore, in the words of Lord Hoffmann, no reason to conclude that this discrimination 'was ever justified.'[49]

There needed to be a rational connection between aim and discrimination caused: 'If the aim of the government and Parliament could properly be described as legitimate, I accept that there would be a rational connection between the aim and the delay in addressing the discrimination.'[50] Lord Kerr was clear that the government could have avoided discrimination by pursuing other options which 'would have allowed the aim to be pursued with less, indeed no, discriminatory impact.'[51] Lord Kerr then considered the fourth limb, 'If the interference with the appellants' rights could be regarded as being in pursuit of a legitimate aim, I would have no hesitation in concluding that a fair balance between their rights and the interests of the community has not been struck.'[52]

16.3.3 The approach post *Daly*

Lord Bingham in *A v. Secretary of State for the Home Department*[53] observed:

> In Smith and Grady v. United Kingdom (1999) 29 EHRR 493 the traditional Wednesbury approach to judicial review . . . was held to afford inadequate

protection (by the ECtHR). . . . It is now recognised that 'domestic courts must themselves form a judgment whether a Convention right has been breached' and that 'the intensity of review is somewhat greater under the proportionality approach.'[54]

Thus, in *A v. Secretary of State for the Home Department* the House of Lords held that the Home Secretary's decision to detain suspected foreign terrorists without trial breached the ECHR. Thomas Hickman reviewing the introduction of proportionality post *Daly*, has commented (making reference to decisions such as *R [Begum] v. Governors of Denbigh High School*[55]) that '[t]he House of Lords has established that proportionality is concerned only with the outcome of the process of decision-making, not the manner in which it was conducted.'[56]

PUBLIC LAW IN PRACTICE

The government has announced that any openly homosexual member of the armed forces will be dismissed. The government's legal advisor has informed the Secretary of State for Defence that following the decision of the Court of Appeal in *Ex p. Smith* the department could go ahead with this policy.

Lieutenant Oakes is homosexual and has recently had her sexuality made public by a former partner. She was questioned by her superior officer and in line with governmental policy dismissed. Lieutenant Oakes wishes to bring an application to judicially review the decision to dismiss her.

Lieutenant Oakes will be able bring an application for judicial review and can argue that the decision was not proportionate. Applying the test for proportionality, there needs to be a legitimate aim which the government policy is trying to achieve, that the decision to dismiss Lieutenant Oakes is connected to the legitimate aim, and that the measure does not violate rights beyond what is really necessary to achieve the objective. Finally, it is necessary to consider the fourth limb and balance the importance of the legitimate aim against the impact on the individual whose rights have been violated.

16.3.4 The role of proportionality beyond violations of the Convention rights

Having two tests, depending on whether or not Convention rights are involved, has been criticised and many commentators, both judicial and academic, have questioned the confinement of proportionality to cases involving ECHR violations. Nicholas Dobson has considered the status of *Wednesbury* unreasonableness after the decision in *Daly*.[57] Commenting on the aftermath of *Daly*, Dobson observed that, 'Wednesbury essentially concerns proper adherence to statutory discretion and to that extent its core principles would seem still to be relevant.'[58] Lord Slynn *in R v Secretary of State for the Environment, Transport*

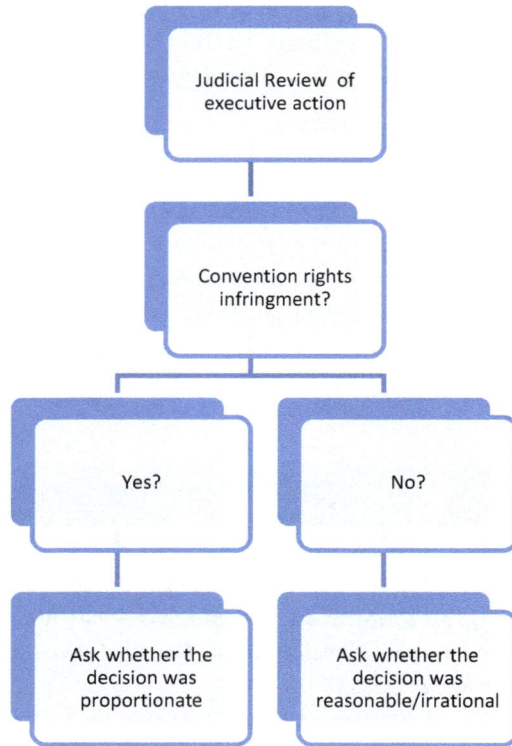

Figure 16.4
When to use proportionality as a ground for judicial review

and the Regions, ex parte Alconbury Developments Ltd[59] had rejected the need to distinguish *Wednesbury* unreasonableness and proportionality:

> The European Court of Justice does of course apply the principle of proportionality when examining such acts and national judges must apply the same principle when dealing with Community law issues. There is a difference between that principle and the approach of the English courts in *Associated Provincial Picture Houses Ltd v Wedensbury Corporation* [1948] 1 KB 223. But the difference in practice is not as great as is sometimes supposed. The cautious approach of the European Court of Justice in applying the principle is shown inter alia by the margin of appreciation it accords to the institutions of the Community in making economic assessments. I consider that even without reference to the Human Rights Act the time has come to recognise that this principle is part of English administrative law, not only when judges are dealing with Community acts but also when they are dealing with acts subject to domestic law. Trying to keep the *Wednesbury* principle and proportionality in separate compartments seems to me to be unnecessary and confusing. Reference to the Human Rights Act however makes it necessary that the court should ask whether what is done is compatible with Convention rights. That will often require

that the question should be asked whether the principle of proportionality has been satisfied.'[60]

What was Lord Slynn saying here? We can see:

1   Proportionality was used as the test by the European Court of Justice within the European Union;
2   Reasonableness was used as the test in England and Wales when reviewing a decision made by a public body;
3   The two tests when they are used were not that different;
4   The European Court of Justice accorded a margin of appreciation to institutions when assessing economic factors, i.e., gave them the benefit of their expertise when considering the conclusions that they had reached;
5   The two tests need not be kept separate as this causes confusion; and
6   Under the Human Rights Act 1998 it makes sense that proportionality is used to gauge whether there has been a contravention of Convention rights.

Following the key decision in *Daly*, the Court of Appeal in *R (Association of British Civilian Internees: Far East Region) v. Secretary of State for Defence*[61] questioned the justification for retaining *Wednesbury* unreasonableness as a ground for judicial review. The Court of Appeal in *R (Association of British Civilian Internees: Far East Region) v. Secretary of State for Defence* is an example of judicial willingness to use proportionality as a ground for review beyond breaches of the ECHR. Dyson LJ had stated that:

> Support for the recognition of proportionality as part of English domestic law in cases which do not involve Community law or the Convention is to be found (in Daly and Alconbury Developments). . . . It seems to us that the case for this is indeed a strong one. . . . The criteria of proportionality are more precise and sophisticated. . . . It is true that sometimes proportionality may require the reviewing court to assess for itself the balance that has been struck by the decision-maker, and that may produce a different result from one that would be arrived at on an application of the Wednesbury test. But the strictness of the Wednesbury test has been relaxed in recent years even in areas which have nothing to do with fundamental rights. . . . The Wednesbury test is moving closer to proportionality and in some cases it is not possible to see any daylight between the two tests. . . . Although we did not hear argument on the point, we have difficulty in seeing what justification there now is for retaining the Wednesbury test. . . . But we consider that it is not for this court to perform its burial rites.[62]

For decisions where there are no violations on Convention rights, then the traditional *Wednesbury* unreasonableness test must be used. We can see that the Court of Appeal was clear that the continued use of the *Wednesbury* test had little justification, given the sophisticated application of proportionality as a ground for review.

ACADEMIC DEBATE
WHAT IS WRONG WITH UNREASONABLENESS AS A GROUND FOR JUDICIAL REVIEW?

Lord Lester and Professor Jeffrey Jowell criticised *Wednesbury* unreasonableness and argued that it should be replaced by proportionality.[63] They criticised unreasonableness as permitting the court to hide the reasons for its decisions under the vagueness of the test, which permits the court to find rational decisions as irrational and the test is 'confusing and tautologous.' However, there are some academics that support the retention of *Wednesbury* unreasonableness. Paul Daly has argued that despite strong judicial and academic criticism, *Wednesbury* unreasonableness has survived as a ground for judicial review in non-Convention rights cases.[64] Daly argues after reviewing its application and responding to criticisms, that unreasonableness still has a place in the 21st century and needs to be better understood rather than be condemned. Commenting on the decision in *R (Association of British Civilian Internees: Far East Region) v. Secretary of State for Defence*, Sir Philip Sales observed that,

> [t]here may be an assumption, in light of [this] . . . decision, that the Supreme Court will, when given the opportunity in a suitable case, change the rationality standard of review derived from Wednesbury and GCHQ into a general proportionality standard of review. I suggest, however, that there should be serious pause for reflection before such a step is taken.[65]

Sales had criticised the suitably of proportionality as a suitable ground for review in all circumstances and had stated that that rationality is quite often a better test. The problem is that proportionality requires the court to engage in a heightened review of the decision and to ask whether it could have been achieved in some other less drastic way. Whilst this is appropriate where Convention rights are infringed, it may be constitutionally inappropriate to do this where the decision involves political decisions and policy matters. Heightened review risks offending the separation of powers and may lead to accusations of judicial activism. Therefore, unreasonableness would permit the courts to permit the executive suitable discretion.

In 2014, when speaking extra-judicially at an academic conference, Lord Carnwath observed:

> So, it seems, almost 30 years after [*GCHQ*], proportionality has crept into the English common law by the back door – not by the explicit addition of a fourth ground to Lord Diplock's trilogy, as he anticipated, but by the transmutation of the Lord Greene's strict reasonableness test into something which I suspect neither he nor Lord Diplock would have recognised, a flexible but structured test which is much better adapted to the task of effective and practical judicial supervision of executive action. To complete the circle, where does this leave Wednesbury? . . . A lot has been said since then about Wednesbury, in recent years much of it critical, but it has never been overruled. In Daly (2001) 51 Lord Cooke thought the day would come when it would be recognised that Wednesbury

was an 'unfortunately retrogressive decision in English administrative law.' In [*R (Associ-ation of British Civilian Internees: Far East Region) v. Secretary of State for Defence*] Dyson LJ had 'difficulty in seeing what justification there is now for retaining the Wednesbury test,' but thought that it was for the House of Lords, rather than the Court of Appeal, to perform 'its burial rites'. Eleven years on those rites remain unperformed.[66]

16.4 Illegality as a ground for judicial review

We shall now look at illegality as a ground for judicial review and see how this can be used to review decisions where the decision-maker has outside of the powers conferred on them by Parliament or the prerogative. Lord Diplock in *GCHQ* had observed, '[b]y "illegality" as a ground for judicial review I mean that the decision-maker must understand correctly the law that regulates his decision-making power and must give effect to it.' This essentially means that the decision-maker must act within his powers. This also means that the decision-maker must have regard to how he uses his powers, that he exercises these in a manner that takes into account relevant considerations, and it is used for the proper purpose for which it was intended.

Put simply, the decision-maker must use their decision-making powers lawfully and must not:

- act outside of the powers given to them by statute or the prerogative;
- abuse the discretion given to them by statute or the prerogative by:
- use the powers given for improper purposes
- delegate their decision-maker powers
- fetter their discretion and introduce a rigid policy without exceptions
- take into account irrelevant considerations and ignore relevant considerations
- reach a decision by making errors as to the law or facts

16.4.1 Acting outside of the powers given to a minister by statute or the prerogative

The courts will review the purported use of powers by the executive. In *R (on the application of Child Poverty Action Group) v Secretary of State for Work and Pensions*[67] the issue was whether the executive was able to change the law. The High Court was clear that it would be lawful for the executive to do this, unless it had been authorised to do so by Parliament. Mr Justice Singh had observed:

It is important to recall certain fundamental constitutional principles. The first is that under our constitutional system the executive has no power to make law save in those circumstances where it is granted power to do so by primary legislation. As has often been observed, the executive enjoys no sovereignty. . . . The executive is perfectly entitled to invite Parliament to change primary legislation. It may, if there is an urgent need to do so, invite Parliament to legislate very quickly, for example by way of a paving Act. . . . However the executive enjoys no power to amend or repeal primary legislation in the absence of delegation by Parliament itself.[68]

The government is not above the law and the courts will review executive decision-making to see if it is *ultra vires*, which means illegal. A classic example of this is the Home Secretary's decision to order his agents to search Mr Entick's house in *Entick v. Carrington*.[69] The court could not find any lawful authority for the Home Secretary to issue a valid search warrant. Therefore, the consequence of this was that the agents had committed trespass. A decision which is *ultra vires* cannot stand and it will be quashed by the courts. In *Entick* the Home Secretary was acting to prevent the distribution of material by people regarded as dangerous to the state, whereas his successor some 200 years later in *Congreve v. Home Office*[70] attempted to revoke television licences where these licences had been taken out with the intention of avoiding a planned price increase. The Home Secretary had acted to prevent people surrendering their licences in order to apply for new licences, with the sole intention of avoiding the planned increase in the price of a licence fee. Lord Denning MR stated that there was no statutory power to revoke the licence. His Lordship emphasised the courts' constitutional role,

> [to revoke the licences] would be a misuse of the power conferred on him by Parliament: and these courts have the authority – and, I would add, the duty – to correct a misuse of power by a Minister or his department, no matter how much he may resent it or warn us of the consequences if we do.[71]

Clearly, the courts cannot legitimise executive illegality in the interests of expediency.

Often the courts will look at both the literal wording of the statutory provision being relied upon by the decision-maker and the intention that Parliament when enacting the provision. The decision in *Attorney General v. Fulham Corporation*[72] concerned a scheme by the local authority to start up a laundry service. The local authority was relying on various Baths and Wash-houses Acts to operate the laundry service. Until the middle of the 20th century many people did not have their own bathrooms or facilities for washing clothes and had to rely on facilities provided by their local authority. Local bath houses enabled people to wash and washing facilities often provided there meant that people could clean their clothes more quickly than they could do at home. It was argued that the Acts were concerned with washing clothes and the laundry service was not excluded by the Act, but rather it was consequential. Indeed, it was argued by counsel for the local authority that '[t]here is no practical difference between the case of a woman bringing her clothes to the wash-house and washing them there and the case of her bringing the clothes in a bag and having them washed for her.'[73] However, the court held that the laundry scheme was not directly authorised by the legislation, and it was not something consequential to what Parliament had intended.

We can see that the courts will look beyond the literal meaning of a provision and look at the intention of Parliament, and therefore ask whether the decision-making is acting *ultra vires*. An example of the courts is the decision in *R v. Secretary State for Foreign and Commonwealth Affairs ex p. World Development Movement Ltd*[74]. The court ruled that the Foreign Secretary could not use his statutory powers under section 1 of the Overseas Development and Co-operation Act 1980 to fund economically unsound projects. Section 1(1) stated that:

> The Secretary of State shall have power, for the purpose of promoting the development or maintaining the economy of a country or territory outside the United Kingdom, or the welfare of its people, to furnish any person or body with assistance, whether financial, technical or of any other nature.

The court held the Foreign Secretary had no power to invest in the project and therefore was acting illegally. The court was willing to read into the statute the fact that Parliament would not intend for the Foreign Secretary to use the statutory powers to invest in unsound projects. Rose LJ was clear that:

> As to the absence of the word 'sound' from section 1(1), it seems to me that, if Parliament had intended to confer a power to disburse money for unsound developmental purposes, it could have been expected to say so expressly. Accordingly, where, as here, the contemplated development is, on the evidence, so economically unsound that there is no economic argument in favour of the case, it is not, in my judgment, possible to draw any material distinction between questions of propriety and regularity on the one hand and questions of economy and efficiency of public expenditure on the other.'[75]

16.4.2 Abuse of discretion by the decision-maker

An application can be made to judicially review a decision where the decision-maker has abused their discretion. The courts provide a check and balance against the executive abusing the powers conferred by Parliament.

16.4.3 Using the powers given for improper purposes

The courts will ask whether the decision-maker's exercise of the powers given to him have been used for the purposes which were intended by Parliament. Examples of situations where the court held that powers have not been used for the intended purpose include *Wheeler v. Leicester City Council*[76].

In *Wheeler v. Leicester City Council* the local authority had used their statutory powers to prevent Leicester Rugby Football Club from using grounds owned by the local authority for one year. This was because some of the players had ignored the local authority's policy on boycotting South Africa and had gone on a tour of South Africa (in the apartheid era when it was ruled by a white minority). Until 1994, South Africa was ruled by a white minority and non-whites were not permitted to vote. Since the late 1940s a system of apartheid divided white and non-white South Africans. It was an extremely controversial policy and led to many people, including musicians and athletes, boycotting South Africa. However, some high-profile people did go to South Africa to play music or take part in sporting competitions. This racial divide only ended when Nelson Mandela became President, having been elected in the first election where all adult South Africans were entitled to vote.

In *Wheeler v. Leicester City Council* the House of Lords ruled that the local authority had misused the statutory power under section 71 of the Race Relations Act 1976 to penalise the club. Lord Templeman stated: 'In my opinion, this use by the council of its statutory powers was a misuse of power. The council could not properly seek to use its statutory powers of management or any other statutory powers for the purposes of punishing the club when the club had done no wrong.'[77] In *Wheeler v. Leicester City Council* the House of Lords held that this was illegal as the powers conferred had not been intended to be used in such a way to punish a club. However, the powers could have been lawfully used to prevent a racist group from using its facilities. The House quashed the decision.

In *Porter v. Magill*[78] several members of the conservative controlled Westminster City Council were held to have abused their powers. These councillors had misused their statutory powers to sell council homes by deliberately selling houses in marginal wards in order to gain additional support from voters. The House of Lords was clear that powers conferred by statute must be used only for the purposes for which the power was conferred. Here there had been a politically motivated misuse of power. The House of Lords observed that: 'Sometimes misconduct may consist of a single decision made on behalf of a local authority by an individual acting under delegated powers, the decision being formally correct but invalid because made for improper and legally irrelevant reasons.'[79]

In *R v. Port Talbot Borough Council ex p. Jones*[80] a housing officer was found to have misused his power when allocating housing, because he had given priority to a councillor. Therefore, the power conferred had been used for an improper purpose. Another example is *R v. Somerset CC ex p. Fewings*[81] where a decision was taken to ban hunting on the local authority's land. The Court of Appeal held that the decision had to be based on the local authority's statutory power and banning hunting solely because it was considered morally repugnant amounted to an improper purpose.

An interesting example of a local authority using its powers to pursue a policy is the House of Lords' decision in *Roberts v. Hopwood*[82]. Here section 62 of the Metropolis Management Act 1855 stated that the local authority, 'shall . . .

employ . . . such . . . servants as may be necessary, and may allow to such . . . servants . . . such . . . wages as (the Council) may think fit.' The local authority used their power under section 62 to introduce a minimum wage for both female and male employees. The House of Lords held that the statutory power had been used for an improper purpose as it was not the intention of Parliament that section 62 would be used to introduce a minimum wage. Rather it was there to ensure that the local authority could perform its services. Lord Atkinson was clear the use of the council's statutory powers to pay such a wage to all employees was a breach of the fiduciary duty that the council owed to the ratepayers and an improper purpose:

> The council would, in my view, fail in their duty if, in administering funds which did not belong to their members alone, they put aside all these aids to the ascertainment of what was just and reasonable remuneration to give for the services rendered to them, and allowed themselves to be guided in preference by some eccentric principles of socialistic philanthropy, or by a feminist ambition to secure the equality of the sexes in the matter of wages in the world of labour.[83]

PUBLIC LAW IN CONTEXT
R (ON THE APPLICATION OF BANCOULT) V SECRETARY OF STATE FOR FOREIGN AND COMMONWEALTH AFFAIRS (NO.3)

In *R (on the application of Bancoult) v Secretary of State for Foreign and Commonwealth Affairs (No.3)*[84] it was argued that the creation of a Marine Protected Area by the Foreign Secretary around the British Indian Ocean Territory, otherwise known as the Chagos Islands, was undertaken for an improper purpose, that is to prevent the resettlement of the Chagossians, who had been removed from their homeland in the late 1960s and early 1970s. The Chagos islanders had been removed so the British government could allow the United States to construct a military base on Diego Garcia, which was the largest island in the territory. The islanders had been arguing to return home for many years and Mr Bancoult, who had been born on the Chagos Islands, had been involved with legal action against the British government since the late 1990s. Mr Bancoult's legal team had relied on purported diplomatic cables that had been published by Wikileaks, that purported to record a meeting at the US Embassy with the British official, Mr Colin Roberts, who was responsible for the Chagos Islands. The cable recorded the discussion with the British official purported to have said:'

> Roberts stated that according to the HGM's [*sic*] current thinking on a reserve, there would be no 'human footprints' or 'Man Fridays' on the BIOT's uninhabited islands. He asserted that establishing a marine park would, in effect, put paid to resettlement claims of the archipelago's former residents. . . . Establishing a marine reserve might indeed, as

FCO's Roberts stated, be the most effective long-term way to prevent any of the Chagos Islands' former inhabitants or their descendants from resettling in the BIOT.

Bancoult's legal team had argued that this gave rise to an improper purpose for the creation of the Marine Protected Area. The Court of Appeal had previously rejected the argument that the Marine Protected Area was created for an improper purpose.[85] The Court of Appeal were clear that the decision to create the Marine Protected Area was the Foreign Secretary's, and that:

> For the claimant's case on improper purpose to be right a truly remarkable set of circumstances would have to have existed. Somewhere deep in government a long-term decision would have to have been taken to frustrate Chagossian ambitions by promoting the MPA. Both the administrator of the territory in which it was to be declared, Ms Yeadon, and the person who made the decision, the Foreign Secretary, would have to have been kept in ignorance of the true purpose. Someone – Mr Roberts? – would have been the only relevant official to have known the truth. He, and whoever else was privy to the secret, must then have decided to promote a measure which could not achieve their purpose, for the reasons explained above, while explaining to all concerned that the MPA would have to be reconsidered in the light of an adverse judgment of the Strasbourg Court. Those circumstances would provide an unconvincing plot for a novel. They cannot found a finding for the claimant on this issue.[86]

A majority of the Supreme Court were of the view that the Marine Protected Area was not created for an improper purpose. In his judgment Lord Mance was sceptical about the accuracy of the purported cables and what they purported to show Mr Colin Roberts saying: 'On the face of it, it seems very unlikely that a British civil servant would have disclosed an improper motivation of this nature, rather than have been outlining the practical consequences of an MPA which is what would have concerned the Americans.'[87] Lord Mance was of the view that even *if* we could imagine that the civil servant had an improper purpose in supporting the creation of the Marine Protected Area, then this did not make the Secretary of State's decision improper, as it was made independently of any purported improper purpose. It is interesting to consider what Lord Mance said:

> The final matter for consideration on this basis is whether any relevance could attach to improper motivation on the part of one or more civil servants, when there is no indication whatever that it shaped or in any way influenced ministerial thinking. The answer must in my opinion be negative. If the Secretary of State as the ultimate decision-maker, the actual decision-making process and the decision were unaffected by an improper motive held by a civil servant, on a proposal bound because of its significance to be put up to the Secretary of State, the decision can and should stand by itself. That would on all the evidence be the present position, even if one assumes that the cable discloses, or would if deployed have led to a conclusion, that there was, some improper motivation on the part of Mr Roberts and/or Ms Yeadon in (or after) May 2009.[88]

Lord Kerr dissented from the majority of the Supreme Court. His Lordship was of the opinion that you could not say a purported underlining improper purpose would have no influence on the Secretary of State when making his decision to create the Marine Protected Area. Therefore, at the original hearing the civil servants needed to be cross-examined on what was purported to be contained within the purported US diplomatic cable.

> The circumstance that the decision to make the MPA rested with the minister does not immunise the process by which that decision was made from the possible taint of improper motive. If those who advised the minister were actuated by such a motive but tailored their advice to the minister so as to conceal it, the fact that the minister took the decision does not render the underlying collateral purpose of no consequence. The contrast between the advice given to the minister and the contents of the cable incidentally reinforces the need for an unrestrained cross examination of the witnesses, particularly because, as Lord Mance observed in para 40, the Divisional Court did not address the contradiction in the evidence of Mr Roberts and that of Ms Yeadon as to whether the former did in fact say that an MPA would put paid to resettlement.[89]
>
> Lord Mance has suggested (in paras 41–43) that even if Mr Roberts and/or Ms Yeadon had an improper motive, there is no conceivable reason to conclude that this affected the ultimate decision-maker. I am afraid that I cannot agree. True it is, as the Court of Appeal observed in para 91 of its judgment, that the decision was personal to the Foreign Secretary. True it may also be, as the Court of Appeal found, that the Foreign Secretary believed that the declaration of an MPA would 'redound to the credit of the government and, perhaps, to his own credit', although I am not at all clear as to the evidence on which the court drew to support that conclusion. But, if the minister had been aware that the civil servants were recommending the establishment of an MPA with the covert purpose of ensuring that the Chagos Islanders' ambition to return to their homeland would never be fulfilled, can it be said that his decision would be immune from challenge? Surely not.[90]

The Prime Minister was alleged to have been motivated by an improper purpose when he advised the monarch to prorogue Parliament in 2019. This was accepted as correct by the Inner House in its judgment, finding that the Prime Minister purpose was to stymy Parliament's attempts to hold the executive to account.[91] The Supreme Court in *R (on the application of Miller) v Prime Minister (No.2)*[92] accepted that the decision to prorogue Parliament was unlawful; however it did not rule on the Prime Minister's motive, just the affect that prorogation would have inter alia on parliamentary accountability.

There is a risk that where power is given to do X in order to achieve Y, that the decision-maker will do X, but will do so in order to achieve Z. It might appear that if X is done, then why should the purpose matter? However, it is important that the power is used for the purpose intended by Parliament, as

Consider power given to decision maker	Has decision maker acted within literal reading of powers?	Has decision maker used powers but for an improper purpose?
• Statutory or prerogative powers	• If yes continue, if no equates to simple ultra vires	• Consider why power has been given to the decision maker.

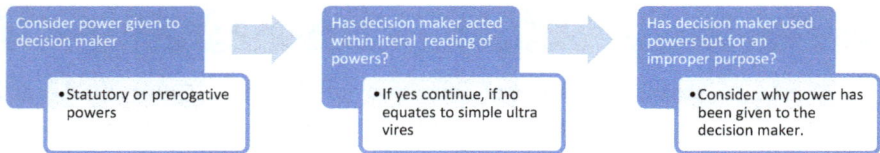

Figure 16.5
Using powers for an improper purpose

otherwise a decision-maker could be pursuing its own policy, i.e. punishing those who defy its policies on playing sport in a particular country. It matters because the power should only be used for the purpose for which it was given; otherwise, the power is open for abuse, whether it is political (*Porter v. Magill*), or is being exercised to benefit associates (*Ex p. Jones*).

16.4.4 Delegation of discretion

If a decision-maker has statutory powers to make a decision regarding a particular subject-matter, is he able to delegate the actual decision-making to another person (see Figure 16.5)? In a government department a minister can delegate powers to civil servants. Where this delegation occurs, the validity of the civil servant's decision cannot be challenged on the grounds that there has been unauthorised delegation. This is because the civil servant is considered the minister's alter-ego. This is known as the *Carltona* principle and was established by the Court of Appeal in *Carltona Ltd v. Commissioners of Works*[93]. When we consider the sheer size of modern government departments, it would be completely unrealistic to expect the minister in charge of that department to make every decision. Therefore, a minister may delegate a decision to a civil servant, even where statute expressly delegates discretionary powers to him.

It should be remembered that where a civil servant makes a decision which has negative consequences (such as resulting in a scandal which affects the minister's department), that the minister depending on the circumstances should take responsibility. In Chapter 8 we explored the convention of individual ministerial responsibility and the role it served in holding the government to account. However, government departments can be very large and employ many people. For example, the Home Office (or Home Department) is responsible for security, counter-terrorism, immigration and passports, the police and the criminal records bureau. In 2010, there were over 27,000 civil servants working for the Home Office.

16.4.4.1 Is there any limitation on who a minister can delegate to?

In *R v. Governor of Brixton Prison ex p. Enahoro*[94] the Home Secretary had the power to deport fugitives under section 7 of the Fugitive Offenders Act 1881. The Home Secretary ordered a fugitive to be deported to Nigeria. However, a

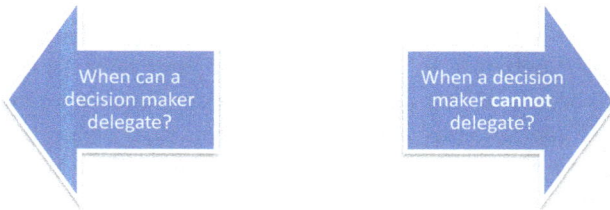

Figure 16.6
When can a decision-maker delegate his discretion?

deputation from Parliament asked that the Home Secretary reconsider his decision. Consequently, it was argued that the Home Secretary had unlawfully delegated his discretionary powers to Parliament. In his judgment Lord Parker CJ stated that:

- A person making a judicial decision cannot delegate the decision-making.
- In certain types of administrative decisions the decision-maker has no power to delegate the actual decision-making.

Parker CJ categorised the decision as an administrative decision with no power to delegate. However, His Lordship did not find that the Home Secretary had delegated the decision to Parliament. All that the Home Secretary was doing was listening to Parliament's opinion and he was permitted to take this into consideration when he made his decision. His Lordship stated:

> I think, to be realistic, he was inviting Parliament to express a view as to whether his decision that it was just was the view also of the majority of the House. . . . [T]here is no reason why he should not invite the expression of further opinion, and, if influenced by it, change his mind. Looked at in that way, I cannot see that by inviting Parliament or by allowing Parliament to express an opinion on his decision, he was in any way surrendering or sharing with Parliament what was his statutory responsibility.[95]

The issue of whether the Home Secretary could delegate his power to deport an individual arose again in *R v. Secretary of State for the Home Department ex p. Oladehinde*[96]. The decision whether to deport immigrants under section 3 of the Immigration Act 1971 had been delegated to immigration inspectors. The House of Lords ruled that the Home Secretary could delegate this power to suitably senior and qualified immigration inspectors, even if they were not classified as civil servants working within his department, but rather employed under statutory powers. The House of Lords made reference to Parliament's intention and found that there was no implied limitation on the Home Secretary's power to delegate.

An example of a decision-maker exercising a judicial function occurred in *R v. Secretary of State for the Home Department ex p. Doody*[97]. Here the Home Secretary had the statutory discretion to determine the sentence tariff for a life prisoner. The House of Lords held that despite the sentencing decision being a judicial function, the Home Secretary could delegate the actual decision-making, but only to a junior minister within the Home Department. Therefore, the exercise of a judicial function will restrict the *Carltona* principle.

Finally, a minister cannot delegate his statutory discretionary powers to a minister responsible for another government department. Although, it is possible to seek advice from that minister before reaching the decision.[98]

16.4.5 Fettering of discretion

We have seen that there are limitations on who a decision-maker can delegate his powers to. If a decision-maker has discretionary powers then it is important that he exercises this discretion properly. It is not valid to fetter (i.e. restrict your discretion), as Parliament has given the decision-maker discretion and intends that the discretion will be properly exercised.

In *R v. Port of London Authority ex p. Kynoch Ltd*[99] the court held that there would be nothing wrong in an authority adopting a policy for legitimate reasons and refusing to hear someone making an application which fell outside the policy, unless there is something exceptional regarding his application. This would not amount to a fettering of discretion, because there is always scope for the decision-maker to take into account exceptional circumstances. However, there will be fettering of discretion if the decision-maker refuses to ever listen to and consider any application which falls outside their policy. We can see that a decision-maker when exercising their discretionary powers will adopt a policy to help him apply his discretion in a consistent and fair way. The decision of the Board of Trade in refusing an investment grant was challenged in *British Oxygen Co Ltd v. Minister of Technology*[100]. The Board of Trade had a policy that it would not consider applications where the cost of the units was under £25. British Oxygen's application was refused because its units cost £20 each. The Court of Appeal held that there was nothing wrong with the Board of Trade adopting a policy, but that they must be willing to consider exceptions to their general policy. Karminski LJ held that a policy could be lawfully adopted but that the decision-maker must always be willing to keep the door ajar. If the policy permitted no flexibility, then it would amount to an unlawful fettering of discretion:

> As a matter of law there is nothing to prevent the Board of Trade adopting or publishing such a policy, providing that it is ready to consider reasons in suitable cases for departing from that policy. . . . I do not think that in the present case the Board of Trade, though they may seek to adhere to their policy decision, have closed the door on reconsidering the application on its merits in the exercise of their discretion. In my view declaration is wrong and should be set aside.[101]

16.4.6 Irrelevant and relevant considerations

When reaching his decision, what considerations should the decision-maker take into account? Conversely, what considerations are irrelevant and should not be taken into account? This is a question for the courts and a decision can be challenged where improper considerations have been taken into account. This is because when Parliament gives a minister statutory powers to determine policy, it will often state that in reaching a decision the minister must consider all relevant considerations.

The decision of the council in *R v. Somerset CC ex p. Fewings*[102] was challenged because the decision-maker had taken into account the consideration of preventing animal cruelty. The Court of Appeal held that animal cruelty could be a relevant consideration, but that the decision was invalid as the local authority had failed to take into account relevant statutory considerations. The Court of Appeal held that the decision-maker's moral views as to the repugnancy of stag hunting were an irrelevant consideration. The decision was quashed by the Court of Appeal. In order to determine what considerations should be taken into account, it will depend on whether the statute expressly states that a consideration must be taken into account, must not be taken into account or that it gives the decision-maker the discretion to take into account 'yet to be identified' (or implied) considerations.[103]

In *CREEDNZ Inc. v. Governor-General*[104] Cooke J considered the correct approach:

> What has to be emphasised is that it is only when the statute expressly or impliedly identifies considerations required to be taken into account by the authority as a matter of legal obligation that the court holds a decision invalid on the ground now invoked. It is not enough that a consideration is one that may properly be taken into account, nor even that it is one which many people, including the court itself, would have taken into account if they had to make the decision.[105]

PUBLIC LAW IN PRACTICE

The Airport Expansion Act 2021 (fictitious) repeals all existing statutes relating to the power to expand airports and gives the Secretary of State for Transport the power to decide whether to expand airports in England and Wales. Section 13(2) of the Act states, 'In deciding whether to expand an airport the minister must take into account the view of local authorities, other government infrastructure and transport projects and environmental policy and all other relevant considerations.' Lutchester Airport Ltd is seeking to expand and the Secretary of State has refused its application. The Secretary of State has reached his decision after considering the fact that Lutchester Airport is located next to Downville House and the increased flights would disturb visitors, and as a new airport will be built 50 miles away there is no need to expand Lutchester Airport. Lutchester Borough Council is annoyed as it was not consulted about this decision. We can see that the Secretary of State took into account the effect that airport expansion would have on visitors to Downville House. This would be an irrelevant consideration. He had failed to take into account the views of the local authority which was a relevant consideration. However, he did take into account a relevant consideration which was government transport projects, i.e. the construction of a new airport.

16.4.7 Errors of law and fact

The courts can review a decision where the decision-maker has made a mistake as to the facts. Judicial review is permitted where the decision-maker wrongly believes the facts permitted him to make a decision. This is known as error of precedent fact or jurisdictional error. The question here is whether the decision-maker has made an error of law and does not legally have the power to make the decision. In *Anisminic v. Foreign Compensation Commission*[106] the decision-maker was held to have made an error of law, as there had been a misinterpretation as to the criteria for compensation. The error could be reviewed.

Errors of fact which are material to the decision reached can also be reviewed by the courts. This is because there was no evidence to support the decision. In *R v. Criminal Injuries Compensation Board, ex p. A*[107], A was a victim of rape and other sexual offences and had applied for compensation from the Criminal Injuries Compensation Board (CICB). The CICB had informed A that she would have to prove that she was a victim of a violent crime. The CICB held that A had not demonstrated this. When the CICB reached its decision it had not been shown a report which suggested that the injuries caused to A's rectum were consistent with buggery. Although the burden was on A to establish that she was a victim of violent crime, the CICB's decision was quashed because it had not requested appropriate evidence from the police and therefore its decision amounted to an error of fact.

In *R (Connolly) v. Havering LBC*[108] the Court of Appeal quashed the decision of a planning inspector, who had granted planning permission and was under the mistaken belief that she was in possession of the full history of the site. The Court of Appeal applied the approach from *E v. Secretary of State for the Home Department*[109] and quashed the decision because it is clear that the fact was not contentious and that it was objectively verifiable, and the applicant challenging the decision was not responsible for the mistake and that the mistake proved material in the decision-maker's reasoning.

16.5 Legitimate expectation as a ground for judicial review

A decision can also be reviewed where the applicant had a legitimate expectation that the decision-maker would exercise his powers in a certain way.

Legitimate expectations can be procedural or substantive. A legitimate expectation is procedural where it is expected that a procedure will be followed in a particular way, and it is substantive where it is expected that a particular decision will be reached.

The term *legitimate expectation* originated from the judgment of Lord Denning MR in *Schmidt v. Secretary of State for Home Affairs*[110]. Lord Denning had stated that an administrative decision-maker could be bound to allow a person affected by his decision to make representations. However, '[i]t all depends on whether he has some right or interest, or, I would add, some legitimate expectation, of which it would not be fair to deprive him without hearing what he has to say.'[111] We shall see that there is an overlap here with procedural fairness.

Procedural legitimate expectation relates to a policy or practice which gives the claimant an unambiguous and clear representation that the decision-maker will follow a policy in exercising his powers. To put it another way, the claimant should not be in any doubt what the decision-maker meant. In *Council of Civil Service Unions and Others v. Minister for the Civil Service* [GCHQ][112] the trade unions representing civil servants working at GCHQ (the government agency responsible for intelligence gathering) challenged the decision of the Prime Minister, in her capacity as Minister for the Civil Service, to prevent civil servants from being members of trade unions. The decision was taken without consulting employees or trade unions. The trade unions argued that the long-term practice of consultation had created a procedural legitimate expectation that consultation would be carried out before a decision such as this would be taken. The House of Lords held that the decision was unfair because of the lack of consultation and that there had been a legitimate expectation that there would be consultation. However, national security considerations could outweigh the need to give effect to the legitimate expectation. Therefore, the decision not to consult was valid.

In *Attorney General of Hong Kong v. Ng Yuen Shiu*[113] the Hong Kong government had issued a policy which stated that before deporting illegal immigrants who had entered Hong Kong, each immigrant would be invited to make representations before the decision to deport them would be taken. The government of Hong Kong decided to deport the claimant without inviting him to a hearing. Lord Fraser stated that:

> The justification for (making the decision-maker honour its promise) is primarily that, when a public authority has promised to follow a certain procedure, it is in the interest of good administration that it should act fairly and should implement its promise, so long as implementation does not interfere with its statutory duty.[114]

Here there was nothing to justify not honouring the claimant's legitimate expectation, as the consultation and hearing were not inconsistent with the government's statutory duties.

A clear and unambiguous representation can also create a substantive legitimate expectation, which rather than stating that a policy will be followed, will instead amount to an undertaking that the decision-maker will exercise his powers in a particular way. In *R v. North and East Devon Health Authority ex p. Coughlan*[115] the Court of Appeal held that a decision to close a nursing home and move the residents elsewhere was unfair and would not be permitted by the court. The residents had been promised that they would have a home for life at the premises and this was held to amount to a clear and unambiguous representation, which created a substantive legitimate expectation. Therefore, the decision-maker was prevented from going back on this previous promise because there was no overriding public interest which justified the change of policy. It was held that:

> Where the court considers that a lawful promise or practice has induced a legitimate expectation of a benefit which is substantive, not simply procedural, authority now establishes that here too the court will in a proper case decide whether to frustrate the expectation is so unfair that to take a new and different course will amount to an abuse of power. Here, once the legitimacy of the expectation is established, the court will have the task of weighing the requirements of fairness against any overriding interest relied upon for the change of policy.[116]

On balance in *Ex p. Coughlan* there was no overriding public interest to justify the decision-maker changing its policy. The reasons stated by the Court of Appeal were:

- the importance of the promise which had been made to the residents;
- the promise had only been made to a few residents and not to a large number of people; and
- there would only be financial consequences in forcing the decision-maker to honour its promise.

The unfairness in the decision made by the decision-maker to go back on its promise amounted to an abuse of power and the decision could be quashed by the court. However, it must be noted that substantive legitimate expectation operates on a limited basis.

16.5.1 Could a pre-election promise give rise to a legitimate expectation?

In *R v. Secretary of State for Education and Employment ex p. Begbie*[117] a child had been offered a place at an independent school under a state-funded scheme. After the 1997 General Election the Labour government decided to end the scheme. The Secretary of State decided to stop funding the education of children beyond the age of 11. It was argued that the child had a legitimate expectation that their schooling would be funded by the state until they reached the age of 18. This was because the Labour party in its pre-election manifesto had stated that whilst it would end the scheme, it would permit children currently on the scheme to continue to be funded. This position had been confirmed by the local MP who had received confirmation of this from the then Shadow Secretary of State. This argument was rejected by the Court of Appeal because a pre-election promise could not be regarded as giving rise to a legitimate expectation.

Five propositions regarding legitimate expectation were accepted by the Court of Appeal:

1   'the rule that a public authority should not defeat a person's legitimate expectation is an aspect of the rule that it must act fairly and reasonably';
2   'the rule operates in the field of substantive as well as procedural rights';
3   'the categories of unfairness are not closed';
4   'the making of an unambiguous and unqualified representation is a sufficient, but not necessary, trigger of the duty to act fairly'; and
5   'it is not necessary for a person to have changed his position as a result of such representations for an obligation to fulfil a legitimate expectation to subsist.'[118]

The Court of Appeal accepted that substantive and procedural rights can be protected; therefore, the courts can compel a decision-maker to exercise his power in a certain way to give effect to a promise made. The need for an unambiguous and unqualified representation is important to establish legitimate expectation, but its absence may not be fatal to a claim. Finally, detrimental reliance by the claimant is not required. However, Peter Gibson LJ was clear that reliance must not be understated as '[i]t is very much the exception, rather than the rule, that detrimental reliance will not be present when the court finds unfairness in the defeating of a legitimate expectation.'[119]

16.5.2 Will a lack of detriment be fatal?

In *R (on the application of Bibi) v. Newham London Borough Council*[120] the applicant successfully argued that the decision should be set aside on the ground that their legitimate expectation had not been taken into account. The local authority had wrongly believed that refugees who were homeless were entitled to security of tenure. This had been communicated to the applicant. The Court of Appeal held that detrimental reliance was not a perquisite to establish a legitimate expectation. The reason for this according to Schiemann LJ was that:

> To disregard the legitimate expectation because no concrete detriment can be shown would be to place the weakest in society at a particular disadvantage. It would mean that those who have a choice and the means to exercise it in reliance on some official practice or promise would gain a legal toehold inaccessible to those who, lacking any means of escape, are compelled simply to place their trust in what has been represented to them.[121]

16.5.3 *The effect of a qualification?*

We can see that legitimate expectation can be created from an unambiguous and unqualified assurance to the applicant. This can be given personally or through a circular, policy or government statement. The claimant in *R (on the application of Bancoult) v. Secretary of State for Foreign and Commonwealth Affairs (No.2)*[122] had argued that the Foreign Secretary had created a legitimate expectation that the Chagos islanders would be allowed to return home to their homeland. The islanders had previously been deported by the British authorities to permit the building of a United States airbase on the largest island, Diego Garcia. After the Divisional Court ruled against the government, the Foreign Secretary had stated in a press notice:

> [t]he work we are doing on the feasibility of resettling the (islanders) now takes on a new importance. We started the feasibility work a year ago and are now well underway with phase two of the study. Furthermore, we will put in place a new Immigration Ordinance which will allow the (islanders) to return to the outer islands while observing our Treaty obligations. This Government has not defended what was done or said 30 years ago.[123]

The majority of the House of Lords held that this public statement did not amount to a legitimate expectation and the government would not be prevented from changing its policy. According to Lord Carswell this was because there was an on-going feasibility study about resettling the islanders and therefore, the statement could not be regarded as unequivocal. His Lordship noted that that the Foreign Secretary's press statement was directed to a large number of people and was 'not an assurance directed towards one individual or a small number of people, whereas in Coughlan . . . the Court of Appeal regarded such a limitation as a significant feature in favour of the applicant's claim.'[124] The relevance of this is that the impact of forcing the government to be bound by the press notice would have a significant impact on resources.

Lord Carswell also noted that, 'if the Government were obliged to resettle the Chagossians, the consequences could be more than financial, as it could give rise to friction with the United States.'[125] This is important because the Court of Appeal in Coughlan had stated that a legitimate expectation needed to be balanced against the public interest in permitting the decision-maker to depart from its promise. As we have seen in *Coughlan*, the Court of Appeal stated that because the only consequences were financial there was no public interest to prevent the decision-maker honouring its promise of a home for life. Whereas, in *Bancoult*, the enforcement of the press notice would have significant foreign policy considerations. The minority in *Bancoult* argued that the Foreign Secretary's press notice could give rise to a legitimate expectation as it was capable of amounting to a clear and unambiguous representation. Lord Bingham argued that the notice was 'devoid of relevant qualification' and that '[t]he Government could not lawfully resile from its representation without compelling reason, which was not shown.'[126] In any event, His Lordship held that the claimant did not need to demonstrate that there had been detrimental reliance.

16.5.4 Judicial consideration of how a legitimate expectation would arise

Laws LJ in *R (Bhatt Murphy) v Independent Assessor*[127] was clear that in his opinion 'The doctrine of substantive legitimate expectation plainly cannot apply to every case where a public authority operates a policy over an appreciable period. That would expand the doctrine far beyond its proper limits.'[128] The Supreme Court *In the matter of an application by Geraldine Finucane for Judicial Review (Northern Ireland)*[129] considered the case law on legitimate expectations and observed that:

> [I]t can be deduced that where a clear and unambiguous undertaking has been made, the authority giving the undertaking will not be allowed to depart from it unless it is shown that it is fair to do so. The court is the arbiter of fairness in this context. And a matter sounding on the question of fairness is whether the alteration in policy frustrates any reliance which the person or group has placed on it. This is quite different, in my opinion, from saying that it is a prerequisite of a substantive legitimate expectation claim that the person relying on it must show that he or she has suffered a detriment.[130]

It is the task of party seeking to establish that there was a legitimate expectation to show that there was a representation. In *Paponette v Attorney General of Trinidad and Tobago*[131] Lord Dyson was clear that,

> The initial burden lies on an applicant to prove the legitimacy of his expectation. This means that in a claim based on a promise, the applicant must prove the promise and that it was clear and unambiguous and devoid of relevant qualification. If he wishes to reinforce his case by saying that he relied on the promise to his detriment, then obviously he must prove that too.[132]

In *R (on the application of Sandiford) v Secretary of State for Foreign and Commonwealth Affairs*[133] the applicant was unsuccessful in arguing that the refusal to pay her legal fees when facing execution in Indonesia did not amount to a breach of legitimate expectations, this was the case because there was a clear policy which said who would and would not be assisted, and she was not within the category of individuals who would be assisted. Recently in *R (on the application of RD (A Child)) v Worcestershire CC*[134] the court considered whether there was a legitimate expectation in respect of a benefit that was taken away in breach of a promise made to a limited number of individuals. The court was clear that in the circumstances, 'The strength and weight to be attached to the promise is substantial' and

> Recognising the legitimate expectation is consistent with, and reflects, the principles that public authorities should not act arbitrarily and should implement their stated policies unless they determine, on a rational basis, not to do so, or that the relevant policy should be withdrawn, amended or replaced.[135]

16.5.5 The risk that a decision-maker will fetter their discretion

If the courts prevent the decision-maker from changing a policy or from going back on a promise, then this approach would risk fettering the decision-maker's discretion.

16.6 Procedural impropriety as a ground for judicial review

Procedural impropriety requires that the procedure used to make a decision must be fair. The level of fairness will depend on the type of decision which is being made. We shall see that procedural impropriety will be a ground for judicial review where it is alleged that one of the requirements is missing. Lord Diplock in *Council of Civil Service Unions and Others v. Minister for the Civil Service [GCHQ]*[136] had stated that procedural impropriety was a ground for judicial review:

> I have described the third head as 'procedural impropriety' rather than failure to observe basic rules of natural justice or failure to act with procedural fairness towards the person who will be affected by the decision. This is because susceptibility to judicial review under this head covers also failure by an administrative tribunal to observe procedural rules that are expressly laid down in the legislative instrument by which its jurisdiction is conferred, even where such failure does not involve any denial of natural justice.[137]

His Lordship was clear that this ground was wider than just the obligation to observe the common law requirements of natural justice or procedural fairness. The common law has developed the concept of natural justice and the requirements needed to ensure the decision is fair.

16.6.1 Should natural justice apply to administrative decisions?

The controversial decision in *Local Government Board v. Arlidge*[138] concerned the exercise of statutory powers under the Housing, Town Planning Act

1909, which permitted the local authority to declare a dwelling-house unfit for human habitation. A person affected by a decision made pursuant to the Act appealed. The Board dismissed the appeal without allowing the appellant to be heard orally before reaching its decision, or without permitting the appellant to see its report. The House of Lords was clear that natural justice did not extend to administrative decisions. The decision-maker must comply with his statutory duties, but other than complying with the statute, the procedure it adopted was a matter for the decision-maker. Lord Shaw's judgment in *Local Government Board v. Arlidge* stated that the courts should not impose the requirements of natural justice which arose when legal issues were determined to be administrative decision-making. His Lordship stated:

> Judicial methods may, in many points of administration, be entirely unsuitable, and produce delays, expense, and public and private injury. The department must obey the statute. For instance, in the present case it must hold a public local inquiry, and upon a point of law it must have a decision of the Law Courts. . . . [I]f administration is to be beneficial and effective, it must be the master of its own procedure.[139]

We can see that His Lordship had acknowledged that there were some basic requirements for the procedure which the decision-maker had adopted. The decision-maker must permit both sides to speak before reaching its decision: 'For it must always be borne in mind that its procedure if not in defiance of elementary standards – say, by hearing one side and refusing to hear the other – is simply the plan which it adopts to satisfy itself that the decision come to by a local authority was a good or a bad decision.'[140] Lord Shaw had criticised the Court of Appeal for applying judicial standards to an administrative decision, as this approach was regarded as a usurpation of the decision-maker's role by the courts.

16.6.2 Natural justice applies to both judicial and administrative decisions

The House of Lords decision in *Ridge v. Baldwin*[141] is an important one because their Lordships held that the requirements for natural justice applied to administrative decisions, rather than just judicial or quasi-judicial decisions. A Chief Constable had been charged with conspiracy to obstruct the course of justice and had been acquitted by a jury. Nonetheless, as a result of negative comments made by the trial judge regarding the Chief Constable's character, the watch committee decided to dismiss him. The majority of the House of Lords held that the decision to dismiss him was void because of the failure to observe the rules of natural justice. This was because the watch committee had not informed the Chief Constable of the charges against him and he was not allowed a chance to be heard.

In *Ridge v. Baldwin* the House of Lords held that natural justice applied to an administrative decision. Lord Hodson had stated: 'The cases seem to me to show that persons acting in a capacity which is not on the face of it judicial but rather executive or administrative have been held by the courts to be subject to the principles of natural justice.'[142]

Lord Devlin had observed that:

> I do not find it necessary to determine whether before 1919 the power to dismiss for neglect of duty could be exercised administratively and without any sort of judicial inquiry. Nor do I need to decide whether or not the power to dismiss for inadequacy is purely administrative. I am satisfied that in all matters to which the regulations apply the power to dismiss must be exercised in accordance with them.[143]

16.6.3 Right to a fair hearing

Natural justice means that when the decision-maker exercises his decision-making powers the procedure used to reach this decision must be fair. A decision, or hearing to decide the issue, must be carried out in a fair way.

PUBLIC LAW IN CONTEXT
ARTICLE 6 OF THE ECHR

Article 6(1) of the European Convention on Human Rights (ECHR) states that: 'In the determination of his civil rights and obligations or of any criminal charge against him, everyone is entitled to a fair and public hearing within a reasonable time by an independent and impartial tribunal established by law.'

Article 6(3) ECHR outlines the minimum rights of someone charged with a criminal offence. These are:

1 to be informed promptly, in a language which he understands and in detail, of the nature and cause of the accusation against him;
2 to have adequate time and the facilities for the preparation of his defence;
3 to defend himself in person or through legal assistance of his own choosing or, if he has not sufficient means to pay for legal assistance, to be given it free when the interests of justice so require;
4 to examine or have examined witnesses against him and to obtain the attendance and examination of witnesses on his behalf under the same conditions as witnesses against him;
5 to have the free assistance of an interpreter if he cannot understand or speak the language used in court.

We can see that in both civil and criminal matters decisions reached using procedures which are not fair will breach Article 6. We are concerned here with administrative decisions and the requirements of natural justice. It should be noted that the decision and the consequences for a person affected by it will be important factors when the courts determine the extent of the requirements needed to satisfy natural justice.

The chapter is concerned with common law requirements, rather than the statutory requirements. If statute requires the procedure to be carried out in a certain way then this procedure must be followed. In *Agricultural, Horticultural and Forestry Industry Training Board v Aylesbury Mushrooms*[144] the issue was that the minister had failed to consult a growers association before establishing the training board. The requirement to consult was required by section 1(4) of the Industrial Training Act 1964.

16.6.4 The extent of fairness required?

Lord Bridge in *Lloyd v. McMahon*[145] observed that 'the so-called rules of natural justice are not engraved on tablets of stone.' The level of fairness required will depend on the type of decision and the circumstances behind it. In *McInnes v. Onslow Fane*[146] Meggary VC observed that there was a distinction between a person who had made an application which was then refused, and on the other hand where someone had been granted a right and this right was now being revoked. In revocation cases the applicant was entitled to notices of the charges against him and the right to be heard at a hearing. We can see that there is a sliding scale of what is required by the requirement of procedural fairness.

The level of fairness required was considered by the House of Lords in *R v. Secretary of State for the Home Department ex p. Doody*.[147] This case concerned prisoners who were serving a mandatory life sentence. The Home Secretary fixed the period which each prisoner would have to serve until their imprisonment could be reviewed. The Home Secretary had consulted the trial judge and the Lord Chief Justice for their recommendations, but had not revealed these recommendations to the prisoners and had not given the prisoners an opportunity to make representations before he reached his decision. The House of Lords in *Ex p. Doody* quashed the Home Secretary's decision and held that the prisoners were entitled to:

- make written representations;
- know the judicial recommendations; and
- know the reasons why the Home Secretary had chosen not to follow the judicial recommendations.

Lord Mustill stated, 'The only issue is whether the way in which the scheme is administered falls below the minimum standard of fairness.'[148] According to Lord Mustill, the key question for the court will be to determine, '[w]hat does fairness require in the present case?'[149] His Lordship outlined six propositions from established case law:

1   Where an Act of Parliament confers an administrative power there is a presumption that it will be exercised in a manner which is fair in all the circumstances.
2   The standards of fairness are not immutable. They may change with the passage of time, both in the general and in their application to decisions of a particular type.
3   The principles of fairness are not to be applied by rote identically in every situation. What fairness demands is dependent on the context of the decision, and this is to be taken into account in all its aspects.
4   An essential feature of the context is the statute which creates the discretion, as regards both its language and the shape of the legal and administrative system within which the decision is taken.
5   Fairness will very often require that a person who may be adversely affected by the decision will have an opportunity to make representations on his own behalf either before the decision is taken with a view to producing a favourable result; or after it is taken, with a view to procuring its modification; or both.
6   Since the person affected usually cannot make worthwhile representations without knowing what factors may weigh against his interests, fairness will very often require that he is informed of the gist of the case which he has to answer.'[150]

It is clear that the common law will require a decision-maker to exercise the power given to him fairly. Fairness will not demand the same procedural requirements for every decision. Each decision, depending on the circumstances, will require differing requirements to meet the minimum level of fairness required. Lord Mustill held that a life prisoner would have the right to make representations to the Home Secretary before the decision was reached. His Lordship acknowledged that there is no general duty to give reasons for an administrative decision. However, the circumstances of the decisions might imply such a right. His Lordship, given the seriousness of the decision, considered that there was an implied right here.

The requirements of common law fairness were considered in *R (on the application of Manchester College of Higher Education and Media Technology Ltd) v. Secretary of State for the Home Department*[151]. The case concerned the suspension of the claimant's licence to sponsor overseas students. The factors identified by Lord Mustill in *Ex p. Doody* were considered, especially the point that the level of fairness would depend on the circumstances. It was held that where a decision was taken to suspend the claimant's licence without prior consultation then there would be a breach of the common law duty of fairness. Mr Justice Pelling QC stated, 'that the common law rule of fairness required in the circumstances of this case that the claimant would be consulted before such a draconian step was taken.'[152]

16.6.5 The right to know the case against you and time to prepare your defence

It is important to know the case against you. Unless you are aware of the allegations or alleged breaches, then how can you counter these at the hearing or in written representations? There must be suitable time for a defence to be prepared and sufficient notice should be given before the hearing takes place. In *R v. Thames Magistrates Court ex p. Polemis (The Corinthic)*[153] a ship's master was summoned at 10.30 a.m. to appear before the Magistrates' Court at 2.00 p.m., after there was an accusation that oil had leaked from the vessel. The fact that there had been insufficient time to prepare a defence meant that the defendant had lost the right to be heard.

16.6.6 The right to be heard and to make representations

The right to be heard does not as a general rule entitle the applicant to an oral hearing, as the applicant could put across his representations through written representations. In *R v. Army Board of the Defence Council ex p. Anderson*[154] Taylor LJ stated that the right to make oral representations will depend 'upon the subject matter and circumstances of the particular case and upon the nature of the decision to be made. It will also depend upon whether there are substantial issues of fact which cannot be satisfactorily resolved on the available written evidence.' Whether an oral hearing is required will depend on the subject matter (whether a person is having a right deprived or merely making an application) and whether the court considers that the degree of fairness requires it. Where the level of fairness required is low, then unless there is sufficient evidential ambiguity, written representations can satisfy the minimum requirement of fairness. However, at a hearing there is no general right to legal representation. Lord Denning MR took the view in *Enderby Town Football Club v. Football Association*[155] that: 'In many cases it may be a good thing for the proceedings of a domestic tribunal to be conducted informally without legal representation. Justice can often be done in them better by a good layman than by a bad lawyer.'[156] This is because a good layman might be better than a lawyer at understanding the regulations in dispute.

In *R v. Secretary of State for the Home Department ex p. Tarrant*[157] it was stated that fairness may require legal representation in circumstances which include:

1   the seriousness of the charge faced;
2   whether points of law were likely to arise; or
3   that the prisoner is not competent to present his own case.

16.6.7 The right to know the decision-maker's reasons

In *Ex p. Doody* it was accepted that as a general rule the decision-maker is not required to give reasons for his decision. However, where the decisions concern something as fundamentally important as personal liberty, then reasons must

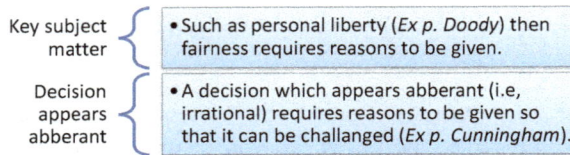

Key subject matter	• Such as personal liberty (*Ex p. Doody*) then fairness requires reasons to be given.
Decision appears abberant	• A decision which appears abberant (i.e, irrational) requires reasons to be given so that it can be challanged (*Ex p. Cunningham*).

Figure 16.7
When must reasons be given?

be given. The Court of Appeal in *R v. Civil Service Appeal Board ex p. Cunningham*[158] had to decide whether the decision-maker was right not to give decisions. The majority held that although there was no general duty at common law to give reasons for why an administrative decision was made, however, where the decision appeared irrational because of the low figure which had been awarded, then a reason as to why the Board had reached this decision must be given. The reduction of a research grant was challenged in *R v. Higher Education Funding Council ex p. Institute of Dental Surgery*[159]. The Council had given no reasons as to why it had decided to reduce the amount of funding. The court held that academic decisions did not generally require reasons to be given. Sedley J clarified the law as to when a decision must be given. Reiterating that at common law there is no general duty to give reasons, he stated that reasons would need to be given in certain circumstances.

Whether reasons will have to be given is a question to be determined on a case by case basis. Even if reasons have to be given then there is no requirement that they are sufficiently detailed. An example of this is *R v. Secretary of State for the Home Department ex p. Al-Fayed (No.1)*[160]. Mr Al-Fayed is an Egyptian national who had lived in the United Kingdom for many years and had been refused a British passport. He is a famous businessman who once owned Harrods, a world-famous department store in Kensington, London. He challenged the decision of the Home Secretary to refuse him a passport. The Court of Appeal in *R v. Secretary of State for the Home Department ex p. Al-Fayed (No.1)* held that although there was no statutory requirement requiring the Home Secretary to give reasons, the Home Secretary must inform the applicant of the areas which weighed against his application. Lord Woolf MR stated that the applicant did not require the full reasons for the refusal, just the areas of concern. This was because the applicant could not argue that the decision was wrong unless he knew the broad areas of concern.

16.7 The rule against bias

Imagine that you have made an application for planning permission to build an extension on your home and the decision whether to allow or reject your application was to be made by a planning committee. The committee is chaired by your next-door neighbour, who had indicated that he objects to his garden being overshadowed by your proposed extension. You are then informed by the committee that your application has been refused. In these circumstances, you could seek to judicially review the decision on the ground that the decision was potentially biased. It is important that in circumstances such as this that decisions made by public bodies are seen to be fair.

In *R v. Sussex Justices ex p. McCarthy*[161] the clerk who was advising the magistrates on a point of law was also a member of the firm of solicitors who were representing one of the parties in the case. The magistrates convicted the other party, and on appeal the court held that his conviction must be quashed. The issue was not whether the clerk has been biased or had advised upon whether to convict, rather it was not proper that he should be acting as a clerk in the circumstances. Lord Hewart CJ stated that:

> [A] long line of cases shows that it is not merely of some importance but is of fundamental importance that justice should not only be done, but should manifestly and undoubtedly be seen to be done. . . . The question therefore is not whether in this case the deputy clerk made any observation or offered any criticism which he might not properly have made or offered; the question is whether he was so related to the case in its civil aspect as to be unfit to act as clerk to the justices in the criminal matter. The answer to that question depends not upon what actually was done but upon what might appear to be done. Nothing is to be done which creates even a suspicion that there has been an improper interference with the course of justice.[162]

It is clear that Lord Hewart CJ was concerned that justice should be seen to be done, rather than whether on the facts it had been done. Citizens must have faith in the legal system and judges cannot be seen to be biased, even if they are not.

The rule that a judge or administrative decision-maker must not be biased and should be seen to be impartial is very important. This is covered by Article 6 of the ECHR.

The Lord Chancellor's judicial role was regarded as potentially being incompatible with Article 6 because of his position in government. This meant that Lord Irvine only sat in cases where there government did not have an interest, so as to avoid the appearance of bias. His successor, Lord Faulkner declared that he would no longer sit as a judge. In Chapter 9 we discussed the importance of judges not being viewed as biased and that judges should be seen to be independent of the government.

16.7.1 Types of bias and consequences on the decision and the decision-maker

Where actual bias is proved then the decision-maker must step down and the decision will be quashed:

• Where the decision-maker has a direct interest in the issues involved, then there will be presumed bias and the decision-maker is automatically disqualified and any decision taken will be quashed.

- Where the decision-maker has an indirect interest in the issues involved, then this will not give rise to automatic disqualification.

We will now look at each of the above in turn and look at examples where the court has had to consider whether the decision-maker was biased. It is important to note that these apply not just to judges, but to other types of decisions made by public bodies, such as government ministers and local authorities. A person affected by an allegation of bias can judicially review the decision.

16.7.2 Actual bias

An example of actual bias would be where it is proved that a judge or administrative decision-maker had taken a bribe. In this case the decision would be quashed as there was clear evidence of bias.

16.7.3 Presumed bias: direct interest

There is no need to prove actual bias, just that the decision-maker has a direct interest in the matter. According to Kate Malleson, 'Once a judge is shown to have a direct interest no examination of the circumstances of the alleged bias will be required and disqualification will follow automatically.'[163] Traditionally, the direct interest needed to be financial. The most famous example of this was the case of *Dimes v. Grand Junction Canal Proprietors*.[164] In this case the Lord Chancellor, Lord Cottenham, had an investment of several thousand pounds in the claimant company. In the 1840s this was a considerable sum. The Lord Chancellor had not declared this interest when he had upheld the decision of the Vice-Chancellor who had ruled in the claimant's favour. The decision was appealed, and the House of Lords held that the Lord Chancellor should have been disqualified because of his direct financial interest and held that his decision be quashed. The question was whether the decision of the Lord Chancellor could be challenged on the grounds of bias? In *Dimes v. Grand Junction Canal Proprietors* Lord Campbell stated that:

> No one can suppose that Lord Cottenham could be, in the remotest degree, influenced by the interest that he had in this concern; but, my Lords, it is of the last importance that the maxim that no man is to be a judge in his own cause should be held sacred. And that is not to be confined to a cause in which he is a party, but applies to a cause in which he has an interest. Since I have had the honour to be Chief Justice of the Court of Queen's Bench, we have again and again set aside proceedings in inferior tribunals because an individual, who had an interest in a cause, took a part in the decision. And it will have a most salutary influence on these tribunals when it is known that this high Court of last resort, in a case in which the Lord Chancellor of England had an interest, considered that his decree was on that account a decree not according to law, and was set aside. This will be a lesson to all inferior tribunals to take care not only that in their

decrees they are not influenced by their personal interest, but to avoid the appearance of labouring under such an influence.[165]

It is worth considering what Lord Campbell was stating here:

- That no one is questioning the Lord Chancellor's integrity nor is anyone saying that he had actual bias.
- The court must prevent any appearance of bias arising from the decision-maker's direct interest in the case.
- No person can be a judge in their own cause.
- This case sets an example at the highest level that decision-makers must be seen to be impartial.

Another important case concerning presumed bias was *R v. Bow Street Metropolitan Stipendiary Magistrate ex p. Pinochet Ugarte (No.2)*.[166]

PUBLIC LAW IN CONTEXT
R V. BOW STREET METROPOLITAN STIPENDIARY MAGISTRATE EX P. PINOCHET UGARTE (NO.2)

In *R v. Bow Street Metropolitan Stipendiary Magistrate ex p. Pinochet Ugarte (No.2)* the former Chilean dictator Augusto Pinochet had come to the United Kingdom seeking medical treatment. Amnesty International and other groups had sought to extradite Pinochet to Spain to face charges for the crimes that were committed by the state during his rule. The House of Lords in *R v. Bow Street Metropolitan Stipendiary Magistrate ex p. Pinochet Ugarte (No.1)*[167] ruled that as a former head of state he did not have immunity and could be extradited to face trial in Spain. One of the judges, Lord Hoffmann, was an unpaid director of a company which was owned by Amnesty International. The House of Lords agreed that Lord Hoffmann's position amounted to a direct interest in the case, since the company's role was to 'to procure the abolition of torture, extra judicial execution and disappearance' and this was the issue in the case. It was not possible to distinguish the company from Lord Hoffmann in his capacity as a director. Additionally, Lord Hoffmann's wife, Lady Hoffmann, worked for Amnesty International. Neither Pinochet's lawyers nor the Law Lords believed that Lord Hoffmann was personally biased against Pinochet.

Lord Goff considered whether Lord Hoffmann's association with one of the parties in the case could have been regarded as giving rise to bias:

The effect for present purposes is that Lord Hoffmann, as chairperson of one member of that organisation, [the company], is so closely associated with another member of that organisation, [Amnesty International], that he can properly be said to have an interest in the outcome of proceedings to which [Amnesty International] has become party. This conclusion is reinforced, so far as the present case is concerned, by the evidence of [the company] commissioning a report by [Amnesty International] relating to breaches of human rights in Chile, and calling for those responsible to be brought to justice. It follows that Lord Hoffmann had an interest in the outcome of the present proceedings and so was disqualified from sitting as a judge in those proceedings.

It is important to observe that this conclusion is, in my opinion, in no way dependent on Lord Hoffmann personally holding any view, or having any objective, regarding the question whether Senator Pinochet should be extradited, nor is it dependent on any bias or apparent bias on his part. Any suggestion of bias on his part was, of course, disclaimed by those representing Senator Pinochet. It arises simply from Lord Hoffmann's involvement in [the company]; the close relationship between [Amnesty International] . . . and [the company], which here means that for present purposes they can be regarded as being, in practical terms, one organisation; and the participation of [Amnesty International] in the present proceedings in which as a result it either is, or must be treated as, a party.[168]

The consequence of *R v. Bow Street Metropolitan Stipendiary Magistrate ex p. Pinochet Ugarte (No.2)* was that the decision in *R v. Bow Street Metropolitan Stipendiary Magistrate ex p. Pinochet Ugarte (No.1)* was quashed and the question of whether Pinochet could be extradited was reconsidered by the House of Lords in *R v. Bow Street Metropolitan Stipendiary Magistrate ex p. Pinochet Ugarte (No.3)*.

Lord Hoffmann subsequently defended his decision not to recuse himself from the appeal (i.e., stand down). The BBC reported that Lord Hoffmann had defended his decision by arguing that as a judge he was not biased. It was irrelevant that his wife worked for Amnesty International:

For his part, Lord Hoffmann has said that standing down from the hearing never entered his mind. 'The fact is I'm not biased. I am a lawyer. I do things as a judge. The fact that my wife works as a secretary for Amnesty International is, as far as I am concerned, neither here nor there,' he told the *Daily Telegraph* newspaper. Indeed, Lord Hoffmann does not have a record of toeing the Amnesty line. As recently as mid-October he made a ruling opposing an Amnesty position while serving on the judicial committee of the Privy Council. He decided that a convicted killer in the Caribbean, Trevor Fisher, could be legally executed – a sentence which was duly carried out.[169]

Looking at the decision of the House of Lords it is apparent that:

- Direct interest can apply to non-financial interests, such as being involved with a company that has an interest in the decision. This is very important as the decision extended the nature of interest beyond a pecuniary one. However, in *Locabail (UK) Ltd v. Bayfield Properties Ltd*[170] the Court of Appeal held that a minor interest, if it was too small to have an effect on the decision-maker, would not give rise to automatic disqualification bias.
- There need not be evidence that Lord Hoffmann was personally biased. It was sufficient that his connection with the company and its connection with Amnesty International gave rise to automatic-disqualification bias.

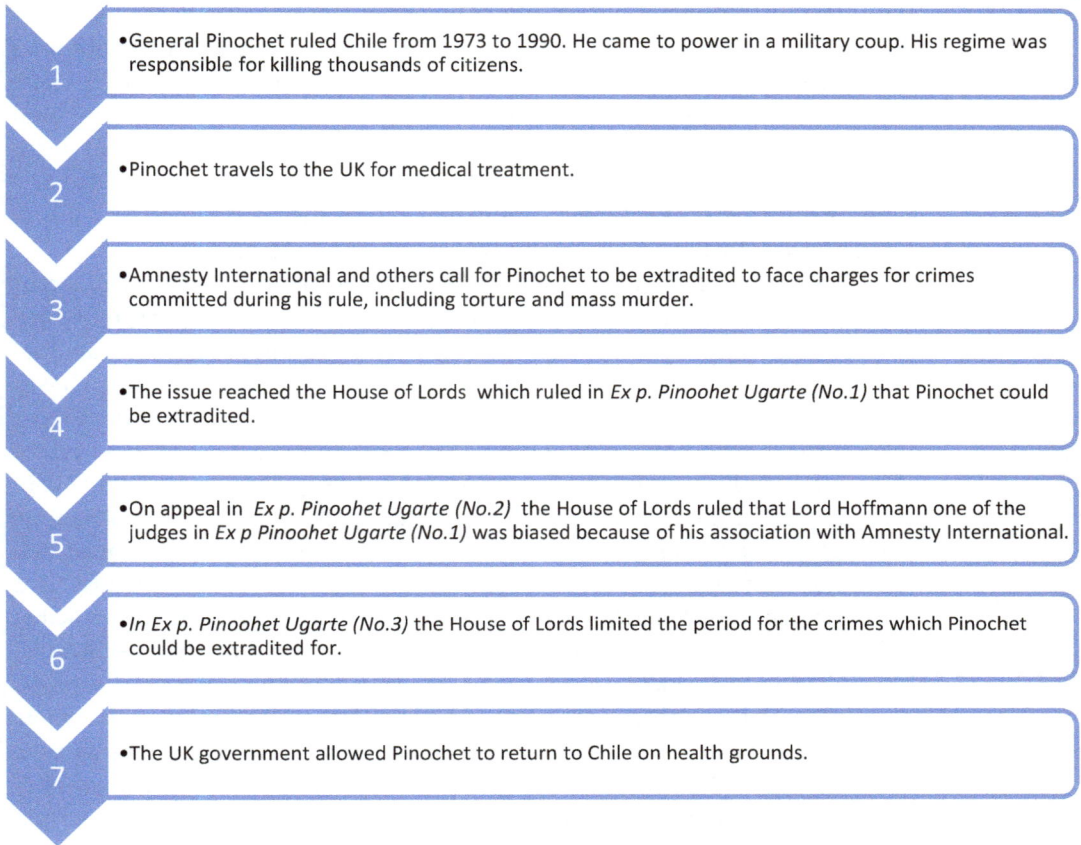

Figure 16.8
Pinochet and the three House of Lords decisions

16.7.4 Apparent bias: indirect interest

Where there is an allegation of apparent bias the decision-maker is not automatically disqualified. Instead the question for the court to decide is whether an indirect interest existed which could lead a reasonable and fair minded observer to believe that there was a real possibility of bias. There is no need to prove that the decision-maker was actually biased. It is important to appreciate that an indirect interest is an interest which exists, but is one which does not affect the decision-maker personally.

The test used for whether there is apparent bias comes from the case of *Porter v. Magill*,[171] where Lord Hope had stated that '[t]he question is whether the fair-minded and informed observer, having considered the facts, would conclude that there was a real possibility that the tribunal was biased.'[172] Therefore, only where this test is satisfied can the decision-maker be disqualified for apparent bias.

The case of *R (on the application of Kaur) v. Institute of Legal Executives Appeal Tribunal*[173] is an example of apparent bias. In this case the vice-president of ILEX and other council members had sat on a disciplinary panel where an ILEX member was accused of cheating in an exam. The Court of Appeal held that the panel was biased. Rix LJ giving judgment argued that the court should not have to make a choice between automatic direct interest bias and apparent indirect interest bias, as both doctrines have the same requirement that a judge should recuse themselves or be disqualified from sitting, 'where there is a real possibility on the objective appearances of things, assessed by the fair minded and informed observer (a role which ultimately, when these matters are challenged, is performed by the court), that the tribunal could be biased.'[174]

The decision in *Davidson v. Scottish Ministers (No.2)*[175] concerned an applicant who was a prisoner and who was arguing that his treatment in prison amounted to a breach of Article 3 of the ECHR. Originally, he had been refused an application for a declarator that his treatment was incompatible with Article 3. One of the reasons given for refusing his application was that section 21 of the Crown Proceedings Act 1947 prevented the court from granting an interim order for specific performance against a Scottish minister. The applicant believed that Lord Hardie, one of the judges who had refused his application, had been biased. He appealed to the Court of Sessions and then the House of Lords. He argued that the Extra Division had not been impartial, because Lord Hardie, whilst Lord Advocate, had made statements to Parliament about section 21 and the remedies which would be available post devolution. In his then capacity as a minister, Lord Hardie had helped to shape the Scotland Act 1998 and had been a promoter of the legislation which was at issue here. The House of Lords held that there was apparent bias and that the decision of the Extra Division should be vitiated. On the facts in *Davidson*, Lord Bingham observed that there was a real possibility that Lord Hardie would be subconsciously influenced by the need to avoid undermining the assurances which he had previously made to Parliament:

[T]hat a risk of apparent bias is liable to arise where a judge is called upon to rule judicially on the effect of legislation which he or she has drafted or promoted during the parliamentary process. Since in the present case there is no issue as to the facts, no issue as to the legal test to be applied and (in my opinion) no significant misdirection by any member of the Second Division, I should for my part be very reluctant to disturb its unanimous decision. I am however of the clear opinion that its conclusion was justified by the nature and extent of Lord Hardie's involvement in the passage of the Scotland Act. The fair-minded and informed observer, having considered the facts, would conclude that there was a real possibility that Lord Hardie, sitting judicially, would subconsciously strive to avoid reaching a conclusion which would undermine the very clear assurances he had given to Parliament.[176]

In *Lawal v. Northern Spirit Ltd*[177] the House of Lords held that there could be apparent bias where a barrister who was appearing for one of the parties in an employment dispute, had sat as a judge in the Employment Appeal Tribunal and knew one, or more, of the lay members of the tribunal which had heard the present appeal. Lord Steyn held that there was a real possibility of bias on the part of the lay members of the tribunal, because they might have subconsciously been biased towards the barrister who had served with them. Lord

Steyn stated that the observer from the test in *Porter v. Magill* would be influenced by the fact that the lay members would have previously looked to the barrister for instructions on the law, and there would be likely to exist 'a fairly close relationship of trust and confidence with the judge.'[178]

It is interesting to consider some recent examples of bias that were related to the judiciary and a judge's handling of a trial.

There was an allegation that the decision of a district judge was tainted with presumed or apparent bias in *United Cabbies Group v Westminster Magistrates' Court*[179]. The initial decision concerned whether Uber should be given a licence by Transport for London. Opponents of this decision, the United Cabbies Group, argued that the judge was biased in favour of Uber because her husband had a financial link to Uber. This was because he the company he consulted for represented a major investor in Uber. The judge denied that she or her husband knew about this at the time of the initial decision.[180] The Court of Appeal rejected the argument that there was bias:

> We do not consider that the facts even begin to show that there was a link between the judge's interest and the interest of her husband 'so close and direct' as to render the interest of her husband indistinguishable from her interest. But the argument fails at an earlier stage. Lord Arbuthnot cannot sensibly be said to have a financial interest in the parent company of Uber, and through them Uber in London.[181]

In *C (A Child)*[182] the Court of Appeal considered whether a judge should have agreed to recuse herself from hearing a case. The issue concerned care proceedings and the proceedings took place online due to the Covid-19 pandemic. During a break in proceedings the judge, not realising that she was still being recorded and could be heard by the parties, had a conversation with her clerk and made pejorative comments about one of the parties, 'including that she was pretending to have a cough and was trying "every trick in the book." '[183] When the court resumed the judge refused to agree to an application that she should recuse herself. The Court of Appeal accepted that the test from *Porter v Magill* was satisfied and that there was a real possibility that the judge was biased. The judge should have recused herself:

> We have considerable sympathy with the judge. We have, however, no hesitation in concluding that her comments did indeed fall on the wrong side of the line. The fact that the comments were intended to be private does not salvage the situation in circumstances where those comments were, unhappily, broadcast across the remote system and were made during the course of the Appellant's evidence.[184]

The way that a judge conducts a trial could give rise to allegations of apparent bias as in *M&P Enterprises (London) Limited v Norfolk Square (Northern Section) Limited*.[185] In this decision the allegations of apparent bias were not successful.

The issue of bias arose in *R v Usman*[186] where a juror had sung the song 'Tell me lies, tell me sweet little lies' after leaving the courtroom once the defendant had given evidence. The trial judge had discharged the juror and the trial had continued. The Court of Appeal held that this ensured that the defendant, who was then convicted by the jury, received a fair trial.

The importance of a judge or where tried on indictment a jury, as the tribunal of fact, being impartial and able to determine the case in a fair manner is of considerable importance. Allegations of judicial bias are not new, and critics of the judiciary are often quick to argue that judges are biased. Following on from the High Court's decision in *R (on the application of Miller) v Secretary of State for Exiting the European Union (No.1)*, one government minister, Kwasi Kwarteng, said that people might believe that the judges were biased:

> On Wednesday, Mr Kwarteng – who campaigned for Brexit in 2016 – told Andrew Neil that there was concern about the extent to which judges are 'interfering in politics.' He said: 'I think that they are impartial, but I'm saying that many people, many Leave voters, many people up and down the country, are beginning to question the partiality of the judges. That's just a fact. People are saying this all the time, they are saying, 'Why are judges getting involved in politics?' We've got to be honest about the debate.

Finally, one judge who had been accused of bias was Peter Smith J. We shall consider this now.

PUBLIC LAW IN CONTEXT
JANAN GEORGE HARB v HRH PRINCE ABDUL AZIZ BIN FAHD BIN ABDUL AZIZ[187]

We will be considering the Court of Appeal's judgment in *Janan George Harb v HRH Prince Abdul Aziz Bin Fahd Bin Abdul Aziz*[188], but first it is necessary to look at the particular facts that gave rise to an allegation of apparent bias.

In *Emerald Supplies Ltd v British Airways*[189] Peter Smith J was hearing a case involving British Airways and had made comments about the airline losing his own baggage. This resulted in Smith J recusing himself after an application was made for him to do so. Smith J's decision is interesting as it shows that the judge did not believe that there was a risk of apparent bias:

> I do not believe for one minute that the reasonably minded observer, which is the test, as Mr Turner has reminded me of, would think that merely because I have raised issues over the non-delivery of my luggage of itself should lead to the possibility of bias. . . . Almost within a matter of hours of the meeting, [BA and its solicitors] decided that I should recuse myself. Now, I do not accept that the correspondence justifies that application. And I am afraid to say that it is, in my view, an opportunistic application, made by a party that has wanted to get me off this case before. . . . I however cannot allow my presence in the case and its difficulties to distract the parties from this case. And therefore,

regretfully, I feel that I have no choice, whatever my feelings about it, but to recuse myself from the case, and that is what my decision is; not for the reasons put forward by BA, but for the reasons that I have said. So I will recuse myself.[190]

After the recusal decision Lord Pannick QC, a senior barrister at Blackstone Chambers, had written an article criticising the judge. In response, Peter Smith J wrote to the chambers and inter alia stated:

The article has been extremely damaging to Blackstone Chambers within the Chancery Division. I am extremely disappointed about it because I have strongly supported your Chambers over the years especially in Silk Applications. Your own application was supported by me and was strongly supported by me to overcome doubts expressed to me by brother Judges concerning you. I have supported other people. It is obvious that Blackstone takes but does not give. I will no longer support your Chambers; please make that clear to members of your Chambers. I do not wish to be associated with Chambers that have people like Pannick in it.

The applicant argued that Peter Smith J had been biased against him for a number of reasons. The allegations of bias related to apparent bias. These included the fact that the applicant's lawyers were from Blackstone Chambers and that he had previously been represented by Lord Pannick QC and that the judge had failed to rectify a material discrepancy in his judgment and the judgment was inconsistent with the evidence.[191]

The Court of Appeal in *Janan George Harb v HRH Prince Abdul Aziz Bin Fahd Bin Abdul Aziz* when considering the test for apparent bias from *Porter v Magill*, was clear that the test related to an objective fair-minded observer and not the subjective opinion of the applicant who had known that the judge had criticised Blackstone Chambers:

The court does not ask whether a litigant who is being represented by a member of Blackstone Chambers and knows of the Article would be content to have his case heard by Peter Smith J. We have little doubt that most, if not all, litigants represented by a member of Blackstone Chambers, knowing of the Article, would prefer to have their case heard by another judge. We are prepared to accept that some, indeed many, might have very strong feelings on the subject. But the litigant is not the fairminded observer. He lacks the objectivity which is the hallmark of the fair-minded observer. He is far from dispassionate. Litigation is a stressful and expensive business. Most litigants are likely to oppose anything that they perceive might imperil their prospects of success, even if, when viewed objectively, their perception is not well-founded.[192]

Therefore, the Court of Appeal held that the appeal could not proceed on the basis of apparent bias being established, although it did succeed on other grounds:

We are prepared to assume that the informed and fair-minded observer, knowing of the Article, would conclude that there was a real possibility that the judge was biased against all members of Blackstone Chambers, at least for a short period after the publication of the Article. But for the reasons we have given, the observer would not conclude without more that there was a real possibility that this bias would affect the judge's determination of the issues in a case in which a party was represented by a member of Blackstone Chambers.

But there is a further reason why this ground of appeal must fail. The assessment of whether an informed and fair-minded observer, having considered the facts, would conclude that there was a real possibility of bias depends on an examination of all the relevant facts. It is fact sensitive. In our view, the facts in the present case show that the possibility that Peter Smith J was actuated by bias against the Prince is unrealistic.[193]

Public Law in Practice

A High Court judge has been having an on- off affair with a barrister. The judge is very professional and when this barrister represents a client before her, she always makes sure that her judgment is impartial. In a personal injury claim before the judge, the barrister is representing the defendant and the judge dismisses the personal injury claim and finds in favour of the defendant. The claimant, Mrs De Keyser, hears rumours about the relationship between the judge and the barrister, and consequentially alleges that the judge was biased. It would be difficult to establish that the judge was actually biased, however if the judge had a direct interest it would be possible to presume that he was biased (*Ex p. Pinochet Ugarte*). It would be difficult to establish here that the judge had a direct interest and therefore Mrs De Keyser could argue that the judge had an indirect interest. We would need to see if the test in *Porter v. Magill* is satisfied before we can establish that there is apparent bias.

16.8 Practical application

Question One

Smudge J is a High Court judge and historian of the Roman Empire. He is a shareholder in A Ltd and his wife is a trustee of Save the Kangaroos, a charity seeking to promote the protection of kangaroos in the wild. Last week Smudge J heard a case between A Ltd and its rival B Ltd, over a dispute over intellectual property ownership. Smudge J found in A Ltd's favour. Three days ago, Smudge J heard a judicial review application from Save the Kangaroos, to challenge the United Kingdom government's proposed grant of £45,000,000 to the Australian government to cull the wild kangaroo population. Smudge J held that Save the Kangaroos had shown that the government's decision was *ultra vires*.

Smudge J lives in Bovis Town. His elderly mother, Joan, lives in a care home owned by Bovis Town Council. When Joan had first considered moving to the care home, she had been informed that she would have a home for life and would not be moved to another care home.

Due to a severe recession Bovis Town Council have decided to close down the care home where Joan lives and move her to another care home.

Smudge J applied for a licence to fish at Bovis Town Council's fishing reservoir and his application was refused and no reasons were given.

The remains of a Roman theatre were discovered in Bovis Town centre whilst building works were being undertaken. Bovis Town Council is obliged under the Local Heritage Act (fictitious) to hold a consultation with experts as section 8 of the Act states, 'Where Roman ruins are discovered the relevant local authority must consult experts to ascertain how best to preserve the ruins.' Smudge J had contacted Bovis Town Council as he would like to be involved with the consultation. However, he was informed that he would not be included in the consultation as he was not an expert.

Please explore the issues relating to judicial review in the above scenario. Your answer should include whether judicial review proceedings could be brought and by whom, the remedies that are available and the grounds that could be relied on.

Question Two

The Local Arts Fund Act 2018 (fictitious) was enacted to encourage the cultivation of arts and associated activities in England and Wales. Each local council was instructed to establish a fund using money given by central government, and local residents could apply for grants from the fund.

Rita applied for a grant from Bovis Town Council to establish an arts and crafts group in local church hall. Maurice Smith, the council employee who is administering the fund from which grants will be awarded, had written to Rita informing her that her application was unsuccessful. Rita is concerned as no reasons were given for the decision, despite all other applicants being given reasons when they were unsuccessful and the council's social media account posting that reasons would always be given. Rita contacted Maurice by email and was informed that no reasons would be given. She also found out that the decision had been made by Ross Town Council, as it had very recently agreed to help Bovis Town Council administer the fund.

Rita decided to do some investigating. She found out that prior to Ross Town Council being asked to make decisions concerning the allocation of grants from the fund, four members of Bovis Town Council had successfully applied for £5,000 each to improve their art appreciation skills. The grant was for the purpose of taking a five-star package holiday around Italy. This decision had been taken two months ago.

Rita then applied again for a grant of £3,000, for the original purpose of establishing an arts and crafts group. Two days later Maurice Smith telephoned her to inform her that her application was refused because the policy by which the fund was administered would only consider applications where the money sought was over £3,500. Furthermore, Maurice informed her that because she had applied twice, she was considered to be wasting council time and that was also why her application had been refused.

Please advise Rita as to whether she could bring a claim for judicial review, the grounds that she could rely on and the remedies that would be the most appropriate.

16.9 Key points to take away from this chapter

- Judicial review has an important constitutional significance.
- There are a number of different grounds for judicial review: illegality, procedural impropriety, legitimate expectation, unreasonableness, irrationality, proportionality and bias.
- There are many sub-elements to illegality, including unauthorised delegation and simple *ultra vires*.
- It is possible to give rise to both a procedural and substantive legitimate expectation.
- If Convention rights have been violated the courts will use proportionality as a ground for review, rather than unreasonableness.
- There are different types of bias, including actual bias and direct interest (automatic disqualification) bias.

Notes

1 [1985] AC 374.
2 [1948] 1 KB 223.
3 ibid 230.
4 [1926] Ch 66.
5 [2020] EWCA Civ 1466.
6 [2014] EWHC 3749 (Admin).
7 ibid 24–25.
8 [1985] AC 374.
9 ibid 410.
10 ibid 411.
11 ibid 410.
12 [2009] EWHC 3060 (Admin).
13 ibid 36.
14 [2013] UKSC 17.
15 ibid 14.
16 [1986] AC 240.
17 ibid 251.
18 ibid 247.
19 ibid 267.
20 [1987] AC 514.
21 ibid 531.
22 [1996] QB 517.
23 ibid 554.
24 (33985/96) (2000) 29 EHRR 493.
25 [1991] 1 AC 696.
26 ibid 17.
27 [2001] UKHL 23.
28 ibid 51.
29 [2001] UKHL 26.
30 ibid 23.

31 [1996] QB 517.
32 [1999] 1 AC 69.
33 ibid 25.
34 [2001] UKHL 26 [32].
35 [1996] QB 517.
36 [2001] UKHL 26, [27].
37 [2013] UKSC 39.
38 ibid 72.
39 [2007] UKHL 11; [2007] 2 AC 167.
40 ibid 19.
41 [1986] 1 SCR 103.
42 [2013] UKSC 39.
43 ibid 76.
44 [2011] UKSC 45; [2012] 1 AC 621.
45 ibid 45.
46 [2018] UKSC 32.
47 ibid 41.
48 ibid 42.
49 ibid 46.
50 ibid 47.
51 ibid 49.
52 ibid 52.
53 [2004] UKHL 56.
54 ibid 40.
55 [2006] UKHL 15.
56 T Hickman, 'The Substance and Structure of Proportionality' [2008] PL 694.
57 N Dobson, 'The Long Trek Away from Wednesbury Irrationality?' [2003] JLGL
    129.
58 ibid.
59 [2001] UKHL 23.
60 ibid 51.
61 [2003] EWCA Civ 473.
62 ibid 35.
63 P Daly, 'Wednesbury's Reason and Structure' [2011] PL 238.
64 P Sales, 'Rationality, Proportionality and the Development of the Law' [2013]
    LQR 223.
65 ibid.
66 Lord Carnwath, 'Judicial Review in a Changing Society: From Rationality to
    Proportionality in Modern Law' 16–17 (14 April 2014) <www.supremecourt.uk/
    docs/speech-140414.pdf>.
67 [2012] EWHC 2579 (Admin).
68 ibid 29–31.
69 [1765] EWHC KB J98.
70 [1976] QB 629.
71 ibid 651.
72 [1921] 1 Ch 440.
73 ibid 449.
74 [1995] 1 WLR 386.
75 ibid 402.

76 [1985] AC 1054.

77 ibid 1080.

78 [2001] UKHL 67.

79 ibid 432.

80 [1988] 2 All ER 207.

81 [1995] 1 WLR 1037.

82 [1925] AC 578.

83 ibid 594.

84 [2018] UKSC 3.

85 *R (on the application of Bancoult) v Secretary of State for Foreign and Commonwealth Affairs (No.3)* [2014] EWCA Civ 708.

86 ibid 76.

87 [2018] UKSC [40].

88 ibid 45.

89 ibid 116.

90 ibid 117.

91 *Cherry v Lord Advocate for Scotland* [2019] CSIH 49.

92 [2019] UKSC 41.

93 [1943] 2 All ER 560.

94 [1963] 2 QB 455.

95 ibid 466.

96 [1991] 1 AC 254.

97 [1994] 1 AC 531.

98 See *H Lavender & Son Ltd v. Minister of Housing and Local Government* [1970] 1 WLR 1231.

99 [1919] 1 KB 176.

100 [1969] 2 All ER 18.

101 ibid 198.

102 [1995] 1 WLR 1037.

103 ibid 1050.

104 [1981] 1 NZLR 172.

105 ibid 183.

106 [1969] 2 AC 147.

107 [1999] 2 AC 330.

108 [2009] EWCA Civ 1059.

109 [2004] EWCA Civ 49.

110 [1969] 2 Ch 149.

111 ibid 170.

112 [1985] AC 374.

113 [1983] 2 AC 629.

114 ibid 638.

115 [2001] QB 213.

116 ibid 57.

117 [2000] 1 WLR 1115.

118 ibid 1123–24.

119 ibid.

120 [2002] 1 WLR 237.

121 ibid 55.

122 [2008] UKHL 61.

123 ibid 17.

124 ibid 134.

125 ibid.

126 ibid 73.

127 [2008] EWCA Civ 755.

128 ibid 35.

129 [2019] UKSC 7.

130 ibid 62.

131 [2012] 1 AC 1.

132 ibid 37.

133 [2014] UKSC 44.

134 [2019] EWHC 449 (Admin).

135 ibid 93.

136 [1985] AC 374.

137 ibid 411.

138 [1915] AC 120.

139 ibid 137.

140 ibid 137–38.

141 [1964] AC 40.

142 ibid 130.

143 ibid 136.

144 [1972] 1 WLR 190.

145 [1987] AC 625.

146 [1978] 1 WLR 1520.

147 [1994] 1 AC 531.

148 ibid 560.

149 ibid.

150 ibid.

151 [2010] EWHC 3496 (Admin).

152 ibid 25.

153 [1974] 1 WLR 1371.

154 [1991] 3 WLR 42.

155 [1971] Ch 591.

156 ibid 605.

157 [1984] 2 WLR 613.

158 [1991] 4 All ER 310.

159 [1994] 1 WLR 242.

160 [1998] 1 WLR 763.

161 [1924] 1 KB 256.

162 ibid 259.

163 K Malleson, 'Safeguarding Judicial Impartiality' (2002) 22(1) Legal Studies 53, 55.

164 (1854) 10 ER 301.

165 ibid 793–94.

166 [2000] 1 AC 119.

167 ibid 61.

168 ibid 139.

169 You can read the entire article at <http://news.bbc.co.uk/1/hi/uk/235456.stm>.

170 [2000] 2 WLR 870.

171 [2001] UKHL 67.
172 ibid 494.
173 [2011] EWCA Civ 1168.
174 ibid 45.
175 [2004] UKHL 34.
176 ibid 17.
177 [2003] UKHL 35.
178 'Kwasi Kwarteng Criticised for "Biased Judges" Comment' *BBC News* (12 September 2019) <www.bbc.co.uk/news/uk-politics-49670901>.
179 [2019] EWHC 409 (Admin).
180 ibid 12.
181 ibid 41.
182 [2020] EWCA Civ 987.
183 ibid 8.
184 ibid 30.
185 [2018] EWHC 2665 (Ch).
186 [2021] EWCA Crim 360.
187 [2016] EWCA Civ 556.
188 ibid.
189 [2015] EWHC 2201 (Ch).
190 ibid 26, 31–32, 41–42.
191 [2016] EWCA Civ 556, [56].
192 ibid 69.
193 ibid 74–75.

Further reading

Carnwath L, *Judicial Review in a Changing Society: From Rationality to Proportionality in Modern Law* (Hong Kong University 14 April 2014)

Daly P, 'Wednesbury's Reason and Structure' [2011] PL 238

Dobson N, 'The Long Trek Away from Wednesbury Irrationality?' [2003] JLGL 129

Endicott T, 'Why Proportionality Is Not a General Ground of Judicial Review' (2020) 1 KLR 1

Hickman T, 'The Substance and Structure of Proportionality' [2008] PL 694

Lester L and J Jowell, 'Beyond Wednesbury: Substantive Principles of Administrative Law' [1987] PL 36

Malleson K, 'Safeguarding Judicial Impartiality' (2002) 22(1) Legal Studies 53

Sales P, 'Rationality, Proportionality and the Development of the Law' [2013] LQR 223

Wade HWR and C Forsyth, *Administrative Law* (10th edn, OUP 2009)

The Ombudsman, tribunals, inquiries and executive liability

In this chapter we will

- consider the role of the ombudsman and the process in bringing a complaint;
- explore the different types of tribunals that exist and the legislative framework;
- evaluate the use of public inquires and why they might be established; and
- debate the ways in which the executive can be liable in private law.

17.1 Introduction

Administrative justice is important in the 21st century. The government, ministerial departments, executive agencies and local authorities have such an important role in our dailyy lives and consequently they have considerable power over us. How are they held to account? How can you the citizen challenge the action of a government department or seek redress for poor service, poor decision making or rudeness? The Ombudsman and public inquires provides administrative accountability and review. No legal remedies can be imposed, rather recommendations will be made. However, the redress available by the Ombudsman and the transparency through the report delivered by an inquiry is extremely important in allowing the individual redress or holding governments to account. Tribunals developed in response to the growth of the state and were established to allow individuals to challenge administrative decisions. In the 21st century there have been major reforms to tribunals which will enable tribunals to play a much more effective role in ensuring that there is administrative justice. Finally, the Crown (government, ministerial departments etc.) and local authorities can be sued for breach of contract or for tort

DOI: 10.4324/9780429293498-19

Figure 17.1
Overview of the chapter

which they or their employees commit. We shall see that this does not necessarily mean that where you have suffered as a result of a local authority breaching its statutory duty, that you can sue in private law for damages by way of compensation.

17.2 Parliamentary and Health Service Ombudsman

Individuals are able to make a complaint to the Ombudsman concerning United Kingdom public bodies, governmental departments and the NHS in England. The role of the Parliamentary and Health Service Ombudsman (PHSO)] is to investigate complaints that governmental departments or the NHS in England have acted unfairly, improperly or have provided the complainant with a poor service.

The PHSO combines the roles of the Parliamentary Ombudsman and the Health Service Ombudsman. These roles were created by the Parliamentary Commissioner Act 1967 and the Health Service Commissioners Act 1993. The PSHO is independent from government and is an important form of administrative redress.

17.2.1 The Parliamentary Commissioner Act 1967

The Parliamentary Commissioner Act 1967 was intended to help individuals get redress where administrative acts affected them negatively. Richard Kirkham observed that:

> By the 1960s, it had become very apparent that redress mechanisms in the UK had not kept up with the growth of government that had taken place during the 20th century. In comparison with today, applications for judicial review were rare. . . . The tribunal system was a more accessible redress mechanism and had recently been reformed, but large areas of executive

activity were left outside its scope. As a result, citizens were too often left with no alternative but to pursue their grievances against the government through political or parliamentary channels.[1]

The Parliamentary Ombudsman as Kirkham notes was not designed to act as 'the citizen's defender' but as 'an aid to Parliament.' The fact that individuals had to make a complaint to their local MP, rather than making their compliant directly to the Parliamentary Ombudsman was controversial.

17.2.2 Current Ombudsman

The current PHSO is Rob Behrens. One of his predecessors, Ann Abraham, outlined her role in 'The Parliamentary Ombudsman: Withstanding the Test of Time' in 2007:

> The Ombudsman is not a court or tribunal, certainly not a court or tribunal of the sort familiar to lawyers of a common law jurisdiction. Ombudsmen and courts are like chalk and cheese: superficially similar, but of very different texture and ingredients. Liberated from the burden of imposing enforceable remedies, with wide discretion, the Ombudsman is free to establish a very different relationship between the disputing parties, based upon trust and shared understandings, not formal compliance. It will remain the task of the office to uphold its distinctive tradition and practice whilst simultaneously forging stronger links with the rest of the system of administrative justice, including the courts and tribunals.[2]

Ann Abraham emphasised that:

- the Ombudsman was not intended to act like a court or tribunal;
- the Ombudsman could not impose enforceable remedies on a public body; and
- it has a wide discretion unlike a court or tribunal.

There is a separate legislation governing the devolved powers in Northern Ireland, Scotland and Wales.

17.2.3 Ombudsman's principles

The Ombudsman has developed six key principles which should be observed by public bodies. These are:

These principles are not meant to replace the public bodies' own guidance nor will failure to follow these amount to the Ombudsman finding that there has been maladministration or service failure. As the Ombudsman's website notes:

> The Principles are not a checklist, nor are they the final or only means by which we will assess and decide individual cases. The statutory test we

Figure 17.2
The Ombudsman's general six principles

apply remains the same as it has always been: is there maladministration or service failure (or failure to provide a service in the case of health bodies and practitioners) and, if so, has this led to an unremedied injustice? If we conclude that a public body has not followed the Principles, we will not automatically find maladministration or service failure. We will apply a broad test of fairness and reasonableness, taking into account the circumstances of each particular case, not a test of perfection. We will apply the Principles fairly and sensitively to individual complaints, which we will, as ever, decide on their merits.[3]

We can see that the Ombudsman's approach is to act fairly and be flexible in looking at whether there has been an unremedied injustice.

17.2.4 *Bringing a complaint*

However, the ombudsman requires that the individual attempt to resolve the despite with the department before seeking their assistance. Individuals cannot bring a claim directly to the ombudsman concerning governmental departments and need to contact their local MP, who will then need to contact the ombudsman on their behalf. An individual has no right under statute that the PHSO will investigate the complaint. It is important to note that the PSHO will decline jurisdiction to investigate if upon their assessment of the complaint it is apparent that the proper complaint procedure with the department concerned has not be followed. The PSHO will only investigate if there is evidence of maladministration or of service fault which has caused injustice or hardship. Often an investigation might not be needed if it is possible to resolve the issue with the complainant and the relevant public body. If it is unable to resolve the issue, then it might be necessary to carry out an investigation. This investigation may well lead to a report being presented to Parliament where there has been a serious example of maladministration. These reports will highlight serious failings which can then result in action being taken to prevent this hopefully from occurring in the future.

PUBLIC LAW IN CONTEXT

An example of a report presented to Parliament is 'Defending the Indefensible' in 2011 which concerned people who had been imprisoned by the Japanese during the Second World War. The government established an *ex gratia* scheme to compensate those who had suffered as prisoners of war. The problem with the scheme was that there was little guidance on exactly who could qualify. This lack of clarification led to many complaints which resulted in legal action. This led the government to introduce two new schemes. The third scheme was based on injury to feelings and it was that scheme where the report found that there had been maladministration. The failures were found not to be isolated instances and had led to injustice.

The outcome of a report will lead to recommendations of how to remedy the maladministration. It is important to note the PSHO cannot impose a remedy on the public body.

In the 2011–12 annual report the PSHO received 23,846 enquiries from members of the public and most were about the National Health Service. There are 4,732 enquiries which the PSHO looked closely at and found that in the vast majority of cases there was no case to answer. Only 421 cases resulted in a formal investigation.

In 2011–12 the result of the PSHO's work resulted in the following remedies:

Remedies 2011/12

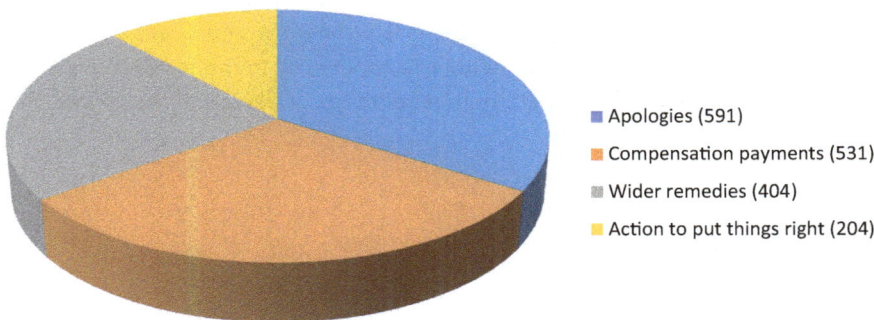

- Apologies (591)
- Compensation payments (531)
- Wider remedies (404)
- Action to put things right (204)

Figure 17.3
Outcome of PSHO's work in 2011/12

In the annual report for 2019–2020 the PSHO received 103,965 enquiries and of these 30,895 were complaints. Of these complaints only 5,236 were taken forward, which resulted in 659 investigations where the complaint was fully or partly upheld, 472 investigations where the complaint was not upheld, 3,742 assessment decisions and 372 resolutions.[4]

The recommendations made by the PSHO for 2019–20 were as follows:

Table 17.1

Recommendation	Number
Formal Apology	507
Compensation	297
Service Improvements	491
Actions to put things right	71

PUBLIC LAW IN CONTEXT
THE OUTCOME OF ONE COMPLAINT

An example of a complaint being made to the PSHO is that of Miss L, who died by suicide whilst a patient at an NHS Trust. The complaint was made by Miss L's sister, Mrs J. It was upheld by the PSHO who found shortcomings in the treatment that Miss L had received from the NHS Trust. The PSHO concluded that if the shortcomings had been addressed then this would have reduced the likelihood of Miss L committing suicide. In terms of recommendations the PSHO said,

> We recommended that the Trusts write to Mrs J to acknowledge the failings we identified and apologise for the impact they had. The Trusts should produce action plans to explain how they will ensure that similar failings do not occur in the future. We also recommended that the Trusts pay Mrs J £10,000 in recognition of the injustice suffered.[5]

17.3 Tribunals

In the United Kingdom there are many different types of tribunals and common examples include the Employment Tribunal and the Asylum and Immigration Tribunal. The procedures used in these tribunals will be different to the procedure used in the courts. The tribunal may be comprised of legal and non-legal members. A tribunal will specialise in a particular area of law and is the procedure used is less formal than the procedure used in court. We are concerned here with the vast majority of tribunals, which involve government decisions being challenged by a party affected. The tribunal will be less formal than courts and developed in response to the growth of government in the 20th century. One example of the importance of tribunals was introduction of pensions and benefits in 1906. Professor Gavin Drewry notes that:

> By definition, those seeking justice in the welfare field tend to be drawn disproportionately from the poorer and less well-educated sections of society: so one great virtue of tribunals operating in this area, apart from their specialist expertise, has always been their perceived relative informality (e.g. a fairly relaxed approach to applying formal rules of evidence) and the fact that applicants could appear without legal representation, and hence at little or no cost to themselves.[6]

The tribunals were viewed 'as alternatives to courts – "court-substitutes" as they are sometimes called.'[7] This was important as although they had developed as part of the state they were merely part of a government department. According to the Frank Report in 1957, 'Tribunals are not ordinary courts, but neither are the appendages of Government Departments. . . . (rather on the whole it would appear) that tribunals should be properly be regarded as part of the machinery of administration.'[8]

According to Carnwath,

> Tribunals have come to play a central part in the UK civil justice system, particularly in relation to administrative law. Their principal distinguishing features, as compared to the courts, are flexibility, specialisation, and accessibility. The present system is the result of piecemeal and incoherent development over many decades.[9]

Considering Carnwath's observation that the tribunal system prior to the reforms introduced in 2007 had been the product of 'piecemeal and incoherent development' it is important to note the impetus for reform.

17.3.1 Leggatt Review

The Leggatt Review of Tribunals was established in 2000 and was headed by Sir Anthony Leggatt. It followed the Franks Report in 1957 which had made important recommendations some 40 years before. Peter Cane notes that:

> Although the Franks Committee considered that courts should generally be preferred to tribunals as providers of administrative adjudication, it accepted that tribunals had certain 'practical' advantages over courts that gave them the edge in certain types of case. Tribunals – so the argument goes – can provide 'administrative justice' more quickly, cheaply, accessibly, flexibly, informally and expertly.[10]

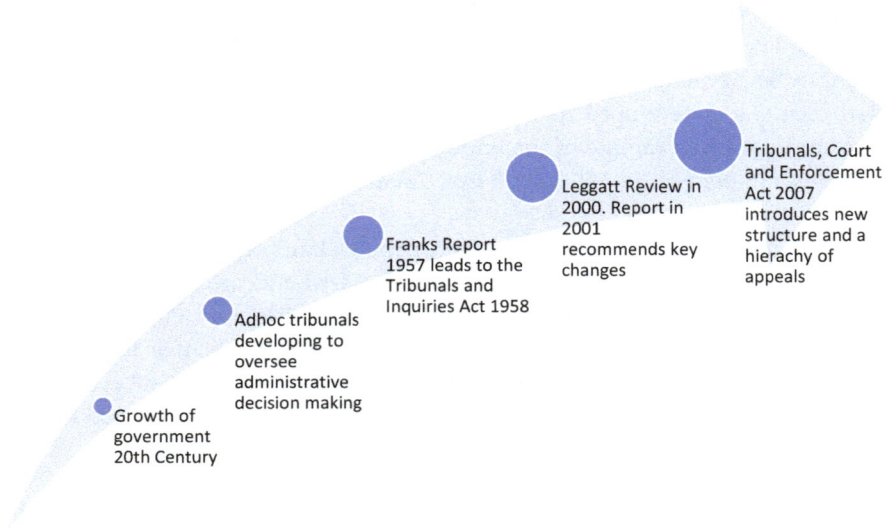

Figure 17.4
The development and reform of tribunals in the 20th and 21st centuries

Following the Franks Report the Tribunals and Inquiries Act 1958 was introduced to reform tribunals. However, the system was not very clear as there were numerous tribunals and little structure in terms of appeals and procedure actually used. In 2001 the Leggatt Report criticised tribunals as:

- having old fashioned methods
- not independent of government departments as salaries paid by the department which might be a party itself at the tribunal – possible Article 6 (1) ECHR breach as risks there not being a fair hearing
- perception that individuals cannot represent themselves without needing a lawyer
- cases before the tribunals taking too long to be resolved

17.3.2 Recommendations

A number of recommendations were made in the Leggatt Report. Amongst the recommendations was that tribunals needed greater independence. It should no longer be acceptable that government departments can appoint members of a tribunal and fund them, whilst expecting that very tribunal to test its decisions. The task of appointing tribunal members should be the responsibility of the Lord Chancellor, which at that time would have resembled the appointment of judges (please note that this was prior to the reforms introduced by the Constitutional Reform Act 2005). There was a view that there were too many separate tribunals and so there needed to be a single system overseeing all the tribunals. This reflected the fact that tribunals had developed in an ad hoc manner. The Leggatt Report recommended setting up a separate Tribunal Service to oversee the running of tribunals and ensure that the service provided should be 'of the highest quality and responsive to the use.'[11] Recommendations were made about the structure of tribunals and that training should be given to its members.

A Tribunal Service was established in 2006. The Tribunals, Courts and Enforcement Act 2007 was introduced to give effect to many of the Leggatt Report's recommendations and it created the First-tier Tribunal and the Upper Tribunal. This would produce a clear appeals system. Carnwath argued that the reforms introduced would help improve procedure used in tribunals and would also help rationalise 'the confused and illogical network of appeal routes which tribunal claimants have to negotiate under the present law.' Decisions of the First-tier Tribunal may only be appealed on points of law to the Upper Tribunal. The Upper Tribunal is then able to quasi-judicially review the decisions of public bodies. This means that there are similarities between the Administrative Court which hears applications for judicial review and the Upper Tribunal. It should be noted that tribunals play a very important role in providing individuals with administrative redress and that many thousands of cases are heard every year by tribunals.

The specialism associated with tribunals allows tribunals to hear disputes in complex matters such as asylum and immigration. It is possible to appeal the tribunal's decision to the First-tier Tribunal, whose decision in turn can be appealed to the Upper Tribunal. Finally, a decision can be appealed to the Court of Appeal. Finally, it may be possible to appeal to the United Kingdom Supreme Court.

17.3 Public inquiries

Inquiries are administrative in nature rather than judicial. No judicial sanction will flow from an inquiry; rather the inquiry will make recommendations which may indirectly lead to legal sanction. An important aspect of administrative justice and indeed executive accountability are public inquiries. Inquiries are viewed as an important review of government policy or to investigate a specific event such as a national emergency, accusations of corruption or the background to military action. An inquiry is an administrative form of review rather than 'judicial.' Inquiries are often led by judges as they are perceived to be sufficiently independent of the government which has made the decision to hold a public inquiry. An example of this is Lord Justice Leveson who recently held an inquiry into the practices of the British press. Because of the perceived closeness between the press and politicians, a senior judge was viewed as sufficiently independent to review the matter. Holding a public inquiry is often a way for the government to show that it is accountable or that it wishes to avoid similar mistakes being made in the future. A public inquiry will make recommendations which can then be implemented.

Public inquiries can take three forms. The first is a statutory public inquiry established under the Inquiries Act 2005, an ad hoc non-statutory public inquiry, and a committee of privy counsellors which is a non-statutory public inquiry.

Examples of public inquiries include:

- The Leveson Inquiry into the culture, practice and ethics of the press. The Inquiry was led by Lord Justice Leveson and came about after allegations of phone-hacking by national newspapers and improper relationships between the press and the police and politicians in governmental positions. Leveson LJ delivered his report in 2012 and recommended regulation of the press. The recommendations were controversial and were subject to intense political debate between the main political parties. For more details on the workings of the Leveson inquiry see: www.levesoninquiry.org.uk/.

- The Iraq Inquiry is chaired by Sir John Chilcot and consists of members of the Privy Council. The inquiry considered British involvement in Iraq from 2001 to 2009 and looked at what lessons could be learnt. The former Prime Minister Tony Blair was questioned by the inquiry and this was televised and broadcast on national television. The inquiry presented its report in 2013. The inquiry will only make recommendations and has no judicial function and it cannot impose sanctions. For more information see: www.iraqinquiry.org.uk/.

- The Hutton Inquiry into the Circumstances Surrounding the Death of Dr David Kelly CMG was led by Lord Hutton. Lord Hutton was a senior judge and his report looked into the death of Dr David Kelly who had supplied the press with information about the intelligence claims that Saddam Hussein has weapons of mass destruction. The Hutton report which was delivered in 2004 was heavily criticised upon its publication.

- The Saville Inquiry explored Bloody Sunday, which concerned the killing of 14 people by the British Army in Northern Ireland in 1972. The inquiry was chaired by Lord Saville and lasted 11 years. The inquiry cost more than £200 million and was criticised as being far too slow and expensive.

- The Grenfell Tower Inquiry is chaired by Sir Martin Moore-Blick a retired Court of Appeal judge. The inquiry was established under the Inquiries Act 2005. The inquiry was established to investigate the causes of the Grenfell Tower fire in 2017, in which a large number of people were killed. For more information see: www.grenfelltowerinquiry.org.uk

- The Scott Inquiry was established in response to the sale of British military equipment to Iraq in the 1980s, when it was ruled by the dictator Saddam Hussein. The inquiry was chaired by Sir Richard Scott, a serving Court of Appeal judge. The inquiry was criticised for taking too long, being too wide in its scope and for not clearly allocating fault. The inquiry was established as an ad hoc non-statutory public inquiry and not using the Tribunals of Inquiry (Evidence) act 1921. One of Sir Richard Scott's main findings was that the convention of individual ministerial responsibility was ineffective.

- The Butler Review looked into the intelligence available to the UK government about Saddam Hussein's alleged weapons of mass destruction. The inquiry was chaired by Lord Butler, a retired senior civil servant. It was established as a committee of privy counsellors.

We can see that the above inquiries resulted in a series of one-off events which necessitated in the government's opinion a public inquiry. The subject-matter of the inquiries is often extremely controversial. The above examples include the decision to commence military action, the killing of United Kingdom citizens by the armed forces and the phone-tapping of members of the public, the royal family, politicians and celebrities by national newspapers.

PUBLIC LAW IN CONTEXT
DENNING, SALMON AND SCOTT

The Tribunals of Inquiry (Evidence) Act 1921 (now superseded by the Inquires Act 2005) was intended to avoid the mistakes that had been made by the use of a parliamentary select committee during the Marconi Scandal. The Select Committee established in the case of the Marconi Scandal has been regarded as partisan and not fair, in the sense that pure arithmetic determined the outcome. The Marconi Scandal originated in the award of a lucrative contract to the English Marconi Company by Herbert Samuel, the Liberal Government's Postmaster General. However, the award of the contract led to accusations that members of the Liberal Government had profited from the award. To investigate the claims, a Select Committee was established and 'The majority report by the Liberal members of the committee exonerated the members of the government concerned whereas a minority report by the Conservative members of the Committee found that these members of the Government had been guilty of gross impropriety.'[12] It was hardly surprising that given the numbers[13] in the House of Commons, that 'When the reports came to be debated in the House of Commons, the House divided on strictly party lines and exonerated the Ministers from all blame.' Donaldson observed that 'the mechanical majority moved into action and the day was won, the Ministers' careers saved, by a vote of 346 to 268.'[14] This was the rationale for the enactment of the 1921 Act.

Despite the 1921 Act, the inquiry undertaken by Lord Denning MR in response to the Profumo Affair of 1963, whereby John Profumo, the Minister of War, had denied an affair with Christine Keeler, was an ad hoc inquiry. The decision not to use the 1921 Act was taken by the government who had appointed Lord Denning.[15] This meant that the procedure was determined by Denning and under statute. The procedure has been criticised as no witnesses were questioned on oath and there were no consequences if they lied when interviewed. Given the subject-matter of the inquiry, Denning's report, despite the excitement surround its publication, was ineffective. Denning's handling of the inquiry has been criticised and it has been argued that the only reason why the inquiry was able to satisfy the public was the fact it was chaired by Lord Denning and his reputation proved a distraction to the problems with the inquiry. In response, a Royal Commission led by Lord Salmon proposed six principles that had to be observed for fairness and that the ad hoc inquiry should not be used again. The Salmon Report's assessment of the Denning Inquiry is significant:

This task he performed with conspicuous success despite the *difficulties inherent in the procedure which he followed*. The inquiry was conducted behind closed doors. None of the witnesses heard any of the evidence given against him by others or had any opportunity of testing such evidence. The transcript of the evidence was never published.[16]

Unlike the Tribunal of Inquiry under the 1921 Act there was no requirement of openness and the public did not have the ability to follow the course of the inquiry. It was hardly surprising that the eventual publication of the report was greeted with such public interest, as evidenced by *British Pathe* newsreels from the time[17]. The Salmon report's assessment continued,

> Lord Denning had in effect to act as detective, solicitor, counsel and judge. In spite of the many serious defects in the procedure, *Lord Denning's report was generally accepted by the public*. But this was *only because of Lord Denning's rare qualities and high reputation*. Even so, the public acceptance of the report may be regarded as a brilliant exception to what would normally occur when an inquiry is carried out under such condition.[18]

A key issue considered by Lord Salmon was whether the Tribunal of Inquiries (Evidence) Act 1921 was fair. This led to the identification of six cardinal principles. The Salmon Report was clear that the inquisitorial method under which the Tribunal of Inquiry operated could be regarded as contrary to the adversarial system and its safeguards:

> Normally persons cannot be brought before a tribunal and questioned save in civil or criminal proceedings. Such proceedings are hedged around by long standing and effective safeguards to protect the individual. The inquisitorial procedure is alien to the concept of justice generally accepted in the United Kingdom.[19]

However, the report was clear that it was in the public interest to use this method to when in 'the very rare occasions when crises of public confidence occur, the evil, if it exists, shall be exposed so that it may be rooted out.'[20] The report was conscious that the inquiry process could 'expose the ordinary citizen to the risk of having aspects of his private life uncovered which would otherwise remain private, and to the risk of having baseless allegations made against him. This may cause distress and injury to reputation.'[21] The solution to this 'difficulty and injustice … can however be largely removed' if the inquiry followed the six cardinal principles laid out in the report.[22] The cardinal principles will be discussed below with reference to civil administrative and criminal law. Whilst a tribunal of inquiry is not a court of law, it could significantly damage an individual's reputation and lead to criminal prosecution or civil liability; therefore it is important to consider the six cardinal principles within a broader context. The principles were:

1   Before any person becomes involved in an inquiry, the Tribunal must be satisfied that there are circumstances which affect him and which the Tribunal proposes to investigate.[23]
2   Before any person who is involved in an inquiry is called as a witness he should be informed of any allegations which are made against him and the substance of the evidence in support of them.[24]

3   (a) He should be given an adequate opportunity of preparing his case and being assisted by legal advisors; and (b) His legal expenses should normally be met out of public funds.

4   He should have the opportunity of being examined by his own solicitor counsel and of stating his case in public at the inquiry.

5   Any material witnesses he wished called at the inquiry should, if reasonably practicable, be heard.

6   He should have the opportunity of test by cross-examination conducted by his own solicitor or counsel any evidence which may affect him.

The Scott Inquiry – another case of fairness denied? The fairness of public inquiries was a key point in the criticism of the Arms to Iraq Inquiry that was chaired by Sir Richard Scott, a Lord Justice of Appeal. This inquiry has proved controversial for a number of reasons, with fairness being one of these. In terms of fairness the Scott Inquiry has been criticised for firstly not being established under the Tribunal of Inquiries (Evidence) Act 1921, and instead operating as an adhoc inquiry. However, did fairness require that it operate under the statute? The Salmon Report was clear that

> We recommend that no Government in the future should ever in any circumstances whatsoever set up a Tribunal of the type adopted in the Profumo case to investigate any matter causing nation-wide public concern. For the reasons we have stated, we are satisfied that such a method of inquiry is inferior to, and certainly no acceptable substitute for, an inquiry under the Act of 1921.[25]

So was fairness compromised? Importantly not all of the six cardinal principles were followed. The Salmon report had been clear: 'We consider it to be of the highest importance that the six cardinal principles which we have stated in paragraph 32 of this Report should always be strictly observed.'[26] However, in the Scott inquiry these were not all followed. Whilst the Salmon report was critical of the procedure adopted in the Denning inquiry, however, the six cardinal principles are presented as what should be done in addition to the statutory minimum as established by the 1921 Act. Context is important and it is the Tribunal of Inquiries (Evidence) Act 1921 that was regarded as being a risk to individuals. So the question which must be addressed is this: did Sir Richard Scott's decision not to follow the six principles render the process unfair or give rise to the perception of a real and sensible risk of unfairness?

The Inquiries Act 2005 allows the government to create a public inquiry and establishes the procedure to be used. A government may establish an inquiry where under s.1(1):

1   particular events have caused, or are capable of causing, public concern, or
2   there is public concern that particular events may have occurred.

There is no need for Parliament to approve the establishment of a statutory enquiry. Section 2(1) states that, 'An inquiry panel is not to rule on, and has no power to determine, any person's civil or criminal liability.' The Leveson Inquiry was set up under the Inquiries Act 2005.

In addition, an Act of Parliament may stipulate that a statutory inquiry could be held into a specific area.

PUBLIC LAW IN PRACTICE

A faulty helicopter crashes into London and 100 people are killed as a result of the accident. There are allegations made in national newspapers that the helicopter was unsafe due to a flaw in the tendering process used to acquire the helicopter from a large arms manufacturer. The government decides that there should be a public inquiry to investigate and if necessary, to make recommendations to reform the tendering process. The inquiry could be held under the provisions in the Inquiries Act 2005. It is important to note that the inquiry will only make recommendations and will not determine civil or criminal liability. However, if there is evidence that the tendering process was subject to bribery and that there were inadequate safety checks on the equipment supplied, then the police could subsequently investigate.

17.4 Executive liability

Historically the Crown enjoyed Crown privilege and therefore had immunity from being sued. In order to bring an action against the Crown it was necessary to obtain the permission of the Attorney General, who is the government's chief legal officer, to obtain a prerogative writ to obtain damages. This was known as the Petition of Right. The problem with this system, as identified by Jacob, was that

> [w]ith few exceptions, it was available only in contract and restitutory claims. Its problems included delay. Most seriously, it did not lie in tort. Here, the Crown was not liable: individual Crown servants were if they could be identified. By 1920 it had become the practice for a government department to give the name of the relevant officer to a potential plaintiff if the circumstances were such that an ordinary employer would have been liable.[27]

We can see that even if permission was given to sue the Crown, it would not be possible to sue the Crown directly where a tort had occurred. This was problematic as the Crown therefore could not be sued for example, in its capacity as the occupier of land. Additionally, there was a 'rule that the Crown is not bound by statute except expressly or by necessary implication.'[28] This meant that the Crown had a privileged status and could be perceived to be above the law which applied to everyone else.

The Crown Proceedings Act 1947 (CPA 1947) was intended to reform the liability of the Crown. The CPA 1947 applies to both the Crown (government departments etc.) and local authorities. However, under s.40(1) the monarch still retains a personal immunity from being sued in her personal capacity.

It is no longer necessary to obtain permission of the Attorney-General. Section 1 of the CPA 1947 permits individuals to sue the Crown as a matter of right. This is an extremely important reform. The Crown has the power to enter into contracts and will be liable upon breach of contract. The Crown can also be liable in tort for the acts of its employees and agents, it can also be liable for breach of the duties owed to its employees and it will be liable for torts committed on its land (s.2). It is no longer necessary to identify the individual Crown servants who had committed the tort before the innocent party can obtain a remedy in tort, but only against those particular individuals Examples of this include *Entick v Carrington*,[29] where an agent of the government was sued for the tort of trespass and *Adam v Naylor*[30], where a solider was sued personally in tort for injuries arising out of the failure to properly secure a bombsite.

An example of the loss of immunity is *Welsh v Chief Constable of Merseyside*[31] where the Crown Prosecution Service were liable in tort for its administrative acts. It was held that the CPS had been negligent as there had been a duty of care owed to the claimant, which had been breached when the CPS had failed to inform a magistrates' court about an arrangement made between the CPS and the claimant, which led to the claimant being wrongly held in custody for two days.

The Crown is also now bound by statutory duties where an individual would also be bound by these (s.2[2]). This no longer permits the Crown to have a privileged status in this regard, unless a statute expressly states that the Crown will not be bound by a particular statutory duty. This means that as a general rule the Crown will be bound by those statutes which apply to private individuals.

17.4.1 Can an individual sue for a breach of statutory duty?

Where a statute imposes a statutory duty on the Crown or local authority, it will not necessarily mean that someone affected by a breach of the duty owed under statute will be able to obtain damages in tort. This is because the statutory duty is intended to protect the public at large and not give a right to private individuals to sue. In *X (Minors) v Bedfordshire CC*[32] child abuse had been committed by an employee of the local authority. The question was whether the local authority could be sued for breach of statutory duty under s.17(1) of the Children Act 1989. The House of Lords held that unless Parliament intended for individuals to have a right to sue in private law, such a right will not exist. Even if such a right exists it is still necessary to establish that a duty of care is owed. Lord Browne-Wilkinson distinguished between public law right which does not entitle anyone to claim damages and a claim for damages in private law. His Lordship held that a 'breach of statutory duty does not, by itself, give rise to any private law cause of action.'[33] However, a right to recover damages in private law could exist where it can be shown 'that the statutory duty was imposed for the protection of a limited class of the public and that Parliament intended to confer on members of that class a private right of action for breach of the duty.'[34] The courts will look at when this intention can be inferred, and the right to sue in private law could arise where there is 'no other remedy for its breach and the Parliamentary intention to protect a limited class is shown.'[35]

The decision in *X (Minors) v Bedfordshire CC* was doubted by the House of Lords in *Phelps v Hillingdon LBC*.[36] It was held that a blanket policy which gave immunity to a local authority could not be justified, and that a local authority could be vicariously liable for the tortious acts of its employees. In *Barrett v Enfield LBC*[37] the decision in *X (Minors) v Bedfordshire CC* was distinguished. Their Lordships held that a duty of care was owed. Lord Slynn stated:

> I do not think that the speech of Lord Browne-Wilkinson in the Bedfordshire case precludes a ruling in the present case that although the decisions of the defendant were within the ambit of its statutory discretion, nevertheless those decisions did not involve the balancing of the type of policy considerations which renders the decisions non-justiciable.[38]

However, in *Cullen v Chief Constable of the RUC*[39] a majority of the House of Lords held that a breach of statutory duty which was intended to protect the public should not give rise to a right to sue in private law. The correct remedy was in private law and the decision could be challenged in public law by way of judicial review.

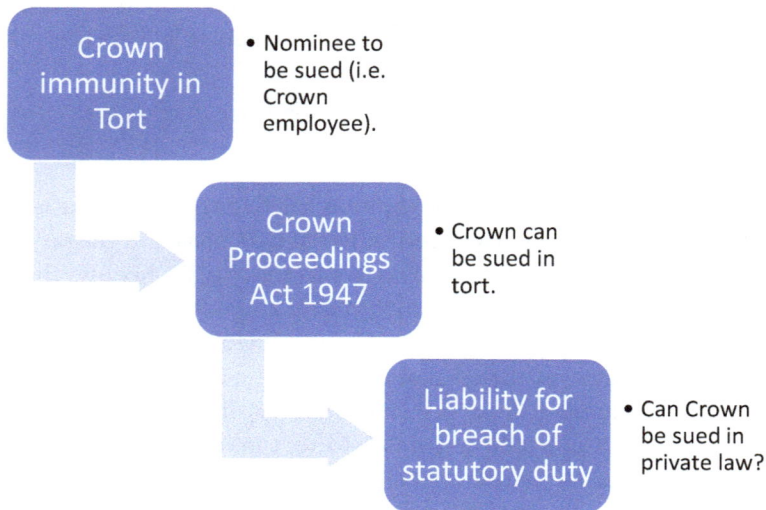

Figure 17.5
Crown's liability in tort

17.5 Practical application

You have been approached by a leading educational charity to produce a poster on the strengths and weaknesses of the use of public inquiries. The poster will be distributed to schools, colleges and universities. In your poster you will need to:

- define what is a public inquiry
- give three examples of where inquiries work well
- give three examples of where inquiries do not work well
- make reference to recent high-profile public inquiries

17.6 Key points to take away from this chapter

After reading this chapter you should now be able to:

- appreciate the development of the Ombudsman and the purpose that it serves;
- understand the use of public inquiries and in what circumstances will an inquiry occur;
- distinguish between a court and a tribunal;
- analyse the effectiveness of the reforms relating to tribunals; and
- understand the importance of the Crown Proceedings Act 1947 and the limits on executive liability.

Notes

1 R Kirkham, 'The Parliamentary Ombudsman: Withstanding the Test of Time' Parliamentary and Health Service Ombudsman, HC 421 (2007) <https://assets.publishing.service.gov.uk/government/uploads/system/uploads/attachment_data/file/231357/0421.pdf>.
2 ibid.
3 <www.ombudsman.org.uk/about-us/our-principles/ombudsmans-introduction-principles>.
4 See <www.ombudsman.org.uk/sites/default/files/The%20Ombudsman's%20Annual%20Report%20and%20Accounts%202019-2020_Website.pdf>.
5 ibid.
6 G Drewry, 'The Judicialisation of "Administrative" Tribunals in the UK: From Hewart to Leggatt' (2009) 28 TRAS 45.
7 P Cane, 'Judicial Review in the Age of Tribunals' [2009] PL 479.
8 Franks Report [40].
9 R Carnwath, 'Tribunal Justice – a New Start' [2009] PL 48.
10 Cane (n 7) 479.
11 Leggatt Report [5.3].

12 P. 11 [11].

13 The General Election in December 1910 saw the Liberals with 275 seats, the Conservatives with 273. However, the Liberals despite not having a majority in the House of Commons were supported by 82 Irish Nationalists MPs. See 'A Century of Hung Parliaments' BBC News (7 April 2010) <http://news.bbc.co.uk/1/hi/uk_politics/election_2010/8572796.stm>.

14 F Donaldson, The Marconi Scandal (Hart-Davis 1962) 230.

15 Royal Commission on Tribunals of Inquiry: Report of the Commission under the Chairmanship of The Rt. Hon. Lord Justice Salmon, November 1966. Cmnd. 3121 [14].

16 Salmon Report [21].

17 See <http:// www.britishpathe.com/video/denning-report>.

18 Emphasis added. Salmon Report [21]. In his report, Lord Denning acknowledged the difficulties that he faced and the perception that a privately held inquiry might have on popular perceptions of justice, 19–20 [37].

19 Salmon Report [28].

20 ibid.

21 ibid.

22 ibid 32.

23 ibid.

24 ibid.

25 ibid 42.

26 ibid 48.

27 JM Jacob, 'The Debates Behind the Act: Crown Proceedings Reform, 1929–1947' [1992] PL 452.

28 ibid.

29 (1765) EWHC KB J98.

30 [1946] AC 543.

31 [1993] 1 All ER 692.

32 [1995] 2 AC 633.

33 ibid 731.

34 ibid.

35 ibid.

36 [2001] 2 AC 610.

37 ibid 550.

38 ibid 585.

39 [2003] UKHL 39.

Further reading

Blom-Cooper L, Public Inquiries: Wrong Route on Bloody Sunday (Hart Publishing 2017)

Cane P, Controlling Administrative Power: An Historical Comparison (CUP 2016)

——, 'Judicial Review in the Age of Tribunals' [2009] PL 479

Carnwath R, 'Tribunal Justice – a New Start' [2009] PL 48

Drewry G, 'The Judicialisation of "Administrative" Tribunals in the UK: From Hewart to Leggatt' (2009) 28 TRAS 45–64

Jacob JM, 'The Debates Behind the Act: Crown Proceedings Reform, 1929–1947' [1992] PL 452

Kirkham R, *The Parliamentary Ombudsman: Withstanding the Test of Time* (Stationery Office 2007)

Laurie E, 'Assessing the Upper Tribunal's Potential to Deliver Administrative Justice' [2012] PL 288

Leyland P and G Anthony, *Textbook on Administrative Law* (8th edn, OUP 2016)729

Index

Note: Information in figures and tables is indicated by page numbers in **bold** and *italics,* respectively.

Lightning Source UK Ltd.
Milton Keynes UK
UKHW052058200322
400359UK00005B/21

9 780367 260774